GOVERNMENT ADMINISTRATION
IN AUSTRALIA

GOVERNMENT ADMINISTRATION IN AUSTRALIA

R. N. SPANN

Professor of Government and Public Administration,
University of Sydney

Sydney
GEORGE ALLEN & UNWIN
London   Boston

First published in 1979 by
George Allen & Unwin Australia Pty Ltd
8 Napier Street
North Sydney NSW 2060

National Library of Australia
Cataloguing-in-Publication entry:

Spann, Richard Neville, 1916–
    Government administration in Australia

    Index
    Bibliography
    ISBN 0 86861 233 2
    ISBN 0 86861 241 3 Paperback

    1. Public administration. 2. Australia—Politics
    and government. I. Title

354'.94

Library of Congress Catalog Card Number: 79-83554

Set in 10.2 on 11 point Times Roman
by Academy Press Pty. Ltd.
Printed in Australia at Griffin Press Limited, Netley, South Australia

CONTENTS

Preface   7
Notes on Other Contributors   8
Abbreviations   9

Part I   INTRODUCTION   11

    Chapter One Government Administration—Scope
      and Problems   13
    Chapter Two The Australian Environment   33

Part II STRUCTURES   41

    Chapter Three Structure and Functions of Govern-
      ment   43
    Chapter Four The Division of Work: Guiding
      Factors and Principles   80
    Chapter Five Non-departmental Agencies   113
    Chapter Six Administration and Law   153
    Chapter Seven Federal Relations I—Constitution
      and Finance   164
    Chapter Eight Federal Relations II—Adminis-
      trative Co-operation   189
    Chapter Nine Local and Regional Government   215

Part III THE PUBLIC SERVICES   245

    Chapter Ten The Australian Public Services and
      Policy   247
    Chapter Eleven Central Personnel Management   286
    Chapter Twelve Staffing the Public Service   312
    Chapter Thirteen Classification, Pay, Industrial
      Relations   360

5

Part IV SOME PROBLEMS OF POLICY
AND MANAGEMENT   385

Chapter Fourteen Policy-making and Planning   387
Chapter Fifteen Co-ordination   411
Chapter Sixteen Budgeting and Financial Man-
    agement   436
Chapter Seventeen Public Administration and the
    Public   463
Chapter Eighteen Administrative Reform, Ac-
    countability and Efficiency   481

Further References   511

Index   515

Preface

This book is an almost wholly rewritten version of one originally published twenty years ago under a different title. The first intention was only to revise details; but the enterprise grew, and the result is a new book, though one that inherits some material from its predecessor. The old book began as a symposium. For this one I have myself written most of the text, and also amended and brought up-to-date the contributions of others. Changed emphasis has made it necessary to shorten or eliminate some chapters, as well as add new ones. In all this, I am most grateful to the early contributors for their co-operation, and their original contribution is acknowledged below. However, the detailed revision has been my own work, and I bear full responsibility for factual errors in the new text, as well as for opinions and faults of style, and the use of 'he' where 'he or she' would often be more correct, but clumsier.

A number of past and present officers from the Commonwealth and State Public Services and statutory authorities have kindly read and commented on drafts; I thank them collectively and anonymously, in accordance with their service traditions. I owe very particular thanks to my colleagues Bernard Carey and Dr Helen Nelson, who have assisted me in innumerable ways at every stage, seeking out information, querying interpretations, and helping to see the book through the press. I am also specially indebted to my colleague, Dr Ross Curnow, for shrewd advice and to John Nethercote, a former student, for much stimulating comment and conversation. I must thank Margaret McAllister and successive secretaries, particularly Jane Clark and Mary Pollard, who have greatly assisted in checking and handling draft chapters.

I am indebted to the University of Sydney, whose granting of a period of study leave in 1978 enabled me to complete this book. For generous hospitality in London during the final stage of writing, I have to thank the Policy Studies Institute and the University of London; and Rose Parton for secretarial assistance.

Notes on Other Contributors

RUTH ATKINS, formerly Associate Professor in the School of Political Science, University of New South Wales, wrote the original version of Chapter Nine.

A.J.A. GARDNER, Chairman of the Public Service Board of Victoria, wrote the original version of Chapter Eight when he was Lecturer in Public Administration, University of Melbourne.

T.H. KEWLEY, formerly Senior Lecturer in Government, University of Sydney, wrote the original study of Statutory Corporations, now part of Chapter Five.

K.W. KNIGHT, formerly J.D. Story Professor of Public Administration, University of Queensland, and now Registrar of the University of Sydney, wrote the original version of Chapter Sixteen.

BARRY MOORE, then of the Consultant and Research Division, Public Service Board of New South Wales, wrote material which now forms part of Chapters Twelve and Eighteen.

R.S. PARKER, Professor of Political Science, Institute of Advanced Studies, Australian National University, wrote the original version of Chapter Three.

A number of other scholars contributed material to the first edition, parts of which remain in amended form in this book. They include Dr A.J. Davies, the Hon. Mr Justice R. Else-Mitchell, Professor Howard A. Scarrow, and the late J.O.A. Bourke.

Abbreviations

AGPS   Australian Government Publishing Service, Canberra. Where the place of publication of a reference is given as Canberra without further addition, it may be assumed that the AGPS is the publisher. Similar references to Adelaide, Melbourne, Sydney, and so on, may be taken to refer to the Government Printer of the relevant State.

HMSO   Her Majesty's Stationery Office, London

RIPA   Royal Institute of Public Administration

RCAGA   Royal Commission on Australian Government Administration. The AGPS published its Report and four Volumes of Appendixes in 1976.

Part I
INTRODUCTION

Chapter One

Government Administration— Scope and Problems

A main purpose of this book is to describe and appraise recent developments in the structures and processes of Australian government administration. It is not directly concerned with issues of 'public policy', that is, it does not examine in any detail the changing content and outcomes of government activities, nor does it attempt to evaluate achievements and possibilities in particular policy areas. But policy comes into the picture. Changing governmental structures both reflect and react upon changing policies. Different policy fields may require different kinds of administrative solution; objectives affect the nature of authority systems, create pressures for centralisation or decentralisation, or suggest the need for new types of government agency. So we inevitably refer a good deal to policy issues, which is as it should be; policy is in the end what administration is about.

Part I is introductory. Chapter One gives a broad account of the book's scope, mentions some general problems and recent trends in government administration. Chapter Two discusses the environmental setting of the Australian administrative system.

Part II deals with Structures. Chapter Three opens with an account of the main structures of Australian government and administration and of their growth in this century, and also describes the distribution of functions between different departments and agencies, at both Commonwealth and State levels. Chapter Four discusses some of the considerations of principle and policy that have influenced this distribution of work, both horizontally (between various units at the same level) and vertically (between different levels). These chapters show the growing complexity of Australian government.

Administrative Trends and Problems

Pluralism

One reflection of this complexity is increasing pluralism, the proliferation of government agencies, and growth of many different centres of power and initiative. It is misleading to suppose that government (any more than business, or education, or religion) marches steadily towards unification and

13

centralisation. In many respects countries are becoming more pluralistic and harder to govern from the centre, not easier. In Australia this political and administrative pluralism is most clearly illustrated by the various power-centres of the federal system. In Chapters Seven to Nine we explore the web of relationships, competitive, co-operative and coercive, between the different levels of government in the federation, and indicate varying ways of answering questions such as: What should be the respective roles of Commonwealth, State, local and regional authorities? How adaptable has the federal structure been to changing needs?

There is a wider sense of 'federal' in which relations at each level of government have a federal character, if we mean by federalism a system whereby sovereignty is divided. Not merely are many ministerial departments important centres of power, but alongside them have developed a great mass of 'non-departmental agencies', as they are called in Chapter Five—administrative boards and commissions, statutory corporations, advisory and investigatory bodies. Some of these are semi-independent powers in the land, and the number of these has multiplied, as most government agencies are difficult to kill off once created.[1] What has led to this multiplication of agencies? What problems does it create for the control and co-ordination of government, and for democratic accountability?

Similar questions arise in Part III, on the Public Services. For example, in Chapter Ten we make the point that senior public servants are not in practice the mere agents and subordinates of ministers, they have resources of their own which can be mobilised. The balance of power between minister and officials, and what role each plays in policy and administration, are influenced by many factors. There is a similar balance to be struck between general administrators and the rising group of professionally and technologically trained government employees (also discussed in Chapter Ten); and between the operating units performing the substantive tasks of government, and the special agencies set up to regulate and co-ordinate aspects of their work, notably Public Service Boards (see Chapter Eleven) and Treasuries or Departments of Finance (see Chapter Sixteen). How far do personnel and financial management need to be centralised in one agency? Or is it better to disperse these controls as much as possible to individual departments?

The growth of public service unions and staff associations (briefly described in Chapter Thirteen), and demands for a greater right to comment, criticise and participate by public employees, add another element to administrative pluralism. There is a more pervasive movement towards 'debureaucratisation', referred to in Chapter Four, which has been well summarised by Dwight Waldo:

> Hierarchy is less strict, or to put the matter differently, there are more recognized sources of authority (unions, for example) and principles of authority (expertise, for example) that impinge upon official authority.

There is more personal mobility, both within organizations and between organizations. The pace of organizational change (reorganizations, recombinations, and so forth) has accelerated. More attention is given to feeling —to the springs of motivation and even to 'fulfilment'—as against purely economic and rational consideration. And interorganizational relations have assumed greater importance, with managers becoming more sensitive to the complex environment to which they must respond.[2]

There is more concern for methods of staff management (see Chapter Twelve) and types of organisations designed to encourage good human relations and a sense of common interest. As mentioned in Chapter Four, the former Department of Urban and Regional Development under the Whitlam government attracted favourable publicity when it was said to be organised into project teams and problem-solving groups, in which hierarchy was somewhat at a discount.

Interdependence

At the same time that government is growing in plurality, there is also (as the Waldo quotation indicates) increasing interdependence. Different policy areas once thought distinct increasingly have effects on one another—consider the current interactions in Australia of minerals policy, Aboriginal policy, environmental policy and foreign policy. Policy sectors, such as energy policy or welfare policy or general economic policy, that used to be left to a mixture of private interests, government departments and the semi-independent activities of statutory commissions, now more and more need co-ordinated attention, intelligent anticipation of interactions, calculation of the points at which government can most usefully intervene. Governments, whatever their political complexion, have to design and implement reasonably consistent and coherent programmes. Realisation of this has already been reflected in organisational structures, as outlined in Chapters Fourteen and Fifteen on Policy-making and Co-ordination. We have tried to illustrate in both cases some of the complexities, and to show that good policy-making is not just a question of creating new 'policy units', and that setting up a new co-ordinating unit is as likely to complicate the problem of co-ordination as to solve it. Modern governments find it difficult to·control themselves, let alone the societies they govern. 'Government is not omnipotent in respect of its own policy-making process. It is as much as it can do to co-ordinate one channel with another.'[3]

It is significant that the 1970s have also seen the creation of a number of commissions and committees of inquiry into government administration and the public services. One important recent trend in Australian government is for it to become more self-conscious, more prone to look critically at itself, or to invite outsiders to look, even if it remains cautious about radical change. It used to be said that the force of inertia was very strong in government organisations—and this is still true of some sectors—but we live more and more in an era of hyperactivism, of constant change and reorganisation of administrative structures, the costs and benefits of which are rarely evaluated (see Chapter Four).

Some features of this era of Administrative Reform are discussed in Chapters Seventeen and Eighteen. One major issue that came up in some of the inquiries was that of public accountability. Can a more pluralistic, interdependent, complex system of government administration also be made 'responsible'? Accountability and responsibility are words with several meanings, and the question was raised in at least two different ways by the most famous of recent inquiries, the Royal Commission on Australian Government Administration (the 'Coombs Commission'). The first is the issue of Accountable Management. How can we improve the ways in which government agencies are focussed on clear objectives, have control over the tools they need to do the job, and can be subjected to tests of efficiency and effectiveness in achieving their aims? This is touched on in Chapter Eighteen.

The second issue is that of responsibility and 'responsiveness' to the public. For example, the Coombs Report argues that government administration needs to review not only its relations at Top Level (to use the Schaffer categories mentioned later in this chapter) and its Inner Man, but also its links with the Outer World, especially in distributing goods and services to its clients. The modern official cannot just be the anonymous agent of ministers and boards, 'often he must do his work in the full light of public awareness, be accessible, attentive and responsive to those seeking to influence the processes of government and to those whom he serves'.[4] Among other issues this raises the problems of Information and Access discussed in Chapter Seventeen, on 'Public Administration and the Public'. There are also controls imposed on administrative discretion by parliament, by courts and tribunals and by ombudsmen, some of which are dealt with in Chapter Six. Can we hope for a better-informed and more influential citizenry in a democracy, concerned for equity and the public interest? Or is this an illusion? Is the best, or worst, we can expect to have an active and vocal collection of pressure groups? Or are these spurious alternatives?

The Character of Government Administration

Definitions

Can a general definition be given of the scope of Government Administration or Public Administration (these two terms are used as synonyms in this book) as a field of study? The scope of Government in this context is not easy to define. Clearly it applies to bodies such as the Department of Foreign Affairs and Departments of Education. It also applies to statutory corporations such as TAA and the State Electricity Commissions, sometimes referred to in Australia as 'semi-government' or 'semi-governmental' authorities. But many people would not apply it to a wide range of public bodies that have some special links with government, such as the universities. It is arguable that these bodies should be called governmental on the ground that they were established by Act of Parliament and/or receive regular government grants. However, the first test is much too general. It would bring in the Australian Gas Light Company, which is certainly not thought of as a government body. The second test, that of the source of funds, also has difficulties. To suggest that all bodies receiving regular government grants are government bodies would involve including the Academy of Social Sciences of Australia and the many cultural groups and voluntary social welfare agencies that are publicly subsidised, and nobody could reasonably make such a claim. A better test would be to inquire whether the managing authority, or a majority of its members, is appointed by Commonwealth or State parliaments or cabinets or by a minister,[5] or by local councils, or by some combination of these; or by some other government body appointed in this way. Even this criterion lets us down in a few cases; the dividing line between governmental and non-governmental is bound to be hazy in the modern world, where the relations between public and private sectors are varied and complicated. We return to this point later in this chapter.

Politics, Policy and Administration

Defining the special field of Administration within the total context of Government is also difficult. It was once common to draw a neat distinction between policy and administration, or between political decisions about government policy, and the administrative task of implementing those policies. Through such mechanisms as political parties, elections, parliaments and cabinets the basic objectives of government are shaped. But further structures are needed to put these policies into action, and this is the task of public administration and the various public services. On this definition, the study of Administration is the study of Means, of the structures and processes involved in carrying out policies, and in trying to achieve the objectives embodied in them.

This concept of Administration as Means is attractive to countries such as Australia, which claim to be representative democracies, in which elected persons are supposed to determine policy and have the final say between elections. In modern societies, such democracies have found it necessary to operate through large career public services, or bureaucracies, which a new government has to accept more or less unchanged. It is convenient to argue that these permanent officials can be loyal servants of changing governments because they are, or should be concerned with a politically 'neutral' expertise, that of devising the most efficient means of carrying out the policies set for them by the people's representatives. So democracy and bureaucracy can be happily combined, as there is no need for public servants to become involved in politics.

Various approaches to the study of Government Administration have been associated with this concept of Administration as Means, such as the legal approach and the scientific management approach. The former sees administration as a way of 'carrying out the law', which may involve certain kinds of subordinate legislation (or rule-making) or adjudication (deciding particular cases under the rules). There is some discussion of this in Chapter Six. In Continental Europe the study of Public Administration is closely associated with the study of Law, and it is a pity that the two subjects have become so separated in English-speaking countries.

Scientific Management, on the other hand, has made use of various analogies drawn from the army, business, engineering and so on. It has seen administration not so much as a system of rules, but more as a 'line of command', with policies fed in at the top as instructions; or a scientifically planned structure which could ideally be designed and blue-printed in advance like a machine, so as to achieve desired outputs with maximum efficiency. Management theory, like Law, still has much to teach the working administrator.

Administrative Politics

However, if we look at what public servants actually do, the distinction between policy and administration becomes blurred. First, senior public servants are often concerned with policy formulation—indeed, they influence policy decisions far more than do most members of parliament, and they inevitably have their own ideas about what policies should be. Many of the initiatives in shaping Australia's national objectives spring from the experience of the public service.

Secondly, implementing policies often involves wide discretion, and many of the decisions involved in turning general policies into something concrete and specific are certainly not neutral or value-free. 'Implementation and enforcement are not clear-cut invariant processes; instead, they are subject to various interpretations and degrees of intensity.'[6] Implementation takes place in a political context, and is itself affected by the changing political and social climate, from outside pressure groups trying to influence departments, to subtler indications that now is the time to act quickly, or to go slow. As well as external pressures, there are political factors within the administrative process itself. We must expect to find departments competing for resources for their cherished projects, seeking greater control over trade policy or child-care policy, making bargains and arranging compromises. Bureaucrats must often also be diplomats, manipulators and warriors.

This is not meant to imply that the public servants concerned are necessarily power-hungry or in some way immoral, but simply that power is sought, and often needed, to secure what may be perfectly legitimate objectives. Political resources are often a prerequisite of effective administrative action. 'A structure of interests friendly or hostile, vague and general or compact and well-defined, encloses each significant centre of administrative discretion. This structure is an important determinant of the scope of possible action.'[7] This was written in the American context, but is not only true of

America. When we ask how efficient or effective a government agency is in achieving its objectives, we have to take account both of the political environment in which it operates, and of the various pressures generated within the administrative system itself not necessarily at all connected with its ostensible aims.

It is true that 'bureaucratic politics' have a special character that makes them different from, say, party politics. For one thing, they operate in the context of large departments with many established procedures, social norms and settled views on policy; organisations that have developed their own corporate life and which constitute a stabler environment than that in which many other political battles are conducted.

Administrative Sociology

This point reminds us that public administration has an important sociological aspect. A government agency is not just a machine designed to serve certain purposes but a human community with its own culture and style of working. A department often has its departmental philosophy or 'line', a body of established policy and a characteristic approach, to which new recruits will be assimilated. Even what looks like a purely technical matter, such as a change in structure or procedures, will be judged not only by scientifically ascertained canons of efficiency, but by its effects on preferred policies, on relative status, and on customary methods that have come to be thought sacrosanct. Government departments are to some extent organisms that are born, grow and adapt like human beings. This biological analogy has been explored by modern systems theory (see Chapter Fourteen). Much interesting research remains to be done on the sociology of the Australian public services. There is, for example, valuable source material in the research and transcripts of evidence of the recent Royal Commission on Australian Government Administration.

The Nature of Administrative Work

Whatever the limitations of the Administration as Means approach, it remains true that much official work is of a relatively neutral and technical character. It is also important to preserve the idea that government administration is a subordinate activity, one that is finally answerable to non-administrative processes and purposes, even if it sometimes involves wide-ranging discretions. The Latin word from which 'administer' and 'administration' derive already had two distinct meanings that bring out these two aspects of administration—to assist or serve; and to manage or direct.[8] The first suggests subordination, the second superiority. Administration is still able to accommodate these two ideas. It may involve very important decision-making and managerial functions, but we still think of it as 'completing a process someone else has started, or running someone else's show, or seeing to the consequences of someone else's purposes. Or, if not someone else's, then one's own, arrived at by some act that is not 'administration'.[9]

It is interesting that business usage has tended to think of Administration as applying to ancillary 'housekeeping' and accounting routines, as contrasted with the major policy-making and production activities, there called Management. In 1888 Henry Gyles Turner, general manager of the Commercial Bank of Australia, wrote with pride: 'A Bank manager is, as a rule, paid a much higher salary than the head of any Government department, because his work is something more than mere administration'.[10] Government has on the contrary often treated Management as only one aspect of the more inclusive activity of Administration, where the latter also covers policy formulation and advice to ministers. It is true that some writers argue that the word administrator suggests a rather passive arbitrator, who stresses procedures and responsibilities, while manager implies a task-oriented activist, concerned with changing the environment rather than working within it.[11] To some *avant-garde* writers, both words sound a bit rigid and stuffy. In this book, we treat Administration and Administrator as the more inclusive terms.

When we try to delimit the field of Administration, we are not merely interested in the distinction between administration and politics, or administration and policy, but in distinguishing between administration and various other technical and specialist activities that go on inside government agencies. This is what a former Chairman of the Commonwealth Public Service Board had in mind when he wrote:

> We believe that top administration and management is a distinct and integrated function and that even where a Second Division position has professional or technical content the choice of appointees should, in high degree, be on the basis of administrative and managerial abilities.[12]

This is sometimes expressed in the distinction drawn between generalists and specialists, or administrators and professionals. It is true that there is no sharp line between administrative and professional work. Most administrative work involves some specialist knowledge of the subject matter of a particular branch, or enough knowledge of a professional skill at least to know what the professionals are talking about. Nevertheless there seems to be a category of work and skill that can be called administrative, even if it is often found combined with knowledge of a specialised field or technique. It is sometimes said that administrative work falls into two main categories, policy formulation and management.

Policy formulation is an important part of the work of senior public administrators. Much of it takes place under ministerial and cabinet direction. It includes preparing plans and advice on policy, collecting and interpreting the data required for a new defence or social services or trade programme, briefing a minister for a parliamentary debate or an international conference. It may sometimes include preparing legislation or regulations (the actual drafting of these in final form is a task involving technical legal expertise). Policy formulation and planning are not once-for-all jobs; policies and plans need regular review. There is also what the Fulton Committee calls 'high-level casework arising from the detailed application of policy',[13] that is, decisions about how existing policy shall apply in particularly difficult cases, where a standard answer is not available. This is one point at which policy making and management are closely interpenetrated.

Management involves the implementation of policy and the oversight of the department's staff and work. This includes both its internal management services (personnel, finance, etc.) and the control of its executive activities and major programmes—the organisation of work, the direction of staff, setting standards of attainment and criteria of performance, measuring results, and so on.

Schaffer makes a slightly different distinction between two kinds of administrative work (he calls the second kind executive). 'The one type is essentially argumentative, the other measurable'.[14] The first type is concerned with decisions which there are no standard rules for making, and where there are no conclusive tests of right and wrong. The second type of decision, though it may involve considerable discretion and skill, is more self-contained. It is made according to standards and procedures provided for within the organisation itself, and its results are more open to objective assessment. It is the kind of work that could in principle be hived off from a normal ministerial department, handed over to a separate agency, and subjected merely to some basic controls over performance.

There are several good accounts of the policy work of Australian public servants, but nothing as good on management and implementation. Nor have there been any really successful attempts to analyse and classify systematically the tasks of administration. One such attempt has been summarised in the term POSDCORB—planning, organising, staffing, directing, co-ordinating, reporting and budgeting. Later writers have criticised and played around with this list. Koontz has reduced it to: planning, organising, staffing, direction and control.[15] Gross talks of: planning, activating, evaluating, which is a version of Henri Fayol's three processes—preparing operations, seeing that they are carried out, watching the results.[16]

These are not useless exercises in sorting out the categories of administrative work, and some use is made of them later. But they are troublesome to use because they overlap. 'Planning' is intended to describe the whole process of systematic forethought—defining objectives and targets as precisely as possible, estimating the resources involved, formulating a programme that will match resources and objectives, forecasting difficulties likely to arise, and the collection and analysis of the data required by these activities. 'Organising' is a useful term for the activity of creating or changing a structure or a set of administrative arrangements. 'Controlling' is sometimes used with reference to checking and evaluating results in relation to forecasts, and taking necessary corrective action, as illustrated by budgetary control and other kinds of measurement of performance. But many administrators do not find it easy to categorise their work in such terms. For example, part of planning itself is 'control', that is, evaluating plans and revising them periodically when made. Part of the process of organising is 'planning' the organisation; and so on. Administration and management are a seamless garment that resists the attempt to take it to pieces in this way.

Such accounts may also treat an administrative agency as more static and closed than is the case. They do not readily provide for Innovation or the initiation of new activities. Nor do they bring out the vital fact that many public servants, and not simply those at the top or behind the counter, spend a great deal of time dealing directly with the outside world—broadly interpreted to include other departments, statutory authorities, local councils, staff associations, as well as industry and commerce, farmers and their organisations, the general public and other countries. These external contacts are of many kinds—handling applications for grants, licences, approvals of various kinds; procurement, obtaining approval of expenditure, recruiting staff; serving on committees; giving advice, persuading, communicating information and policies; as well as more ordinary contacts with the public, including the distribution of goods and services. They are the important boundary activities of an organisation.

Indeed, rather than merely distinguishing between policy work and management, we could adopt another of Schaffer's formulations,[17] and say that public administration is concerned with three different, if overlapping, worlds:
1. The Top Level—providing support for, and responding to the demands of political leaders.
2. The Inner Man—managing its own staff, providing incentives, and so on.
3. The Outer World—from handling procurement and making contracts, to distributing its goods and services to its clients.

Public and Private Administration

Another way of investigating the nature of government administration is to compare and contrast it with the administration of the private sector. Some writers maintain that there are fundamental differences between the two, others emphasise the similarities.[18] A common fault in such comparisons is to ignore the many different types of function and organisation to be found in both sectors. For example, the working of a Department of Productivity factory or of TAA is more akin to that of many private firms than to a Treasury or an Education Department. Some of the outputs of government are similar to those of the private sector—a broadcasting station or a scientific research laboratory or a kindergarten will present similar problems of organisation, whether it is public or private. Other functions of government, such as law and order, public health regulation, economic planning, have few or no close parallels in the private sector.

The Market Mechanism and Central Direction

One way of approaching the differences between public and private sectors is to distinguish between two different ways of preserving equilibrium and allocating resources within a society—the market mechanism and central direction.[19]

The market and its associated price and profit system function through the reactions of consumers, producers and investors, which is often a convenient and flexible method. Central direction, and the administrative hierarchy associated with it, involve action by some overriding authority. The two mechanisms overlap, because many decisions in private organisations are taken in a hierarchical way as in government, while some publicly provided goods and services are priced and sold on the market.

However, many government services are not charged for, and the profit test cannot be used to decide whether customers are getting what they want or would prefer something different. Even if a department has some rough way of knowing whether its clients (say, pensioners or primary producers) are reasonably satisfied, this is no test of efficiency. They may be satisfied because the department has been well-supplied with funds by the budget. If teachers' salaries were to be doubled tomorrow, they would feel very pleased, but other departments might feel that more urgent needs were being neglected.

So the broad allocation of resources has to be determined centrally by the government and its advisers. But how can they decide? Sometimes one can assess the relative costs and benefits of competing projects in the common denominator of money. But even in these cases political gains and losses are also important to governments, and in many instances monetary calculations of profit and loss are impossible or inappropriate. It is not easy to determine whether a new high school is more needed than a new geriatric ward in a public hospital, or a new university more than a new main road. Those concerned may try to judge the relative strength of departmental demands, public and pressure group complaints, how marginal voters will be feeling at the next election, or they may indulge their own preferences and notions of relative urgency. At an election the customers can speak their minds— though it will still remain unclear why they returned or failed to return the government. Was it the promise of tax cuts? Or the cost of living? Or deficiencies in public transport? The signals of favour and disfavour are hard to interpret and weigh.

Business has a simpler and less ambiguous test of the correctness of its actions, the level of profits. Firms have to meet market tests of efficiency, and these are what ultimately control the flow of resources to them. A related way of exploring this problem is to talk in input–output terms, and to say that a government department's inputs are less closely and directly related to its outputs. The monetary fruits of special efforts do not accrue readily to the organisation making the efforts. It is harder to say whom a government department must satisfy to stay in business. Its activities may improve someone else's income (pensioners) or earning capacity (education), not its own. Some observers have even discerned a perverse relationship between the outputs and inputs of government, by which failure is rewarded and success penalised. One way of getting a larger allocation of funds is to establish that you have not succeeded—in providing adequate education, public transport, and so forth; in public administration, as in defence, 'it is the points of failure to which reinforcements are rushed',[20] and rarely are the successes reinforced. In business, failure is more regularly penalised by a drying-up of the flow of inputs. Clients and investors shift their resources elsewhere, and in extreme cases the firm ceases to exist.

However, this contrast should not be overdrawn, as profits are by no means always a satisfactory test of 'social efficiency'. They can be an index of monopoly or tariff protection, as well as of public satisfaction. Many firms prefer a small safe profit to a large but risky and troublesome one, which may make them as conservative as any government agency. Nor do profits take account of social costs. Economists often distinguish between private and social costs and benefits. Some activities have costs to society that greatly exceed the personal cost to the individual or group undertaking the activity —for example, they may cause considerable pollution or congestion. In such cases, the profit criterion may be a very imperfect guide to the cost to society, because the activity has 'spill-over' effects or 'externalities', social costs not counted in the private costs. This can, of course, apply to government activities as well as to those of private business—but firms find it somewhat easier to ignore the consequences of their actions.

Similarly the benefits of some goods and services are mainly private, that is, they are enjoyed exclusively by the individual receiving them, without direct or conspicuous effects on others. 'Public goods', on the other hand, have spill over or external benefits, the benefits also flow on to other people. Some government services are pure public goods, necessarily available to everyone, as are defence services. If the Australian armed forces defend me, they cannot help but defend most other Australians at the same time. Many goods are a mixture of 'private' and 'public', as is education, which benefits individuals, but there is also some spill-over to society. Education could be charged for; if it is provided free, or below cost, it is partly as one way of redistributing incomes, partly because the government considers it knows best how much education children should have (and of what kind), and partly also to take advantage of supposed spill-over effects. Governments are expected to, and sometimes do, take account of externalities, including the indirect effects of their own outputs, though this is hard to do and rarely done successfully. Even a government commercial enterprise is expected to have regard to general social policy—make a contribution towards development, or take account of the social implications of retrenching its staff or its services in a particular region.

Special problems also arise because government agencies often produce services rather than physical goods. This makes them, like middlemen, appear to be unproductive and may lead to undervaluation of public sector services, especially 'contingent services' such as vacant hospital beds or peacetime armies. Services also have vaguer boundary lines than goods, and even the identity of the product may be uncertain.

Modern governments also undertake long-term speculative ventures in technology, urban planning, infrastructures, and may sometimes want to engineer a major structural change in the economy. Similar ventures by business might have no more certain tests of worthiness; but governments do seem to be more regularly tempted into large-scale errors, such as the Ord River Scheme or Concorde. This is partly because they are often not governed by economic calculation, but by considerations of political necessity or prestige. Again, ministers and governments are apt to feel that they must make their mark quickly, also they are not in the job for sufficient time to know the difficulties and are rarely there long enough to be held personally responsible for long-run failures; the last point is sometimes also true of officials. The secrecy and anonymity of government administration helps to hide failures and does not promote good feedback and learning processes; of course, there is also plenty of secrecy in business.

As was mentioned earlier, there are competing pressures for resources from the various public agencies and their pressure groups. Some writers see an analogy between this kind of political competition and the economic competition of the market. However, it is an imperfect analogy. In the battle for government resources, almost every department and activity has its supporters, and there are no good tests for discriminating between them, so there is a tendency to follow precedent, and to favour 'continuity of policy'. Resource allocation in government is often incremental, concerned with marginal changes on last year's figures. It is true that from time to time there may be sudden bursts of new expenditure on particular projects or services; but budget economies tend to be 'across the board', and because it is normal for departments to be under pressure to economise, there is a constant tendency for public resource allocation to become conservative and undiscriminating. In particular, it is very hard for governments to kill anything off. Peter Self makes the point that governments are often concerned more with 'market compression' (limiting demands that cannot be met) than 'market innovation', and it is a relief to them when a demand is met by someone else. Innovation 'must make its way against a sluggish headstream of numerous existing commitments'.[21] The same phenomenon may be observed in universities.

A related point is that a government agency tends to have a limited field of competence within a defined structure. Its purposes are authorised by parliaments or governments, and indirectly controlled by finance departments. It has only a limited power to change its own policies; even public business enterprises usually have a limited charter, which sometimes greatly restricts them in developing new activities. A government agency has little power to displace other government agencies (there is an occasional takeover bid). The scope for defence and stonewalling is much greater than that for aggression, so a department is often protected not merely from outside competition, but from more than marginal competition by other departments.[22] Private business is usually less protected, freer to invade the territory of others and to practise the 'succession of goals' (replacement of one objective by another). An efficient business may even see its task as 'mobilising resources to create wealth', in terms of which a unit producing a particular product is wholly dispensable, and the organisation may, perhaps initially through diversification, end by producing a wholly different range of products. Even a university department or a voluntary association has more room to promote the succession of goals, though it may in practice be conservative. There is obviously a danger, in their delimited and protected situation, that government agencies will not be flexible enough in meeting changing needs.

The Public Interest and Political Constraints

Whereas private organisations are expected primarily to satisfy their own 'publics', customers, shareholders and employees, a public department tends to be regarded as part of a larger unit, the government, which serves the needs of the whole community. In short the administrator is expected to act in the public interest. Governments are supposed to integrate the various activities of society. To help them to do this they have many compulsory and coercive powers, including the powers to tax, arrest and make war. Yet in a democratic society they are at the same time supposed to be controlled by us, and their public servants are our servants.

This has many consequences. One is that the public sector is subject to more formal controls. This is a matter of degree; nowadays the private sector is increasingly controlled by law, government policy and public opinion, and some large firms have to go through much the same balancing act as government agencies in meeting the many claims on them. Conversely public enterprises have a certain freedom to follow business principles in dealing with customers, and other government agencies may in practice act with a good deal of independence. (An extreme view is that politicians often have less effective control over government agencies than they do over the private sector).[23]

Still, in general the public administrator is more completely the servant of political decisions. Ministers may be appointed or removed for reasons not related to efficient administration. A sudden change of policy or of political leadership may occur, to which the administrative system must adapt. Parliamentarians, unlike shareholders, meet often, ask questions and write letters—and the Opposition has a vested interest in criticism. The very allocation of functions between departments may be based on political considerations, rather than what is administratively sensible (in December 1977 the Department of Trade and Resources was designed not by any logical process but for Mr Anthony, the National Country Party leader). When departmental decisions are on matters of potential controversy, this can lead to fear of letting more than a small number of experienced public servants take them, which may mean that the senior people are overworked, while the discretion of their juniors is severely limited by departmental rules. Short-term issues may take up a disproportionate amount of time.

There is also a special demand for fairness and justice from government agencies—because of the power of government, and the belief that it should act in a unified way and have higher ideals than business. This induces a special concern for consistency, that is, similar cases being treated similarly. The attempt to avoid charges of favouritism and inconsistency is strong in government, and partly accounts for the great reliance on rules and precedents. People's fear of being imposed on by government also makes it harder for public organisations to advertise themselves without attracting charges of propaganda and misuse of public money. There is a tendency to over-rate the power of government and to hold it responsible for matters over which it has little or no control.

Parker and Subramaniam argue that the overall responsibility of government for integration tends to produce within government itself a more intense integration than is common in private organisations with many different activities; and this can be carried to irrational lengths. In government administration there is often elaborate machinery for co-ordination, for seeing that one part does not step out of line with another, and that decisions pay regard to all interests. This produces the characteristically labyrinthine form of administration, as it has been called. Thus a public school or hospital, unlike its private equivalent, is treated as part of a larger State or regional organisation, with various lines of managerial and policy control and provision of specialised services.[24] The operating unit sometimes has little say in activities very important to it; as has been said, its top management looks up to a bureaucracy as well as down to one. One authority may have fixed its functions, a second its staff, a third the funds it gets, a fourth the building it occupies, and so on. Decision-making is bound by many rules of consultation and objection; many policies have lost their cutting-edge at the hands of an interdepartmental committee. This extends into the organisation of the public service itself, where recruitment and promotion tend to become encased in a similar framework of central control.

All this explains many characteristics of government departments, including so-called red tape, once defined as 'the application of a rule to the exception'. Files expand partly because every expenditure has to be justified, and partly to provide materials for answering questions, as any decision may be challenged sooner or later. There is less room for acting on hunches, because the basis of a hunch cannot be explained on paper. The emphasis on the need to avoid mistakes promotes a certain reluctance to take risks.

Nothing said in this chapter should be taken as implying a judgment about the relative merits of public servants and businessmen, or of public and private enterprise. The conclusion we may validly draw is that government is different from business in important ways, though many problems overlap; and that, to the extent that it is different, different talents are needed to operate it successfully. Most of the points we have made suggest that government is the harder sphere in which to achieve assured success. However, there are factors that tell in the other direction. At its best government can call upon a high degree of loyalty and devotion to the public interest. In Australia much research and developmental work that brings long-term advantages depends on the initiative of government, not simply because it commands the resources, but because it is less blinkered to their use. Some of the disadvantages that confront the public administrator can be reduced by public attitudes that encourage enterprise and experiment among public authorities, and do not judge them mainly by their mistakes; as well as by doing everything possible to introduce measures of efficiency into the public service, and incentives to economical working.

Convergence

There is also evidence that these distinctions are being eroded, and public and private sectors are moving closer together. Government, traditionally associated with regulatory functions, is entering into many new fields, and having to adapt its methods to them. There is a belief that methods that have improved efficiency and flexibility in the private sector, such as decentralised management, modern techniques of financial control and so on, are also applicable to the public sector. Conversely business is being pressed to accept social responsibilities, is coming more and more under the eye of law and opinion, and older models of the capitalist entrepreneur are more disfavoured. Within private organisations, the notion of a 'career service', once a characteristic mark of public services, is spreading, while there are signs of greater openness of recruitment in the public sector. (To note this convergence is not necessarily to approve it.)

There is the beginning of greater movement between public and private sectors, though it has not yet proceeded very far. Businessmen and a few trade unionists sit on the boards of government corporations; public servants sometimes join boards of directors on retirement, or less commonly resign to join private firms or trade associations, or are seconded for a period to the private sector. This closer contact does not only apply to the business world. The pattern of recruitment into public service is starting to change, to draw more widely on the outside world, whether into new types of permanent positions or as temporary consultants. The growing importance and changing composition and role of professional groups should be mentioned here—a variety of professionals, including architects, various kinds of natural scientist, sociologists, political scientists, lawyers and town-planners, are increasingly being drawn into the governmental orbit; and many of them move more readily than their predecessors between government, universities and other parts of the private sector. The relation between government and the professions has in other ways become close—governments take more interest in the educational system that produces them, and play an increasing part, directly or indirectly, in determining their pay and conditions of service.

The relations between public and private sectors are often market or trading relations, as well as ones involving central direction and control. Governments regulate and coerce industry through taxation, credit policy, tariffs, control of land use, and so on: but they also buy and sell to the private sector, and provide subsidised or free goods and services. In the nineteenth century Australian governments already sold land, built roads and railways, provided some port facilities and banking services, subsidised hospitals, made and sold electricity. In this century they also provide research aid, employment services, airport facilities and subsidised technical education; and in addition they assume part of the risks of enterprise in fields such as mineral exploration, export insurance and prices of farm produce.

Nowadays, typically 'a private firm mines public coal or oil, and sends it by private ships using public docks and navigational aids, or by public pipelines or freight railways, to a private gasworks or a public power generator'. The product may then pass to 'a private brickworks . . . to produce bricks, which go by private truck over public roads to (say) a Housing Commission building site. There a private contractor puts the bricks into a house which a public agent then sells to a private buyer . . . '.[25] This is one example of an intricate network of market interdependencies.

There is also a growing variety of 'intermediate' and liaison forms of organisation—statutory corporations, mixed enterprises, government-subsidised but semi-autonomous institutions such as universities, government agencies providing the facilities to the private sector mentioned above, or regulating the giving of financial aid to non-government institutions. Many private undertakings now work on contract to government, constructing public works or supplying equipment. In the two-airline system, Ansett is private, TAA public, but in terms of external regulation and internal organisation the similarities are more important than the differences. In all these ways, the relation between public and private sectors is becoming very different from the common stereotypes, and the dividing line between the two is becoming harder to draw. The two shade into one another, and the criteria for drawing lines are inevitably multiple: Who appoints to the governing board? Who controls finance, staffing, and so on? Who has the power to issue directions or monitor decisions? Behind these are even more difficult questions such as: What constitutes autonomy (see the discussion in Chapter Five)? Where does real (as opposed to formal) power lie? Is the occasional exercise of critically important power more significant than the regular exercise of more routine forms of influence?

One important kind of intermediate organisation—the statutory corporation—is discussed at length in Chapter Five. In Australia the term 'semi-government' was early applied to such bodies. In the literature of public administration, they are now classed among 'quasi-governmental organisations' (quagos). On the other hand, there are bodies that, though we still want to treat them as non-governmental, have acquired some special relation with government. These have been christened 'quasi-nongovernmental organisations' (quangos).[26] Such bodies still have the form of, and have often started as private agencies, but now heavily depend on government involvement to survive. The government may give them large subsidies, appoint some members of their boards, use them as its agents for certain purposes, as is true of many voluntary bodies in the field of the social services; or it may be that much of their work is on government contract. So a quango may range from a large private firm or voluntary hospital through 'scientific research institutes and welfare associations to a small Aboriginal self-help health care group spending Australian government money . . . '[27] Such bodies raise interesting new problems of public control and accountability.

It is likely that there will be more cases where the public and private sectors work together on shared projects. For example, Australian governments have not on the whole, unlike some other countries, sought private sector co-operation in what they regard as their own investment preserves, such as highways and public transport. A quite different kind of case is social welfare services where, if countries are not to be engulfed by a vast bureaucracy, governments will need to move somewhat away from the direct provision of services to facilitating community self-help. One future task of modern government administration will be to invent new ways of combining the efforts of government agencies and private concerns, from large corporations to consumer groups. There are resistances to co-operation on both sides, the latter on guard against government 'interference', while it has seemed one of the achievements of honest and efficient government administration to segregate the 'public' service from potentially embarrassing links with the private sector. But mixed-up the two will become, whether this is desirable or not and whether it be called market socialism, or neo-capitalism, or whatever.

Notes

1. cf. Herbert Kaufman, *Are Government Organizations Immortal?*, Brookings Institution, Washington, 1976.
2. Dwight Waldo, 'Does Management have a Future?', *Dialogue*, 10, 4, 1977, 102.
3. H.V. Emy, *Public Policy: Problems and Paradoxes*, Macmillan, Melbourne, 1976, 16.
4. Royal Commission on Australian Government Administration, *Report* (henceforth Report, RCAGA), AGPS, Canberra, 1976, 16.
5. Or, 'on the advice of', as cabinet appointments are formally made by the Governor-General, or Governor, in Council.

6. J.M. Pfiffner and R. Presthus, *Public Administration*, 5th edn, Ronald Press, New York, 1967, 15.
7. Norton E. Long, 'Power and Administration', *Public Admin. Review*, 9, 4, 1949, 257–8. Two valuable Australian articles are L.F. Crisp, 'Politics and the Commonwealth Public Service' and T.H. Rigby, 'Bureaucratic Politics', reprinted in R.N. Spann and G.R. Curnow (eds), *Public Policy and Administration: A Reader*, Wiley, Sydney, 1975.
8. See A. Dunsire, *Administration: the Word and the Science*, Martin Robertson, London, 1973. An appendix lists fifteen meanings of the word!
9. *ibid.*, 1.
10. *cit.* Geoffrey Blainey, 'The Politics of Big Business', *National Times*, 26–31 December 1977.
11. Desmond Keeling, *Management in Government*, Allen and Unwin, London, 1972, 27–8.
12. Sir Frederick Wheeler, 'Providing for Future Management Needs in the Commonwealth Service', *Public Admin.* (Sydney), XXX, 1, March 1971.
13. *Report*, (Fulton) Committee on the Civil Service, HMSO, London, 1968, I, 51.
14. B.B. Schaffer, 'The Distinction between Administrative and Executive Work', *Public Admin.* (Sydney), XVII, 2, June 1958, 118, reprinted in B.B. Schaffer, *The Administrative Factor*, Frank Cass, London, 1973.
15. H. Koontz and C. O'Donnell, *Principles of Management*, 3rd edn, McGraw–Hill, New York, 1964, 1.
16. B.M. Gross, *The Managing of Organizations*, Free Press, New York, 1964, II, 758.
17. B.B. Schaffer, 'Comparing Administrators, Research and Reforming', *Public Admin. Bulletin*, 22, December 1976.
18. Two books agreeing that there are great differences, though one is anti- and one is pro-government, are L. von Mises, *Bureaucracy*, Yale University Press, New Haven, 1962, and Paul Appleby, *Big Democracy*, Russell, New York, 1949. Three discussions that tend to stress similarities are in H.A. Simon, D.W. Smithburg and V.A. Thompson, *Public Administration*, Knopf, New York, 1961; R.S. Parker and V. Subramaniam, ' "Public" and "Private" Administration', *International Review of Administrative Sciences*, XXX, 4, 1964, 354–66; and Sir Geoffrey Vickers, 'Criteria of Success', in *Towards a Sociology of Management*, Chapman and Hall, London, 1967. See also Peter Self, *Administrative Theories and Politics*, Allen and Unwin, London, 1973, 261 ff.
19. For a sophisticated discussion, see Parker and Subramaniam, *op. cit.* and R.A. Dahl and C.E. Lindblom, *Politics, Economics and Welfare*, Harper, New York, 1953.
20. Keeling, *op. cit.*, 94.
21. Self, *op. cit.*, 266–7.
22. For the view that more competition between bureaucrats would promote efficiency, see W.A. Niskanen, *Bureaucracy: Servant or Master?*, Institute of Economic Affairs, London, 1973.
23. See James Q. Wilson and P. Rachal, 'Can the government regulate itself?', *The Public Interest*, 46, Winter 1977, 3–14.
24. cf. Self, *op. cit.*, 263.
25. Hugh Stretton, 'Business and Government', *Aust. J. Public Admin.*, XXXVI, 1, March 1977, 68.

26. For recent discussion, see D.C. Hague, W.J.M. Mackenzie and A. Barker, *Public Policy and Private Interests: The Institutions of Compromise*, Macmillan, London, 1975; articles by Desmond Keeling and Peter Self, 'Beyond the Ministerial Department: Mapping the Administrative Terrain', *Public Admin.* (London), 54, Summer 1976; articles by Roy Forward and R. Plehwe, *Aust. J. Public Admin.*, XXXV, 3, September 1976.
27. Forward, *op. cit.*, 248.

Chapter Two

The Australian Environment

An administrative system is not 'closed'; it lives within an environment by which it is influenced and on which it has effects. In the case of public administration, this environment includes the constitutional and political system, as well as the physical, economic, social and cultural setting.

The British Connection and Some Differences

Many features of this environment have set their mark on Australian government administration. First, Australian public life still bears many traces of the British connection. Administration works within the framework of a parliamentary and cabinet system. The public services share many features of British administration, including pragmatism, relative honesty and secretiveness, though there are also important differences. Australia was until modern times less concerned with foreign affairs, defence and the external world generally; on the other hand, it was earlier and more deeply involved in national development—already in the 1870s and 1880s public investment represented 30–40 per cent of total investment, about the same proportion as it does today. In 1900 public authorities in Australia employed about 10 per cent of the national workforce, which seems to have been twice the percentage employed by British and United States governments.[1] As well as building and operating the railways, Australian governments were providing many other forms of social overhead capital and employing a fair amount of direct labour in the process. Since then, though the public sector has continued to expand in Australia, it has grown faster elsewhere. Nowadays in Australia about 20 per cent of the working population are government employees, in Britain over 25 per cent, in the United States over 15 per cent.

This had its reactions on the characteristic forms of Australian public administration. For example, the professional expert and the manager played a relatively more important role, and the higher policy-maker and top-level negotiator a lesser role, than in Britain. Nowadays Australia has established its own group of policy-makers and international negotiators. Another consequence of the stress on physical development is that in earlier days the heads of the major State agencies concerned with public works, transport, agriculture seem to have counted for more than those who looked after health, welfare and education. Railways, in particular, dominated State budgets for a long period, and still accounted for nearly half of State government employment in 1939. Primary producers, manufacturers, mining companies and small towns anxious to grow have been in favour of 'economic development'; and this has been the main economic concern of the States, who have left the broader issues of economic management to Canberra and then concentrated on maximising the resources available to them for expenditure on their own plans. In recent years, the development ethos has been under attack in State politics, prominently from the environmentalist lobby, but more importantly and pervasively from the competition of consumerism and the welfare state.[2] This is reflected in many fields, from the creation of Departments of Consumer Affairs to the pressures on governments to expand educational, cultural and social welfare programmes.

One important result of the British connection is that Australia did not develop an American 'spoils system' in public employment. Many of the obstacles that the British system of government placed in the way of this also applied in Australia.[3] Nor did self-government, achieved as it was without great trouble, leave a legacy of political suspicion or hostility directed towards the bureaucracy, such as has existed in many new countries. It is also noteworthy that what Australians were asking for in the mid-nineteenth century was 'self-government'—transfer of power from London to the colonies, and in some quarters more democratic elections. There was little demand for 'responsible government', a notion still fairly novel in Britain itself, indeed most Australians still thought of the Governors as choosing the executive and many, as in South Australia, positively feared the prospect of short-lived ministries answerable to parliament and faction, wielding patronage and trying to run the departments.[4]

In fact Australians got responsible government, and did not receive it unwillingly. But some features of the old system survived. The existing structure of departments was only imperfectly assimilated to the new ministries (see Chapter Three). The practice of giving public officials their own statutory powers, common before self-government, continued after it, and it was not an established convention that official heads of departments were subject in all matters to a minister.[5] Indeed, in certain respects this has survived until the present day (see Chapter Three).

Public Attitudes

It has been argued that Australians have distrusted the State less than most peoples, and viewed it in a utilitarian way 'as a vast public utility, whose duty it is to provide the greatest happiness for the greatest number'.[6] This may be partly a question of scale. Government presents itself as a more controllable enterprise in a sparsely populated country—or six countries, as Australia still was in 1900 and remained, for most purposes, until the Second World War. There was also the inhospitable physical character of much of the country; the small and (outside the capital cities) scattered population often looked to governments for the funds for development. The image of government was a fairly pedestrian one, as none of the six colonies had much of the glamour and prestige of a nation-state, even less of a great power. The main accusation made against officials was their failure to be business-like, to practise 'economy and efficiency', and they were sometimes much criticised by the established classes. On the other hand, their fairly democratic promotion system and centralised character offered some of the best chances for an able person without money or influence to rise to the top of a great organisation.

In fact Australian attitudes to government have been more complex than the Hancock quotation suggests. Kewley, for example, speaks of paradoxical elements in nineteenth century views, 'a powerful demand for State action to promote development and later, to regulate the collective conditions of labour, combined with some reluctance to accept State action to relieve individual need'.[7] The supply of social welfare services above the level of minimum means-tested cash benefits has often been left to the private sector; such services as public housing have remained at a modest level, and much of that sold off to occupiers, so that under 5 per cent of dwellings are rented from public authorities.

Australia has often been regarded as an egalitarian society, with a disrespect for 'tall poppies'. The classic statement of this view is also in Hancock's *Australia*. 'The ideal of mateship, which appeals very strongly to the ordinary good-hearted Australian, springs, not only from his eagerness to exalt the humble and meek, but also from his zeal to put down the mighty from their seat.'[8] Even those who point to objective inequalities of wealth and status that seem to go against this account, would still claim that in their social attitudes Australians have had a strong sense of human equality. Russel Ward[9] has attempted to trace the historical origins of this, though his particular version has been challenged; and its distinctive character is probably being eroded, as the country is subjected to the same forces that operate in all prosperous societies. Still, there remain some economic and social facts that underpin the feeling of equality. Inequalities of wealth, though considerable, are in fact less than in most countries. Outside Aboriginal communities, there are few territorial zones of blatant under-privilege; differences of income per head between the States are remarkably small (see Table 7.2, Chapter Seven), and no federation does more to equalise conditions between its units.

The disrespect for authority is harder to establish than the sense of equality. It is true only at a superficial name-calling level, but the theory that Australians are a lawless, even a violent people dies hard in some overseas countries. This theory is not borne out by attitude surveys, nor by statistics of behaviour. Indeed some sociologists, with equal exaggeration, have maintained that Australia is a highly authoritarian and conformist country.

Whatever the truth about attitudes, Australians have shown a considerable disposition to accept official authority in practice. Some writers have argued that this is the other face of equality. Bureaucracy 'is the very model of the regime which acts by the rule of equality'.[10] It is true that pressure groups have been active in seeking safeguards or special privileges for their clientele, but even the latter have often exhibited less than the normally low rank-and-file activism, and have passed fairly readily under the control of their own institutional elites. This is in part the product of the Australian easy-going nature and pragmatism—a general disposition, so long as directly felt injustices and problems can be mitigated, to allow leaders to run the country's higher affairs and to argue with and check one another.

Indeed, pressure group activity has contributed to bureaucratisation; governments have responded by making regulations or setting up a board to protect the group concerned or to settle group differences. Miller and Jinks have spoken of the Australian tendency 'to put the force of the *state* to work for the adjustment of group demands and to do this without overtly involving the *government*, in the sense of the ministry of the day'.[11] The best examples are the Commonwealth and State arbitration courts that make wage awards with the force of law. Respect for their judges has contributed to the success of these courts. Though strikers may from time to time defy their rulings, powerful forces operate to maintain the system.

As in other spheres, Australian aggressions sometimes look menacing or anarchical, but soon blow over, or decay into the defence of petty gains. This seems to derive in part from the homogeneous character of the population (with the important exception of Aborigines) through much of its history, in terms of ethnicity, class and general way of life, and the widely spread view that impartial and fair ways of settling differences exist. It is significant that judges have not only ruled arbitration tribunals and the ordinary courts, but have been called upon to make findings as sole Royal Commissioners on a wide variety of topics, from fluoridation to whales, regarding which they have no special claim to expertise. This homogeneity is now under challenge as a result of post-war immigration, though visible signs of the challenge are still small.

The Role of the Public Service

Among the institutional elites of Australian society, public servants occupy an important place. Australia has an executive-biased political system, in which Prime Ministers and State Premiers play a key role. Parliaments rarely have a large supply of able members, and operate fewer formal controls on administration than in most countries. Ministers have often had political skills and interests, rather than executive capacity or experience. This has helped to give senior departmental officers and the executive heads of the large statutory corporations considerable influence, especially when they have worked with a strong head of government.

Public officers have played a major part in Australian history; if their names are often forgotten it is because all names fade that leave no conspicuous monument and fail to interest historians. Even so, 'educational policy in Victoria is identified with the name of Frank Tate, and in New South Wales with those of Peter Board and Harold Wyndham'; the 'building of railways, of great bridges, of water supply projects, electricity generating enterprises . . . with names like Speight, O'Connor, Bradfield, Hudson and Monash. In other cases, leading officials have become dominant figures over the whole range of State administration . . . like J.D. Story, in Queensland, and Wallace Wurth in New South Wales.'[12] There is also the remarkable place of the economist–public servant in modern Australia.

The federal system has helped in this process. The constitution has been hard to amend, and much of the burden of adapting it to changing needs has fallen to the administrator, devising and operating schemes of federal assistance to the States, negotiating other forms of inter-governmental co-operation in the background of Premiers Conferences and Loan Council meetings, and at interstate official gatherings. The working of Australian federalism at the official level is still a relatively unexplored subject.

One reflection of the strength of the bureaucracy has been that between 1928 and 1973 no major outside inquiry into any Australian public service, or into public administration generally, took place.[13] There was no equivalent of the United States Hoover Commissions or the Canadian Glassco Commission; the Commonwealth Committee on Recruitment, which reported in 1959, is a partial exception, but it had limited terms of reference. Some credit must be given to the fairly smooth progress of Australian affairs after the Second World War. Things changed in the 1970s when three States and the Commonwealth undertook wide-ranging investigations.

Geographical Factors

An important factor has been Australia's geography and the political, economic and demographic patterns related to it. The early emphasis on opening-up the continent, or its more exploitable parts, made Departments of Lands and Mines and Railways strategically important in the nineteenth century, and gave administrations a special concern for development. In this process the government corporation has, since the 1880s, played a striking part (see Chapter Five).

Geography has influenced the federal system itself. Federation had no basis in heterogeneity of population, nor were there major differences of economic interest between the units. The need for a federal solution arose mainly because the present States and their capital cities were on the scene first, and the case for even limited formal unity was only slowly accepted in an isolated and dispersed country. As late as 1939, 82 per cent of government employees still worked for State and local authorities, a figure that fell to 70 per cent as a result of the war but has since remained remarkably stable.

Geoffrey Blainey has analysed the impact of distance on Australian history,[14] both physical isolation from the great world centres and the problem of internal communications. Australia has a land area of nearly eight million square kilometres, more than half as large again as Europe excluding the USSR and approaching the size of the United States. Yet its population had only reached three million by the late 1880s, six million by the late 1920s, twelve million by the late 1960s, and over fourteen million in 1978. The population has always been concentrated in the capital cities; a quarter lived in the cities in 1871, and this figure had risen to over 60 per cent by 1971.

A good account of the effects of isolation and distance on Australian government is lacking (Blainey deals mainly with its economic impact). It helped to promote some experiment and novelty, at least up to the early twentieth century. It encouraged self-reliance and a practical approach to immediate problems, but may also have led to some failure to learn lessons in the light of inescapable comparisons with others. Isolation has helped Australia to have a peaceful history. The wars in which it has taken part were until 1942 far away, and there have been fewer internal conflicts than in most countries. By international standards it has had to face little in the way of major crises in economy or society involving fundamental adjustments. This has been a happy circumstance, but it deprived the country of another stimulus to self-criticism and reform. The Australian States were none too anxious to learn lessons even from one another, and mutual isolation helped this, as borders were mostly not drawn where contact mattered. All this is now changing.

Isolation went along with a land mostly resistant to closer settlement and a population either widely scattered or concentrated in a few capital cities, on or near the coast, far distant from one another. Each capital became the centre of export and import for its colony, attracted manufacturing industry, was the seat of centralised government, the developing professions and the main newspapers. Indeed according to some historians, metropolitan–country relations have been characterised by 'closeness' rather than 'distance'.[15] The country has often depended on services supplied in and from the city; city and country interests in each State have acted together, as well as been opposed. From the city, the education and police services were run, as were lands and mines and railways. Outside the cities, the main public services were provided by officials 'whose roots were not in the area . . . and who looked to 'head office' or the 'department' for promotion and a change of scene'.[16] They owed no direct allegiance to local MPs or local councils clamouring for new roads, schools or hospitals.

The dominance of capitals had some good results. It made possible reasonably efficient and powerful State governments, and Australia has not suffered, as America has, from grave administrative weakness at this level of the federal system. On most matters the writ of government ran effectively through each colony, even in the days of 'landtaking'. The national government, when it was created, could draw on the services of an experienced bureaucracy. The States have provided a more uniform service to rich and poor areas, town and country, than smaller units would have done. On the other hand, dominant capitals helped to bureaucratise administration. One of the continuing problems of Australian administration is to create viable units of decentralisation, regional or local, able to some degree to stand on their own feet and flexibly adapt their methods to the communities they serve. Local government has had a chequered history.

One can only speculate on the interactions of large capitals and long distances. In some ways the former have mitigated the effects of the latter. They were, as we have said, effective bases for centralised government of each colony. Some capitals were large enough to develop an intellectual life and vitality of their own. Of course, there has been much parochialism bred by distance, with each small country town wanting its own local council and its own share of the State's pork-barrel. But there has been enough traffic linking the main centres with one another, and with their hinterland, to limit the degree of provincial isolation and income-variation that might otherwise have existed, and that did come to exist in parts of America and Canada. However, the focussing of each colony on its own capital also encouraged a different kind of separatism engendered by distance and promoted a form of 'metropolitan provincialism', capitals which (so far as they looked outside) looked to London rather than to one another.[17]

Much of this belongs to the past. New ideas and devices now reach Australia as quickly as they do most other countries. Sydney knows as much of Melbourne as Manchester does of Birmingham, and more than London knows of Glasgow, or New York of Chicago. Air travel has revolutionised inter-elite contacts. But Canberra politicians still commute to distant coastal cities and country towns, university students still rarely get their education outside their own State capital. Distance, in spite of television, has lessened public awareness of the problems of controlling new mineral enterprises or of the plight of Aborigines—until recently, almost as exotic to Australians as to foreigners. Australia's physical isolation as a western country nearer (but still not very near) to Asia than to the countries with which it has most in common, still has important effects on its external policies.

Notes

1. A. Barnard, N.G. Butlin and J.J. Pincus, 'Public and Private Sector Employment in Australia', *Aust. Econ. Review*, 1st qtr, 1977, 45.
2. cf. Martin Painter, 'New Forces in State Politics', *Current Affairs Bulletin*, 53, 8, January 1977, 16.
3. For discussion, see Henry Parris, *Constitutional Bureaucracy*, Allen and Unwin, London, 1969, 29–33.
4. See John M. Ward, 'The Responsible Government Question in Victoria, South Australia and Tasmania, 1851–1856', *J. Royal Aust. Hist. Soc.*, 63, 4, March 1978.
5. See R.L. Wettenhall, 'The Ministerial Department', *Public Admin.* (Sydney), XXXII, 3, September 1973, 233–60.

6. W.K. Hancock, *Australia*, Benn, London, 1930, 72.
7. T.H. Kewley, *Social Security in Australia*, 2nd edn, Sydney University Press, Sydney, 1973, 7.
8. *op. cit.*, 74.
9. *The Australian Legend*, Oxford University Press, Melbourne 1958. For a summary of relevant writing, see S. Encel, *Equality and Authority: A Study of Class, Status and Power in Australia*, Cheshire, Melbourne 1970, ch. 4.
10. John H. Schaar, 'Some Ways of Thinking About Equality', *J. Politics*, 26, 4, 1964, cit. S. Encel, *op. cit.*, 57.
11. J.D.B. Miller and Brian Jinks, *Australian Government and Politics*, 4th edn., Duckworth, London, 1970, 115.
12. S. Encel, *op. cit.*, 71.
13. cf. R.L. Wettenhall, 'A Brief History of Public Service Inquiries', in R.F.I. Smith and Patrick Weller (eds), *Public Service Inquiries in Australia*, University of Queensland Press, St Lucia, 1978, 21.
14. Geoffrey Blainey, *The Tyranny of Distance*, Macmillan, Melbourne, 1966.
15. On the dominance of capital cities, see the excellent discussion in J.B. Hirst, *Adelaide and the Country 1870–1917*, Melbourne University Press, Melbourne, 1973, ch. 3; and cf. I.H. Burnley (ed.), *Urbanization in Australia*, Cambridge University Press, Cambridge, 1974.
16. J.D.B. Miller, *Australia*, Thames and Hudson, London, 1966, 12.
17. Sean Glynn, *Urbanization in Australian History, 1788–1900*, Nelson, Melbourne, 1970, 37, 48.

Part II
STRUCTURES

Chapter Three

Structure and Functions of Government

Parliament

The Commonwealth Parliament is easily the largest in Australia (in 1978 it had 188 members in its two Houses, compared with 144 in New South Wales); and its ministry is also the largest, usually now with twenty-five or more ministers (there are nineteen in New South Wales, eighteen in Victoria), though for much of the period since 1956 only about half of these have been included in the Commonwealth Cabinet.

Parliamentarians can and do intercede with administrative agencies to consider the individual claims and grievances of their constituents. Apart from this, the direct influence of parliament in most administrative fields is not great. Members are free to state their view on administrative matters in debate, ask questions of ministers, and can sometimes be influential on a particular issue, especially if it affects individual rights or the member's electorate. But governments usually keep firm control over legislation and policy-making, and in general have discouraged the development of parliamentary committees to inquire into administrative questions. Discussions of the reports of government agencies are rare, and some departments are not even required to publish an annual report. (The Coombs Commission thought that they all should, and suggested what might be included.)[1]

There is always a handful of members who take an interest in administrative questions[2] and there have been a few parliamentary committees concerned with such matters. Probably the most important has been the Commonwealth Parliament's Joint Committee of Public Accounts (see Chapter Sixteen)—set up in 1951 to examine government accounts and to report to Parliament—which had issued over 160 reports by 1977. Several States have similar bodies. The Senate Committee on Regulations and Ordinances scrutinises delegated legislation (see Chapter Six). The role of parliamentary committees of inquiry expanded in the later 1960s and early 1970s, especially because the Senate experimented in the wider use of committees, and was able to do so because for some years governments had uncertain political control of that body.

The Coombs Report discussed some ways in which parliamentary scrutiny of administration might be improved, but made no strikingly original suggestions.[3] Indeed, no one has thought of any very convincing method of giving parliaments more effective control than they have at present. There is even dispute about whether direct parliamentary control of administration should be increased. Critics argue that it easily becomes 'tinkering', and reduces administrative efficiency by leading to excessive fear of minor error, elaborate record-keeping and hindering decentralisation and long-term planning.[4] Whatever one's views on this, the quality and realism of parliamentary intervention are improved when members are well-informed on administrative issues. One important virtue of parliamentary committees on specialised aspects of administration is their role in educating members.

Cabinets

The major instruments of administrative control in Australia are the Commonwealth and State cabinets. The cabinet is, in Bagehot's words, 'a *hyphen* which joins, a *buckle* which fastens politics and administration'. While it holds its parliamentary majority, it is very powerful. Parliament approves legislation affecting government agencies, including the budget; but the initiative in introducing this legislation rests largely with ministers, acting with cabinet approval. On many important matters of policy and planning that do not involve legislative changes it is usually the final authority. In the administrative area, it is the final arbiter on the basic structure and organisation of departments, which in Australia is mostly settled by executive action not by legislation, and on many of the most senior administrative appointments.

It is sometimes hard to distinguish the cabinet's role from that of its chairman, the Prime Minister or (in the States) Premier, especially as its proceedings are secret. He certainly has a major voice in many appointments, including the allocation of ministerial portfolios. When the cabinet meets, he has the normal power of a chairman, fortified by his prestige as party leader and head of the government. How he uses it also lies partly within his discretion—for example, he may develop an informal 'inner cabinet', encourage or discourage discussion of emerging policy issues, make more or less use of committees, and so on. In Australia, Prime Minister and Premiers play a special part in federal relations, through agencies such as the Premiers Conference (see Chapter Eight). However, the cabinet still has substantial collective importance. Because it is a political as well as an administrative body, its size and composition cannot be determined only by administrative considerations.[5]

In 1978 the Commonwealth cabinet had fourteen members. A large number of ministers (thirteen) were not in the cabinet, mainly because of the desire to keep it to a manageable size; for example, the Ministers for the Northern Territory, Construction, Health, Immigration were not in the 1978 cabinet. Such ministers were still responsible for their own departments; they could attend meetings when summoned, as when the business of their own departments is under consideration; they could sit on cabinet committees, and there were occasional meetings of the full ministry. The size of the cabinet is usually at the Prime Minister's discretion, though in 1972–75 the large Whitlam Cabinet of twenty-seven represented Caucus preference, not that of the Prime Minister. The six State cabinets include all ministers, and vary from 19 (New South Wales), and 18 (Queensland and Victoria) to 10 (Tasmania).

In Australia there is nothing to prevent the States from appointing salaried assistant ministers solely to help other ministers, on British lines, but they rarely see the need. In the Commonwealth government, there is said to be a constitutional obstacle, as a minister must according to section 64 of the Constitution have a department to administer, but it appears that this could be got around.[6] Some unsalaried posts of this kind have been created by the Commonwealth from time to time; and some regular ministers, in addition to having their own departments, also assist the more heavily-burdened ministers, such as the Prime Minister, the Minister for Trade and Resources, or the Minister for Defence. Thus in 1978 the Minister for Aboriginal Affairs was also designated Minister Assisting the Prime Minister, including Public Service Matters.

The cabinet meets when the Prime Minister or Premier summons it, usually weekly, and he decides the agenda, though a minister or ministers may have taken the initiative in getting a particular item discussed and circulated written submissions on the matter. Especially in the Commonwealth, the administration of these proceedings (circulating papers, drafting the agenda and minutes, and so on) has become a major task, and the Department of the Prime Minister and Cabinet services the cabinet and its committees, including taking minutes at meetings. A modern cabinet may well deal with several hundred items a year—between December 1972 and October 1974 the Commonwealth cabinet received 1304 submissions.[7] The States have less complex machinery, though the Premier's Department may prepare a draft agenda and papers, and follow up decisions. In New South Wales, at least under Liberal–Country Party government, the Under Secretary of the Premier's Department attended meetings and recorded decisions. In Victoria and Western Australia a member of parliament is appointed as Parliamentary Secretary to the Cabinet to do this job. Most State Cabinets still prefer to meet without officials being present.

The Commonwealth and some State cabinets make use of committees. Their existence and membership may be unpublished, though this secrecy is rarer than it used to be. This topic is dealt with more fully in Chapter Fifteen, but one or two examples may be quoted here. There has been for some years in the Commonwealth a Foreign Affairs and Defence Committee, though its importance has fluctuated. A Legislation Committee examines draft bills and regulations; a General Administrative Committee and a Machinery of Government Committee are concerned with administrative matters, departmental functions, and so on. *Ad hoc* cabinet committees may be set up from time to time to deal with particular current issues. In the Commonwealth both kinds of committee include ministers from outside the cabinet, and they sometimes have power to make decisions without referring them to the cabinet. Such committees can complicate the life of the Prime Minister or Premier, who finds it necessary to chair the most important ones himself; this is one reason why they sometimes fall into desuetude. At times a parallel committee of officials will service a ministerial committee.

One important function the cabinet can play is that of a confidential forum for the settlement of major interdepartmental disputes, and a body that helps to keep the various departments in step with one another; it can play this role, but often it does not (on the limitations of cabinets as co-ordinators, see Chapter Fifteen). It is also the main formal source of major policy decisions, to which ministers will bring problems and proposals of consequence in their own fields of activity, or to which the Prime Minister or Premier himself will bring matters he wishes to raise and have discussed or decided. There is no code that lays down what ministers should take to cabinet rather than decide themselves—one can only say, in a general way, that they include important new policies; major disagreements that require resolution at the highest level; issues, not necessarily major, likely to lead (or which have led) to outside controversy or serious public criticism; all proposals involving legislation as, even if uncontroversial, these will take up parliamentary time so a case must be made for their priority.[8] A new policy may involve large new expenditures, in which case both budgetary authority and cabinet will have to be satisfied; or it may, for example, be likely to have a major impact on Commonwealth–State relations, or on unemployment. These are the sorts of matters that should be dealt with by cabinet, though they by no means always are. A strong Prime Minister or Premier may have views to the contrary, and prevent an item from reaching the agenda. Conversely, quite minor matters may get there, if a minister digs in his heels; just as important issues may not get there, if the relevant departments are agreed on policy or prefer to settle the matter 'out of court'.

Since the Second World War, the Prime Minister's position has been reinforced in a number of ways and one example especially relevant to this chapter is the growth of his own staff of public servants. We have already mentioned the Department of the Prime Minister and Cabinet. As well as servicing the cabinet, it also has a group of senior officers responsible for assisting the Prime Minister in his co-ordinating and policy-forming functions. The growth of this staff has given him an independent source of policy advice, distinct from the regular departments. This topic is further discussed in Chapter Fifteen. In the States, the Premier is often also Treasurer, so the Treasury is his Department, but Premier's Departments have also developed to assist him. The influence of these has also been increasing, as has that of personal assistants to some Premiers. In both Commonwealth and States, there is some trend to a more Presidential style of government.

Administrative Responsibility to Parliament

What is meant by the statement that 'a minister is responsible for all the operations of an ordinary department'? Primarily it means that in this realm powers and duties are conferred by statute, or by virtue of the Royal prerogative, upon ministers, and not upon 'departments' or public servants. In performing their departmental duties the latter are simply exercising the powers of a minister. For this reason it is ministers and ministers alone who can report, explain and defend in parliament, whether in answer to questions or in ordinary debate, what is done in the exercise of their powers and duties. (It is true that public servants as well as ministers may be answerable in the courts for illegal acts under certain circumstances.) Because this is one of parliament's main ways of exercising control over administration, it expects ministers to answer politically for departmental acts. This is still an important form of control, as ministers do not like being made fools of in public, and their reputations will be damaged if their departments are regularly in trouble.[9]

It has often been said that ministerial responsibility also involves the liability of a minister to resign if parliament disapproves of some act or omission of his department, whether or not the minister knew or approved of what the public servant in question had done. However, this view has been questioned, not only because parliaments have excused ministers when officials acted without their approval or knowledge, but also because enforced resignations, even when the minister's personal responsibility was clear, have been very rare.[10] In the complex modern world it seems to be accepted that public servants are bound to do many things without the minister's approval or knowledge, and with which the minister could not reasonably have been expected to concern himself. It is even nowadays not unknown for Australian ministers publicly to censure officials if something goes wrong, though such open attempts to disclaim responsibility are liable to backfire. Some people argue that public servants should be open to such public criticism for their misdoings. If so, they should presumably also be allowed to reply to criticism, which at present they are not; and perhaps also to claim public praise for their achievements, and not let these be credited to the minister!

There are some exceptions, or partial exceptions, to the general rule of ministerial responsibility as stated above. There are cases where certain public servants are vested with statutory powers and responsibilities in their own right, by legislation which does not always declare that the exercise of these powers is subject to ministerial direction. There are, of course, a few 'non-ministerial' officials on whom parliaments have conferred statutory powers, such as the Auditor-General (see Chapter Sixteen), the Solicitor-General and the Public Trustee. But their special position is well-recognised and not in dispute. The Auditor-General is deliberately freed from ministerial control so that he can make an independent report to parliament on irregularities in the government accounts. The more interesting case is where an officer normally regarded as subordinate to a minister, such as the permanent head of a department, is given some power or duty of his own by legislation, as happens in a few instances.

The origins of this practice have been traced back to the period before responsible government, when there were no ministers in whom to vest powers.[11] It has been argued in such cases that there is an implied qualification that the official should act in accordance with ministerial policy. However, though this may sometimes be true, 'there can certainly be no universal rule' to this effect,[12] and Australian governments and courts have not behaved as though there was such a rule. In one well-known Australian case, which concerned the statutory power granted to the Director-General of Civil Aviation (then the permanent head of his department) to issue licences for the import of aircraft, the judges were divided in their view of the weight that he might properly give to ministerial policy.[13]

There is one example of a very broad statutory power vested in permanent heads. Section 25(2) of the Commonwealth Public Service Act says that:

> The Permanent Head of the Department shall be responsible for its general working and for all the business thereof, and shall advise the Minister in all matters relating to the Department.

There is dispute about how far this constitutes a legal limitation on a minister's authority to intervene in matters of departmental management, but some writers maintain that it does.[14]

It should also be noted that the quotation with which this section began referred to 'ordinary departments'. But there are also many non-departmental agencies. Many Acts of Parliament (statutes) give powers and duties to so-called statutory authorities, or various types of administrative boards or commissioners—ranging from those in charge of public enterprises such as TAA or the State electricity commissions, through executive agencies such as the Health Insurance Commission managing new programmes, to regulatory bodies such as the Trade Practices Commission, and to marketing boards for primary products and registration boards set up to maintain standards in the trades and professions. Such statutory authorities (on which see Chapter Five) have no right to appear in parliament to explain or defend their acts and policies. In some cases it is public policy that they should be as independent as possible in carrying out their functions, provided they do not exceed the powers conferred on them by statute. It is true that the power of granting money constitutes an indirect form of parliamentary and governmental control over many non-departmental agencies (even those with a large degree of formal independence like the universities). So does the government's power to appoint all or some of the members of their controlling bodies. They may also be subject to other kinds of control by a minister, but often this falls well short of the control that the minister has over his own department.

The question of the actual relationship of Australian ministers and permanent officials is discussed in Chapter Ten. Detailed ministerial control of administration is probably more effective in the States than in the Commonwealth, and more effective in a small State like Tasmania than in a large and populous one like Victoria or New South Wales. Adequate knowledge and control of the working machinery of their departments is made more difficult for Commonwealth ministers, not only by the dispersal of their staff throughout Australia and by the fact that one or two departments still have main offices in Melbourne, but also because their own offices are concentrated in Parliament House in Canberra, so that often they do not work inside their own departments as is generally the practice in the States (and also in Britain). The State parliaments sit less often, and the ministers are nearer home, so they tend to be more closely involved with their departments than in Canberra. A State minister may do much work that would be left to the permanent head of a Commonwealth department.

Departmental Structure

The Nature of Departments

According to section 64 of the Commonwealth Constitution, the 'department of state' is the main agency of executive government, though what this is is nowhere defined. A special legal enactment is not usually required to create, abolish, subdivide or reorganise a department, the executive government has wide power to do this without consulting parliament. In the Commonwealth, the power derives partly from section 61 of the Constitution, but also from section 64 which implies that the Governor-General in Council has the authority to create departments of State. More generally, the power is inherent in the notion mentioned earlier that departments are merely the instruments of ministerial action.

This illustrates the fact that Australian governments do not depend for their power simply on legal authority given them by parliament. They have their own 'executive power', which includes the residue of the old prerogative powers vested in the Queen and her representatives, the Governor-General and Governors, now normally exercised on the advice of ministers. This enables governments to take various kinds of actions having legal consequences without parliamentary sanction. Some interesting examples of this occurred during the period of the 1972–75 Whitlam Labor government.[15] Apart from new departments created by executive action, many other agencies and programmes were established in this way, without supporting parliamentary legislation, such as the Australian Legal Aid Office and the Australian Assistance Plan. Most Commonwealth departments have been established by order of the Governor-General in Council, embodied in an Executive Council minute, and departments in the States may similarly be created by the Governor in Council. When the Whitlam government came to power, an Administrative Arrangements Order of 20 December 1972 abolished fourteen existing departments, and created a large number of new ones; this was all done (so to speak) by a stroke of the pen. However, departments have in the past sometimes been established by Act of Parliament or, on the other hand, simply by a cabinet minute.

If any official definition of a department existed, it would probably refer to a group of public servants organised under a single permanent head responsible directly to a minister. In the Commonwealth the number of such departments usually corresponds closely to the number of ministers. In the States, ministers are more often each in charge of several departments, as well as of other types of government agency. This situation derives from the beginnings of responsible government, when in many colonies the cabinet system was grafted on to a pre-existing structure of departments and boards; though there have been many consolidations since, there have also been Premiers who enjoyed multiplying the number of government agencies. So in 1975 eleven South Australian ministers supervised forty-six departments, though this number has since been cut to thirty-two. In New South Wales and Victoria there has been more consolidation, though even there the picture is diverse. In New South Wales some ministers look after more than one department, others have no department to look after, only statutory author-ities; in the case of the Department of the Attorney-General and Justice two ministers of equal standing share one department.

Of course, creating or rearranging administrative departments does not in itself increase the total range of legal powers available to ministers. However, Australian statutes granting powers to, or imposing duties upon ministers commonly refer to 'the Minister', without further specification. The allocation of these powers and duties to particular ministers is thus left to be determined by the Prime Minister or Premier or by cabinet decision, and may be varied from time to time by executive action. So the jurisdiction of a particular minister can be altered as well as the scope of departments, within the ambit of the powers available to the government as a whole from acts of parliament or the royal prerogative. In this respect, as in others, the Australian department is a very flexible and adaptable instrument of government. An interesting example of this flexibility is to be found in an Executive Minute and Administrative Arrangements Order of 22 December 1975, to be found in the Gazette of that day. The Department of Administrative Services was abolished—but a new Department of Administrative Services was created, with a different permanent head. This was not merely a way of changing the permanent head, but also of considerably altering the department's functions.

So one may say that two general features of Australian departments are that they are each responsible through a permanent head to a minister; and that their existence and the division of functions between them may be, and often is, determined by executive action not legislation. A third feature discussed later in this book is that they are fully subject to 'Treasury control' of their finances, Public Service Board control of staffing, and the standard controls exercised by common service agencies over building, accommodation, equipment and so on. This serves to differentiate them from some, though by no means all, statutory authorities (see Chapter Five).

There is no word to describe the total jurisdiction of a minister, where this includes more than one department, or a department and a variety of other units. The word Ministry has been suggested but there are difficulties about this, especially as it is used in some Australian States to describe small staff units or secretariats set up to aid ministers in their co-ordinating, supervisory and policy-guiding functions; or co-ordinating departments super-imposed on existing agencies, often statutory authorities. Thus in New South Wales there are Ministries in such fields as transport and education, and in Victoria for transport, planning, the arts, and so on. These are often areas where important executive functions are carried out by statutory corporations, or where largely autonomous bodies such as universities and colleges of advanced education are involved.[16]

Departmental Organisation

Under the minister, the permanent official head of a department is often called the Secretary in Commonwealth departments, or Under Secretary in some States; but other titles are also used nowadays, such as Director-General or Director. The permanent head usually combines the role of chief official adviser to the minister with that of a kind of general manager of the department.[17] In many Commonwealth and some State departments, there will be one or more Deputy Secretaries or Deputy Under Secretaries to assist the permanent head in supervising the department, and to relieve him of part of his workload.

Then come the main divisions and branches of the department. In many Commonwealth departments, there are five to seven First Assistant Secretaries in charge of the major operating units of the department, called divisions; in a few departments, more than ten. Below them come Assistant Secretaries who head the Branches into which each division is divided. Below branch level, forms of organisation differ widely between departments. The basis of the divisional and branch structure naturally varies a good deal, and generalisations are hazardous. There is quite commonly a management services unit, in charge of personnel, finance and organisa-tion matters throughout the department. Although the First Assistant Secretary (Management Services) or his equivalent may have close contact with Public Service Board and Treasury, he is wholly responsible to the permanent head. There may be a separate policy and research division, or planning and research division. Then there are likely to be some major subdivisions based on the main substantive responsibilities of the depart-ment, for example, in 1978 the Department of Social Security had divisions for Benefits, Rehabilitation, Social Welfare and a separate Office of Child Care.

The rest of the organisation varies according to the character of the department. For instance, there are comparatively small 'policy' departments such as the Commonwealth Department of Industry and Commerce or 'co-ordinating' departments such as the New South Wales Ministry of Transport, whose staffs are largely accommodated in a single office in a capital city. In contrast are the big departments that operate extensive services to the public or to other government agencies and may have large regional organisations, such as the Department of Social Security or the State Departments of Agriculture, Lands or Public Works. The big Commonwealth departments generally use State boundaries for purposes of territorial decentralisation, and each State division will be headed by a State Director or equivalent senior officer, with a large office controlling operations within the State. Similarly among New South Wales State departments, for example, there is decentralisation to regional directors in Education, Public Works, and so on. In other departments, there are directors of specialised bureaux, such as the Bureau of Agricultural Economics in the Commonwealth Department of Primary Industry.

In the States, the heads of divisions and branches may have very various titles. This is partly because professional officers are more important in State administration. In New South Wales a division is sometimes headed by a 'Chief of Division' or 'Director', but the title of a branch or divisional head may be occupational, such as accountant, chief architect, chief inspector, chief engineer, legal officer, and so on.

Collegiality

Some departments have formal provision for some 'collegiality', collective discussion or decision-making, at or near the top of the agency. The 'weekly morning prayer meeting' is becoming quite common. The importance of many such arrangements should not be exaggerated—they usually still leave the permanent head free to go away and do something different if he wants. Some departments have, at least on paper, boards of management or collective executives, but their role is often less exalted than their title. The formal groups vary in size from relatively small meetings confined to a few immediate subordinates of the permanent head, a kind of inner cabinet, to larger weekly meetings of all second division staff or their equivalents. The latter kind of group may be mainly for information exchange and informal discussion, but one or two are more formal bodies that keep minutes and even take certain decisions.

There have been suggestions that this growth of 'collegiality' should be formally recognised by the creation of some kind of executive board or corporate management structure for departments, and there are a few cases in the States where an important ministerial department has been 'put into commission'. An interesting example is the five-member Health Commission of New South Wales, set up as a result of the 1969 Report into Community Health Services, to replace the Department of Health. It was a 'functional' board, with both medical and non-medical members, but in 1978 the requirement was dropped that each should have a designated office. The next layer is largely decentralised to regional directors. Health commissions of varying composition have since been established in some other States, such as South Australia and Victoria. One alleged advantage of a board is that it is possible to introduce a representative element. The New South Wales Teachers' Federation has been agitating for years for an Education Commission with executive powers on which it would be strongly represented, and in 1978 it seemed close to achieving this.

However, it is hard to imagine many Australian ministers wishing to operate through boards. They are mostly firmly conditioned to want one individual whose clear responsibility it is to be the minister's principal adviser and to manage the department, even if they also want to be able to consult more widely (as they can) in particular cases. Certainly in departments working under heavy pressures of time, an executive board can be a clumsy instrument. But some new experiments in corporate management are likely to be made. The Commonwealth Department of Education began one in 1977, with a management group made up of the Secretary, his Deputy and four First Assistant Secretaries, with two Assistant Secretaries serving in rotation.[18] The former Department of Urban and Regional Development made some interesting experiments in corporate management, including a weekly Executive Meeting attended by the Permanent Head, First Assistant Secretaries, the Head of the Information Services, a staff representative, and others called in from time to time. It was given certain decision-making powers, though the 'aim is for consensus decisions and where this is not possible the decision rests with the Secretary'.[19] There was also a weekly staff meeting.

Departmental Growth and Change

Commonwealth

Table 3.1 shows the growth in size and number of Commonwealth departments up to the beginning of the Second World War and then to 1977. The first group of seven were the original departments formed at federation, the first three absorbing the corresponding departments transferred from the States. In addition to the 11 661 permanent officers of these seven departments in 1904, there were 1765 temporary employees, and about 9000 manual workers, making a total of around 22 000 employees. The dates opposite the other departments indicate when they were established roughly in the form in which they appear in the table. The story has been very greatly simplified, as it is really too complicated for a single table. In many cases there were previous departments under similar names, which had been abolished, subdivided or absorbed elsewhere. Not all the departments had a continuous existence between the dates for which figures are given. For example, External Affairs, which in 1904 was really concerned with Territories, was absorbed partly into Prime Minister's and partly into a Department of Home and Territories in 1916, emerged as a separate unit again in 1921, then disappeared in 1924 into Prime Minister's and reappeared as an independent foreign relations department in 1935.[20]

TABLE 3.1

Growth of Commonwealth Departments

Department		1904 Permanent	1939 Permanent	1939 Total	June 1977 Permanent	June 1977 Total
Postal[a]		10323	25314	35066	621	657
Trade and Customs[b]		1099	1671	1886	—	—
Defence		124	1029	1291	19108	27848
External Affairs[c]		16	29	30	2314	4646
Home Affairs[d]		48	—	—	—	—
Attorney-General		10	375	437	1997	2160
Treasury		41	1746	2109	15522	16382
Prime Minister's	1911	—	360	398	2070	2339
Health	1921	—	313	576	5336	7390
Commerce[e]	1932	—	589	953	—	—
Interior[f]	1932	—	907	4051	—	—
Civil Aviation[g]	1938	—	90	240	—	—
Employment and Industrial Relations[h]	1940	—	—	—	4931	5322
Capital Territory[i]	1941	—	—	—	1677	3518
Northern Territory[i]		—	—	—	1136	1907
Social Security[j]	1941	—	—	—	8964	9687
Construction[k]	1945	—	—	—	5681	13260
Immigration	1945	—	—	—	1378	1471
Veterans' Affairs[l]	1947	—	—	—	7407	11746
National Development	1950	—	—	—	1333	1442
Transport[m]	1951	—	—	—	9957	11098
Primary Industry	1956	—	—	—	2930	3152
Trade and Resources[n]	1956	—	—	—	1048	1092
Education[o]	1966	—	—	—	2300	2468
Science[o]		—	—	—	1902	3316
Aboriginal Affairs	1972	—	—	—	685	1102
Administrative Services	1975	—	—	—	5624	9289
Business and Consumer Affairs	1975	—	—	—	5710	5861
Environment, Housing and Community Development[p]	1975	—	—	—	722	743
Industry and Commerce[q]	1975	—	—	—	375	389
Finance[r]	1976	—	—	—	1609	1935
Productivity	1976	—	—	—	3686	4192
Special Trade Representative	1977	—	—	—	—	—
Totals		11661	32429	47043	116023	154412

[a] The former Postmaster-General's Department was decimated in 1975 when two statutory commissions were established, and the remnant became Postal and Telecommunications.
[b] Now part of Business and Consumer Affairs, and Trade.
[c] Called Foreign Affairs after 1970.
[d] Re-established in December 1977.
[e] Now Industry and Commerce; Trade and Resources, etc.
[f] Now Construction; Transport; Northern Territory; etc.

Table 3.1 shows a departmental service of 47 043 in 1939, working in eleven departments. It also illustrates an important point—that up to the Second World War, the Post Office had always accounted for at least three-quarters of all Commonwealth departmental employees, and well over four-fifths of the permanent staff. By 1977 there had been a striking trans-formation. The Post Office had dwindled away, with the transfer of most of its functions and over 100 000 employees to two statutory corporations. In spite of this, total departmental staff had multiplied over three times. There were sixteen more departments. At least half of these had existed in embryo in the 1939 group; nevertheless some of the latter, such as Social Security, had opened up fresh fields of Commonwealth activity just as much as wholly new departments like Education and Immigration.

States

The States have shown a less spectacular, but still striking, development in this departmental field. In Victoria, there are fifteen main departments and six 'Ministries'. The basic pattern—Agriculture, Chief Secretary's, Crown Lands, Education, Health, Law, Mines (now Minerals and Energy), Public Works, Treasury—was largely consolidated before federation. Major changes since then have included new departments such as Labour and Industry (a factory inspectorate inside the Chief Secretary's Department until 1915), Premier's (until 1936 also inside Chief Secretary's), Local Government (until 1958 a branch of Public Works), Social Welfare (until 1970 another part of Chief Secretary's), State Development (a Division of the Premier's Department until 1971) and Youth, Sport and Recreation. The six 'Min-istries' are mostly not clearly distinguishable from departments, though the original idea seems to have been to apply the term to fairly small units superimposed on existing agencies (often statutory corporations) with the aim of co-ordinating policy in related areas. This was true of the Ministry of Transport, created in 1951 and whose staff is still very small, and the Ministry for Planning. However, the Ministries for the Arts, for Conservation, of Consumer Affairs and of Housing, although they partly fit this pattern, employ staffs as large as many normal departments.

g Absorbed by Transport in 1973.
h Originally Labor and National Service.
i Originally in the Department of Territories.
j Originally Social Services.
k Originally Works and Housing, then Housing and Construction.
l Originally a Repatriation Commission outside the Public Service Act (1920–47).
m Originally Shipping and Transport.
n Originally Trade, then Trade and Industry, then Overseas Trade.
o Originally in the Department of Education and Science, until 1972.
p By amalgamation of Department of Environment, Department of Urban and Regional Development (both 1972) and Housing (from Housing and Construction).
q Originally Secondary Industry (1972), then Manufacturing Industry.
r Separated from Treasury in 1976.

TABLE 3.2

Growth of NSW Departments
(Permanent and Temporary Employees Under Public Service Act)

Department[a]		1904	1939	June 1977
Chief Secretary's[b]		2047	405	—
Treasury		1459	2497	1225
Attorney-General and Justice		1375	1762	3181
Lands		813	717	3265
Public Works		960	1351	4523
Public Instruction (now Education)[c]		6132	12626	11347
Mines[d]			176	553
Agriculture[d]		489	756	3284
Premier's	1909	—	222	3444
Labour and Industry[e]	1910	—	585	892
Transport, Ministry of	1932	—	21	80
Social Services (now Youth and Community Services)	1933	—	339	2476
Public Health (now Health Commission)	1938	—	3205	13869
Local Government[f]	1941	—	—	182
Tourism	1946	—	—	176
Technical Education[g]	1949	—	—	5761
Decentralisation and Development	1965	—	—	179
Services	1975	—	—	14242
Consumer Affairs	1976	—	—	241
Sport and Recreation	1976	—	—	207
Employees under Public Service Act Not included above:				
Planning and Environment Commission		—	—	463
State Pollution Control Commission		—	—	302
Public Service Board		—	34	374
Housing Commission		—	—	1792
Soil Conservation Service		—	—	553
Forestry Commission		—	218	829
Registry of Cooperative Societies		—	—	71
Government Insurance Office		—	—	1406
NSW State Fisheries		—	—	249
Totals		13275	24914	75166

[a] Departmental figures include a number of closely related agencies.
[b] Abolished in 1976.
[c] Includes small staff of 'Ministry of Education'; 1904 and 1939 figures include teachers.
[d] Originally in Department of Mines and Agriculture, so one figure for 1904.
[e] Became 'Industrial Relations and Technology' in 1978.
[f] Local Government was also a separate Department from 1915–36, when it was amalgamated with Public Works.
[g] Now 'Technical and Further Education'.

The situation in New South Wales is a little different in form but similar in principle. Table 3.2 shows seven ministerial departments in 1904 (Mines and Agriculture was then a single department), with a staff of 13 275. The number of major departments had risen to thirteen by 1939, and the staff doubled—but nearly half of them were schoolteachers, now no longer under the Public Service Act for most purposes. Of the new departments, some had been operating modestly within other departments—the health function in the Chief Secretary's Department, for example. Social Services was a new departure, as was the co-ordinating Transport Ministry superimposed on existing statutory bodies. Other expansions of State activity had been accommodated in the traditional departments.

Changes in New South Wales since 1939 have been greater. The number of major departments has risen to nineteen, though this was partly the result of separating off existing subdepartments. Child and youth welfare has been withdrawn from Education and combined with Social Services in a single new Department of Youth and Community Services; Technical Education has been separated from Education, Local Government from Works; a new Department of Services has assembled together a number of 'service functions' and other tasks from the old Chief Secretary's Department, the Treasury and elsewhere; the Department of Consumer Affairs grew out of the Consumer Affairs Bureau in the Department of Labour and Industry. Small co-ordinating Ministries of Housing and Education were superimposed on existing agencies. The Ministry of Housing was abolished in 1976. The increase in total staff to three times the 1939 figure is comparable with the growth of Commonwealth employment.

Developments in New South Wales and Victoria are reasonably indicative of the role of State departmental administration generally; but it would be wrong to attempt quantitative summaries for the States as a whole—detailed differences in structure, and in the kinds of functions and employees included in ministerial departments, make it impossible to present comparable statistics.

Non-departmental Agencies

Among agencies of this kind, developments have been spectacular in both the Commonwealth and States. The significant change is not so much in the number of these bodies, because they have always been so numerous that it is impossible to count them precisely. There are over two hundred Commonwealth statutory authorities, and several hundred in the States.

What is important is the growth in large public utilities and business undertakings under the corporate form, and the way in which they came to dominate the politics and public finance of some States. The Commonwealth has been under less pressure than the States to extend its activities in these directions. Nevertheless, when it has done so, it has almost invariably resorted to the device of this statutory corporation. Before the Second World War the Commonwealth had established, in addition to a number of commodity marketing boards, many regulatory and quasi-judicial agencies, such as Taxation Boards of Review, the Tariff Board, the Commonwealth Grants Commission, the Court of Conciliation and Arbitration, and the Public Service Arbitrator. However, its only large public utility or service corporations in 1939 were the Commonwealth Bank (1912), the Commonwealth Railways (1917), the Australian Shipping Board (1923), the Council for Scientific and Industrial Research (1926) and the Australian Broadcasting Commission (1932). Total direct government employment in non-departmental agencies in 1939 was 20 820, compared with 47 043 in the ministerial departments. By 1977, Commonwealth non-departmental employment had risen more than tenfold, to over 220 000. The main postwar statutory corporations are listed in Chapter Five.

Employees of non-departmental agencies in New South Wales numbered over 180 000 in 1977. The largest single employers were the Public Transport Commission with a staff of over 48 000; the Metropolitan Water Board with over 16 000; the Department of Main Roads, over 9000; the Electricity Commission, over 8000.

Functions of Government

The Government Machine

No simple summary, whether in words, figures or diagrams, can faithfully represent the complexity of relations between the institutions of government.

For example, for purposes of budgeting and some aspects of ministerial responsibility (e.g. introducing legislation and answering questions in Parliament), the Public Service Boards and Auditors-General are treated as though they are part of the Prime Minister's Department (Commonwealth) or Premier's Department (NSW), although their heads are independent authorities. Again, 'non-departmental employment' is generally equated in the statistics with 'employment not subject to the Public Service Act'. But there are a few ministerial departments that have some staff outside the Public Service Act, and there are public corporations whose staff is wholly or partly employed under that Act. Chapter Five shows the degree of control by ministers, the Treasury, the Public Service Board and the Auditor-General over general policy, specific actions, staffing and finance of many non-departmental agencies. Because these different forms of control are not associated in consistent patterns with particular kinds of agencies, the relationships cannot be summarised in any simple form.

All that can be said about structure in this sense is that not only departmental units but nearly all government agencies are 'associated', in one or other of the ways mentioned, with some particular minister or department. So it is possible to present a broad picture of the scope of governmental institutions by simply listing departments, together with associated agencies, including statutory bodies and standing advisory committees.[21]

The following are such lists of Commonwealth and New South Wales departments, subdepartments and agencies. They cannot pretend to be exhaustive.

TABLE 3.3

Machinery of Commonwealth Government, 1978

Parliament:
  Governor-General
  Senate, 64 members
  House of Representatives, 124 members

Parliamentary 'Departments' (i.e. officials):
  Senate, headed by Clerk of the Senate
  House of Representatives—Clerk of the House
  Joint House Department—Secretary
  Parliamentary Reporting Staff—Principal Parliamentary Reporter
  Parliamentary Library—Parliamentary Librarian

Courts
  High Court of Australia—Chief Justice and 6 Justices
  Federal Court of Australia—Chief Judge and 22 Judges
  Australian Conciliation and Arbitration Commission—President, 10 Deputy Presidents, 25 Commissioners
  Family Court of Australia—Chief Judge, 8 Senior Judges, 27 Judges
  Trade Practices Tribunal—President, Deputy President, 4 lay members
  Administrative Appeals Tribunal—President and 2 members
  Supreme Court of the ACT—Chief Judge, 2 Judges
  Supreme Court of the Northern Territory—Chief Judge, 2 Judges
  There are also Courts of Norfolk Island, Christmas Island, Cocos (Keeling) Islands and minor Territorial Courts

Executive Government
  Governor-General
  Federal Executive Council: Ministers of the day, and all surviving ex-Ministers. But the latter are not 'under summons' for current meetings

Ministry (June 1978)
  Cabinet Ministers (14):
    Prime Minister
    Deputy Prime Minister and Minister for Trade and Resources
    Minister for Industry and Commerce
    Minister for Primary Industry
    Minister for Administrative Services
    Minister for Employment and Industrial Relations
    Minister for Transport
    Treasurer
    Minister for Education
    Minister for Foreign Affairs
    Minister for Defence
    Minister for Social Security

TABLE 3.3—*continued*

Minister for Finance
Minister for Aboriginal Affairs
Other Ministers (13):
  Minister for Health
  Minister for Immigration and Ethnic Affairs
  Minister for the Northern Territory
  Minister for Construction
  Minister for National Development
  Minister for Science
  Minister for Post and Telecommunications
  Attorney-General
  Minister for Productivity
  Minister for Business and Consumer Affairs
  Minister for Special Trade Representations and Minister for Veterans Affairs
  Minister for Home Affairs and Minister for the Capital Territory
  Minister for Environment, Housing and Community Development

Departments and Agencies

Departments and Subdepartments	Associated Agencies*
Department of Aboriginal Affairs:	
Central Office (Canberra)	Aboriginal Hostels Ltd
Regional Offices	Aboriginal Land Commissioner, NT
	Aboriginal Land Fund Commission
	Aboriginal Loans Commission
	Applied Ecology Pty Ltd
	Australian Institute of Aboriginal Studies
	Central Land Council
	Northern Land Council
	Australian Aboriginal Affairs Council
	National Aboriginal Conference
	Council for Aboriginal Development
	National Aboriginal Sports Foundation
Department of Administrative Services:	
Central Office (Canberra)	Academic Salaries Tribunal
Regional Offices (States and Territories)	Remuneration Tribunal
Australian Government Publishing Service	Australian Electoral Office (and State and Territory Offices)
Australian Information Service	Commonwealth Police Force (and District Offices)
Australian Government Advertising Service	
Honours Secretariat	Commonwealth Fire Board
Protective Services Co-ordination Centre	Commonwealth Grants Commission
Attorney-General's Department:	
Central Office (Canberra)	Solicitor-General

---

* The list excludes most Federal–State Ministers Councils (see Chapter Eight) and *ad hoc* committees.

TABLE 3.3—*continued*

Departments and Subdepartments	Associated Agencies
Northern Territory Office and Overseas Representation	Office of Parliamentary Counsel
Crown Solicitor (and State and Territory Deputies)	Australian Institute of Criminology
	Australian Security Intelligence Organization (ASIO)
Commonwealth Reporting Service (and State and Territory Offices)	Commonwealth Practitioners Board
Australian Legal Aid Office (and State and Territory Offices)	Criminology Research Council
	Film Censorship Board
	Films Board of Review
	Institute of Family Studies
	Legislative Drafting Institute
	Legal Aid Commission (ACT)
	Office of Commissioner for Community Relations
	Administrative Review Council
	Family Law Council
	Law Reform Commission

Department of Business and Consumer Affairs (including Bureau of Customs):

Central Office (Canberra)	Company Auditors Board of the ACT
State and Territory Administrations (Bankruptcy and Bureau of Customs)	Industries Assistance Commission
Customs Representatives Overseas	Temporary Assistance Authority
	Prices Justification Tribunal
	Trade Practices Commission (and State Offices)
	National Consumer Affairs Advisory Council
	National Standing Control Committee on Drugs of Dependence

Department of the Capital Territory:

Central Office (Canberra)	National Capital Development Commission
City Manager's Office	
Jervis Bay Territory (Regional Director)	Agents Board of the ACT
	ACT Architects Board
	ACT Bushfire Council
	ACT Electricity Authority
	ACT Fire Brigade
	ACT Milk Authority
	ACT Police (Commissioner)
	ACT Surveyors Board
	Building Review Committee
	Canberra Commercial Development Authority
	Canberra Retail Market Trust
	Canberra Theatre Trust
	Commonwealth Brickworks (Canberra) Ltd.

TABLE 3.3—*continued*

Departments and Subdepartments	*Associated Agencies*
	Design and Siting Review Committee
	Land Commissioner
	Liquor Licensing Board
	Valuation Review Board
	ACT Historic Sites and Buildings Committee
	ACT Legislative Assembly
	ACT Nature Conservation Advisory Committee
	Building Industry Advisory Council
	Canberra National Memorials Committee
	Consumer Affairs Council
	Emergency Housing Committee
	Small Business Advisory Committee
Department of Construction:	
Central Offices (Canberra and Melbourne)	Snowy Mountains Engineering Corporation (SMEC)
Regional Offices (States and Territories)	
	Building Research and Development Advisory Committee
	SMEC Advisory Committee
Department of Defence:	
Central Office (Canberra)	Chiefs of Staff Committee
Regional Offices (States)	Council of Defence
Overseas Representation	Defence Committee
Australian Defence Scientific Service	Defence Force Development Committee
Joint Intelligence Organisation	Australian Defence Force Academy Development Council
Natural Disasters Organisation	Defence Industry Committee
Air Force Office	Committee of Reference for Defence Force Pay
Army Office	Defence Force Ombudsman
Navy Office	
Department of Education:	
Central Office (Canberra)	Tertiary Education Commission
Regional Offices (States and Territories)	Schools Commission
	ACT Apprenticeship Board
	ACT Schools Authority
	ACT Standing Committee on Further Education
	Commonwealth Teaching Service
	Curriculum Development Centre (Council)
	Australian National Commission for UNESCO

TABLE 3.3—*continued*

Departments and Subdepartments	Associated Agencies
	Education Research and Development Committee
	National Aboriginal Education Committee
Department of Employment and Industrial Relations:	
Central Office (Melbourne and Canberra)	Industrial Registrar (and States and Territories)
Regional Administration (States and Territories)	Public Service Arbitrator
Overseas Representation	Coal Industry Tribunal
	Flight Crew Officers Industrial Tribunal
	Industrial Relations Bureau
	National Committee on Discrimination in Employment (and State committees)
	Australian Trade Union Training Authority
	Commonwealth Hostels Ltd (and State Managers)
	Stevedoring Industry Finance Committee
	Australian Apprenticeship Advisory Committee
	National Labour Consultative Council
	Stevedoring Industry Consultative Council
	National Training Council
Department of Environment, Housing and Community Development:	
Central Office (Canberra)	Australian National Parks and Wildlife Service
State Offices	Housing Loans Insurance Corporation
	Australian Heritage Commission
	Great Barrier Reef Marine Park Authority
	Indicative Planning Council for Housing Industry
	Non-Residential Building Consultative Committee
	Sports Advisory Council
Department of Finance:	
Central Office (Canberra)	Australian Government Retirement Benefits Office (Superannuation Commissioner)
Accounting Offices (State and Territories)	
Overseas Representation	Superannuation Fund Investment Trust
Controller of Enemy Property	
Royal Australian Mint	
Department of Foreign Affairs:	
Central Office (Canberra)	Australia–Japan Foundation

TABLE 3.3—*continued*

Departments and Subdepartments	Associated Agencies
State Offices	
Overseas Representation	
Australian Development Assistance Bureau (and Regional Offices)	
Department of Health:	
Central Office (Canberra)	Commonwealth Serum Laboratories Commission (and State Offices)
Regional Offices (States and NT)	Health Insurance Commission (and State Offices)
Overseas Representation (London)	Capital Territory Health Commission
	Australian Drug Evaluation Committee
	National Health and Medical Research Council
	Registration Boards of the ACT (Dental, Medical, Nurses, etc.)
	Australian Dental Services Advisory Council
	Hospital and Allied Services Advisory Council
	National Health Services Advisory Committee
	National Tuberculosis Advisory Council
	Pharmaceutical Benefits Advisory Committee
	Therapeutic Goods Advisory Committee
Department of Home Affairs:	
Central Office (Canberra)	Australia Council
Office of Women's Affairs	Australian Archives
	Australian Film and Television School
	Australian Film Commission
	Australian National Gallery (Council)
	Australian War Memorial (Trustees)
	Christmas Island, Cocos Island, Norfolk Island Administrations
	National Library of Australia (Council)
	National Women's Advisory Council
Department of Immigration and Ethnic Affairs:	
Central Office (Canberra)	Committee on Overseas Professional Qualifications
Regional Offices (State and NT)	Australian Ethnic Affairs Council
Overseas Representation	Australian Population and Immigration Council
	National Ethnic Broadcasting Advisory Council

TABLE 3.3—*continued*

Departments and Subdepartments	Associated Agencies
Department of Industry and Commerce:	
Central Office (Canberra)	Australian Tourist Commission
Bureau of Industry Economics	Australian Shipbuilding Board
	Australian Manufacturing Council
	Industry Advisory Councils (Automotive, Footwear, Textiles, etc.)
Department of National Development:	
Central Office (Canberra)	Albury–Wodonga Development Corporation
State Offices	
Bureau of Mineral Resources	Ministerial Council for Albury–Wodonga
	Australian Atomic Energy Commission**
	National Mapping Council
	Ord Project Co-ordinating Committee
	Pipeline Authority
	River Murray Commission
	Snowy Mountains Council
	Snowy Mountains Hydro-Electric Authority
	Decentralisation Advisory Board
	National Coal Research Advisory Committee
	National Energy Advisory Committee
Department of the Northern Territory:	
Central Office (Darwin, and ACT Secretariat)	Administrator of the NT (and Executive Council)
Regional Offices (2)	Northern Territory Public Service
Postal and Telecommunications Department:	
Central Office (Canberra)	Australian Broadcasting Commission (Head Office, Sydney; State Managers)
	Australian Postal Commission, and
	Australian Telecommunications Commission (both Head Office, Melbourne; State Managers)
	Overseas Telecommunications Commission (Sydney)
	Australian Broadcasting Tribunal
	Special Broadcasting Service
Department of Primary Industry:	
Central Office (Canberra)	Marketing Boards (Canned Fruits, Dried Fruits, Egg, Honey, Tobacco, Wheat, Wine Boards)
State Branch Offices	
Overseas Representation	

** Nuclear commercial functions are the responsibility of the Minister for Trade and Resources.

TABLE 3.3—*continued*

Departments and Subdepartments	Associated Agencies
Bureau of Agricultural Economics	Australian Apple and Pear Corporation
Bureau of Animal Health	Australian Dairy Corporation
	Australian Meat and Livestock Corporation
	Australian Wool Corporation
	Export Sugar Committee
	Research Committees (Dairying, Dried Fruits, Meat, Poultry, etc.)
	Australian Wool Testing Authority
	Australian Dairy Industry Advisory Committee
	Australian Meat Industry Conference
	Australian National Dairy Committee
Department of the Prime Minister and Cabinet:	
Central Office (Canberra)	Auditor-General's Office
	Public Service Board
	Office of National Assessments
	Commonwealth Ombudsman
	Historic Memorials Committee
	Advisory Council for Inter-Government Relations (Hobart)
	Australian Science and Technology Council
Department of Productivity:	
Central Office (Canberra)	Australian Industrial Research and Development Incentives Board
Regional Offices (States)	
Aircraft and Guided Weapons Establishments	Board of Examiners of Patent Attorneys
Munitions Factories	Production Board
Patent, Trademarks and Designs Office	Australian Inventions Advisory Committee
National Materials Handling Bureau	
Department of Science:	
Central Office (Canberra)	Commonwealth Scientific and Industrial Research Organisation (Canberra; Regional Offices and State Committees)
Bureau of Meteorology	Anglo–Australian Telescope Board
	Australian Biological Resources Study
	Australian Institute of Marine Science (Council)
	Australian Research Grants Committee
	Metric Conversion Board
	National Standards Commission
	Astronomy Advisory Committee

TABLE 3.3—*continued*

Departments and Subdepartments	Associated Agencies
Department of Social Security: Central Office (Canberra) State Headquarters Overseas Representation (Geneva)	Social Welfare Policy Secretariat Commissioner for Employees Compensation Commonwealth Employees Compensation Tribunal Social Security Appeals Tribunals (States and Territories) National Advisory Council for the Handicapped National Consultative Council on Social Welfare Womens Welfare Issues Consultative Committee Homeless Persons Advisory Committees
Department of the Special Trade Representative: Central Office (Canberra)	
Department of Trade and Resources: Central Office (Canberra) Regional Offices (States) Trade Commissioner Service	Export Development Grants Board Export Finance and Insurance Corporation Joint Coal Board Lamb Industry Council Pea and Bean Industry Council National Coal Research Advisory Committee Overseas Trade Publicity Committee Joint Australia–New Zealand Committees (Dairy, Forest Industries, etc.) Trade Development Council Multilateral Trade Negotiations Industries Consultative Group
Department of Transport: Central Office (Canberra) Regional Offices Overseas Representation Bureau of Transport Economics	Australian National Airlines Commission (TAA) Australian National Railways Commission Australian Shipping Commission (Australian National Line) Qantas Airways Ltd Maritime Services Advisory Committee Transport Industries Advisory Council

TABLE 3.3—*continued*

Departments and Subdepartments	Associated Agencies
Department of the Treasury:	
Central Office (Canberra)	Australian Industry Development Corpo-ration
Overseas Representation	Australian Loan Council
	Commonwealth Banking Corporation
	Reserve Bank of Australia
	Australia Bureau of Statistics
	Australian Taxation Office (Com-missioner; State Offices)
	Taxation Boards of Review and Valuation Boards
	Australian Government Actuary
	Insurance Commissioner and Life Insur-ance Commissioner
	National Debt Commission
	Australian Statistics Advisory Council
	Economic Consultative Group
	Financial Corporations Act Advisory Bodies
	Foreign Investment Review Board
	Government Economic Panel
	Insurance Consultative Committees
Department of Veterans Affairs:	
Central Administration (Canberra)	Repatriation Commission
State Administration	Repatriation Boards (States)
	Defence Service Homes Corporation
	Office of Australian War Graves
	Assessment Appeal Tribunals
	War Pensions Entitlement Appeal Tri-bunals

TABLE 3.4
New South Wales Machinery of Government, 1978

Parliament:
  Governor
  Legislative Council, 45 members
  Legislative Assembly, 99 members

Parliamentary 'Departments' (i.e. officials):
  Clerk of the Parliaments
  Clerk of the Legislative Assembly
  Parliamentary Librarian
  Joint Services-Building Manager
  Parliamentary Reporting Staff—Editor of Debates

TABLE 3.4—*continued*

Courts
  Supreme Court of NSW—Chief Justice, President, 20 Judges of Appeal, 14 other
    Judges, 3 Masters
  District Court—Chief Judge and 30 Judges
  Courts of Petty Sessions—Stipendiary Magistrates
  Licensing Courts—Stipendiary Magistrates
  Court of Marine Inquiry—District Court Judges
  Wardens' Court (Mining)—Stipendiary Magistrates
  Land and Valuation Court—Chief Justice and 2 Supreme Court Judges
  Industrial Commission—President and 7 other Judges
  Crown Employees' Appeal Board—Chairman
  Chief Industrial Magistrate's Court
  Workers' Compensation Commission of NSW—Chairman and 8 Judges
  Coroners' Courts—Stipendiary Magistrates
  Children's Courts—Stipendiary Magistrates

Executive Government
  Governor
  Executive Council: Ministers of the Day*

Ministry (December 1977) (all Ministers are members of Cabinet, as in other States)
  Premier
  Deputy Premier and Minister for Public Works and Ports
  Treasurer
  Minister for Transport and Highways
  Attorney-General
  Minister for Industrial Relations, Minister for Mines and Minister for Energy
  Minister for Planning and Environment and Vice-President of the Executive Council
  Minister for Decentralisation and Development and Minister for Primary Industries
  Minister for Education
  Minister for Local Government
  Minister for Lands
  Minister for Health
  Minister for Consumer Affairs and Minister for Co-operative Societies
  Minister of Justice and Minister for Housing
  Minister for Sport and Recreation and Minister for Tourism
  Minister for Conservation and Minister for Water Resources
  Minister for Youth and Community Services
  Minister for Services and Minister assisting the Premier

Departments and Agencies

Departments and Subdepartments	*Associated Agencies*
Department of Agriculture:	
Central Administration	Dairy Industry Authority
Regional Offices	Dairy Industry Prices Tribunal
Agricultural Colleges	Grain Elevators Board

---

* In the case of Victoria and Tasmania, as with the Commonwealth, ex-ministers remain Executive
  Council members but are not summoned to attend meetings.

TABLE 3.4—*continued*

Departments and Subdepartments	Associated Agencies
Biological and Chemical Research Institute	Institute of Rural Studies
Research Stations	Marketing Boards (Egg, Rice, Tobacco Leaf, etc.)
	Meat Authority
	Pastures Protection Boards
	Prickly Pear Destruction Commission
	Royal Botanic Gardens and National Herbarium
	Sydney Farm Produce Market Authority
	Board of Tick Control
	Board of Veterinary Surgeons
	Artificial Breeding Advisory Board
	Dairy Produce Factories Advisory Committee
	Poultry Advisory Board
	Rural Advisory Council

Department of the Attorney-General and of Justice:

Head Offices	Barristers Admission Board
Court Offices	Companies Auditors Board
Crown Solicitor's Office	Corporate Affairs Commission
Parliamentary Counsel's Office	Council of Law Reporting
Protective Office	Licenses Reduction Board
Public Trust Office	Public Accountants Registration Board
Sheriff's Office	Public Defenders and Public Solicitor
Commissioner for Legal Aid Services	NSW Superannuation Office
Bureau of Crime Statistics and Research	Railway Service Superannuation Board
	NSW Retirement Board
	State Superannuation Board
	Local Government Superannuation Board
	Solicitors Admission Board
	Privacy Committee
	Corporate Affairs Advisory Committee
	Bureau of Crime Statistics and Research Advisory Committee
	Law Reform Commission

Department of Consumer Affairs:

Head Office	Registry of Co-operative Societies
Rent Control and Strata Titles Office	Consumer Affairs Bureau
Prices Commission	Fair Rents and Strata Titles Board
	Council of Auctioneers and Agents
	Consumer Affairs Council
	Co-operative Societies Advisory Committee
	Credit Union Advisory Committee

TABLE 3.4—*continued*

Departments and Subdepartments	Associated Agencies
Department of Decentralisation and Development:	
Head Office	Albury–Wodonga (NSW) Corporation
Small Business Agency	Bathurst–Orange Development Corporation
	Committee on Commonwealth Tariff Inquiries
	State Development Co-ordinating Committee
	Regional Advisory Councils
Ministry of Education:	
Minister's Staff	Board of Adult Education
Adult Migration Education Service	Board of Teacher Education
	Higher Education Board
	Conservatorium of Music (Board of Governors)
	Teacher Housing Authority
Department of Education:	
Head Office	Bursary Endowment Board
Regional Offices	Secondary Schools Board
Teachers Colleges	Board of Senior School Studies
	Education Advisory Commission
	Health Education Advisory Council
Department of Technical and Further Education:	
Head Office	Examining Board of Plumbers, etc.
District Councils	
Technical Colleges	Council of Technical and Further Education
	Vocational Instruction Advisory Board
*Health Commission:**	
Central Administration	Drug and Alcohol Authority
Regional Offices	Institute of Clinical Pathology and Medical Research
State and Psychiatric Hospitals and Clinics	Institute of Psychiatry
Community Health and Nursing Centres	Medical Practitioners Disciplinary Tribunal
	Mental Health Tribunals
	Registration and Licensing Boards (Medical, Nurses, Pharmacy, etc.)
	State Cancer Council
	Ambulance Services Advisory Council
	Fluoridisation of Public Water Supplies Advisory Committee

* In effect, a Ministerial Department in 'Commission' form.

TABLE 3.4—*continued*

Departments and Subdepartments	Associated Agencies
	Committee on Patient Care
	Community Health Education Advisory Council
	Drug Education Advisory Council
	Health Advisory Council
	Hunter Regional Advisory Committee
	Medical Appointments Advisory Committee
	Poisons Advisory Committee
	Professional Services Advisory Council
	Pure Food Advisory Committee
	State Consultative Committee in Child Care
	Therapeutic Goods and Cosmetics Advisory Committee
Department of Labour and Industry:	
Head Office	Factory and Industrial Welfare Board
Apprenticeship Directorate	
District Inspectorates	Apprenticeship Council
Vocation Guidance Bureaux	Bread Industry Advisory Committee
	Retail Trade Advisory Committee
Department of Lands and Registrar General:	
Crown Lands Office	Crown Land Agents
Registrar General's Office	Local Land Boards
Western Lands Commission	Geographical Names Board
Central Mapping Authority	Lord Howe Island Board
National Parks and Wildlife Service	Park Trusts
Valuer-General's Department	Board of Surveyors
	Zoological Parks Board
	Valuation Boards of Review
	Aboriginal Relics Advisory Committee
	National Parks and Wildlife Advisory Council
Department of Local Government:	
Head Office	Metropolitan Waste Disposal Authority
	Sydney Cove Redevelopment Authority
	Local Government Appeals Tribunal
	Local Government Boundaries Commission
	Local Government Grants Commission
	Examination and Qualifications Committees (Clerks, Health Inspectors, etc.)
	Building Regulation Advisory Committee
	Noxious Plants Advisory Committee

TABLE 3.4—*continued*

Departments and Subdepartments	*Associated Agencies*
Department of Mines:	
Head Office	Electricity Commission
Chemical Laboratory	Electricity Authority
Geological Survey of NSW	Energy Authority
Geological and Mining Museum	Coal Mining Qualifications Board
	Mines Rescue Board
	Mine Subsidence Board
	Petroleum Committee
	Prospecting Board
	Lightning Ridge Advisory Committee
Premier's Department:	
Head Office	Auditor-General's Department
Policy Co-ordination and Analysis Bureau	Police Department (Commissioner)
Women's Co-ordination Unit	Public Service Board
Industrial Development Unit	Government Actuary
Overseas Offices (London, NY, Tokyo)	Anti-Discrimination Board
	Archives Authority
	Art Gallery of NSW (Trustees)
	Australian Museum (Trustees)
	Museum of Applied Arts and Sciences (Trustees)
	Counsellor for Equal Opportunity
	Development Corporation
	Ethnic Affairs Commission
	Film Corporation
	Office of Ombudsman
	Review of N.S.W. Government Administration (Commissioner)
	State Library of NSW (Council)
	Sydney Opera House Trust
	Crown Employees Appeal Board
	Promotions Appeal Tribunal
	Arts Advisory Council
	Building and Construction Industry Consultative Committee
	NSW Consultative Council on Ethnic Affairs
	Manufacturing Industries Advisory Council
	Museums and Galleries Committee
	NSW Government Overseas Trade Authority
	NSW Science and Technology Council
	Women's Advisory Council

TABLE 3.4—*continued*

Departments and Subdepartments	Associated Agencies
Department of Public Works:	
Head Office	Maritime Services Board
District Offices	Metropolitan Water Sewerage and Drainage Board
Government Motor Garage	
State Brickworks (Board of Management)	State Dockyard Board
	Water Boards (Broken Hill, Hunter District, etc.)
Department of Services:	
Head Office	Department of Corrective Services
ADP Service Bureau	Parole Board
Cleaning Service Branch	Board of Fire Commissioners
Industrial Engineering Group	Government Printing Office
Government Information and Sales Centre	Government Stores Department
	State Contracts Control Board
Letter Delivery Bureau	State Electoral Office
Publishing Advisory Service	State Emergency Services
Registry of Births, Deaths and Marriages	
Department of Sport and Recreation:	
Head Office	Greyhound Racing Control Board
Regional Offices	Sydney Cricket and Sports Ground Trust
	Trotting Authority
Department of Tourism:	
Head Office	Travel Agents Registration Board
Regional Offices	Regional Tourism Promotion Committee
Ministry of Transport:	
Head Office	Public Transport Commission of NSW
	Department of Main Roads
	Department of Motor Transport
	Traffic Authority
	Omnibus Advisory Committee
	Taxi Advisory Council
	Urban Transport Advisory Committee
Treasury:	
Head Office	Government Insurance Office
Land Tax Office	Rural Bank
Pay Roll Tax Office	Rural Assistance Board
Stamp Duties Office	Totalizator Agency Board
State Lotteries Office	
Department of Youth and Community Services:	
Head Office	Children's Courts
District Offices	Association of Youth Organisations
Aboriginal Services Branch	Bushfire and Flood Relief Committees
Immigration Division	Duke of Edinburgh's Award Scheme
Institutions and Establishments	Home Help Service
	Family and Children's Services Agency

TABLE 3.4—*continued*

Departments and Subdepartments	*Associated Agencies*
	Aborigines Advisory Council
	Child Welfare Advisory Council
	Consultative Council on the Handicapped
	Youth Advisory Council

Other Agencies:

(1) *Under Minister for Conservation and Water Resources*
  State Fisheries
  Fish Marketing Authority
  Forestry Commission
  Soil Conservation Service (Commissioner)
  Water Resources Commission

(2) *Under Minister for Housing*
  Housing Commission
  Builders Licensing Board
  Land Commission
  Board of Architects

  Housing Advisory Committee

(3) *Under Minister for Planning and Environment*
  Planning and Environment Commission
  State Pollution Control Commission
  Macarthur Development Board

  Air Pollution Advisory Committee
  Clean Waters Advisory Committee
  Height of Buildings Advisory Committee
  Heritage Council
  Noise Advisory Committee
  Parking Advisory Committees

Commonwealth versus State Administration

It has become fashionable to say that Commonwealth administration has grown in scope and stature, in power and prestige, while State administration has been reduced to the level of a county council in Britain. On the other hand, it is also suggested that Commonwealth administration is remote from the people, relatively abstract, and centralised in Canberra, while State administration more closely concerns the daily lives of citizens and is more directly in touch with the economic and social activities of the community. Other related contrasts are sometimes made. It is said that Commonwealth administrators tend to be more concerned with broad policy issues, requiring constant and rapid adjustment to changing circumstances, while those of the States are mainly engaged in routine management of long-standing, stable regulatory functions, public utilities and social services. Finally, it has been observed that federal programmes are generally better financed than those at State level.

Only the last of these contrasts can safely be applied as a generalisation about Australian government today. By the introduction of uniform income tax in 1942, the Commonwealth claimed the lion's share of all government revenues. But it is precisely this relative impoverishment of the States that has helped to bring the Commonwealth increasingly into certain fields of domestic legislation and administration. With the State governments lagging for want of funds, the Commonwealth has had to provide much of the incentive, the financial means and sometimes the administrative machinery for the improvement of education, for extended social services, better roads and even the encouragement of the arts. Thus Commonwealth predominance in finance has helped to blur any broad distinction between Commonwealth and State functions. How far can such a distinction be made?

An important basis for the distinction is the distribution of the fundamental 'constituent functions' of government—those that are bound up with the nature of political government itself. At federation, the Commonwealth Parliament was inevitably made exclusively responsible for defence, external relations, the government of territories, the control of migration into and out of the country, and the control of external trade and of trade between the States. On the other hand, the States retained almost complete control of one of the basic constituent functions of government—the preservation of internal law and order, including the administration of common law and statute law, both civil and criminal, with all their varied influences on the personal, economic and moral relations between citizens. This responsibility alone is enough to raise State government above the level of local authorities. Thus there is a fairly clear-cut division of the constituent functions between the Commonwealth and the States, and it is broadly true that in this field the latter more intimately touch the private affairs of individuals; even here there are now important exceptions such as family law.

Beyond this field we must recognise that, especially since the Second World War, the Commonwealth has become involved in every one of the broad categories of regulatory and service functions that have been undertaken by State governments in Australia and unitary governments abroad. As a result, Commonwealth public employees are not concentrated in remote Canberra, nor detached from the direct impact of government policies. They are widely dispersed through the continent in the conduct of grass-roots administration. Of the 154 512 Public Service Act employees in 1977, only 33 787, or less than a quarter, were working in Canberra. The rest were distributed throughout the States roughly in proportion to their population, or were overseas.

As to the distinction between flexible policy functions and more routine service functions, most Commonwealth employees fall into the latter group. They include over 12 000 engaged in services to air, land and sea transport from lighthouses to weather stations; about 30 000 paying out social security and health benefits and administering repatriation benefits; and over 15 000 collecting taxes and customs duties. To these should be added the many thousands of employees of non-departmental agencies running Commonwealth post offices, railways, airlines, shipping lines, banks, migrant hostels, telecommunications, power generation and broadcasting services.

In fact, under a half of departmental employees are serving in departments concerned with external affairs, immigration, defence, economic and trade policy, and the development of resources, and this includes much routine work in defence factories and building construction. A substantial proportion of these activities is devoted to the promotion of economic development, marketing of primary products and building of public works—functions that are also carried out by State governments.

Thus, apart from the constituent functions, it is difficult to make any clear distinction between the nature of Commonwealth and of State functions. But some rough lines can be drawn.

In the field of long-term economic development and conservation of natural resources, the Commonwealth's role has been relatively restricted and indirect, though it is now seeking to influence not only the total scope of development programmes (so far as they are dependent on loan expenditure) but also the priorities among them. However, its own works are mostly for its own enterprises and for defence purposes, though there are striking exceptions such as the Snowy Mountains scheme. The States must initiate, plan and carry out most of the detailed programmes for extending harbours and highways, encouraging industrial and mining development, building dams and controlling floods, providing power and light, conserving soil and forests. The Commonwealth helps some of these projects by making grants of money. Two other examples may illustrate this relationship. The Commonwealth Scientific and Industrial Research Organisation aids primary industry, mostly by carrying on basic research and publishing the results. The State Departments of Agriculture do some similar work, but primarily they must ensure, through their extension services, that new knowledge and techniques are understood and applied in practice by primary producers. (This, incidentally, seems to have been a singularly fruitful division of labour.) The direct responsibility for long-term economic development is the second major State function (the first being the making of criminal, commercial, industrial and social law) that quite clearly distinguishes the States from local governing bodies.

In the field of short-term economic policy for maintaining a high level of employment and controlling fluctuations, the Commonwealth necessarily has a major role to play through its taxation powers, the central bank's regulation of credit, and so on. The State parliaments have more specific powers which can contribute to the regulation of the economy; for example, they can impose price controls and alter wage levels and working conditions. However, this is an area in which the constitutional distribution of powers can still hinder coherent and co-ordinated action, especially in a crisis, when monetary and fiscal measures may need to be dovetailed with price and wages regulation, and with import and taxation policy. Some of these functions can only be exercised by the Commonwealth government, some only by the States, some are shared between them, and many wages are fixed by Commonwealth arbitration tribunals judicially independent of any government's direction. And economic policy is so closely bound up with the political convictions of governments that even in the depth of the Great Depression it was not possible to secure unanimous concerted action.

In the field of social services the Commonwealth administers the major benefits that involve monetary payments. It also pays large sums to help the States to carry on certain services, such as the provision of housing, education and hospitals. The States and voluntary bodies are still responsible for most social services requiring not merely money payments but detailed administration and personal attention, though the Commonwealth has come to intervene much more in this area since the 1950s (see Chapter Eight).

Finally, in the field of public enterprise and public utility services, while both Commonwealth and States conduct some services of the same kind, these activities are less important to the Commonwealth; in the States, on the other hand, they have tended to dominate the budgets, the employment picture and political life itself. Together with education, conservation and economic development, the work of the great corporations providing transport, power, and water supplies has in the past constituted what A. F. Davies has called the fast-running current of State politics and administration.

Notes

1. Report, RCAGA, 76.
2. G.E. Caiden, *The Commonwealth Bureaucracy*, Melbourne University Press, Melbourne, 1967, 176, says that between 1939 and 1965 the Commonwealth Parliament included 67 members who had been public servants, most of them Labor members. This ensured that certain matters relating to public service conditions had, for better or worse, some parliamentary attention. Of 185 federal Members of Parliament in 1973, only 20 were government employees just before election including 7 teachers; 18 of these were Labor members, and 3 had been senior Commonwealth officers (information supplied by Dr T.V. Matthews).
3. Report, RCAGA, 108–21, 90–3.
4. Some of the issues are discussed in the Fulton Report. See *Report*, Committee on Civil Service, HMSO, London, 1968, Vol. II, paras 20–7, 305–15.
5. For political problems of cabinet-making, see S. Encel, *Cabinet Government in Australia*, 2nd edn, Melbourne University Press, Melbourne, 1974, and C.A. Hughes (ed.), *Readings in Australian Government*, University of Queensland Press, St Lucia, 1968, pt II.
6. See G. Sawer, in Hughes, *op. cit.*, 63–8, and Enid Campbell, 'Ministerial Arrangements', Report, RCAGA, Appendix Vol. One, 191–209.
7. Report, RCAGA, Appendix Vol. Four, 208.
8. See A.H. Birch, *The British System of Government*, Allen and Unwin, London, 1967, 198; and Report, RCAGA, Appendix Vol. Four, 198–9.

9. David Butler, *The Canberra Model*, Cheshire, Melbourne, 1973, ch. 7, 'Ministerial Responsibility', 51.
10. See Butler, *op. cit.*, and S.E. Finer, 'The Individual Responsibility of Ministers', *Public Admin.* (London), XXXIV, Winter 1956. The formal position of a minister in relation to his own department was stated in the British House of Commons at the time of the Crichel Down affair. See Frank Dunhill, *The Civil Service: Some Human Aspects*, Allen and Unwin, London, 1956, 122; and G. Marshall and G.C. Moodie, *Some Problems of the Constitution*, 4th edn, Hutchinson, London, 1967, 67–74.
11. R.L. Wettenhall, 'The Ministerial Department', *Public Admin.* (Sydney), XXXII, 3, September 1973, 241; and 'Modes of Ministerialisation, Pt. I', *Public Admin.* (London), 54, Spring 1976.
12. Enid Campbell, 'Ministers, Public Servants and the Executive Branch', in Gareth Evans (ed.), *Labor and the Constitution, 1972–1975*, Heinemann, Melbourne, 1977, 149.
13. *R.* v *Anderson; Ex parte IPEC–Air Pty. Ltd.*, (1965), 113 C.L.R. 177; and Wettenhall, *op. cit.*, 245–8.
14. See Report, RCAGA, 61–2, and Appendix Vol. One, 219–20, 234–9.
15. cf. Enid Campbell, 'Ministers, Public Servants and the Executive Branch', Federal Anniversary Paper, Faculty of Law, University of Melbourne, Melbourne, August 1976.
16. See R.L. Wettenhall, 'Concepts of Ministry', *Public Admin.* (Sydney), XXIX, 4, December 1970, and 'The Ministerial Department', *Public Admin.* (Sydney) XXXII, 3, September 1973; and cf. First Report, Board of Inquiry into the Victorian Public Service, Government Printer, Melbourne, 1974, 45.
17. See J.G. Crawford, 'The Role of the Permanent Head', *Public Admin.* (Sydney), XIII, 3, September 1954.
18. See 'Administrative Chronicle—Federal Government', *Aust. J. Public Admin.*, XXXVI, 3, September 1977, 275–7.
19. *Australian Government Administration, A Submission to the Royal Commission,* Department of Urban and Regional Development, Canberra, November 1974.
20. Fuller details of departmental histories are to be found in G.E. Caiden, *Career Service,* Melbourne University Press, Melbourne, 1965, Appendix. For departmental changes 1972–78, see charts by Peter Coaldrake in *Aust. J. Public Admin.*, XXVII, 4, December 1978.
21. For an interesting attempt at more systematic analysis, see R.L. Wettenhall, *A Guide to Tasmanian Government Administration*, Platypus, Hobart 1968.

Chapter Four

The Division of Work: Guiding Factors and Principles

The extent to which any complex structure can be planned in advance is limited. Most administrative structures have not been designed as a whole, but have grown up historically, by the combination, subdivision or rearrangement of existing units, or by adding new units to old ones. The history of structures is an important and neglected study. It may explain some apparent illogicalities in present arrangements, and throw light on what will be relatively easy or hard to change in the future.[1] It is unfortunate that, for most governmental units in Australia, there is not even a comprehensive survey of such structural changes as are currently happening. Builders of administrative structures usually depend on past example, they add a little here and there, or copy some other agency. Without such precedents, planning a new organisation would be virtually impossible; the problem of prefiguring the whole complex range of tasks and their interrelations would be too great, especially when the desired outputs are multiple and interrelated, or have not been (or cannot be) clearly defined.

Administrative reorganisation is a continuous process. Often it is a product of feedback from current operations, as the members of the organisation become aware of gaps between actual and desired performance; or the gradual development of existing tasks may attract new supporting functions which have to be provided for; nowadays a change of management techniques (a new system of financial control, or the introduction of computers) sometimes demands a corresponding change in structures. This kind of internal process has sometimes been distinguished from the more difficult kind of administrative reform, which is 'the artificial inducement of administrative transformation, against resistance'. An example is change brought about on external initiative, perhaps to make an organisation serve new political and social values. The demand for 'economy and efficiency', influential in both Australian and British administrative reform in the nineteenth century, was once a new value of this kind.[2] A similar process may now be starting in the late twentieth century, when demands are being made on the bureaucracy for more openness, more concern for participation and access.

Whether that is the intention or not, reorganising a structure is quite likely to alter policy and programme emphasis. For example, the creation of a special unit to deal with an existing field of activity may, designedly or otherwise, have the effect of promoting its importance. A change in administrative structure may also affect the power structure, so putting some people in a better position to influence results. Some changes are, of course, deliberately designed to do this.

Finally, a major structural change involves considerable cost. The time and disruption involved can sometimes be considerable and such costs are easily underrated. Because the benefits are often uncertain, conservatives in these matters may have a rational case and should not be regarded as necessarily sunk in inertia.[3] Of twelve cases of reorganisation that F.C. Mosher studied, he rated only half as really successful (one at considerable cost) and two as very costly failures. Such postmortems are rare in administration, and may be inconclusive, as other things will also have changed since the reorganisation took place. All this helps to explain why reorganisation, at least at the highest levels of administration, is a rather crude and *ad hoc* business. There is no equivalent to the more advanced techniques that exist for deciding such problems at lower levels. On major matters everyone thinks he or she knows best. Sometimes considerations are so evenly balanced that the best result is a decision acceptable to all parties as final,[4] especially as much time can be wasted on such problems.

Reorganisation often has a pendulum-like motion, with alternating tendencies of proliferation and merger. There is always 'rivalry between forces seeking greater standardization, closer integration in the activities of government . . . and forces seeking greater flexibility, more independence for the various parts'.[5] At different times, one or other will be in the ascendant. In a period of change, new agencies, new divisions within agencies or new forms of delegation may emerge, followed later by demands for consolidation. Sometimes proliferation and merger go on together, as they did in the early period of the Whitlam government.

Specialisation

The problem of the division of work is the problem of specialisation.[6] Of course, some units may be given interchangeable tasks and in that sense are not 'specialised'—for example, if ten men in a licensing department that is dealing with a thousand applications a day are each given a hundred to deal with on a random basis. But most divisions of work have a higher rationale, they give each unit a specialised task—one that makes use of, or helps towards the acquiring of special skills. Even if ten typists are each assigned to a different individual, they at least learn about particular quirks and methods of working, and something about the content of the particular job, and so cease to be fully interchangeable.

Why are some forms of division of work more efficient than others? This arises from interdependencies in the tasks to be performed. In simple terms the performance of one task may aid or impede the performance of another. There are, for example, 'changeover costs'. If I have to type a letter and file a copy, this involves moving from typewriter to file; on the other hand, I already know the contents of the letter, so find it easier to file when I get there. Estimating the relative importance of these two factors helps one to decide whether a typing–filing combination of tasks is better or worse than having separate typists and filing clerks.

This is a very crude example. What the appropriate combinations of tasks are usually depends on many factors. People bring into organisations resources of habit, knowledge and skill which can be made use of; they also acquire these in the course of performing tasks. Some task combinations facilitate, some impede, the full use of human resources and the improvement of performance—they are more, or less, 'skill-eliciting'. Some skills combine better than others, or are already found in certain combinations. Much the same applies to machines and technologies; some task combinations exploit their potentialities more fully than others. There are also problems of morale. Some forms of specialisation conflict with the psychological needs of individuals or work groups. It has sometimes been argued that there is a conflict between the forms of modern organisation and the need for individual fulfilment and the performance of a 'meaningful task'.[7] Thompson distinguishes between the specialisation of tasks and the specialisation of persons; the former relating to making tasks more specific, the latter to the process by which an individual acquires self-valued skills.[8]

Co-ordination

The problem of the division of work cannot be discussed separately from that of co-ordination; one of the aims of dividing work between units is to minimise costs of co-ordination between the units so created. Indeed it is another aspect of the same problem, as the need for co-ordination arises from the same facts of interdependence between tasks.

Some ways of dividing up work leave little need for co-ordination. One way of cultivating an area of land is to divide it into small blocks, and give a block to each person. This might involve very little co-ordinating machinery, but it might also be a poor way of maximising production. However a more complex way of dividing up the work could involve more administrative effort to see that the workers did not get in one another's way. So, in the division of tasks, account has always to be taken of which divisions will make it easier to relate tasks to one another. Not long ago an Australian government agency converted certain activities from a 'regional' basis, where each officer had a variety of tasks in his area, to a 'functional' basis, in which each had a more specialised task. It looked efficient, but had unfortunate results. The new structure turned out to require an intricate specification of procedures to co-ordinate the various specialist functions as they impinged on the clients; it also made the jobs more boring for those concerned. In other words, specialisation and co-ordination may pull in opposite directions and, if so, some advantages of the one must be sacrificed to promote the other. 'It is not very easy to thread a needle if one person holds the thread and another the needle'.[9] Some problems of co-ordination are discussed in Chapter Fifteen.

The Structure of Administrative Agencies: The Horizontal Division of Work

'If any minister or senior civil servant were asked why the work of the central administration is arranged in its present form . . . he would probably have no ready reply'.[10] In Australia, as in most countries, the present departmental structures of the Commonwealth and States have never been planned as a whole, but grown in an incremental way; and many factors have been involved in structural change—political and personal factors as well as administrative. Here, following Chester and Willson, we briefly discuss some factors involved under two headings: the Number of Units, and the Grouping of Functions.

The Number of Units

One of the important factors tending to increase the number of government units is growing workload. It helps to explain the increase in the number of Commonwealth departments from twelve in 1939 to twenty-eight in 1978. The biggest change happened during the Second World War which produced at least thirteen new departments, though some had disappeared by 1950 and others have been added since.

However, workload is a slippery criterion. For example, at what point does it enforce the need for a new department? Is it when the normal day throws up 'more business than can flow smoothly across the desks of the minister and his permanent secretary'?[11] Some ministers and senior officials can, or think they can, carry larger and more complex responsibilities than others; and there may be other and conceivably better ways of coping with workload than by adding new units, whether new departments or new divisions. An obvious alternative is to delegate more, or to increase the amount of high-level staff work. This can sometimes be implemented more smoothly than a subdivision, and without the existing unit wholly surrendering control of a function. Delegation is easiest when much work is routine or where it can be broken down into distinct groups of activities, many of which can be 'hived off' to others to run, with a few policy directives and simple controls; that is to say, where an increase in work does not add proportionately to the burdens of policy-making and co-ordination. Some departments are mainly concerned with policy-making or high-level control and co-ordination of other agencies, while others are directly involved in operational detail. The latter tend to be much larger than the former, and generally find it easier to expand without overstrain at the top.

The hardest problem to deal with is when a field is much too large for one minister to deal with, but at the same time its various subfields are so closely interrelated that they cannot be easily hived off to different agencies. This is true of economic policy. No single minister can possibly concern himself with government taxation and spending, looking after international trade and finance, keeping in touch with farm problems, trade unions and wages, the problems of manufacturing industry, and resources development. In fact, these are currently thought to need the attention of Canberra of at least seven or eight departments and various statutory authorities. Yet decisions in one subfield closely affect others, and delegating them to a variety of units is fraught with difficulty.

Even when workload seems clearly to call for an increase in the number of departments, other considerations may stand in the way. Existing ministers or senior officers may dislike losing powers, in spite of overburden. An increase in the number of ministers makes the cabinet unwieldy or involves excluding less important ministers from the cabinet. One trouble is that increasing the number of units at one level may increase co-ordination difficulties higher up. Indeed, the demand for closer co-ordination sometimes leads to pressure to reduce, not increase, the number of units. The Second World War saw a sharp increase in the number of departments concerned with defence questions, but there followed demands for a unified Department of Defence, finally achieved in 1973. It is true that this was not simply an argument about the number of units, but about the grouping of functions —that is, separate Army, Navy and Air Departments were thought to stand in the way of a more logical rearrangement of defence tasks. In the same year the Commonwealth created a unified Department of Transport.[12] At the State level, New South Wales had already combined several statutory agencies in a Public Transport Commission.

A few years ago there was a worldwide fashion for the giant government agency. This was partly to achieve so-called economies of scale, because larger departments were thought to have the specialised resources to manage themselves more efficiently; but it was also to promote co-ordination, to favour 'the resolution within a single Department of the differences that arise— notoriously—between separate and competing Departments' (to quote Mr Whitlam, though as Prime Minister he was ambivalent, and created new agencies faster than he amalgamated others).[13] However, there are some difficulties about this view. Small departments may complicate problems of overlap and conflict, but they are easier to control by their own ministers and top officials. They may even sometimes be easier to control by the central co-ordinating agencies as, although there are more of them, each by itself is less powerful. There are other factors involved, such as spread and scope of functions. If a large department consists of a number of disparate sections, each of which has a good deal of internal coherence—and possibly also has 'political' significance—the department will find it hard to co-ordinate them effectively and will became a loose conglomerate. On the other hand:

> If the spread and scope are too small, the department either becomes an enclave carrying on its work in a backwater of public affairs or becomes the voice of a sectional interest.[14]

A factor that may add to the number of units is programme emphasis. A new department or a new division may give recognition to the special status of an interest group, or give impetus to a new programme. An instance of the former is the Commonwealth Department of Veterans' Affairs, with its concern for ex-servicemen and their dependants; an instance of the latter is the creation of a Commonwealth Department of Immigration in 1945, and of Aboriginal Affairs in 1972. These overlap in their activities with other agencies dealing with health, social welfare, education and so on. Sometimes such a unit disappears again when the need for special status declines or the programme settles down. However, a new activity does not always benefit by being given its own department; on the contrary, it may do better in the friendly environment of a larger unit with the power and prestige to launch and finance it. But sometimes there is no existing agency able or willing to perform this function.

One obvious way of giving importance to an activity is to put it in the Prime Minister's or Premier's Department. This happened to the Australia Council, which advises on support for the arts, and to its equivalents in some States; heads of government often seem to enjoy presiding over such cultural largesse. Aboriginal Affairs was also first handled in this way, when the national government began to show interest in the 1960s. But there generally comes a point when heads of government have to resist their departments being cluttered up with special tasks, and start pushing them out again to other agencies. If we study the evolution of the Department of the Prime Minister and Cabinet, we see it regularly divesting itself of responsibilities as well as absorbing them. In December 1977 Mr Fraser, in the flush of electoral victory, shed not only the Australia Council but also the Office of Women's Affairs.

Another factor that may lead to a new department is a growing heterogeneity of functions, or alleged incompatibility between the various functions of an existing agency (though this may not constitute a case for more units, but for a functional regrouping). For example, it may sometimes be thought wise to separate a major policy-advising function from one that involves large-scale routine executive responsibilities, as when Commonwealth trade policy and customs functions were placed in different hands in 1956.[15] There were those who welcomed the splitting of the Department of Trade and Industry in 1972, on the ground that an overseas trade agency should not be hindered in its work by the presence within it of a 'self-proclaimed lobby group for manufacturers . . . only interested in higher tariffs'.[16] However, heterogeneity is a somewhat question-begging word, and there are those who see positive merit in it.

There is also a certain unreality about talking of the number of departments in this elementary way, as it refers only to the formal structure. As we have indicated, formally unified agencies may in practice be loose holding companies of semi-autonomous units. There are also a number of alternatives to creating a wholly new department, such as setting up a statutory authority still controlled in some respects by an existing minister, or establishing a unit inside a department but with a special title and status, called perhaps 'Office' or 'Bureau of . . . ' and with some direct access to Minister or permanent head.

What is there to say about the present position in Canberra? Twenty-seven or more departments, which seems to have become the norm, is almost certainly too many. In a society where interdependence is growing, having so many artificial lines of division does seem unduly to complicate the problems of co-operation. As indicated above, it also increases the chances that some will align themselves with narrow sectional interests. However, there have been some bad experiences overseas with very large departments.

It is also worth remembering that there is no reason why departments should not be of varying size and 'weight' (indeed, they already are), as ministers vary a good deal in capacity and there are few ministers or permanent heads who can make a success of a really big job. Small departments are a good training-ground for larger ones. Rather than have so many departments, it would be better if some ministers became assistant ministers in the large departments, such as Defence or Transport or an integrated Department of Social Welfare, or a reintegrated Treasury or Department of Trade and Industry. This seems to be the view of the Coombs Commission whose 'inclination is towards reducing rather than increasing the number of departments'. It also suggested a few experiments in grouping departments in functional clusters with a co-ordinating minister (see Chapter Fifteen).[17]

There is some inertia about major changes in the formal structures of government. Such changes may be sparked off by a major crisis, such as war. A new government sometimes leads to new emphases, as with the flurry of Commonwealth change in 1972. The Commonwealth Department of Health was born in 1921 out of the postwar influenza epidemic. The establishment of the Department of Trade (now Trade and Resources) owed something to 1954–55 balance of payments deficits. It is often easier to create a new department for a large new function, or a suddenly expanded one, than to take the same action to cope with a slower increase of workload and heterogeneity. But we should not only speak of inertia, there can also develop a mania for change or 'hyperactivism',[18] as a symbol of reformist intentions or in the pursuit of short-term goals. The Labor government of 1972–75 increased the number of departments from twenty-seven to thirty-seven, then reduced it again by stages to twenty-eight. Its successor abolished ten departments and established as many, accompanied by considerable reshuffling and renaming. Governments rarely count the administrative or human costs of their re-arrangements. An example is the dismemberment of the Department of Immigration after December 1972, when it was amalgamated with the Department of Labour—absurdly enough, the two were divided again three years later. 'A significant impact, particularly at higher levels, was a loss of identity and uncertainty as to the future. In addition, many . . . saw the fragmentation of their activities as having serious effects on career prospects. Their response was to form staff committees to protect their interests and to seek assurances . . . that Immigration staff would not be disadvantaged'.[19] The Career Service survey of the Coombs Commission revealed some very low morale in departments when major change or reconstruction had taken place.

The Grouping of Functions

It seems an elementary observation that some administrative tasks are more closely related than others; that the various levels and kinds of education have more links with one other than they have with social welfare or agriculture or immigration (but we may run into more arguments about child-care services or agricultural colleges or migrant adult education). Most countries have recognised this by having separate Departments of Education, Health, Agriculture, and so on. There is a broad assumption that 'similar' tasks should be grouped together. But to be told that tasks are similar prompts the questions: 'Similar in what respects?' and 'How are these similarities related to good administration?' The same problem arises if one is told that the main criterion should be homogeneity or 'coherence of subject matter'. What does homogeneous mean in this context? And suppose there are competing forms of coherence, which does one choose? One Australian permanent head's justification of certain functions being gathered within his department was that it led to a 'more synergetic result from a total societal point of view than against their scattering amongst departments and bodies with which they have no symbiosis whatsoever'![20]

A famous statement of principles was that of Luther Gulick.[21] This has aroused much criticism, mainly destructive, but little empirical research has been done to follow up his insights. Gulick said that there were four main alternative ways of grouping functions, according to similarity in respect of (i) service rendered; (ii) processes used; (iii) people served; (iv) area served. These are called below: objective, process, clientele, region. Most government agencies embody some mixture of these various ways of dividing work.

The term 'functional' is often used, but seems to have no precise meaning; it is sometimes used to describe (i), sometimes more loosely to cover both (i) and (ii) in contrast to a 'regional' or 'geographic' or 'area' basis of organisation. Thus the Australian Army in 1972 was described as in process of a switch from command headquarters, based on the States, to three functional commands—field force, logistics (transport, supply and repair) and training—though some matters would continue to be dealt with on an area basis.

(i) Objective   One can try to classify the functions of government in terms of major social objectives. An elementary typology is protection and welfare (Adam Smith, the economist, spoke of defence and opulence). A further breakdown could be: external affairs, defence, law and order, economic

development, social services. The last might subdivide into education, health, social security, and so on.

This criterion has been widely used for grouping governmental functions, though with more reservations than appears from the titles of departments. The main advantage of organising by objective arises from the simple fact that a major test of good government is the end result. The gathering together under one responsible authority of the resources and processes that are needed in order to achieve a particular social purpose has obvious merits. It makes it easier to enforce responsibility for a bad result and to discourage buckpassing. An equally obvious disadvantage of this method, if carried to the limit, arises from the need to duplicate ancillary services in all the agencies. Is each to recruit, train, pay, promote its own staff, buy its own stores and equipment, acquire and allocate its own finances? Will not this lead to major diseconomies? So in practice most government departments are only to a limited extent organised according to objective.

Another difficulty is that it is hard to describe the task of government in terms of a few major objectives. In practice there are many different goals, which may also vary over time and overlap or conflict with one another. An apparently similar group of objectives may turn out to be heterogeneous. Police and courts are both concerned with law and order, but catching offenders and giving them a fair trial call for different methods and attitudes of mind, so it is widely accepted that police and court control should be placed in different hands. Similarly, when the Commonwealth Attorney-General acquired for a time (under Labor) control over the ACT Police and the Commonwealth Police and Customs, this raised the question of whether the minister responsible for the government's litigation and for framing its laws should also be deeply involved in their enforcement; all three enforcement units are now (1978) in different hands. The field of economic policy teems with such difficulties. How far should Treasurers and Treasuries have a dominant voice in economic policy? Some say that their concern for short-run economy and economic stability renders them insensitive to long-term issues of economic development, or that their impartial role as controllers and 'economisers' consorts ill with their value-laden role as formulators of economic policy. Others deny this, or say that if you strip finance departments of counterbalancing concerns of this kind, they revert too much to being pure ministries of economy.

Objectives also overlap, though some are more self-contained than others. An objective that is currently popular and not at all self-contained is that of protecting and improving the environment. The Commonwealth has a department with 'the Environment' in its title, and most States have created similar bodies. But many fields relevant to this objective are already handled by other departments, such as Health, Agriculture, Mines, water and sewerage authorities, planning authorities, forestry commissions, harbour boards, local councils. Many of these are themselves organised around some 'objective'—such as town planning or health. There is clearly room for conflict about how far the planning agency should deal with land-use problems, or the health agency with pollution problems, or how far these are matters for a Department of the Environment.

There are various ways of resolving such problems. One is to carve up the area as best one can. Another might be to charge the Environment agency with mainly research, policy-advice and co-ordinating functions, leaving most operational tasks to other agencies; but others might argue that the Planning agency should do the co-ordinating. A third solution would be to combine environmental control and some closely related tasks in a single department. Thus the Commonwealth (1975–8) had a single Department of the Environment, Housing and Community Development, and New South Wales has a single Minister for Planning and Environment, and a Planning and Environment Commission, but also under the same Minister a separate State Pollution Control Commission which 'sets environmental standards and supervises their implementation'.[22] A different kind of example is scientific research. This has some natural links with higher education; but pure and applied research also need linking, applied research has to be related to developmental work, development to production and general economic policy. No simple analysis of objectives will inform one exactly at which points on this continuum it is proper to draw departmental boundaries.

(ii) Process   This is a grouping of functions according to the methods or techniques employed in achieving objectives. It has been found convenient to group together many financial processes in a Treasury or Department of Finance, and in a Finance Division or Accounts Branch within departments. The personnel process has similarly been partly centralised in Public Service Boards. A 'process' may involve a recognised type of skill—for example, engineering, medical, legal, statistical, accounting or scientific research. It may be a set of procedures, such as issuing licences or checking income tax returns, which it is convenient to have done in the same office. This method of grouping functions has particular relevance to so-called common services, or those required by many different departments—such as to stores and equipment, printing and publishing, legal advice, building maintenance. How far should these tasks be brought together in one agency, how far left to the departments that use the service?

A unified 'process' agency can make good use of specialist skills and take advantages of economies of scale. Examples in Australian government include government stores units, public works departments, and so on. In the Commonwealth the Department of Administrative Services, and in New South Wales the Department of Services, are agencies that look after a number of 'common service' functions of this kind. In the case of the former, this includes such fields as property management, purchasing, publishing and information services. Another interesting area is legal services, which the Commonwealth has largely concentrated in the Attorney-General's Department, while States such as New South Wales leave more to legal officers spread among the departments. How far does the advantage of legal advice from a specialised department compensate other agencies for the extra delay involved? Some Commonwealth agencies have indeed managed to acquire their own departmental sources of legal advice. It has been argued that skill alone rarely justifies a special overhead unit of this kind, because of the clear advantage of relating particular skills more directly to the other activities of a department.[23]

An agency organised round an objective can (as we have seen) claim advantages for its own control of the various processes that go to fulfil its aims, and it may argue that a common service agency is less likely to meet its particular needs. Sometimes a compromise may be reached in which a single agency controls those parts of a process where the advantages of uniformity, special skill and large-scale operation seem relatively high, while individual departments control other aspects of the process. We have introduced the word 'uniformity', and this reminds us that some process departments also play a co-ordinating role. The case for a specialised Treasury or Department of Finance is not only that it represents a desirable concentration of skills, but that it is needed to keep the other departments in step with one another. Similarly a central legal or personnel or purchasing agency may concentrate certain techniques, but it may also meet demands for uniform treatment or procedures.[24]

A criticism made of some specialists in process is that they are apt to become ritualists who bother more about how things are done than about what is achieved. Process specialisation has other complications. A serious weakness in one agency may render ineffective all other agencies depending on it. But its basic weakness as a basis for grouping tasks is the difficulty of ensuring that the various units so created all work together effectively to produce the desired outputs of government.

Two important variables are size and change. For example, if the total number of governmental activities is small in relation to the number of objectives and processes involved, organising by objective may make it hard to get maximum value out of process. If the units based on objective are bigger, process specialisations can be made subdivisions of these units. In rapidly changing and complex situations, where the pattern of interdependencies cannot easily be programmed or reduced to routines, some of the economics of process specialisation may have to be sacrificed, in favour of units based clearly on responsibility for an objective, or 'project', or 'operation'. Both points are illustrated by the 1970 reorganisation of the Commonwealth Department of Works (now Construction), which is concerned with the planning, execution and maintenance of government buildings and public works. It had been mainly subdivided on the basis of various professional skills, architectural, engineering and so on, and also as between design and construction—in Gulick's terms, on a process basis. However, with a growing volume of work and 'an increasing incidence of large, complex and urgent projects', changes were needed 'to ensure effective planning, co-ordination and control, and to provide for more complete participation of individual specialized staff in the more important projects'.[25] So the project became the basis of organisation, at least where large projects are concerned. Among other things, a project leader is designated to be responsible to the client, and to lead a team for both the design and construction phases. The 'project' approach became fashionable in the 1970s, but like all good ideas in administration, can be overdone; the National Capital Development Commissioner has been reported as reacting strongly against it.[26] When the former Department of Urban and Regional Development was created under the Whitlam government, most officers formed part of a project pool from which they were allocated to particular project teams. This was combined with various devices for encouraging more staff participation. This seems to have worked best while the department was defining its aims and launching novel projects. After a while, 'it just lost its initial stimulus value. A variety of pressures moved the department towards a more traditional bureaucratic way of working.'[27]

(iii) Clientele The clientele or 'client group' method of grouping tasks has usually been regarded as inconvenient, wasteful and making poor use of specialised skills, but it is a possible method—say, a children's department or commission dealing with the very young for a whole variety of purposes (education, health, protection, welfare). A mild approach is made by the Department of Veterans Affairs, which provides pensions, medical treatment, housing finance and even graves for ex-servicemen and women, and various services for their dependants. The Defence Department also provides a variety of services for the armed forces. The New South Wales Education Department was at one time not only responsible for the education of children but also for child welfare and school medical services, though it has lost both functions to other agencies. Now each State meets the needs of schools for guidance, counselling, social work and health and career services through four agencies—Education, Community Welfare (under various titles), Health and the Commonwealth Employment Service—and there is not much co-ordination in the approach to the various needs.[28] Some functional agencies may develop a 'clientele' approach, as do Departments of Agriculture which tend to identify more generally with the concerns of the farmers.

Many departments that are primarily organised on some other basis need to pay regard to clientele—human beings are not conveniently divided into parts for administrative purposes—and administrators have become more aware lately of the problems of access of clients to a complex bureaucracy. An agency may sometimes attract a function because it already has the closest links with the clientele concerned (this was why the Education Department initially became involved in child welfare and school health). Certain groups, such as Aborigines or migrants or deprived children, may need some undivided attention to, or special sponsorship of their needs, and special units may be established for this purpose. But such groups may also suffer if the various services provided for them become too isolated from similar services rendered to the rest of the community. This problem may be partly resolved by creating a clientele agency with policy-forming, co-ordinating subsidy-giving functions, but assigning its executive responsibilities in particular areas to the regular departments, or insisting that it makes the fullest possible use of the latter. The Commonwealth Department of Aboriginal Affairs has been largely a failure, partly because it was asked to be expert on too wide a range of projects.

Another concession that governments sometimes make is to set up a special unit to inform people where they can have all their various needs attended to—the information and referral centre, or citizens advice bureau—or delegate some departments to perform this referral function, as the Immigration Department might be expected to do with newly settled migrants. A more ambitious effort in this direction is the 'one-stop shop', an attempt to provide a variety of government services, especially welfare services, 'in one place, at one visit, and with members of the public having to deal with not more than one or two different officers'.[29] In 1975, the Coombs Commission sponsored a two-year experiment in a Melbourne suburb, the Northwest-one-stop Welfare Centre (NOW) where federal, state and local officials and representatives of voluntary agencies have tried to work as a team to provide a comprehensive welfare service.[30] In practice it has been mainly an information or referral service for clients, as there are great practical difficulties about locating a variety of services in one office, and some agencies have been reluctant to delegate decision-making power to the staff. However, it has also stimulated the work of local community groups, and in a mild way seems to have improved co-ordination between departments. A less ambitious method is simply to encourage the regional and local offices of different agencies to locate themselves in the same building. This example overlaps with the next basis of subdivision: region or area. Indeed an 'area' division of work is often defended on similar grounds to clientele—for example, that it enables the problems of particular communities to be treated in a unified way, or that it can be the basis of making government more accessible by decentralisation. Against this it can be argued that, like a clientele agency, it sacrifices the advantages of functional specialisation.

(iv) Region or Area   A federal system itself embodies an important regional or area division of functions and much of the discussion of federalism turns on which jobs can best be done on this basis, which not. Problems also arise within States in relation to local government and regional decentralisation, or from the need to give unified attention to the problems of metropolitan areas. Indeed Function and Area have often competed as a prime basis for governmental systems;[31] the former largely reflected in the division of work between ministers, and in the great statutory corporations; the second in the structures of federalism, local government and regionalism. It has been held that Area as a basis for government is in decline (as mobility increases, local

communities break up) and the advantages and economies of functional specialisation increase. On the other hand, there are also signs of some revival of community feeling in Australia and distrust of expanding functional bureaucracies. Some of the issues are discussed elsewhere in this book.

Sometimes a government agency makes region an important basis of its internal structure. For example, the New South Wales Health Commission has been largely regionalised, save at the very top. The Commonwealth Department of the Capital Territory is an agency based on region; it manages the ACT (and Jervis Bay) except for such matters as health, education and the making and enforcement of some laws. However, it also has to accommodate itself to the presence of a number of statutory authorities, including the influential planning body, the National Capital Development Commission, and there are now proposals for giving more power to an elected Assembly (see Chapter Nine).

An abortive case of a 'regional' department is the former Commonwealth Department of Northern Development.[32] In the early 1960s the Labor Party promised to create a department especially concerned with the development of Northern Australia (north of the 26th parallel). Menzies went only as far as establishing a Northern Division in the Department of National Development, but this achieved little, and the Whitlam government kept the promise to establish a full department in 1972. However, no one was prepared, both for political and administrative reasons, to give the agency the power and resources to compete effectively with its 'non-regional' rivals—particularly the Department of Minerals and Energy (now National Development)— or its 'regional' rivals, including two States. This reluctance continued even after it combined with another regional rival, the Department of the Northern Territory, to become the Department of Northern Australia. With the next change of government, the latter disappeared and the Northern Territory reappeared, and the notion that the whole northern region needed a special agency to cope with its problems seemed once more dead.

For some purposes overseas countries need to be treated 'as a whole'. Australian embassies play this role, and the Department of Foreign Affairs gives considerable weight to geographic divisions in its departmental structure.

(v) Other criteria   The four alternatives mentioned so far are not quite exhaustive. For example, another possibility is to organise in terms of the physical resource that is dealt with such as forests or, more generally, land. Thus in 1972, the old Commonwealth Department of National Development was reorganised into a Department of Minerals and Energy, renamed National Resources in 1975. Its main task is to 'provide advice on matters related to mineral, water and energy resources including evaluation and balanced development . . . '[33] However, the concept of a unified resources agency was no sooner achieved that it began to be eroded in 1977, when some resources issues, especially regarding uranium, went to Trade and Resources, and a separate Department of National Development reappeared.

Political and Sociological Factors

Power and Culture

The above account is in many ways naive. As we have seen, the structure of government and administration is not simply a monolith of rational design, but a political structure of competing powers and interests, and a society with its own culture and subcultures. Some writers would put it differently, and say that 'political rationality' was as relevant to structure as 'administrative rationality'.[34] Some political factors in reorganisation are obvious. A department may be created to find a job for a minister, for instance. A function may be given to a department for any of several reasons: such as because a particular powerful minister or senior officer is interested in it, or sees it as important to his status, or as a vehicle for his policies; or because the department's clientele or other supporters like it that way. Some clienteles want to have their 'own' agency, at least if a separate unit will have enough power to achieve what they want it to achieve. However, power considerations sometimes suggest the value of having a particular function sponsored by a major department. 'If foreign aid is to hold its own . . . it needs an influential voice to represent it in Cabinet and at interdepartmental meetings.'[35] This is part of the case for attaching the responsibility for aid to developing countries to the Department of Foreign Affairs, which can also stress the link between aid and the national interest. Of course, Foreign Affairs may tend to see overseas aid as an extension of diplomacy, as a contributor to goodwill, rather than in economic terms; or the function may become neglected because it is not central to the Department's interests.

There are political and cultural factors operating within the administration itself. Treasuries and Public Service Boards were not simply products of the view that it was desirable to specialise the financial and personnel processes; they also saw themselves, and were seen, as part of a balance of power. Treasuries stood for the principle of economy against departmental pressures towards wasteful spending, and Public Service Boards were the protectors of the merit system against pressures for patronage. The nature of this balance has changed over time, as Treasuries have emerged as supporters not merely of economy in the narrow sense, but also as general co-ordinators of government economic policy, often seeing themselves, rightly or wrongly, as detached guardians of the public interest against the various sectional demands of other departments and their social partners, the interest groups sponsored by them. Leon Peres has argued that there needs to be a balance between departments of 'principle' and departments of 'interest', and that it is dangerous to divide up functions so that most government agencies can readily become channels of self-interested demands, leaving the task of central regulation and the expression of broader viewpoints to a few overburdened hands.[36]

Each government agency has also its own departmental philosophy, conception of its role, and style of administrative behaviour. This too may influence the decision about whether it should be given a particular function. Thus it has been argued that the problems of higher education require an administrative style different from that normal in dealing with school education—a different 'feeling for the reins'—and cannot simply be left to a Department of Education primarily concerned with schools. This is one reason why special agencies have developed to oversee universities and tertiary education colleges.

Fringe and Neglected Areas

A particular division of work may enable certain functions to establish a solid power base and to maintain a firm self-image. On the other hand, it also tends to create a number of fringe or twilight areas, which are either not central to anybody's responsibility and so become neglected, or which are the object of competition and overlap, or leave those in charge of them uncertain of their role. One symptom of the need for administrative reorganisation is when such neglected or disputed or anomalous areas begin to proliferate and fester. There are several examples of this in the field of education. Thus until recent years technological education was a neglected area, lost between structures primarily designed to deal with other forms of education. Adult education is still to some extent in this position.

The structures of government themselves generate objectives, and act to encourage certain demands and to repress others, so helping to mould the society they are supposed neutrally to serve. To quote another example from education, technical schools have been a much more important part of public secondary education in Victoria than they ever were in New South Wales. An important reason is that the Victorian Education Department established a separate technical education branch at the secondary level when the latter was developing before the First World War, which proceeded vigorously to build its own empire.[37] Our very notions of what constitutes education, or social services or urban planning, are partly conditioned in this way, by what they have been taken to be by administrators.

The federal division of powers has generated its own areas of neglect, and non-decision taking. Consider the great emphasis in Australian social services on cash grants that are easy to control from the centre; or the very specific forms of Commonwealth aid to particular, easily defined fields; or the difficulty that the Whitlam Government found in underwriting flexible programmes that allowed of varied multi-purpose plans to suit complex situations. More generally, it could be argued that a main effect of the federal system, perhaps more important that those 'distorted' priorities beloved of economists, has been to widen the area of 'non-decision-taking' or 'policy vacuum'. Thus Australia cannot be said to have a social welfare policy, because no one has regarded it as their business to look at the system as a whole.

There are also what have been called 'precarious values';[38] that is, social values and demands that are hard to formulate precisely, or to legitimise, or to quantify, because they depend on 'soft data'. Such values will tend to be neglected unless they can be given an especially secure organisational base. Such are some of the less tangible objectives of higher education and urban planning.

Machinery of Government Questions

It will be clear that no simple principles are available to determine major issues concerning the machinery of government. Many factors, including political factors, are involved and there is also the need for continuous adjustment to changing circumstances. The objectives and technologies of government are constantly shifting and priorities change. Such issues are unlikely to be settled once and for all by a committee of inquiry or by teams of management experts. Decisions are more likely to be an amalgam of cabinet and ministerial initiatives, the advice of permanent heads, or of senior officers in important co-ordinating departments such as the Prime Minister's or Premier's Department or the Public Service Board, and pressures from outside interests.

Governments themselves have sometimes stressed the political character of major decisions regarding departmental functions. When the Commonwealth Government in 1957 seemed for once to be taking a major initiative in reviewing the functions of departments (the impetus was not maintained), it set up a Cabinet subcommittee for the purpose.[39] The Prime Minister stated that:

It is only the Government, acting under the control of Parliament, which can decide what functions are to be performed by the various departments. The decision is a peculiarly political one . . . The subsequent and different question, which concerns the administration, efficiency and internal organization of any department is one which does not require a political decision, but administrative skill and judgment. It is to deal with such matters that we have a Public Service Board.

Planning the basic structure of departments certainly raises important political issues, but it also requires administrative skill and judgment if it is to be done well, and also more time than the politicians are able to give. A recent study suggests that major Commonwealth decisions of this kind are still taken mainly at the political level, by the Prime Minister consulting more or less with his colleagues (sometimes there are commitments in the election platform); and 'there seems to be little or no evidence of any attempt . . . at systematic evaluation of other possible rearrangements'.[40]

In Britain much work has been done by committees of permanent heads and by a machinery of government unit, now in charge of an Under Secretary in the Civil Service Department.[41] In Canberra, the Public Service Board has a clear responsibility for promoting efficiency within departments, including reviews of their structure, and it regards advice on broader machinery of government questions as one of its tasks; but there is no direct reference to this in the Public Service Act, and in this area it has maintained a low profile. On major issues, such as the creation of a new department, the Board's advice may be sought, but it has often had to make the best of decisions arrived at politically; it seems to have had some influence on the Labor Government's changes in December 1972.[42] Of course, the Board plays an important part in implementing change once it has been decided. The Department of the Prime Minister and Cabinet also has interests in this field, and among its functions is: 'Government administration including administrative arrangements'. In New South Wales, there has been a stronger tradition of Board consultation by the government, not so in Victoria.

The Commonwealth Board recommended to the Coombs Commission that an advisory unit should be set up within the Board's office to provide for continuous and systematic study of machinery of government problems, including statutory authorities.[43] The Commission did not support this. It thought that the Public Service Board and the Prime Minister's Department should both offer advice on such matters, but it agreed with Menzies that the allocation of ministerial functions was 'a highly political exercise'. Major changes were intermittent and 'often arise from unpredictable political events or considerations', on the other hand, in the more continuing tasks of adjustment, a separate unit would only duplicate work that was better seen as growing out of the day-to-day operations of the Public Service Board and other co-ordinating agencies.[44]

The points made by the Coombs Report help to explain why the method of public inquiry by an outside committee or royal commission has not been a successful way of handling machinery of government questions. A number of inquiries have taken place in various countries that touched on these matters since the British Haldane Report,[45] which itself had more impact on theory than practice, including the Brownlow and Hoover Reports in America and the work of the Glassco Commission in Canada. There have also been one or two good research studies by outsiders, such as the one in Britain by Chester and Willson aided by a study group of public servants, the analysis of Tasmanian government by Wettenhall with the support of the Royal Institute of Public Administration,[46] and studies done for the Coombs Commission.

New South Wales in 1974 initiated a largely internal review of the machinery of government,[47] operating through nine study groups mainly composed of officials with ministerial chairmen (but with separate chairmen for the detailed work), supervised by a cabinet subcommittee and with staff assistance from a machinery of government unit in the Premier's Department. This attempt to obtain acceptable proposals by involving politicians and top officials in the review seems to have been successful, and a fairly large number of changes were effected, though some critics have held that they were mainly 'bureau shuffling'. The Administrative Review committee set up by Mr Fraser (see Chapter Eighteen) was close to being a committee of insiders, and its reports were not intended for publication.

The Vertical Division of Work

Formal and Informal Structure

In administrative agencies levels of responsibility differ; individuals and units form a hierarchy, in which each subordinate unit is responsible to a superior at the next level. So there is what is sometimes called a chain of formal authority or 'line of command' running from top to bottom.

In many organisations, public and private, there are the following levels:
1. Criticism, review, final control. Parliament, shareholders.
2. Governing authority. Cabinet, board of directors.
3. Link between policy-making and operations. Departmental minister, active director.
4. Operating authority. Permanent head, director-general, managing director/general manager.
5. A variety of supervisory grades down to those who have no authority over anyone else.

The functions of each level can rarely be neatly categorised and the descriptions above, which derive from L.F. Urwick,[48] are themselves highly imperfect. For example, permanent heads could, at least as much as ministers, be described as linking policy and operations.

In the past, books on administration and management laid great emphasis on the importance of a clear line of command, and of precise definitions of authority. There are many situations where this is still relevant, but in recent writing the stress falls rather differently. First, many positions in organisations cannot be adequately characterised in these terms. A subordinate officer's role is not in practice defined by a single superior giving orders, but by a much more complex set of interdependencies which may be with several superiors and with his own subordinates, with colleagues outside his own line of command and with clients outside his department —all of whom he relies on, or who rely on him, to some degree.[49] In some instances it must be unambiguously clear who has the final word, but often the reality is much less rigid and well-defined, and rests on a complicated set of understandings and mutual expectations.

The point is sometimes made by distinguishing between the 'formal' and the 'informal' structure of organisations. Some writers go further and describe organisations as having a number of 'overlays', or different patterns that we can imagine as superimposed on the pattern of formal authority. These include:
1. *The power overlay*. Patterns of actual power and decision-making, which may not follow the pattern of formal authority.
2. *The communication overlay*. The nature of the regular communication network.

3. *The functional overlay.* The pattern of specialised contacts arising from the need for various forms of expert assistance.
4. *The sociometric overlay.* Broadly, the pattern of personal likings and dislikings within the group.[50]

Each does not simply co-exist with the other, but modifies it, though they never quite coincide. For example, we may come to like those whom we consult, or vice versa, and this reinforcing relationship may alter the regular network of communications, and possibly in due course the structures of power and authority,

Secondly, many organisations operate in practice very little on the basis of commands or orders. The problem is one of arranging the division of tasks between different levels, and training individuals to perform them, so that everyone understands what is required of him and does the right thing without being told.[51] Dwight Waldo has christened this 'built-in rationality'.

If administrative hierarchies are looked at in this way, the problem of dividing work between levels begins to look more like that of dividing it between formal equals. It becomes the problem of 'vertical division of work', and the same general criteria apply as in any division of work: to create units in which tasks are grouped so that one facilitates another, and to minimise the problem of co-ordination between levels; that is, to minimise order-giving, buckpassing and fruitless conflict.

Authority

In administration, the word 'authority' is commonly used as an attribute of office in a hierarchy, as when we say that someone occupying a particular office or position has authority to approve expenditure up to a certain amount, or to supervise a group of persons or set of tasks. This is sometimes called formal authority; a more accurate term is 'official authority' or 'positional authority'. The word 'power' is sometimes used, but 'authority' is better, as it conveys the notion that this is legitimate power. A person with authority is seen as having the right, not merely the power, to make certain decisions.

If we ask what is the source of this authority, one kind of answer is the formal legal kind, that it is given by a higher authority, deriving from some ultimate source in Crown, Parliament or Constitution. But authority also carries with it the notion that it is habitually obeyed: we normally think of administrative authority as existing in situations where subordinates follow a rule that they obey, doing so as a matter of routine and not because they have chosen to in the particular case. Authority in this sense is a certain kind of regular relationship between persons in different positions in an organisation.

So in looking for the sources of authority, we need also to look at the basis of this obedience. Clearly it depends partly on the power of superiors to manipulate material rewards and punishments, from promotion to dismissal. In public administration these rewards and punishments exist, though weakened by diffusion of their control and often hard to invoke. In the private sector there may be a clearer boss. But the contrast can be overdrawn, as the essence of the negative sanctions at least is that they are rarely used, and authority does not rest only on material rewards and punishments. There is an element of willing and habitual compliance with what is seen as legitimate.

The sociologist Max Weber thought that modern organisations had a distinguishable kind of legitimacy, different from that of traditional institutions or groups depending on the charisma of leaders believed to possess exceptional powers. It was an authority that belonged (so to speak) to the organisation as such, because it presented itself as a rational system of impersonal rules, precise, stable and reliable, within which individuals had a defined set of tasks, and through which they could progress according to rational criteria. Weber called this 'rational–legal' or 'bureaucratic' authority —using the word 'bureaucratic' in a neutral sense, not as a term of abuse.

Bureaucracy

What are the main characteristics of a bureaucratic structure? Weber included the following:

1. *Specialisation of function.* The members of a bureaucracy are 'officials' —that is, they fill offices or positions with fairly fixed duties attached to them. The discretion of each unit is prescribed and limited, so as to produce a high degree of specialisation of skill and function.
2. *Hierarchy.* Offices form a structure, with different levels, so that each lower office is under the control and supervision of a higher one.
3. *Rules and regulations.* These define the responsibility of members and the relations between them.
4. *Impersonality.* This is the elimination of personal bias or attachments from work.
5. *Qualifications for office.* For example, a career service recruited on a merit basis, with promotion by objective criteria of seniority or merit, or both. (The members of a bureaucracy do not own the assets of the organisation, or have any property rights in their job.)[52]

Weber is setting up a model, what he called an 'ideal type', and no actual bureaucracy wholly fulfils his criteria. However, government departments and large business firms have many of these characteristics.

Bureaucracy is only one of a number of ways in which people can act together. There are non-hierarchical modes of co-operation, where decisions are made on a basis of formal or actual equality, by voting, bargaining, discussion and informal kinds of mutual adjustment. There are also non-bureaucratic forms of leadership, as Weber pointed out, where leaders exercise influence mainly through some form of personal or customary authority. Most actual bureaucracies incorporate some of these non-bureaucratic elements, otherwise they would be unworkable. Many current features of existing government departments are unbureaucratic; if there are rigid hierarchies in some, in others one may find much informal consultation on a basis of equality, or the use of the team approach to deal with a particular problem.

Costs of Bureaucracy

The bureaucratic method has enabled all kinds of things to be done that would have been difficult or impossible without it, but it also carries various costs, which have to be measured against its advantages. What are these costs?[53] It uses people and resources not to give clients what they want or need, but to see that other people do this. The best educational administrator is not teaching anybody, though he may be helping teachers to teach better. It raises control and enforcement problems. Bureaucracies are hard to control from outside. Outsiders (think of shareholders or backbenchers) are generally ill-informed, relatively ill-organised, and run up against the solidarities of bureaucracies. They are also hard to control from inside. Decisions have to be communicated through many persons, rules and regulations have to be made, and someone has to see that they are carried out. They tend to be inflexible and to promote rigidity of conduct.

To make a large organisation work, jobs and procedures have to be more or less prescribed, or no one knows where they are. But this may mean that decisions are made slowly or are poorly adapted to individual cases. It may evoke a formalistic attitude of mind obsessed with procedures, regardless of how they work; mistaking means for ends, the process known to sociologists as the 'displacement of goals'; or as Bagehot said, thinking of the machinery 'as a grand and achieved result not a working and changeable instrument'. There may be too many obstacles to mobility and the free flow of communications. There may be neglect of twilight areas that fall between the various jurisdictions. Changing needs may make the prescriptions out-of-date, but those members of the hierarchy protected from the direct impact of the world outside may not see the need for change. A bureaucracy tends to become overcentralised—the top people may be too confident of their own superiority or too insecure to delegate or, having worked their way up slowly, still have the concern for minor detail appropriate those people lower down.

The fact that bureaucracy involves so much definition of duties and subordination of one person to another is sometimes held to be destructive of human freedom, equality, spontaneity and morale. There may be many highly specialised routine tasks, which are boring and leave no sense of achievement. In a recent State employees' attitude survey, half thought their job 'routine', and over half the clerical assistants found their jobs boring and conveying little sense of achievement.[54] The hierarchy that accompanies bureaucracy also has its human costs (see below). Many people view with distaste the extension of bureaucratic control, as a threat to human values. It also promotes irresponsibility and buckpassing. As much decision-making is fragmented, perspectives are narrow and no individual feels responsible for final outcomes. There is often too much distance between the planning and execution of tasks. A pathological case is a bureaucracy running concentration camps in which the people at the bottom carry out the orders of a long chain of officials, each in turn more and more remote from what actually happens as a result of their activities. It may concentrate power in too few hands, or only work by developing 'pockets of illegitimate power'. It may create a mentality concerned with advancement in institutional status, not with solving substantive problems.

Such criticisms can be taken too far. For example, bureaucracies are often criticised, as we have seen, for impersonality, slowness and poor adaptation to individual cases. However, impersonality does not imply, though it may sometimes lead to, lack of human warmth—it simply means that involvement is restricted to the needs to which the specialised function is relevant. As for slowness, when action involves the co-operation of a number of persons, it inevitably takes time. As for individual cases, there must be provision for dealing with exceptions, but every case cannot be treated as an exception.

As for resistance to change, many institutions resist change, not only bureaucracies. It is perhaps more cogent to argue, not that bureaucracies resist change, but that they tend to be 'incremental' rather than innovating —that is, they favour small changes of policy at the margin and disfavour major novelties. This may hinder them in coping with rapidly changing demands. Their relatively rigid structure also encourages compartmentalised thinking. The characteristic expertise of the administrator is to know his own organisation and how it can be used; but this very skill may render him insensitive to problems for which unusual and experimental approaches are needed.[55]

There are broadly two ways of improving a bureaucracy which may appear, and sometimes are, contradictory; some paragons claim they can mix both in ideal proportions. The first is to make it a more perfect bureaucracy— for example, clarify lines of authority, improve accountability to superiors, standardise procedures, and improve the design of forms or the classification of jobs. The second is to make more use of non-bureaucratic ways of acting —keeping formalities to a minimum, encouraging individuals or small groups to act on their own initiative, even at some expense to orderly routine and strict control of expenditure, and to be responsive to 'more diverse sources of stimulus' (to quote the Coombs Commission).[56]

Tom Burns has recently published a study of the growth of bureaucracy in the British Broadcasting Corporation, from which the ABC could no doubt also learn lessons. The growth is reflected, for example, in the steady increase in the proportion of revenue that goes to the regular staff as opposed to the artists; and in the way in which professionalism has tended to replace the 'public service' ethic of an earlier period, so that the staff come to think that only they can judge their own efforts, and that the public are moronic. Interesting links are also brought out between the growth of bureaucracy and that of trade union power—for example, the complex grading of jobs has raised the level of discontent, and as it has become harder to bring about change through normal channels, so only trade unions have been able to get results; but this brings about further rigidities.[57]

Costs of Hierarchy

Some of the costs of bureaucracy arise from its hierarchical character, the existence within it of many differences of formal power and status. We deal with this problem separately, as many hierarchies are not bureaucratic, and to rid oneself of bureaucracy would by no means rid one of hierarchy.

An important cost of hierarchy is often said to be that it blocks certain valuable kinds of communication. Hierarchical structures sometimes develop a heavily skewed status system, in which prestige accelerates sharply as we go up the hierarchy,[58] and this may be reflected in power, deference, inside knowledge, interesting work and pay. Large status differences (it is argued) can block the free communication within a group that is needed to solve certain kinds of problem. Hierarchy not only encourages and condones the withholding of information by superiors, but high-status people underestimate the need for discussion. In turn lower-status officers avoid really telling criticism, or communicate only what is consistent with their interests or sense of personal security. Barriers to communication in turn help to differentiate perceptions of reality and attitudes towards objectives.

All this has some plausibility. On the other hand, it can be argued that formal leadership and formal status differences have their uses, especially when they correspond broadly to differences of talent or experience. In many groups communications flow more easily with formal leaders, at least those leaders who use their status to counter inhibiting group-influences, including the rough kind where majorities stifle minorities. A formal leader can assume a role officially signalled as exempt from the partialities of ordinary members, and can also reduce debilitating disputes about what the status order is.[59]

Secondly, it is only at some problems that a number of minds work better than one. As R.L. Thorndike put it, groups tend to beat individuals at solving crossword puzzles but not at constructing them. In the latter case, the problem is not to find each uniquely right word in succession, but to co-ordinate earlier with later steps; within certain limits, any word will do that agrees with earlier choices and does not obstruct later ones, the major problem being to get a good 'fit', a consistent result. This is in line with some evidence that groups with a recognised hierarchy find it easier to reach internal agreement, and this has advantages where co-ordinated action is important but also fairly difficult to achieve.

Arguments of these kinds represent the essence of the case for and against visible authority in organisations. The results of status difference are emphasised by those who stress the poor communications, dependence, apathy or alienation that results from hierarchy and who argue for more co-operative and participatory structures. Those who lay the stress on formal authority emphasise its value in structuring the situation for others, or in restructuring it to emancipate them from inhibiting structures, and its usefulness in promoting agreement and co-ordinated action when other devices fail.

The Future of Authority

It should be added that:

1. Different kinds of organisation differ in the sources of their authority. For example, some place a high value on free individual participation in important decisions, and lose their power over members if they become too bureaucratised and (on the face of it) rationally administered. Some organisations have objectives that are attractive, and lose their authority when their aims lose their attractiveness. Some depend more than others on material incentives to the individual. The roots of authority are as various as the roots of incentive.[60]

2. There are degrees of compliance with authority, varying from the minimal and evasive, through neutral obedience, to enthusiastic identification. It is less clear that modern organisations promote the last of these rather than the first two; yet it makes a good deal of difference what degree of compliance we are talking about.

3. Some writers have argued that bureaucratic authority is now losing its legitimacy. First, it is not evident that bureaucratic hierarchies are the most rational mechanism for dealing with many current problems; and this is reflected in the amount of administrative experiment taking place in both public and private sectors. Secondly, the authority of bureaucracies has rested in part on the special security they offered to employees in a world of poverty and unemployment; on habits of deference to superiors, supported by the status symbols of superiority (large pay differentials, big offices, tightly controlled access, secrecy and other forms of play-acting); and on a compulsive interest in order and discipline shared by all ranks. These supports seem to be sagging, though this is far from certain. (Some writers have argued that the symbols of office become more important with the relative decline in other forms of social status.)

Those who believe that conventional bureaucratic or positional authority is losing its legitimacy, tend to argue that organisations will need to depend more and more on 'functional authority' or the 'authority of knowledge', and on 'participation'—the precise mix and interpretation of these terms varies with the writer. The former is authority based on clearly exhibited professional competence and problem-solving expertise. 'Participation' may be seen in many different ways (see also Chapters Thirteen and Seventeen). An optimistic version sees it as involving a real extension of democratic control inside organisations. Those who regard any large amount of democratic control as undesirable, or incompatible with the complex character of modern organisations, talk more in terms of human relations skills or 'mobilisation'—the techniques involved in making employees and clients feel that they are being given reasons for what is done, that their views are being considered, and that their job is pleasurable or worthwhile; and in other attempts to capture the values of friendship and community for organisational purposes.[61]

Australian government agencies have done something about this state of affairs (the Commonwealth and South Australia get the best publicity), but have still a long way to go—it surprises an outside observer still in the 1970s to hear intelligent and well-motivated younger officers in departments complain of the defensiveness of their superiors, the lack of opportunity for free discussion of departmental issues, and the suspicion attaching to a public servant regarded as pushful. In New South Wales the Wilenski report gives good marks among others to the Department of Agriculture and the Planning and Environment Commission.[62]

Levels

Just as in the horizontal division of work, there were two questions—How many subunits? How shall functions be grouped?—so in the case of the vertical division of work, there are the questions: How many levels? What shall each level do?

(i) The Number of Levels   The problem of relationships between levels has arisen in various ways in administrative theory. One is in connection with the old doctrine of the 'span of control'. This is the view that because the difficulty of co-ordination increases disproportionately with an increase in the number of directly controlled subunits, the latter should be kept down to a low figure. This always looked oversimple; it was pointed out that because there is also a problem of communication between levels, and because for any given organisation narrowing spans of control involves increasing the number of levels, the principle cannot be one of an absolute kind.

Thus if, to lessen co-ordination problems at the top, a cabinet were to consist only of six ministers, their departments would become bigger than they could look after in the old way. This might lead to their handing some powers to a new layer of junior ministers; or to their leaving more to the permanent head, who would then find the burden intolerable and so might appoint a new layer of deputy heads. In the effort to simplify the cabinet's problem, we have complicated things lower down. It is clear that some balance between the number of units at any level, and the number of levels, is involved.

It has been argued that in public administration there is some presumption that a tall narrow pyramid is not a good substitute for a broad flat one. Long hierarchies exacerbate communication problems. They often make more difficult the precise allocation of responsibility and authority, and encourage buck-passing, because it is hard to define the tasks of different levels. The British Fulton Committee criticised the long hierarchies of some Whitehall departments on this ground; and one can make a similar point to those who favour multi-tier governmental systems—for example, the Commonwealth, State, regional and local governments all having a finger in a good many pies.

(ii) Delegation and Decentralisation   'Delegation' strictly refers to the act by which a political or legal authority transfers the right to exercise powers to a subordinate authority, that 'acts for' the superior authority. Here it is used more broadly to refer to any formal transfer of authority to lower levels of a hierarchy. 'Decentralisation' sometimes has the same meaning, but more commonly refers to territorial decentralisation, such as creating regional branches with powers formerly exercised by head office. This latter process need not involve more 'delegation', as the regional officer's powers may be no greater (or even less) than those formerly held by headquarters officers at the same level. Where decentralisation involves creating new legal or political authorities, it is sometimes called 'devolution'.[63]

The arguments for and against delegation and decentralisation cannot be stated in black and white; as with the number of levels, a balance of advantages and disadvantages is involved, the commonly used criteria are hard to quantify, and sometimes contain paradoxes. Thus more delegation may in one case be said to enable problems to be dealt with by those most knowledgeable about them, who are able to adapt solutions to the particular case; in another to increase the possibility of error, by resulting in less knowledgeable people taking decisions. Clearly it all depends on circumstances, on policies, personnel and the nature of the environment.

Some terms in the argument need careful definition. If a senior officer finds that instead of dealing with many individual cases, he can promote a rule that largely determines their outcome, which he leaves to his subordinates to apply, is that 'delegation'? It is clearly 'delegation of workload', but there is not much 'delegation of power' involved. The latter is much harder to achieve, as people rarely favour the deconcentration or dispersal of their own powers on matters that they regard as important.

It is true that certain conditions favour a dispersed control system. The more an organisation depends on a highly technical and professional staff, the harder it may be for the top to control their work. This is also true if an organisation greatly depends for important information on the initiative of staff further down the line, or depends for other 'resources' on lower-level units. It may be an agency reliant on voluntary or highly motivated workers who object to being ordered around; or one whose subunits have access to important independent sources of finance; or have established strong affiliations with influential clientele or other outside groups. Sometimes an organisation's success depends on achieving centrally determined goals by the clear structuring and control of tasks from the top down. In others the important objectives may be set at lower levels, and the top may be mainly concerned with settling disputes or liaison activities. As Peter Self has said, it is important for a government agency to decide whether it is operating a unified service, or is more like an 'overhead unit' or 'holding company' for the various operating units.[64]

There is also a distinction between delegating authority in substantive decision-making, and increasing a unit's command over those common services needed for the decisions it already has formal power to make. The latter might seem to present the clearer case—if a unit has to perform certain tasks, surely, in the interests of clarity of responsibility, speed and flexibility, it should have a large command over the resources (finance, personnel, material equipment and supplies) needed for them? In practice, it is not so simple. There are many cases where central control of finance and personnel is properly used as an effective, if a little covert, control on substantive decision-making, especially when the limits on a subordinate unit's discretion are hard to define precisely, or it is inexpedient to define them.

The clear delegation of decision-making powers has some special problems in government agencies. Ministerial responsibility to parliament means that some decisions have to be taken at a higher level than they would otherwise. Departments and branches are so organised that many decisions involve more than one of them, and can only be taken after consultation. In some fields of work, it is hard to define in advance the precise discretion that can be allowed to each level.

Decentralisation and delegation in all their forms can be made easier by good training—both in the sense of widely spread skill and of a widely shared habit of co operation; and by exploiting to the full the possibilities of control through fairly simple devices, so that a few central decisions provide a framework within which a good many people can exercise discretion without engendering major conflicts or disharmonies.

Hiving Off

This term has been used lately to describe a form of delegation by which some field of activity that can be made largely self-contained is handed over to a largely autonomous authority, over which the main department exercises only a general control. This is said to reduce the workload of the latter, so that it can concentrate on policy-forming functions; and to encourage the hived-off agencies to adopt modern criteria of efficient and accountable management.

The example of Sweden is often quoted, where ministerial departments are small, and mainly act to advise the minister and provide a central secretariat. Execution of policy lies with separate Agencies, usually public boards, subject to certain controls given to the ministries by legislation, including budgetary approval and written 'guidelines'. The Agencies can make policy and budgetary recommendations to the ministries, which are made public, and reasons must be given for accepting or rejecting them. Senior ministry officials are often fairly young and often move out later to become managers in the Agencies.[65] The directors-general of the latter are appointed for a term of years, but usually reappointed, and they normally have wide decision-making powers.

A good deal of hiving off has already taken place in Australia, notably to statutory authorities (see Chapter Five). There are a few cases in the States of small co-ordinating ministries (see Chapter Three), and a number of cases (fifty or more in New South Wales) where fairly large units within ministerial departments, other than statutory corporations, operate with a fair measure of independence. At Commonwealth level, over the years the Treasury hived off various functions not central to its control and policy-making functions. The Australian Taxation Office (working through its own Commissioner to the Treasurer) is largely left to its own business, though tax policy is the separate concern of a departmental branch. There are a number of other 'outrider shows', as they are familiarly called, now associated with the Department of Finance, like the Royal Australian Mint and the Retirement Benefits Office. The Australian Bureau of Statistics was recently hived off as a statutory authority. However, in most cases the relations between Australian departments and semi-autonomous agencies within them are regulated more by convention and are not exposed, as in Sweden, to the law and to public scrutiny; and most have less staffing freedom.

The Fulton Report recommended more hiving off in Britain, though it would 'raise parliamentary and constitutional issues, especially if they affected the answerability for sensitive matters such as social and education services'. In Sweden the checks of courts, Ombudsmen and enforced publicity are more important mechanisms of answerability than in most countries, and there is no tradition of ministerial responsibility for detailed administration. Hiving off seems most attractive where the field is relatively uncontroversial, reasonably self-contained, and specially suited to 'accountable management' (control by setting a few general standards and targets). There is always the danger of producing a mass of petty empires, poorly co-ordinated. The Coombs Report was less attracted to the idea than might have been expected. It thought that a reasonably flexible departmental administration could probably achieve most of the advantages of formal hiving off without its defects. Australia still holds to the British tradition that policy and administration ought not to be sharply separated; and permanent heads are not keen on having their authority reduced.

Territorial Decentralisation

This turns up nowadays in many political and administrative contexts—in Commonwealth–State relations, in questions of decentralisation away from capital cities (regionalism, growth centres) or even within capital cities. Some useful lessons have been learnt. One is that success is more likely if the number of centres chosen is fairly small. 'Scatteration' tends to be wasteful and unproductive, whether it be the attempt to stimulate growth by putting a little money into many country towns, or dispersing offices to many different locations in a capital city. As has been said (with some exaggeration) of office dispersal in Canberra, 'You have public servants . . . making an eight mile car ride every time they want to have a conference with someone from another department'.[66] Many of the issues are pursued further, as they affect intergovernmental relations, in Chapters Seven to Nine.

Notes

1. On the conditions of successful reorganisation, see F.C. Mosher (ed.), *Governmental Reorganisations*, Bobbs–Merrill, New York, 1967.
2. G.E. Caiden, *Administrative Reform*, Allen Lane, London, 1970, 65; and cf. B.C. Smith, 'Reform and Change in British Central Administration', *Political Studies,* XIX, 2, June 1971.
3. On the 'liability of newness', see the good discussion in A.L. Stinchcombe, 'Social Structure and Organizations', in J.G. March (ed.), *Handbook of Organizations,* Rand McNally, Chicago, 1965.
4. W.J.M. Mackenzie and J.W. Grove, *Central Administration in Britain*, Longmans, London 1957, 365.
5. R.L. Wettenhall, 'Government Department or Statutory Authority', *Public Admin.* (Sydney), XXVII, 4, December 1968, 352.
6. For fuller discussion, see H.A. Simon, D.W. Smithburg and V.A. Thompson, *Public Administration*, Knopf, New York, 1950, ch. VI.
7. For example, see C. Argyris, *Personality and Organization*, Harper and Kew, New York, 1957; for a modified view, see E.L. Trist, *Organizational Choice*, Tavistock Publications, London, 1963.
8. V.A. Thompson, *Modern Organization*, Knopf, New York, 1961, ch. 3, 'Specialization'.
9. H.A. Simon, *Administrative Behavior*, 2nd edn, Macmillan, New York, 1957, 238.
10. D.N. Chester and F.M.G. Willson, *The Organization of British Central Government*, 2nd edn, Allen and Unwin, London, 1968, 390.
11. Chester and Willson, *op. cit.*, 392.
12. C.C. Halton, 'Change from Within: the Australian Department of Transport', *Aust. J. Public Admin.*, XXXV, 1, March 1976.
13. E.G. Whitlam, 'Australian Public Administration under a Labor Government', Robert Garran Oration, 1973.
14. Sir Richard Clarke, *New Trends in Government*, HMSO, London, 1971.
15. cf. R.P. Deane, *The Establishment of the Department of Trade*, ANU, Canberra, 1963, 71 ff.
16. Peter Samuel, *The Bulletin*, 8 July 1967.
17. Report, RCAGA, 77–8.
18. cf. K. Minogue, 'Hyperactivism in Modern British Politics', in Maurice Cowling (ed.), *Conservative Essays*, Cassell, London, 1978.
19. R. van Munster, 'Changes in Administrative Arrangements and their Implementation', Report, RCAGA, Appendix Vol. One, 423.
20. *The Age*, 27 October 1974.
21. In a paper for the US President's Committee on Administrative Management, reprinted in L. Gulick and L.F. Urwick, *Papers on the Science of Administration,* Institute of Public Administration, New York, 1937. Some of the principles were derived from the British (Haldane) Report on the Machinery of Government,

HMSO, London, 1918. See also H.A. Simon, *Administrative Behavior*, ch. II; D.N. Chester and F.M.G. Willson, *op. cit.*, especially ch. XI; and V. Subramaniam, 'Machinery of Government Investigations: Fifty Years after the Haldane Report', *Public Admin.* (Sydney), XXVII, 3, September 1968.

22. *The Government of N.S.W.: Directory of Administration and Services, 1977–78*, 220.
23. P. Self, *Administrative Theories and Politics*, Allen and Unwin, London, 1972, 137.
24. Self, *loc. cit.*
25. Report, Commonwealth Public Service Board, Canberra, 1970, 13. For a further account, see Peter Saul, 'Changing Organisations', in Report, RCAGA, Appendix Vol. Three, 418.
26. See Bruce Juddery, *Canberra Times*, 31 March 1978.
27. Saul, *op. cit.*, 427–9, gives an interesting account of these pressures.
28. cf. M. Craft, *School Welfare Provision in Australia*, Commission of Inquiry into Poverty, Canberra, 1977.
29. Report, RCAGA, 161.
30. *ibid.*, 161–3, 340; in Appendix Vol. Two, 371 ff., there is an interesting account of the difficulties involved in such a project.
31. J.M. Power and R.L. Wettenhall, 'The Organisation of Government: The Place of Function and the Function of Place', paper to the Canberra Seminar on Administrative Studies, August 1976.
32. cf. Bruce Juddery, 'Farewell to Vision of Northern Region', *Canberra Times*, 18 February 1976.
33. *Commonwealth Government Directory*, Canberra, 1977, 171.
34. cf. David Corbett, 'The Glassco Commission and the Machinery of Government', *Public Admin.* (Sydney), XXIII, 3, September 1964, 263–7.
35. A.H. Boxer, *Experts in Asia*, ANU Press, Canberra, 1969, 171.
36. Leon Peres, 'Principle or Interest? Changing Roles within Australian Government', *Melbourne J. Politics*, 3, 1970; and see also the interesting article by Sir Richard Clarke, 'The Number and Size of Government Departments', *Political Quarterly*, 43, 2, April–June 1972.
37. M. Bessant, 'Education and Politics in . . . New South Wales and Victoria, 1900–1940', Ph.D. thesis, Monash University, Melbourne, 1971.
38. See B.R. Clark, 'Organizational Adaptation and Precarious Values', *Amer. Sociological Review*, 21, 1956, reprinted in part in A. Etzioni, *Complex Organizations*, Holt Rinehart Winston, New York, 1961, 159–67.
39. See G.E. Caiden, *Career Service*, Melbourne University Press, Melbourne, 1965, 405–7.
40. R. van Munster, 'Changes in Administrative Arrangements and their Implementation', Report, RCAGA, Appendix Vol. One, 410.
41. Chester and Willson, *op. cit.*, 333–8, and 1st Report, Civil Service Department, HMSO, London 1970.
42. van Munster, *op. cit.*, 414.
43. See *Canberra Times*, 6 September 1975.
44. Report, RCAGA, 387.
45. Report, Committee on the Machinery of Government, HMSO, London, 1918.
46. Chester and Willson, *op. cit.*; R.L. Wettenhall, *A Guide to Tasmanian Government Administration*, Platypus, Hobart, 1968.

47. See Barry Moore, 'Machinery of Government Changes in New South Wales', *Public Admin.* (Sydney), XXXIV, 2, June 1975.

48. See L.F. Urwick, *Elements of Administration*, 2nd edn, Pitman, London, 1950, 63–4.

49. I owe some points to an unpublished paper on 'Role Analysis' by Mr Barry Moore.

50. See J. Pfiffner and F. Sherwood, 'Organizational Overlays', in R.T. Golembiewski *et al.* (eds), *Public Administration: Readings in Institutions, Processes, Behavior*, Rand McNally, Chicago, 1966.

51. An important early proponent of this view was Mary Parker Follett. See her essay, 'The Giving of Orders', in H.C. Metcalf and L. Urwick (eds), *Dynamic Administration: The Collected Papers of Mary Parker Follett*, Management Publications Ltd, London, 1941. She stresses the need to depersonalise orders, and make the subordinate feel that the so-called order is given in obedience to the 'law of the situation'. The perfect product of such methods, with co-operativeness built-in, has been under fire since W.H. Whyte published *The Organization Man*, Simon and Schuster, New York, 1957.

52. This account of Weber's model does not always use his own words. On Weber, see H.H. Gerth and C.W. Mills, *From Max Weber: Essays in Sociology*, Routledge and Kegan Paul, London, 1948: P.M. Blau and M.W. Meyer, *Bureaucracy in Modern Society*, 2nd edn, Random House, New York, 1971, ch. 2; and M. Albrow, *Bureaucracy*, Macmillan, London, 1970.

53. Some of the following is based on R.A. Dahl and C.E. Lindblom, *Politics, Economics and Welfare*, Harper, New York, 1953. The classic account of the dysfunctions of bureaucracy is R.K. Merton, 'Bureaucratic Structure and Personality', *Social Forces*, 18, May 1940, reprinted in *Social Theory and Social Structure*, Free Press, Glencoe, Ill., 1949.

54. Interim Report, Review of New South Wales Government Administration, Sydney, 1977, 160–1.

55. cf. B.B. Schaffer, 'The Deadlock in Development Administration', in Colin Leys (ed), *Politics and Change in Developing Countries*, Cambridge University Press, Cambridge, 1969.

56. Report, RCAGA, 27.

57. Tom Burns, *The B.B.C.: Public Institutions and World*, Macmillan, London, 1977.

58. V.A. Thompson, *Modern Organization*, Knopf, New York, 1961, 69. See also P.B. Blau and W.R. Scott, *Formal Organizations*, Chandler Publishing Co., San Francisco, 1962, 116–28.

59. Chester Barnard, *Organization and Management*, Harvard University Press, 1948, 223; and cf. G.C. Homans, *Social Behaviour*, Routledge and Kegan Paul, London, 1961, 251.

60. On different forms of compliance in organisations, see P.B. Clark and J.Q. Wilson, 'Incentive Systems: A Theory of Organizations', *Admin. Science Quarterly*, 6, 2, September 1961; and A. Etzioni, *A Comparative Analysis of Complex Organizations*, Free Press, New York, 1961.

61. For discussion, see A.F. Davies, 'Politics in a Knowledgeable Society', *Public Admin.* (Sydney), XXIX, 2, June 1970; A. Etzioni, *The Active Society*, Free Press, New York, 1968; H.S. Kariel, *Open Systems*, Peacock, Illinois 1969, and references in the Davies article.

62. *Review of New South Wales Government Administration: Directions for Change* (Wilenski Report), Sydney, 1977, 163.

112 GOVERNMENT ADMINISTRATION IN AUSTRALIA

63. J.W. Fesler, 'Centralization and Decentralization', *International Encyclopedia of the Social Sciences*, Macmillan and Free Press, New York, 1968.
64. Self, *op. cit.*, 74.
65. See e.g. T.H. Caulcott and P. Mountfield, "Decentralised Administration in Sweden", *Public Admin.* (London), Spring 1974.
66. *Australian Financial Review*, 28 June 1975.

Chapter Five

Non-Departmental Agencies

We use this negative term to apply to all those Associated Agencies listed in Chapter Three that differ in one way or another from the pattern of the normal ministerial department. The main group discussed in this chapter are the so-called Statutory Authorities, in particular Statutory Corporations; but there is also a short section on Advisory Bodies, some of which are also 'statutory', but many of which are appointed by executive action.

Statutory Authorities

Definition

If asked to define a 'statutory authority', most Australians would probably reply by giving an example—the Public Service Board of New South Wales or the Australian Broadcasting Commission. This caution is warranted, as such bodies conform to no single pattern and their functions are diverse. Indeed, the only feature common to them all is that they are created by special statute. Many are also expected to behave with somewhat more independence from political control than a normal ministerial department, though the degree of this varies considerably. They frequently have their own governing board. There is an important group of statutory bodies, usually called 'statutory corporations', to which much of this chapter will be devoted, and which have the legal status of corporate bodies with independent legal personality, which enables them to own property and to sue and be sued in their own name.

The first characteristic of statutory authorities—that they are set up by an Act of Parliament, which lays down the nature of their governing body and its powers and functions—is one way in Australia of distinguishing them from normal ministerial departments, which can commonly be created, reorganised or abolished at the will of the government, without parliamentary sanction. Though this distinction works pretty well at Commonwealth level, it is not as clear when we look at the States, where many ministerial departments are also creations of statute. Among other things, establishment by special legislation gives such a body a certain status and prestige.

The second characteristic is that many statutory authorities are given some independence. A minister is supposed to be fully and directly responsible to parliament for all the activities of his department (though Chapter Three has indicated problems about this view). The Act that sets up a statutory authority generally provides for some ministerial control, sometimes a high degree of control; all the same, it is often accepted that such a body will have greater freedom of action than the ordinary department under a minister. Indeed, if a statutory authority is not to have some independence, there seems little point in setting it up. This freedom may be reinforced by exempting its staff partly or wholly from the provisions of Public Service Acts; that is, giving the statutory body more control over its personnel. It may be empowered to organise its finances on commercial lines, separate from consolidated revenue, and less subject to treasury control.

Here is a description of a fairly independent statutory corporation, the Australian National Airlines Commission that operates TAA. A small part-time board 'determines major policy questions within the framework of the creating act, . . . its officers are not public servants in the legal sense, and they are recruited independently of the Public Service Board. Its receipts do not flow into consolidated revenue; it holds its own funds and spends them free from the restrictions of the normal governmental budgetary process. Certain of its decisions are subject to ministerial approval, but the minister is not its head in the departmental fashion. The minister fixes a profit-target, and the annual dividend payment, the return on the public investment, goes into the Treasury. The enterprise is not subject to detailed questioning in parliament (though the British House of Commons is more consistent about this than Australian legislatures), but will present annual reports and financial statements on which judgements about performance may be made'.[1]

However, this is by no means representative; there are many variants, and a large 'grey area' between the normal ministerial department and a fully fledged statutory corporation such as the Australian National Airlines Commission.[2] At one extreme, there are a few sections of departments covered by specific legislation, and in that sense 'statutory', yet which have few or no powers in their own right and which are staffed in the normal departmental fashion. On the other hand, one very important category of statutory body operates virtually as an independent department, staffed under the Public Service Act and with a chief executive who has the same status as permanent head, and more independence, as the powers of the minister concerned are nominal. Such 'quasi-departments' include the Public Service Boards and Auditors-General. There are bodies such as Qantas Airways Ltd, which is no more 'statutory' than any other company incorporated under ordinary state law, yet 'seems for many governmental and administrative purposes to be indistinguishable from a statutorily created business enterprise, such as TAA or the Commonwealth Serum Laboratories'.[3]

Development of Statutory Authorities

The non-departmental agency has a long history in Australian government.[4] Before the days of self-government, Land Boards were set up to report on applications for land, and Boards of Education ran the school system; trustee savings banks were established in several colonies; Aborigines Boards, Central Boards of Health and Harbour Boards were created, and some have survived to the present day. Commissioners were used as early instruments of local government. These early boards were mostly amateur part-time bodies, a convenient way of getting special jobs done, especially where there were interested parties ready to act. Many statutory bodies of this kind still exist, such as library boards and a variety of other small regulatory bodies.

However, the major activities of government, if sometimes at first farmed out to boards, tended in the later nineteenth century to be absorbed into regular ministerial departments fully responsible to Parliament. The old amateur board proved inadequate to run major services, and by the 1880s 'there was a strong movement towards centring all administrative functions in ministerial departments . . . accompanied by another seeking to integrate all the departments in a single uniformly regulated and patronage-free public service for each colony'.[5]

This tendency to unify governmental functions in ministerial departments in turn generated a counter-tendency, which has produced the modern types of statutory authority. Some administrative theorists have argued that this is part of a regular oscillatory movement in government. There are periods when a unified departmental system appears constricting, and there are strong pressures to cut loose from it, and to hand over new or ailing governmental functions to novel kinds of agency. But such a trend can produce a very complex and confused structure, with many diverse centres of power; and this creates a demand for simplification and integration of government activities under a few clear heads of responsibility. A recent example of the latter is the Bland Report's criticism of Victoria's 'disorderly organisational structure', with its mass of commissions and boards, and his view that the functions of government should be brought together under a smaller number of ministerial departments.[6]

In a less dogmatic way, the Coombs Commission has also criticised the proliferation of statutory authorities at the federal level, and thought that it should be possible 'to reduce the number of independently operating statutory bodies by using instead the established machinery available to departments'.[7] In 1976 the government endorsed the Commission's conclusion favouring the ministerial department unless 'a clear necessity' for using a statutory authority can be demonstrated,[8] and a working party is to draw up guidelines.

Functions

Certainly the number of Australian statutory authorities is very large and greatly exceeds the number of ministerial departments. The State of Victoria has about 150. A New South Wales survey listed 244, and some items included a number of separate authorities. A recent incomplete Commonwealth survey covered 170 statutory authorities (of these, 89 were statutory corporations, and another six registered as companies),[9] and the true figure probably exceeds 200. They vary greatly as to their functions, area of jurisdiction, membership, financing, staffing, relations with ministers and departments. Table 5.1 gives an incomplete list, showing the kinds of bodies operating in New South Wales in 1978.

TABLE 5.1
NSW Statutory Boards and Commissions

1. Public Utility and Business Undertakings
Transport
Main Roads Commissioner
Maritime Services Board
Public Transport Commission
Power and Fuel
Electricity Commission
Other Commercial Undertakings
Rural Bank
Government Insurance Office*
Sydney Farm Produce Market Authority
Totalizator Agency Board
Water Supply and Conservation
Water Resources Commission
Forestry Commission*
Metropolitan Water Sewerage and Drainage Board
Hunter District Water Board
Broken Hill Water Board
Housing and Urban Development
Albury–Wodonga (NSW) Corporation
Bathurst–Orange Development Corporation*
Housing Commission*
Sydney Cove Redevelopment Authority

2. Regulatory and Co-ordinating Authorities
Electricity Authority*
Commissioner for Motor Transport
Joint Coal Board
Public Service Board*
Auditor-General*
Corporate Affairs Commission*
Planning and Environment Commission*
State Pollution Control Commission*

3. Quasi-departmental Administrative Agencies
Board of Fire Commissioners
Health Commission*

TABLE 5.1—*continued*

       Police Commissioner
       Grain Elevators Board
       State Superannuation Board*
       Western Lands Commission*
       Bursary Endowment Board*

4. Quasi-judicial Tribunals
       Industrial Commission*
       Workers Compensation Commission*
       Crown Employees Appeal Board*
       Fair Rents Board*
       Licenses Reduction Board*
       Local Land Boards*

5. Commodity Marketing Boards
       Dairy Industry Authority
       Marketing Boards (Egg, Lemon, Rice, Tobacco Leaf, etc.)
       Fish Marketing Authority

6. Educational, Cultural, and Recreation Trusts
       Art Gallery Trustees*
       Australian Museum Trustees*
       Museum of Applied Arts and Sciences Trustees*
       National Trust of Australia (NSW)

7. Professional Registration and Examining Boards
       Board of Veterinary Surgeons*
       Medical Board*
       Dental Board*
       Architects Board
       Surveyors Board*
       Public Accountants Registration Board*
       Pharmacy Board*
       Nurses Registration Board*
       Physiotherapists Registration Board*

---

* Statutory authorities with staff under Public Service Act.

For many years the Commonwealth, with its more limited responsibilities in the fields of development, economic regulation and community services, was under less pressure than the States to establish new forms of government agency. Up to the Second World War, it had established a handful of statutory corporations, as described later in this chapter, but its largest business undertaking, the Post Office, was operated as a ministerial department, and remained so until the 1970s. The Commonwealth had also created a number of regulatory agencies, such as the Public Service Board and the Tariff Board (now Industries Assistance Commission); and one or two quasi-judicial tribunals, such as Taxation Boards of Review, the Conciliation and Arbitration Court, and the Public Service Arbitrator.

After the war there was a great expansion in Commonwealth statutory authorities. A large number of business, public utility and service enterprises were created by both Labor and non-Labor governments, starting with TAA (1945) and the Snowy Mountains Hydro-Electric Authority (1949). These are discussed in more detail below. There was also a significant growth in other kinds of statutory authority, among which we may specially note bodies concerned in various ways with planning, research and advice on federal financial aid—such as the Australian Universities Commission (1959) and the National Capital Development Commission (1958). In the twenty-five years after 1939, Commonwealth government employment in non-departmental agencies rose from 20 000 to over 100 000—a figure more than doubled since then by the creation of the Postal and Telecommunications commissions.

The Labor government of 1972–75 had a special predilection for statutory bodies, and created or reconstituted more than sixty.[10] They included:

1. Commercial and semi-commercial corporations, such as the Pipeline Authority, the Postal Commission and the Telecommunications Commission.
2. Executive agencies to manage special projects or new programmes, such as the Albury–Wodonga Development Corporation and the Health Insurance Commission.
3. Regulatory and quasi-judicial agencies, such as the Prices Justification Tribunal and the Administrative Appeals Tribunal.
4. Cultural agencies, such as the Australia Council and the Film Commission.
5. Consultative bodies concerned with planning, financial aid, and so on, such as the Social Welfare Commission (now defunct) and the Schools Commission.

As noted earlier, there is now some reaction against the statutory authority. However most of Labor's creations have survived, and its successor has added a few. A notable example is the Office of National Assessments (1977), which is concerned with assessing international intelligence and is a statutory body free of departmental control, or of any external control of the contents and conclusions of its reports. It is 'subject to policy control and managerial oversight through the Committee of Ministers on Intelligence and Security assisted by a committee of permanent heads'.[11]

Reasons for Creation

The advantages over normal departmental administration claimed for the statutory authority may be summarised[12] as follows:

1. The advantage of administration free from political control, making it easier for the authority to act impartially; or to provide an independent judgment; or to develop policies appropriate to the activity; or to concentrate on technical and managerial efficiency.
2. The possibility of representing on governing boards various functions, interests or outlooks appropriate to the activity—the expert, the producer,

the businessman (one form of this has been characterised as 'putting the activity where the talent is'); of bringing an outside element into management.

3. The chance of building up a personnel system appropriate to the activity and free from some of the rigidities of ordinary public service rules.

4. The advantage of giving the agency some degree of self-contained financing and budgetary control, especially where it engages in revenue-earning activities.

5. The belief that separate statutory identity helps an agency to develop its own institutional pride and *esprit de corps* by virtue of its distinct and separate existence, which leads to more effective work.

In the case of a statutory body with corporate status, there is also

6. The technical legal advantages of an entity with perpetual succession, capable of suing and being sued by ordinary processes of law and of owning property free from the restrictions and immunities of Crown law (this has become less important with the reform of Crown law in general).

Lists of 'advantages' of this kind have their uses; but they by no means all apply to any particular authority, nor do they cover all cases, for example, some statutory bodies have been set up with the mainly negative aim of freeing a minister or a department from overload, especially from detailed involvement in a relatively self-contained area of the department's work. Some facilitate joint government control of a function, as do the Joint Coal Board and the Albury–Wodonga corporations (see Chapter Eight). There are also various reasons for creating statutory authorities that may be broadly termed political. Some of these may be subsumed under the so-called 'back-double' theory, which maintains that people who cannot get where they want to under the existing system will back-double (a phrase of English cabdrivers) and set up new routes outside the system.[13]

For example, the Labor government's statutory authorities referred to above served several objectives. They were channels for new initiatives in policy-making, relatively uncluttered by the debris of the past.[14] They widened the scope for patronage, especially in the relatively benign sense of direct and speedy appointment to key positions of persons with relevant expertness and drive, thought to be broadly sympathetic to ministerial aims. They were a way of giving some power to professionals at the expense of generalist administrators. They were sometimes a means, believed to be politically more acceptable than a ministerial department, of extending federal intervention in State affairs. This is a special case of a quite common motive for creating a statutory agency, to make a new venture more palatable to the interests concerned, by reducing direct government control and appointing a more trusted group to run it; the latter act as a kind of middleman, or buffer, to allocate resources or deal with some other controversial area without directly involving the government. This is the principle long involved in the arbitration system and some marketing boards.[15] Of course, there is always the danger that such buffers and brokers will also disintegrate government, each of them becoming the assessor and advocate of particular needs, without regard to broader priorities and policies.

The central arguments for and against the statutory authority tend to be related to its supposed greater autonomy. Thus it may be argued that 'goal effectiveness' will be maximised if some function can be taken outside the normal bureaucratic system and given to a special agency solely concerned with its performance and with power to get on with the job. Against this it may be argued that more autonomy for particular agencies weakens co-ordination. To grant a high degree of independence is easier where the function is reasonably self-contained, and where it can be adequately controlled by a few general policy guidelines.[16] Thus a main roads authority is likely to do a better job for road-users if it has a fair amount of freedom, but the co-ordination of roads with general planning may suffer, as some say has happened in Australian States with Main Roads Boards or Commissioners. How far we are prepared to let the highway function become autonomous depends on how important we think this co-ordination is, and how far it can be achieved by exercising a few broad ministerial controls.

Certain fields of government are often said to be best suited to statutory authorities,[17] such as

1. For commercial activities.
2. Where impartiality needs safeguarding, and close party-political links are considered undesirable, as in judicial and quasi-judicial tasks, certain kinds of grant-aid, or in informational and opinion-forming activities, such as broadcasting and television.
3. For creative activities of a research or cultural kind (CSIRO, the universities, broadcasting).
4. Where the case for strong interest-group participation is widely accepted (marketing boards), or for the representation on the governing body of a variety of community interests.
5. Where a separate channel of advice or separate evaluation of policies is needed.

The logic of this is not as clear as it might be. One reason for this is that it assumes a clearer distinction than often exists in practice between the working of statutory authorities and that of ordinary government departments. It cannot be taken for granted that the former always, or even commonly, have more autonomy than the latter. This matter is discussed below in relation to the statutory corporation. Nor is it clear how far one can stretch the concept of 'impartiality' and freedom from politics. Mr Whitlam has said that bodies such as the Commonwealth Grants Commission and the Universities Commission have shown how effective national policies are possible 'through processes of systematic, impartial and objective inquiry followed by establishment of national priorities and the provision of appropriate funds'.[18] This suggests a broad function for independent bodies in investigation, followed by public advice to governments on long-term planning. But this assumes that they will behave with considerable discretion, and not move far out of the line that they think will be acceptable to government.

When they want to go further than this, it can lead to trouble, unless their public prestige is very great. The independent-mindedness of some statutory authorities was well demonstrated in 1977. Within the course of a few weeks the Prices Justification Tribunal was ignoring the stated policy of the government,[19] the Conciliation and Arbitration Commission made it clear that it took little account of the government's view that wage increases were the major cause of inflation and unemployment, while the Industries Assistance Commission (IAC) was under attack by the Prime Minister for its free-trade inclinations. The Schools Commission, having been given guidelines by the Commonwealth government on its allocations, said in its 1977 Report that it viewed 'very seriously the implications of such prescriptive guidelines', which pre-empted the nature of the commission's advice, and threatened the consultative processes by which it made up its mind.[20] Even the Public Service Board allowed itself some fairly sharp criticism of government policy on staff ceilings in its 1977 Report.

Some of these cases illustrate how a body whose powers are no more than investigatory and advisory can nevertheless embarrass the government, if its reports are published. This was often shown by the former Tariff Board, and more recently by its successor, the Industries Assistance Commission. The latter is a statutory authority whose task is to advise the government on assistance to be given to domestic industries. Sir John Crawford, in recommending its establishment in 1973, spoke of two advantages of such a body; it could 'because of its independence, be expected to provide advice . . . which is disinterested' and it could also 'facilitate public scrutiny' of government policies.[21] The Commission consists of from five to nine commissioners who are appointed for renewable terms of up to five years. Its advice is given in published reports based on public inquiries, and it has its own research staff. Some matters, such as variations in long-term tariff or financial assistance to primary and secondary industry, have to be referred to the commission for report before the government can act, and it also has some power to initiate its own inquiries.

Its reports have often worried governments, as did those on the textile, clothing and footwear industries in August 1977, which led the Prime Minister to speak of the paradox of a body designed to assist industry which 'some believe is dedicated to the destruction of industry'.[22] As a result the government is to add a section to the Act reducing the considerable discretion of the commission, by laying down new guidelines—such as requiring it to indicate in its reports the assistance needed to maintain present activity and employment in an industry and, if a lower level of protection than this is recommended, to justify this proposal. It is doubtful whether this would really stop the commission embarrassing governments from time to time. The only effective way to do this would be to appoint tame-cat commissioners, or to deprive them of their research staff. Even a general report, such as the position paper on *Some Issues in Structural Adjustment* (September 1977) is in effect a criticism of the government for the inadequacy of its measures to help manufacturing industry adapt to changing conditions. This is not to say that outspokenness is necessarily the same as effectiveness. Some would argue that the Treasury operating anonymously has often been a more effective anti-protectionist voice than the IAC, which has to act mainly in public. Such a body has to strike a difficult balance between its investigatory work, its longer-term 'educational' function, and the political forces that threaten it from time to time.

Concept of Autonomy

As Peres has argued, most writers on this subject have far too simple-minded a notion of what constitutes autonomy, or independence. A government agency may be independent but uninfluential, or very independent from one point of view, not at all from another.

The central issue is often taken to be control of 'policy'. But, as has been indicated elsewhere in this book, how policy is determined is a complex matter. The formal structure of the organisation may be of little importance. In some fields, the policy decisions made at the top are inevitably vague and general, and many of the significant operational policy decisions are made lower down, whether we are talking of a ministerial department or an 'independent' board. Also, if a minister has no control or only imperfect control over policies, this is no guarantee that they will be made autonomously by the board or commission concerned; sometimes a government agency may be more exposed to outside pressures by not having a minister to defend it.

In any case, an agency with a strong operational side may be much more interested in controlling its own options in the implementation of policy, than in controlling policy itself. Alternatively, a statutory authority may be mainly concerned with control of its own incentives; that is, of its capacity to attract contributors to its work. To take a simple example, an agency with greater financial resources has more freedom in the sense of more power to buy the contributions it wants. But what if more ministerial control of policy also means that an agency gets more money for its activities? Is it more or less 'free'? Of course, it may be an important non-material incentive to some groups to take part in policy-making, as with research workers; it seems to be important to bodies like CSIRO to have a good deal of this kind of freedom to distribute around. Finally, what some organisations, such as universities, partly seek is power to preserve their own character and style of behaviour, and this is yet another criterion of independence.

The Statutory Corporation

Development

The statutory corporation as an instrument of government enterprise may well have been invented in Australia, where it has long been a familiar agency

of government. Towards the end of the last century some awareness developed
of the political and administrative advantages of such agencies. This arose
chiefly in relation to railways, which had been government-owned and
operated in Victoria and New South Wales since the 1850s, and had provided
considerable opportunities for patronage and corruption. In 1883 Victoria
took the first deliberate step to provide a suitable instrument for government
in business, when legislation created a statutory corporation to operate the
Victorian railways. It consisted of a Chairman and two Commissioners,
appointed by the Governor for seven-year terms. The Commission was
granted a large measure of managerial autonomy, including authority over
the appointment and control of staff. However, the government did not fully
honour either the law or the intent behind it, so that by 1890 the experiment
looked like failing. This led to some rethinking, and a reduction in 1891
of the formal autonomy of the Commission.[23]

The New South Wales railways legislation of 1888 was initiated by Sir
Henry Parkes, who had carefully reviewed Victorian experience, and it
avoided some of the pitfalls of the Victorian legislation. Parkes' determination, shared by later ministries, to defend the Railways Commission's
autonomy against the pressures of pettifogging local members contributed
to its early success.[24] The device was later adopted in the other States.

Other fields in which it was early used include ports (the Sydney Harbour
Trust, set up in 1901, and the Melbourne Harbour Trust, reorganised as
a statutory authority in 1912); savings banks (e.g. the NSW Government
Savings Bank, 1906); developmental activities such as irrigation (the Victorian State Rivers and Water Supply Commission, 1905); and some public
utility services ordinarily associated with local government. A number of such
boards were established in Victoria after 1902, when the Liberal Premier,
Sir William Irvine, launched a policy of State development. The aim was
to separate out the province of the expert, eliminating direct political control
from undertakings that served a political consensus.[25] This phase culminated
in the 1919 Act which established the State Electricity Commission.

Other Forms of Public Enterprise

Not all government enterprises are operated by statutory corporations. The
Commonwealth Department of Productivity manages several munitions and
ordnance factories. In the States, too, there are examples of departmental
administration of business enterprises, though fewer than was once the case.
This has been specially true of Queensland, though it has also often happened
there that the permanent head of the department concerned with industry
has been incorporated as a corporation sole for the purpose of running a
particular activity. When, during the second decade of this century, a Labor
government in New South Wales embarked upon a number of business
ventures, including fishtrawling, brickworks, tileworks, sawmills, timberyards
and shipbuilding, it enacted an Industrial Undertakings Act in 1912 laying
down an administrative and financial code to be followed by all undertakings

brought within its provisions. Several undertakings functioned under this legislation, but they have since passed from the scene, and the blanket enactment has been repealed.[26] Two business undertakings at present in existence are the State Brickworks and the Government Engineering and Shipbuilding Undertaking (the State Dockyards). Although established by special statute, these have not been incorporated, but are run by a manager or board of management under the control of the minister. Both are in a shaky condition.

Another device of which some use has been made is the publicly owned or controlled company. This has sometimes taken the form of a mixed undertaking, in which there is a shareholding partnership between government and private enterprise. Comalco Aluminium (Bell Bay) Ltd, in which the Tasmanian government is a partner, is an example. Two other, wholly government-owned, agencies incorporated under the company laws are Commonwealth Hostels Ltd (1951), the migrant hostels authority; and Qantas Airways Ltd, a public company registered under the Queensland Companies Act, all the shares in which were bought by the Commonwealth in 1947. In the latter case the only statutory action needed was to appropriate the funds to buy the shares. The extent to which the company form has been adopted for operating public enterprises is, however, very limited. Commonwealth Hostels Ltd was set up at a time when a new Liberal–Country Party Government was pledged to reduce the size of the public service, and this influenced the form chosen; it also owed something to British and American example. An interesting recent example is Law Courts Ltd, which owns and operates the Commonwealth–State law courts building in Sydney. Each government appoints three directors, and the Articles of Association enable the two ministers concerned to give policy directions to the directors. However, like Britain, Australia has been mainly faithful to the statutory corporation form.

New South Wales

In the Australian environment, the energetic pursuit of development has always been a vital matter to governments, whatever their politics. An important group of statutory corporations in New South Wales are those operating services such as transport and conservation, which have played an important role in the development of the State. The fact that these undertakings are, on the face of it, of a business kind, should not obscure their developmental character. On business criteria they might be expected at least to return direct revenues equal to their annual cost, including capital servicing charges. However, they often fail to do so.

The corporations that may be grouped together under this head are the Public Transport Commission, which replaced the Railways Commissioner and Government Transport Commissioner in 1972, and operates railways and some other public transport services; the Maritime Services Board, established in 1936 to operate the Port of Sydney (formerly the responsibility of the

Sydney Harbour Trust) and the other main ports in New South Wales; the Water Resources Commission, which is concerned with the conservation of water resources and their use in irrigation projects; and the Forestry Commission (1916).

A development authority with an interesting history is the so-called 'Department' of Main Roads (1925), in fact a statutory corporation headed by a Commissioner. Roadbuilding had been the responsibility of local councils, which had neither the finance nor the engineering competence to meet the demands of the motor-car age. In 1923 the Commonwealth provided matching grants to assist road construction. This helped to evoke a New South Wales Act in the following year which established a statewide main roads authority. The intention was that local councils would continue to do the job, though the authority would 'tell them what to do and pay them for doing it'.[27] However, the Main Roads Board (as it was then called) had power to construct and maintain highways itself, if necessary. In fact, within three years of its foundation, after fending off a rival claim from the Public Works Department, it had become the chief road construction authority in the State, and Bruxner saw it as an instrument of the Country Party's decentralisation policy. For many years, 'with a strong sense of mission and a succession of powerful commissioners',[28] it went its own way on many matters. This became less true in the 1970s, when it passed from the relaxed care of the Minister for Local Government into the co-ordinating hands of the Ministry of Transport and Highways, and found itself required to make submissions to the minister for approval. (It returned to Local Government in 1978.)

Another corporation in this group is the Rural Bank of New South Wales (1933), which emerged from the collapse in the depression of the Government Savings Bank, as a rural and homes lending institution.[29] Its charter has since been extended to include general banking business. Another is the Electricity Commission of New South Wales (1950) whose prime function is to generate and supply electricity in bulk to the distribution authorities, mostly local authorities.

These corporations operate over the whole State. Partly for that reason, the Metropolitan Water Sewerage and Drainage Board, which operates in the Sydney metropolitan area and its environs, has not been included in this group, although it has a long record of developmental activities; in 1977 it had over 16 000 employees, an annual revenue of $250 million and supplied water to over three million people. It may be grouped with other corporations which provide, mainly in the metropolitan area, a public utility service of a kind often associated with local authorities. Local council areas in Australia have been too small for the effective operation of many services. Indeed, it was partly their deficiencies that led to the creation in the later nineteenth century of statutory boards for water supply, ports, fire protection and other services. Other localised corporations are the Sydney County Council (1935), which distributes and sells over a wide area electricity purchased in bulk from the Electricity Commission; the Sydney Cove Redevelopment Authority

(1968), set up to plan and control the redevelopment of an inner area of the city; and the Sydney Farm Produce Market Authority (1968), which owns and manages public markets and also has a promotional task for the farm produce sold in them (it took over from the City Council). A recent addition is the Metropolitan Waste Disposal Authority.

A few corporations, including the Metropolitan Water Board and the Sydney County Council, differ from the others in retaining a formal link with local government. The members of the Sydney County Council are elected by the aldermen and councillors of the relevant municipalities; the chairman is elected by and from the members. The statute under which it operates makes provision for dividing administrative responsibility between the Council and the General Manager, on American council-manager lines. Three of the six part-time members of the Metropolitan Water Board are chosen by the minister from a panel nominated by the Local Government Association; the full-time President and Vice-President are appointed by the government.

The statutory corporations mentioned above are nearly all operating monopoly undertakings or services, though some of them are subject to indirect competition such as that between railways and road hauliers. An exception is the Rural Bank, in respect of its general banking activities. There is a third group of statutory corporations which operate enterprises that are in competition, to a greater or lesser degree, with private undertakings. The oldest of these is the Public Trustee (1913) who was constituted as a corporation sole with power to carry on the business of executor and trustee. Another is the Government Insurance Office, established in 1926 as a sub-branch of the Treasury, primarily to provide employers with a means of insuring their liability under the Workers' Compensation Act of that year. A wider charter was granted in 1941, when it was constituted as a body corporate under a general manager, empowered to carry on any class of insurance business.

A number of trusts have been established to manage and protect public amenities and cultural activities. The members are appointed by the Governor and serve in a voluntary capacity, though in some cases certain privileges have been enjoyed by the trustees. A large number of those concerned with national parks and historic sites were wound up, with the creation in 1966 of a National Parks and Wildlife Service under the Minister for Lands. Various outside conservation bodies pressed for an independent statutory authority but the government, perhaps wisely, preferred to retain full ministerial control.

In New South Wales, as in other States, numbers of boards have been established for the purpose of registering and disciplining members of the professions, or of trades in which only registered persons are permitted to practice after proof of competence, and subject to deregistration for loss of competence, criminal conviction and such matters. Some of these, such as the Pharmacy Board, have been incorporated; others, like the Medical Board, have not.

It should perhaps be stressed that this chapter is concerned only with 'governmental' corporations.[30] The main test applied has been to ask whether all or a majority of its governing board are appointed by a minister or the government, or elected by local authorities, or both. For example, there is little reason for treating the marketing boards established under the New South Wales Marketing of Primary Products Act (and similar legislation in other States) as governmental; the initiative in creating such a marketing board lies with the producers of the relevant commodity, and all or the majority of board members are elected by the producers. Moreover, on the vote of enough producers the board may be disbanded. There are one or two exceptions, such as the Dairy Industry Authorities of New South Wales and Victoria, which are constituted by special statute and whose chairman and members are appointed by the Governor. The others are perhaps 'quasi-nongovernmental' (see Chapter One).

An unusual addition to New South Wales administrative agencies was made by the 1966 State Development and Country Industries Assistance Act, which constituted the minister a corporation sole under the name of Minister for Decentralisation and Development. There was also established a Development Corporation of New South Wales, but this has only investigatory and advisory powers. The minister in his corporate role is charged with the duty of encouraging the establishment, extension or development of country industries. The corporation sole took over a previously established decentralisation fund, the recourses of which were derived from appropriations by Parliament. The Authority is also empowered, subject to the concurrence of the Treasurer and the approval of the Governor, to borrow money by the issue of debentures, bonds or inscribed stock.

This raised interesting questions about ministerial responsibility. In exercising his functions as a development corporation, the minister may enjoy some limited autonomy in relation to expenditure projects, but it appears that he must answer parliamentary questions on his activities. The corporate role may have justification in the removal of the legal impediments attending the Crown and in the flexibility with which development projects can be handled. That it is assigned to a minister may be to ensure that government policy is closely followed. The arrangement is by no means unique to New South Wales; in four Western Australian departments, including Education, the relevant minister is a body corporate in the name of the department, with powers to sue and be sued.[31]

Other States

The general character of statutory corporations in other States does now show any marked differences from New South Wales, and in some cases there is a close parallelism. For example, three States appointed Railways Commissioners about the same time as New South Wales, and the others followed with some time-lag. In some they have likewise been superseded by a transport commission with wider functions. Victoria created a Board to deal with main roads (the Country Roads Board) in 1912, and three other States set up Main Roads Boards or Commissioners in the 1920s, as did New South Wales. Most States have Electricity Commissions or Trusts, which control the bulk of generation and have extended in varying degrees into the field of sale to the final consumer. Victoria's State Electricity Commission (1919) and Tasmania's Hydro-Electric Commission (1930), itself preceded by a State Department, were earliest in the field, and have the widest functions.

Harbours are generally controlled by harbour boards or trusts, most public housing by State Housing Commissions or Trusts.[32] Many States operate savings banks and rural banks and insurance institutions. The Victorian Savings Bank engages in regulated competition with other banks. Victoria's State Rivers and Water Supply Commission (1905) pioneered the idea of a statewide corporation for water supply and irrigation.[33] State boards or trusts operate public transport services in Adelaide, Hobart, Melbourne, Perth and Sydney. Only in one State capital, Brisbane, is passenger transport in the hands of a municipal authority, the Brisbane City Council.

There are some differences. Victoria's Gas and Fuel Corporation (1950) is the only public body in Australia created specifically to reorganise gas supply. In Western Australia the State Energy Commission provides both electricity and gas. In most other States gas is supplied by private enterprise or local government (municipal ownership is strong in rural New South Wales).[34] The Melbourne and Metropolitan Board of Works (1890) has the functions of Water Boards in other capitals, but also has town planning powers. In some States forestry is controlled by a statewide commission, in others by a ministerial department or subdepartment. Many States have several harbour boards or trusts, not a single authority. Queensland's Public Service Act covers a somewhat wider scope than that of other States, where corporations are not usually subject to the Public Service Board, though there are important exceptions. Management by a single Commissioner is also most popular in Queensland. Individual states are still pioneering new types of enterprise, such as the very successful South Australian Film Corporation.

Commonwealth

Because of its fairly limited activities during the earlier years of federation, the Commonwealth Government made little use of the statutory corporation. An early experiment was the Commonwealth Bank, created in 1911 by a Labor Government.[35] In its original form there was no Board: the powers were given to a Governor appointed for seven years. In 1917, the Commonwealth-owned railways were unified under a single Commissioner, since replaced by the Australian National Railways Commission. The same model was used in the next year when the ill-fated War Service Homes Commission was created.[36] The principle of the one-man commission was thus established in the early days, and was favoured by Labor.

The 1920s was a more active period in the creation of statutory bodies.

The corporations established in the 1920s by the Bruce-Page non-Labor Government were usually of the multi-member kind, and intended to resemble boards of company directors. This was true of the Australian Shipping Board, which operated a shipping line from 1923 to 1928; the reconstituted Commonwealth Bank (1924); the Council for Scientific and Industrial Research (1926), forerunner of the Commonwealth Scientific and Industrial Research Organisation; and the three short-lived development corporations —the Federal Capital Commission, the North Australia Commission and the Development and Migration Commission.[37] The new model that emerged was the board of part-time members, with a full-time chief executive; though there were some minor exceptions. The Australian Broadcasting Commission (1932) was a part-time body, with a full-time General Manager. Here the model of the British Broadcasting Corporation was followed. Most Commonwealth government business undertakings still mainly consist of part-time members.

The post-war period really begins with the 1942 Report of the Joint Parliamentary Committee on Broadcasting, which made the first notable study in Australia of the principles that should be adopted in creating a statutory corporation. Most of its recommendations were embodied in the reorganisation of the Australian Broadcasting Commission that followed, and they also influenced the character of some of the post-war corporations. The first of these was the Australian National Airlines Commission (TAA), set up in 1945. In the following year the Overseas Telecommunications Commission and the Joint Coal Board were established. Later creations have included the Snowy Mountains Hydro-Electric Authority (1949)[38]; the Australian Atomic Energy Commission (1953); the Australian Shipping Commission (1956), which operates the Australian National Line; the Export Finance and Insurance Corporation (1956, 1975); the National Capital Development Commission (1958); the Commonwealth Banking Corporation and the Reserve Bank of Australia (1959—out of the former Commonwealth Bank); the Housing Loans Insurance Corporation (1965, 1977); and the Australian Industry Development Corporation (1970). The Labor Government of 1972–75 added appreciably to the number of statutory bodies of this kind, including the Pipeline Authority, the abortive Petroleum and Minerals Authority, and the two bodies hived off from the Postmaster-General's Department—the Australian Postal Commission and the Australian Telecommunications Commission. There were also statutory agencies set up to develop growth centres, such as the Albury–Wodonga Development Corporation.

The extensive use of the statutory corporation by the Commonwealth does not mean that it has been employed as an 'instrument of nationalization' as in the United Kingdom. There are constitutional limitations on this, as witness the fortunes of the 1947 banking legislation.[39] Of the Commonwealth corporations involved in commercial enterprises, only a few monopolise the field in which they operate. For example, in neither broadcasting nor television has the Australian Broadcasting Commission been granted a monopoly, though it does not compete with commercial stations for advertising revenues, but is financed from government funds. The 'rationalised' competition between statutory corporations and their rivals in private enterprise—in fields such as internal airlines, coastal shipping, banking and insurance—has become a notable feature of the Australian public enterprise scene. Australia's two-airline system (TAA and Ansett Airlines) has been advanced as something of a model for such 'metaphytic' industries.[40] Others argue that some of the benefits either of really vigorous competition or of full State ownership are being lost. A small dent in the two-airline policy was made by a 1977 High Court decision permitting IPEC and Air Express each to import two aircraft for the Bass Strait freight run. The minister had given permission, but Ansett claimed that this breached the 1952 agreement on which the two-airline system is based.

Constitutional Aspects

The constitutional aspects of statutory authorities are of special concern, as these throw light on an allegedly important common feature, independence or autonomy. Key points at which political control may be exercised are: the constitutions of the governing boards, finance, staff and those matters over which the minister is granted statutory powers. The statutes go into a fair amount of detail on such matters. The discussion that follows mainly deals with statutory corporations engaged in trading and commercial activities.

Boards: Appointment and Tenure

The usual provision is for boards to be appointed by the Governor-General or Governor, acting with the advice of the Executive Council, which means that the cabinet determines appointments. Statutory provisions relating to the tenure of board members are far from uniform. Sometimes the period for which the appointment is to be made is specifically stated, or the legislation may merely state the maximum period, in both cases normally subject to renewal. There are statutory disqualifications from continuance in office, mental illness, bankruptcy, unjustified absence and so on. The appointment may usually be terminated for inability, inefficiency or misbehaviour, or even in some cases 'for any cause which appears [to the Governor] sufficient'.

Mostly provision is made for a reasonably secure tenure during the specified period, which tends to be three to five years, though often a longer period, such as seven years, for the chairman, or where the appointment is full-time. In a very few cases, tenure is until retiring age. There is provision in some cases for parliamentary review of any government action to suspend members of governing bodies, usually as a protection against arbitrary political interference. This is particularly noticeable in older-established corporations, for example Railways Commissioners, whose status was originally seen as falling little short of that of Auditor-General.[41] The NSW Railways Commissioner, for example, could not be dismissed from office during his seven-year term without a vote by both houses of parliament. He was also the State's highest paid officer, as is his successor, the Chief Commissioner of the Public Transport Commission.

These provisions regarding tenure are important as they can influence the independence of the board. Where appointments are made for short periods or may be terminated at the will of the minister, the influence of the latter can be considerable. During the earlier years of the Australian Broadcasting Commission members were sometimes reappointed for very short periods.[42]

Composition

The size and character of the governing body of statutory authorities has varied. Three main patterns have been followed:

1. The part-time board, with a full-time chairman, who is also the executive head. In some instances there may also be another full-time member, often vice-chairman or deputy, as is now the case with some major New South Wales corporations, and with the Reserve Bank of Australia (Governor and Deputy Governor).

2. The wholly part-time board, with a general manager as executive head. This is true of a number of Commonwealth corporations, including the Australian National Airlines Commission (TAA) and the Australian Broadcasting Commission, and it is also used in Western Australia. (The executive head may attend board meetings, or even occasionally have a formal seat on the board, as have the General Managers of the Australian Atomic Energy Commission and the Western Australian State Housing Commission.)[43]

3. The 'corporation sole', or one-man corporation, with a single commissioner, as is still the case with one or two railways authorities, and with such bodies as the New South Wales Forestry Commission and the Tasmanian Government Insurance Office. In some cases the single Commissioners, in whom the statutory powers are vested, are aided by full-time Assistant Commissioners. The one-man commission seems to be going out of fashion.

The part-time board is the commonest pattern in most States. The Commonwealth has been more attracted by the notion of a part-time chairman, drawn from the private sector, as a help-mate and sometimes counterbalance to the general manager. But it uses all three, as well as special patterns, such as that of CSIRO with three (formerly five) full-time members, including the Chairman, who is also the chief executive, and three to five part-time members. However, most boards are mainly part-time, they have been 'policy', not 'executive' (or 'functional') boards. Part-time boards have one advantage for public accountability, as it is easier to get rid of such members at the end of their statutory term. It also makes it possible to represent wider groups than are commonly found at the top of a normal department. The size of boards varies. In most instances provision is made for a small compact membership, varying from three to seven, but some are larger; the membership of the Australian Broadcasting Commission was increased from seven to nine members in 1967. The deficiencies of a very large board are well-illustrated by the history of the Metropolitan Water Board in New South Wales between 1925 and 1935.[44]

The Australian statutes do not usually specify qualifications for members. In this they differ from the statutes creating boards for the British nationalised industries, where members are normally required to have had wide experience in specified fields. Commonly statutes include little more than a provision about the appointee being a 'fit and proper person'. It is sometimes contended that this makes it easier for party political appointments to be made and that some such appointments have been made in the past is beyond question.[45] However, the quality of appointees depends more on the rectitude and ability of political leaders than on specifying qualifications. The Commonwealth government has recently laid down guidelines for full-time statutory appointments which involve the minister in consultation with the Public Service Board and Prime Minister, and in some circumstances a selection committee.[46]

As well as the fear that political appointments will deprive the boards of independence, there has also been the belief that they may give boards too much independence. Labor members used to worry more than others about the independence of boards, partly in the belief that non-Labor governments saw it as a means of preserving 'continuity of policy' and frustrating the 'wrecking' activities of Labor governments.[47] With the general growth of managerialism, this controversy now seems to be dead. Indeed, one motive behind the many statutory authorities created by the Labor government of 1972–75 seems to have been to take initiatives that a successor would find it hard to undo. By this time Labor seemed to have thoroughly shed its earlier suspicions of the statutory body, while the Liberals were expressing the desire to reduce their number.

Some statutes provide for the representation of various interests on the board. The State Energy Commission of Western Australia, for example, has members representing consumers, including commercial consumers, and employees. Four of the seven Commissioners of the Maritime Services Board of New South Wales are part-time members appointed to represent shipping and other maritime and commercial interests.

The members of some harbour trusts are elected by interested parties, as are those of many marketing boards. There are a few examples of legislation providing for staff representation, as is true of the Postal and Telecommunications Commissions. But there has been little substantial discussion of the general question of employee representation, such as has taken place in Europe. The legislation of the Chifley Labor government establishing the earlier post-war Commonwealth corporations did not provide for this. It seemed to be thought that, for the efficient running of commercial undertakings, the conception of the board as a meeting place for interests was mistaken. The knowledge that the official view of the British trade union movement and Labor Party at that time was opposed to the direct representation of employees, or their trade unions, on public enterprise boards may have influenced this decision. However, the Labor government of 1972–75 made some appointments of this kind; Mr Hawke (President of the ACTU) joined the Reserve Bank Board, the general secretary of the Waterside Workers' Federation was appointed to the Australian Shipping Commission, and there are other examples.

In Britain the absence of direct representation has been partly offset by the establishment of advisory committees, formal machinery for joint consultation between employer and employees, and consumers councils. In Australia less attempt has been made to establish such machinery; with a few exceptions, notably the Australian Broadcasting Commission, little use has even been made of advisory committees, but some discussion of employee and consumer participation is now beginning (see Chapters Thirteen and Seventeen).

An interesting judgment on the responsibilities of part-time members of statutory boards was delivered following a conflict in 1967 between the New South Wales Board of Fire Commissioners and the Board member elected by the permanent firemen. (Of its seven members, two are elected by fire insurance companies, and one each by local councils, volunteer and permanent firemen. The President and his Deputy are appointed by the government.)

> The object of providing for interested groups to nominate the members of such a Board as this might be said to be threefold: first, one can be confident that an interested group will select a man whose personal qualities and competence equip him for membership; second, it promotes the confidence of that particular group in the Board, and provides a means of liaison between that group and the Board; and third, it ensures that the Board as a single entity has available in its deliberations the views of all the interested groups . . . Once a group has elected a member he assumes office as a member of the Board and becomes subject to the overriding and predominant duty to serve the interests of the Board in preference, on every occasion upon which any conflict might arise, to serving the interests of the group which appointed him. With this basic proposition there can be no room for compromise.[48]

At times serving public servants (and especially Treasury officers) have been made part-time members of boards. Over 20 per cent of the members of Western Australian corporations are public servants.[49] Since the 1940s, the Tasmanian Treasury has gained representation on the boards of most of the newer corporations of that State. A Treasury officer sits on a number of New South Wales boards, sometimes specifically as a representative of the Treasury; in other cases the intention is simply to bring to the authority some financial and administrative expertise. Senior public servants sometimes also move to full-time positions with statutory bodies; the full-time Presidents of the Metropolitan Water Board and of the Rural Bank of New South Wales were both (1978) former Under Secretaries of the Treasury. There is an obvious advantage to be gained from drawing on the wide experience in government administration of such individuals and it certainly represents a significant widening of career opportunities for top public servants.

In the Commonwealth, the broadcasting legislation of 1948 specifically provided for public service appointments. The Act, repealed in 1956, increased the membership of the Australian Broadcasting Commission from five to seven in order to include serving officers of the Treasury and the Postmaster-General's Department. During the period of the Chifley Labor Government public servants were appointed as part-time members of a number of other boards, though this practice did not meet with favour by the Menzies government; illustrations of the confusion of loyalties and conflict of interests sometimes liable to be caused were revealed by the Public Accounts Committee during 1954, in the course of its inquiry into the affairs of the now-defunct Australian Aluminium Production Commission.[50] However, the Secretary to the Treasury is a member of the Reserve Bank Board and of the Board of the Commonwealth Banking Corporation. The Secretary to the Postal and Telecommunications Department is a member of the Postal and Telecommunications Commissions. Two permanent heads sit on the Australian Industry Development Corporation. Senior officers of the Commonwealth Department of Transport are on a number of boards (e.g. TAA, Qantas). The Coombs Commission said there was no evidence that serious problems had arisen from such arrangements.[51]

The chairmen, general managers and other prominent members of statutory bodies have in general been less anonymous than top public servants, and more readily defend or advertise their activities in public, even sometimes criticise government policies with regard to the undertaking, as we have already seen.

Staff

Control over the appointment and conditions of employment of staff has generally been regarded as an important element in the independence of statutory corporations. It has been argued that corporations operating commercial enterprises should as far as possible follow the pattern of business management. Conversely, it might be expected that the staff of purely regulatory bodies would form part of the ordinary public service, but this is not invariably the case. Nor have all commercial corporations been granted formal freedom in controlling their staffs; for example, the staff of the New South Wales Government Insurance Office, save for the General Manager, are subject to Public Service Board control, and in 1951 the Queensland Public Service Act was widened to bring in virtually all the salaried staffs of non-departmental agencies. Mostly, however, the staff of commercial corporations are excluded from the provisions of the Public Service Acts.

This does not necessarily imply great diversity in methods of recruitment, salaries and other conditions of employment. In matters of pay and conditions, there seem to be few major departures from public service norms, though a corporation is occasionally accused of being a pace-setter, especially where it can pass higher costs on to the public. In New South Wales, for example, there is no great difference between the normal recruitment and promotion methods of the corporations and those of the Board, though they may find it easier to achieve flexibility in particular cases, from altering their managerial structure to getting a new typist if they want one. Some co-ordination is achieved from time to time through conferences of corporation heads and the Chairman of the Public Service Board, and regular meetings are held between the industrial officers of the various authorities. In Victoria a ministerial subcommittee tries to co-ordinate industrial issues, including pay, within all State employing authorities. However, no comprehensive study has been made of conditions of employment or personnnel practices in statutory bodies.[52]

One important result of controlling their own staff has been a tendency for statutory authorities each to create their own little career service and to fill most senior positions from inside the authority. They can easily become 'insular and introspective' in this respect, as the federal secretary of ACOA recently remarked.[53] Sir Henry Bland, in his report on Victorian statutory corporations, and the Wilenski report in New South Wales, have both commented on this.[54] It may help to give the staff a strong sense of commitment, but also leads to undue immobility. Statutory authorities tend to have a higher percentage of senior officers who have spent their whole career in the agency, and well-worn promotion routes. In recent years more statutory bodies have gone outside their organisations for new blood, especially for top positions, but there is still too much inbreeding, and too much security of tenure even in bodies like the Australian Broadcasting Commission, where it is singularly inappropriate.

Post-war legislation imposes a number of restrictions upon Commonwealth corporations in staff matters. Many statutes require them to recruit on the basis of open competition, except for specified classes of positions; and provide for ministerial approval of the appointment, transfer or promotion of an officer where the salary exceeds a specified amount. In a good many cases, terms and conditions of employment must be approved by the Public Service Board.[55] Of course, this still leaves a good deal of freedom to appoint and promote within the Board's standards. Many business enterprises (such as the Postal and Telecommunications Commissions and the Commonwealth Banking Corporation), or especially prestigious bodies (like the Reserve Bank of Australia), or ones with powerful political backing at the time of their creation (such as the Australian Industry Development Corporation) control their own staffs, though they may where appropriate follow public service practices; in some cases (e.g. TAA) the Minister has certain powers, and in practice seeks the Public Service Board's agreement to higher posts before approving them. In research agencies, such as CSIRO and the Atomic Energy Commission, many employment conditions have been formalised under Public Service Board rules, but they have retained, by law or convention, flexibility with research staffs. The government may from time to time impose staff ceilings on statutory bodies.

State corporations also have relationships with their counterparts in other States, and pay awards sometimes reflect this—for example, the one award covers railwaymen in several States, even though there is also a separate section of the award for each State. States compete for skilled staff, say as between Electricity Commissions, which tends to keep pay and conditions of employment in line; indeed this kind of competition may sometimes be as important as that with other public service groups within the State itself.

Finance

Financial control is often the most important of all forms of control. The degree of financial autonomy enjoyed by statutory corporations tends to be related closely to their financial self-sufficiency. Other things being equal, a corporation that has independent sources of revenue from sales (TAA) or from assigned revenues (the New South Wales Department of Main Roads) is likely to be subject to less external control than one financed wholly out of annual parliamentary appropriations. Of course, words like 'control' beg some questions. In one sense, financial control over a commercial corporation may be stronger, if it has an obligation to match expenditure with revenue, than over an agency that has a guarantee of automatic government support when deficits emerge. There are considerable variations in the degree of financial autonomy enjoyed by Australian statutory corporations. The following outline of the situation in New South Wales is, however, broadly indicative of the situation in other States.

New South Wales

With the exception of one or two financially self-sufficient enterprises, most statutory corporations fall into one of two categories: those whose capital is wholly or almost wholly provided by the government, and those where it is partly raised through loan issues. Important in the first category are the railways, bus services and so on operated by the Public Transport Commission. The latter now has minor power to raise loans, but the bulk of its capital is allocated by the State government. However, the appropriation process when applied to a business enterprise lacks some of the force it has in relation to departmental expenditures; operational needs and outcomes more clearly determine the volume of expenditure. Other authorities that are wholly capital-financed by the government (for example, the Government Insurance Office) are excluded from the budget. Their operating funds are kept in the Treasury, but they are available for expenditure simply on requisition by the authority, not like railway expenditure appropriated for specific purposes by parliament.

Of the corporations in the second category—those having some independent borrowing powers—the most important are the Electricity Commission, the Metropolitan Water Board, and (since 1966) the Maritime Services Board. The first two directly control their own funds outside the treasury system. Their operations are not included in the budget, and are not subject to the processes of parliamentary appropriation. Corporations with independent borrowing powers are not subject to formal Loan Council restraint, but use of their powers is regulated by a 'gentleman's agreement', which in practice means that large loans are approved by both State government and Loan Council (see Chapter Seven). State control of loan-raising is laid down by statute. The provisions applying to the Electricity Commission of New South Wales may be regarded as broadly typical. The Act sets out, among other things, the purposes for which capital may be borrowed, requires that the government's approval first be obtained, that a reserve for loan repayment be created, and stipulates the measures for the custody, investment and use of the reserve for loan repayments. Securities are to be in the form of debentures, bonds or inscribed stock. The loans are declared to be secured on the income of the enterprise, and are guaranteed by the government. However, such enterprises can also accumulate reserves from their own revenues, and in the past there has been little control over this process.

Mostly the New South Wales statutes are silent as to the contingency of profit or loss, and in many cases losses fall automatically on general revenue. In one or two minor cases, provision is made for surpluses to go into general revenue; there may sometimes be a requirement that undertakings pay over the equivalent of income tax arising from their operations. Otherwise practice has mostly been influenced by the course of events. Most profitable corporations have retained their profits, and one or two State corporations have been able to accumulate substantial reserves; but on occasion, especially when the government has been seeking budget assistance, legislation has been enacted for the transfer of some of the surplus of the more affluent authorities.

The powers of statutory corporations regarding the fixing of rates and charges vary considerably. The Sydney County Council, in common with other county councils distributing electricity, fixes rates on its own authority. The Electricity Commission likewise, under its general powers, may determine its charges, and is not required by the Act to seek the approval of the minister in this matter (though the minister is given a general power of direction and control). A different arrangement applies to the Metropolitan Water Board, the Maritime Services Board and the Public Transport Commission, where the authority is empowered to determine rates, but the decision has to be promulgated by regulation or by-law. This means that ministerial consideration of the matter is required before it goes to the Executive Council and also that the regulations may be subject to disallowance by parliament.

In practice, decisions about railway and bus fares are made by the cabinet, any changes normally forming part of the budget.

The corporations are required to submit annual reports, accompanied by statements of account. Accounts of the corporations are, with very few exceptions, subject to audit by the Auditor-General who is usually required by the governing legislation to report to the corporation and to the relevant minister. It has been the practice over many years for the New South Wales Auditor-General when reporting to Parliament to include comment on the accounts of those public authorities that have financial links with the Treasury.

Commonwealth

Most Commonwealth corporations (unlike many State corporations) lack independent borrowing powers; this difference probably arises from the fact that the Commonwealth has regularly been able to finance its capital works from revenue. The permanent capital they require is appropriated by Parliament and advanced to the corporation on terms and conditions decided by the Treasurer. Where a Commonwealth corporation has a temporary need for capital to supplement funds provided by parliamentary appropriation, its recourse is to bank overdraft. One or two corporations, such as the banks and the Australian Industry Development Corporation, have borrowing powers.

The expenditures of some Commonwealth corporations, such as the ABC and CSIRO, form part of the budget and are appropriated annually like those of an ordinary government department. The ABC, for example, depends largely on annual government decisions. It is true that most of its current expenditure is derived from a 'one-line' appropriation, not broken down under specific heads. But its detailed budget proposals will have been scrutinised by the Minister for Post and Telecommunications, and more particularly by the Department of Finance, before going to the cabinet, much as though it were a normal department. Like the latter it faces the prospect of detailed criticism, proposed cuts and negotiations. Its main advantage over a ministerial department is that flexible arrangements appear to exist for it to vary expenditure on individual items within the global figure approved by parliament. But the government can still veto a particular service, as it did in June 1977 when it said that funds would not be provided to continue the Melbourne ethnic radio station.

The finances of most corporations have been separated from the budget and are not subject to annual appropriation. Each corporation is authorised to maintain its own bank account, into which are paid capital moneys and revenue, and from which it has substantial freedom to make drawings to meet capital and operating expenditure. The Australian National Airlines Commission (TAA) may be taken as an example of the kind of provisions which may apply where a corporation is in competition with a private enterprise. The funds required to carry out its functions are provided mainly by capital advanced from parliamentary appropriations, nominally repayable but not subject to any sinking fund conditions; partly by overdraft accommodation with the Commonwealth Banking Corporation, subject to a statutory limit. Operating profits or losses are carried in the commission's account; in place of a fixed interest charge on its capital, the Australian National Airlines Act requires it to aim at making enough profit to meet a yearly target set by the Minister for Transport. This payment is in the nature of a dividend paid into public funds. The commission is required to submit to the responsible minister annual estimates of receipts and expenditure; to keep its accounts in approved form; and to submit to Parliament an annual report and statement of accounts, the latter certified by the Auditor-General. In practice, the accounts are kept on a commercial basis. It is subject to income and other taxes, and in most respects its finances parallel those of its private enterprise competitor.

A somewhat different approach to the financing of corporations has been adopted with a non-competitive undertaking. It is charged interest on moneys advanced to it, and enjoys immunity from income taxation (but not other Commonwealth taxes), the basic idea being that its charges should be related to the real cost of providing the service, including interest on capital employed. During the developmental stages of such an undertaking, the decision might be that interest will be charged but payment deferred until it is producing revenue.

Many differences have resulted less from statutory prescription than from decisions made by the Treasurer under discretionary powers conferred on him in the relevant statutes. The latter do, however, contain a number of detailed provisions regarding financial methods. They usually specify, for example, what may be done with any profits and also the conditions under which money may be invested. Most corporations are empowered, subject to the approval, to set aside such sums as they think proper for reserves and depreciation of assets. Some are required to keep their accounts in an approved form. The statutes also require that the accounts of the corporation shall be inspected and audited at least once yearly by the Commonwealth Auditor-General. A striking exception is the Australian Industry Development Corporation, the accounts of which are not subject to such scrutiny and which in other ways was given a remarkably high degree of independence.

A restriction on the autonomy of the corporations in financial management that deserves special notice is the statutory requirement that certain transactions be reserved for the approval of the minister. Thus in a number of cases, the corporation may not without ministerial approval purchase or dispose of assets for an amount exceeding, say, $100 000. This means, in effect, that the minister reserves the right to approve major contracts. The statutes also mostly require that the approval of the minister must be obtained before changes are made in the prices charged by corporations.

As we have seen, many statutes relating to State corporations say nothing about profits or losses. In some cases, such as TAA and the Australian

National Line, Commonwealth corporations are charged to operate commercially, and may be expected, as in the case of TAA quoted above, to pay a dividend, with the balance going to reserves. Some are only expected to break even, as is the case with the Australian Postal Commission and the Export Finance and Insurance Corporation.

Other Economic Issues

There has been controversy about the pricing and investment policies of public enterprises. For example, a recent study of the electricity supply industry, over 90 per cent of which is controlled by public authorities, concludes that it is reasonably efficient on the generating side.[56] But it casts doubt on the economics of hydro-electric schemes in Tasmania and the Snowy Mountains, and there is some criticism of distribution, especially in New South Wales, and of a general failure to devise pricing systems that relate prices closely to costs. This, and other studies, seem to suggest that Australian public enterprise has had better engineers than economists, or at least that the former have often been more influential in policy-making. Another problem of pricing is how large a contribution to investment public enterprises should make from their own revenues. Some are accused of drawing too heavily on the public purse, others of over-investing or accumulating excessive reserves at the expense of consumers. Much depends on how far they monopolise their field. It is clearly easier for postal and telecommunications services to maintain profits than public transport services. For some transport undertakings raising prices may not only be politically unpopular, but also worsen their financial condition; one of the alternative remedies, cutting out uneconomic services, may also be difficult for social and political reasons.

The financial arrangements of statutory corporations raise many other economic issues, which it would not be appropriate to discuss here. Should a public enterprise have access to capital funds on more favourable terms than can be obtained in the ordinary capital market? To what extent, if any, should corporations be given relief from taxation? Do their investment programmes represent the best allocation of national resources? If they have a 'developmental' or 'welfare' function as well as a strictly business one, should specific provision be made for this in their budgets?

The last two points have some special relevance to transport. For example, it is sometimes argued that State governments with a vested interest in their own railway systems have not concerned themselves objectively with the economic problems of transport, but have preferred to protect railways by subsidy and by restrictive policies towards transport competitors. On the other hand, the railways argue that they bear more of the construction and maintenance costs of their track and operating facilities than do their rivals, who get interest-free capital grants for roads, subsidised airports, and so on. Railways are also widely used to give assistance to country industries and country dwellers, exporters, suburban travellers and so on, and many of their losses arise from this. The Victorian Railways Commission, for example, has argued that it should be reimbursed not just by deficit financing with its undisclosed cross-subsidisation, but by a conscious decision to allocate funds for each main social purpose for which the corporation is required to desert purely business criteria.[57] The case for this is to help the government (and interested groups outside) understand exactly what is happening; and to improve morale within the organisation itself.

Control by Ministers and Parliament

Ministers

Statutory corporations differ in the extent to which they are legally and in practice, independent of ministerial control. In some cases the statute may say nothing about the minister's role; but in many instances the minister is empowered to exercise certain controls over the operation of the corporation. Some kinds of ministerial powers have already been noted. Often the statute requires that the minister's approval be sought before the authority purchases or disposes of assets above a specified value, or pays a salary above a specified amount, or varies its rates and charges. Sometimes statutes empower the minister to give directions generally, or on policy issues only, or on specific matters. For example, the minister may direct the Australian National Airlines Commission (TAA) to establish, alter or continue to maintain, any specified airline service; but if the service shows a loss, and the whole corporation shows a loss, the latter must be reimbursed by the government to the extent of the lesser of the two losses. A similar principle is embodied in the recent postal legislation. In certain cases, if a ministerial direction is given, it has to be in writing, and perhaps be published in the authority's report or the Commonwealth Gazette, or even tabled in parliament within a specified period, as with the ABC and the Reserve Bank. In the latter case the government can only enforce its views on policy by a formal direction from the Governor-General in Council, and the Treasurer must present to parliament within fifteen sitting days a copy of the direction and statements by the government and the Bank on the matter in respect of which the difference of opinion arose.[58] This has never been necessary, though the Bank has certainly been influenced on occasion by the government's views. There are a few cases where an authority is not subject to any ministerial direction, but is required by statute to have regard to policies or principles laid down in the statute itself.[59]

There has been a tendency to increase the minister's formal powers of control over governing boards. New South Wales statutes generally contain a provision that 'in the exercise and discharge of its powers, authorities, duties and functions' the corporation shall be subject to 'the control and direction of the Minister', (a formula modified in some cases by adding, 'except in relation to the contents of a report or recommendation made by it to the Minister'). In Victoria, some statutes contain general declarations that operations shall be subject to the approval, or subject to the direction and control, of the minister; however in many cases, there is no such general power but only a number of more specific ones. In Tasmania the Hydro-Electric Commission has often been accused of being a State within a State.[60] As the head of one statutory body has been reported as saying: 'It says in the Act that if the minister directs me to do something I have to do it—but there's nothing in the Act to say that if I want to do something myself I have to consult the minister first' (actually, as we have seen, there sometimes is).[61]

In theory ministers are responsible to parliament for the exercise (or the non-exercise) of all their statutory powers and duties. Thus the greater the statutory powers of control possessed by a minister in respect of a particular board, the more in theory the affairs of the board are directly the concern of parliament. This does not work out in practice, as a sponsoring minister may wish to protect a board from parliament or from all outside interference other than by himself. Little or nothing is known about how much ministerial intervention takes place. Wettenhall, in his 1975 survey of Commonwealth statutory authorities (not only corporations), found that although 53 per cent thought they were subject to 'substantial' control of policy and functions by legislation, under one-fifth felt themselves to be so controlled by ministers; and almost none felt themselves to be controlled by departments; while control from outside of 'day-to-day administration' was generally seen as insignificant. Although 38 per cent thought that the Public Service Board had substantial control of staff and organisation, only 10 per cent of the business undertakings took this view.[62] Even when ministers do intervene, it is not by exercising their formal powers of direction and control but by informal pressures and consultations.

Where a minister has powers regarding a statutory authority, the question also arises of the relation between his permanent head and the authority. Usually the latter reports direct to the minister and has no formal link with the permanent head. But it is natural for a minister to look to his own senior officers as an independent source of advice; there are areas where they may be better informed than the authority, as on questions of broad government policy; and sometimes (see Chapter Three) the department may have an explicit 'co-ordinating' role, as does the Ministry of Transport in New South Wales. Yet there are dangers of building up a departmental staff to 'second guess' the statutory bodies associated with it, with the potential duplication of work involved, and in some cases the department may be a rival of the statutory body.

Parliament

Neither at Commonwealth nor State levels have there been established special parliamentary committees, such as the United Kingdom Select Committee on Nationalised Industries, designed to improve accountability to parliament. Following the report of the Parliamentary Joint Committee on Wireless Broadcasting in 1942, the Commonwealth Parliament established a Standing

Committee on Broadcasting with a view to reconciling 'the Australian Broadcasting Commission's independence with the political conception that all activities of government or quasi-government authorities should be subject, in the final analysis, to parliamentary control'. This committee was in existence for a number of years, but was not successful in securing the objects for which it was appointed and was abandoned.[63] Wettenhall has argued that parliaments should have a special statutory review committee to inquire into a group of statutory authorities each year, which could build up a body of expertise in this form of activity.[64] The authorities might come to welcome this; it is arguable that the British Select Committee on Nationalised Industries has reduced, not increased political pressure on the boards.

The statutes require the corporations to render annual reports and financial statements to the minister who is usually, but not always, required to transmit these to parliament. Usually neither these reports, nor the Auditor-General's report on the financial statements, provide an occasion for debate in parliament upon the affairs of the corporation. Often they are of a formal kind, and make little attempt to raise issues of concern to the authority, or to answer criticisms.

There is no consistent practice about parliamentary questions about the activities of corporations. They often seem to be treated in much the same way as questions about the activities of ministerial departments. Sometimes the minister will give information supplied to him by the Board on matters for which he will not accept responsibility. Thus he may say: 'The question concerns the internal administration of the bank, which is a matter for the bank to determine. However, the Governor of the Bank has informed me that the total cost of the bank's new Hobart premises was . . .' In Victoria, the State Electricity Commission and the Railways have by statute to supply information to the minister to enable 'answers to be made to all questions in Parliament'; but ministers still at times exercise some discretion in answering. A former Premier of New South Wales has said about 'semi-autonomous' bodies: 'Any government organization must be prepared at any time to give an explanation if a question is raised from either side of the House, or by a minister. I refer not so much to a criticism as to a question about a course of action.'[65] No thorough study has been made of Australian conventions in this field, nor have there been any well-considered and authoritative rulings on the subject, as in the United Kingdom (perhaps this is just as well, as the rules there are somewhat restrictive).[66] There is no evidence that parliamentary questions play a significant part in making statutory corporations more accountable to parliament.

While that is the general position, the role of the Joint Committee of Public Accounts in the Commonwealth Parliament requires special mention (see also Chapter Sixteen). The Committee has some responsibility for inquiring into the accounts of statutory corporations. An inquiry of special importance was made during 1954 into the Australian Aluminium Production Commission, which led to a general examination of the nature and status of such bodies.

However, in recent years the Committee has been much less lively. Senate Estimates Committees have also taken some interest in statutory bodies. Indeed the head of the National Capital Development Commission has complained of excessive parliamentary scrutiny.[67]

Problems of Control

The tendency to restrict the formal autonomy of statutory corporations has been lamented by some writers, who have suggested that it results from the inherent inability of politicians and public servants to leave well alone. However that may be, there appear to be other and more important reasons for this trend, which is also to be observed in many other countries, including the United Kingdom, Canada and the United States. It has occurred during a period in which the economic activities of governments have greatly increased and in which new kinds of responsibility for national welfare have been assumed by governments. These developments have encouraged attempts to co-ordinate the policies of corporations, so that the policy of the government as a whole might be free from international contradictions.

The 1968 report of the Select Committee on Nationalised Industries in the United Kingdom pointed to some potential weaknesses of control.[68] Ministers may sometimes be tempted to interfere too much in detail, or in an arbitrary way with particular decisions of policy, such as pricing decisions. Alternatively, or even at the same time, they may be quite ineffective in checking on the general policies of corporations. Ira Sharkansky has argued that in some Australian States, the very variety of ministers and plethora of statutes concerned with statutory corporations may hinder attempts to control them, and that there is a tendency for Australian controls to be formalised and legalistic. Often the Treasury seems to have been the only body that has effectively queried the soundness of the investment programmes of statutory bodies. Sponsoring ministers may indeed act as a cover for corporations, instead of revealing their shortcomings; parliaments, as we have seen, have few effective ways of investigating the affairs of such bodies, even if they suspect that all is not well. There is sometimes a case for independent policy review of very large investment schemes.

There are also some respects in which the statutory authority may be less flexible than a department, or section of a department. As conditions change, governments may be stuck with a body with a legally defined structure and functions that it is harder to abolish or reorganise than those of a department. A possible example might be the Australian Atomic Energy Commission, which has survived as an independent unit within a statutory framework in many ways ill-adapted to changing circumstances since the 1953 Atomic Energy Act was passed.

However, there can still be great benefit to a commercial, cultural or research enterprise in escaping partly or wholly from standardised staffing and budgetary practices, and from the tradition of anonymity within the public service. There is a fashion now for recommending that statutory corporations be brought back under the bureaucratic co ordination of Treasury or Prime Minister's/Premier's Department or Public Service Board, and equipping the latter with more sophisticated units to do the job. But it is also arguable that governments need to set themselves a self-denying ordinance in relation to many of their enterprises—lay down the main objectives, establish a clear management structure, appoint a good board with a reasonably long tenure, and leave them to get on with the job. There will, of course, still be a need for periodical efficiency audits (see Chapter Eighteen) and for special arrangements and subsidies where enterprises are required by government to pay regard to public objectives that form no part of their normal criteria for efficient operations.

Advisory Bodies

Outside groups and individuals may sometimes be formally incorporated into the administrative process by gaining representation on the board of a statutory authority with executive powers. Some examples of this are given earlier in this chapter. However, a commoner method of formal involvement is through advisory bodies, some of whose members quite often come from outside interest groups, though they will also include persons chosen for their individual expertise or standing. Producer groups have the advantage. The 199 Commonwealth advisory committees at work in 1975 included representatives of 243 associations, and 203 of these were producer groups.[69] The ACTU was on fifteen. Other kinds of interest group were relatively poorly represented. Some of this representation is ritualistic, and the advisory body is sometimes a device for 'educating' its members, enlisting their support and 'co-opting' them into the administrative machine as a peculiar kind of public servant. However, to some groups advisory bodies are an important means of access to government.

Types of Advisory Body

The term Advisory Body is used to cover certain government bodies that consist of or include members from the outside world, and are established to give advice, not to carry out executive tasks. Advisory bodies help to link government agencies with two kinds of knowledge and experience: outside expertise and the views of people being regulated or receiving services. They are very numerous. We have already quoted some Commonwealth figures; a recent survey in New South Wales revealed the existence of no fewer than 550 government committees and boards that included non-government members—some of these had executive functions, but many of them were purely advisory.[70] They may be standing committees, or *ad hoc*; standing advisory bodies are set up to give continuing advice in their field, usually in private; *ad hoc* bodies are established to report on a particular matter, after which they cease to exist, and their reports are frequently published. Although in the discussion that follows they are referred to as 'committees', they may have a variety of titles, and occasionally consist of one person only. Even the line between a standing and an *ad hoc* body is sometimes blurred —at the time of writing, New South Wales has appointed an outside Commissioner to review government administration who is not only to make reports but help to implement them.

(i) Standing Committees   The formal title Advisory Committee or Advisory Council is often reserved for standing advisory committees, and *ad hoc* bodies are sometimes called Committees of Inquiry; but a wide variety of other terms is used, Commission, Consultative Council, Working Party, Task Force and so on. The lists of Associated Agencies in Chapter Three, which contain many standing advisory bodies, will be seen to include the National Women's Advisory Council, the Industry Advisory Councils associated with the Department of Industry and Commerce, and the National Labor Consultative Council (which has employer and union representatives, with the Minister for Employment and Industrial Relations in the chair). But it also includes such widely differing titles as the National Aboriginal Conference, the Tertiary Education Commission, and the Defence (Industrial) Committee, all of which are advisory bodies. At State level, the Development Corporation of New South Wales, in spite of its name, is a standing body set up to give advice to the State government 'on matters relating to the balanced development of the State'.

Standing committees may meet infrequently and be mere sounding boards for opinions in some broad field, or they may be in much closer and more continuous touch with the minister or department. One rough index of this is size; another is how much time the chairman and others are expected to devote to the committee's work. A nine-man body such as the Tertiary Education Commission, which advises the Commonwealth government on the whole post-secondary area—and which has a full-time chairman and three other full-time members, and a staff of around ninety—is clearly intended to be far more active and influential than the quite common part-time advisory council of twelve or thirteen; and the latter likely to be collectively more active than some committee with thirty-odd members. Indeed, the Tertiary Education Commission is in practice a sort of mini-department. How an advisory body is staffed is also an important factor. Usually the secretariat is provided by the relevant government department, and the quality, size and continuity of this staff are another index of the committee's importance and effectiveness. Another factor is the size of its budget. Occasionally an advisory body will include public servants on the committee along with outsiders, as does the National Parks and Wildlife Council which advises the New South Wales Minister for Lands. Sometimes an Advisory Council will do its effective work through a number of subcommittees, so the character of these may be another clue to its importance. A body like the New South Wales Ethnic Affairs Commission, with its own staff, a proper budget and direct access to the minister, has more chance of being effective than some amorphous group that meets occasionally with a single part-time secretary provided by the department.[71]

(ii) Ad hoc Bodies   *Ad hoc* advisory bodies are set up to complete a specific task, and die when they have reported. They often take oral and written evidence, and in some cases employ a research staff. The most exalted form is the Royal Commission, but in this century Australian governments have not often used this device to obtain advice on broad policy, but rather to investigate some alleged scandal or charge of maladministration. Royal Commissions have commonly been one-person or three-person bodies, with judges and lawyers well-represented.[72] A distinguished exception was the recent Royal Commission on Australian Government Administration (1974–6), a five-member body with broad terms of reference.

The so-called Committee of Inquiry is the more usual way of assembling a group of outsiders to make recommendations. Even this seemed to have fallen into disrepute before Labor returned to Commonwealth office in 1972. There had been a brief era of committee activity in the few years after the successful report in 1957 of the Murray Committee on Australian Universities, but on the whole experience seemed to confirm Australian governments in their dislike of authorising and assisting a group of outsiders to investigate and report publicly on their activities and policies; and they were supported in this by public services confident of their own capacity for fact-finding and policy formulation.

One or two signs of a change of heart were apparent in the last years of Liberal–Country Party rule.[73] The Commonwealth set a few outside inquiries on foot, including a Committee on Tax Reform and the Henderson inquiry into poverty, soon to be expanded by the Labor government into a much larger affair. In South Australia, the Karmel Committee reported on the State education system. In New South Wales, there had been inquiries into the health services, and in 1971 the Barnett Committee on Local Government Areas and Administration was established. But the big change came after 1972. By late 1973 the Prime Minister was able to list sixty-five *ad hoc* committees of inquiry and 'task forces' reporting to the Commonwealth government.[74] The most famous of the 'task forces' was that led by Dr H.C. Coombs on Continuing Expenditure Policies, which reviewed the spending programmes current when Labor took office, to see what could be cut back to make room for the government's own priorities.[75] With the full co-operation of the Treasury, it reported in ten weeks. Many committees of inquiry were appointed in the welfare field, on poverty, legal aid, rehabilitation and compensation, and so on.

This activity by no means ceased after the government changed in 1975. In its first eighteen months the Fraser government set up over twenty inquiries involving advisory bodies.[76] There were, however, some changes of approach. A number of so-called Review Committees were established to look critically at the internal organisation of government services, and in several cases no report was published. The best-known was the Administrative Review Committee, whose members were an ex-public servant, a serving State official and a businessman. The reason seems to have been not mainly the desire for secrecy, but a severely pragmatic view that the aim of such inquiries was to make speedy and immediately practicable recommendations to the government, rather than to draw up an impressive report for public discussion. This is not to say that the Administrative Review Committee was a particularly successful enterprise. Some other investigations were basically one-person affairs, though with official assistance. In general, they were pointed more towards promoting efficiency and better co-ordination within existing objectives than to recommending new forms of intervention.

In some cases no advisory body in our sense was used at all, but a public servant was appointed to report. When existing resources are deficient, it appears commoner now to create new policy and research units inside government itself, or to seek external advice by informal consultation or from persons whose views can be obtained in private. There is nothing novel about this; previous governments, including the Whitlam government, handled many of their problems in just this way.

The appointment of an advisory body is not, of course, only to draw on the expertise and opinions of its members and their helpers. It has sometimes been a useful way of delaying action on a matter; conversely, a published report may also help to 'legitimate' and to mobilise opinion in favour of changes that the government already desires, or at least to provoke discussion in some field where there is a vague government impulse to do something, or some pressure on it to act. An inquiry also stimulates other groups and individuals both inside and outside government, to give their views. Much of the material on which the Coombs Commission on Australian Government Administration based its findings came from the Public Service Board and from other sources inside government, as well as from its own research staff. It is often said that in this way an outside inquiry has an educational function; but it may, of course, mobilise opposition as well as support—and that can make change harder, not easier.

A committee of inquiry may run into difficulties on problems where extensive or sophisticated research is needed. It can commission this, as did the Vernon Committee and the Coombs Commission: but it may meet too intermittently (especially if its members are part-timers) or the research may not be completed quickly enough, for it to make full use of research findings. Finally, because a report is not immediately accepted or only in very modified form, this does not mean that the effort has failed; it may have helped to create the atmosphere in which change becomes possible, even if not as quickly as, or in the precise form that it hoped. Sometimes an outside report clarifies the problems, even if it does not get the answers quite right, or make them acceptable enough. Geoffrey Vickers has some useful passages on the value of certain commissions in providing a new 'appreciation' of a situation, in educating the reader in relevant facts, values and possible new initiatives, and in inviting government and public to modify their categories of thought.[77] The Coombs Report may serve this purpose, though some critics have argued that its insights are too scattered and that it has not provided a firm enough outline of the problems with which it attempts to deal.

Notes

1. R.L. Wettenhall, 'Public Ownership and Public Service', in H. Mayer (ed.), *Australian Politics: A Second Reader*, Cheshire, Melbourne, 1969, 629–70.
2. R.L. Wettenhall, 'Report on Statutory Authorities', in Report, RCAGA, Appendix Vol. One, 315.
3. Report, RCAGA, 82.
4. See R.L. Wettenhall, 'Administrative Boards in Nineteenth Century Australia', *Public Admin.* (Sydney), XXII, 3, September 1953, and 'Savings Banks, Bureaucracy and the Public Corporation', *Aust. J. Political History*, 10, 1, 1964.
5. Wettenhall, 'Administrative Boards in Nineteenth Century Australia', 267.
6. First Report, Board of Inquiry into the Victorian Public Service, Government Printer, Melbourne, 1974, 45.
7. Report, Royal Commission on Australian Government Administration, Canberra, 1976, 82.
8. *Com. Parl. Deb.* (H. of R.) v 102, 9 December 1976, 3592.
9. On Victoria, see list in Jean Holmes, *The Government of Victoria*, University of Queensland Press, 1976, 57–60; on New South Wales, *Statutory Bodies in New South Wales: A Checklist*, 2nd edn, NSW Parliamentary Library, Sydney, 1969; on the Commonwealth, Wettenhall in Report RCAGA, Appendix Vol. One, 329. Another RCAGA survey located 193 Commonwealth bodies.
10. See Enid Campbell, 'Ministers, Public Servants and the Executive Branch', in Gareth Evans (ed.), *Labor and the Constitution, 1972–1975*, Heinemann, Melbourne, 1977, 139–40; and Aust. Parl. Deb. (H. of R.), 8 September 1977, 998–1010, 'Statutory Authorities established since 1972'.
11. Prime Minister, during the Second Reading, Office of National Assessments Bill, *Com. Parl. Deb.* (H. of R.), 15 September 1977, 1179.
12. cf. G. Sawer, 'The Public Corporation in Australia', in W. Friedman (ed.), *The Public Corporation*, Carswell, Toronto, 1954, 12–13; see also for discussion in the Australian context, F.W. Eggleston, *State Socialism in Victoria*, P.S. King and Son, London, 1932, 41–8; Report, Royal Commission on Australian Government Administration, Canberra, 1976, 84–6; and Peter Bailey, in Cameron Hazlehurst and J.R. Nethercote, *Reforming Australian Government*, ANU Press, Canberra, 1977, 33.
13. Wettenhall, *op. cit.*, 320; I owe the analogy to Professor W.J.M. Mackenzie.
14. C.J. Lloyd and G.S. Reid, *Out of the Wilderness: The Return of Labor*, Cassell, North Melbourne, 1974, 256; see 255–8 for a good general account of Labor's statutory bodies.
15. J.D.B. Miller and Brian Jinks, *Australian Government and Politics*, 4th edn, Duckworth, London, 1970, 115.
16. For general discussion, see Peter Self, *Administrative Theories and Politics*, Allen and Unwin, London, 1972, 89–92.

17. For discussion in an Australian context, see L.C. Webb, 'Freedom and the Public Corporation', *Public Admin.* (Sydney), XIII, 2, June 1954; R.L. Wettenhall, 'Government Department or Statutory Authority?', and Leon Peres, 'The Resurrection of Autonomy', both in *Public Admin.* (Sydney), XXVII, 4, December 1969, both reprinted in R.N. Spann and G.R. Curnow, *Public Policy and Administration in Australia: A Reader*, Wiley, Sydney, 1975; R.L. Wettenhall, in Report, RCAGA, Appendix Vol. One, 319–21.

18. E.G. Whitlam, 'A New Federalism', *Aust. Quarterly*, 43, 3, September 1971, 13.

19. David Haselhurst, 'The Unjust Prices Tribunal', *The Bulletin*, 30 July 1977.

20. As quoted by Bruce Juddery, *Canberra Times*, 23 September 1977.

21. As quoted by *Australian Financial Review*, Editorial, 29 August 1977.

22. Report of address to NSW Chamber of Manufactures, *Journal of Industry and Commerce*, October 1977, 3.

23. R.L. Wettenhall, *Railways Management and Politics in Victoria, 1856–1906*, Royal Institute of Public Administration, Canberra, 1961, 19–67. On the ups and downs of its first chairman, Richard Speight, see Geoffrey Blainey, *The Tyranny of Distance*, 1968 edn, 255–6.

24. R.L. Wettenhall, 'Early Railway Management Legislation in New South Wales', *Tasmania University Law Review*, I, 3, 1960, 462–74.

25. Eggleston, *op. cit.*, 19, and Jean Holmes, 'The State Electricity Commission of Victoria—A Case Study in Autonomy', M.A. thesis, University of Melbourne, Melbourne, 1969. The first SEC included George Swinburne, who had been Minister for Water Supply when the Rivers and Water Supply Commission was established, and who also represented Victoria in the negotiations that led to the River Murray Commission. See E.H. Sugden and F.W. Eggleston, *George Swinburne*, Angus and Robertson, Sydney, 1931.

26. Some were part of a conscious policy of State enterprise espoused by W.A. Holman, as Attorney-General and Premier, and the Minister for Public Works, Arthur Griffith. See R.S. Parker, 'Public Enterprise in New South Wales', *Aust. J. Political History*, IV, 2, November 1958, and H.V. Evatt, *Australian Labour Leader*, Angus and Robertson, Sydney, 1942, Ch. XLII.

27. Don Aitkin, *The Colonel: A Political biography of Sir Michael Bruxner*, ANU Press, Canberra, 1969, 83.

28. Martin J. Painter, 'New Forces in State Politics', *Current Affairs Bulletin*, 53, 8, January 1977, 22.

29. On its predecessor, see N. Griffiths, *A History of the Government Savings Bank of N.S.W.*, W.T. Baker and Co. Ltd, Sydney, 1930.

30. See the discussion of this term in Chapter One.

31. Martyn Forrest, *The Organisation of Government in Western Australia*, Department of Politics, University of Western Australia, Perth, 1977, 21.

32. On the history of port control, see Glen Lewis, *A History of the Ports of Queensland*, University of Queensland Press, St Lucia, 1973; and Olaf Ruhen, *Port of Melbourne, 1835–1976*, Cassell, North Melbourne, 1976, especially ch. 9.

33. The Act creating it, the (Swinburne) Water Act, 1905, was a very advanced measure for its day (cf. F.W. Eggleston, *op. cit.*, 75). A separate Board supplies Melbourne's water.

34. On the gas industry, see J.D. Keating, *The Lambent Flame*, Melbourne University Press, Melbourne, 1974.

35. See R. Gollan, *The Commonwealth Bank of Australia: Origins and Early History*, ANU Press, Canberra, 1968, ch. 7–8.
36. R.L. Wettenhall, 'Administrative Debacle, 1919–23', *Public Admin.* (Sydney), XXIII, 4, December 1964.
37. For an account, see R.L. Wettenhall, 'Federal Labour and the Public Corporation under Matthew Charlton', *Labour History*, no. 6, 1964, 10–24.
38. See D.J. Hardman, *Snowy Scheme Management and Administration*, West Publishing Corporation, Sydney, 1970; and above, Chapter Three.
39. See A.L. May, *The Battle for the Banks*, Sydney University Press, Sydney, 1968.
40. See D.C. Corbett, *Politics and the Airlines*, Allen and Unwin, London, 1965; S. Brogden, *Australia's Two-Airline Policy*, Melbourne University Press, Melbourne, 1968; R.L. Wettenhall, 'Australia's Two Airline System under Review', *Aust. Quarterly*, 34, March 1962; and D.G. Davies, 'The Efficiency of Public versus Private Firms, the Case of Australia's Two Airlines', *J. Law and Econ.*, 15, 1, April 1971.
41. For the career of one well-known Commissioner, see R.J. Jennings, *W.A. Webb: South Australian Railways Commissioner 1922–30*, Nesfield Press, Adelaide, 1973. There is a good short account of his Victorian contemporary, Harold Clapp, in *The Age*, 14 June 1975.
42. Joan Rydon, 'The Australian Broadcasting Commission', *Public Admin.* (Sydney), XI, 4, December 1952, 191. The broadcasting legislation has since been amended to provide for terms of three years. For another example, see Barry Cole, 'The Australian Broadcasting Control Board, 1948–1966', *Public Admin.* (Sydney), XXIX, 3, September 1970.
43. Martyn Forrest, *op. cit.*, 34.
44. See J.W. Goodsell, 'The Metropolitan Water Sewerage and Drainage Board', *Public Admin.* (Sydney), XVI, 3, March 1957.
45. See *Sydney Morning Herald*, 27 February 1956, and R.S. Parker, in S.R. Davis (ed.), *The Government of the Australian States*, Longman, Melbourne, 1960, 166. Practice is better now than formerly; and cf. 'Mr Wurth's Estate', *Nation*, 22 September 1962.
46. See Report, Commonwealth Public Service Board, 1977, 94.
47. See an Opposition critic, J.G. Latham, *Com. Parl. Deb.* v 123, 21 March 1930, 386–7; and R.L. Wettenhall, 'Federal Labour and the Public Corporation under Matthew Charlton', *Labour History*, 6, May 1964.
48. Street, J., in *Bennetts* v. *The Board of Fire Commissioners of New South Wales* (1967) 87 W.N. (Pt 1) (N.S.W.) 307.
49. Martyn Forrest, *op. cit.*, 34
50. Twenty-first Report, 13–14 and Twenty-second Report, 71–72. See also S. Encel, 'Public Corporations in Australia: Some Recent Developments', *Public Admin.* (London), XXXVIII, Autumn 1960, 235–52.
51. Report, 90.
52. For a short account of Commonwealth practices, see G.E. Caiden, *The Commonwealth Bureaucracy*, Melbourne University Press, Melbourne, 1967, 117–27.
53. *Canberra Times*, 14 July 1977.
54. First Report, Board of Inquiry into the Victorian Public Service, Government Printer, Melbourne, 1974; Interim Report, Review of New South Wales Government Administration, Government Printer, Sydney, 1977.

55. For details, see Report, RCAGA, Appendix Vol. One, 365–74.
56. G.D. McColl, *The Economics of Electricity Supply in Australia*, Melbourne University Press, Melbourne, 1976.
57. *Report*, 1968–9.
58. Reserve Bank Act, sections 10 and 11.
59. e.g. Australian Industry Development Corporation Act 1970, section 8; and cf. Report, Royal Commission on Australian Government Administration, Canberra 1976, 88.
60. On its powers, see W.A. Townsley, *The Government of Tasmania*, University of Queensland Press, St Lucia, 1976, 124–7.
61. cf. Interim Report, Review of New South Wales Government Administration, 55.
62. R.L. Wettenhall, Report, Royal Commission on Australian Government Administration, Appendix Vol. I, 323, 351.
63. See Joan Rydon, 'The Australian Broadcasting Commission, 1942–1948', *Public Admin.* (Sydney), XI, 4, December 1952, 194 ff.
64. R.L. Wettenhall, in Report, Royal Commission on Australian Government Administration, Appendix Vol. I, 334.
65. The first and third quotations are from *Com. Parl. Deb.* (Senate), V.S. 4, 905, 21 October 1954, and *N.S.W. Parl. Deb.* (Leg. Ass.), V. 81, 1975, 22 October 1969.
66. For fuller discussion, see D.N. Chester and N. Bowring, *Questions in Parliament,* Oxford University Press, Oxford, 1962, 301–5; Sir B. Cocks (ed.), *Erskine May's Treatise on . . . Parliament*, 17th edn, London, 1964, 335–6; and House of Commons Debates, V. 682, 1962–63, 449–55 (statement by Mr McLeod).
67. Evidence to Royal Commission on Australian Government Administration (*Canberra Times*, 24 January 1975).
68. *Ministerial Control of the Nationalised Industries*, 3 vols, HMSO, London, 1968. The Government's reply to this report is in Cmnd. 4027 of May 1969, with the same title.
69. T.V. Matthews, 'Interest Group Access to the Australian Government Bureaucracy', Report, RCAGA, Appendix Vol. Two, 339.
70. P.J.D. O'Meagher, *Community/Government Participation*, Administrative Research Committee, Public Service Board of NSW, 1977 (mimeo).
71. cf. Interim Report, Review of New South Wales Government Administration, 307.
72. On an earlier 'golden age of royal commissions', see G.N. Hawker, *The Parliament of New South Wales, 1856–1965*, Government Printer, Sydney, 1971, 88–9, 284–5. On the powers of Royal Commissions, see Report, RCAGA, Appendix Vol. Four, 340–70.
73. cf. Report, RCAGA, Appendix Vol. One, 402.
74. E.G. Whitlam, 'Public Administration in Australia: Changes under the Labor Government', *The Round Table*, 253, January 1974, 81–3.
75. See Report, Task Force on Continuing Expenditure Policies, Canberra 1973. Though Dr Coombs was assisted by senior public servants and ministerial advisers, he took sole responsibility for the recommendations.
76. *Com. Parl. Deb.* (H. of R.), 26 May 1977, 2019.
77. Geoffrey Vickers, *The Art of Judgment*, Chapman and Hall, London, 1965, 50 ff.

Chapter Six

Administration and Law

This chapter deals with certain limited aspects of the relation between administration and the law—in particular, with the growth of various special procedures for checking and controlling the discretionary acts and decisions of government administration. There are a number of routes by which individuals may seek redress against the administration, some of which are discussed in other chapters. For example, they may appeal to their local member (and parliament itself has some collective ways of controlling administrative discretions); they may form a pressure group (see Chapter Seventeen), or raise the matter individually with the government agency concerned. Most departments have some procedures for reviewing past decisions. In this chapter we confine ourselves to two special areas: first, methods of controlling 'delegated legislation'; and secondly, the use of special tribunals and courts to review administrative action.

Delegated Legislation

In complex modern societies parliaments have neither the time, the expertise, nor adequate processes to undertake the detailed formulation of every necessary law. Usually they must content themselves with declaring the policy or outline of legislation and empowering some administrative authority to prescribe most of the machinery by which, and the circumstances in which, that policy is to be implemented. This is done by conferring power in the Act on a minister or other authority to make regulations, orders, rules or by-laws, which when made are 'delegated legislation', sometimes also called 'subordinate legislation'.[1]

Delegated legislation may take a variety of forms. In Australia, Acts of the Commonwealth Parliament usually give the power to the Governor-General in Council. In most States, including New South Wales, the delegation of power is to the Governor in Council, or to special statutory authorities such as the Public Transport Commissioners. The power is usually to make regulations, but terms such as order, warrant, rule and ordinance are also used. Local government legislation generally authorises the making of ordinances or by-laws by the Governor in Council, and local authorities themselves in some States have power to make rules or by-laws of limited application within their own districts. In Britain, it is common to give the power to some particular minister or department, but this is much rarer in Australia; in Britain 'statutory instrument' is the term used nowadays to describe delegated legislation made by ministers and government departments.

Sometimes, as in Australia by the National Security Act 1939 and the Defence Preparations Act 1951, power has been conferred to make regulations that in turn may authorise the making of orders and giving of directions by others; this entails a double delegation of power. But the courts have been careful to limit the right of subdelegation by subordinate authorities and have seized on even minor indications in an Act of Parliament to confine power to the hands of the primary repository. Thus it has been held that the Sydney City Council cannot delegate the power to levy a rate of make by-laws.[2] In Victoria the Supreme Court for similar reasons restricted the right of a shire council to delegate its power to manage and control a town hall.[3] In New South Wales a 1945 amendment to the Local Government Act (section 530A) extended the power of local councils to delegate powers to other persons, but expressly excluded such actions as the fixing of any rate or charge, the voting of money for expenditure, transactions in land, and other basic powers.

Control by the Courts

In Australia, legislative powers are distributed between the Commonwealth and the States, and each parliament has sovereign power within its own sphere of activity. Any legislative power granted by statute to any other law-making body is not sovereign but subordinate in character. This means, among other things, that the courts can scrutinise its exercise and determine the validity of any such exercise. The main grounds on which they will do this are that it is *ultra vires* (beyond power).

Delegated legislation is *ultra vires* and invalid when it exceeds the powers granted by the Act of Parliament to the subordinate authority. This entails an examination of the law in the light of the powers granted. It follows that the wider the grant of power the less possibility there is of holding any subordinate legislation to be invalid. But a grant of power, even in absolute terms, will be construed by the courts as limited to the specific purposes for which the Act was passed. In Australia the regulation-making powers conferred by Commonwealth and State Acts usually refer to specific matters that are mentioned in the Act or must necessarily arise thereunder; in addition it will often be found that a general power is conferred to make regulations or by-laws 'as may be necessary or convenient . . . for giving effect to this Act'. It might seem that such a provision gives extremely wide powers to the subordinate authority, but a series of decisions in Australia has imposed important limitations on its scope. Except in time of war or other emergency, the High Court has been careful to limit the delegated power to the 'filling in of the outline' of the Act. Some statutes have conferred power to make regulations in terms that seek to preclude any challenge to their validity by the courts, though it has been rare in Australia for parliaments to try to do this. One device that has been used is for the Act to declare that 'any regulations or by-laws made under this Act shall have effect as if enacted in this Act'. But the Australian courts have not in general treated this as precluding inquiry into the validity of a regulation.[4]

Other Forms of Control

Some problems can be avoided by careful attention to the drafting of delegated legislation. In New South Wales, for example, it is the practice to submit drafts of proposed delegated legislation to the parliamentary draftsman, who can give expert advice on their wording, and the Attorney-General also gives an opinion on their validity. Commonwealth delegated legislation is drafted by officers of the Attorney-General's Department.

It has sometimes been held that particular interests who are specially affected by delegated legislation have some right to consultation before the law comes into force. An obvious method would be to give prior public notice of intention to make regulations pertaining to a particular subject and to make draft copies of the proposed regulations freely available. This procedure was formerly provided for in Britain by the Rules Publication Act 1893, but that Act did not apply to orders nor to any rules certified to be urgent. Its piecemeal character deprived it of real value. There is provision for prior notice (with loopholes) in the United States.

The Role of Parliament

Nowadays in Britain most statutes require that delegated legislation shall be laid before parliament. The commonest form of provision is that it comes into immediate effect, but may be annulled by resolution of either House. However, sometimes an affirmative resolution is needed before the regulations operate, or to allow them to continue to operate beyond a limited time. The Statutory Instruments Act 1946 lays down procedure for delegated legislation required to be laid before parliament. Where it is subject to annulment, this must be done within a period of forty sitting days. This procedure gives a chance for representations to be made by interested parties to their parliamentary representatives or the minister. It is too much to expect members to look at instruments for themselves; they are too numerous and technical and, in any case, members spend all their time perusing regulations and orders. However, the Select Committee on Statutory Instruments sits regularly to review all instruments that are laid before parliament and draws the attention of the House to particular instruments.

In Australia there was once provision for sixty days' prior notice of Commonwealth Regulations. In 1916, this was superseded by section 48 of the Acts Interpretation Act which requires that, unless a contrary indication appears in the empowering Act, regulations shall be notified in the *Gazette* and shall be laid before each house of parliament within fifteen sitting days, failing which they will be void and of no effect. Notice of intention to move a resolution of disallowance may be given within a further fifteen days after tabling. In the States there is no uniform procedure with respect to checks upon delegated legislation. Most States have general Acts similar to the Commonwealth Acts Interpretation Act.[5] For example, the New South Wales law provides for publication in the *Gazette*, laying before parliament within another fourteen days, and notice of motion to disallow by either house within fifteen days after laying. Victoria has less satisfactory arrangements—most regulations are tabled, but without parliament having any general power to disallow.[6] There is no general provision or practice in the States requiring advance notice of delegated legislation but in some instances such a procedure is mandatory, such as where a local authority proposes to exercise compulsory powers regarding the acquisition of property. The charge has often been made that the obligation to table regulations is an empty formality, which results in their becoming effective by default. However, in these days, when all sections of industry and employees are highly organised into trade associations and unions, and pressure groups are on the watch for any infringement of their rights, it rarely happens that the persons affected do not make full representations to the responsible authority, if not before, at least very promptly after, any law comes into force.

It is necessary, of course, that there should be adequate publicity of delegated legislation; and the requirement of publicity is not adequately satisfied by merely providing, as many of the laws do, that regulations or orders 'shall be published in the Gazette'. This is important as a means of recording the regulation in accurate and permanent form, but it does not necessarily bring its terms to the notice of the public. There is a need for delegated legislation to be accompanied by a memorandum explaining its effect in simple terms and for more official publications setting out concisely the purport of regulations that affect members of the public.

Parliamentary Committees

There is also a case for a body to review and report to parliament on all delegated legislation, a course that was recommended in the 1932 report of the UK Committee on Ministers' Powers. Nothing was done in Britain to implement this recommendation until 1944, when the Select Committee on Statutory Instruments was established. The reports of this committee were responsible for the passing of the Statutory Instruments Act, 1946. The Act and the committee now operate as an important safeguard in ensuring that all delegated legislation is reviewed by a competent independent body before the lapse of the period allowed for annulment after tabling in parliament. The committee's terms of reference authorise it to draw the attention of the House to any statutory instrument on any of the following grounds:

1. It imposes a charge on the public revenues.
2. It is made in pursuance of an enactment containing specific provisions excluding it from challenge in the courts.

3. It appears to make unusual or unexpected use of powers conferred by statute.
4. It purports to have retrospective effect without specific statutory sanction.
5. There appears to have been unjustifiable delay in the publication or in the laying of it before parliament.
6. There appears to have been unjustifiable delay in notifying it to the Speaker under the provision of the Statutory Instruments Act, relating to instruments which have come into operation before tabling in parliament.
7. For any special reason its form or purport calls for elucidation.

The committee has had a salutary effect on the form and substance of delegated legislation, and the number of instruments that it has found occasion to report to the House has steadily declined. There is no doubt that the mere existence of such a body operates as a substantial check on any excess or abuse of power.

Regulation-making bodies in Australia usually have full power to amend or revoke regulations so as to achieve flexibility. The Commonwealth and some States have also created machinery for the review of delegated legislation. In 1931 the Senate set up a Standing Committee on Regulations and Ordinances to which delegated legislation tabled in the Senate is referred. The committee scrutinises regulations to ascertain that:

1. They are in accord with the statute.
2. They do not trespass unduly on personal rights and liberties.
3. They do not unduly make the rights and liberties of citizens dependent upon administrative and not upon judicial decisions.
4. They are concerned with administrative detail and do not amount to substantive legislation, which should be a matter for parliamentary enactment.

These terms of reference suggest that, unlike the UK committee, it could concern itself with wider questions of 'policy', but it has not done so in practice. It is assisted by an outside legal adviser, and seems to have been a success in a modest way. It can call officials before it; and give a department the chance of withdrawing the offending regulations, or report to the Senate recommending disallowance. 'In practice the former course has proved more successful'.[7]

Joint parliamentary committees with similar functions exist in South Australia, Tasmania and Victoria, and in the single-chamber parliament of Queensland. In 1960 the New South Wales Legislative Council set up a Committee of Subordinate Legislation, whose terms of reference combine those of the Senate Standing Committee and the British Scrutiny Committee. 'If one is to judge the Committee solely by its reports, the appearance given is of a not particularly active body.'[8] In 1976 Western Australia legislated for a non-parliamentary committee to keep an eye on delegated legislation.

Administrative Tribunals and Courts

W.A. Robson wrote in 1927 that 'one of the most striking developments in the British Constitution during the last half-century has been the acquisition of judicial power by the great departments of State and by various other bodies and persons outside the courts of law'.[9] The nature of this development must be examined against the historical background of British institutions, in which the ordinary courts were almost the only bodies having power to make decisions that affected the personal or proprietary rights of the individual. Most disputes, claims and rights were determined by the courts in accordance with accepted judicial methods.

However, the trend towards government control of trade, commerce and industry led to a wide range of legislation. Decisions about how this mass of law applied in individual cases had to be made by someone—who better than a governmental agency which knew the policy of the legislation? Moreover, the fields into which such legislation penetrated were often, because of their social content, quite foreign to the courts, and the remedies called for were alien to established judicial processes. Finally, considerations of time and cost made judicial procedures unsuitable for determining matters that had to be settled informally, quickly, and with minimum expense. So a tendency developed to give the power of decision on individual cases in certain fields to administrative agencies.

Many such decisions are part of the day-to-day routine of public servants. But in a number of areas of special sensitivity, special kinds of tribunal have developed, either to make the decision or to review it on appeal.

Types of Tribunal

The principal types of decision involving tribunals in Australia have been classified as follows, but the field is constantly expanding:[10]
1. Regulation of industrial conditions—industrial arbitration, terms and conditions of employment, etc.
2. Public Service tribunals—terms and conditions of service of Crown and semi-government employees.
3. Award of benefits, pensions and other grants—social security payments, pensions to discharged servicemen, public servants and others, workers' compensation, etc.
4. Supervision of social conditions affecting the community—regulation of buildings, health and sanitation, factory conditions, theatres, rent control, etc.
5. Licensing of occupations involving special skill or public responsibility—medical, dental, and other professions, electrical contractors, estate agents, moneylenders.
6. Supervision of trade, commerce, and transport—marketing of primary products, licensing of distributors of primary and other products, licensing of transport operators, protection of consumers, etc.

7. Assessment of taxes, rates, and duties—income and other taxes, valuations for rating purposes, etc.
8. Legal protection of industrial property—patents, copyrights, trade marks, etc.
9. Compensation for interference with private property rights in the public interest—town and country planning, valuations of property acquired by public authorites.
10. Various matters of State policy—surcharge of public and semi-governmental officers, immigration, regulation of Crown lands, prickly-pear control, etc.

The machinery set up to deal with these matters does not follow any single pattern. The initial decision may be made by a regular administrative department or board, sometimes with provision for reference to or an appeal to some administrative tribunal or to a court. Thus, in the case of land valuation in New South Wales, the Valuer-General makes the initial valuation, but there is an appeal to a Valuation Board of Review, and further appeal is possible to the Land and Valuation Court, and (on a question of law) to the Supreme Court. In the Commonwealth, three-member Taxation Boards of Review have been established to review decisions of the Commissioner of Taxation and his Deputy Commissioners, with a further appeal to the High Court possible on a question of law. In other cases, a special tribunal deals with the matter, but there may be provision for further reference to an administrative authority, or for appeal to a court.

The nature of administrative tribunals itself varies greatly, from ones that are named and that operate in ways very similar to the ordinary courts (for example, the Australian Conciliation and Arbitration Commission), to bodies that operate in a much more discretionary fashion, such as milk boards or film censors, or where informality has been a major aim. Thus the Social Security Appeals Tribunals established in 1975 are planned to operate as informally as possible. Each tribunal consists of two independent members, usually a lawyer and a social worker, and an officer from the Department of Social Security; departmental instructions leave procedures to their discretion but forbid legal representation, and tell them to ensure that a court room atmosphere does not exist at hearings. They cannot themselves overturn decisions, though the Director-General of the Department of Social Security nearly always accepts their views. Striking examples of informality are the Small Claims Tribunals that deal in most States with certain consumer complaints—no costs are allowed and professional advocates are largely barred from appearing.

The members of the tribunal may be wholly appointed by the government or in some more independent way. They may or may not choose their own chairman. They may or may not include 'representatives' of the interests concerned, including employees. They may or may not include members of the legal profession. The composition of bodies dealing with the same kind of matter may vary considerably between States. Inspection of the legislation relating to Australian administrative tribunals reveals few or no clear and consistently applied principles. Some writers have urged the creation in a much more systematic way of administrative courts to review decisions affecting individual rights.

Recent Developments

This question was taken up by the Franks Committee on Administrative Tribunals and Enquiries, set up in Britain in 1955.[11] It rejected the idea of a general administrative appeals tribunal, but recommended the creation of a Council on Tribunals which would keep the constitution, organisation and procedure of administrative tribunals continuously under review and advise on such matters whenever a new tribunal was to be created. This was provided for in the Tribunals and Inquiries Act 1958, and had a marked effect on the tone and procedures of such bodies, and of administration generally. The committee also expressed its own views about composition and procedure. It thought that the independence of tribunals would be assisted if the members were not appointed by the minister concerned. The chairman should normally have legal qualifications. Though procedures were bound to vary, tribunals should normally meet in public and follow some of the basic rules evolved by judicial bodies for protecting the individual. Reasons for decisions should be given to the fullest practicable extent. There should usually be an appellate tribunal, and an appeal to the courts on a point of law.

The United States has faced similar problems, but dealt with them in a somewhat different way. Two important and long-established features of American administration have influenced policy in that country. First, there exist guarantees of individual rights in the various constitutions, which have been held to require a fair hearing in many cases of interference with liberty and property. Secondly, as well as ordinary government departments and statutory enterprises, an exceptionally large number of major statutory agencies have been established expressly to deal with regulatory matters, bodies such as the Interstate Commerce Commission, the Federal Communications Commission, and the Federal Trade Commission, which adopt judicial procedures in the course of their normal administrative business. This has encouraged a strong tendency to 'judicialise' administrative procedures more generally, culminating in the Administrative Procedures Act 1946, and similar legislation in many States, in which the attempt has been made to draft codes of administrative procedure to be adopted in reaching decisions affecting individual rights.

Not everyone would accept the view that Australian administration should be made more judicial in character and some writers think that Australia has already gone quite far enough in this direction. A notable feature of public administration in this country is the extent to which parliament has provided for direct judicial or administrative tribunal review of official action.

Some administrators would argue that efficiency has been too often sacrificed to fair play, and that the emphasis in administrative adjudication and tribunals should be on skill, cheapness, informality and effectiveness rather than legal membership and court-like procedures.

The most interesting recent developments have been at Commonwealth level. An Administrative Review Committee, under the chairmanship of John Kerr, reported in 1971, and recommended the creation of a federal administrative court and other machinery, including an Administrative Review Council, which was finally appointed in 1976. It has the task of keeping under examination the whole range of administrative discretions and recommending those in respect of which there should be provision for review by a court, tribunal or other body and what mechanisms are most appropriate. It can also play the same watchdog role over existing tribunals as the United Kingdom Council on Tribunals. In the same year an Administrative Appeals Tribunal, with a judge as President and (in 1978) two other members, came into operation. The tribunal reviews only those actions and decisions of ministers or officials taken under legislation that provides for such an appeal; but in these cases its powers are very extensive, it can review the whole matter on its merits and if necessary change the decision. In contrast, the new Federal Court, which also has powers of administrative review, is not supposed to be concerned with the substantive merits of an administrative decision, but (putting it broadly) can act only if the decision is *ultra vires,* or if proper procedures have not been followed in making it a decision. The council also hears appeals on a point of law against decisions of the tribunal. So the Commonwealth now has the makings of a systematic body of administrative courts.

The procedures of the Administrative Appeals Tribunal are intended to make it a reasonably accessible body.[12] Legal representation is allowed at the option of the parties, and hearings are held in public unless the tribunal decides otherwise in a particular case. In this respect it is like a court, but the Act also says that procedures shall involve 'as little formality and technicality' as proper consideration of the case permits, and it is not bound by the rules of evidence. There is also provision for conferences which may settle matters without the need for a formal hearing. The tribunal must give written reasons for its decisions. It may give advisory opinions. The President must be legally qualified, but the other members need not be. It can summon people to give evidence or to produce documents (the Attorney-General may certify that disclosure would be contrary to the public interest, but the tribunal has certain powers to inspect them itself). Although the tribunal only deals with matters where legislation provides for such an appeal, it seems likely to end up with a very wide jurisdiction. As well as new fields, some existing rights of appeal to other kinds of tribunal will probably be transferred to it. At present its scope is limited though various—from customs matters to appeals against deportation orders or by pilots who have had their licences revoked.

Ombudsmen

Another kind of check on administration is the Parliamentary Commissioner or *Ombudsman*, an idea derived from Scandinavia.[13] This shares some features of both parliamentary and judicial control. An *Ombudsman* is a full-time commissioner appointed by the government to receive individual complaints about administrative decisions and actions, to investigate them in private and to make representations to the government agency concerned if he thinks the action was wrong. Such commissioners have been appointed recently in several Commonwealth countries and elsewhere. The New Zealand Commissioner investigated nearly 2000 complaints in his first six years, and 20 per cent were held to be fully justified; the Australian average seems to be at least this.

Western Australia legislated for an Ombudsman, called there Parliamentary Commissioner, in 1971. Since then all the mainland States, and the Commonwealth, have appointed Ombudsmen, and Tasmania is (1979) to do so. Ombudsmen need not be lawyers, and some States have appointed ex-public servants. In 1977 the Commonwealth appointed an academic lawyer, but one with considerable experience of government service. In Australia Ombudsmen have no power to change any decisions, the only sanction is their critical comment in private reports to the head of department or, if necessary, to the Prime Minister or Premier; in their published reports to parliament, or (occasionally) other kinds of publicity. Most complaints are dealt with satisfactorily without Ombudsmen having to report formally at all. They may subpoena witnesses and examine government files, subject to certain limitations, for example, where disclosure of cabinet proceedings or prejudice to security is involved. In Australia Ombudsmen are not supposed to concern themselves with the 'policy' involved in actions or decisions, but are restricted to investigating complaints relating to a 'matter of administration'—that is, maladministration of policy. This means that the decisions of ministers are not subject to review by Ombudsmen and in this respect their scope is more restricted than that of the Administrative Appeals Tribunal, which can examine ministerial decisions and also has the power to change decisions. On the other hand, the Ombudsmen are not confined to specified fields of administration, though they may be excluded from particular areas, such as complaints against police.

A Note on Access

Another interesting recent development concerns 'access' to the courts, especially by individuals affected by the regulations or decisions of government agencies. In the past the law has often denied 'standing', or the right to go to court, where the complainant cannot show that the effect on his interests is substantial, or the harm suffered direct and personal. Hence someone seeking a court order declaring a regulation invalid has often to show that, say, his property is specially affected, and has not been allowed to challenge a council by-law that affects him no more than anyone else in the community, such as one that has a generally adverse effect on the environment. A related question is that of 'class actions'—in the United States, for example, an individual or group can sue not only for themselves but on behalf of the whole class of people affected by some wrongdoing and obtain redress for the class. The Commonwealth Law Reform Commission has been looking into such questions, and in December 1977 issued a discussion paper recommending that citizens should have wider access to the courts on 'public interest' matters.

Notes

1. The standard work is now D.C. Pearce, *Delegated Legislation in Australia and New Zealand*, Butterworths, Sydney, 1977. See also D.G. Benjafield and H. Whitmore, *Principles of Australian Administrative Law*, 4th edn, Law Book Co., Sydney, 1971.
2. *Bailey* v. *Municipal Council of Sydney* (1927) 28 S.R. (N.S.W.) 149.
3. *Morrison* v. *Shire of Morwell* (1948) V.L.R. 73.
4. cf. Pearce, *op. cit.*, 273.
5. Some significant differences are noted by Pearce, *op. cit.*, 86–8, 90–1.
6. Pearce, *op. cit.*, 109.
7. Report, RCAGA, 112; cf. Pearce, *op. cit.*, 32–40. The committee's 43rd Report discusses how it applies its principles.
8. Pearce, *op. cit.*, 105.
9. W.A. Robson, *Justice and Administrative Law*, Stevens, London, 1928, xxviii.
10. Benjafield and Whitmore, *op. cit.*, and for accounts of some tribunals, 345–60. For a list of Commonwealth tribunals, see *Com. Parl. Deb.* (H. of R.), 15 October 1968, 1978–81, and the account in Report, Administrative Review Committee, Canberra, 1971, 6–7.
11. See *Report*, Committee on Administrative Tribunals and Enquiries, Cmd. 218 (1957). The work of the Council on Tribunals is vividly described in J.F. Garner, 'The Council on Tribunals', *Public Law*, Winter 1965, 321–47.
12. For a brief account, see H. Whitmore and M. Aronson, *Review of Administrative Action*, Law Book Co., Sydney, 1978, ch. 2; and the first Annual Report of the Administrative Review Council, Canberra, 1977.
13. On the topic generally, see G. Sawer, *Ombudsmen*, 2nd edn, Melbourne University Press, Melbourne, 1968; on Australia, J. Disney, 'Ombudsmen in Australia', *Aust. Quarterly*, 46, 4, December 1974; Whitmore and Aronson, *op. cit.*, 5–9; and the Annual Reports of Ombudsmen.

Chapter Seven

Federal Relations I— Constitution and Finance

Federalism has been defined as 'the method of dividing powers so that the general and regional governments are each, within a sphere, co-ordinate and independent'.[1] In a federal system, most citizens are subject to two governments, and neither government is the subordinate of the other, they are 'co-ordinate'. They are not necessarily equals in power and influence, but each has appreciable powers of its own, protected by a written constitution. So in Australia, local governments are formally subordinate to the States—the clearest indication of this is that local councils could be abolished by the State legislature—but the existence and powers of the States are not owed to the Commonwealth parliament.

Most federal systems have been unstable, on the way towards unification or disintegration.[2] This is usually because the structure of political interests and demands has come to differ from the territorial division of powers. National divisions (say, between two national parties) may be much more important than regional differences, or regional differences may dominate national politics. In either case, even if federal institutions survive, they do not work as planned. The two levels of government tend to become different arenas for the same set of demands, with both governments responding to what are essentially the same electoral pressures. Most people would agree that Australia has moved a fair distance in the former direction, in which national divisions tend to dominate State differences, though there would be dispute about just how far this process has gone, and how likely it is to continue.

In federations where regional differences still matter (and they are still of importance in Australia),[3] an important factor in determining how the federal system works is inequalities of population and resources between the various units. An unstable situation is where well-populated poor regions use their voting power to mulct small rich regions—the latter then have good reason for discontent. Australia has been fortunate in the past that its richer units have also been relatively well-populated. Even if they have sometimes felt like milch-cows, they have valued the influence that their size gives them in national affairs; while the smaller units have been reconciled to Commonwealth power at least partly by the financial advantages to their regional

164

interests that have accrued. However, nowadays Queensland and Western Australia feel more like potentially rich but exploited peripheries, which seems to be leading to rather more federal instability.

Another important factor in determining the federal balance, and one especially relevant to this book, is the relative strength of the administrative services at the two levels of government, the quality of advice available to ministers and the skill with which the various government services are operated and managed.

The Constitutional Framework

Before federation, Australia was a group of six colonies, independent of one another and largely self-governing. Each of them had, and has, its own constitution, originally embodied in statutes of the British Parliament. The State Constitutions are simple documents. In particular, they impose few restrictions on the power of the State legislatures. However, in 1900 another constitution placed some serious limitations on State powers. The six colonies federated, and the United Kingdom Parliament passed the Commonwealth of Australia Constitution Act. How does his affect the six States?

A few powers were given solely to the Commonwealth parliament. These are known as exclusive powers of the Commonwealth and include: customs and excise, postal services, control of federal Territories, and most defence matters. For example, only the Commonwealth may have armed forces, make treaties and declare war, though the States still conduct some active 'resources diplomacy' with overseas countries. In many cases, the Commonwealth parliament was given concurrent powers; that is, both it and the States can legislate on the matter. Such powers include taxation (other than customs and excise), banking, divorce and many others. Section 109 of the Constitution provides for the supremacy of Commonwealth over State law in concurrent fields, in case of conflict; so this is an area in which the Commonwealth has gradually been able to extend its powers by legislation. However, provided that Commonwealth law does not cover the field, there is nothing to prevent both the Commonwealth and the States legislating on such topics. For example, both may constitutionally levy income taxes, and both did so between the two World Wars.

On matters on which the Commonwealth parliament was not given exclusive powers, and has not exercised its concurrent powers, the States retain those powers which they had at the time of federation. These are nowhere listed. The New South Wales Constitution Act, for example, says only that the State parliament 'shall, subject to the provisions of the Commonwealth of Australia Constitution Act, have power to make laws for the peace, welfare and good government of New South Wales in all cases whatsoever'. The States simply have the residue of public powers not given to the Commonwealth. These residual powers are important ones; they include most internal law and order (police, courts, prisons), most powers over agriculture, mineral resources, secondary industry, the main public utilities (power, water, most transport) and many social services, including education. It should be added that, as local government is weakly developed in Australia, the States have also continued to provide many services that in countries such as America and Britain would be mainly the responsibility of local authorities. Of course, the Commonwealth has all these powers in its own Territories.

Legal disputes between Commonwealth and States are normally settled by a federal court, the High Court of Australia. Section 71 vests the judicial power of the Commonwealth not only in the High Court, which decides most constitutional cases and acts as a national court of appeal, but 'in such other federal courts as the Parliament creates, and in such other courts as it invests with federal jurisdiction'. For most purposes, the Commonwealth did not set up its own system of courts, but allowed the State courts to act. In recent years this policy has shown signs of changing, with the creation of the Family Court (1975) and the Federal Court (1976).

Main Trends since 1900

The main changes that have occurred in federal relations may be considered under the following headings:

Constitutional Amendment

Section 128 of the Commonwealth Constitution provides a method of changing the Constitution. Proposed alterations must be agreed to at a popular referendum by an Australia-wide majority of those voting, and also by a majority vote in a majority of States. This has been hard to achieve, as Australians are reluctant to vote 'Yes' in constitutional referenda. The voters have considered thirty-six amendment proposals since 1901, but agreed to only eight, and of these only two seem to have been important in increasing Commonwealth power. Section 105A allowed the Commonwealth to make agreements with the States regarding their debts and future borrowing, and paved the way for legislation giving the Loan Council statutory authority. Section 51 (xxiiiA), added in 1946, enlarged and clarified the Commonwealth's social services powers.[4] In recent years the Commonwealth has been reluctant even to attempt a major extension of its powers by this method, though it tried unsuccessfully to get control over prices and incomes in 1973.

The Constitution also allows the State parliaments to refer their legislative powers to the Commonwealth on any matter, but this has been almost a dead letter. Two States have referred powers regarding intrastate air transport. Tasmanian railways and South Australian non-metropolitan railways were transferred to the Commonwealth in 1975. The most ambitious attempt was in 1942 in connection with certain powers claimed to be necessary for the Commonwealth to deal with problems of post-war reconstruction. At a convention in Canberra, State representatives agreed to ask their parliaments to refer 'adequate' powers for five years from the end of hostilities; a referendum was later to decide whether this should be permanent.[5] New South Wales and Queensland passed the Powers Bill as agreed, South Australia and Western Australia amended it. Victoria's Act was made dependent on all States passing uniform laws. In Tasmania the Upper House refused assent to the legislation, though it was the Tasmanian Premier who had moved the convention motion on the transfer of powers. The Commonwealth government then tried in 1944 to obtain the powers by referendum, but was unsuccessful.

High Court Decisions

Decisions of the High Court have had an important effect on Commonwealth–State relations. If the words of the Constitution are hard to change, their interpretation may be changed. Members of the first High Court said in *The King* v. *Barger*:[6] 'Our duty is to declare the law as we find it, not to make new law'. But the Court cannot avoid making new law. Many sections of the Constitution are vague, and more than one interpretation can be given to them. Which interpretation is chosen may depend on earlier court decisions, the prevailing social climate, and the general outlook of judges.

In the early years of judicial interpretation, the High Court tended to argue that certain restrictions on Commonwealth power were implied by the very nature of a federal constitution; one version was that the Commonwealth could not use its powers to interfere with the States' machinery of government. In practice, this tended to go along with the view that Commonwealth powers should be given a narrow construction. Opposed to this has been the view that one should not read any such implications into the Constitution. Its words should be given their full, ordinary, natural and grammatical meaning (whatever that is deemed to be); and if this involves allowing the Commonwealth some power which drastically upsets the federal balance, this cannot be helped. This view became current after 1920 when, in the *Engineers' Case*,[7] it was held that the Commonwealth arbitration system could in certain circumstances make awards binding on State employees and therefore on State governments. The view was re-emphasised in 1942, by the *Uniform Tax Case*,[8] where legislation was upheld that, though not prohibiting the States from levying income tax (which would have been plainly unconstitutional), made it so difficult as to drive them from this field.

This controversy is not yet dead, and we cannot go into its complications here. In general, the High Court has been far more cautious than the United States Supreme Court in directly subverting State powers; all the same, its interpretations have helped the Commonwealth Constitution to adapt to changing circumstances. For example, the defence power has been given a broad construction, so as to permit very wide Commonwealth government controls over the economy in wartime and some use of such controls even in peacetime. The same is true of the Commonwealth's power in section 51 (xx) with respect to foreign, financial and trading corporations, which has been interpreted so as to make possible restrictive practices legislation and other controls over companies.[9] The Commonwealth government has been recognised as having exclusive authority over the territorial sea. Some sections of the Constitution have got the courts into a tangle. A well known example is section 92, which states that 'trade, commerce and intercourse among the States . . . shall be absolutely free'. Its main aim was to stop the States from erecting tariff barriers between one another; but the wording has led to interpretations that greatly limit both Commonwealth and State regulation of interstate trade. The section was used in 1948–49 to invalidate the bank nationalisation legislation of the federal Labor government, and in 1954 to invalidate New South Wales road transport legislation and taxes.[10]

Finally there should be mentioned certain sections of the Commonwealth Constitution that concern financial matters. Section 81 permits Commonwealth spending 'for the purposes of the Commonwealth'. No one has finally decided what this means, and it could be said to refer only to purposes related to federal powers under the Constitution. However, the Commonwealth does not restrict its spending in this way, in particular it gives grants for many specific purposes quite outside its own powers. It has been difficult legally to challenge Commonwealth government expenditures as such, if they are not accompanied by controls that directly interfere with people's property or freedom; and the High Court gives no interpretation unless a case is brought before it, and maintains that it is not permitted to give advisory opinions. Indeed, the Commonwealth has done many things that might have been disallowed if they had ever been brought to court.

The Australian Assistance Plan Case of 1975[11] clarified some matters, but left others obscure. Under the Plan, the Commonwealth government had provided for direct financial aid to Regional Councils for Social Development with power to assess social welfare needs in various regions. Victoria challenged the validity of this appropriation of funds. A High Court majority upheld the Commonwealth, but on varying grounds; and, even if the Commonwealth spending power is unlimited, which remains doubtful, it is even more doubtful whether it can regulate the bodies who get the money, unless the purposes involved are covered by Commonwealth powers. Some of the cases mentioned above illustrate two other features of judicial review of the Constitution worth mentioning. The first is that the process continually leaves great areas of uncertainty about just what are the limits of Commonwealth power. The second is that judicial review is slow and expensive. One reason the 1965 Trade Practices Act (now replaced by later legislation) never got off the ground was that it was subject to two lengthy challenges in the courts.

Two other financial sections have been interpreted by the High Court so as to affect State power. Section 96 permits the Commonwealth parliament to give grants to the States 'on such terms and conditions as the Parliament thinks fit'. On a literal interpretation, which the High Court has largely accepted, the Commonwealth may attach any conditions it likes to such grants. They now form a very large item in State budgets, so there is nothing in the Constitution to prevent the States from being turned mainly into administrative agencies of the Commonwealth. If this has not happened, it is for political rather than constitutional reasons. The High Court has also interpreted the excise power of the Commonwealth so as to hinder the States in levying sales taxes, an important form of regional taxation in other federations; however, a 'franchise tax' was held valid in 1974, and is now levied by several States.[12]

Commonwealth powers seem to have been adequate, at least until recently, to the task of controlling and developing a capitalist economy, and of providing a fairly high degree of welfare. The Commonwealth regulates the main forms of taxation and has the predominant influence in determining the level of government borrowing. It has assumed that it may grant money freely for most purposes. It controls imports and exports and, through its exclusive power to make tariffs, can manipulate one of the main economic variables that affect Australian industry. The Reserve Bank of Australia has wide powers to control banking and credit. Labor government fears in the 1940s that these powers would be eroded or subjected to legal attack, which led to the abortive attempt at bank nationalisation, were not justified. One limitation on the Commonwealth is that in peacetime it has had little direct power to control wages and prices, an important restriction in a period of inflation; and, mainly because of section 92, a Commonwealth government that wished directly to control the internal production and flow of goods, or to nationalise industry, would be likely to run into constitutional difficulties. However, the High Court decision in the 1971 *Concrete Pipes Case*[13] seems to have accepted a considerable power of the Commonwealth to regulate the activities of financial and trading corporations, the limits of which are still unclear, but which permits restrictive practices legislation, probably a uniform companies act, and perhaps more extensive controls.

Changing Needs and Policies

The main reason why federal relationships have changed since 1901 is that the situation of Australia has changed; new needs have arisen and new policies have been adopted to meet them. In 1901, 32.5 per cent of the workforce was employed in primary industry (including mining). By 1975, this figure had fallen to 6.7 per cent. At federation, each State was absorbed in its own problems. Now many industries work on an interstate basis, and many national controls of economic life are thought to be necessary. The concept of the welfare state has emerged, and with it a demand for something close to equality of social provision across the nation. There has been much more emphasis on foreign policy, international trade policy and defence. These changes have involved a considerable growth of national policy-making, especially since the Second World War. Thirty years ago it appeared to some observers that there was an inevitable trend towards full or virtually full unification.

However, this has not happened. It may be partly the product of a conservative electorate and of Liberal predominance in federal government from 1949 to 1972. But it is also because the State governments still control important activities, and can rally political support for such control—a striking case is that of (onshore) mineral resources. State governments have become more active in planning and development, and sometimes more innovatory in style than used to be the case. They retain important bargaining powers, and are still significant forces in the federal system, far removed from the mere administrative agents of the Commonwealth that they are sometimes said to be becoming. They have their own breed of effective politicians: and State politicians rarely move into federal politics, or *vice versa*. The State political and administrative establishments have become a powerful vested interest in their own right. There is still a State sentiment that can be mobilised, at least in some parts of Australia. Although there are national parties cutting across State lines, each party machine is itself federal in character. Most of the press is State-based.

Federal Finance

Federalism is, as we have seen, a system of dual government, in which governmental powers are divided between two main levels. On paper, the Australian States still have wide powers, but the translation of powers into effective policies depends on command over financial resources. At present, there is a wide disparity between the financial resources available to the Commonwealth and the States.

Public finance in a federal system involves three basic decisions: the relative size of public and private sectors, mainly a function of the level of taxation; the allocation of public expenditure between different services; and the allocation of public expenditure between different regions.

Size and Distribution of Public Expenditure

The relative importance of government expenditure in general, Commonwealth, State and local, is much greater than it was before the war. In 1938–39 total government expenditure represented about 22 per cent of gross national product; by 1968–69 this share had risen to 31 per cent; and by 1975–76 to 38 per cent. If we exclude simple transfers of money, such as national debt interest, and cash benefits under social security schemes, government expenditure on goods and services rose from about 13 per cent before the war to about 26 per cent of gross national product in 1975–76.

Part of this increase in the relative importance of government was a result of the war itself. A recent account is as follows:

Why should the war have produced a permanently higher plateau of government spending? Several reasons may be suggested. First, it was only to be expected that after the war, and as a consequence of the war, expenditure on war and defence (including repatriation payments and interest on war debt) should absorb a larger share of the community's resources than in the 1930s. Secondly, the greater concern for social security, which has been a distinguishing feature of the postwar period, can be traced back to the war years themselves. Immediate practical considerations made it necessary during the war to extend social security benefits—for example, in the fields of child endowment and widows pensions. These were also disturbing years emotionally and intellectually, producing a strong resolve that the postwar economic world should be a better place for all to live in. Thirdly, the Government gained considerable administrative experience during the war, thus facilitating—and to some extent probably even encouraging—a higher peacetime level of government spending. Finally, mention should be made of what two English economists, Peacock and Wiseman, have called the 'displacement effect'. From a study of British data, they have come up with the hypothesis that government spending is held in check mainly by the community's reluctance to approve the extra taxes required to finance higher expenditure. However, war forces higher taxes on the community, in the first instance as an emergency measure; but in time people become accustomed to paying more, so that the tolerance limit on government spending is permanently lifted.[14]

Another factor has been the rapid rise in money incomes. When money incomes are rising steadily, the Commonwealth government has not needed to increase income tax rates in order to collect a higher proportion of the national income, as most people have been automatically shifted to a higher tax bracket. Personal income tax has now been indexed to take account of changing price levels, so this trick will be harder for future governments to play.

Table 7.1 has been presented in very round figures, and not according to good accounting practice. Its aim is simply to give a broad picture of the financial position of the Commonwealth in relation to other governments, and to highlight such facts as that:

1. The Commonwealth received (in 1975–76) nearly 80 per cent of the 'independent income' of all Australian governments.

But:

2. Nearly one-third of this was paid in current grants to the States, and another third in social service and other cash benefits. These 'transfer payments' (and there are others) are not a direct call on the national resources by the Commonwealth government itself. As well as providing $5530m in current grants, the Commonwealth was able to provide another $2940m in capital grants and advances to the States, some of which went to local councils.

TABLE 7.1

Commonwealth and State/Local Revenue and Expenditure
1975–76 ($m)

	Commonwealth	State/Local	Total
Current Revenue—			
Taxation	16960	4310	21270
Public enterprise income[a]	410	440	850
Other	120	500	620
Total	17490	5250	22740
Grants to States[b]	−5530	5530	—
Revenue after Grants to States	11960	10780	22740
Current Expenditure—			
Defence	1580	—	1580
Social, education, health, housing, etc.[c]	1090	5640	6730
Cash benefits to persons	6090	240	6330
Other	2440	3260[d]	5700
Total	11200	9140	20340
Surplus in Current Account	760	1640	—
which helps meet			
Capital Expenditure	4720[e]	5360[f]	

[a] As defined in *Australian National Accounts: National Income and Expenditure, 1975–76*, Australian Bureau of Statistics, on which this table is based.

[b] Includes $100m in direct grants to local authorities.

[c] Final Consumption Expenditure as defined in *Australian National Accounts*, i.e. excludes capital expenditure and cash benefits to persons. Much of it consists of salaries to government employees.

[d] Includes $1300m in interest payments.

[e] Includes $1070m by Commonwealth enterprises (especially communications) and $2940m in capital grants and advances to States.

[f] Includes fixed capital expenditure on roads ($1240m), power ($680m), education ($630m), and around another $250m each on water supply, railways, health and housing.

3. Commonwealth grants to the States represented over half the income available to them for current expenditure

4. The States, their statutory authorities and local councils have very heavy capital commitments, around $5360m in 1975–76. Where did they raise this? There was $2940m in Commonwealth grants and advances, and $1640m from the surplus on current account; the rest came mainly from the sale of government bonds or from internal funds.

Problems of Federal Finance

There are two main problems involved in federal finance: (1) the 'vertical' balance—that is, the relation between the functions allocated to the two levels of government, and their revenue sources; and (2) the 'horizontal' balance

—that is, the amount of redistribution between States required, for example, to meet demands for equalising capacity to perform, or actual performance.

(i) Functions and Revenue—the Vertical Balance   If the expenditure obligations and the revenue-raising capacity of States in a federation get out of balance, as they have in Australia, there are several possible ways of remedying the situation. They include:

1. Cutting expenditure, by reducing standards of service or by improving efficiency.
2. Transfer of functions to the federal government.
3. Increasing taxation, including finding new sources or taking over federal sources.
4. Increasing federal grants.

All these solutions have been tried at various times. The most impracticable at the present time is (1), for three main reasons. First, though there is always room for improving efficiency, most State governments seem to find that there are no simple ways of making large savings by this method; the greatest scope for improvement is probably in the allocation of capital resources, by working out better systems for determining investment priorities. Secondly, much State expenditure is fairly inflexible, committed to servicing debts, paying salaries and wages, and providing essential services. Thirdly, there has been a rapidly growing demand for the most expensive State services, including education.

Transfer of functions is possible under the Constitution but, as indicated earlier, the States have not in the past been anxious to divest themselves of powers. Part of the State railway systems has been transferred to the Commonwealth, which has also taken over financial responsibility for tertiary education. The third possibility—increases in State taxation—is touched on below. Some steps have been taken in this direction, though scope is limited under the present division of taxing powers.

The easiest and commonest solution has been to increase Commonwealth grants, but this has disadvantages. First, it is said to lead to political irresponsibility; each level of government can blame the other for short-comings, and States may find it politically easier to demand more Commonwealth money than to raise taxes or cut liabilities. Grants may also distort the pattern of government services, as compared with what would have happened under a unitary form of government. Commonwealth control over revenue often leads to its services being more readily and better financed than State services. The States are encouraged to switch into services that qualify for Commonwealth grants at the expense of those that do not. In particular, the widespread use of specific-purpose grants may produce some areas of fairly rapid development, and alongside them other activities rubbing along on inadequate funds.

One problem about arriving at a proper balance of functions and revenues is that there is no agreement about what constitutes adequate performance of a function. If the States say they cannot meet their education or hospital needs, this depends on some definition of what these needs are, which there is no precise way of calculating. A more complex example is the Commonwealth claim that it needs to have a high degree of financial control in order to carry out its task of regulating the general level of economic activity, reducing unemployment, controlling inflation, and so on. There is room for great controversy about what degree of control of resources is necessary to carry out these functions adequately. Needs and demands also change over time, so that a balance deemed proper at one time can soon be upset.

There are related disputes about who should properly bear the responsibility for certain outlays or financial shortcomings, about what should be of purely State concern, and what of 'national' concern. 'It is tempting to say that a problem becomes national if it cannot be effectively handled by any one region, and that this is due to an inter-relation of factors extending over at least two regions. The integration of industry, commerce and finance has hence made a good deal of economic regulation inevitably national in all the affluent societies. However, there is a tendency for problems to be treated as national merely because they are *common* to many regions, even though there is no *integration* involved.'[15] Thus, as Professor Sawer points out, it is often said that problems of urban development in our large cities are 'national', though the difficulties of Sydney and Melbourne are not inter-related. Nor is there evidence that noticeable economies of scale accrue through tackling such problems from Canberra, which might be another argument for treating them on a national basis. For the most part, there do not exist satisfyingly objective and operational criteria for distinguishing between matters of national, regional and local concern, or for showing what such distinctions imply in terms of the legislative, financial, or administrative responsibilities of the various levels of government.

(ii) Redistribution between States—the Horizontal Balance   In the claim for a correction of the vertical balance, the States tend to be united against the Commonwealth, though some might be slightly happier to surrender functions and others keener on increasing revenue. The second problem, that of redistribution between States, usually ranges States against one another. It also influences their general attitudes to the increase of Commonwealth power. The Commonwealth is the agent of redistribution. So the richer States will be more likely, other things being equal, to seek greater financial independence of the Commonwealth, while other States try to exploit Commonwealth financial power in their own interests.

The demand for redistribution arises mainly from the fact that revenue resources, and also the cost of providing an equal standard of government services, vary between States. The disparities are less in Australia than in most federations; on the other hand, the demand for equalisation has been strong and effective. (For a comparison of State incomes per head, see Table 7.2). Some of the so-called disparities of need are debatable. It is often thought, for instance, that States with small populations suffer from the diseconomies of small scale; but States with large metropolises like Sydney and Melbourne might argue that they need compensating for the diseconomies of large scale, as the cost of providing a given standard of service in these cities rises disproportionately as they grow. Nor is the existence of very large unpopulated areas an index of need; having a number of country centres big enough to create a sizeable demand for government services may be a much more difficult situation to deal with than empty spaces.

Redistributive demands of this type tend to merge into demands of a different kind—that it is the duty of the relatively developed parts of Australia to help finance the underdeveloped parts. However, the two kinds of argument should not be confused. The demand that a State should get special financial treatment in the interests of uniform standards and social justice, is different from the demand that it should get special treatment in the interests of balanced national development. It is arguable that the main criterion in the latter case should not be redistributive, but simply whether the expenditure will yield a higher net national return if spent on one service rather than another, irrespective of their location. However, when States make demands, the criteria of equity and of economic growth tend to get mixed. States consider they have a right to grow, as well as to receive a fair share of the profits of growth; and such demands may form part of a federal consensus that has to be recognised, as well as subjected to informed criticism.

In Australia one also needs to take special account nowadays of States such as Western Australia and Queensland, which have turned out to be rich in natural resources and have close links with overseas mineral markets and financial centres, but which are underdeveloped in secondary industry and claim that they are exploited in various ways.[16]

TABLE 7.2

Population and Income per Head, 1976–77

	Population (millions)	Income per head (dollars)
New South Wales	4.91	5070
Victoria	3.75	5222
Queensland	2.11	4565
South Australia	1.26	4857
Western Australia	1.17	4765
Tasmania	0.14	4697
ACT	0.20	6316
NT	0.10	4856
Australia	13.92	4995

Source: June 1976 census and 1976–77 National Income Figures published by Australian Bureau of Statistics.

(iii) Commonwealth and State Revenues   The Constitution gave the Commonwealth Parliament exclusive power to levy customs and excise duties, which had been the main source of State finance. At first the States got three-quarters of these revenues back from the Commonwealth, and were fairly well off, but after 1910 they had only such grants as the Commonwealth saw fit to give them. Other tax powers were concurrent, and the States had now to depend on taxes other than customs and excise, including income tax. During the First World War the Commonwealth entered the fields of death duties (1914) and income tax (1915) alongside the States, and between the wars both levied income tax. Though the economic depression of the early 1930s forced the States into large budget deficits, they still had a fair measure of financial independence in 1939, when State taxes yielded $101 million, and federal grants amounted to only $31 million.

During the Second World War there was a large increase in Commonwealth taxation, especially income tax. This created a problem. State income taxes differed greatly in structure and level. The Commonwealth had hitherto waived its (section 109) right of priority in concurrent fields of taxation, and allowed State taxes to be deducted from income before the federal tax was assessed. This helped to reduce the disparities in the combined rates of tax. But the Commonwealth was stopped from going further in this direction by the constitutional bar (section 99) to discrimination between States in its tax rates. As a result the practicable limit of taxation was fixed by the most highly taxed State, which left many people in other States undertaxed in terms of wartime requirements. State revenues were also benefiting from rising wartime incomes, and the States were reaching a position where they could make increasing demands on resources for their own purposes.

After trying to solve these problems by negotiation, the Commonwealth parliament passed legislation in 1942 that forced the States out of the income tax field. It imposed new uniform rates of tax on incomes, and insisted that the federal tax be paid before State income tax. It also offered income tax reimbursement grants to the States, provided that they did not impose an income tax. Some States challenged the legislation, but the High Court upheld its validity. (In fact, in 1959 the condition that income tax be not levied ceased to appear in the Grants Act, though it continued to exist in practice.)

This wartime measure was placed on a permanent basis in 1946–47. The intention was for the reimbursement grant to be modified progressively over the next few years, until its total and distribution would bear no relation to former tax revenues, but be based on some calculation of needs. Even so, the Commonwealth regularly had to pay large supplementary grants. In 1959, an application by Queensland for special grants brought about a major revision of the scheme. A new grant was fixed for each State in the base year (1959–60), which was to vary in future with the increase in State population, and with the increase in average wages for Australia as a whole, with the addition of a 'betterment' factor.

The grant per head varies considerably between States, so that the general revenue grants contain an important redistributive element. In 1975–76, New South Wales and Victoria received about $200 per head, Western Australia $319 and Tasmania $383. (If we look at Commonwealth grants as a whole, the first two States receive back only about 60 per cent of the personal income taxes paid by their citizens to the Commonwealth, while Tasmania gets close to 130 per cent.)[17] The general purpose grants lost any link with income tax collections and became the subject of five-yearly bargains at Premiers Conferences, with modifications at shorter intervals.

On the whole, though they from time to time requested the right to re-enter the income tax field, the States have not been eager to do so, even with the Commonwealth's blessing. This was shown by their reaction to the important change of Commonwealth attitudes after 1975, in accordance with the New Federalism policy of the Liberal–National Country Party government. In 1976 it was provided by statute that the States as a whole should receive a specified share of Commonwealth income tax revenue (see below). The next stage (still in progress) was to allow each State to levy its own percentage surcharge, or to give a rebate, on the Commonwealth income tax. The States have not given this latter proposal a warm welcome.

Table 7.3 gives the main tax sources of the various levels of government; Commonwealth income taxes in 1975–76 represented over half the total tax-bill.

The main State tax sources were various forms of motor taxation, stamp duties, probate, gift and succession duties, land taxes, mineral royalties, racing, liquor, lotteries and (in New South Wales) poker machines. Sales taxes, an important source of revenue in the American States, have been regarded as unconstitutional, as a form of excise reserved to the Commonwealth. By 1969 all States had introduced some form of business turnover or receipts tax, which they hoped would escape this ban, and be a fruitful source of revenue. The Commonwealth government did not object to this, provided it remained small and did not include wages and salaries. However, High Court decisions in 1969–70 declared much of this tax invalid, as an 'excise', and the Commonwealth had to agree to compensate the States for the lost revenue. (In 1971 payroll tax was also transferred to the States.) Since then the High Court has looked with more favour on certain kinds of State tax deemed to be taxes on 'consumption' not sales.

Commonwealth Grants

These fall into two main groups: first, general purpose grants such as the present General Revenue Funds made available to all States, and the Special Grants that have in the past been paid to the weaker States; and, secondly, specific purpose grants, made on condition that they are used for particular objects of expenditure.[18]

General purpose grants still form the major part of Commonwealth aid

TABLE 7.3
Government Taxation ($m)

(a) Commonwealth Taxation	1972–73	1975–76
Income Taxes:		
Individuals	4084	9213
Companies, etc.	1617	2600
Estate Duties, etc.	73	87
Customs and Excise	1782	3375
Sales Tax	765	1408
Other	149	254
Total	8470	16937
(b) State Taxation		
Payroll Tax	451	1163
Motor Taxes	347	551
Stamp Duties	351	549
Estate Duties	163	226
Land Taxes	107	202
Racing, Liquor, Lotteries	176	340
Other	129	341
Total	1723	3371
(c) Local Taxation		
Indirect Taxes (mainly Rates)	492	845
Direct Taxes, Fees, etc.	5	7
Total	497	852

Source: Public Authority Finance, Federal Authorities 1976–77 and Public Authority Estimates, 1976–77, Australian Bureau of Statistics.

to the States. They have the advantage that they can be spent on any purpose within State powers. On the other hand, their large size makes the States very dependent on Commonwealth handouts. The States (Personal Income Tax Sharing) Act 1976 provided for the first time that the States should get a specified share of Commonwealth personal income tax collections—currently (1978) almost 40 per cent of the previous year's revenue. Another statute provides a further share for local government, which is to rise gradually to 2 per cent. There is no particular rationale about this, except as an earnest of good intentions. If the Commonwealth wishes to raise or lower income taxes to stabilise the economy or to meet a greater or smaller defence commitment, or to change the balance between direct and indirect taxation, this creates no automatic case for changing the level of State grants. Nor with the introduction of tax indexation will personal income tax be quite the growth tax that it once was and that the States have hoped for. In any case, the general purpose grant based on income tax provides under half of total grants to the States, so there is still considerable room for manoeuvre by the Commonwealth, even without changing the percentage. The Commonwealth Treasurer has also made it clear that he may declare any part of the income tax to be a 'surcharge', in which case it will not be part of the base that determines the States' share. The States could well end by being more uncertain about what they will get than they were under the old arrangements.

TABLE 7.4

Commonwealth Payments to States and Local Authorities ($m)

	1975–76	1978–79 (est.)
(1) *For Recurrent Purposes*		
General grants[a]	3073	4777
Special grants	39	22
General Revenue Funds	3112	4799
Specific Purpose Payments	2316[b]	3075[b]
Total for Recurrent Purposes	5428	7874
(2) *For Capital Purposes*		
General Purpose[c]	1291	1434
Specific Purpose	1836	1446
Total for Capital Purposes	3127	2880
Total funds	8555	10753
less Repayments	198	260
	8357	10493
Payments direct to Local Authorities	106	19
Total Net Funds to States and Local Authorities	8463	10512

Source: Adapted from figures in *Payments to and for the States, the Northern Territory and Local Government Authorities*, Budget Paper no. 7, Canberra, 1978.

[a] Formerly called Finance Assistance Grants, now (apparently) Personal Income Tax Sharing Entitlements.

[b] Includes Assistance to Local Government paid through States of $80m in 1975–76, $180m in 1978–79.

[c] Includes capital grants, but also Loan Council borrowing by State governments. Excluding the latter, general purpose capital grants were $430m in 1975–76, $478m in 1978–79. The figure *excludes* Loan Council borrowing by State semi-government and local authorities, $1738m in 1978–79.

Special grants have been made to States believed to be economically weaker, the so-called 'claimant' States, which at various times have included every State except New South Wales and Victoria. As an equalising device, these grants now seem to be on the way out. Since 1933, they have been assessed by the Commonwealth Grants Commission, an advisory body of up to four members appointed by the Commonwealth government.[19] It established principles that made its recommendations acceptable, and removed the matter from direct political controversy, if not from sophisticated bargaining between the Commission and experts from the various State Treasuries. It has always been independent of the Commonwealth Treasury, and sometimes shown its independence. Its smallness seems to have helped towards unanimity of recommendation, and it made a point of establishing close friendly relations with the claimant States. Its determinations have been based on variations in revenue-raising capacity and in the cost of providing comparable services. The Commission has more recently played a part in grants to the States for local government purposes (see Chapter Nine), and in 1977 it was agreed that the chairman and two members should undertake periodical reviews of a wider range of questions, including general State relativities in grants, being joined for this purpose by three associate members nominated by the States. The general purpose grants are now designed to do the main job of redistribution between States, which has made the special grants largely redundant; Queensland has been the only applicant in recent years.

Specific purpose grants. Both types of grant discussed above are given to the States for general revenue purposes. But many Commonwealth grants are for specific purposes. There are many tasks that the Commonwealth has no power or no inclination to undertake itself, but which it is pressed by the States or private groups to support, or alternatively finds it convenient to encourage the States (or voluntary bodies) to undertake by offering subsidies. Indeed, the States regard some specific purpose grants not as aid to State policies but as a way of using the States as agents of Commonwealth policies. They began in 1923, with aid for main roads, and nowadays include also aid to education, housing, health and welfare services, local government, rural development, urban public transport and a variety of other matters. Many of these concern fields right outside Commonwealth powers. In one or two cases, the Commonwealth has taken over full financial responsibility for a State function, as in the case of universities and other institutions of advanced education.

Specific purpose grants can affect State independence in three main ways: first, unless it is prepared to refuse the grant, the State is committed to the indicated programme; secondly, grants sometimes require the State to 'match' the grant from its own budgetary resources; thirdly, the Commonwealth may administer the grant so as to gain some control over both policy formation and implementation within individual departments of the State government. However, States receiving new special purpose grants can partly reassert their own priorities by reallocating those revenues (including general purpose grants) over which they still have full control. For example, when in 1977 the Commonwealth increased its allocation to local roads but reduced funds for urban arterial roads, Victoria compensated by reducing its own funding of local roads. States can also juggle around as between capital and current expenditure or draw on internal reserves. In 1977 the Premier of New South Wales 'found' some $230 million in the reserves of government agencies and statutory authorities, especially the State Electricity Commission and the Metropolitan Water Board, and used this to complement funds raised elsewhere.

Specific purpose grants may be capital grants, or for current expenditure. They may be based on formulae, or on detailed inquiry into a particular need. They may be embodied in a special Commonwealth–States agreement. They are sometimes conditional on a State 'matching' the whole or part of the Commonwealth grant by monies from its own resources. Grants may be made for a period of years or negotiated annually. They may be part of a continuing policy of assistance, or made *ad hoc* to particular States to meet a special emergency or short-run political contingency. In the early 1960s, when the Menzies government was in political trouble following the credit squeeze, there was a sharp rise in specific purpose grants, especially to Queensland.

Specific purpose grants may be regarded as a way of getting a higher or more uniform national standard in some service, beyond the resources or natural inclinations of particular States. They may 'distort' the distribution of State expenditures; that is, as compared with what States might do if given the same amount to spend as they wished. The States complained in a 1970 White Paper that such grants often ran 'counter to the order of priorities for expenditures in the States', and that they could 'increase rather than decrease State obligations', especially by encouraging capital works that involve higher running costs.[20] The States also fear that the Commonwealth government will try to regulate such expenditure in detail, at some cost to efficiency and adaptation to local conditions. Such grants can act to disintegrate Commonwealth government, especially where a special department or statutory authority is given the job of assessing needs in the particular area, without much regard for general priorities or budgetary constraints.[21] They can also disintegrate State government, as the receiving agencies come to depend more and more on their functional links with the dispensing bureaucrats, leading to the phenomenon sometimes called 'functional federation'. In general, a multiplicity of grants makes it harder to judge and to control their overall effect.

Others argue that the Commonwealth is more aware than at least some States of what are new national priorities, and has been on the whole more innovative than State and local governments. It is also said that some State-provided services, such as education and health, generate spill-overs, or externalities. Their benefits are nationwide, so the level at which they are provided cannot be the exclusive concern of the State government. General purpose grants help to equalise 'capacity' as between States—that is, enable States to provide a certain standard of service in a given field if they so wish; but specific purpose grants may aim also to enforce more equality of 'performance', as do, for example, the school grants of the Education Commission. The Commonwealth government may also be more willing to unloose the purse-strings if it can specify the object of expenditure, which not only gives it more control but also political credit for an identifiable result.

It is sometimes argued that specific purpose grants give flexibility to the grants system. Once a State gets a certain percentage of a general grant, it is politically difficult to revise that percentage downwards. It may be easier to manipulate specific purpose grants so as to change the distributive balance; for example, it may become clear that what you have to give States to do justice to their hospital needs, or transport needs, or welfare needs, by no means corresponds to the existing formulae for general purpose grants.

The proportion of grants paid as specific purpose grants rose sharply under the Labor government of 1972–75 to about 45 per cent of total grants— the precise percentage depends on what one counts as specific, and how far capital grants are included in the calculation. For example, federal education grants rose from $259 million (1972–73) to $1455 million (1975–76), there were many new grants for welfare, and so on. The Liberal–National Country Party government of 1975 wished to reduce the importance of specific purpose grants, and to absorb many of them into general purpose grants. The future role of the former was seen as 'to initiate programmes in agreed areas of national need, to encourage innovation and to meet special situations'.[22]

However, it seems likely that whatever the political complexion of future federal governments, they will wish to have a strong voice in the spending of their own funds, at any rate in areas they regard as important. Apart from this being the natural reaction of any piper-payer, it is a disadvantage to the Commonwealth to get no credit for having financed any particular activity, which is what operating by general purpose grants amounts to. It is also clear that the present Commonwealth government (1978) intends to go on having an education policy, a health and welfare policy, a minerals policy, and a policy about many other fields where important powers remain in State hands and that this will have implications for the allocation of financial resources.

Government Borrowing and the Loan Council

Most borrowing in Australia is done by the sale of long-term securities, or government bonds.[23] The States and their statutory bodies make fairly heavy use of loan finance for public works and developmental projects, as indicated earlier. The Commonwealth since the war has been able to finance most of its capital expenditure out of revenue, though this may be less true in the future. Even the States have met a good deal of capital expenditure, especially for roads, out of current revenue, including Commonwealth grants. State government departments and statutory bodies are still the big capital spenders; they accounted for over 60 per cent of total public investment in 1975–76, the rest being shared by the Commonwealth and local authorities.

The Australian Loan Council

Up to the 1920s, the Commonwealth and the States each borrowed money as they saw fit, though during the First World War, the Commonwealth government (which did little borrowing before 1914) had conducted borrowing in London on behalf of all States, save New South Wales. After the war, worried at the renewed outburst of State activity, the Commonwealth proposed the creation of an advisory Loan Council to co-ordinate public borrowing. This was established in 1923. The 1927 Financial Agreement redefined its powers and functions, and a constitutional amendment (section 105A) was approved by referendum in 1928, giving the Commonwealth power to make agreements with the States with regard to their public debts. Following this, the Australian Loan Council was given statutory authority.[24] It was the first major move towards 'co-operative federalism'.

The Loan Council members are the Prime Minister and Premiers, or their nominees. In practice nowadays it consists of the Commonwealth Treasurer (Chairman) and the State Premiers, who are usually also State Treasurers. It meets about twice a year; the main meeting is usually in June, at the same time as the Premiers Conference. The difference between the two is that Loan Council decisions have statutory force. The Commonwealth has two votes and a casting vote, so needs the support of only two States to obtain a majority. All seven governments submit to the Loan Council a proposed borrowing programme for the financial year. If the Loan Council decides that the total sum cannot be raised 'at reasonable rates and conditions', it fixes by majority vote the total amount that may be borrowed by all seven governments. It may also by unanimous decision allocate that amount between the Commonwealth and each State. If unanimity is not achieved, the Commonwealth is entitled to one-fifth and the States get the rest in the proportion that each of their net loan expenditures 'in the preceding five years bears to the net loan expenditure of all the States during the same period'.[25] This formula has never been used, as the Commonwealth has usually had enough power to obtain unanimity; perhaps this is just as well, as applying it would raise some difficult problems of interpretation.

Certain types of loan are not subject to the agreement. It does not apply to Commonwealth borrowing for defence, or to any borrowing 'for temporary purposes'. Nor does it formally cover borrowing by local governments or statutory authorities, though major programmes are in practice submitted to the Loan Council under a so-called 'gentleman's agreement'. When loans are approved, these authorities issue their own securities, whereas the Commonwealth handles other State borrowing. The question of what 'for temporary purposes' means was raised when the Commonwealth government used this escape clause in December 1974 to try to borrow $4000 million from Arab sources without going through the Loan Council; the intended outlays seem to have been largely for long-term development projects. However, the deal fell through.[26]

The Commonwealth has tended to dominate Loan Council proceedings, and not only, or even mainly, because of its voting power. Even if it is outvoted by the States, as happens occasionally, it has enough control of the money supply through other channels to make its views pretty effective. For many years after the Second World War it made up the shortfall in the agreed borrowing programme from its own revenues, in the form of interest-bearing loans to the States or, in the 1970s, partly as capital grants. This has clearly given it the final voice.

Loan Council meetings are *in camera*, official releases tell little, and no annual reports are made to Parliament; a certain amount leaks out to the press through Premiers' statements and in other ways, and there seemed to be a distinct decline in the secrecy of its proceedings in 1976. The Australian Loan Council is responsible to no one, and its decisions are final.

Development

There is one important limitation on the Loans Council's activities. It was designed to settle global financial totals, and has played little part in fixing priorities for particular forms of public investment. The States have still much freedom to determine their own development programmes within the total allotted to them, added to what they may choose to finance from their own revenues or internal reserves. The Loan Council method of allocation has also been relatively inflexible, commonly with only minor adjustments taking place from year to year—so it has been hard to cater for special needs or to readjust the balance between States. However, the Commonwealth government has been making more use of specific purpose capital grants outside the Loan Council machinery. This has enabled it to play a larger role in determining the direction of State investment; on the other hand, it has had the effect of multiplying the points of decision-making. During the Second World War, a Co-ordinator-General of Works and later a National Works Council, representing Commonwealth and States, were set up to co-ordinate public works programmes. The latter soon ceased to be effective after the war and ceased to meet in the early 1950s. There has continued to be a Co-ordinator-General of Works, now a senior Treasury official, who reports to the Loan Council on State programmes. Otherwise, the Loan Council has had no staff other than secretarial, and hence no machinery (even if it wanted to) to appraise particular projects.

There has been some criticism of the weakness of the machinery for settling investment priorities; and of the extent to which development schemes have been governed not by economic criteria, but by mythology, technology or short-term electoral calculation. The position is complicated by the fact that many major investment decisions are taken by semi-independent statutory bodies. The States can claim that rational long-term planning on their part is hindered by their dependence on annual handouts by the Loan Council and through other Commonwealth-dominated channels, though in a few cases (e.g. roads) the Commonwealth has entered into longer-term commitments.

For much of the post-war period the Commonwealth seemed to have no positive development policy, outside some of its own Territories (Canberra, Papua and New Guinea) and a few special fields (such as universities, scientific research). In general, it has let the States take the initiative in making demands and has then bargained with them.[27] The Vernon Committee of Economic Enquiry recommended the creation of a Special Projects Commission 'to investigate proposals for major development projects, wherever they are located, to advise governments on them, and to publish its findings'.[28] The Commonwealth government has been unwilling to allow either an independent body, or one in which the States are powerful, to have an important voice in settling development priorities. However, it has improved its procedures in other ways. In the 1969 reorganisation of the Treasury, the machinery for dealing with federal financial relations and development was considerably strengthened. The Revenue, Loans and Investment Division now deals not only with borrowing and Loan Council affairs, but with State and local government finances generally, and also with special development projects. New Commonwealth bodies to appraise particular areas of capital expenditure such as the Bureau of Transport Economics have been established. The Labor government of 1972–75 attempted more positively to control national development in certain areas, for example, in relation to minerals and energy resources. The Commonwealth has quite wide powers to control development, if it wishes, through taxation, by use of the trade and commerce power and the corporations power, and through its control of imports and exports.

State Capital Programmes

State machinery for co-ordination and determination of investment priorities varies, but broadly rests on the fact that the annual allocation of funds or borrowing authority for capital works and services is determined by the Treasurer, after a review of all proposals submitted. For this purpose each State has a Co-ordinator of Works. In four States the office is held by a senior Treasury officer, in Queensland and Tasmania, though the office is in another department, the Treasury still plays an important part in allocation. Each department and statutory body is required to provide the State Co-ordinator of Works with detailed programmes of works already in progress and new works proposed, giving their individual estimated cost and anticipated period for completion. These are reviewed by the Co-ordinator, though the review is often of a limited kind. In New South Wales, for example, 'Budget Branch officials examine agency programmes, but in general do not question the priority given to items', and are mainly concerned with 'correctness in presentation and the determination of an aggregate Loan Council bid'.[29] These programmes are passed on to the Commonwealth Co-ordinator-General of Works, who prepares a report on them for submission to the Loan Council. He does not report on Commonwealth programmes, though he may refer to them; nor does he critically review State programmes, though he reports on the capacity of the economy to sustain them.

As total State requirements are unlikely to be met by Loan Council allocations, each State has to review its programmes in the light of these. In New South Wales, for example, where the permanent head of the Treasury is also State Co-ordinator of Works, this review is undertaken by the Treasury. In most fields, needs are so obvious and pressing that the main problem is to determine priorities among known needs. Schools and hospitals must be built to meet known population increases, water and sewerage services, power stations and railway rolling-stock and harbour facilities must keep pace with growing industrial demands. Nowadays it has become customary for the Treasury to call for 'forward planning' programmes and (where appropriate) to assure the agencies concerned of a minimum allocation for one or two years ahead, to help them in their own forward planning. It is now part of the formal budget process that departments submit forward expenditure estimates for capital works for each of the three years ahead.

From time to time major new projects, some with considerable political backup, are approved and must somehow be fitted into the State's development plans. The decision to proceed with such a project is taken by the government, after a review by the Treasury of the extent to which it can go ahead without unduly upsetting the progress of the enormous number of smaller projects that make up the total works programme. In these matters, and others of special political significance, Treasury views may not prevail; it is still important that its voice should be heard, or that of some other agency with a comparable concern for general priorities. In the normal run of smaller projects, details about individual works will be left to the agency concerned. For example, the location of particular school buildings is decided by the Education Department, within the fund allocation determined by the Treasurer.

Statutory corporations such as the Electricity Commission and the Metropolitan Water Board have their own internal funds and have often in the past been able to fix their own priorities. They have not had to give the Treasury details of their whole capital programme, only of projects for which they cannot find the funds themselves, so the Treasury has not been in a position to undertake a full critical appraisal. The New South Wales government has lately been trying to impose its own priorities more firmly on statutory bodies, and there have been proposals for new machinery to make a State 'capital budget' effective.

There is a difference between Commonwealth and State attitudes to capital expenditure, arising from the greater control the federal government has had over its investment programme.

Commonwealth procedures tend to be based on the evaluation and selection of particular projects 'while State government policies are more decades-long developmental programmes'.[30] As described above, States are always heavily over-committed to improving the provision of essential services; at the same time, financially they are used to living from hand to mouth, and adapting to annual changes in the flow of funds. So they tend to see any capital they can get hold of as a way of injecting more money into continuing programmes, not as a way of financing a particular high-priority project.

Notes

1. K.C. Wheare, *Federal Government*, 4th edn, Oxford University Press, Oxford, 1963, 10.
2. See R.J. May, 'Decision-making and Stability in Federal Systems', *Canadian J. Political Science*, III, 1, March 1970, 74; and R.J. May, *Federalism and Fiscal Adjustment*, Oxford University Press, Oxford, 1969, ch. 1, from which the general argument of this section is drawn.
3. On some regional differences, see Jean Holmes and Campbell Sharman, *The Australian Federal System*, Allen and Unwin, Sydney, 1977, chs 2–3.
4. Some would add a third—the changes approved in the 1967 referendum concerning Aborigines. But there is dispute about whether these were really necessary for the Commonwealth to act. For a short history of referenda, see J.E. Richardson, 'Reform of the Constitution: The Referendums and Constitutional Convention', in Gareth Evans (ed.), *Labor and the Constitution, 1972–1975*, Heinemann, Melbourne, 1977, 76–101.
5. For an account of the convention, see G. Greenwood, *The Future of Australian Federalism*, Melbourne University Press, Melbourne, 1946, ch. VI. On reference of powers to 1972, see J.E. Richardson, *Patterns of Australian Federalism*, Centre for Research on Federal Financial Relations, Canberra, 1973, 95–6.
6. (1908) 6 C.L.R. 41; see C. Howard, *Australian Federal Constitutional Law*, 2nd edn, Law Book Co., Sydney, 1972, ch. 2, 'Balance of Power'.
7. *Amalgamated Soc. of Engineers* v. *Adelaide Steamship Co. Ltd*, (1920) 28 C.L.R. 129.
8. *South Australia* v. *Commonwealth* (1942) 65 C.L.R. 373.
9. *Strickland* v. *Rocla Concrete Pipes Ltd.* (1971) 124 C.L.R. 468.
10. *Bank of New South Wales* v. *Commonwealth* (1948) 76 C.L.R. 1 (H.C.); (1949) 79 C.L.R. 497 (P.C.); *Hughes and Vale Pty. Ltd.* v. *New South Wales* (1954) 93 C.L.R. 1.
11. *Victoria* v. *Commonwealth (A.A.P. Case)* (1975) 7 A.L.R. 277. For discussion, see M. Crommelin and G. Evans, 'Explorations and Adventures with Commonwealth Powers', in Gareth Evans (ed.), *Labor and the Constitution, 1972–1975*, Heinemann, Melbourne, 1977, 41–5.
12. *Dickensons Arcade Pty. Ltd.* v. *State of Tasmania* (1974) 130 C.L.R. 177.
13. *Strickland* v. *Rocla Concrete Pipes Ltd.* (1971) 124 C.L.R. 468.
14. A.H. Boxer (ed.), *Aspects of the Australian Economy*, Melbourne University Press, Melbourne, 1965, 21.
15. Geoffrey Sawer, *Modern Federalism*, 2nd edn, Pitman, Carlton, Victoria, 1976, 107.
16. See Garth Stevenson, *Mineral Resources and Australian Federalism*, Centre for Research on Federal Financial Relations, ANU, Canberra, 1977.

17. Russell Mathews, 'Issues in Australian Federalism', *Quadrant*, February 1978.
18. On Commonwealth grants, see the latest edition of *Payments to or for the States, the Northern Territory and Local Government Authorities*, published annually as a Commonwealth Budget Paper. A more summary account is in the Official Year Book.
19. See R.J. May, *Financing the Small States in Australian Federalism*, Oxford University Press, Oxford, 1970; J.A. Maxwell, *Commonwealth–State Financial Relations in Australia*, Melbourne University Press, Melbourne, 1967, ch. 2; W. Prest, 'Maxwell on Federal–State Finance', *Economic Record*, 44, 106, June 1968; for recent changes, see Grants Commission Reports.
20. cit. W. Prest, 'Fiscal Significance of the 'New Federation' ', in Dean Jaensch (ed.), *The Politics of 'New Federalism'*, Aust. Political Studies Assoc., Adelaide, 1977, 62.
21. Russell Mathews suggests that this happened with the Labor government's statutory commissions in 1942–45. See R. Mathews, *The Changing Pattern of Australian Federalism*, Centre for Research on Federal Financial Relations, ANU, Canberra, 1976, 45.
22. Liberal and National Country Parties, *Federalism Policy*, September 1975, section 10.
23. Governments also borrow from the banks by the issue of treasury bills and by overdraft.
24. For a more detailed account, see R.S. Gilbert, *The Australian Loan Council in Federal Fiscal Adjustments 1890–1965*, ANU Press, Canberra, 1973; Maxwell, *op. cit.*, ch. 4; R.L. Mathews and W.R.C. Jay, *Federal Finance*, Melbourne, 1972, 186–7, 202–7; C.G. Headford, 'The Australian Loan Council—Its Origins, Operation and Significance in the Federal Structure", *Public Admin.* (Sydney), XIII, 1, March 1954, reprinted in Colin A. Hughes (ed.), *Readings in Australian Government*, Queensland University Press, St Lucia, 1968.
25. Financial Agreement Validation Act, 1929, the Schedule, pt. I, 3 (i) (ii).
26. On the 1936 'gentleman's agreement', see R.S. Gilbert, *The Future of the Australian Loan Council*, Centre for Study of Federal Financial Relations, ANU, Canberra, 1974, ch. III. On the Arab loan, see Geoffrey Sawer, *Federation under Strain, 1972–1975*, Melbourne University Press, Melbourne, 1978.
27. cf. K.J. Walker, 'Development Politics', M.A. thesis, University of Melbourne, Melbourne, 1966, for a discussion of attitudes.
28. Report, Committee of Economic Enquiry, Canberra, 1965, I, 17, 21.
29. Interim Report, Review of NSW Government Administration, Government Printer, Sydney, 1977, 32.
30. Holmes and Sharman, *op. cit.*, 202.

Chapter Eight

Federal Relations II— Administrative Co-operation

Not much provision was made for Commonwealth–State co-operation in the Commonwealth Constitution, though a few sections envisage this, such as those concerning justice (section 51, xxiv), railways (section 51, xxxiv) and prisons (section 120). According to some theories, in an ideal federal system each government is independent of the other and exercises sovereign powers in its own field. This is not the case in practice, and especially not in Australia, where the number of concurrent powers implies that there are many areas in which Commonwealth and State governments both operate; and where the growing financial power of the Commonwealth, among other factors, has led to a continuous re-adjustment of relationships between the two levels.[1]

There have also been important changes in relations between the States. These can hardly be discussed separately from Commonwealth–State relations, as developments in the two have been closely linked. For a long time the six States did not have much incentive to promote joint action in the field of their own powers. Mostly their borders were not drawn where contact counts and their capital cities are widely separated. Well over half the population lives in New South Wales and Victoria, and this has promoted some resentment of their alleged dominance, and rivalry between the two giants. The other States have promoted their own forms of isolationism and have often preferred to let the central government take the initiative in promoting co-operation.

All the same, numbers of interstate links have developed in recent years. In some cases they have been closely related to changes in Commonwealth–State relations, either because the Commonwealth has stimulated closer relations, or because the States have drawn together in response to growing Commonwealth power. Aims have been various.[2] Sometimes it has been simply to improve the flow of information and exchange of views, or to avoid overlapping in the provision of some service. Sometimes there was a need for uniformity, or the pooling of resources, or at least for close interstate contacts, complementary action or reciprocal arrangements. The imbalance between finance and functions described in the last chapter has resulted in much intergovernmental action to overcome its consequences.

So there has developed what has been termed co-operative federalism, both 'vertical', between Commonwealth and States, and 'horizontal' co-operation, in which some or all States work together without necessarily involving the federal government at all—what in the United States has been called federalism without Washington. Some writers regard the word co-operative as a misnomer for those Commonwealth-State relations that have arisen mainly from what they regard as Commonwealth bribery or coercion. A more neutral term is 'interdependent federalism'. 'Coercive federalism' may exist, for example, when the States feel that they are being coerced by specific grants into policies that do not suit them, politically or otherwise, while still being left to bear an appreciable share of the cost. There are also areas where 'competitive federalism' might be the appropriate term, as the two levels of governments represent rival centres of power. Thus they compete in their demands on taxable resources, and for the political credit of spending the money. This competition and confrontation can be highly intense and visible, especially when different parties are in power at the two levels.[3]

Growth of Commonwealth Activities

In 1901, there were only seven Commonwealth departments. By the 1970s governments usually provided for at least twenty-seven regular departments, and there were many other statutory agencies. Here are examples of fields where new or largely new Commonwealth activities have developed, all impinging in some way on the States:

1. Agriculture—Department of Primary Industry, Australian Agricultural Council, Marketing Boards.
2. Education, Science and Culture—Department of Education, Department of Science and the Environment, Tertiary Education Commission, Schools Commission, Commonwealth Scientific and Industrial Research Organisation, Australia Council.
3. Employment and Industrial Relations—Departments of Employment and Industrial Relations.
4. Environment and Planning—Department of Science and the Environment, Housing and Construction, Commonwealth–State Housing Agreement, Australian Heritage Commission, Albury–Wodonga Development Corporation.
5. Export Policy—Departments of Primary Industry, Trade and Resources.
6. Foreign Affairs—domestic implications of international discussions and agreements.
7. Health and Social Services—hospital and medical benefits, social service benefits; assistance to States for hospitals, social welfare services, etc.
8. Immigration—Department of Immigration and Ethnic Affairs, Commissioner for Community Relations.
9. Minerals and Energy—Department of Trade and Resources, Department of National Development, Bureau of Mineral Resources, Australian

Minerals and Energy Council, Snowy Mountains Scheme, Australian Atomic Energy Commission, Pipeline Authority.

10. National Development—Department of National Development, Australian Forestry Council, Australian Water Resources Council, Australian Fisheries Council, Commonwealth Development Bank, Australian Resources Development Bank.

11. Secondary Industry—Department of Industry and Commerce, Department of Business and Consumer Affairs, Department of Productivity, Australian Industry Development Corporation, Trade Practices Commission.

12. Transport and Roads—Department of Transport, Australian Transport Advisory Council, Commonwealth Aid Roads Agreement, Bureau of Transport Economics, Australian National Railways Commission.

Types of Co-operation

Five main areas of co-operation may be distinguished:[4]

1. The Commonwealth has the main power, but the States act in part of the field, or have closely related powers.

2. Neither Commonwealth nor State power alone suffices.

3. The States have the main power, or Commonwealth power is uncertain, and a scheme overlaps the State boundaries.

4. The States have the main power, but there is need for uniformity or parallel legislation or close interstate contacts or reciprocal arrangements.

5. The States have the main power, but Commonwealth financial or other help is needed.

Some examples from widely different fields are briefly described below, to indicate the variety of techniques involved, and some of the problems that may arise.

(a) Off-shore Oil and Natural Gas   Australia is unlike most federations in that the main power over mineral resources belongs to the States. The States control exploration and production in their own land-area and internal waters, the Commonwealth in the Territories. Off-shore areas have been the subject of dispute, at least since it became clear that nearly all Australia's known oil reserves and most of its natural gas is in such areas, adjacent to Victoria and Western Australia.

The disputes over off-shore oil and natural gas are only one facet of wider disputes about mineral resources and about energy policy, which we can only mention briefly.[5] The Commonwealth played a minor role in this field before the Second World War. It gave a few exploration subsidies and tax concessions; its Bureau of Mineral Resources was a technical body set up to obtain, study and provide information; it used its trade powers to ban iron ore exports. After the war, it set up a small Department of National Development, but the States continued to control most mineral developments, which were left largely to private enterprise.

The great expansion in mining and mineral exports in the 1960s led to demands for more national planning and policy-making. In particular, it was thought that competing States had given overseas interests too free a hand, and that there was a case for raising the Australian share of benefits by influencing export prices, and by increasing Australian ownership and taxation—all areas where the Commonwealth had relevant powers. New initiatives led to sharp conflict with some States, especially under the Gorton government in 1970 and under the Whitlam government after 1972. There was centralist contempt for alleged incompetence and parochialism in State administrations. By 1972, there was also an active and enlarged Commonwealth department dealing with minerals and energy problems, many of whose senior officers tended to 'ignore the States and to consult them as little as possible'.[6]

It was fortunate for some States that five years earlier they had made a deal with a less activist Commonwealth government over offshore oil and gas. After conferences and discussions between ministers and officials, an Agreement had been signed, and embodied in parallel legislation passed by the Commonwealth and State parliaments in 1967.[7] The question of their respective constitutional powers was by-passed, both sides agreeing to put their joint legal authority behind an agreed system for regulating exploration and production. The administration of the scheme was largely left to the States, though the Commonwealth was to be consulted on major issues, could veto State decisions on certain specific grounds, and was to have a share of royalties. The Agreement was generally welcomed at the time as a neat solution to a problem that had caused jurisdictional disputes in other federations, though there was already some criticism that the Commonwealth had given too much away, and also that the State ministers concerned would really be responsible to no one, certainly not to the Commonwealth parliament whose legislation was the main basis of their powers.

However, the potential scope of off-shore minerals exploitation widened in the later 1960s, and legal opinion hardened in favour of the view that the States had no jurisdiction over off-shore areas (even within the old three-mile limit of territorial waters). But there was no decisive judicial opinion on the matter. In 1970 the Gorton government introduced a bill asserting federal control from low-water mark to the edge of the continental shelf, with the intention that the States should challenge this and so get a court ruling; the existing off-shore oil and gas agreement was preserved from the possible consequences of the legislation. Even so, the proposed bill was treated by the State governments as an unnecessary challenge to their authority; they contended that a co-operative arrangement like that applying to oil and gas could and should be negotiated for all off-shore mining. A sufficiently strong group in the federal Liberal–Country Party coalition shared this view for the legislation to be postponed. In 1973, under a Commonwealth Labor government, the Seas and Submerged Lands Act purported to give the Commonwealth control of the territorial sea. The States contested this in the High Court, which decided in favour of the Commonwealth,[8] and confirmed that the latter had exclusive authority regarding off-shore areas. By this time, however, the Labor government had fallen, and its successor upheld the 1967 Agreement. During this period of legal uncertainty, much of the interest of the private sector in exploration evaporated, though it has since revived.

Two lesser accompaniments of the conflict were the temporary demise of the Australian Minerals Council, which had been established in 1968 to represent Commonwealth and State ministers; and the infanticide of the Petroleum and Minerals Authority, set up in 1974 to acquire a Commonwealth equity in off-shore oil, natural gas, uranium mining and so on, but whose statute was found invalid on procedural grounds by the High Court in the following year. Federal–State conflict was also aroused by the Commonwealth's establishment of the Pipeline Authority (1973) to build a national pipeline grid, and to buy and sell natural gas. Several States were already exploiting natural gas fields. The largest was the off-shore field in Bass Strait, developed by Esso-BHP, and mainly controlled by Victoria under the 1967 Agreement. The Australian Gas Light Company in New South Wales (the only mainland State without natural gas), after unsuccessful negotiations to import Bass Strait gas, turned to the Cooper Basin in South Australia and started to build a pipeline to Sydney. The Pipeline Authority took over the operation in 1974. New South Wales could have stopped such construction within its own land-area as other States managed to do. But equally the Commonwealth could have hindered the private operation by using its power to control overseas borrowing and imports. Those States with their own gas continue (1979) to control it, onshore and off-shore.

(b) Marketing of Primary Products   A more genuinely 'co-operative' area is the marketing of primary products (in the old Australian meaning of that term). Agricultural marketing boards exist in every State and also at the federal level, on which primary producers are strongly represented. The Commonwealth boards are mostly concerned with regulating exports; concern with internal production, marketing and price-fixing involves Commonwealth agreement with the States, which have most of the constitutional powers. Compulsory marketing schemes exist for many products, such as wheat, butter and cheese. These involve parallel Commonwealth and State legislation and joint administration because the Commonwealth controls exports and supplies finance, but only the States can, for example, compel wheatgrowers to sell through the Australian Wheat Board. Sometimes there are also Commonwealth price guarantees, met partly by fixing home-consumption prices in co-operation with the States, and partly by subsidy. The State boards act mostly as marketing pools within each State. In most cases the majority of members are elected by the producers, and the Board is established at their request, though under State legislation. The Commonwealth Boards are somewhat less producer-dominated.

Lately the Commonwealth has become involved with more general problems of rural reconstruction. It has raised levies and provided finance, which it is able to do, but a scheme that involves more extensive interference requires agreement with the States. An important role in Commonwealth–State negotiations has been played by the Australian Agricultural Council and the Standing Committee on Agriculture (see below). From 1970–75 the Commonwealth provided over $300m for various schemes, most of which went in loans to farmers. The major programme was administered by the States, and complementary laws were passed by each State parliament.

(c) Civil Aviation   No general power regarding civil aviation has been conferred on the Commonwealth, though it can make laws with respect to international air services, services within a Territory, and (subject to section 92) interstate air services. Following apparent agreement at a Premiers' Conference, the 1920 Air Navigation Act purported to give the Commonwealth a more general power extending to services within States, but this was successfully challenged in 1936.[9] The Commonwealth then tried and failed to obtain the power by referendum. Next, Commonwealth and States met in 1937 and the States agreed to pass uniform legislation adopting the Commonwealth air navigation regulations as State laws, and giving Commonwealth officials the necessary powers to act.

The States seemed once again to have accepted the principle of federal control and licensing of all air services, though some also required State licences for intrastate services. In 1963 the New South Wales government decided to cancel some State licences held by an Ansett subsidiary and reallocate them to East-West Airlines. The former challenged this action in the High Court. The Airline Cases[10] of 1964–65, taking account of the vast growth of air transport and of the complexities resulting from technological advance, upheld the Commonwealth's power to regulate the safety, regularity and efficiency of air navigation, even when it impinged on intrastate air services; at the same time, the Court upheld a wide area of State power over the latter, so co-operation is still needed.

Two other strengths in the Commonwealth's position are that it provides and controls the major airports, and in this and other ways gives a subsidy to air services, though this is smaller than it used to be; and that it controls imports of aircraft.

(d) Social Welfare   At one time an intelligible relationship seemed to be emerging between Commonwealth and States in the social services. The former became mainly concerned with cash benefits to broad social categories, and other similar money payments. It paid means-tested invalid and age pensions from 1909–10, and by 1946 had acquired clear constitutional power to make laws regarding family allowances, widows pensions, unemployment benefits, medical benefits, benefits to students, and so on. The States were responsible for most environmental and preventive services and for institutional and personal care services. This was not a bad working arrangement,

because as a rule the more a function needs to take account of varying local and individual needs in ways not readily categorised, the closer it should be to the grassroots. There were some exceptions to this general rule, the most striking being that the Commonwealth had for many years operated through the Repatriation Department (now Veterans' Affairs), an extensive system of hospital and related welfare services for ex-servicemen and their dependents.

During the last generation the situation described above has greatly changed, and the Commonwealth has intervened more directly in many social welfare fields. Some of this resulted from the Second World War, for example, a Commonwealth Rehabilitation Service for handicapped civilians grew out of an initial concern for ex-servicemen, just as federal involvement in tertiary education developed out of wartime and post-war reconstruction schemes. It was partly because the States lacked the money. However, in the personal social services we also have a clear case of Commonwealth intervention because the States and local government were backward and unenlightened in coping with many areas of social need. They had grown accustomed since the nineteenth century to letting the main weight in many personal care services be borne by voluntary agencies, often subsidised in a fairly haphazard way by the government (even the so-called 'voluntary' hospitals have been heavily subsidised by government for well over a century; by the 1860s the New South Wales Treasury already provided about half the costs of the hospital service).

State social welfare departments developed, but they were mainly concerned with child care and protection, and with benefits in cash or kind to people awaiting determination of claims or who for some other reason fell through the Commonwealth network; even these people often got more care and attention from voluntary agencies. The State departments have begun to move into wider fields of community welfare, such as family case-work, but in general their activities have been unenterprising in relation to needs, their welfare departments have counted for little in State policies, and no State ever seems to have had anything that could be dignified as a 'social policy'. State education and health departments have been more vigorous in their own fields. A good deal was also done by the States to protect employed workers, from arbitration to factory welfare and generous workers' compensation schemes; but many of those citizens most in need of help, from the elderly to Aborigines, were poorly provided for.

For this and other reasons, the Commonwealth began to move into the personal social services. A good example was the Aged Persons Homes legislation of 1954 by which voluntary, especially church-based, agencies received matching grants towards building special accommodation for the elderly. This later extended itself to many other fields, such as nursing homes, sheltered workshops and even home care services. The Commonwealth also acquired in 1967 a clear constitutional power to provide services for Aborigines outside its own Territories. Most of this happened under non-Labor governments but the process was accelerated after 1972, when a great variety of Commonwealth agencies sprang up to administer new schemes, and there was often a more deliberate effort than previously to by-pass the States (see also Chapter Nine).

There also began to be much Commonwealth talk in the social policy field about 'experiment', 'model', 'pilot' and 'trial'.[11] In the article cited, Peachment lists twenty-seven policy areas in which one or other term was used, from mobile home parks to Aboriginal self-development. One form was for the Commonwealth to take the initiative in its own Territories. Another was to start a wider programme but with provisions for early evaluation, and sometimes without final commitment. The Australian Assistance plan (see Chapter Nine) was to be a three-year experiment, 'to test pilot programs and evaluate the need for alternative and supplemental measures'.[12] This approach was often genuinely intended to promote an innovative frame of mind; but, as Peachment says, there was also the paradox that one associates experiment with variety, but in this case it was also used by those wanting to obtain greater unity of legislative provision through Commonwealth action. A 'model' can mean a first attempt to be tested out, or a small-scale design on which to base some final result; it can also indicate a plan already perfected by experts, there to be copied by lesser mortals.

One of the most successful and flexible Commonwealth-aided enterprises has been the Community Health Program begun in 1973. This has been called 'the first well-considered attempt'[13] in Australia to develop a comprehensive health and welfare service, with community health centres providing various nursing and home care services. The scheme has channelled Commonwealth funds into a great variety of welfare projects, made a genuine effort to involve local people in decisions, and provided for continuing evaluation. By 1977 over seven hundred projects had been approved, mostly now supervised through State health departments or commissions. The Commonwealth is now leaving the detailed administration of this programme more in State hands, and has tightened-up its subsidy policy.

This is a very crude and incomplete picture of a complex situation in the social welfare field. The Bailey report and other inquiries have tried to sort out the situation.[14] In general, they see the Commonwealth as continuing to finance social welfare programmes, though in a broader way, and also playing a policy and 'monitoring' role, with the States becoming the main co-ordinators of welfare services delivery. One trouble is that the States are often not much closer to the grassroots than the Commonwealth. Whether they can enlist and support the more localised initiatives involved in good welfare provision remains to be seen.

In some related areas, such as legal aid, special formal Agreements have been concluded, by which the Commonwealth Legal Aid Commission is given an advisory, co-ordinating and monitoring role, and provides funds to State Legal Aid Commissions, each of which includes a Commonwealth nominee, as well as representatives of the State government, legal profession and consumer or welfare bodies. This is only one example of a number of new arrangements that are currently being worked out as part of the so-called New Federalism.

Techniques of Co-operation

As these examples indicate, techniques of co-operation have followed no fixed pattern. They include: formal and informal councils and conferences at ministerial and official levels; formal and informal agreements; seconding of officers, and exchange of information and day-to-day contact between officers engaged in the same field of administrative activity. Some examples of these have already been given, others are mentioned below.

Councils and Conferences

(i) *The Premiers Conference*[15]   Even before federation the Australian colonies found it necessary to send political representatives to intercolonial conferences to discuss matters of mutual concern and common interest. Since federation, conferences of State Premiers have been held at frequent intervals. The first, held in November 1901, was called by Edmund Barton, the Commonwealth Prime Minister; under his chairmanship all States except Western Australia met to discuss such matters as the acquisition of State properties for Commonwealth purposes, quarantine, lighthouses and postal arrangements. Each State was represented by the Premier and a minister. The next conference was held in May 1902, under the chairmanship of the Premier of New South Wales. Western Australia and Tasmania were represented by ministers and the other States by their Premiers. The conferences had soon taken the place of Senate as the real 'States House'. Discussion was wide-ranging, and reports long and detailed.

For some years Premiers Conferences were called on the initiative of the States and were confined largely to the Premiers, though a Commonwealth minister was often present for at least some sessions, and the Prime Minister was sometimes there by invitation. They rotated between State capitals, though Melbourne soon became the commonest venue, and remained so until 1937. Even when the Commonwealth government took the initiative, the State Premiers and ministers met privately outside the main conference. In 1908 New South Wales undertook to provide a secretariat which would act as a link between successive conferences, and Holman (Premier of New South Wales from 1913 to 1920) tried to establish his State's leadership.

From 1919 onwards the practice developed, with some exceptions, of the Commonwealth arranging the conferences. Since 1929 the Prime Minister's Department has provided the staff and the name 'Premiers Conference' (which strictly applies to a meeting of State Premiers, summoned by one of them) has dropped out of official use. The regular meetings are referred to as 'Conference of Commonwealth and State Ministers'. The present position is that a conference is called by the Commonwealth Prime Minister either on his own initiative or at the request of a State Premier. The State Premiers often hold informal meetings between themselves before meeting together with the Commonwealth in the main conference; and lately have had one or two formal meetings without the Commonwealth, rather like the old-style Premiers Conferences.

Representation at the regular conference varies. The Commonwealth is represented by the Prime Minister (in the chair), the Treasurer and, where appropriate, by the minister concerned with any important item to be discussed. Each State is represented by its Premier, and usually its Deputy Premier or Treasurer (in many States, the Premier is also Treasurer) and sometimes another minister. They are backed by official experts, who will be called upon to do detailed bargaining at the official level. There is now at least one conference a year, lasting two days and held in Canberra in June; further conferences are sometimes called if it is necessary to deal with special problems between the annual meetings. Thus in 1976 there were also meetings in February and April to settle the outlines of the New Federalism policy.

The early conferences did not achieve much, but during the depression years of the 1930s the Premiers Conference became an important means of securing co-ordination in economic policy between Commonwealth and States, and the States played an influential part. After the war the question of the size and distribution of grants to the States came to overshadow the proceedings.

Premiers Conferences usually meet at the same time as the Australian Loan Council, as they have an almost identical membership; this tends to reinforce concentration on financial matters. However they deal with other problems. Here are the main topics of the June 1975 Conference:[16] grants to the States, which took up all the first day; co-operative planning and regionalism; wage indexation; State legislation to extend the scope of the Prices Justification Tribunal; common procedures for the calling of tenders; restrictive trade practices; and joint Commonwealth–State environmental impact statements. Traditionally the Prime Minister begins by reading a long statement, and the debate is opened by each State speaking in order of size. The conference has no executive powers, and its decisions are only effective if the cabinets and parliaments concerned agree. The proceedings are informal, motions are not put nor votes taken. Most Prime Ministers and Premiers nowadays are in a position to commit their governments, and even though the Commonwealth's position is often very much predetermined, something still depends on individual bargaining skill at the conference table.[17] Officials will have helped to decide on the Commonwealth's opening offer, 'coupled with a number of fall back positions depending on the response of the States . . . [In 1975] Treasury preparation included such detailed tactical matters as estimating the rate of progress through the agenda, and when calls for consultations with officials were likely to occur.'[18]

No doubt the Premiers Conferences, and the informal discussions that accompany them, do on balance tend to promote co-operation and have encouraged thinking in wider terms. At the very least they are a forum for the expression of varying State concerns. On the other hand, they are a rather inefficient way of allocating money. The formal sessions used often to be open and widely reported; but the conferences may at any time decide to go into closed session, and in recent years has regularly done so for important business. Each head of government has a veto on what appears in official press releases, but unofficial versions of the proceedings become known, and the conferences are generally also good publicity grounds for some State Premiers, less so for the Prime Minister.

In 1976 the Premiers Conference agreed to the Commonwealth's establishing an Advisory Council for Inter-Government Relations, including Commonwealth and State MPs, local government representatives and private citizens. Its powers are advisory and investigatory, and will (it is hoped) develop issues for debate at future Premiers Conferences. Its secretariat is in Hobart. Queensland has not joined the Council.

(ii) Federal–State Councils　　The term 'Council' is used to describe a number of joint agencies, mostly of an advisory character, though some, such as the Australian Loan Council and the Ministerial Council for Albury–Wodonga (mentioned below), have wider powers. Generally a Council consists of the appropriate Commonwealth and State Ministers, who have a formal meeting once or twice a year.[19] However, the Council is usually paralleled by a Standing Committee of senior Commonwealth and State officials, which is a permanent technical body to consider and report on matters referred to it by the Council, and which may meet more frequently.

The Australian Agricultural Council was the prototype. It was established in 1934 to help co-ordinate agricultural policies, hitherto mainly the affair of the States. Its regular membership consists of the Commonwealth Minister for Primary Industry (in the chair), the Minister for the Northern Territory, and the State Ministers for Agriculture or Primary Industry. It has no statutory authorisation, and no power to make binding decisions. Its functions are 'generally to promote the welfare and development of agricultural industries', to consider proposals about marketing policies and financial assistance, and so on. It is assisted by a Standing Committee on Agriculture, consisting of the permanent heads of the Commonwealth Departments of Primary Industry and of Trade and Resources and of the relevant State departments, and representatives of other Commonwealth departments concerned and of the CSIRO. This committee, in addition to advising the council, is charged with securing co-operation in research and on animal and plant quarantine. The council generally meets in private, four or five times a year, rotating between capital cities. Secretarial services are provided by the Department of Primary Industry.[20]

This has generally been regarded as among the more successful examples of Commonwealth–State co-operation. A former member of the Standing

Committee once commented that: 'In agriculture we have enjoyed a very great advantage in recent years in comparison with other fields of policy in that we have had an established piece of machinery for Commonwealth–State collaboration.'[21] Among other things, the council has promoted national conferences on particular topics; has encouraged a number of co-operative research projects, and uniform State action or legislation in various fields; it has also helped towards the establishment of marketing bodies, and of joint Commonwealth–State schemes such as those for dairy stabilisation.

It has been a model for similar bodies created since, such as the Australian Transport Advisory Council, the Australian Water Resources Council, the Australian Forestry Council, the Australian Fisheries Council, and the Australian Minerals and Energy Council. These arrange the exchange of information, often promote research, and formulate and recommend national policies in their fields. Thus the recommendations of the Australian Forestry Council in favour of increased softwood planting led to formal Commonwealth–State Agreements involving State schemes financially assisted by the Commonwealth (see, for example, the New South Wales Forestry Agreement Act, 1968). An Australian Education Council consults on education policies.

Bodies of this kind have their limitations. They are purely advisory, and their decisions are not binding on the governments concerned. As they are confined to the Commonwealth and State ministers and officials in their field, they are rarely good vehicles for reforms and changes that do not meet with fairly ready agreement. The Australian Minerals Council (as it was originally called) became defunct for some years, after getting involved in the off-shore minerals debate. However, such councils encourage co-operation; they help the various State and Commonwealth ministers and officials to get to know one another better; their unanimous decisions carry weight. The creation of such a body is an indication of special Commonwealth concern for the field involved, and is often followed by greater national provision for research and financial aid.

(iii) National Health and Medical Research Council   This is one of several bodies at, or mainly at, the official level. It began as the Federal Health Council, set up in 1926 following the report of a Commonwealth Royal Commission, to advise the Commonwealth and State governments on health questions and to promote co-operation. This was a purely official body, but in 1936 it was absorbed into the National Health and Medical Research Council, with an enlarged membership.

The council at present has twenty-four members. It consists of the Commonwealth Director-General of Health (Chairman) and three other Commonwealth representatives; the chief administrative medical officer of each State; representatives of outside bodies; and a laymen and laywoman appointed by the Commonwealth government. It will be noted that this body, unlike those mentioned earlier, includes outside members. It advises

Commonwealth and State governments on general health questions and on medical research grants, but has no laboratories of its own. The Commonwealth Department of Health provides the secretariat. The council has appointed a number of committees, on which outside experts serve, to deal with specialised aspects of its work.

(iv) Snowy Mountains Council   The Snowy Mountains Council was set up in 1959, following an agreement ratified by the relevant parliaments. It has a Chairman and Deputy Chairman appointed by the Commonwealth, two members each from New South Wales and Victoria, and also represents the Snowy Mountains Hydro-Electric Authority. It controls the operation of the permanent works of the Authority, and also the allocation of loads to the generating stations manned by State Electricity Commissions, and advises and reports on various matters. A Deputy Secretary of the Department of National Development was chairman in 1978.

The Snowy Mountains Hydro-Electric Authority was a purely Commonwealth body, established in 1949 by the Commonwealth parliament (relying tenuously on the defence power[22] and more confidently on State and popular support) to construct dams, generating stations and so on, in the Snowy Mountains area. However, New South Wales and Victoria played an important role in the planning stages, and many State agencies helped with technical advice, with the design and construction of various works associated with the scheme, and with providing housing, schools and so on. Having completed its task, it was largely disbanded, though some staff were retained to form the Snowy Mountains Engineering Corporation (1970), available for specialist engineering consulting services to governments and private bodies, both within Australia and overseas.

(v) River Murray Commission   The River Murray, which borders three States, was once the subject of much interstate strife. The work of the River Murray Commission (1917) is based on an Agreement ratified in 1915 by Commonwealth legislation and that of the three States concerned. The four part-time Commissioners represent the Commonwealth, New South Wales, Victoria and South Australia. Till 1972 a Commonwealth Minister normally presided, with the Secretary to his Department as Deputy Commissioner; the three State Commissioners are senior officers of rivers and water supply agencies. When Dr Cass (as Minister for Environment) became the responsible minister, he thought it better that the national government, like the States, should be represented by a senior officer, and his permanent head took over. Now (1979) the Commissioner of the Snowy Mountains Authority is President. The Agreement, which the commission is required to put into effect, provides for the construction of works by, and allocation of water between, the three States concerned, which are also responsible for maintenance. One odd provision of the Agreement is that in the event of certain kinds of disagreement, the Chief Justice of Tasmania may appoint an arbitrator.

(vi) Australian Tourist Commission   This was established in 1967, and has nine Commissioners, including representatives of the Commonwealth and State governments and the tourist industry. It has a Commonwealth grant, which it uses to encourage overseas visits to Australia and travel in Australia. The State governments are mainly concerned with domestic travel, though they also do some overseas promotion.

(vii) Australian Apprenticeship Advisory Committee   In 1957, following a Commonwealth–State inquiry and conference, the Australian Apprenticeship Advisory Committee was established to make recommendations on apprenticeship matters, and also to arrange for the conduct of research and to provide an information service. It represents the Commonwealth Department of Employment and Industrial Relations, senior officers from each State Labour Department, and from other apprenticeship and technical training authorities. The Commonwealth provides the staff. The committee operates mainly through Working Parties, and has brought in 'Advisers to the Chairman' from trade unions, employers associations, and other bodies.

(viii) Hospital and Allied Services Advisory Council   This was established by the 1970 Australian Health Ministers Conference. The council consists of officers from relevant Commonwealth and State agencies and makes recommendations for joint consideration by the various Health Ministers. It has subcommittees on construction planning, uniform costing, computers, nursing homes and so on.

(ix) Standing Conferences and Committees   There are also a large number of conferences and meetings held between ministers and officials responsible for specific fields. During 1969, for example, close to three hundred formal conferences and meetings took place between Commonwealth and State ministers and/or officials.[23] There are over twenty standing conferences, councils and committees of Ministers, often attended also by officials; and over ninety bodies at the official level. The former usually meet once or twice a year, a few of the latter may meet more frequently.

The work of the Standing Committee of Attorneys-General is discussed below. Another useful instrument of co-operation is the annual Conference of Health Ministers, to which they are accompanied by their senior officers, and to which the Minister for Social Security, and on occasion other ministers, are invited. In 1969, for example, the Health Ministers endorsed a code for drug manufacturers prepared by a working party of Commonwealth and State representatives. In 1970 it agreed to establish the Hospital and Allied Services Advisory Council (see above). Other matters on which ministerial conferences are held regularly include Aboriginal affairs, housing, immigration, local government, national parks, police, tourism, transport and welfare. At the official level, there is the Australasian Public Service Commissioners Conference, held every two years,[24] and conferences of Auditors-General, Directors of Education, Police Commissioners, and port, railway and road authorities. The Bailey Report has identified fifty-six formal arrangements for Commonwealth–State consultation in the welfare and health fields alone.[25]

As already indicated, there are limitations on representative bodies of this kind, especially when they simply represent Commonwealth and State ministers and officials. Though they do much to promote co-operation in areas where interests do not radically diverge, they are less easily made vehicles of major reconciliations of policy and, unless they build up their own permanent staff, it is hard for them to do sophisticated and impartial research.

So the Commonwealth has also set up some independent research and advisory agencies of its own, on which the State governments are not represented, especially to advise it in fields where it makes grants. The Grants Commission has already been mentioned. Other examples are the Tertiary Education Commission, a nine-member body that advises on the needs of higher education; the Bureau of Transport Economics, the work of whose research staff is helping to promote a major rethinking of roads and other transport programmes; and the Australia Council (for the arts). Such bodies have been said to work best when they are dealing with a fairly small number of organisations, with the six States, or (as the original Universities Commission did) with a few Universities. When they have many more units to cope with, they tend to get bogged down, or have to resort to formulae, in the manner of the Schools Commission.

One of the advantages to the Commonwealth that flows from its financial strength is that it has more resources to devote to research. For example, it has built the Commonwealth Scientific and Industrial Research Organisation into an impressively large government research agency (for a fairly small country in terms of population), with a current annual budget of $141 million (1978–79). The Bureau of Agricultural Economics, now in the Department of Primary Industry, was another important pioneering unit of this kind.

One abortive part of the Constitution is contained in sections 101–104, which provided for an independent interstate commission that parliament could empower to adjudicate and administer the trade and commerce provisions. The Inter-State Commission was appointed in 1913 with wide powers in the economic field, which turned out to be mainly investigatory, as the High Court disallowed its judicial role. It conducted some important inquiries but was allowed to lapse in 1920, and has never been revived. The Labor government legislated for its re-establishment in 1975, but the succeeding government failed to proclaim the Act.[26]

Agreements

Many instances of joint action have resulted from formal Commonwealth–State or interstate Agreements, usually signed by the Prime Minister and Premiers concerned. These may be agreements to pass parallel legislation, or to take other kinds of co-operative action. Many Commonwealth subsidies, to which complex conditions may be attached, are paid under such arrangements, such as the housing subsidies paid under the Commonwealth–State Housing Agreement. These agreements may be on a three to five-year basis, and renegotiated at the end of their term.

One case discussed earlier in this chapter is that of off-shore oil and gas, where the device was used in the attempt to by-pass complex disputes about the ambit of Commonwealth and State powers. Following an agreement, both sides enacted parallel legislation, and the States were given fairly full control. The status of such agreements is a little obscure, and it is not clear what legal remedies, if any, are available if one party refuses to carry out its side of the bargain.[27] The agreement on off-shore oil expressly stated that the governments involved 'acknowledge that this agreement is not intended to create legal relationships judiciable in a Court of Law . . . ' (clause 26).

A complex example of co-operative federalism that partly depends on an Agreement is the Albury–Wodonga Development Corporation, set up to plan and develop two adjacent towns, Albury in New South Wales and Wodonga in Victoria, as a growth centre. The principal corporation was established by Commonwealth statute in 1973 as amended. It is subject to a Ministerial Council of three, one from each government concerned, whose decisions must be unanimous. As many of the powers involved belonged to the two States, an Agreement was made with them as a result of which all three governments passed necessary legislation. In fact the corporation is legally three corporations, which in practice work as a single entity with a common staff— the main task of the State corporations is to acquire land, which can be done more readily under State powers. The Corporation has a chairman nominated by the Commonwealth minister, two deputies nominated by the two States ministers, and five part-time members representing the local communities and other interests.

Agreements are a good example of how the federal system tends to increase the power of the executive. An arrangement made after prolonged executive negotiation and involving agreed legislation by all parliaments is a striking case of using the latter as a rubber stamp. Of course, any of the parliaments can reject or amend legislation—but that would wreck the whole carefully negotiated scheme, an exercise no legislature would lightly undertake. Agreements have been a flexible and reasonably amiable form of co-operation, and an interesting example of Australian administrative pragmatism.

There are also more informal kinds of agreement. A good example is the arrangements between Restrictive Practices Commission staff working in the consumer protection area, and State agencies in the same field. Following discussions at the official level in 1976, a set of guidelines for concurrent administration was drawn up. They recognised, for example, that 'State and Territory agencies were in the best position to deal with the problems of individual consumers and that those agencies should provide the principal complaint-handling mechanism. State authorities would be the prime agencies in relation to problems that can be resolved by action in one State.'[28] The

Trade Practices Act Review Committee (the Swanson Committee) recommended in 1976 that the 'major responsibility for the day-to-day enforcement' of the consumer protection section of the Commonwealth statute should be handed over to the States.

Other Forms of Co-operation

There is also the daily reference between public authorities on all kinds of subjects from arbitration to personnel practices. Police departments co operate widely, carry out investigations and serve summonses for one another, even sometimes have powers to arrest in adjoining States. The Commonwealth still relies greatly on State police for general law enforcement, though there has been a Commonwealth police force of sorts since W.M. Hughes became concerned about wartime civil disturbance in 1917, and some recent attempts to expand its role have caused friction. One Public Service Board from time to time may act as an agent for another; Crown Solicitors and Public Trustees act for one another. There are many other examples of co-operation—from interlibrary loans to electricity supplies, interstate railway arrangements, education services in border areas, and so on. For example, by reciprocal agreement New South Wales and Queensland give financial aid to parents whose children cross the State border to attend school.

However, there are still many fields where co-operation is limited, or where there is a need for better reciprocal arrangements or more joint or uniform provision. A good example is superannuation schemes that limit mobility of government employees.

Uniformity of Laws

As we have seen, the six Australian States have each wide legislative powers. Now that interstate movement and contact are increasing so rapidly, the case for reasonably uniform laws has become stronger. Uniformity is not a good in itself; part of the case for States has rested on the argument that a plurality of governments promotes experiment, and experiment involves variety and difference. Again, when State governments have agreed to a policy of uniform legislation in some area, further progress then depends on continued agreement, and each can blame the others if no further improvements in the law are made, or if piecemeal amendment reintroduces variety. All the same, one might expect that successful innovations in one State would tend to be copied by others. There is also a wide field in which reasonable uniformity has virtues that outweigh possible curbs on experimentation, just as in modern industry there are basic forms of standardisation that are highly economical, and that even facilitate variety of product.

In many respects State law has been reasonably uniform.[29] The Australian colonies inherited the English common law, and have been largely faithful to its later development and attitudes, including the organisation and attitudes of the legal profession. Many United Kingdom statutes were applicable to, or copied by Australia. Successful innovations in one State, from 'Torrens title' in South Australia to recent examples such as environmental protection laws, consumer protection and small claims tribunals, have sometimes been widely adopted in other States. In a few fields where the advantages of common standards are reasonably obvious, such as civil aviation, the achievement of reasonable uniformity has not been too difficult. More uniformity has also been achieved by Commonwealth occupancy of some field of concurrent power, such as family law. There are Commonwealth codes on such matters as bankruptcy, copyright, patents and life insurance (though not in contracts, property or criminal law).

Nevertheless, progress to the mid-1950s was very limited, and is still slow. State laws are full of pointless variety, and differences that mainly reflect indefensible backwardness and inertia. A breakthrough came in the field of economic regulation. During the boom years of the late 1950s, with Victoria taking the lead, a largely uniform hire purchase law was achieved after lengthy meetings between State representatives. Further discussions followed, with the Commonwealth playing a larger role, on uniform company laws; these achieved something at the time, but on the whole the States missed their opportunity to regulate companies (and stock markets) by mutual co-operation. However, at the time of writing (1979) Commonwealth–State agreement on national company law and securities industry regulation seems to have been reached. Much work has been done by the Standing Committee of Attorneys-General, backed by the staff work of departmental legal officers, commissioned outside experts and bodies such as the Australian and New South Wales Law Reform Commissions. The Standing Committee has been a useful source of co-operative action since it was formally constituted in 1961. Among other things, it worked out the joint arrangements, later embodied in a formal agreement, regarding off-shore oil and natural gas. However, it has had various limitations, including lack of any staff of its own, though there are now bodies such as the various Law Commissions that can undertake research on projects for uniform laws.

In the 1960s the uniform law movement spread into other fields, especially where some machinery already existed to promote the cause and where the problem had no strongly political cast—such as adoption laws, control of drugs and so on. Of course, it is harder to achieve results in areas where the advantages are not strikingly clear or which are politically sensitive. Even in fields where the case for uniformity seems overwhelming, there are pointless differences, from food laws[30] to workers' compensation and the law of defamation. Even though the States agreed to have uniform adoption laws, the various acts passed were not in fact uniform, and later amendments made them even less so. The Australian Transport Advisory Council has been seeking for years to achieve uniform laws relating to road traffic and motor vehicles; some progress has been made. Governments and their senior advisers, like most people, do not relish the thought that other people have better ideas than themselves. Sometimes there is a case for varying views.

States may be faced with different local circumstances, or different constellations of interests. The process is also technically complex, and demands concentrated attention and considerable negotiating skill. It has depended very much on the drive and energy of a few individual ministers, public servants and law reformers.

Duplication and Overlapping

Duplication and unnecessary overlapping of Commonwealth and State activities are always possible in a federal system where many powers are concurrent, and where Commonwealth powers have been capable of wide extension by constitutional interpretations and the centralisation of financial power. As activities expand, and points of contact on administrative boundaries multiply, these possibilities increase, and become point of attack for critics of federalism. Investigations of this have been made from time to time. In the past they have generally shown that a good deal of the so-called duplication or overlapping was more apparent than real;[31] but the problem seems to have grown worse in the 1970s. Of course, another way of putting this is that so long as the Commonwealth confined itself to fairly routine kinds of intervention through general grants without strings, or to a few specific grants of a rigid kind, there were necessarily fewer problems of overlap—but also many social problems remained untackled.

It should also be said that there have been a number of arrangements for joint working in particular fields. The Commonwealth Electoral Act provides for the joint preparation of electoral rolls. Commonwealth and State statistical services were largely amalgamated, following the Statistics (Arrangements with States) Act 1956. Animal and plant quarantine policy is implemented by State Departments of Agriculture acting as agents for the Commonwealth government.

One area especially liable to duplication of work is where the Commonwealth is providing money for particular activities administered by the States, especially by some form of specific purpose or tied grant. Scrutiny and control by the Commonwealth may tend to become too rigid and detailed. Commonwealth administrators may come to regard themselves as the superior authority and, even where the States present expert evidence, insist on duplicating the work. The reaction of the States may be resentful.

There have for a long time been complaints by the States about the administration of specific purpose grants, though perhaps less in volume than about some of the grants themselves, when they have been treated by the Commonwealth as a politically attractive alternative to increasing general aid, or where they appear to distort State priorities. In 1970 it was reported that a 'secret' memorandum detailing cases of Commonwealth interference in State affairs had been prepared by the New South Wales Government.[32] It allegedly referred to Commonwealth insistence on making its own classification of Australian roads in connection with roads grants; the requirement of detailed statements and multiple plans in relation to education grants; duplicating Commonwealth and State inspectorates in some health institutions, including private hospitals. In spite of this, detailed control of grant-aid, at least up to 1972, was less than in most federations. One reason is that the Australian States have had competent and well-established public services already accustomed, before the federal government became powerful, to administering a wide range of functions. Campbell Sharman quotes a senior State Treasury official as saying that before the advent of the Labor government in 1972 working relationships had been good, 'on the basis that the Commonwealth had the cash and ideas while the States had the expertise'.[33] However, the Labor government of 1972–75 combined increased use of specific purpose grants with the creation of new departments and statutory commissions to collect data and make plans. This led to an increased demand on State agencies for information, often asked for in new forms, in greater detail, by more different agencies and sometimes by relative newcomers to the game of dealing with the States. There was a greater Commonwealth disposition to develop its own plans and projects, sometimes without the experience or feedback facilities to operate them effectively.

Relations were not helped by the fact that four of the six States had non-Labor governments. Some States reacted in 1975, as New South Wales and Victoria did, by appointing a Minister for Federal Affairs and/or creating a unit to deal with federal matters in the Premier's Department, in order to keep a check on Commonwealth activities (the new Labor government in New South Wales has abolished both). The four non-Labor States also formed a Council of States, from which New South Wales has since withdrawn.

Certain Commonwealth agencies learned to co-operate with their own State clienteles, and created various contacts with State departments that by-passed traditional channels, based on a joint concern with maximising resources for the particular function; a step to which Commonwealth and State Treasuries sometimes responded with their own forms of 'mild collusion', to retain financial control and to find out just what was going on in the more flexibly administered programmes in, say, education or Aboriginal affairs.[34] This is one way in which the greater variety of federal interventions has raised new problems of co-ordination at State level. South Australia has a Coordination Branch in the Policy Division of the Premier's Department, whose task it is to monitor all Commonwealth government activities affecting the State and to help ensure that it responds to them in a consistent and co-ordinated way.

Public Service Attitudes

Australia, like most federations, has 'dual' public services, not a single bureaucracy serving both levels of government—and this is sensible, given the close link between ministers and public servants at each level. Occasionally, as mentioned earlier, there have been amalgamations. For example, there is a single statistical service in each State, operated by Commonwealth officers under the Australian Statistician, who holds office under both Commonwealth and State governments. But in general each service looks after its own government's affairs.

However, because the affairs of the two levels of government have become entwined, this has inevitably had reactions at the official level. One is a much greater tendency for senior officers to meet together. State under treasurers and their staffs have prepared data and briefs for Premiers Conference and Loan Council meetings, or for the Grants Commission. This has made them more sophisticated, encouraged the development of staff and research units inside the treasuries, and drawn them together in regular meetings. As we have seen, a network of Commonwealth–State Councils also exists, with parallel committees of officials.

There are many other important contacts. When the Commonwealth gives a conditional grant, its administration involves a good deal of negotiation with State public servants, both from Treasuries and from the functional area involved. Not much is known in detail about the character of these relations, nor about what part co-operativeness, rivalry and resentment play.

> The fact of Commonwealth affluence does have an effect on the style of bureaucratic interchange. While it is no longer true that there is a large margin . . . Commonwealth officials still have a certain smugness about their superior pay, conditions of work, perks, opportunities for advancement and about the superior Commonwealth organizational resources . . . Early in the Whitlam ministry this was accentuated by the policy of making the Commonwealth public service a pacesetter in pay and conditions and by the belief that the new, innovative Commonwealth broom was about to sweep away the conservatism and parochialism of state policies.[35]

The State official will naturally lay more stress on the virtues of State independence, and on his greater experience about and sensitivity to the needs of his part of Australia.

It has been claimed that permanent officials in federations see intergovernmental relations in more co-operative terms than do politicians.[36] If so, this may in part be because the growth of complexity in intergovernmental relations tends to increase bureaucratic influence, by encouraging a disposition to let many problems be settled at the official level. There has been no full study of the attitudes of Australian public servants to the federal system.[37] One has the impression that few Australian State officers want to see an increase in federal administrative supervision, and that their State loyalties are often strong. There is no regular flow of officers between State and Commonwealth services, such as might promote mutual confidence, though (as indicated above) a good deal of meeting now takes place and some organised interchange is now beginning. The Leach survey showed 76 per cent of State officials responding to his questionnaire as seeing Commonwealth–State relations more in terms of 'conflict' than 'co-operation', as compared with 61 per cent of Commonwealth public servants.

There is probably a fair amount of difference between departments. Particular ministers and agencies have often been reasonably free to negotiate their own relationships with their opposite numbers, so one can have areas of harmony alongside others of bitter conflict. Public servants can be very critical of the federal government, and at the same time strongly in favour of getting federal money. In the mid-1970s some State education and health authorities could be accused, rightly or wrongly, of having 'sold out' to the Commonwealth government, whose finance had partly liberated them from State treasuries. Professionals may learn to work closely with their colleagues at other levels of government, and their private sector supporters, to promote expansion in their particular field.

The chief danger to the States at the administrative level is that if they continue to attract less administrative talent than the Commonwealth, a bureaucratic imbalance will come to match the present financial imbalance. 'As matters stand, because it [the Commonwealth] has a better equipped bureaucracy, it is more powerfully placed to give effect to the role it has ordained for itself and to press its initiatives.'[38] This is a touchy question. The States think they are at least as good if not better than the Commonwealth at 'operations', getting a job done, even if not always able to compete as well at the game of policy argument. Some States are now actively trying to improve recruitment and training, developing policy and research units, and so on.

The Future of Federal Relations

It is clear that within the limits of the federal system and the constitution, politicians and administrators have not been inactive in developing agencies and procedures capable of dealing with new problems. Assessment of the result is difficult and, especially as so little serious research has been done on the topic, largely depends on the political approach of the assessor. The centralist is impatient with the complex techniques of Commonwealth–State co-operation and hopes, by concentrating political power in Commonwealth hands, to render most of them unnecessary. Professor Greenwood, for example, claimed thirty years ago that:

> Superficially . . . the record of co-operation in Australia seems to be an imposing one. However . . . the results which have flowed from these contacts have been meagre and unusually disappointing. The test by which the principle of co-operation must stand or fall is the speed and efficiency with which it secures action upon problems of major significance. Measured by such a standard, the record of co-operation is seen to be dilatory and ineffective.[39]

Some centralists argue that the advantages of unified decision-making on major issues and of decentralised administration can both be secured. As the former Leader of the Labor Party in the Commonwealth Parliament put it some years ago:

> If we were devising anew a structure of representative government for our continent, we would have neither so few State Governments nor so many local-government units. We would have . . . an assembly for the affairs of each of our dozen largest cities, and a few score regional assemblies for the areas of rural production and resource development outside those cities.[40]

The argument runs that, in a culturally homogeneous country like Australia, the so-called demand for 'States' rights' is really only a demand for decentralised administration, for a system that gives people some sense of participation in and control over their own affairs.

> It is now a classic case, not for cooperative federalism (which involves an almost total loss of effective political responsibility), much less for . . . coordinate federalism . . . , but for organic federalism. A Bill of Rights and a guarantee of decentralised administration would reconcile Australians to the concentration of policy control, economic control and fiscal strategy in Canberra which the country so obviously needs.[41]

It is not certain that the word federalism can usefully be applied to such a system, nor does it seem likely that it will come about. Australia is not, as Mr Whitlam recognised, 'devising anew a structure', there already is one, with its own powerful vested interests, and it has not been shown to be unworkable. Nor is it clear that the power of the States is being eroded.

There are two other problems with this kind of solution. One is that the policy–administration, or thinker–doer, dichotomy works no better in federal relations than anywhere else. Often when both sides are involved in some field, it is better for each to have its own activities, and meet to deal with the interface (I owe the words to an officer of the Commonwealth department concerned with urban affairs). Some people have a different fear of the unholy alliance between the new centralism and the new localism that Professor Sawer recommends. It has been argued by Samuel Beer and others[42] that in some federations a series of 'intergovernmental lobbies' is emerging, of bureaucrats and activists at the different levels, each pressing for more government intervention in their own field, promoting the steady growth of public expenditure and the loss of firm control over general priorities.

Some observers of the present federal system, who are also critical of its growing complexities, argue that greater simplicity can be restored by new financial arrangements. They say that many of the recent developments described in this chapter, including a growing resort to specific grants and agreements, would be unnecessary if a proper balance between responsibilities and financial resources could be re-established. Some have not abandoned hope of re-creating 'co-ordinate' federalism, in which the division of functions between Commonwealth and State is reasonably clear and unambiguous, and the States can stand firmly on their own feet. The New Federalism policy of the 1975 Fraser Government represents a small move in this direction. The States are being encouraged to levy their own income tax, though most of them do not appear anxious to do so. Some specific purpose grants are to be replaced by general purpose funds under the tax-sharing arrangements described earlier; and the Commonwealth government is trying to stage a retreat from interference in detailed administration.

A third view is that the present complexities of co-operation are likely to continue and must be coped with. It is arguable that co-operative federalism is simply one symptom of the growing interdependencies of modern societies, which will defeat all simple-minded attempts to sort them out. Modern government, federal or otherwise, will continue to be involved in very complex systems of co-operation, in which it will be harder and harder to assign specific powers and responsibilities. Co-ordination and control will still be necessary, will have to be sought through an increasing variety of methods, and will always be incomplete.

Notes

1. On constitutional aspects of co-operation, see J.E. Richardson, *Patterns of Australian Federalism*, ANU, Canberra, 1973, especially Appendixes B and C.
2. For a useful account, see K.W. Wiltshire (ed.), *Administrative Federalism: Selected Documents in Australian Intergovernmental Relations*, University of Queensland Press, St Lucia, 1977, 5–8.
3. cf. Jean Holmes and Campbell Sharman, *The Australian Federal System*, Allen and Unwin, Sydney, 1977, 27.
4. The classification is a modified version of that used in A.F. Davies, *Australian Democracy*, 2nd edn, Longmans, Melbourne, 1964, 89–90.
5. For a fuller account, see Garth Stevenson, *Mineral Resources and Australian Federalism*, Centre for Research on Federal Financial Relations, ANU, Canberra, 1977, on which this section has drawn heavily.
6. *ibid.*, 30.
7. The Agreement is reprinted in K.W. Wiltshire, *op. cit.*, 207–13. See also Report, Senate Select Committee on Off-Shore Petroleum Resources, Canberra, 1971.
8. *New South Wales* v. *Commonwealth* (Offshore Sovereignty Case) (1976) 8 A.L.R. 1.
9. *The King* v. *Burgess; Ex parte Henry* (1936) 55 C.L.R. 608.
10. *Airlines of N.S.W. Pty Ltd* v. *New South Wales* (1964) 113 C.L.R. 1; *Airlines of N.S.W. Pty Ltd* v. *New South Wales* (No 2) (1965) 113 C.L.R. 54.
11. cf. A. Peachment, 'Experiments in Decisionmaking: The Whitlam Legacy', *J. Commonwealth and Comparative Studies*, October 1976.
12. *Australian Assistance Plan*, Discussion Paper No. 2, 28.

13. By Michael Jones, in his case-study of Australian social services in Barbara N. Rodgers (ed.), *The Study of Social Policy: A Comparative Approach*, Allen and Unwin, 1979 (Forthcoming).

14. See, for example, First and Second Reports, Task Force on Co-ordination in Welfare and Health, Canberra, 1977, 1978; Report, Committee on Care of the Aged and Infirm, Canberra, 1977.

15. K.N.J. Bernie, 'The Premiers' Conferences', *Public Admin.* (Sydney), VI, 8, December 1947, gives an account of the development of the Premiers Conference up to 1930. Campbell Sharman, *The Premiers' Conference: An Essay in Federal State Interaction*, ANU Press, Canberra, 1977, has good general discussion and bibliography.

16. Sharman, *op. cit.*, 34–39. For earlier conferences, see the *Reports*, Proceedings of the Conference of Commonwealth and State Ministers. These reports have not been available since 1974; for a checklist, see Sharman, *op. cit.*, 60–75.

17. For a famous occasion, see *Public Admin.* (Sydney), XXVIII, 1, March 1969, 91–2; Sharman, *op. cit.*, 34 ff. gives an account of the June 1975 Conference. For 1976, see Andrew Clark, 'What Went On At the Premiers Conference", *National Times*, 23–28 February 1976; and A. Peachment and G.S. Reid, *New Federalism in Australia: Rhetoric or Reality?*, Flinders University, 1977, 20–28.

18. Sharman, *op. cit.*, 15–17.

19. For a list of Federal–State Councils, see Answer to Question, *Com. Parl. Deb.* (H. of R.), V. 105, 2 June 1977, 2545–2553.

20. F.O. Grogan, 'The Australian Agricultural Council', *Public Admin.* (Sydney), XVII, 1, March 1958; Leach, *op. cit.*, 49–53; Wiltshire, *op. cit.*, 215–20.

21. J.G. Crawford, 'Administrative Aspects of Food and Agricultural Policy', *Public Admin.* (Sydney), XI, 3, September 1952, 106.

22. See D.P. Derham, 'The Defence Power', in R. Else-Mitchell (ed.), *Essays on the Australian Constitution*, 2nd edn, Law Book Co., Sydney, 1961.

23. Based on Answers to Questions, *Com. Parl. Deb.* (H. of R.), V. 68, 12 June 1970, 3619–27. This excluded meetings at which only one State was represented.

24. For the reprinted report of the first conference in 1937, see K.W. Wiltshire (ed.), *Administrative Federalism*, University of Queensland Press, St Lucia, 1977, 157–68.

25. 2nd Report, Task Force on Co-ordination in Welfare and Health, Canberra, 1977, 52.

26. See J.A. La Nauze, "The Inter-State Commission", *Australian Quarterly*, IX (1937), reprinted in Colin A. Hughes (ed.), *Readings in Australian Government*, St Lucia, Queensland, 1968; and Inter-State Commission Act, 1975. The Senate refused to pass a Bill with broad powers, and the Labor government accepted that the Commission should be only an investigatory body in the transport field.

27. cf. G. Sawer, *Australian Federalism in the Courts*, Melbourne University Press, Melbourne, 1967, 146.

28. See J.V. McKeown, 'Protecting the Consumer', *Aust. J. Public Admin.*, XXXVI, 1, March 1977, 30–31; and Second Annual Report, Trade Practices Commission, Canberra, 1969.

29. For a general survey of Australian law, see Geoffrey Sawer, *The Australian and the Law*, 2nd edn, Penguin Books, Harmondsworth, Middlesex, 1972. See also Ross Cranston, 'Uniform Laws in Australia', *Public Admin.* (Sydney), XXX, 3, September 1971.

30. Federal and State governments are said to be drafting national food legislation to replace the varied food controls that are now in force (*Canberra Times*, 3 September 1977).

31. cf. S.R. Davis, 'The Problem of Overlapping and Duplication between Commonwealth and State Public Services in Australia', *Public Admin.* (Sydney), X, 3–4, September–December 1951. For a recent example of duplication, see Report, RCAGA, Appendix Vol. Two, 'Meat Inspection in Australia', 450–6.

32. *Sydney Morning Herald* and *The Australian*, 8 January 1970.

33. Campbell Sharman, *The Premiers' Conference: An Essay in Federal State Interaction*, ANU Press, Canberra, 1977, 19; I have drawn widely on this study in what follows.

34. Sharman, *op. cit.*, 18–22.

35. Sharman, *op. cit.*, 18–19.

36. By E.W. Weidner, in A.W. MacMahon (ed.), *Federalism: Mature and Emergent*, Doubleday, New York, 1955, 363 ff.

37. The study carried out by R.H. Leach, *Perceptions of Federalism by Canadian and Australian Public Servants*, ANU Press, Canberra, 1973, is based on too undifferentiated a sample, with a poor response rate.

38. First Report, Board of Inquiry into the Victorian Public Service, Melbourne, 1974, 47.

39. G. Greenwood, *The Future of Australian Federalism*, Melbourne University Press, Melbourne, 1946, 299.

40. E.G. Whitlam, *An Urban Nation*, Leslie Wilkinson Lecture, University of Sydney, 1969. Much the same words are used in E.G. Whitlam, 'A New Federalism', *Aust. Quarterly*, 43, 3, September 1971.

41. G. Sawer, 'Australian Federalism: A Sketch', a paper presented to the World Congress on Philosophy of Law and Social Philosophy, Sydney, 1977, 9. See also Sawer, *Modern Federalism*, 2nd edn, Pitman, Carlton, Victoria, 1976, especially 104–8 and ch. 11.

42. See e.g. Samuel Beer, 'Political Overload and Federalism', in V. Schuck and J. Milburn (eds), *New England Politics*, Schenckman, Cambridge, Mass. (forthcoming).

Chapter Nine

Local and Regional Government

Local government in Australia has always been primarily an administrative arrangement devised by colonial and then State governments to deal with specific local tasks. At no stage has there been any general demand for local self-government, nor have the conditions ever been favourable to its easy growth. The influences that fostered equality and uniformity in Australian life did not encourage strong local government. We do not find—as in parts of Britain, the United States, or in some of the cities of Europe—a long history of local independence or survivals of special privilege, distinctive organisation, localised sources of income, or particular responsibilities. Once established the local council has sometimes become the focus of local pride, the leader of local development. But the characteristic feature of local government history in Australia has been the attempt by higher authorities first to persuade and then to require local groups to accept financial and administrative responsibility for bread-and-butter tasks.

Even though each State has its own system of local government, the similarities are more important than the differences. In each case the local council is the creation of State government, dependent for its power on State legislation and ordinances. The States direct and control local authorities in a fairly detailed way, usually through a department of local government. What they may or must do does not vary strikingly. The practical possibilities include the same fairly narrow range of housekeeping tasks—local roads, sanitation, garbage disposal, street lighting, building control, protection of food supplies, in some areas water supply and sewerage, gas and electricity supply—and much the same possible excursions into recreational, welfare and cultural activities. There has been some variation between States. In Victoria, for example, local councils have been more involved in personal health and welfare services than in, say, New South Wales and Queensland, and much less concerned with public utility services such as water supply. However, local government functions in all States would seem strangely restricted to British or American observers. Education, police, housing, transport and other major services are State government responsibilities. Local councils are much less powerful and less significant politically than many of their counterparts elsewhere. In America expenditures of federal, state and local authorities in the early 1970s were in the ratio of 60:14:26; in Canada equivalent figures were 40:32:28; in Australia 48:44:8.[1]

In the whole of Australia there are over 850 ordinary local councils, with another 52 indirectly elected county councils in New South Wales, and a few similar bodies elsewhere. Tasmania does not distinguish between urban and rural authorities, the whole State is divided into municipal districts. The mainland States make this broad distinction. The urban councils are usually known as cities, municipalities or towns, the rural councils as shires or districts—there is some variation between States. New South Wales has (1978) 205 councils, of which 81 are municipalities and 124 shires. Their average population in 1973 was only 22 000, and in many the population is actually falling. (In some States the average is 8000 or less.) The New South Wales municipalities include 23 city councils, an honorific title granted to urban councils with more than a certain population and revenue. The county councils are joint committees of neighbouring local authorities, usually with a specific responsibility to provide electricity or water, or to manage an airport, or to destroy noxious weeds. They are not, as in Britain, second-tier authorities; there is no hierarchical structure in Australian local government, and the various types of council have broadly similar structures and powers.[2]

What is 'local' is a matter of custom rather than logic. Where, as in Australia, there develops an early trend towards uniformity, opposed to the creation or maintenance of special local advantage or disadvantage, the centralising of authority is inevitable. 'Independent' local government means local differences and local inequalities. For example, 'independent' local education authorities involve a noticeable variation in standards and equipment between schools in different areas. In Australia the central governments of the colonies began the public schools, financed them, decided their location and their curricula on a colony-wide basis; they organised teacher training.[3] Australian local government has not given much opportunity for lively local experimentation in important things. But there are compensating advantages in not having locally controlled police forces, or local school boards, or boundary disputes about the responsibilities of fire brigades.

Development to 1900

Conditions in Australia did not favour strong local government. In this new country scattered settlements spread tentatively from coastal bases to hinterlands which were usually drier and less fertile than the coastal fringe. These inland settlements were always linked to the headquarters city, the base of operations, the centre of administration and trade. Moves for self-government were directed towards gaining power at the colonial centre. Without participation in central government there seemed little point in seeking self-government at the local level, as later seekers after colonial freedom have also argued. Moreover, the developmental tasks were much too great to be financed by the tolls and rates that were used in Britain.

Even there they were found inadequate, although there at least some of the roads, bridges, hospitals and prisons were already built. In contrast, Australian central governments had access to the proceeds of land sales and customs duties. 'One very good reason why the colonists were happy for the central government to undertake so much . . . was that it did not appear to cost them anything.'[4]

The first stage was an attempt to reproduce something akin to English highway boards and municipal corporations, and to persuade local citizens to take responsibility for providing roads, streets and bridges in the few main towns. Parish Road Trusts and District Councils were provided for in New South Wales in 1840 and 1842, Adelaide had the first elected municipal council in Australia in 1840; Sydney and Melbourne were incorporated in 1842.[5] In 1838 and 1841 provision was made for Town Trusts in Western Australia. Hobart Council was established in 1852, Brisbane in 1859. For the most part there was little demand for or enthusiasm about these developments. Most schemes 'reflected the desire of the Home Authorities to lessen the cost of such services [roads and bridges] to the Imperial Government'.[6] Local groups could scarcely be expected to share this desire. The new authorities were short of resources, and sometimes found their legal powers inadequate to enforce the payments on which their work depended. Those who were elected or appointed to them, and the staffs they employed, were inexperienced in the work of local government.

An 1842 New South Wales statute for the compulsory incorporation of district councils, with powers to provide roads and schools, and which were to pay half the cost of the police, was ineffective. Sydney's first council ran into grave difficulties soon after its establishment, and was replaced by appointed commissioners from 1854–57. In Perth the Town Trust of 1842 'practically ceased to function' in the later 1840s, and in 1856 'was again entirely without finance or labour to carry out local works'.[7] There was a parallel story in Adelaide, and the *South Australian* bewailed that 'the advantages of the representative principle are at a terrible discount in South Australia'.[8] Things were not helped by the economic depression of the mid-1840s. However, Melbourne's Council managed to set an example that encouraged in Victoria a readier acceptance of the opportunities of the permissive system of local incorporation. By 1875 a general pattern of local government was firmly established in that State.

Between 1854 and 1871, starting with Victoria, each of the Australian colonial parliaments adopted a Municipalities Act (under varying titles) that permitted, but did not require, the formation of a municipal corporation if certain conditions were fulfilled. Some improvements were made to the 1858 New South Wales Act by further legislation in 1867, and important steps were taken in that State in the 1880s when loans and other assistance were authorised for water supplies, gasworks and the construction of town halls and council chambers.[9] However, large areas of New South Wales remained unincorporated, their needs supplied (if at all) by the Department of Public

Works, under pressure from the local member of parliament. In default of local government, *ad hoc* statutory authorities, wholly or partly appointed by the colonial government, started to multiply, especially in the metropolitan area.[10] Some States moved from permissive to compulsory incorporation in the later nineteenth century, as Queensland did in 1878. In the suburbs of capital cities and some country towns there had developed by the 1880s communities stable and prosperous enough to encourage successful attention to civic affairs. However, there were many places where the area incorporated, the funds available and the quality of the persons elected or employed were hopelessly inadequate. As late as 1906 in New South Wales, only 56 per cent of the population, and less than 1 per cent of the area of the State, were within the local government system.

The establishment of local government was a long and painful process. It had little political drive behind it. In Britain new political contenders, such as Labour and Socialist groups, fought some of their early battles in the local field. What local authorities controlled or provided was important enough to make this challenge worthwhile, and the height of the barriers in national politics made it expedient to take some local hurdles first. In Australia's more open political society such groups moved with relative ease into wider political arenas. The development of local government continued to lack popular impetus. It waited until a higher level of government decided that local authorities should be built into the governmental system, whether the citizens were enthusiastic or not.

Developments and Problems since 1900

All the same, by the turn of the century the future outlook for local government appeared reasonably promising. The development of a general system of local government in New South Wales followed the passing of the Local Government (Shires) Act, 1905, and the Local Government (Extension) Act, 1906, later embodied in the Local Government Act, 1919. The first of these tackled the problem of sparsely settled rural areas by empowering the government to divide into shires the whole of the State outside the City of Sydney, existing municipalities, and the Western Lands Division (which acquired local government only in the 1950s); and to compel the incorporation of those shires for specific tasks. It was expected that the State government would have to subsidise shires because the latter were to take over jobs of roadmaking and maintenance and so on, which were beyond their financial powers and which had formerly been a State responsibility. Their functions, it was hoped, would be gradually extended. The 1906 Act repealed the permissive system and laid the basis for a general municipal system with a detailed statement of rules about formation, procedure, financial organisation and functions. At the time the aim was stated in wide and generous terms as being to provide for the perfectly natural and free growth of the local governing body in powers, functions and responsibilities *pari passu* with the needs caused by growth and development of the district and the State.[11]

Future plans were also announced to concentrate all local administration in one local authority by handing over many of the functions performed by harbour trust, fire board, traffic commissioners, as well as some jobs done by State departments. Local authorities were expected to increase in importance over the years. Queensland passed a new Local Authorities Act in 1902, under which statute and its amendments most of the State has been incorporated. Tasmania did the same in 1906. Western Australia legislated several times between 1892 and 1911.

The expectations of this period have not been fulfilled, though there have been positive gains, and talk of the decline of local government is not justified. In the field of community welfare and cultural affairs, for example, local authorities have made creditable advances in recent years. In New South Wales, for example, the provision of community centres, child health centres, special facilities for old people and a network of local libraries all belong to the last generation. Moreover the local government services in every State are much better organised and professionalised than they were early in this century. Qualifications are usually now laid down for appointment as town clerks, engineers, health officers and so on; training schemes have been developed; associations of local government employees, and of elected members of councils, have encouraged administrative and technical improvements. Town halls are more efficient institutions than they were. The occasional scandal that is headlined, or the petty stupidities and narrow attitudes that still exist, should not prevent us from recognising real achievement.

The Area Problem

Of the three levels of government, Commonwealth, State and local, only local governments face the periodical threat of changes in their territorial areas. When services become expensive to provide, or when uniform or larger-scale provision or regulation is desired, State governments have several possible lines of action open to them. They can take this function away from local government and manage it themselves, either departmentally or by establishing a special authority. They can encourage or require the formation of some joint organisation, through which existing local authorities can act co-operatively. Or they can adjust the boundaries of local units to give them greater size and financial capacity. In all States the generation of electricity, and sometimes its distribution, have become State responsibilities. In most metropolitan areas the provision of water, sewerage and drainage is the responsibility of some special authority, such as the Metropolitan Water Sewerage and Drainage Board in Sydney, or of a State government department. In all States the tendency has been to decrease the number of local authorities, though the number of local councils in Australia fell by only about 15 per cent between 1911 and 1971. In New South Wales the number of municipalities halved between 1920 and 1970, but there was only a 2 per cent reduction in the number of shires.

This question is one of the touchiest in the whole field of State–local relations. Methods of making such decisions vary, though they are usually tackled piecemeal. In some States, a Local Government Boundaries Commission examines proposals put before it, and makes recommendations to the Minister for Local Government. Some local authorities are certainly too small to be efficient. They fail to use fully the executive skills of their staff, or cannot provide proper support-staff. In small councils, the Municipal Commission of Tasmania said, in 1974,[12] the council clerk

> will be required to perform many functions other than those of the administrative head of an organisation. He will also be the clerk, the accountant, the works overseer, perhaps the building inspector and even the dog inspector and noxious weeds inspector.

In 1974 only 13 of the 137 local authorities in South Australia could support full-time engineers.[13] The position is not so bad in New South Wales and Victoria. However, even many of the larger councils find it hard to maintain a good town planning staff and to provide the various kinds of specialised talent needed to cope with the problems of, say, an expanding industrial suburb. There is also unnecessary duplication of buildings and equipment. Many shire councils now depend on large grants-in-aid to survive, even though they are often providing only a narrow range of services to the local community.

> It was said that small areas provide the greatest opportunity for public participation in local government. The right of local individuals and groups to participate in local government is, of course, fundamental to a democratic society. . . . At this stage, we wish only to make the point that this right is of little value *if there is no real government in which to participate.*[14]

It is true that local councils have co-operated for some purposes. Apart from the New South Wales county councils, there have been a few wider groupings. Regional library services are quite common, and some States have encouraged the growth of regional planning authorities with local government representation, as mentioned later in this chapter. There is now some co-operation in using heavy equipment, and some local authorities are learning to take advantage of economics of scale by contracting out to other councils or private contractors. In 1977 New South Wales local councils, with aid from the State government, established a Management Services Unit within the Local Government and Shires Associations. Local councils are finding it harder to pay for the specialist help they need, and 'to build up groups of officers of a size adequate to provide for good teamwork and really expert advice, in a manner that matches the expertise of other levels of government'.[15]

No State has sponsored as thorough an investigation as that undertaken by the Royal Commissions on Local Government in Greater London, and on Local Government in England and Wales. Such inquiries were concerned with more than areas and boundaries, because recommendations on these cannot be effectively dissociated from questions of function and finance, and they were also given the means to organise their own research. Local government inquiries in Australia have usually had restricted terms of reference, and sometimes been open to the charge that the State government is manoeuvring to suit itself. In 1945 a Royal Commission on Local Government Areas in the County of Cumberland (i.e. in Sydney's metropolitan region) was appointed. But the terms of reference were so narrow, and the assumptions and attitudes of the three Commissioners so dissimilar, that three different sets of recommendations were made.[16] All that happened was a series of amalgamations that reduced the number of metropolitan councils from 68 to 39. One of these changes, enacted by a State Labor government in 1948, extended the area of the city of Sydney to embrace eight adjoining authorities. The inclusion of industrial suburbs, and some re-districting of the city for local electoral purposes, were seen by many critics as intended to ensure Labor control of the council. In 1967, a new non-Labor government redrew the boundaries of the city so that it lost the industrial suburbs added in 1948. One view of this change was that it was also politically inspired; another that the central city area has its own problems that justify a separate authority. The scheme was based on an extremely restricted inquiry by the Local Government Boundaries Commission. Given the limitations of their terms of reference, the Commission's recommendations may have been as good as they could manage.

There has recently been a spate of more impartial local government inquiries, including the (Barnett) Committee of Inquiry into Local Government Areas and Administration in New South Wales; the South Australian (Ward) Royal Commission into Local Government Areas; the Report of the Municipal Commission of Tasmania; and of the Local Government Assessment Committee in Western Australia. These have in part reflected a growing concern with the financial and administrative inadequacies of local councils at a time when new demands are being made on their services. The recommendations all proposed a sharp reduction in the number of local authorities, from 223 to 97 in New South Wales, from 137 to 74 in South Australia, and so on. Their terms of reference prevented much discussion of functions, though some were able to make recommendations on internal administration. 'Faced with widespread opposition the State governments, without exception, have failed to proceed with the implementation of the various proposals for reform.'[17] At times there has seemed to be an unholy alliance of conservative council members and 'progressive' action groups preaching that 'small is beautiful'. Further attempts at statewide reform now seem to be unlikely, and there has been a reversion to piecemeal change through Boundaries Commissions.

222 GOVERNMENT ADMINISTRATION IN AUSTRALIA

Metropolitan Planning and Metropolitan Government

The great metropolitan area is a modern phenomenon in all countries and under all economic and social systems. Some common developments can be observed in London, Moscow, New York, Tokyo, Bombay, and dozens of other major cities. The pattern is recognisable also in the major cities of Australia.[18] But there is a special feature of the Australian scene, though there may well be roughly comparable problems in some other parts of the world, such as Canada, South America, Northern Ireland or even Scotland (no one has been interested in exploring such comparisons). Each State is a kind of city-state, with the capital as metropolis and no other town remotely comparable with it. In Victoria, Melbourne—with a population of 2.66 million (72 per cent of the State's population)—is in a strong position of leadership; and the next biggest city, Geelong, is close enough to make likely a great urban area linking the two. In New South Wales the dominant position of Sydney—with a population of 2.92 million (61 per cent of the State's population)—is almost as unchallengeable.* The two other most flourishing urban centres, Newcastle and Wollongong, are both on the coast, and have important links with Sydney. The one really significant urban centre not on the Australian coastline is Canberra, the national capital, though the Bathurst-Orange complex is expected to reach 70 000 in the early 1980s.

This situation has had important consequences for the government of major cities. The State government is always an active participant in the management of the capital's affairs. In Brisbane, where in 1925 there was created a Greater Brisbane Council, as one product of an era of local government reform which also gave Queensland adult franchise, compulsory voting, and direct election of mayors, there have been difficulties in establishing a workable relationship between State and city government. The uneasy relations between State and metropolitan authorities are also illustrated by the history of the former Cumberland County Council in New South Wales.

(i) New South Wales   Other Greater City schemes in the capitals have come to nothing. The creation of the London County Council (1888) aroused interest in Sydney at the turn of the century, when the City Council was being charged with mismanagement and the need for some metropolitan provision had already produced a Metropolitan Water Board. Sidney Webb visited Australia in 1898, lecturing on municipal government in Britain and especially on the London County Council.[19] Legislation was promised in 1902 but did not appear. Ten years later, a bill providing for a convention to plan Sydney's government was introduced, delayed by Legislative Council opposition, and then dropped. A Royal Commission on Greater Sydney was appointed in 1913 and its findings resulted in a Greater Sydney Bill, but this also failed, as did proposals made in 1927 and 1931.[20]

---

* Adelaide is another striking case, as it contains about 73 per cent of the population of South Australia. Metropolitan figures are for the relevant 'Statistical Division' in 1975.

Immediately after the war there was the Report of the Royal Commission on Local Government Areas in the County of Cumberland, already mentioned, which led to some reduction in the number of municipal areas. More important was the establishment in 1945 of the Cumberland County Council as the land-use and planning authority for the Sydney metropolitan area.[21] This body was itself the product of compromise. The original bill made the Minister for Local Government, with an Advisory Committee, the metropolitan planning authority. Pressure from local government led to the creation of the Cumberland County Council (CCC), the ten members of which were elected by local councils, and which shared planning powers with the minister. Some people hoped that it might have its functions extended beyond those of town planning, to become a multi-purpose second-tier local authority. But even its planning responsibilities proved very difficult to fulfil. For the first time there was a government authority specifically responsible for examining the Sydney area, estimating its future needs, and making plans to meet them; and much good work was done. However, the CCC had neither staff nor authority nor resources to resist pressures, or to do the things that might have relieved the pressures on it, such as acquiring land and planning new towns. Its composition meant that some members were slow to appreciate or support what its professional planning staff proposed. The State government was not united in supporting the Council, nor could it regard a group of local council members as entitled to make policy for it. The Department of Local Government was itself poorly staffed and the great statutory authorities mostly unhelpful. The rapid rate of population growth compounded the problem.

A good example of Sydney planning deficiencies in this period is Mount Druitt, to which the Housing Commission of New South Wales was attracted by the existence of virgin land on which it could build large numbers of houses cheaply. From the planning point of view, the Cumberland County Council would have preferred to see more consolidation of existing urban areas, and in the longer run was looking further afield to Campbelltown as a satellite. The Minister of Local Government settled the dispute in favour of the Housing Commission. At the same time it was agreed that Mount Druitt should be more than a housing estate. However, though more comprehensive plans were prepared, the CCC lacked the power and resources to see that they were implemented, and the local council could not cope with the task. As a result land values were inflated, many community needs remained unfilled and local employment opportunities were poor. The State Planning Authority, which replaced the CCC, finally built a town centre. Some of the lessons of Mount Druitt have been applied to the Macarthur Growth Centre in the Campbelltown–Camden area, where the State Planning Authority achieved much better co-ordination of the plans of the various agencies involved.

The State Planning Authority (1964) was another product of compromise, which in its final form had a Chairman, Associate Chairman and fourteen part-time members, including five local government representatives and the

heads of various State government agencies. It was not concerned only with
the Sydney metropolis, but had statewide responsibilities.[22] It saw itself as
an overall co-ordinator, but the task was for the most part too great for
a largely part-time committee and its subcommittees, and it had too little
political backing at cabinet level. However, it had some achievements to its
credit. For the first time important statutory bodies like the Water Board
and even the transport authorities found themselves agreeing on the need
for co-ordinated action, even if actual results left much to be desired.

The State Planning Authority was replaced in turn (1974) by a Planning
and Environment Commission with three full-time commissioners and only
two part-time members. It has proposed a regional planning scheme for the
State,[23] but nothing much has happened at the time of writing. A new minister
has taken over the functions of the Minister for Local Government in the
planning field, the Minister for Planning and Environment.

Within this changing framework, local councils have prepared planning
schemes, and have for some years been encouraged to appoint planning
officers. This has meant that in some areas for the first time comprehensive
studies have been made of urban centres, topography, traffic and so on. But
not all local councils appoint full-time and fully qualified planning officers,
there has been a shortage of experienced planners to appoint, and few councils
able to build up a reasonably large group of planners.

In some respects, the large Australian cities are less desperately in need
of metropolitan government because schools are not locally controlled or
provided, nor are police or fire protection or public transport or public
housing. The lack of a metropolitan authority does not mean that one locality
necessarily has far more generous welfare services than another (though there
are differences and areas of special need are sometimes under-provided). This
does not mean that all these services are adequately supplied, nor that the
activities of the various State agencies, many of them statutory corporations,
are well co-ordinated. One of the problems is to ensure that separate State
agencies concerned with transport, roadbuilding, harbours, water and sewerage, power, education, housing—some of them powerful, and used to going
their own way—work within a common strategy. The course of urban
development has often owed more to the decisions of water boards, housing
and transport authorities, than to overall planning decisions. Some have
argued that a change in local government is not the primary need if we want
to have better social services or urban redevelopment, but new governmental
arrangements in which State and Commonwealth agencies play an important
part.

Others believe that the political impetus needed to achieve results can only
be achieved by the creation of some elected body for the whole metropolitan
area, and having general responsibility for its development; an authority
whose plans could be subjected to public scrutiny and whose leadership would
encourage interest in metropolitan affairs. The metropolis lacks a voice to
speak for it. Short of this, which will be hard to achieve, metropolitan local

authorities should at least combine to set up a central secretariat to promote research, run seminars and maintain high-level contact with State and federal authorities. There does seem to be developing a greater disposition of local councils to co-operate on matters of common interest affecting the metropolitan area. The Barnett Committee considered the notion of a two-tier system of government for metropolitan Sydney, and concluded that local government needed more time and opportunity to demonstrate its ability to undertake major metropolitan functions at present in State hands.[24] They thought that a first step should be a drastic reduction in the number of local councils in the metropolitan area, combined with a joint metropolitan committee to maintain contact and to explore co-operative projects.

An alternative sometimes offered to the continued growth of metropolitan cities is decentralisation. In the past decentralisation policies have been too fragmented to make an appreciable impact, and the political pressures for 'balanced development'—in practice, giving most country towns a bit— remain strong. In 1969, the Development Corporation of New South Wales, set up three years earlier to examine these problems, produced a *Report on Selective Decentralization* strongly favouring the selection of a small number of regional centres where growth might be accelerated to reach a population of a least 100 000–250 000. This policy of concentrating more resources on a limited number of 'growth centres' achieved wide acceptance in the next few years in both federal and State planning circles. The Commonwealth, New South Wales and Victoria co-operated in developing Albury–Wodonga. New South Wales took the initiative over Bathurst–Orange, though a large growth centre on the North Coast might have been more attractive to the average citizen. Development corporations were set up in 1974 for both these projects. However, development funds are likely to continue to be scattered widely, and economic stringency and the slowing-up of population growth have taken some impetus out of these schemes.

(ii) Metropolitan Problems in Other States   In Victoria, Melbourne has had a story not unlike that of Sydney, of a patchwork of over fifty local councils in the metropolitan area and proposals for Greater Melbourne government that 'all foundered at earlier or later stages on the rocks of apathy and the hostility of entrenched interests'.[25] In 1890 the Melbourne and Metropolitan Board of Works, representing metropolitan councils, was given functions similar to those of the Metropolitan Water Board in Sydney. However, the Board of Works had its functions extended; and a 1951 Bill, narrowly defeated in the State Upper House, would have incorporated it and thirty metropolitan councils in a new Greater Melbourne Council. Instead it was made the planning authority for the metropolis, and later the responsible authority for metropolitan main roads, bridges, parks and foreshores, but it lost most of the latter powers in 1974. It has also acquired a government-appointed chairman and deputy, and been (1978) reduced from over fifty to a small body of commissioners chosen by groups of local councils.

Its unwieldy size and conservatism had attracted criticism, as had its plans
for Melbourne's future growth. Meanwhile various intelligent proposals for
amalgamating the Melbourne City Council and adjacent councils have been
made and rejected.[26]

There have been a number of changes in statewide planning machinery
in Victoria. As a result, Victoria now has a State Coordination Council of
twelve, representing the heads of the main State agencies concerned with
planning, and advising a small Town and Country Planning Board, which
in turn advises the Minister for Local Government on strategic planning.
Regional planning authorities have been established in some areas composed
of representatives of local councils. The Board of Works remains the chief
planning authority for the metropolis.

Neither Melbourne nor Sydney has been very successful at coping with
its metropolitan problems. Some writers give the palm to Adelaide, though
not to the official town planners (at least not since Colonel Light laid out
the original plan) so much as to the industrial programme that reshaped
the city after 1934, and 'to the way in which a handful of unusually educated
men came to control a few of its public services in the 1930s'.[27] Though
South Australia passed a Town Planning and Development Act in 1920, a
comprehensive town plan for the Adelaide metropolitan area was not
produced until 1962. At State level there is now a Department of Housing,
Urban and Regional Affairs.

In general one may say that urban planning in Australia up to the 1970s
was a failure, certainly so in the great centres of population. This was partly
because of lack of public support, but also the result of institutional inertia.
It has been argued that what was achieved mainly benefited the more affluent,
and may even have helped to disadvantage the poor.[28]

(iii) The National Capital   Canberra is not yet a metropolitan area in the
same sense as the six State capitals, but its population is over 210 000 (1979)
and until recently was increasing rapidly. It is governed by various Commonwealth departments and agencies (see Chapter Three), including the
Department of the Capital Territory. There is also an advisory Legislative
Assembly of eighteen elected members; and a planning authority, the
National Capital Development Commission (1958), which has a large
responsibility for implementing its own plans, and considerable achievements
to its credit.[29] There is fairly general recognition that the form of self-
government appropriate to Canberra should not be one modelled on existing
Australian councils, mainly because of the special nature of the national
capital. In the Australian Capital Territory, the Commonwealth government
exercises responsibilities elsewhere shared with both State and local governments. So potential functions for a 'local' council include the whole range
of State functions, though it is unlikely that the Commonwealth government
would or should surrender the control of any function that relates mainly
to Canberra's role as a national capital.[30] Following the report of a Task

Force on Self-Government in the Australian Capital Territory, the government decided in 1976 that legislative and executive functions would be 'delegated' to an elected ACT Assembly, and the Minister for the Capital Territory released proposals in September 1977 with the stated aim of encouraging public debate and comment. The delegated functions would include building controls, cleansing and garbage services, cultural and recreational activities, most health and hospital services, housing, police, schools and technical colleges, water supply and sewerage, welfare services, and power to levy local rates and normal State taxes. Many existing statutory authorities would become responsible to the Assembly, but the National Capital Development Commission would remain independent. Government and parliament would retain a veto power over ordinances of the Assembly, and the government would retain power to make ordinances 'in the interests of the national capital or the seat of government'.

Regionalism

In Australia the term 'region' is mostly applied to units intermediate between States and local councils, with the implication that the States are too large for certain tasks, and local councils too small. In contrast, in America it usually applies to units comprising several States, implying that the latter are too small for some purposes, and the federal government too big. This may suggest that no one is ever satisfied with the governmental units they happen to have, and that the search for the ideal 'region' represents some kind of Utopian quest. It is always tempting to imagine that there is some ideal set of areas combining the advantages of the big and the small, of planning and participation.

The distinction is sometimes drawn between the movement 'upwards to region', growing from co-operation between local bodies, and 'downwards to region', where State or federal government has taken the initiative. Most Australian regionalism has been of the latter kind, though there have been one or two spontaneous regional movements such as the New States Movement (which now seems to be dead).[31] Local government can point to little more in the way of collaboration than a few county councils and one or two metropolitan authorities. The typical region in Australia has arisen from the wish of a State, or more recently the federal government, to administer some particular function in a more decentralised way. 'And rarely do the field officers of one central department or corporation talk across the line to their counterparts in the field offices of other central departments or corporations',[32] though efforts have sometimes been made to assist this by locating them in a common centre.

Hence regionalism in New South Wales, for example, mainly means that Departments like Education, Agriculture, Lands, Mines, Works, and statutory authorities such as the Health Commission and the Housing Commission have established regional or area or district or divisional offices, and that towns like Newcastle, Wollongong, Bathurst and Wagga Wagga have come to have quite a large number of regional officers stationed there with varying amounts of delegated power. In one or two cases, such as that of the New South Wales Health Commission, regionalisation of health and hospital services has been extensive, but in most fields regional offices are still mostly thought of as decentralised arms of the central department, not as vehicles for any distinctively regional point of view or interest. It has been regionalisation rather than regionalism, if one uses the latter to refer to a move towards devolution, with regional staffs being in some sense accountable to the regions they serve.[33] The State government has attempted to standardise regional boundaries and nine standard regions have been adopted, though not all agencies have confirmed to them.

It is true that in some States there have been developments that might be growing-points for regionalism. New South Wales has also established Regional Advisory Councils representing State government agencies, local councils and including private citizens from the region. They replaced the Regional Development Committees, which were created in a number of States after the Second World War but mostly achieved little. Officers in various local centres are also being appointed as Regional and Local Co-ordinators of State Administration, to keep in touch with all State government activities at their level, to plan better co-operation and co-ordination and to improve public access. For example, the Regional Director of Education in the Illawarra Region south of Sydney is also Regional Co-ordinator, and Local Co-ordinator for Wollongong. However, a State government proposal to establish Regional Development Corporations seems to have been ill-received and the future of the Advisory Councils is uncertain.

Extensive machinery for regional co-ordination has existed in Queensland. This large and differentiated State might seem to be well-suited to regionalism, and has also had the unique feature of a powerful Co-ordinator-General's Department under the Premier, to co-ordinate the whole State works programme. On this basis, legislation in 1971 provided for standard regions for the various State agencies (again, not all have adopted them), the appointment of Regional Co-ordinators, and of advisory Regional Co-ordination Councils. There were ten regions, and three Co-ordinators, all engineers in 1976 but with broader qualifications as well. Each was a high-level officer with a significant policy-making role in the Department, which gave him 'some leverage over . . . State government colleagues in his own regions';[34] but he was far from being a French prefect, and most lines of authority remained departmental. The ten advisory councils consisted in practice wholly of local government representatives (not the original intention), with a Regional Co-ordinator as chairman. Their main job was to advise the Co-ordinator-General on planned regional development and environmental matters. The Commonwealth government, in its activist 'regional' period (see below) used this machinery for local government grant aid and for the Area Improvement programme.

Local councils initially opposed the Queensland scheme, as a device for undermining local government, but once started it did seem to raise 'regional consciousness', and to improve communications between State and local government, though regional councils that excluded regional representatives of State agencies could not contribute greatly to regional co-ordination. However, the regional councils were disbanded without explanation in 1977. 'The reasons for the move are not clear although it seems that the councils were not functioning well in one or two of the ten regions, local government remained uneasy about a possible fourth tier of government, and the need for a system to counter national government intervention on a regional basis had disappeared following the defeat of the Whitlam Labor government.'[35]

In Western Australia, also large in area, the Court government has become interested in regionalism, stemming initially from its desire to cater for the special needs of the North-West. By 1977 seven Regional Administrators had been appointed or planned—they are mainly seen as 'activators', working with the local representatives of all levels and functions of government, and with outside groups, and helping to define the region's problems. The aim is to improve the delivery of State programmes and to involve the people of the area more in government. The scheme is operated through the Office of Regional Administration and the North-West in the Premier's Department. Regional Development Committees are also being established.

In the more compact State of Victoria, the government announced a policy of regionalisation in 1972–73. Ten regions were planned, grouped into five districts each with an administrative centre, as a basis for decentralising State administration.[36] A few regional planning authorities are also emerging under the Town and Country Planning Act (see above). South Australia is planning closer integration of services at the regional level, and the Public Service Board has appointed its first Regional Co-ordinator.

The Labor government of 1972–75 conducted some interesting regional experiments.[37] One was the Regional Councils for Social Development (RCSDs), created under the Australian Assistance Plan to promote new initiatives in social welfare.[38] They were in appearance highly participatory, with members elected at public meetings, and the initial aim of their more radical backers was to by-pass the existing local government and social welfare Establishment, and to create a new network of grassroots agencies closely linked with the social welfare agency in Canberra. 'While strengthening decentralisation in a social organism, one is at the same time strengthening centralisation and vice versa', as one of the scheme's chief planners wrote.[39] But the Regional Councils never seemed likely to become a permanent new unit of government, and the next government refused to participate in the programme. Mr Whitlam, as Leader of the Opposition, promised to restore the Australian Assistance Plan if re-elected but 'through the auspices of local government' and added that 'we made a mistake in 1973' in administering the scheme through non-local government bodies.[40]

Also under the Whitlam government, the then Department of Urban and

Regional Development (DURD) tried to develop a more comprehensive regional plan for the whole of Australia, which was finally divided into seventy-six regions, many of them corresponding to existing State regions. Within these, local councils were encouraged to form Regional Organisations of Councils (ROCs) to make proposals for federal financial assistance. These groups rarely became more than post offices for the demands of individual councils, though in a few cases there was genuine regional co-operation, as in the Area Improvement Program, an imaginative scheme of DURD to raise the quality of urban facilities and amenities in deprived areas. A number of other federal agencies developed regional schemes under Labor, each with its own regional office, and some serious co-ordination problems were arising by 1974.[41] The relation between RCSDs and ROCs was 'stormy, sometimes bitterly so'.[42] The former are now dead, but some Area Improvement Programs survive in an attenuated form, and a few Regional Organisations of Councils are still active, as in the Western Sydney region.

In all these developments, State and federal, there has never been any real indication that a fourth level of government was emerging in Australia, certainly not one with representative institutions or power to allocate resources. As Power and Wettenhall argue, the 'functional principle' has up to now won out, and regionalism is still viewed as a congeries of more-or-less decentralised programmes of various central departments and agencies.[43] The Coombs Commission saw part of the problem and, in tentative support of one of its Task Forces,[44] recommended as an experiment the appointment of a Commonwealth Government Representative to one or two regions. This official would not (at any rate initially) have many executive powers, but would be there primarily to develop contacts with all government agencies and community groups, to assess general needs and priorities, and to help co-ordinate the work of Commonwealth agencies in the region. The Coombs Report says that its concern is with more efficient administration, not with whether a new tier of regional government is needed.[45]

In 1977 the Fraser government accepted this idea and decided to appoint such a government representative in Townsville, Queensland, as an experiment in regional co-ordination; his authority is still undetermined at the time of writing.[46] There is some doubt, as the Coombs Report admitted, whether such a person can be effective in face of the various departmental representatives, each embedded in a functional hierarchy. He will have few of the powers of a French prefect, and even the latter's ability to control the work of more specialised colleagues is said to be declining. It may be that there is no purely administrative solution to the problem of creating an authority that can really express and co-ordinate regional needs.

Yet the chances of developing a new tier of regional government seem slight; and if it were to be an addition to, not a substitute for, State and local government, it might well leave Australia 'with a complex and unwieldy four-tier system of government'.[47] Another criticism of regionalism is that it can be used to evade what may be a more central problem, that of creating strong basic units of local government. It may be the case that 'a suitable restructuring of the present units of local government would strongly diminish the need for regional authorities',[48] though special provision might still be needed in a few fields. This is not to deny that the region may well become an important unit for research, and for the marshalling of information and advice, and that it will continue to be a basis for the decentralised administration of central government activities.

The Local Government System

Organisation

It is difficult to talk in general terms about local authorities, as they vary so much in area, population and income. In New South Wales, the Sydney City Council had in 1976 a total staff of over 2000, and a rate income of over $25m a year. A small municipality like Narromine had a total staff of only 18½ and a salaries and wages bill of $168 000. Warringah Shire served a population of 170 000 and had a staff of 832. But Windouran Shire had a population of under 600, and a staff of only 21, most of whom were manual workers. Thus some councils are the controllers of large and varied administrative organisations, while others are concerned only with minimum responsibilities, country roads, some health supervision and so on.

The size of Australian local councils usually ranges from five to fifteen members.[49] There are no large councils of a hundred or more, as sometimes exist in Britain, though one or two are larger than normal—the City of Melbourne has a Council of thirty-three. In New South Wales and Queensland, councils are elected every three years, with a turnover in New South Wales of about 30 per cent. In other States there is an annual election, at which one-third or one-half of the council is re-elected. Queensland and New South Wales have a parliamentary franchise—in the latter, owners and rate-paying lessees of land can vote wherever their land is, though only once for the same council. Some States still restrict the local government franchise, often to owners and occupiers of rateable property, and perhaps their spouses. One or two, like Tasmania, still have plural voting. Queensland has compulsory voting. New South Wales had it from 1947 to 1968, though laxly enforced. However, it was said to have caused an increase in party politics in local government; a Liberal–Country Party government abolished it, and the turnout in local elections fell from around 70 to around 30 per cent. Now it has been restored. In Victoria councils may have compulsory voting if they wish. Councils are often divided into wards, ridings or divisions for voting, but sometimes the whole authority is a single voting area. The number of women council members seems to be increasing, but was still only 3 per cent in some States in the early 1970s, though rising to 6 or 7 per cent in urban areas.[50]

The chairman of urban councils is usually called mayor, of rural councils president or chairman (Tasmania calls most chairmen warden). In Victoria, and most of Tasmania, he is elected by and from the council members. In other States, all or many mayors are directly elected by the voters, and in New South Wales some mayors and a few presidents of shire councils. There are no city managers,[51] no Home Rule charters, few or no recent constitutional experiments in local government. Even though most councils are small, they often do much of their work in committee, usually in private; others transact much detailed business in the full council or through 'committees of the whole'. In some States there is limited provision for the co-option of outsiders on to committees, but advantage is rarely taken of this; the Barnett Committee recommended that councils be given more discretion in this matter. The New South Wales Act also allows for 'urban committees', as a kind of smaller community council within council areas, but this scheme has not come to much. The Barnett Committee proposed that in some council areas a sub-area might be proclaimed a 'community', with provision for a community council with minor powers, but mainly to act as a voice for local opinion.[52]

The major political parties are sometimes, but by no means universally, the chief contenders at local elections. The principal cities, especially capital cities, in any country are likely to be prizes that no national party will ignore. But even for these the contest is not always simply between parties, and the existence of purely local competing groups has its effect. In other councils there has been some increase in party politics, but there are still a large number of places where candidates do not even form groups for electoral purposes, but stand as individuals. One study of Victorian local government points to the absence of any ladder from local politics to other levels; in particular, Labor supporters are not plugged into local government in Victoria (and some other States), and the occupational structure of council members is sharply skewed towards the middle class.[53] It is true that experience of strong party divisions in local government has been generally unfortunate. Local elections are not contests for one local body, but for hundreds of different ones. There are common issues, but many more specific to each area. Too much concentration on party affiliations is almost certain to make the councils battlefields for contests on national or State issues, to the detriment of local concerns.

In principle, councillors are voluntary part-time workers for their area; though mayors and other council chairmen have expense allowances, and other councillors can be paid certain out-of-pocket expenses, and sometimes a small attendance fee—they are not salaried, except in Brisbane. However, the work can be time-consuming and involves certain clear duties. Councillors are responsible for all activities of the council and its staff, especially for the custody and proper control of the funds at their disposal. The council as a whole has certain things it must do, many things which it may do and some things that are expressly forbidden. There are obligations on a council concerning how it conducts its business, how its staff are appointed and employed, and the reports it must furnish. New South Wales legislation and ordinances probably give the most detailed listing of powers and duties. In Queensland some detail is avoided by giving councils a general power to make by-laws in all matters not pre-empted by other governments or expressly forbidden. In some States, councils must submit their budgets for examination by the Department of Local Government. Supervision and control of councils is especially thorough in New South Wales, where the drastic step has been taken, on twenty occasions since 1919, of dismissing a council under section 86 of the Local Government Act and replacing it for a period by a State-appointed Administrator. This is a final sanction; it has been used not only in cases of suspected or proven corruption or malpractice, but also in more instances where the offence has been inefficiency. Power may be exerted in other ways, as when in 1977 the New South Wales government told the Botany Council to hand over the processing of a development application by ICI, held up by the council, to the State's Planning and Environment Commission.

In all local authorities the council officially controls policy while an administrative staff, headed by the Town or Shire Clerk or equivalent officer, is the permanent organisation that carries out council decisions. The Clerk is usually the key figure in the local council. He is the secretary of its meetings and responsible for seeing that its decisions are carried out. He is often a well-paid officer, as in States such as New South Wales where his salary is geared to council revenues. In the best councils, he is in effect the chief adviser and general manager, who controls the staff and usually has considerable powers of appointment to all but the most senior positions. An engineer is also appointed, to be responsible for constructional activities, though it is possible for his services to be shared between smaller local authorities. Other key officials are the health officer and building inspector. Planning officers are becoming commoner, as are librarians, even trained social workers. Some reformers believe that local councils should have a chief administrative officer, with certain authority over the whole council staff and able to advise the council on policy as a whole.[54] There are councils in which the clerk already plays this role, though it does not have much formal recognition (in New South Wales, an ordinance under the Local Government Act does designate the clerk as chief administrative servant of the council with some general control over the the staff). In other councils, the clerk and the engineer function as co-equals; this may work well enough in some authorities, especially the smaller ones, but does not appear to meet the need for co-ordination in larger units.

Not much imagination or enterprise has been shown in the training of local government officers, though courses in local government administration are now being improved in the States, helped by the newly developing structure of colleges of advanced education.[55] An educational function (among others) is served by associations of council members—such as the Municipal Association of Victoria (formed in 1879) and the Local Government Association of New South Wales—and of local government officers. There is now also an Australian Council of Local Government Associations with a permanent secretariat in Canberra, one of whose functions is to encourage training and research, though its primary purpose is to be a lobby. The pertinent point has been raised by Donald Purdie whether the present local government structure can adequately use the talents of the officers produced by improved systems of education.[56]

For most purposes local councils are under the supervision of one State government department, usually a Department of Local Government. But councils also have frequent contacts with other departments. A good deal of the engineer's work is concerned with roads, where his staff may be largely working on behalf of the State's main roads department. A health inspector, though responsible to the council, has most of his duties imposed by a State health authority. In providing welfare facilities councils may work closely with the State social service agencies, in local planning with planning authorities. The State Treasury will keep an eye on loans policy.

If councils have enough money, if they are energetic, and if they have support for their policies, there are many things beyond their basic responsibilities that they may do. Among other things, most councils have powers covering the provision of libraries, markets, playgrounds and sporting facilities, art galleries, child care centres, community centres, and so on. There are activities which councils may subsidise, as well as ones they may provide directly. The factors that decide whether any of these powers will be used and whether the local authority will become something more than a local provider of roads and drainage are principally these: how far its area has already been developed; how acceptable its policies are to local ratepayers; how much money it can raise. Money and local support are crucial factors.

Local Finance

The current revenue of local councils is derived from four main sources: rates on local property, grants from the State government, income from public enterprises, and local licences and fees.

Australian local authorities are highly dependent on revenue from rates. Government grants were at one time mainly for roads, though there are now other subsidies for special purposes (e.g. water and sewerage schemes, libraries); and in recent years both Commonwealth and States have also given sizeable general purpose grants. In 1975–76 grants formed 27 per cent of current revenue; some country and shire councils have become heavily dependent on them to survive.

The largest item in council expenditure is on roads and streets; next are council properties (including recreational and cultural facilities) and health, sanitary and garbage services. The importance of council services should not be judged simply by a financial yardstick. Even if only a small percentage of revenue goes to a library service or to maintaining a centre for old people, or towards providing a trained social worker, subsidising an orchestra or improving a city square, the contribution of these to local community life is significant. In fact, the sums involved in such activities have been rising. In New South Wales, for example, local authority expenditure on cultural and recreational activities and social welfare was over $57 million in 1974–75, in Victoria over $47 million. Local councils have been expanding their

TABLE 9.1
Local Authorities: Receipts and Outlay 1974–75 ($m)

Receipts and Financing Items	NSW	Victoria	All States
Receipts—			
Rates	260.1	211.9	674.1
Licences	7.4	5.6	23.3
Income from public enterprises	52.7	3.2	98.9
Property income	24.9	8.0	43.4
State and federal grants	108.3	79.9	314.5
	453.4	308.6	1154.2
Balancing Items—			
Net borrowing	70.8	29.4	199.7
State and federal advances	5.6	0.3	17.3
Reduction in balances	30.6	−0.9	7.2
Other (depreciation allowances, etc.)	19.5	8.5	39.0
	126.5	37.3	263.2
Outlay			
General Public Services	70.8	84.6	240.0
Roads, etc.	190.7	108.2	459.0
Electric and gas	78.2	3.2	91.7[a]
Water supply	11.0	0.4	31.5[b]
Recreation and culture	54.0	40.1	150.4
Health	12.7	12.5	33.0
Environmental protection	40.7	18.4	129.3
Community and regional development	5.3	2.6	12.6
Social welfare	3.1	7.6	12.5
Education	0.2	4.3	4.7
Other expenditures	54.9	42.3	98.5
Interest paid	58.6	21.8	142.0
Total Outlay	579.9	345.9	1417.6
Of which—			
Current outlay	194.6	157.2	539.0
Capital outlay	385.3	188.7	878.6

[a] Local authorities, mostly grouped into thirty-four county councils, still retail electricity in New South Wales. They play little part in other States, save in areas of Melbourne and in some Queensland shires.
[b] New South Wales and Queensland are the only States where local councils play a significant part in water supply.
Source: Official Year Book of Australia, 1975–76.

functions in the personal social services and many have powers in fields such as child care, clinics, home care services, old people's clubs and so on, if they care to use them. In Victoria (1977) about eighty out of two hundred and ten councils employed social workers, but this is more than in most States, and the amount local councils spend on personal care services is still small. The advance in the early 1970s was much of it based on specific Commonwealth grants and now these have dried up, this limits local interest.[57]

The chief source of local government revenue is the 'rate', or property tax. Rates are normally levied on either the unimproved capital value (UCV) or site value* of the land, or on the annual value of land and buildings. UCV is the main basis of rating in New South Wales and Queensland. Annual value has been the main basis in several other States, though often both systems are used. In Western Australia cities and towns generally use annual value, and shires UCV. One of the merits of land value rating is supposed to be that it encourages owners to put their land to full use, or sell it to someone else who will do so, but other factors are probably more important in determining the rate of development. The fact that it disregards the actual use made of a site is sometimes said to offend against the criterion of 'ability to pay'. It can cause some hardships; the increased value of a site may not be realisable except by selling the asset, which may include the ratepayer's home. This effect is mitigated where councils can levy a lower residential use rate, or are allowed to give complete or partial relief from rates to certain categories, such as pensioners. A case can be made for both methods of rating, and for combinations of the two.[58]

Councils may also raise loans for capital works, but the total amount available partly depends on Loan Council allocations (see Chapter Seven) and the distribution among councils is a matter for the State government. Local government spokesmen regret that no one represents them directly at Loan Council meetings. One or two States (not New South Wales) permit the profits from trading undertakings, such as markets, to be used as general revenue, but this is never more than a minor source of income.

For the most part, rates are the only independent source of revenue. In some other countries, especially in continental Europe and North America, local authorities have special local dues to supplement their property taxes, and the latter often have a wider scope. There are taxes on entertainment and motor vehicles, sales and business taxes. In many places a local income tax is imposed. Australian local authorities may seem financially deprived by comparison. However, the European and North American systems are based on a tacit acceptance of local responsibility and local benefit or deprivation. A local income tax may benefit a rich locality: it may leave a poor one inadequately served. Any considerable development of new sources of local revenue, raised at local discretion, must cut across the general policy

---

* UCV has differed from 'site value', by excluding certain other improvements to the site as well as visible structures.

of redistribution between poorer and richer areas that has become firmly embedded in the Australian system.

All the same, local rates are no more popular in this country than in any other. Councils wish they had more flexible and less noticeable taxes to rely on, and assertions are common that local rates have reached the upper limit that property owners can bear. In Australia home-ownership is commoner than in most countries, so a large percentage of the population is immediately conscious of the incidence of rates, even though the percentage they form of personal income is lower than in many countries including America, Britain and Canada. Nor is there evidence that rates in general form a much higher percentage of incomes than they have in the past. Rates and land taxes rose from 1.01 per cent of gross national product in 1949–50, to 1.49 per cent in 1972–73. In 1970 property taxes (other than death duties) in Australia represented only 5.8 per cent of total taxation, as compared with 10.5 per cent in the United Kingdom and 15.5 per cent in the United States,[59] and the percentage has been falling in recent years.

Such grievances were strongly enough expressed in New South Wales for the State government to set up a Royal Commission on Rating, Valuation and Local Government Finance. The Commission considered that rates were still the most convenient local tax, but that they might be supplemented in various ways, such as: a poll tax not exceeding $20 a year on residents over seventeen; a licence fee on businesses and clubs; tourist and entertainment taxes. The report also recommended that most Crown land (except railways) be rateable, and some other kinds of property previously exempt. Most of these recommendations were either formally rejected, or received without enthusiasm. However, in 1968 the New South Wales government agreed to establish a Local Government Grants Commission to distribute an annual Assistance Fund to local councils, now (1979) $8.25 million. Other states have created similar bodies.

In countries such as Britain, America and Canada, grants have formed a larger percentage of local revenue, but their local authorities have much wider functions, especially in social welfare and education. Most Australian grants up to 1973 were still specific purpose grants disbursed by the States, though these included fairly large sums for roads, where the Commonwealth met part of the bill through payments to local councils through the States. Another example of a specific purpose grant is the library grant. In many States library subsidies are provided on a dollar-for-dollar basis up to a certain maximum.[60] However, in general there has been no great feeling in State circles that local councils should be encouraged greatly to expand their functions, or to have more public money at their disposal to spend as they pleased.

The Commonwealth Labor government wished to improve the position of local government, with at least one eye on by-passing the States and creating a framework of regional administration. A referendum proposal in 1974 to give the Commonwealth parliament a general power to finance local

238 GOVERNMENT ADMINISTRATION IN AUSTRALIA

governing bodies on such terms and conditions as it thought fit was defeated. However, the Commonwealth began to make large unconditional block grants available to local government, with a strong equalising element built into them. Non-Labor governments have continued such grants, but on a somewhat different basis. Under the income tax-sharing arrangements (see Chapter Seven) a percentage of personal income tax revenue is earmarked for local government. The Grants Commission recommends how this is to be divided between States, but within the latter it is allocated by State Grants Commissions; each council gets a share of at least 30 per cent of the total, mainly on a population basis; the rest is to be allocated on 'a general equalisation basis',[61] but the precise formula is left to the State commission. Under this scheme local government will get $179.4 million from the Commonwealth in 1978-79.

The Commonwealth Labor government also made new specific purpose grants to local government in the social welfare field, for unemployment relief, and including aid to regional groupings, as under the Area Improvement Program. Some of these have now been ended or greatly reduced. The present reliance on general grant increases may help to freeze the local government structure.

Future Prospects

Local government in Australia does not present an exciting picture of enterprise and enthusiasm. It consists of a large number of administrative units, varying greatly in size and resources, usually discharging with reasonable efficiency a variety of essential jobs. Counterbalancing the occasional failure there is a quite impressive list of areas where the local council has shown leadership in community effort. There are temptations offered by some councils' control of land use and in the contracts they have to offer, and the record of council members (and occasionally of their officials) can show a few bad examples of betrayal of public trust. But the general standard of honesty and responsibility is high. If some councils, or individual members of them, are parochial, narrow-minded, interested in commercial development first and in cultural or welfare activities last—are they singularly unrepresentative of their electors?

For those who are dissatisfied with local council policy, one long-term remedy is to seek election. The new council member may be tamed by finding that decisions are by a majority, to which he may not belong, or by discovering that the council's time and money are not as elastic as previously imagined. Even if the citizen's interest is too spasmodic or short-lived to seek election, there are some other ways of influencing the situation. There is the right to attend council meetings and to have produced certain information, including financial statements. There are circumstances where legal remedies may be sought. There are open the usual political methods of letters, meetings, petitions and deputations. Such channels are generally under-used.

It is true that councillors and their officers do not usually feel that the local public is indifferent to what the council is doing. Most of them are bombarded by individual requests and complaints, and must often pray for a little more apathy. All the same, people are not well-informed about local government, and only a few local councils have done much to encourage them to understand the system and its policies.

Local government is not so obviously the basis of a 'self-governing democracy' as is sometimes assumed by its supporters. Doubt has already been cast on the claim that local government was once in Australia a vigorous form of self-government, from which it has now declined. Even in Britain the contribution of local government to the 'democratic' tradition was not one of wide participation. British local authorities almost until this century were in the hands of privileged local minorities, though they did act as restraints on central power. But Australian local authorities have never been independent in this sense. Indeed local authorities are more effectively part of the general political system than they were fifty years ago. Nor can we identify democracy simply with direct participation in government, liberty of protest and equality of opportunity may be at least as important.

Even if we were to identify democracy with participation, such a democratic tradition has not depended here in any important way on local councils. Self-government, self-determination and responsibility for political decisions can be developed in a number of ways. Because Australian local authorities are in important respects the administrative agents of State government, the politically active may pursue their claims by participation in State or federal politics; or by working through any of the numerous associations and organisations that may present claims at any level of government. Enthusiasm for local councils may wane not because democracy is dying, but because even those interested in participation choose other avenues for their activities.

There are some fairly serious obstacles to local government playing a much wider role that it does at present. One is that many authorities are too small. It is true that there is a wide dispersion, and about half the population live in council areas with a population of over 50 000,[62] mainly in the big cities. But it has never been the practice to discriminate much between authorities in terms of size. Power and Wettenhall have suggested that a more flexible approach is needed by which State and Commonwealth governments would set guidelines for the devolution of resources and functions, which might for example require certain populations to be reached for particular local and regional authorities to qualify.[63] At any rate those who believe that local councils should be more important units of government need to think hard about financial and other strategies for bringing this about. The States need better-staffed and more creative Departments of Local Government, concerned with policy as well as supervision.

In the past local government has concentrated on providing physical facilities, and enforcing building, health and other regulations. This has also

created some attitudes inimical to progress. Engineers have counted for much
more than social workers. Local councils enforce many minor by-laws, from
housing and town-planning regulations to car-parking and dog control, and
have an image of petty coercion.[64] Sometimes the accusation of pettiness is
justified. In housing it has been said that many local councils operating in
the Sydney metropolitan area have created a labyrinth of 'inflexible and
discriminating control codes which . . . make it difficult for many disadvantaged and minority groups to operate in the metropolitan housing market'.[65]
Some councils also make demands on developers which pay small regard to
their effect on costs.

It has been suggested too that local councils have failed to develop
countervailing power in relation to other levels of government, which they
can only do by greater co-operation.[66] Actually local government seems to
have performed quite well as a pressure-group in the last few years. It is
a fairly conservative pressure group, as a majority of local councils are to
be found in small towns and rural areas, and to these we must add the middle-
class suburban authorities of the capital cities.

Notes

1. P.B. Spahn, *Issues of Municipal Reform and the Future Role of Local Governments in West Germany*, Centre for Research on Federal Financial Relations,
   ANU, Canberra 1976. Figures exclude intergovernmental transfers.
2. For a general survey of Australian local councils and their powers, see Margaret
   Bowman, *Local Government in the Australian States*, AGPS, Canberra, 1976.
3. For a case study of the forces making for centralisation, see M.J. Ely, 'The
   Mangement of Schools in New South Wales 1848–1880: Local Initiative Suppressed?', in R.N. Spann and G.R. Curnow (eds), *Public Policy and Administration
   in Australia: A Reader*, Wiley, Sydney, 1975, 247–258. For a different emphasis,
   see J.B. Hirst, *Adelaide and the Country 1870–1917*, Melbourne University Press,
   Melbourne, 1973, ch. 3.
4. J.B. Hirst, *op. cit.*, 145.
5. See F.A. Larcombe, *The Development of Local Government in New South Wales*,
   Cheshire, Melbourne, 1961, 17–24; and cf. Larcombe, *The Origins of Local
   Government in New South Wales, 1831–58*, Sydney University Press, Sydney, 1974.
6. J.R. Johns, 'Development of Local Government in Western Australia', *Public
   Admin.* (Sydney), VIII, 4, October–December 1949, 172.
7. *ibid.*, 176.
8. D. Pike, *Paradise of Dissent: South Australia, 1829–1857*, Melbourne University
   Press, Melbourne, 1957, 240, 245, 462; and Larcombe, *op. cit.*, 31.
9. For some fine examples of town halls and other public buildings of this period,
   see Morton Herman, *The Architecture of Victorian Sydney*, 2nd edn, Angus and
   Robertson, Sydney, 1964.
10. Larcombe, *op. cit.*, 53–66; and cf. Larcombe, *The Stabilisation of Local Government in New South Wales, 1858–1906*, Sydney University Press, Sydney, 1976.

11. Joseph Carruthers, Second Reading Speech, NSW Legislative Assembly, 1905, cited in R.S. Parker, *Highlights of Local Government Legislation in New South Wales*, Local Government Association of NSW, Sydney, 1956, 7.

12. *Report*, cit. D.M. Purdie, *Local Government in Australia*, Law Book Co., Sydney, 1976, 56.

13. Purdie, *op. cit.*, 135.

14. Report, NSW (Barnett) Committee of Inquiry into Local Government Areas and Administration, Government Printer, Sydney, 1973, 27 (referred to below as Barnett Report).

15. Barnett Report, 36.

16. See *Report*, Royal Commission into Local Government areas in the County of Cumberland, 1946.

17. Martin Rawlinson, 'Local Government Reform in Australia: The State Experience', *Public Admin.* (Sydney), XXXIV, 4, December 1975, 329. This article gives a short account of recent inquiries, as does D.M. Purdie, *op. cit.*, 70–89.

18. cf. Bruce Ryan, 'Metropolitan Growth', in R. Preston (ed.), *Contemporary Australia*, Durham, North Carolina, 1969, a good survey of facts and causes; and R.H. Leach, *The Governance of Metropolitan Areas in Australia*, ANU Press, Canberra, 1978.

19. See A.G. Austin (ed.), *The Webbs' Australian Diary, 1898*, Melbourne University Press, Melbourne, 1965, 29–31, 51; and cf. J.D. Fitzgerald, *Greater Sydney and Greater Newcastle* NSW Bookstall, Sydney, 1906. Fitzgerald was later the first New South Wales Minister for Local Government (1916–20).

20. On pre-war schemes, see J.D.B. Miller, 'Greater Sydney, 1892–1932', *Public Admin.* (Sydney), XVI, 2, 3, June and September 1954; and Larcombe, *op. cit.*, 69–77.

21. See Denis Winston, *Sydney's Great Experiment*, Angus and Robertson, Sydney, 1957; Peter Harrison, 'City Planning—What Went Wrong?', in Denis Watson *et al.* (eds), *Australian Cities—Chaos or Planned Growth?*, Angus and Robertson, Sydney, 1966, and 'Planning the Metropolis: A Case Study', in R.S. Parker and P.N. Troy (eds), *The Politics of Urban Growth*, ANU Press, Canberra, 1972; W.G. Clarke, 'Policy Conflict in the Green Belt Controversy', *Aust. Quarterly*, XXXII, 4, December 1960.

22. See Eileen V. Price, 'The Debate on the State Planning Authority Bill', *Public Admin.* (Sydney), XXVI, 3, September 1967; J. Colman, 'Sydney's Second Great Experiment', *Aust. Quarterly*, XLI, 1, March 1969; and Harrison in Parker and Troy, *op. cit.*

23. See *Towards a New Planning System for N.S.W.*, Planning and Environment Commission, November 1974; and *Proposals for a New Environment Planning System for N.S.W.*, June 1975.

24. Barnett Report, 44.

25. A.F. Davies, 'Local Government in Melbourne', *Public Admin.* (Sydney), XIV, 2, June 1955, 66; and cf. Margaret Bowman, 'Local Government in Melbourne', *Public Admin.* (Sydney), XXVIII, 4, December 1969.

26. Margaret Bowman, *op. cit.*, 330, 333; Robert Murray, 'How Local Should Local Government be?', *Australian Financial Review*, 3 October 1969; Report, Board of Inquiry into Local Government Finance in Victoria, Government Printer, Melbourne, 1972; and Holmes, *op. cit.*, 74–5.

27. Hugh Stretton, *Ideas for Australian Cities*, Georgian House, Melbourne, 1970, 142–3.
28. cf. Leonie Sandercock, *Cities For Sale: Property, Politics and Urban Planning in Australia*, Melbourne University Press, Melbourne, 1975.
29. See its annual reports, and Hugh Stretton, *op. cit.*, ch. 3, 'Inventing a City'.
30. For discussion, see Ruth Atkins, *The Government of the Australian Capital Territory*, University of Queensland Press, St Lucia, 1978.
31. But it has been pronounced dead before, and revived. The best survey is by R.S. Parker, in *New States for Australia*, Australian Institute of Political Science, Sydney, 1955.
32. J.M. Power and R.L. Wettenhall, 'Regional Government versus Regional Programs', *Aust. J. Public Admin.*, XXXV, 2, June 1976, 118. For a fuller picture of regional decentralisation, see John Power and Helen Nelson (eds), *The Regional Administrator in the Riverina*, Canberra College of Advanced Education, Canberra, 1976. Dean Jaensch (ed.), *The Politics of 'New Federalism'*, Australian Political Studies Association, Adelaide, 1977, 113–4, has a good reading list on regionalism by Michael Wood.
33. cf. Interim Report, Review of New South Wales Government Administration, Government Printer, Sydney, 1977, 82–3.
34. K. Wiltshire, 'Regional Co-ordination in Queensland', *Aust. J. Public Admin.*, XXXV, 2, June 1976, 136.
35. K. Wiltshire, 'Administrative Chronicle—Queensland', *Aust. J. Public Admin.*, XXXVI, 3, September 1977, 296.
36. Jean Holmes, *The Government of Victoria*, University of Queensland Press, St Lucia, 1976, 77–8.
37. For a summary of Commonwealth regionalism, see C.P. Harris, 'Federalism, Regionalism and Local Government, 1972–3 to 1976–7', in Dean Jaensch (ed.), *The Politics of 'New Federalism'*, Australian Political Studies Association, Adelaide, 1977.
38. See *Australian Assistance Plan: Discussion Papers 1 and 2*, Social Welfare Commission, Canberra, 1973 and 1974; and *A Survey of the Activities of Regional Councils for Social Development* . . . , Department of Social Security, Canberra, 1976.
39. T. O'Brien, 'Social Philosophy of the Australian Assistance Plan', *Aust. J. Social Issues*, 10, 2, May 1975, 139. This journal has printed several useful articles on the Plan. See also Leonard Tierney, *From Vague Ideas to Unfeasible Roles*, Department of Social Studies, University of Melbourne, Melbourne, 1977.
40. *Canberra Times*, 10 November 1977.
41. See the discussion in H.R. Dent, 'IDC on Overlap in Australian Government Grants to Local Bodies', in Report, RCAGA, Appendix Vol. Four, 308–23.
42. Dent, *op. cit.*, 311.
43. Power and Wettenhall, *op. cit.*
44. The Task Force reports are *Regionalising Government Administration*, RCAGA Discussion Paper No. 1, Canberra, 1975; and *A Regional Basis for Australian Government Administration*, RCAGA, Canberra, 1975.
45. Report, RCAGA, 153–6.
46. *Canberra Times*, 28 September 1977.
47. Barnett Report, 40–1.
48. Purdie, *op. cit.*, 161.

49. Their members are usually called councillors; in New South Wales and Queensland the term "alderman" is used in urban areas. In South Australia "aldermen" are additional councillors elected for the whole area, not for wards.

50. Purdie, *op. cit.*, 30, 31; and Margaret Bowman, *Local Government in the Australian States*, AGPS, Canberra, 1976, 30.

51. Launceston (Tasmania) experimented briefly with a city manager. See R.J.K. Chapman, 'An Experiment in Australian Local Government', *Public Admin.* (Sydney), XXVII, 4, December 1968. The Sydney County Council, an indirectly elected electricity board, has the council-manager system; on this topic, see Barnett Report, 52–4.

52. Barnett Report, 45.

53. Margaret Bowman, *The Suburban Political Process*, Department of Political Science, University of Melbourne, Melbourne, 1978, 3.

54. See Barnett Report, 47–54; and Purdie, *op. cit.*, 132–8.

55. For discussion, see H. Maddick, *Education and Training of Local Government Administrators in Australia*, Canberra, 1974; and D.M. Purdie, *op. cit.*, 115–28.

56. Purdie, *op. cit.*, 128.

57. On the general issues, see Social Welfare Commission, *The Role of Local Government in Social Welfare*, Canberra, 1976; and B. Manning, 'The Role of Local Government in Community Development', in *Local Government in Transition*, Centre for Research on Federal Financial Relations, Canberra, 1978.

58. For discussion, see *Report*, Royal Commission on Rating, Valuation and Local Government Finance, 1967, 54–72.

59. D.G. Davies, *International Comparison of Tax Structures in Federal and Unitary Countries*, Centre for Research on Federal Financial Relations, ANU, Canberra, 1976, 50, 24. United States figures are for 1973.

60. For details of these and other grants see, for example, the Annual Reports of Departments of Local Government. On public libraries generally, see Report, Committee of Inquiry into Public Libraries, Canberra, 1976.

61. Local Government (Personal Tax Sharing) Act 1976, section 6 (2)(a).

62. C.P. Harris, *The Classification of Australian Local Authorities*, Centre for Research and Federal Financial Relations, ANU, Canberra, 1975, 120.

63. J.M. Power and R.L. Wettenhall, 'Regional Government Versus Regional Programs', *Aust. J. Public Admin.*, XXXV, 2, June 1976, 128.

64. cf. M.A. Jones, *Organisational and Social Planning in Local Government*, Heinemann, Richmond, Victoria, 1977, 77.

65. James Coleman, letter to *Sydney Morning Herald*, 23 February 1978.

66. Jones, *op. cit.*, 79.

Part III

THE PUBLIC SERVICES

Chapter Ten

The Australian Public Services and Policy

Definitions

A recent British definition of a civil servant—what in Australia is usually called a public servant—is as follows:

> A civil servant is a Crown servant (other than the holder of a political or judicial office or a member of the armed forces) appointed directly or indirectly by the Crown, and paid out of funds provided by Parliament and employed in a Department of government.[1]

In some ways this is a narrow definition. It would exclude employees of many statutory authorities, especially those engaged on commercial enterprises; the latter are often not regarded as Crown servants and not usually paid out of parliamentary funds. However, it broadly defines the group of government employees we are mainly concerned with in the chapters that follow.

A holder of a 'political office' in the Commonwealth government can be defined by reference to sections 44 and 64–65 of the Constitution. Section 44 provides that no one who holds any office of profit under the Crown can be chosen or sit as a Senator or a member of the House of Representatives; but it makes an exception of the Queen's ministers of state. The latter are defined by section 64 as officers appointed by the Governor-General to administer such departments as the Governor-General in Council may establish; according to section 65, the number of such ministers is fixed by parliament. In this way the line is drawn between ministers and other paid servants of the Crown. (The position in the States differs in detail, but amounts to much the same in practice.)

In the Commonwealth and some States, the Constitutions also provide that the ministers must be, or become within three months of appointment, members of parliament; most State constitutions refer explicitly to a category of 'officers liable to retire on political grounds'. Whatever the constitutions say, the modern conventions are clear: Ministers must be members of parliament, and they depend for office on retaining the confidence of parliament; they are responsible to it. In contrast, public servants are holders of non-political office, and are normally protected from political change.

In Australia, a more usual definition of public servants is: 'Those government employees covered by the Public Service Acts.' The six States and the Commonwealth, beginning in the later part of the last century, have enacted such statutes, which govern methods of recruitment, promotion, discipline, dismissal and so on, and place them under the supervision of Public Service Boards. The courts have interpreted these statutes as creating enforceable rights, and they are regarded as an important protection of the non-political character of the public service, and of the rights of established public servants to employment so long as they are not too inefficient and do not misconduct themselves.

However, large groups of civilian government employees are wholly or partly outside the ambit of the Public Service Acts; examples are police, teachers, and the employees of many statutory authorities and semi-government bodies such as TAA, the Reserve Bank and State electricity commissions and transport undertakings. The same is true of local government employees. These groups are often covered by separate legislation, such as police regulation acts. The statutory protections of Public Service Act employees have been extended in this way to employees of many statutory bodies, including local government employees.

In so far as 'Crown servants' are not specially protected by statute, they appear still to be subject to the traditional common law doctrine that they are employed, and can be dismissed, at the pleasure of the Crown.[2]

Internally, the Public Services are classified into divisions, and classes and grades within divisions. The Commonwealth service at present has four divisions, though some changes are under consideration. The First Division mainly consists of permanent heads. The Second Division (a group of about 1200 officers) is broadly aimed at including those senior positions regarded as carrying major policy-forming and management functions, including professional officers who have such a role. The Third Division has a wide spread from fairly senior officers to base-grade clerical officers, and also includes many professionals. The Fourth Division includes typists, clerical assistants, and a large artisan and manual worker group. The pattern is similar in many States, though some have a separate professional division, and no equivalent of the second division. However, what is more important to most public servants is their 'class' or 'grade' within the division (see Chapter Thirteen).

The Growth of Government Employment

Numbers

In June 1975, there were in Australia 1 295 500 government employees, forming about one-fifth of the working population.[3] Table 10.1 shows changes in government employment since 1939. As a proportion of the total workforce, it has grown from 13.5 per cent to 21.3 per cent, though this percentage has not changed markedly since the 1950s. Over the whole period since 1939,

Commonwealth government employment has grown faster than that of the States, especially during the Second World War. In the 1950s total government employment grew much more slowly than in the previous decade, and more slowly in the Commonwealth than in the State governments. After this, the rate of growth increased, especially Commonwealth growth; however, in 1975 about 70 per cent of government employees still worked for State and local governments, a figure not very different thirty years earlier.

The term 'government employees' covers some very varied groups, including teachers and postal workers (about 125 000 each), railway staffs (about 110 000), and police (over 25 000). Only a small percentage is engaged in the kind of clerical–administrative work normally associated with the term 'public servant'. The figures also include the wide variety of professional workers—engineers, architects, scientists, statisticians, town planners, professional social workers, and so on—that is so characteristic a feature of present-day government.

In the ten years between 1959 and 1969, total civilian government employment rose by 32 per cent, total Commonwealth employment by 41 per cent. State government employment also rose quite fast in the decade 1959–69, by 27 per cent; local government, often regarded as the poorest relation in modern government, expanded by 34 per cent. In the States, education was high on the list of rapidly expanding services.

TABLE 10.1

Government Employees 1939–75
(thousands)

	1939	1946	1949	1959	1969	1975	Per cent Increase			
							1939–49	1949–59	1959–69	1969–75
Commonwealth	67.9	149.7	182.2	224.5	315.7	397.7	168	23	41	26
State	275.6	326.3	377.7	492.6	627.5	756.8	37	30	27	21
Local	61.5	53.0	63.0	76.7	103.0	141.0	2	22	34	37
Total	405.0	529.0	622.9	793.8	1046.1	1295.5	54	27	32	24
As per cent of total workforce	13.5	16.6	18.6	19.8	20.1	21.3				

Source: Official Year Books of Australia. Statistics of government employees include semi-government authorities and exclude the defence forces. For estimates of the Australian workforce, see M. Keating, 'Australian Work Force and Employment 1910–11 to 1960–61', Aust. Econ. Hist. Review, VII, 2, September, 1967, and the fuller version in M. Keating, The Australian Workforce 1910–11 to 1960–61, ANU Press, Canberra, 1973; for more recent figures, see the monthly employment statistics of the Australian Bureau of Statistics, and Official Year Book of Australia.
For a detailed survey and commentary, giving figures that differ slightly from those above, see A. Barnard, N.G. Butlin and J.J. Pincus, 'Public and Private Sector Employment in Australia', Aust. Econ. Review, 1st quarter 1977, 43–52.

It is true that in this period the total Australian workforce was growing almost as rapidly as government employment, so the relative importance of the latter only slightly increased. However, the statistics of government employment include large numbers of workers in governmental public utilities and commercial enterprises. A somewhat better, though still only a very rough, index of public 'bureaucratic' expansion might be numbers of Public Service Act employees. For example, between 1959 and 1969, the number of Commonwealth public servants in this narrower sense (and excluding the Post Office) rose from 76 928 to 114 995; that is, by 49 per cent. In the New South Wales Public Service, the number rose from 48 203 to 80 883, or by 68 per cent. After a short period of relative restraint, Commonwealth Public Service Act staff (excluding the Post Office) once again grew by 5 per cent a year in the period 1972–75. This represents a much faster rate of growth than in total government employment, and a rate more in accordance with one's impression that government administrative services, in common with tertiary services generally, have been undergoing a relatively rapid growth rate. This rate of growth has, temporarily at least, been halted. By 1976, as an anti-inflationary measure, a move was on foot to reduce the size of the Commonwealth public service. It was cut by 4.2 per cent in 1975–76 and by 1.7 per cent in 1976–77; a further reduction was planned for 1977–78.

The slowest growing area of public employment in recent years has probably been transport and communications, because of staff economies, increased mechanisation and reductions in certain services (e.g. railways, mail deliveries). In other fields, such as public works, less direct labour is now employed and more is done by private contractors, so changing employment figures are a poor indicator of the numbers employed on government works projects; these are part of the growing body of 'invisible' employees of government, working on a fee basis or employed by private firms working under contract.

Public Service Act Employees

Of a total of about 400 000 Commonwealth Government employees in Australia only about 150 000 are in departments and agencies under the Public Service Act (see Table 10.2).

A rough distinction can be made between relatively large departments and relatively small ones. Thus there are a number of large departments with 10 000 to over 30 000, sometimes including many manual or routine workers, such as Departments of Administrative Services, Construction, Defence, Transport, and the Australian Taxation Office. On the other hand, there are small government agencies, often with a high percentage of senior officers, and concentrated more heavily in Canberra, such as the departmental staffs of Trade (1286 in 1977), Industry and Commerce (466), the Treasury (479), and the Commonwealth Public Service Board (1094). Although

TABLE 10.2

Government Civilian Employment, June 1976
(thousands)

	Commonwealth Public Service*	Total Commonwealth	State	Local	Total
Located in:					
New South Wales	34.3	122.6	306.8	54.0	483.4
Victoria	36.3	97.0	239.7	27.6	364.3
Queensland	14.3	40.9	136.4	21.7	198.9
South Australia	12.7	32.0	105.2	6.8	144.1
Western Australia	8.1	23.2	95.7	8.0	127.0
Tasmania	2.7	8.0	35.0	2.9	46.0
Northern Territory	9.7	14.4	—	0.2	14.6
Australian Capital Territory	34.3	52.9	—		52.9
Total	152.4	391.0	918.9	121.3	1431.2

* Excludes employees overseas, and a small number of part-time Public Service Act employees.
Source: Commonwealth Public Service Board Report, 1976; Australian Bureau of Statistics, *1976 Labour Statistics.*

small in total numbers, the latter group are important 'policy-forming' departments.

If we narrow our scope still further, and restrict ourselves to the main 'policy advisers' and officers-in-charge of major divisions and branches, few Commonwealth departments would have more than fifty such officers. As a broad guide we may take the total number in the First and Second Divisions of the Commonwealth Service in June 1977, which was 1253, spread over twenty-seven main departments. In practice some senior Third Division officers will also form part of this select group, but it is not too misleading to think of thirteen or fourteen hundred public servants as forming something like a 'bureaucratic elite'; over 70 per cent of this group were in Canberra, and only two in Tasmania!

Table 10.3 gives a breakdown of State government employees. The most populous State, New South Wales, employed over 250 000 persons in its departments and statutory bodies (June 1976), of whom under 75 000 were Public Service Act employees. Again, some departments relatively small in numbers were very important in influence; for example, the Public Service Board of New South Wales employed only about 400.

Public Service History

In the early years of New South Wales, the machinery of government was controlled by a Governor, directly responsible to the United Kingdom minister in charge of colonial affairs. Senior officials were usually appointed from Britain; if the Governor wanted to appoint a local man to a senior post, this needed approval from London. The principal civil officer was the Colonial

TABLE 10.3

State Government Employment, 1976
(thousands)

	A	B	
	Public Service Act Employees	Total Government Employees	Percentage A of B
New South Wales	73.9	306.8	24
Victoria	30.1	239.7	13
Queensland	45.5	136.4	33
South Australia	16.0	105.2	15
Western Australia	12.5	95.7	13
Tasmania	6.3	35.0	18
All States	184.3	918.9	20

Source: Figures in Column A are from Public Service Board Reports, in Column B for 1976 Labour Statistics. The latter include semi-government authorities, such as employees of statutory corporations, marketing authorities and non-departmental public hospitals, as well as police and teachers (including university staffs).

Secretary, who was the Governor's chief adviser, and paid £2000 a year after 1825.[4]

By the 1820s a structure of departments was developing. The first Colonial Treasurer, Attorney-General, Auditor were appointed in the mid-1820s. Departments grew up to deal with public works, roads, police, post office, customs and so on. The Australian public services inherited some of the antiquated methods and patronage still current in the United Kingdom. However, 'the absence of indigenous capital, the necessity for exploration, expansion and settlement, the want of protection from local hazards, and the need to support local production and trade, compelled the Crown to assume responsibility for those essential services which the population could not provide for itself. For the size of the population the number of officials in the Australian colonies was comparatively large, and public services played an important part in the life of the community'.[5] Some early public servants were able and well-educated men, though there was also a considerable shortage of talent. In the last thirty years before responsible government there were only two Colonial Secretaries in New South Wales, Alexander McLeay and Edward Deas Thomson, both efficient administrators. It has been said that the earliest tradition of the Australian public services is one of paternal autocracy—in which the public servant was seen as the conservative and disciplined officer of the Crown, at all times supporting authority (but this was hardly true of McLeay), and accustomed to the centralisation of power in his office.

Though this tradition survived, it was for a time challenged by the growth of self-government and the extension of the franchise. As legislatures grew in power, and finally public servants came under the control of ministers responsible to the local parliament, the public services became subject to new political pressures. There were resentments at official privileges. It is common in new countries for the bureaucrats who survive from colonial days to be viewed with some suspicion, and this happened to a moderate extent in Australia. It is equally common in a new country for the public service to expand rapidly as new ministers stretch their wings and there is a popular call for development; and as new kinds of 'democratic' patronage replace or supplement older forms of privilege. At the same time, instability of ministries may act as a new cement of official power, as well as delaying public service reform. All this happened in late nineteenth century Australia, where different forces both stimulated and hampered the fulfilment of demands for better public service management.

The line between political and official posts, though partly provided for in the new Constitutions of the 1850s and 1860s that inaugurated responsible self-government, remained blurred in some cases, and some of the implications of the Westminster model were imperfectly understood. For a short time ministries contained a few senior officials; that was soon sorted out. But there were other forms of blurring the lines. In Tasmania some public servants were also members of the legislature between 1856 and 1870. In South Australia several active politicians were paid members of Boards and Commissions during the 1860s. Peter Lalor, of Eureka fame, combined membership of the Victorian Legislative Assembly with a £600-a-year job as railway inspector, until legislation made this impossible. In 1858, J.H. Plunkett would not vacate, and had to be dismissed from an official post by the Governor of New South Wales.[6]

It could also be argued, in the days before disciplined political parties had emerged, that patronage was necessary in order to buy support in the Legislative Assembly.

> Parliamentary (or as it is fancifully called, Responsible) Government is necessarily to some extent . . . a government by corruption . . . Appoint the sons and nephews of a sufficient number of members of parliament to be clerks of Petty Sessions, or waiters in the Customs, or something on the Roads, or in a Light House, and you will command votes for the Session . . . probably for two next following.[7]

Political patronage was one problem. Another was departmentalism. As the old centre of power, the Governor's office, had declined, it was succeeded by more fragmented departmental control, which now depended on the character and habits of ministers and permanent heads. Treasuries never acquired all the power, prestige and cheese-paring habits of the nineteenth-century British Treasury. Some of the public services grew rapidly in size. In New South Wales, the number of government employees grew from about 2500 in the 1850s to 35 000 in the early 1890s (over 9000 of these were employed on the railways, and about 5000 each in public works, education and the post office). Each department handled its own recruitment and internal management. Along with patronage, there were also symptoms of an inbred service, including promotion by seniority, and public complaint that the bureaucracy was becoming a privileged class. Departmental rivalries were sometimes intense. There were few general rules as to appointments, promotions, dismissals, pay and superannuation.

However, there is another side to the picture. In New South Wales at least, there were distinguished public servants, some of whom owed their advancement to patronage, and the basic structure of the bureaucracy remained intact. Partly because the turnover of governments was rapid and unpredictable, there was never an American 'spoils system', except briefly in Victoria. Though ministers used their powers of patronage, there was no wholesale removal of officers when governments changed, and senior officers in New South Wales and some other colonies seem to have made many appointments themselves, and controlled most other administrative arrange-ments in their departments. Though there was corruption, standards of honesty in most services remained reasonably high.

The latter part of the nineteenth century was one of rapid government growth in many parts of Australia. Governments were responsible for about half the total capital expenditure on railways, roads, harbour works, public buildings, water supplies, and so on. In the absence of a developed system of local government, most public functions were concentrated in the capital-city bureaucracies. Governments established themselves as major employers of labour, and 'attracted skilled and professional personnel directly into public services and enterprises, offering high salaries and importing many from overseas'.[8] Some colonies were already engaged 'in the long-term planning of expenditure and the approval of construction commitments several years ahead'.[9] It is true that there were weaknesses of budgeting and audit control, and overmuch reliance for revenue on overseas loans and land sales.[10] If one were looking for a second source of the traditions of the Australian public service, after the period of colonial autocracy, one might well find it is in the tough-minded officers who ran Treasuries, Departments of Public Works, Lands, Railways in the later nineteenth century, powerful and sometimes arrogant in their own departments, jealous of their prerogatives, and by no means as anonymous as their twentieth-century successors.

The history of this has not yet been written, and there were doubtless important differences between the public services of the various colonies. For example, Tasmania, though in the early years of responsible government it set useful inquiries on foot, did not share in the rapid growth that New South Wales and Victoria experienced. Its service remained disintegrated and less well-paid with little impulse to become more efficient; at the end of the century, there were over forty departments, loosely grouped under a handful of ministers.[11] South Australia's service also led a more placid existence, though there too men of ability emerged.

The twentieth-century public services were the product of a series of reforms that began with the 1859 commission of inquiry in Victoria, and the decisive events in which were the 1895 New South Wales and 1902 Commonwealth Public Service Acts. The effects of these are discussed in Chapters Eleven and Twelve. They set a pattern for the public services with three main features: central control by Public Service Board or Commissioner; recruitment from school at base-grade on the basis of open competition; and a career service, with promotion by a combination of merit and seniority. It was a pattern not without interesting variations, and which never extended itself to all positions. But it came to be the norm—departures from which, however numerous, were felt to need special justification.

So the theory of the Australian public services came to be that they were 'closed' career services recruited from school, except for a limited number of people with special, mostly professional, qualifications. This kind of system has two main problems. It may not recruit enough of the right people at the bottom; and, its success depends on having effective training and promotion machinery which correctly identifies the promising people down below, and gives them the right opportunities before they are too old or too set in their ways to benefit from them.

The system partly worked. There are still a number of able senior officers (especially in the better States) who came in from school and were promoted in time. However, what often happened was that professionally trained people got the top administrative jobs, or they went to outsiders recruited through some loophole in the system, or the clerical recruits achieved responsibility by seniority too late to be really lively. The Commonwealth public service had a great shortage of talent in 1939, though by then it had begun to recruit non-professional graduates. Since then the quality of the higher staff has risen markedly, and the State services have now belatedly realised that they are lagging behind.

Until recent years only the Commonwealth recruited a sizeable number of non-professional graduates. The continuing significance of this for the States is reflected in the number of permanent heads of major departments who entered the service straight from school. All the same, there have always been many who entered in other ways, for example, as professionally trained lawyers, engineers and so on, who moved later into positions with major administrative responsibilities. Some services have also given considerable encouragement to their officers to obtain degrees or other higher qualifications after they entered government employment.

Merit is in theory, and quite often in practice, the primary basis of promotion. But seniority has had a way of creeping in, and in most services a well-developed appeals system has imparted a certain caution to promoting authorities. Lateral recruitment, from outside at later ages and to fairly senior positions, is by no means unknown, but has often been made difficult by the laws and conventions of the Service.

Rights and Obligations: Neutrality and Anonymity

The Doctrine of Neutrality

Formally the relationships between the administrative system and the political system in Australia are fairly clear. As indicated in Chapter Three, the ordinary government department is headed by a minister, who is responsible for its operations to parliament (matters of major policy may be the collective responsibility of the whole cabinet). The minister and his officials apply the statutes passed by parliament, and the policies decided in cabinet or by the minister himself.

This implies that public servants are expected to be politically 'neutral' in their official work.[12] They are permanent, but ministers and parliaments change. Hence they may find themselves having to execute policies with which they disagree. Such disagreement is not supposed to affect their behaviour. This doctrine of neutrality is nowhere fully defined in statutes or regulations, nor could it be effectively enforced by outside sanctions—there are too many subtle ways of hindering or not fully backing a policy one dislikes. It is part of a code of conduct that permanent officials are supposed to follow. Public servants are trained to think of themselves as working out of the limelight and anonymously to implement policies ultimately decided by their political masters, on which they may have offered advice, and which may leave much scope for discretion and feedback, but which they should not consciously distort in response to other viewpoints and pressures, including their own personal preferences.

This is part of the 'culture', or tradition, of the public service, which, like any vocation, moulds its own members. New entrants find themselves playing roles in a well-defined structure with norms of proper behaviour. If such a structure is well-established (as it is, by and large, in Australia) it acts as a powerful influence on the individuals within it. Training is supported by 'self-selection'—individuals who would feel very restive under such constraints tend not to enter the public service, or to get out again if they do. A high capacity for tolerating frustration is regarded as part of the mental kit of a good public servant.

As the Commonwealth Public Service Board has said,

> the concept of neutrality does not imply that public servants have no political views or associations. Rather it is concerned with the responsibility owed by a public servant to the government of the day, irrespective of its political complexion; impartial advice on policy options; and the wholehearted implementation of decisions made at the political level irrespective of whether they accord with the views of the officer.[13]

So neutrality does not mean even-handedness to government and opposition, but on the contrary loyal support of the party in power, whichever that happens to be. The writer's view is that this loyalty means more than giving impartial advice when asked, and following instructions faithfully when received. A public servant has a duty while at work to protect and promote the minister's and the government's interests, as he would if they were wholly acceptable to him personally. So, in making clear policy options, he should indicate how they might be related to the apparent political aims and general outlook of the government; and he should interpret and promote the government's and the minister's policy concerns as best he can, even in the absence of clear guidelines in a particular field of policy. The easiest way for a bureaucrat to trip up a politician is not by non-compliance but by 'withholding positive help'.[14]

The neutrality of public servants is also safeguarded by some legal and institutional checks. Public Service Boards were originally designed partly to prevent political interference in Public Service recruitment and promotion. Public servants are supposed to be recruited on objective criteria of merit, and in practice have job security. There are rules forbidding the disclosure of official information, and restricting public comment by officials.

Rights and Obligations of Public Servants

As we have seen, the Commonwealth and the States have enacted Public Service Acts. These statutes (and the regulations made under them) protect the rights, as well as stating some of the obligations, of large categories of government employees. The courts have interpreted these statutes as creating enforceable rights. It is true that they often leave wide discretionary powers to the executive government, but the body of legal decisions in which the courts have declared or protected the rights of Crown servants is still considerable.

Special procedures have been established under the Public Service Acts to deal with such questions as discipline and dismissal. Though minor punishments, such as reprimand (sometimes a small fine), may usually be imposed by the permanent head or other senior officer, elaborate safeguards are provided for more serious offences. In the States, charges are normally heard by the Public Service Board; in some there is a further appeal to a tribunal—in New South Wales, the Crown Employees Appeal Board, which also deals with appeals by police and employees of many statutory authorities. In the year 1975–76, ninety-six New South Wales employees were dismissed and thirty-four others allowed to resign. These are not large figures in a Public Service of 74 000.

In the Commonwealth, lower division officers are dealt with departmentally, subject to various procedural safeguards; but if the punishment is more than minor, an appeal is possible to an appeal board including a staff representative, and the officer may have legal representation. In case of dismissal, the Public Service Board also retains power to reduce the penalty. Charges against First and Second Division officers would be dealt with by an *ad hoc* Board of Inquiry, likely to be presided over by a judge. Officers convicted of criminal offences by the courts can be dismissed or reduced by the Public Service Board (section 62). In 1976–77, eight officers were dismissed, thirteen reduced or transferred and over a hundred fined or reprimanded.

What are the obligations of public servants?[15] Most of them are the same as those of any employee in the private sector, to keep time, work with reasonable efficiency, obey lawful instructions, keep the employer's secrets, and so on. The Commonwealth Public Service Act (section 55) lists some of these, and adds as an offence, 'any disgraceful or improper conduct, either in his official capacity or otherwise'. The broad wording of this indicates that a public servant has some obligations not shared by private employees, partly arising out of the special security of his employment, but mainly the result of his special position as a servant of the Crown.

Political Rights

A case of special interest is that of political activity. One old view, derived from fear of their voting power, was that permanent officials should be stringently controlled in this respect. In eighteenth-century England, many public servants were debarred from voting; as recently as 1903 in Victoria they were segregated into special electorates, though this was a short-lived experiment. Their claim to form staff associations used to be looked on with suspicion, and in Britain from 1927 to 1946 these associations were debarred from outside affiliations. On the other hand, in Britain: 'Until almost the end of the (nineteenth) century, civil servants could stand for Parliament without giving up their posts'.[16]

In many respects, Australian opinion has accepted trade union and political activity on the part of public servants. Staff associations have mostly preserved their own freedom from obviously party-political links; but they have sometimes had good parliamentary contacts, and at times engaged in their own political pressure-group activities. Views about the political rights of individual public servants have mellowed over the years, with some (usually shortlived) backtracking.

Some limitations on political activities have been thought justified, on the ground that these may become incompatible with the proper performance of official duties. The best argument runs somewhat as follows: effective government requires a permanent bureaucracy that does not change with changing governments; indeed, this is a condition of democratic government in a complex modern state. 'The electorate is at liberty to eject ministers, provided ministers are not free to eject civil servants.'[17] But, the argument proceeds, ministers and cabinets will accept this restriction only if public servants, especially senior public servants, are seen to be impartial; and the political supporters of governments will expect this impartiality from all officials, otherwise strong pressures will develop to replace them. It is important to realise that this is not simply an argument about whether public servants are in fact neutral, but whether they are seen by other people as neutral.

One basic rule in Australia was mentioned earlier: no one can be a public servant while at the same time holding elective office in parliament. The application of this rule varies slightly as between the parliaments. Public servants, Commonwealth or State, who wish to contest Commonwealth elections must first resign (this has been held to follow from section 44 of the Constitution).[18] However, if defeated, they are normally reinstated without loss of entitlements; at least such an application seems never to have been refused, though the Commonwealth Public Service Act (section 47c) only says that the Board 'may' reappoint. Rules as to State elections vary. Sometimes they are broadly as above. New South Wales has since 1916 allowed its public servants to contest State elections without resigning, though they must resign if elected; the same has been true since 1935 in Victoria. More freedom still is allowed to accept elective office in local government, so long as it is deemed compatible with the discharge of official duties. In other respects, public servants are free to engage in active politics outside office hours, subject to the restrictions on public comment discussed below.

These rules are more liberal than those of many countries. In the United States, the Hatch Act places severe statutory restrictions on the political activities of the federal career service. Britain operates mainly through internal service regulations, which greatly restrict senior officers; other officers are allowed more freedom, though rarely as much as in Australia (a good deal of discretion is left to individual departments). Senior and middle-ranking officers can vote and belong to a party, but are debarred from active participation in national politics. At the other extreme there are Scandinavian countries where one can be an MP and a public servant at the same time, and be given time off for one's parliamentary duties; a number of other European countries allow public servants to take leave of absence if elected to parliament, and do not insist on their resigning.[19]

It is clear that national attitudes on the subject vary greatly. The Australian rules might present difficulties with senior officers, if the latter often wished to engage in active politics. In 1965 the Director of the Northern Division of the Commonwealth Department of National Development was endorsed as a Labor candidate for the next federal election. He was transferred to another position in his department, created overnight, at the same salary but of less policy significance. He then resigned to fight a by-election, which he won.[20] On the other hand, when in 1972 the Commonwealth Solicitor-General became an endorsed Liberal candidate, the Attorney-General defended his action.

Such cases have up to now been rare. In a recent Commonwealth parliament, of eighteen members who appeared to have been government employees immediately before election, seven were teachers, two policemen, the others postal worker, inspector, tax assessor, court reporter or on routine duties.[21] Only one seems to have been in a position where he might possibly have influenced policy or had access to policy files. Australian governments have given more than one indication that they do object to the active political involvement of senior officers who are in the policy-forming area. This may seem to conflict with the rule—but Australia, unlike Britain, prefers the rules to be egalitarian, even if the conventions are not.

Public Comment and Disclosure of Information

There has been more controversy about restrictions on public comment and disclosure of information by public servants. The main Commonwealth restrictions are in the Public Service Regulations and the Crimes Act. Regulation 34 provided until recently that:

> An officer shall not (a) use for any purpose, other than for the discharge of his official duties, information gained by or conveyed to him through his connexion with the Service; or (b) publicly comment upon any administrative action or upon the administration of any Department.

The second restriction—on public comment—was removed by the Whitlam government in 1974. Nevertheless, public servants are still required to be discreet. There are guidelines drawn up by the Public Service Board, and the Prime Minister responsible for the repeal of Regulation 34(b) has said that there 'will still be proper observance of the conventions, including the convention which provides that public servants do not justify or propagandize policies. This is the job of Ministers.'[22]

Regulation 35 puts a more specific and stringent limitation on the unauthorised disclosure of official information or papers, 'except in the course of official duty'. The Crimes Act supports these regulations by making it a criminal offence for a Commonwealth officer, or former Commonwealth officer, to publish or communicate a public document that it is, or was, his duty not to disclose; anyone who encourages him to commit such an offence may also be charged. Hence the Commonwealth can deal with certain forms of disclosure either by ordinary disciplinary action or by prosecution.

The more general prohibition on 'disgraceful or improper conduct', which is also to be found in other Public Service Acts, remains in the Commonwealth Act. A former Director of the Commonwealth Serum Laboratories, who publicly criticised and tried to promote opposition to a 1961 Bill relating to his agency, was disciplined on the ground of 'improper conduct'; he was downgraded, and resigned. In March 1969 it was reported that an employee of the Attorney-General's Department had been similarly charged for *inter alia* acting as convenor of a demonstration against the National Service Act; his salary was reduced, and he also resigned.[23]

One likely reason why such cases were not dealt with, or not solely dealt with, under regulation 34(b) is that the public comment was on 'Policy' rather than 'Administration'. The line between the two is hard to draw. Freedom to engage in active politics seems necessarily to involve some freedom to criticise government policies, if not the way they are administered by departments. However, other actions by the Commonwealth government seem to have made it clear that, at least as far as senior officers are concerned, the rules are in practice intended to cover public discussion of government policies.

The rules and conventions have not been invoked very often. Officials in general tend not to comment critically on government matters in public gatherings within press hearing, or write critical letters to the press, even on minor matters; confidential leaks are another question, and are liable to occur from time to time on some matter in which an officer has a very strong interest or about which he feels deeply. In recent years, some observers have detected a 'noticeable easing in the traditional reticence of the Public Service'.[24] Senior public servants do seem more readily go give public addresses and take part in academic seminars, and occasionally let their views on policy be known. On the whole, it is surprising how discreet most Australian public servants are, though the leaking of documents to the press seems to be on the increase.

One absolutist view is that no question of 'freedom' is involved. It is said logically to follow from the principle of ministerial responsibility that what public servants say or do on official matters is at the minister's or the cabinet's discretion, as the latter bear the brunt of outside criticism. However, this argument is inconclusive. It wholly ignores any right the public may have to know what is happening in government other than what governments at present choose to tell them. It also fails to answer the question, given that ministers should have the final say in these matters, what kind of ministerial attitude is most likely to produce a public service of high morale and effectiveness. Lastly, if governments suffer when they are criticised, they also suffer (possibly as often) when they lack the pressure, supportive or critical, of a well-informed public.

It is sometimes argued that the public service itself benefits by being largely removed from the public eye, and that this creates an atmosphere favourable to the detached consideration of issues. Even if this were so, detachment is not the only virtue of a good bureaucrat, and the general quality of the higher public servant possibly suffers from excessive anonymity. Though he may wield considerable power in private, he is credited with few successes, while his kind are (if he is not personally) readily blamed for mistakes. Ministers take the credit for new policies that work, bureaucrats may be blamed collectively for those that are unworkable. There is a case for saying that senior officers should be seen for what they often are—responsible persons who play an important part in policy-formation and the execution of policy. The love of anonymity, discretion and power wielded in private attracts some admirable types, but is not the sum of administrative virtue. Public attitudes to the bureaucracy might improve if it were less anonymous, and seen from time to time on television screens (as now occasionally happens); one must admit that the opposite might be the case! Anonymity and secrecy have also the disadvantage that fewer people know when some costly mistake has been made; they probably make it harder to learn lessons from the recent past.

There is the special question of whether officials attacked (with a fairly high degree of specificity) by politicians, especially by ministers, should have the right to answer back. The Commonwealth Treasury has in recent years been the scapegoat of more than one government, yet its senior officers have no 'right of reply', or at any rate have claimed none—Mr Renouf, a former permanent head of Foreign Affairs, did return fire when attacked by the Leader of the Opposition in 1975, and added that

> The Public Service is rightly no longer the mute figure it used to be . . . Is the department to be denied the right to defend itself when asked how it feels about criticism?[25]

In 1978 the New South Wales Commissioner for Corrective Services was criticised by a Royal Commission for the state of the prison system and also publicly criticised by the Premier, who had already transferred him from his post to the unattached list, although there was a 'responsible' minister in charge of his department.[26] There seem to be occasions when a permanent head or commissioner should have the right to reply publicly to criticism, as departments already do in the case of criticism by the Auditor-General. In the matter of press comment, it is now not uncommon for permanent heads to write to the press, complaining of unfair treatment.

A powerful argument against freedom of comment is that public servants who made use of it would tend to forfeit the trust of their superiors. This applies especially to the senior public servants who advise ministers, who have (or should have) every right to express their views to him confidentially. The argument is that if the minister cannot rely on their discretion he will cease to trust them; and will tend in the long run to take advice from less independently minded persons, 'party political sympathizers or . . . acquiescent nobodies'.[27] This is a strong argument, especially when applied to exposing the advice given to ministers on particular questions; and especially perhaps in Australia, where ministers can be remarkably defensive and tend to overreact to public comment.

The argument clearly has less force when applied to public servants not in the policy area, though it was mentioned above that the public's trust, as well as the minister's, may be involved. Thus it has been argued that if the majority of voters have given their support to a particular government the public espousal, even by less senior officials, of minority viewpoints would tend to erode majority belief that a permanent bureaucracy can be trusted to carry out the public will.

Trust is a complex notion. Ministers already have to trust senior officers whom they know to have definite views on some question, to give them full and fair advice, and faithfully to carry out government policy decisions with which they may personally disagree. Why should they not also trust them not to let any public comment they make affect their work? Perhaps it is simply that ministers are not used to the idea, and we could all by degrees become used to a somewhat freer system. It is hard to believe that more relaxed conventions could not be established without destroying trust; indeed, they already exist in some countries.

The main problem is to safeguard against the irresponsibility and (not unusual, if often unjustified) sense of grievance of some second-rate public servants; and against the self-righteous pronouncements of the ideologists. The public servants most anxious to make public comments may often be those with the lowest professional sense or with strong political commitments, likely to bias their comment. Such pronouncements are as likely to be misleading as instructive to the public. Many public servants are less than fully informed about the reasons for decisions taken inside the administration, yet any comments which they make as insiders will inevitably be regarded as made in full knowledge of the facts.

The mode of publicity is important; for example, a somewhat freer hand can be given, as it sometimes has been in practice, to critical comment in scholarly or professional publications or meetings. An onus is also placed on officers to couch their comment in temperate language, to show that they took trouble to base it on relevant facts, and so on.

As well as the issue of public comment, there is the separate question of regulations or legislation about the disclosure of information. This is discussed later in this chapter. The question of disclosure is linked with the right of public comment, as a comment may involve disclosure of official information relevant to it.

The Role of Public Servant in Policy

The relations between policy and administration, and between ministers and public servants, have been mentioned in earlier chapters. Here we shall attempt to say something more specific about the role of the public servant.

Law and Policy

Some people see the role of public servants as 'executive', as carrying out 'the law'. Parliament passes a statute, and the administration applies it to particular cases. This has been termed the 'milk and water' view of the public service, as opposed to the 'cloak and dagger' view of those who denounce the bureaucratic usurpation of power. It certainly applies to some activities of public servants, provided we remember that most of the laws modern parliaments pass are initiated by governments, and that the ideas embodied in a government bill may come from public servants.

There are two other reasons why 'carrying out the law' is an inadequate account of the bureaucratic task. The first is that typically statutes leave governments and their officials with a great deal of leeway. The best way of seeing this is to read a few Acts of Parliament. A law may, in a general fashion, outline the task and define the powers and duties of the minister or statutory authority; it may provide for certain machinery and finance, lay down some procedures, and so on. But the powers concerned and procedures required are often not stated with precision. Quite often the law does not say that such-and-such must be done, but that it 'may' be done.

The minister or other authority is often given an express power to fill gaps in the statute by making regulations, so-called delegated legislation (see Chapter Six).

The second point is that there are many areas of government little regulated by statute, such as foreign and defence policy and some fields of economic policy, where (provided that the necessary funds are available) there are few legal restrictions on how governments may act. In such areas, public servants are still required to carry out the policies and instructions of minister, but 'the law' may hardly enter into the picture. There are areas where legislation exists, but covers only a fraction of the problems. For example, Mining Acts, however well-devised, are irrelevant to many problems of a modern minerals industry, where governments are dealing with a few concentrated centres of economic power in relation to large-scale projects of a complex and diverse character. Much of Australia's immigration policy has a highly discretionary character and major changes have resulted from decisions made departmentally, or within the cabinet, without benefit of legislation.

So we must widen our earlier statement and say that public servants act within a framework of 'law and policy'. But when ministers make policy, as when they initiate bills, they derive much of their advice from officials; and their policy directives usually leave a good deal to be filled in, and may be open to various interpretations. As a result, senior public servants are inevitably involved in much policy formulation, and will often have considerable discretion in carrying out policy, as even a first-class minister cannot keep an eye on everything.

Ministers, Officials and Decision-making

What will ministers deal with themselves, and what will they leave to officials? As we saw in Chapter One, it is hard to draw the line between policy and administration, or between ends and means. Consider the case of foreign affairs. Within the general framework of Australian foreign policy objectives, there are more specific aims and strategies to be determined, policies about Indonesia, China, America, overseas aid; and within these broad fields, decisions of a more specific kind to be taken. At what point do the ends (to be decided by politicians) become the means (to be decided by administrators)? There is no clear answer to this question. How far the minister concerned and the cabinet will want to go into detail, what they will be ready to leave to career officials, depends on many factors.

First, some policies are easier to reduce to general rules than others. A new policy about pensions can be stated in a general way that is also operational, that is, gives a clear guide to officials about what they are to do in practice to implement it; one test of this is that if they act in ways inconsistent with the policy this will soon become apparent. (It is true that policies about social welfare benefits can sometimes be highly discretionary.) On the other hand, it is much harder to lay down general views about foreign or economic policy and then leave it to someone else to interpret the rules.

Ends and means are much more mixed up together; the making and conduct of foreign policy is a collaborative product of politicians and officials, in which it is hard to sort out the contribution of each. When there is no neat and obvious way of sorting out these responsibilities, a sense of strategy is important to ministers, a good nose to smell out those decisive moments at which they should start taking a personal interest.

A related point is that in government there is often no pre-determined and stable hierarchy of matters more and less politically 'important'. In many cases what is going to matter politically cannot be settled in advance, and may change over time. A normally minor matter can sometimes arouse great public alarm, especially if it affects individual rights or has a whiff of scandal about it. Then it becomes the minister's business, a matter of 'policy', and the minister may suddenly call for papers on the subject. The political importance of a whole field of government may vary over time. Thus conservation and environmental issues have recently become matters of public controversy, and this means that ministers take more interest in them, and leave less to public servants. As Paul Appleby put it: 'The level at which a decision is made . . . may be shifted upward or downward as evaluations point to more or less controversy, or to more or less 'importance'.'[28]

In some situations, it may also be more attractive to elected politicians to intervene in detailed matters or individual cases than to take general policy decisions. It is sometimes said that this is not what they should be doing. However, there may be rational point to their preferences. They may be choosing those matters that they find it easiest to cope with (see below), and they may also have an eye for those that most concern their constituents. It is one traditional and well-understood task of politicians to bring individual claims and grievances to the attention of administrators.

Another factor is the degree of special expertise that is, or is thought to be, required and available to determine a question. Some policies, and some levels of policy, are easier for the average minister to cope with than others. If he has time and inclination to deal with the matter, and thinks that he knows as well as, or better than his departmental officers what should be done, he will be likely to try to decide the question himself. In other cases he may feel baffled by science, and ready to accept the work of the experts. One can treat the relations of ministers and officials as a kind of bargain in which the former offer to share power with the latter in exchange for their skills—the greater the skill, the greater the power.

There is also trust, not simply in the expertise of one's advisers, but also in their loyalty and their determination to put into effect the intentions of the government. If this trust is lacking, then ministers will want to do more themselves or to find someone else they think they can trust.

As indicated already, the inclinations of ministers and the time they are ready to spend on departmental matters are also important. Some ministers are more hardworking or reformist or interventionist than others. They may become specially interested in the detail of those policies that they particularly wish to see implemented. Some writers have argued that the most important factor is scarcity of attention, which arises because there are far more issues to be settled than any government can possibly deal with, and ministers are chronically short of time. Most issues are unattended issues, and are either settled by default at the administrative level, or cheerfully left by politicians to be dealt with by public servants. When an issue attracts the attention of ministers, then the stereotype of political master and administrative servant comes to life. Otherwise the distinction between politician and administrator is simply that the latter deals with all those governmental matters that the former is not bothering about.[29]

These variables apply within the public service itself. Senior officers are faced with situations of the same kind, in which they are more or less willing to delegate or leave matters to their subordinates. Most decisions are necessarily left to institutional processes, to be settled by procedures which have developed over time and which embody the accumulated knowledge and experience of the department. It is the exceptional case that is plucked out for special consideration; and from time to time the processes and procedures themselves are changed. Some departments have extensive formal systems of delegation, that is, written regulations and instructions covering the kinds of financial and other administrative decisions that may be taken at various levels. This is especially true of departments controlling sizeable staffs away from head office, where some regular but limited discretionary powers are needed—say, the Department of Social Security. But much delegation is informal, that is, a department develops a set of unwritten understandings and conventions about what kinds of matters are decided at any particular level. This is especially true of those policy areas where it is hard to define clearly in advance what is of any given degree of 'importance'. So it has to be left to an officer's judgment whether to deal with the matter or to refer it up the ladder.

Australian departments are smaller than their equivalents in more populous countries, or ones without a federal division of powers. One would expect it to be easier for ministers (and permanent heads) to cope with them, and one might expect state ministers to have more personal influence than Commonwealth ones, especially as they are shuffled about less often. But perhaps complexity of business is more important than mere size. The States do seem to throw up more cases where a determined new minister puts fresh life into a department, or occasionally rides roughshod over his public servants. Some ministers often concern themselves with departmental matters that in Canberra would be left to permanent heads. In some States which have had (as is not uncommon) long periods of one-party rule, ministers have been fortified in this role by outlasting their permanent heads.

On the other hand, it is often suggested that it is easier to draw the line between politics and administration in the States because their services are more 'management-oriented'. State public servants are not called upon to play politics as much as their Commonwealth colleagues, and this represents one important difference of administrative style. In some fields senior officers have not even thought it their business to initiate policy. This is partly because many important State activities (railways, roads, water supply, housing and so on) involve much technical expertise, and where there have been wider planning and policy aspects, these have often been imperfectly understood. The cast of mind of State permanent heads is more managerial, and there has been a failure in the past to train enough administrators of broad outlook and with skills in policy analysis. Sometimes neither senior officials nor minister have thought policy-making their responsibility, and a policy vacuum has developed.[30]

Much turns on the relative talents of ministers and officials. If the political system recruits less talent than the administrative system, the balance of power will shift. The Commonwealth administrative system seems to have been more adaptable than the political system to the demands of modern government. Indeed its very adaptability has concealed, or made up for, political shortcomings. The talents of a few really able ministers in cabinets have also helped to protect weaker ministers.

Other factors have tended to increase the influence of the Commonwealth service. Canberra is the permanent home of most policy-making officials, to many politicians it is a distant place where meetings are held. Some ministers seem constantly on the move between Canberra and their home base, often on the distant seaboard. Ministers have other duties to distract them—to attend meetings of the cabinet and its committees, to be in parliament when it is sitting, at question time, during debates and so on; to look after their electoral base, make speeches, conduct other party activities, and meet delegations.

Where a department has had frequent changes of minister, or a succession of poor ministers, the senior public servants are likely to be more influential inside their own agencies. When an able and determined minister heads a department for a long time—as Mr (now Sir Paul) Hasluck did the Department of Territories from 1951 to 1963—he may dominate it. Tasmania had virtually only two Education Ministers between 1948 and 1973. Some ministers have the gift of mastering the affairs of a new department quickly. Even power-conscious officials often like a strong minister who will stand up for their interests in the cabinet—and to the Prime Minister, Treasury and Public Service Board—because a department with a weak minister may lose out in the interdepartmental power struggle. On the whole, most top officials like a minister who makes decisions and gives them clear policy directives, so that they 'know where they are'; provided that he will also listen to their advice and has the capacity to understand it (which involves being able to question it where necessary). They also like a minister who will act fairly by them, and who will not sacrifice the department's interests to his own in a time of crisis or controversy.

One complication is that tensions between a minister and his officials often arise when the minister is getting out of step with his own government, and the public servants know this and choose to take their cue from the latter. The Coombs Commission points out that a departmental head, as well as being responsible to his own minister, has to take account of 'the decisions of other ministers . . . Cabinet decisions, Treasury rulings and Board advice . . . occasions can arise when a departmental head senses conflict between a proposal of his minister and the understood intentions or policy of the cabinet . . .', and he has obligations to both.[31] This issue became of importance in 1975, in the controversy between Dr Cairns, the former Treasurer, and Sir Frederick Wheeler, his permanent head.[32]

Ministers and Permanent Heads

In theory, a minister is answerable for all the operations of his department, and this might be supposed to carry with it a corresponding right to intervene in any aspect of its work, to make the decision himself if he wants to, and to lay down as many rules and give as many instructions as he likes about how things are to be done. It does not work out quite like this. On matters of policy, no one doubts that the minister has the last word in the department but he will in practice have to leave a great deal to others. On matters relating to departmental management and implementation of policy, even his right to intervene may be questioned.

On personnel matters—problems of establishment, appointment, promotion and so on—parliament has given the major powers to Public Service Boards, and sometimes also to permanent heads, and the minister has little say. There is also a widespread view in Canberra, and in some States, that a number of other matters related to the structure and management of the department are not the minister's business. In the Commonwealth, section 25(2) of the Public Service Act is held to give statutory force to this view.[33] This says that:

> The Permanent Head of a Department shall be responsible for its general working and for all the business thereof, and shall advise the Minister in all matters relating to the Department.

In New South Wales the Public Service Regulations provide that:

> The Permanent Head of each Department shall be responsible to the [Public Service] Board for the discipline, efficiency, and economic administration of the Department . . .

Indeed, in Australia there has been a persistent tendency, also to be seen in the prevalence of the statutory authority, to preserve various sectors of administration for expert and impartial management insulated from political interference.

Many Commonwealth ministers accept this conception of their role. They are very 'political animals'. Their offices are in Parliament House, so that often they do not work inside their own departments as is the normal practice in the States. The Minister for Supply in 1971–72, unlike most of his colleagues, worked in his department. He said it was at first 'a great shock to the system', as the public servants were not used to the idea.[34] Most ministers prefer the pleasant informality of the atmosphere of ministerial offices in Parliament House, with personal staffs, girl secretaries and journalists engaging in chatter. Parliamentary arrangements relating to divisions and to question time make it necessary to be more continuously on hand than in most countries. (The Coombs Commission suggested that Parliament should consider revising its arrangements so as to 'enable ministers to become a more effective presence in their departments'.)[35] Ministers also usually have long distances to go to their homes and electorates, and they like to be away from Canberra as much as possible when parliament is not sitting. Even the more hardworking ministers seem to find working in their own departments tedious and unrewarding. This has some disadvantages, the most serious of which is that ministers and cabinets remain more unsophisticated than they need be about administrative problems. It also means that a minister is sometimes in too weak a position in relation to his officials. However, as Curnow has pointed out, there are few incentives for ministers to devote more time to administration beyond some respectable minimum, for public reputations are not made in this way.[36]

Of course, at best there will always be strict limits to a minister's participation in departmental administration. In the United Kingdom, management-oriented ministers are uncommon,[37] though in continental Europe, ministers more often see their main function as the management of a department, and have a decisive influence on senior appointments.[38] A minister's direct contact and influence is bound to be limited to a very few officers. The most important of these is the permanent head.

The permanent head or most senior officer in a department is commonly called the Secretary (in the Commonwealth) or the Under Secretary (in the States). A few have special titles such as Director-General. He has the joint task of being chief official adviser to the minister and general manager of the department. Even if a minister has direct dealings with several other senior officers, as he must have nowadays, the permanent head 'needs to know what ideas his senior officers send or take to the minister so that he may intervene if he wishes'.[39]

In a good department there is also 'some kind of informal machinery which enables a complete and continuous interchange of ideas among senior officials . . . and between them, on the one hand, severally and collectively, and the minister on the other'.[40] Apart from these few very senior officers, a minister's closest working-day associates will be in his own office, with his personal staff (see below). Though Commonwealth ministerial staffs have increased in size and importance, there is little tradition in Australia of a minister using his personal staff as a major instrument of his influence. He is expected to operate largely through a small number of senior permanent officers in the department. All this raises questions of some delicacy, especially in the case where a minister might desire to know for himself more directly what is going on, and what is the state of the debate at lower levels. Of course, a permanent head may also be dependent on his immediate subordinates, but he has, in practice, more chance to take advice where he wants to.

(i) Policy Formulation   A minister does not often put much on paper, mostly a few words of comment, added to a submission prepared for him in his department; though there is nothing to stop him writing long minutes to his officers if he wants (and this occasionally happens). In this sense, he may rarely originate action. Of course, he may have asked for the submission, and mentioned some of the things he wants to see in it. Hence an important task of his senior officers is to prepare submissions, giving their views and perhaps outlining a number of alternative possible courses of action. So we may read in the newspaper that a State Premier went to the Premiers Conference 'armed with a strong case from his own State Treasury', or read in an advertisement for an official post that its duties include 'formulation of a policy or plans concerning . . . ; consideration of new or varied legislation . . . preparation of cabinet memoranda'.

Conscientious ministers will read and fully digest such official submissions and briefings, if they have time. This does not always happen. We have it on the authority of Sir Alan Watt, a former permanent head of the Department of External (now Foreign) Affairs, that few things are harder,

> with certain notable exceptions—than to secure ministerial attention to, understanding of and decisions upon complex submissions before a conference actually begins . . . it has been rare for an Australian Minister of External Affairs attending a conference in person to have read the brief in full in advance . . . [41]

Of course, official briefs are often not concerned with new policy, but with defending existing policies.

Senior officers may in turn look to their juniors for help in policy formulation, or in the preparation of background material. So a fair number of public servants become involved in this activity. There may be oral as well as written discussion of policy matters at various levels; indeed there is a general trend, encouraged by the growth of interdepartmental committees and more 'collegial' notions of administration inside departments, to do more business by word-of-mouth.

Some policy-making depends very much for its success on close contact with the operative levels of government. A change in tax policy, for example, has to take account of the administrative disruption likely to be caused and the practical snags of assessment and collection; the implementers of policies can, of course, also be stimulated or pressed to find ways round some of the alleged difficulties. This is one trouble about trying to draw too clear a line between policy-making and operations.

Policy-advising skill may go along with many different types of personality, some dynamic, some more conservative. It has been held to include 'talents for neat and tactful drafting, good manners, presence of mind in conversation, general good sense, some flair for politics'. A former head of the British Civil Service has mentioned power of rapid analysis, ability to recognise the essential points in a situation, a sense of timing, and power to think of likely developments up to a year ahead.[42]

(ii) Discretionary Application of Policy A public servant often has considerable discretion in interpreting policy and in organising the business of carrying it out. Many of the most important skills of administration are in this field of implementation. Carrying out most policies involves a good many decision-makers at several different levels interpreting statutes or ministerial directions, or exercising judgment in individual cases about what to deal with at their own level or what to send up to a higher level for decision.

There is also the problem of organising and managing the staff and resources required to carry out tasks. Good policy advisers are not always good managers; the Fulton Committee in the United Kingdom criticised permanent heads and senior public servants for tending to think of themselves too much as advisers on policy to the people above them, and not enough as managers of the administrative machine below them.[43] The Coombs Commission in Australia made a similar point when it said that:

> Access to government services has often been badly planned; the work in relation to it has been undervalued, and those involved inadequately trained and supervised . . . The planning, organization and supervision of work of this kind are essentially managerial functions having little in common with the role of the official as the minister's source of information and advice. It is this latter function which is most highly esteemed among officials as well as most highly rewarded and it is to this, rather than to management tasks, that ambition, study and other forms of training are directed.[44]

Neutrality and Policy

One conclusion to be drawn from this is that many public servants are 'men of influence', both in policy-making and in the implementation of policies. As has been said, a good deal in public administration turns not so much on who finally makes a decision, as who is consulted about it; and, when a policy decision is made, what really counts is how policy 'hits the ground'.

It also follows that we must expect to find political pressures operating at the official level as well as at the parliamentary and ministerial levels. Outside interests will seek access to those who they consider can influence decisions that affect them. A public servant's efficiency may depend partly on his capacity to adapt his department's policy to give satisfaction to interested parties, to make its programmes acceptable—at its crudest, 'to keep the department (or his minister) out of trouble'; in the longer run, to help it to adapt to changing needs and pressures.

In countries like the United States, such factors have resulted in some senior administrative posts being treated as frankly political appointments. Patronage is not regarded as a mere political reward, or even simply as a way of bringing in new blood, but as a necessary condition of having loyal and adaptable officers in key positions. The British tradition, which Australia has followed, has (as we have seen) laid great stress on the political neutrality of senior officials.

This emphasis has many virtues. It assists the development of a career service in which the highest posts are open to permanent officers; this in turn gives the public servant a professional status and encourages him to adopt a professional attitude to his work. He can develop pride in his administrative skills, and learn to distinguish his personal view of a matter from the demands placed upon him by his office. In any event it is doubtful whether the conditions exist in Australia for an American-type system, in which a fair number of able outsiders assume temporary office at the top of the bureaucracy. In Australia the attractions of temporary office are less, it being a country where governments have no fixed term, elections are frequent, and where outside career-channels are more rigid and the pool of jobs in the private sector open to former 'political executives' would be very restricted. Even in America there are many difficulties about recruitment, 'true in-and-out careers are much less common than usually thought', and about half the political appointees are transients who stay less than two years.[45] So it may be doubted whether an attempt to break up the top layer of the public service would succeed in replacing it by a race of equally able, but more dynamic and committed individuals. They could just as easily be (as one permanent head has said) 'youthful activists with their own interest to pursue, individuals on the make, and political yes-men'. A former economic adviser to the Whitlam government has argued that the public servants who most damaged Labor were not those who disagreed with ministers, but those who failed to warn of potential dangers.[46]

All the same, it is not a complete description of a good public servant, certainly a senior public servant, that he must do a fair day's work, be personally honest, loyal, discreet and observe the standards of neutrality.[47] The fact that he may have a significant influence on an agency's policies carries with it other obligations. It imposes on him a creative responsibility. Much of the creative work of higher public servants—like that of Sir Tasman Heyes and Sir Peter Heydon, successive heads of the Department of Immigration, on Australia's post-war immigration programme—goes unrecorded, but may be no less effective (in this case, perhaps more effective) for that.

How can this be reconciled with the idea of neutrality? First, this process goes on in private. Even so, does not this mean the public servant is exercising great influence on policy? It is true that the final decision rests with the minister or the cabinet, but senior officers are placed in a strong position to sway the government towards their own point of view.

Secondly, there are some important kinds of critical activity that public servants may engage in regarding policy, which do not involve them in criticising the objectives of governments and ministers. They can help governments to rid policy of ambiguities and obscurities, and to become clearer about what they want. A policy may sometimes contain internal contradictions, which analysis will expose. They can point to some of the consequences in other fields of adopting this policy. They can also ask: now that the aim is clear, is the action proposed really the most effective way of achieving it? What are costs likely to be in relation to benefits? Could some alternative achieve this aim or a better result at lower cost? Is there existing machinery that could be used instead of creating new machinery? or will present administrative resources be hopelessly overstrained?

Of course the line between this kind of criticism and criticising the aim itself is hard to draw; as we have seen, ends and means are often hard to disentangle. Thus, suppose that the Commonwealth wants (as it did in 1978) to limit the growth of health service costs, public servants are likely to be drawn into discussion about alternative ways of doing this. But it is probable that different methods of limiting costs will also have different distributive effects, and may also have some longer-run influence on the whole character of the service; or set some kind of precedent for other kinds of welfare service, or have effects on the government's anti-inflation policies, and so on. The general point is that changing the means is not always a policy-neutral technical problem, but may have all kinds of repercussions on political objectives.

Some people try to delimit the role of the official by drawing a distinction between 'facts' and 'values'. They say that it is the job of the public servant to give the facts, leaving ministers to decide the policy; or (a more plausible account) to indicate all the possible alternative lines of action, estimating the likely costs and benefits, the advantages and drawbacks of each, but leaving ministers to choose between the alternatives so presented. It may even be said that if the permanent official goes beyond this, and indicates his personal preference or that of his official colleagues, he is exercising illegitimate influence.

This is attractively simple, but oversimple. As one senior public servant has written,

> you do not get much change from either ministers or Cabinet these days, busy as they are, if you just dish up about a half-a-dozen alternatives, three of them silly, two of them 'maybe', and one perhaps good . . . I do not think we can run away from, or need run away from the fact of influence . . . If there are available alternatives, which might attract the political thinking of the day . . . I put them in and I think that necessary. But, given a firm belief of my own about the decisions which I want to come out, those are the recommendations I put in. Anything else is waffling . . . [48]

The writer is not, of course, speaking for all senior public servants, but he is drawing attention to three important points. The first is the time factor. Ministers and senior officers are busy people, and many decisions cannot be discussed and debated at great length. Most ministers want public servants who are not afraid to participate, and shortcut the process of choice. A good minister can usually sense fairly quickly if important alternative possibilities are being concealed from him.

Secondly, many alternatives are not politically available. A minister wants advisers with the political sense to know this. This is not necessarily inconsistent with the fact-value dichotomy—all it means is that a successful senior official is aware of political, as well as administrative, economic, and other 'facts'. The political facts may include his minister's personal preferences—a permanent head must 'know the mind' of his minister, and be able to enter into his thoughts on policy. This does not mean that he should not sometimes stand up to him, and indicate his own view of the needs of the situation, if he believes that they are being obscured by political pressure or prejudice. If he feels strongly enough, the final reprisal is 'the honourable economic disaster' of resignation,[49] but this is no part of the conventions of a bureaucratic system, and hardly ever happens.

Thirdly, the number of possible alternatives is often very large indeed. Even if a public servant selects several for discussion, he is selecting; and when he supports them with appropriate facts, he is selecting those facts. His own valuations inevitably enter the process, though he may try to allow for this. Once concrete proposals have been formulated on paper, fresh ideas are less likely to be introduced into the discussion, so whoever has the task of filtering options in this way has a good deal of power. There is a related comment by a former head of the British civil service, who refers to

'an early stage when things are fluid; when, if you are in touch with those concerned and get hold of the facts, it is fairly easy to influence decisions. But after a scheme has been worked on for weeks or months, and has hardened into a particular shape, and comes up for formal decisions, then it is often very difficult to do anything except approve it or throw it overboard.'[50]

The Bureaucracy and Changes of Government

There are some important advantages of a career public service. The officials can become expert in administrative affairs generally, and in knowledge of a particular department. Politicians cannot use jobs as political rewards.

A career service also has some disadvantages. The tradition of neutrality is easiest to maintain where there is a settled system of government and changing governments do not differ too widely on major policy issues. However, the permanency of permanent heads may create problems even when they are thoroughly neutral, if their temperament clashes with that of the incoming minister. It is sometimes said that neutrality is not enough, that governments need advisers who support their policies with the enthusiasm and creative imagination that results only from a thorough commitment to those policies.

It has been argued that the theory of civil service neutrality breaks down completely when there are major differences about policy goals within a society, and that the 'bureaucratic conservatism' of the public service may stand in the way of really radical shifts of policy. A book on European civil services points out that

> 'in the nature of things higher civil servants rightly regard it as their principal duty to safeguard the continuity of the state. They are therefore always likely to consider that what they do is in some way on a higher plane than what politicians do; that they are the protective force of society and politicians the destructive force.'[51]

It is important to distinguish caution and conservatism from party-political bias. Some Liberals thought that the public service in the early 1950s was hindering the Menzies government from taking bold action in an anti-socialist direction, including reducing the size of the bureaucracy itself. Again, the benefits of a politically committed bureaucracy need to be weighed against those of the present system, which does at its best produce a race of senior officers with cool heads, long experience and often with a strong commitment to the long-run concerns of their department. Any system of periodical importation of new talent at the top also tends to damage morale among the career people lower down. Nor should it be assumed that senior public servants are invariably more cautious than ministers; sometimes it is the government's caution that stands in the way of changes evidently necessary to those who are doing the job. The whole idea of a conservative 'guardian bureaucracy', keeping the ship of the state on an even keel, is a bit unrealistic in a situation where new ideas may come from bureaucrats and they may be at least as responsive to underlying conditions as are the politicians. 'The day-to-day horizons and public relations obsessions of most ministers in any administration are no more worthy of reinforcement than the intellectual conservatism of most senior officials.'[52]

A career system does assume that enough able men rise to the top through the service. If the career system is second-rate, it is more desirable to bring in outsiders. During the war a large number of outsiders had to be brought into senior Commonwealth posts, partly because the existing public servants were often mediocre. A public service may also develop the need for new kinds of expertise and experience. There has been a good case in recent years in Australia for making it somewhat easier to recruit from outside, permanently or on a temporary contract, at later ages. There is not as much movement as there should be between the various sectors of Australian life, which remain too departmentalised, with rigid superannuation arrangements and conventional promotion ladders helping to make mobility difficult. Even within the government service, smaller 'career services' tend to develop, as in some statutory authorities; certain departments remain poorly staffed because they are too ingrown (some departments concerned with local government fall into this category).

The Impact of Labor on the Public Service, 1972–75

When a government has been long in power, a political change may seem like a major upheaval to senior public servants. They have become used to the ideas and working methods and habits of a particular body of men, or of a particular Premier or Prime Minister. In Canberra a whole generation of public servants grew up under Liberal–Country Party governments between 1949 and 1972. In New South Wales and South Australia, the same was true under Labor, in power in New South Wales from 1941 to 1965, and under Sir Thomas Playford, in power in South Australia from 1938 to 1965; Mr Dunstan is having a similar impact.

As the new Labor Prime Minister wrote soon after taking office in 1972:

> The question was asked whether the administrative machine that had been controlled by our political opponents for twenty-three years could respond to a significant political change, and the needs of a Government charged with urgently-needed reforms and impelled by a philosophy involving a shift from long-established positions. No doubt the Public Service was equally anxious to see whether we in the Labor Party would be able to adjust effectively to the business of government, and how we would go about the task of governing.[53]

Nor had there been much contact between members of the Opposition and senior officials, though the Public Service Board had done a little contingency planning and Dr Peter Wilenski, a public servant who later became Principal Private Secretary to the Prime Minister, had independently written papers for Mr Whitlam on the machinery of government. The two sides met in December 1972 in a Machinery of Government Committee. (When the Fraser government took office in 1975, the Public Service Board was more trusted, had learned to do better, and had the advantage of contact during the period of caretaker government before the election. The government has since approved guidelines providing for officials to consult with the opposition before elections, especially regarding the administrative and technical problems of implementing policy.)[54]

In spite of some minor flurries, the transition was largely peaceful. There were various reasons for this. One is that new governments, especially when their members have no experience of office, are very dependent on the background knowledge and expertise of their senior public servants. In 1972 no member of the new Labor cabinet had ministerial experience, even at State level (two had been senior public servants). In any case many public servants welcomed a change of government, while others were happy with the promotion chances opened up by new and expanded programmes; between 1972 and 1975 the size of the Second Division rose from 856 to 1267. They could take heart too from this sentence in the ALP platform: 'As the largest single employer of labour, the Commonwealth has the duty to advance the cause of all employees by establishing new and improved standards of employment for its own employees.' In 1973 the public service became for a time a pace-setter in pay and conditions.

Other changes were less unambiguously welcomed, such as what happened to some permanent heads—powerful men in Canberra who (as we have seen) are used to a great deal of say in the running of their departments. Only one or two were conspicuously displaced from the system. All the same, the many changes that Labor made in the structure of departments left scope for reshuffling and new appointments. Of permanent heads serving in December 1972, under half were still in such positions two and a half years later, and many others were unhappily placed in invented posts or left 'unattached' for long periods. However, most of the new appointments were from the career service. Only three outsiders were appointed in the early days, one of them a senior State public servant; two others came later. One of these was Mr John Menadue, from the Murdoch newspaper organisation and once Mr Whitlam's private secretary, who became Secretary to the Department of the Prime Minister and Cabinet in 1974, replacing Sir John Bunting, who was made High Commissioner to the United Kingdom; even Menadue had at one time been a public servant. In one or two cases what might be termed the 'normal succession' was interrupted, as when Mr Alan Renouf, Ambassador to France, was made Secretary to the Department of Foreign Affairs (his predecessor retired early). It was an erosion, but hardly amounted to a revolution.

There was a notable increase in 'lateral recruitment' (direct from outside to senior positions) to the rapidly growing Second Division, and top ranges of the Third Division. Around ninety outsiders were recruited to such positions in 1973, compared with fifty in 1971. A striking case was the newly established Department of Urban and Regional Development (DURD), where nineteen of the twenty-seven Second Division officers appointed by early 1975 had come from outside the public service; five were from statutory authorities, six from universities and eight from private enterprise. But this was an exceptional case. DURD was a wholly new department, built on no existing nucleus; it needed skills in short supply in Canberra; finally, it was intended to be a preeminent and shining example of the novel policy thrusts of the Labor government. Most of the other new departments were based on sections of existing departments, though enlarged in size and status.

Experiments

Even governments wishing to leave the main structure of the career service intact may wish to supplement it by new sources of expert advice, more personal advisers and more planning units outside the normal departmental framework. This happens widely in Europe. There have been moves of this kind under both Labour and Conservative governments in the United Kingdom. It is an old story in America. However, such experiments are hard to make successfully in the Australian context. They tread on bureaucratic toes, affecting morale or inviting mild sabotage; the outsiders may not be all that expert at engaging with and working within an involved administrative context; they may further complicate the works, or tend to pursue their personal interests. Many Australian ministers have not shown great skill at choosing personal staffs, though there have been only a few bad cases of patronage.

The Labor government in Australia made experiments of this kind after 1972. Though the career public service was left mainly intact, there were still doubts about its capacity and drive in putting through major reforms, some wish for a countervailing force, or at least a desire to improve the capacity of ministers to give political direction to the public service, to inject 'a stream of tendency'. Two devices are worth special mention: the appointment of outside advisers to ministers, including larger personal staffs; and the creation of special committees and commissions, drawing all or a considerable part of their membership from outside the public service. Neither of these was novel, but the Labor government extended their use considerably.

Advisers and Personal Staffs[55]

Before 1972 a minister typically had a private secretary, a press officer, and a small clerical staff, but even the senior staff were largely concerned with fairly modest support and housekeeping duties—looking after the minister's personal mail, his public relations, monitoring his daily schedule, helping to write speeches, rarely playing a significant role as policy advisers. Much of this personal staff came from the minister's department, and returned there in due course; others came from outside as temporary employees and their tenure depended, as it still does, on the will or fate of the minister. There had been attempts to promote the British idea of private secretaryships as jobs for able career officers with a promising future in the public service, and a number of appointments of this kind were made under Liberal–Country Party governments. Ministerial staffs, whether seconded from the public service or not, are not subject to instructions from the permanent head.[56]

Under Labor (1972–75), ministerial staffs were still drawn from both sources, but the proportion of outsiders increased, as did the number, pay and status of the senior positions. Each minister could appoint two fairly high-level ministerial officers, a press secretary, a liaison officer with the department and a complement of other secretarial staff. The Prime Minister and Deputy Prime Minister had larger staffs. By 1975 senior staffs had about doubled in number compared with 1972, rising to around a hundred with another 120 juniors (not all the vacancies were filled).[57] Provision was also made for staff assistance to opposition leaders.

Most of these were doing what such people always did; perhaps thirty had some policy skills, but only a minority of these regularly acted as policy advisers to ministers. It is easy to exaggerate their importance; they were there to assist the minister, and not in the line of command, which still passed through the permanent head. Some ministers made no use of non-departmental advice. Still, the more important recruits represented an additional source of policy advice, a staff that the minister could use to confer with, write papers, examine departmental submissions and which enabled him, if he desired, to 'second guess' his own department. The Prime Minister's personal staff included men of significant influence such as Dr Peter Wilenski (who came from the Foreign Affairs Department). Labor's health scheme was to a considerable extent the product of the Minister for Social Security's personal advisers, Dr R.B. Scotton (an economist) and Dr J.S. Deeble. There was also an important group of general economic advisers and consultants—Dr H.C. Coombs (former Governor of the Reserve Bank), Professor Fred Gruen and Mr Brian Brogan; and special units such as the Priorities Review Staff, designed for work on longer-range priorities and planning, though in practice drawn into a number of current issues and controversies.

The reactions of career public servants to the expanded ministerial staffs varied. They were welcome in certain capacities—to help with the more party-political tasks that fall to a minister, so saving career officers from pressures to help in this area; and to conduct the minister's public relations. Otherwise, senior public servants were mainly concerned to see that the minister's staff did not 'interfere with the department'. In this regard, it was suspect both to public servants committed to norms of impartiality and, as a potential rival, to political operators in the bureaucracy; and did not sufficiently realise that it had to make such people aware of the benefits to them of its presence as well as the disadvantages.[58] There were fears that ministerial staffs would isolate ministers even more than normally from their own departments. As indicated above, Commonwealth ministers already look after their departments at a distance, from offices in Parliament House which their personal staffs also inhabit, and sections of the latter formed part of the communications network of Parliament House, which extends to journalists, backbenchers and outside groups (a fair number of staff members were former journalists).

John Edwards has given an account of how this worked in the early days of the Whitlam Government:

I suppose when I walked into Parliament House earlier this year (1973), I would have known half the personal staffs who had already arrived, through nothing more conspiratorial than a left-liberal history in the local Labor party, the Sydney University and N.S.W. Fabian Societies, the anti-Vietnam movement and three years on the *Financial Review*. It was as though a part of a whole generation had marched through Kings Hall and filtered through to the various ministers' offices. It's in the discovery of so many connexions that one realises just what a small country this is, and how important face-to-face groups are.[59]

He goes on to explain how these groups were swift communication channels and arbiters of status. 'In the exchange of information, group members are also likely to develop a common attitude to a political event, which then becomes a critical determinant of how it will appear in the newspapers and to the public.' It should be added that, as such groups were often distrusted by and distrusted the bureaucracy, the images that they made current about senior public servants were hardly flattering ones.[60] However, this is to generalise too broadly. There were staff who had little contact with other offices, and others acted so as to promote ministerial rivalries (a common danger of such staffs). In certain cases the communications network—for example, that between members of the Prime Minister's Office and some other staffs—was a valuable means of co-ordination.

After 1975 the Fraser government retained this concept of an expanded personal staff for ministers, but their numbers were reduced and their activities were lower-key. Private secretaries, press secretaries and advisers initially fell from over a hundred to sixty (April 1976), but seem to have crept up again. Most ministers have a staff of six, two of whom have the senior rank of ministerial officer. A few do a little better, and also have a press secretary, though the number of these has diminished as compared with the days of McMahon and Whitlam. The personal staff establishment of the Prime Minister is over twenty, including twelve important enough to be listed in the Commonwealth Government Directory. About half of these ministerial staffs still have public service backgrounds. There are fewer party activists, especially among the public service recruits, and very few ministerial offices under Fraser,

> house staffers of forceful character and political commitment . . . whereas under Whitlam at least half the ministerial offices housed such person-alities. They were often pompous, sometimes megalomaniac, usually turbulent but supportable in the sense that they provided rivalry to non-responsible bureaucratic power.[61]

New Agencies

The Labor government also experimented with many new agencies. There was a notable increase in the number of committees and commissions—both *ad hoc* task forces and committees of inquiry, and standing commissions that offered continuing advice on, and sometimes managed new government programmes (see Chapter Five). In late 1973 the Prime Minister listed sixty-five of the former and over twenty-five new commissions and similar bodies.[62]

There are dangers in the multiplication of new units of government; if it sometimes promotes vitality, it also encourages confusion of responsibilities and makes co-ordination more difficult. Instead of creating new agencies, it is often more fruitful, if in the short run more troublesome, to find ways of adapting existing machinery to new purposes, by creating an atmosphere and structure within which permanent officers and short-term advisers or staff units can be brought together to work as a team. Under Labor, attempts were made to achieve this co-operation, and some of the more successful enterprises of the Labor government were the product of mixed teams of regular public servants, outsiders on fixed-term contract and part-time consultants. This is easier to achieve nowadays as, within bureaucracies themselves, rigid notions of hierarchy seem to be breaking down, and a more collegial approach is encouraged.

There is a general tendency for outside advisers and new agencies to be most important in the early days of a new government. After that, some 're-bureaucratisation' is apt to set in; the regular public service contrives to reassert itself, the new people leave or are absorbed into more clearly defined roles. This happened under Labor. Indeed, the more lasting contribution of the Whitlam government to public administration may lie in the regular departments—the consolidations of Transport and Defence, and the re-organisation of the Department of the Prime Minister and Cabinet into a major centre of policy co-ordination, a process carried still further by Mr Fraser (see Chapter Fifteen).

Changes under Fraser

When Mr Fraser became Prime Minister there was no upheaval of the kind that occurred in 1972. There were fewer changes in departmental structure, though there was some reshuffling of duties and name-changing. This was partly because the new Prime Minister genuinely desired to restore the old conventions, but also because he wished to avoid the appearance of 'instant' government. Two of Mr Whitlam's appointments as permanent heads were harshly treated, but two other fairly controversial appointees remained at the head of the Prime Minister's Department and of Foreign Affairs for over nine months, when they departed amicably as Ambassadors to Japan and the United States. A few displaced persons of the Whitlam era returned to significant office. The Prime Minister also had his love affair with Sir Henry Bland, as Chairman of the Administrative Review Committee and (until they fell out) as Chairman of the Australian Broadcasting Commission.

It looked like a conservative administration, and a common view was the collapse of Labor had strengthened the position of the permanent public service and of permanent heads in particular. Australia was in for a period of 'sound' government, with ministers depending very much on their official advisers, including the Treasury. There was some truth in this. However as time went on certain changes did not fit this picture. One was the decision to build the Department of the Prime Minister and Cabinet into a major arm of government, and in particular of the Prime Minister; a second, even more striking, was the splitting of the Treasury in 1977, a blow against orthodoxy that Labor had never dared to strike. Though senior public servants have an important place in the present Commonwealth administration, it is also clear that they are expected to 'know their place'; at the time of writing, Australia has an assertive Prime Minister, as well as a number of assertive State Premiers.

Notes

1. S.A. de Smith, *Constitutional and Administrative Law*, 2nd edn, Penguin, Harmondsworth, Middlesex, 1973, 185. For discussion, see W.J.M. Mackenzie and J.W. Grove, *Central Administration in Britain*, Longmans, London, 1957, ch. 2; and W.J.M. Mackenzie, 'The Civil Service, the State and the Establishment', in B. Crick (ed.), *Essays on Reform, 1967*, Oxford University Press, Oxford, 1967. On Australia, see D.G. Benjafield and H. Whitmore, *Principles of Australian Administrative Law*, 4th edn, Law Book Co., Sydney, 1971, ch. 3.
2. For some of the uncertainties of the law on this question, even in Britain, see S.A. de Smith, *op. cit.*, 194–5, and references cited there; on Australia, see C. Arup, 'Security at Law of Public Employment in Australia', *Aust. J. Public Admin.*, *XXXVII*, 2, June 1978.
3. Statistics here and elsewhere exclude the permanent defence forces, estimates at 69 200 in June 1975. The figures include employees of Commonwealth and State statutory authorities, and also local government employees.
4. S.T.A. McMartin, 'The Origin and Development of the Public Service in New South Wales, 1788–1856', unpublished Ph.D. thesis, University of London, London, 1976, contains the best account of these developments.
5. G.E. Caiden, *Career Service*, Melbourne University Press, Melbourne, 1965, ch. I, 'The Colonial Legacy', 34.
6. R.L. Wettenhall, *A Guide to Tasmanian Government Administration*, Platypus, Hobart, 1968, 30; G.N. Hawker, 'The Development of the South Australian Civil Service, 1836–1916', Ph.D. thesis, Australian National University, Canberra, 1967, 208. On Victoria, see G. Serle, *The Golden Age*, Melbourne University Press, Melbourne, 1963, 311–23; on Lalor, the *Australian Dictionary of Biography*, Vol. 5, Melbourne University Press, Melbourne, 1974, 52; on Plunkett, John N. Molony, *John Herbert Plunkett in New South Wales, 1832–1869*, ANU Press, Canberra, 1973.
7. Sir Alfred Stephen, Chief Justice, to Sir Henry Parkes, 31 May 1868. *Parkes Correspondence*, A905, 148 (Library of New South Wales).
8. A. Barnard, N.G. Butlin and J.J. Pincus, 'Public and Private Sector Employment in Australia, 1901–1974', *Aust. Econ. Review*, 1st quarter 1977, 46.
9. N.F. Butlin, 'Colonial Socialism in Australia, 1860–1900', in H.G. Aitken (ed.), *The State and Economic Growth*, Social Science Research Council, New York, 1959.
10. See P.N. Lamb, 'Geoffrey Eagar and the Colonial Treasury of New South Wales', *Aust. Econ. Papers*, September 1962; and 'The Financing of Government Expenditure in New South Wales, 1856–1900', Ph.D. thesis, Australian National University, Canberra, 1963.
11. *Report*, (Tasmanian) Select Committee on the Civil Service, 1902, *cit.* R.L. Wettenhall, *Evolution of a Departmental System: A Tasmanian Commentary*, University of Tasmania, Hobart, 1967; cf. Wettenhall, *A Guide to Tasmanian Government Administration*, Platypus, Hobart, 1968, 216.
12. On the emergence of this doctrine in nineteenth-century Britain, see G. Kitson Clark, 'Statesmen in Disguise: Reflections on the History of the Neutrality of the Civil Service', *Hist. J.*, II, 1, 1959, and H.W. Parris, *Constitutional Bureaucracy*, Allen and Unwin, London, 1969, ch. 3.
13. First Public Service Board Submission to RCAGA, Canberra, 1974, 64.

14. Hugh Heclo, *A Government of Strangers*, Brookings Institution, Washington DC, 1977, 172.

15. See Report, RCAGA, 230–6; G.E. Caiden, *The Commonwealth Bureaucracy*, Melbourne University Press, Melbourne, 1967, ch. 16; and Enid Campbell and H. Whitmore, *Freedom in Australia*, 2nd edn, Sydney University Press, Sydney, 1973, ch. 18. On general duties of employees, see E.I. Sykes and H.J. Glasbeek, *Labour Law in Australia*, Butterworths, Sydney, 1972, 51–63.

16. H. Parris, *op. cit.*, 151.

17. Mackenzie and Grove, *op. cit.*, 155.

18. cf. L.F. Crisp, *Australian National Government*, 3rd edn, Croydon, Victoria, 1965, 428–9; and V. Subramaniam, 'Political Rights of Commonwealth Public Servants', *Public Admin.* (Sydney), XVII, 1, March 1958. For the history of these provisions, see also L.F. Crisp, 'Politics and the Commonwealth Public Service', in R.N. Spann and G.R. Curnow (eds), *Public Policy and Administration in Australia: A Reader*, Wiley, Sydney, 1975, 177.

19. See Brian Chapman, *The Profession of Government*, Allen and Unwin, London, 1959, ch. 14.

20. For an earlier case, that of Dr John Burton, see H.A. Scarrow, *The Higher Public Service of the Commonwealth of Australia*, Duke University Press, Durham, NC, 1957, 154–6.

21. Paul Hasluck, *The Public Servant and Politics* (Garran Memorial Oration) Canberra, 1968, 11. A few senior public servants have later entered politics. For examples, see S. Encel, *Equality and Authority*, Cheshire, Melbourne, 1970, 73.

22. E.G. Whitlam, 'Public Administration in Australia: Changes under the Labor Government', *The Round Table*, 253, January 1974, 79–80.

23. See R.S. Parker, 'Official Neutrality and the Right of Public Comment', *Public Admin.* (Sydney), XX, 4, December 1961, and XXIII, 3, September 1964, who also discusses other cases. On the 1969 case, see *Canberra Times* leading article, 18 March 1969, *Sydney Morning Herald*, 25 March 1969, and other press reports at this time.

24. C.J. Lloyd and G.S. Reid, *Out of the Wilderness: The Return of Labor*, Cassell, North Melbourne, 1974, 219.

25. *Canberra Times*, 12 April 1975.

26. See *Sydney Morning Herald* editorial, 5 April 1978 and comment in succeeding issues.

27. R.S. Parker, 'Official Neutrality and the Right of Public Comment I', *Public Admin.* (Sydney), XX, 4, December 1961, 302.

28. Paul Appleby, *Policy and Administration*, University of Alabama Press, Alabama, 1949, 13.

29. For an early form of this argument, see Appleby, *op. cit.*, 20. A sophisticated version is in Leon Peres, 'Technology, Administration and Politics', *Aust. J. Public Admin.*, XXXVII, March 1978.

30. On this see the comments in the Interim Report, Review of New South Wales Government Administration, Sydney, 1977, 17–18.

31. Report, RCAGA, 62–3, 414.

32. See *Com. Parl. Deb.* (H of R.), V. 95, 9 July 1975, 3558FF; Report, RCAGA, 64, and Appendix Vol. One, 235; and various books such as Laurie Oakes, *Crash Through or Crash*, Drummond, Richmond, Victoria, 1976.

33. For discussion of the legal status of this section, see R.N. Spann, 'Permanent Heads', in Report, RCAGA, Appendix Vol. One, 234–9.
34. R.V. Garland, 'Relations between Ministers and Departments', ACT Newsletter (Royal Institute of Public Administration), August 1976.
35. Report, RCAGA, 66. See also David Butler, *The Canberra Model: Essays on Australian Government*, Cheshire, Melbourne, 1973, and Macmillan, London, 1977, ch. 4, 'Ministers and Their Departments'.
36. G.R. Curnow, 'The New South Wales Machinery of Government Review', in R.F.I. Smith and Patrick Weller, *Public Service Inquiries in Australia*, University of Queensland Press, St Lucia, 1978.
37. cf. Bruce Headey, *British Cabinet Ministers*, Allen and Unwin, London, 1974.
38. cf. Nevil Johnson, *Government in the Federal Republic of Germany*, Pergamon Press, Oxford, 1973, 65.
39. Sir John Crawford, 'Relations between Civil Servants and Ministers in Policy Making', *Public Admin.* (Sydney), XIX, 2 June, 1960, n.9, reprinted in R.N. Spann and G.R. Curnow, *Public Policy and Administration in Australia: A. Reader,* Wiley, Sydney, 1975. The author is a former Permanent Head of the Department of Trade. An earlier article by the same author, 'The Role of the Permanent Head', *Public Admin.* (Sydney), XIII, 3, September 1954, is also well worth reading.
40. Crawford, *op. cit.*, 102.
41. Alan Watt, *The Evolution of Australian Foreign Policy, 1938–1965*, Cambridge University Press, Cambridge, 1967, 79.
42. Mackenzie and Grove, *op. cit.*, 72; Lord Bridges, in A. Dunsire (ed.), *The Making of an Administrator*, Manchester University Press, Manchester, 1956, 12–13.
43. Report (Fulton) Committee on the Civil Service, London, 1968, I, 12.
44. Report, RCAGA, 21.
45. Hugh Heclo, *A Government of Strangers*, Brookings Institution, Washington DC, 1977, 102.
46. Professor F. Gruen, presidential address to ANZAAS conference, May 1976, cit. *Australian Financial Review*, 12 May 1976.
47. The Commonwealth Public Service Board has recently (March 1978) issued as a Discussion Paper, *Draft Guidelines on Official Conduct of Commonwealth Public Servants*. For an earlier attempt to draw up a code see 'Draft Code of Ethics for Public Servants', *Public Admin.* (Sydney), XXIV, 3, September 1965.
48. Sir William Dunk, 'The Role of the Public Servant in Policy Formulation', *Public Admin.* (Sydney), XX, 2, June 1961, 113.
49. T.B. Millar, *Australia's Defence*, Melbourne University Press, Melbourne, 1965, 160.
50. Lord Bridges, 'Whitehall and Beyond', *The Listener*, 25 June 1964.
51. Brian Chapman, *op. cit.*, 274.
52. S. Brittan, 'The Irregulars', in R. Rose (ed.), *Policy-Making in Britain*, Macmillan, London, 1969, 335.
53. E.G. Whitlam, 'Public Administration in Australia: Changes under the Labor Government', *The Round Table*, 253, January 1974, 79–80.
54. *Com. Parl. Deb.* (H. of R.), V. 102, 9 December 1976, 3591.
55. See R.F.I. Smith, 'Ministerial Advisers: The Experience of the Whitlam Government', and Roy Forward, 'Ministerial Staff under Whitlam and Fraser', both in *Aust. J. Public Admin.*, XXXVI, 2, June 1977.
56. Smith, *op. cit.*, 144.

57. In December 1974, 209 were employed, of whom 75 were seconded from public service departments (Report, RCAGA, Appendix Vol. One, 298); but some others had public service experience.
58. Smith, *op. cit.*, 150–2.
59. John Edwards, 'Political Scientists in Politics', paper delivered to the Australian Political Studies Association Conference, August 1973, 3.
60. Compare the tart but apposite comments on the coteries of Parliament House by R.S. Parker (Report, RCAGA, Appendix Vol. One, 277).
61. Peter Samuel, *The Bulletin*, 10 July 1976.
62. Whitlam, *op. cit.*, 81–3.

Chapter Eleven

Central Personnel Management

In government the management function is somewhat dispersed, and in certain areas departmental heads have less control than many managers of equal-sized private firms. Their expenditures are subject to control by Treasury or Department of Finance (see Chapter Sixteen). They are also dependent on other specialised 'common service' agencies; for example, a Department of Works or Construction may be their building authority, the Attorney-General's Department may handle legal matters, there may be arrangements for central purchasing, publishing and so on. This is true not only of ministerial departments, but also of many statutory bodies. Even for an institution such as the Australian Broadcasting Commission, negotiations with Commonwealth finance, construction, legal and other departments may be very time-consuming. All this makes it harder for an individual government agency to 'design itself' for its specific tasks, and to be made accountable for their efficient performance.

One of the most important fields in which such controls operate is that of personnel. The staffing of many government agencies is controlled and supervised by Public Service Boards; and their functions also generally extend into the field of working methods and efficiency, though in the Commonwealth the latter function is now beginning to be shared with the Auditor-General (see Chapter Eighteen). This chapter is concerned with central personnel management, as reflected in the work of Public Service Boards, and begins with a short history of public service reform.

Public Service Reform

The Genesis of Reform

In English-speaking countries, one may conveniently begin the story in the 1780s.[1] One persistent note is first sounded in Edmund Burke's House of Commons speech, *Of Economical Reform*, 'that all offices which bring more charge than proportional advantage to the State' ought 'to be taken away' and 'that it is right to reduce every establishment, and every part of an establishment, (as nearly as possible) to certainty, the life of all order and good management'. The main emphasis of early public service reform was

286

often negative—to clear up a mess, reduce patronage and privilege, save money. In Australia, this was later to become embodied in the catchphrase, 'efficiency and economy', or vice versa. Out of this process, more positive ideas were to emerge.

In late eighteenth-century England, there began a long period of reform, which laid the foundations of modern administrative structure. The executive leadership of the cabinet was established; although much was still left to individual departments, they were expected to work more together. Central control of the budget and finance was increased, with more effective supervision of departmental spending. Attention began to be given to a more logical division of functions between and within departments. Another aspect of this was public service reform, which began in the Indian Civil Service, and culminated in the introduction of competitive recruitment by written examination. This had its reaction on the home Civil Service in Britain. In 1854, there was published the Northcote–Trevelyan Report on the Organisation of the Permanent Civil Service.[2] Here are some quotations from it:

> It may safely be asserted that, as matters now stand, the Government of the country could not be carried on without the aid of an efficient body of permanent officers, occupying a position duly subordinate to that of the ministers who are directly responsible to the Crown and to Parliament, yet possessing sufficient independence, character, ability, and experience to be able to advise, assist and to some extent, influence, those who are from time to time set over them . . .
>
> Admission into the Civil Service is indeed eagerly sought after, but it is for the unambitious, and the indolent and incapable, that it is chiefly desired . . . where their success depends upon their simply avoiding any flagrant misconduct, and attending with moderate regularity to routine duties . . .
>
> The general principle, then, which we advocate is, that the public service should be carried on by the admission into its lower ranks of a carefully selected body of young men, who should be employed from the first upon work suited to their capacities and their education, and should be made constantly to feel that their promotion and future prospects depend entirely on the industry and ability with which they discharge their duties, that with average abilities and reasonable application they may look forward confidently to a certain provision for their lives, that with superior powers they may rationally hope to attain to the highest prizes in the Service, while if they prove decidedly incompetent, or incurably indolent, they must expect to be removed from it.

Among the Northcote–Trevelyan recommendations were that competitive examinations under a central board for the whole service should replace the patronage of departmental heads; that promotion should generally be by merit; and that there should be a division of the service between those concerned with 'intellectual' work and those concerned with the more 'mechanical' (as we should now say, routine) side. By Order in Council of May 1855, the British government established a Board of three Civil Service Commissioners to conduct qualifying examinations. Candidates could not in future be admitted to junior posts without a certificate of qualification by the Commissioners, but the candidates were still nominated by departments, and nine out of ten appointments were still not made competitively. Open competition did not prevail until after 1870, and even then some departments and administrative positions remained for a considerable period exempt from the rule.[3]

The Civil Service Commission was the model for similar bodies in other English-speaking countries, including the United States, though most of these bodies became in time more powerful than their prototype. In Britain the Commission remained a body with limited functions, whose main task was to conduct recruitment examinations; the other central personnel functions were exercised by the Treasury. This arrangement was sometimes criticised, but it was not until 1968 that the British government accepted the recommendation of the Fulton Committee that a Civil Service Department should be established to combine the personnel functions of the Treasury and the Civil Service Commission. The department comes under the Prime Minister, but the latter has delegated day-to-day responsibility to a non-departmental minister; and the permanent head of the Civil Service Department has been designated head of the Home Civil Service.

Little really effective co-ordination of the Australian public services took place until near the end of the nineteenth century. By this time the new doctrine, expressed most strikingly in New South Wales and the Commonwealth was that 'it was possible to divorce personnel administration from financial administration and government policy in general'. Alfred Deakin, at the time Commonwealth Attorney-General, in his Second Reading Speech on the 1901 Public Service Bill, referred to the new occupation of 'business doctors' in the United States of America and 'other members of Parliament expressed repeatedly their belief that it was possible to enact general principles of personnel administration which could be supervised and policed by impartial and objective managers and inspectors'.[4]

Victoria

The movement for public service reform had begun much earlier than this, in Victoria. From the 1850s, Victoria was for forty years the fastest-growing colony, and its public service problems were perhaps the worst. A board of inquiry reported in 1856; its report was almost certainly written by Professor W.E. Hearn, who knew of the Northcote–Trevelyan recommendations in the United Kingdom.[5] (Hearn was Professor of History and Political Economy in the University of Melbourne, and later a member of the Legislative Council of Victoria. His book, *The Government of England* (1867), deserves to be better remembered, and has an interesting chapter on the public service.)

The report proposed an independent central board to conduct open competitive examinations, as proposed in the United Kingdom, and to classify the service, conduct a system of promotion by merit, and so on. The board of inquiry was reconstituted as a Royal Commission, which made less far-reaching recommendations in 1859. The terms of reference of both bodies invited them to recommend such changes as might 'promote efficiency and economy'.

The Victorian Civil Service Act of 1862 provided for qualifying examinations conducted by a Civil Service Board of Examiners, and for other important reforms, but with loopholes that made them ineffective.[6] Another Royal Commission reported in 1873, and was impressed by the recent (1868) Canadian legislation on the subject, even though this turned out in practice to be ineffective. It had provided for a Civil Service Board representing the main departments, both to run an examinations system and, when asked by the government, to report on the general administration of the public service. But Victoria still preferred to swell its service with temporary employees and in the 1970s ran the nearest thing Australia has achieved to the American spoils system. A large 'established' bureaucracy could no doubt be an embarrassment in colonies with widely fluctuating economic conditions and budgets. There were similar ineffective moves in Queensland, New South Wales and South Australia.

Finally in 1883, Victoria passed a new Public Service Act.[7] It provided for a full-time Public Service Board of three to conduct competitive examinations, and to control appointments. Its chairman was a distinguished actuary. The new board was resisted by 'politicians unconvinced that an independent board was the answer to patronage, by staff dissatisfied with the Act for reducing salaries and limiting opportunities, by departments not prepared to accede to the new controls, and by the press which thought the public service too costly'.[8] The outside chairman was forced into resignation and the financial crisis of the 1890s was an excuse for retrenchment: the Public Service Board's duties were transferred to the Audit Commissioners. In 1902, a single Public Service Commissioner was appointed with limited powers, an arrangement which lasted till 1941, when a Public Service Board was re-established.

New South Wales

New South Wales passed a Civil Service Act in 1884 of a less ambitious kind. It provided for a part-time Board of Civil Service Examiners of five members, mostly departmental heads, who met once a week. Its chairmen included well known permanent heads such as Geoffrey Eagar at the Treasury and A.C. Fraser, the Under Secretary for Justice.[9] The board was empowered to conduct qualifying examinations, to recommend appointments and promotions to the Governor, and to grade positions and classify work (ministers retained the right to make temporary appointments). It does not seem to have been a success. However, the depression of the 1890s, so damaging to the Victorian Board, led paradoxically enough in New South Wales to the first really effective public service legislation in Australia.

A Royal Commission, with strong business representation, reported in 1895 that 'the Civil Service of the Colony could be efficiently conducted with a much smaller staff than is now employed; that salaries and wages generally are on a much more liberal scale than is paid for equally responsible work outside; that, owing to the system of promotion by seniority rather than by merit, officers are forced into positions which they are not competent to fill', and so on.[10] The Commission had been a response to demands for public economy, and the charges may have been exaggerated, how much it is now difficult to estimate.[11] The report recommended the creation of 'an independent Board of Commissioners', of three whole-time members, 'to be chosen for their reliability, probity and administrative capacity', not only to conduct examinations but with 'entire control' over the public service. The government, now only too willing to free itself from embarrassing problems, accepted this recommendation, and the 1895 Public Service Act was soon passed. The Premier said: 'If the board tread under feet political patronage, ecclesiastical influences, Potts' Point influences, relation influences, and all other influences . . . [it] will be the most hated board in New South Wales long before it has finished its work.'[12]

The 1895 Act provided for a full-time Board of three Commissioners, appointed for seven-year terms, to control recruitment, promotion, grading and classification, salaries, major disciplinary matters and the employment of temporary staff. The board was also given wide management functions. Section 9 provided that:

> As often as necessary to carry out the directions and provisions of this Act, and ensure the establishment and continuance of a proper standard of efficiency and economy in the Public Service, the Board shall, as far as practicable, personally inspect each department, and investigate the character of the work performed by every officer therein, and the manner in which such officer has performed his duties, and the efficiency, economy, and general working of such department, both separately and in its relation to other departments, and may, for such purpose, examine the permanent head of such department and such other witnesses as may appear to the Board to be necessary.'*

This was the Benthamite principle of 'inspectibility' carried to its limit. Its implications were, and continue to be, enormous. Was the board responsible for managing the service, or was it to ensure that it was well-managed? If the first, what had happened to the principle of ministerial responsibility? If the second, could the board prevail against a minister who insisted that issues of management were inseparable from considerations of policy?

---

* Quoted in the slightly amended form in which it appears in the present Public Service Act. The words, 'and the manner in which such officer has performed his duties', were added later.

The Act also provided for the separation of the service into five Divisions —Special, Professional, Clerical (now Administrative and Clerical), Educational and General. Entry to the Special Division (departmental heads) was to be by promotion on the basis of special qualifications and aptitude. Recruitment to the next three was to be by open competitive examinations organised by the board. The 1895 Act was replaced by a consolidating Act in 1902, with little alteration to its main provisions, and the 1902 Public Service Act is still the main instrument of public service control and management in New South Wales, though it has been amended at various times since then.

The 1895 Board covered most categories of government employee, but the police, railway staff and one or two other groups were exempted from its control. (The number of government employees outside the Public Service Act started to grow again after the First World War when new statutory boards began to be created outside the board's jurisdiction.) The first board included two distinguished public servants, Joseph Barling and T.A. Coghlan; the latter had drafted the 1895 Act. It was active, not least in cutting the size of the public service, and its liveliness is reflected in the outspokenness of its annual reports. Mason Allard later said that its methods had been 'vigorous almost to the point of ruthlessness', but its achievements were great. It may be said to have created the structure of the modern New South Wales service, still in many ways the most professional of the State services. By 1903, it was approaching the University of Sydney for help in providing courses of study suitable for public servants, and proposing Chairs of Economics, Education and Agriculture. However, by the time of the First World War, its energy and influence seem to have waned (Barling retired in 1907); it became preoccupied with routine, less able to assert its authority over the departments, and to win the ear of governments. In Allard's more picturesque language of 1918, 'the Board has drifted along in the uncontrolled current of Service affairs, twisted from time to time in the eddies of expediency'.[13]

Other States

Most other States were passing legislation about the same time as New South Wales, though the permanent results were on the whole unimpressive. A complication was the large transfers of staff to the Commonwealth that took place on federation. Queensland, after abortive legislation in the 1860s, made provision for a Civil (later Public) Service Board in 1889. Tasmania, which had classified its service for promotion purposes as early as 1851, created a part-time Civil Service Board of five in 1900, to be elected by public servants and with a two-year tenure. This early experiment in 'self-government by civil servants' was not successful and was replaced in 1905 by a Public Service Board of three—two full-time 'independent' members, and one elected by public servants (at the same time the Education Department was excluded from its control).[14] Western Australia provided for a Public Service Commissioner in 1904. In South Australia, an advisory board was set up in 1901, to which public servants elected a member, to classify the service. It produced an abortive plan, and disappeared; South Australia had no public service authority until 1916.

All this reflects a significant development taking place in the later nineteenth century—the raising of the organised voice of the ranks of the public service. From this time onwards the views of staff associations, and their political pressures, start to count.

Alfred Deakin, a notable Victorian politician and later federal Prime Minister was reported as expressing this view of the dilemma of the public services at the turn of the century:

> With regard to the civil service, they were between the devil and the deep sea; either men had to be selected and promoted according to the arbitrary device of individuals (which meant political jobbery) or had to be recruited and advanced according to some mechanical process. At the present time it was all a question of seniority and the service was deteriorating in capacity.[15]

It is true that he was speaking in a period of depression and retrenchment.

Commonwealth

Benefiting by the experience of the States, the Commonwealth passed its Public Service Act in 1902. The Act vested control of the service in a single Public Service Commissioner, appointed for seven years and eligible for reappointment; it also provided for up to six inspectors. The Commonwealth service was organised into four Divisions. Admission to it was to be by open competitive examination. The Commissioner was required to make recommendations to the government regarding management and improved methods of work, and also to report annually to parliament on possible improvements, especially for ensuring 'efficiency and economy'.

The Second Period of Reform

Wars are often a source of bureaucratic change. They highlight defects, sometimes bring critical outsiders into the service, and their later stages are liable to evoke widespread reaction against the State and all its doings. The 1914–18 war was no exception, and led to a new series of inquiries into the Australian public services. Businessmen persuaded governments that all that was needed to stop the rot was to enlist their talents and run the bureaucracy on business lines. Many attacks were directed against swollen war-time departments. 'The craze for economy and the admiration for business methods got their second wind . . .'[16]

New South Wales

One service to feel the pressure was that of New South Wales. Mason Allard, a prominent Sydney accountant, was appointed by the government in 1917 as Royal Commissioner to inquire into the 'administration, control, efficiency and economy' of the public service (and also of certain agencies operating outside the Public Service Act). Allard wrote a number of detailed reports. He was very critical of the existing Board, and recommended its dismissal. He complained of its proneness to rely on the permanent heads and on the influence of written regulations. 'There does not appear to be the slightest doubt that the Public Service Act of 1895 contemplated a continuous and close supervision of the Public Service by a Board specially selected for individual capacity.'[17] He recommended among other things that future board members hold office until sixty-five, subject to earlier removal only by a vote of both Houses of Parliament; that the board consist of a Chief Commissioner selected from outside the service with two Assistant Commissioners under his direction; that a staff of 'inspectors or investigating officers' be appointed, to whom the board should delegate powers; that the board establish training classes to assist officers preparing for the various grade examinations which had developed; and that it be put beyond doubt that permanent headships, like other appointments, were subject to the board's jurisdiction.

Amending legislation in 1919 incorporated much of Allard's thinking. The existing board was replaced by a new Public Service Board of three, appointed till the age of sixty-five, and with extensive powers vested in the Chairman. It could be removed only by parliamentary resolution. Five inspectors were appointed in 1919–20,[18] one of whom (Bertram Stevens) was later Premier of New South Wales. The Board now had the independence and authority that has enabled it to play a dominant role in the New South Wales Public Service. In 1955 the number of members was increased from three to four, one of whom was to be a person 'trained as an educationist who has been an officer and who has been directly concerned with or engaged in teaching or the administration of education'.[19] Provision has since been made for one of the members to be designated Deputy Chairman.

The Commonwealth

The Commonwealth fared worse. The first Commissioner, Duncan McLachlan, who had been imported from the New South Wales Service,[20] controlled a service with a solid foundation of officials recruited from the States and made full use of his powers. But after the early years he had to fight hard to keep his authority intact in the face of new democratic and pluralistic pressures from parliament, public service associations and departments, and in a bureaucracy that expanded very rapidly in the years after 1910. When McLachlan left in 1916, his system was beginning to collapse. Thereafter arbitration awards spread, more agencies were made exempt from the Public Service Act, departments in general increased their independence, while recruitment was paralysed by an over-generous scheme of ex-service preference.

The government appointed two Royal Commissions in 1918, one to review the public service, the other public expenditures. The former consisted of

McLachlan, the latter was the so-called Economies Commission—two businessmen and the accountant of the Post Office. As a result, the new Public Service Act of 1922 replaced the Commissioner by a Public Service Board of three (this was a much modified version of the Economies Commission proposal for a Board of Management). The first board appeared to be a strong team with a vigorous policy but, faced with opposition, it let its authority slip away.[21] The Bruce-Page government, though it backed the Board in many respects, preferred to expand government activities through 'business-like' boards and commissions whose staffs were not under the Public Service Act. The depression curtailed many activities, and after 1931 there was again only a single Commissioner, as the two who retired were not replaced. Attempts were made to improve matters in the mid-1930s, but all the same the Commonwealth Public Service was in fairly poor condition in 1939.

As one might expect, some of its best public servants were outsiders, or professionals who had moved across into administration. The Director-General of the Post Office, Sir Harry Brown, was an engineer imported from England. The first secretary to the revived Department of External Affairs, W.R. Hodgson, had spent most of his career with the Army general staff. The secretary to the Defence Department was another graduate and ex-army officer who had been drawn into military administration. J.H.L. Cumpston, the able Director-General of Health, had entered the service as a medical officer before the First World War. Some capable permanent heads had risen from the ranks such as H.J. Sheehan, Secretary to the Treasury (1932–38), and Frank Murphy at the Department of Commerce.

Victoria

In Victoria, the single Public Service Commissioner jogged along. An amending Act in 1912 allowed the appointment of inspectors who could implement the Commissioner's power to investigate the efficiency, economy and general working of the departments. The 1917 Royal Commission on the Victorian Public Service found that an inspector had been duly appointed but 'it was found necessary to transfer his services to another department' and 'the results of the amending legislation were not what might have been anticipated'. Wallace Ross, an accountant and ex-public servant, ten years later made a further report on the Victorian Public Service,[22] and criticised the weakness of the Commissioner in face of ministers and permanent heads. However, Victorian Cabinets preferred to retain a substantial say in public service matters. The public service authority recommended and advised; but the government controlled most personnel matters down to the smallest detail, even to subdivisional promotion within a class.[23] A tolerable system was not achieved until the 1940 and 1946 Public Service Acts were passed, establishing a Public Service Board of three—a chairman, a government member and a staff representative. This late achievement of reasonable authority made things much harder for the new Board. It had a mediocre inheritance.

Other States

Other public service systems were being criticised by the time of the First World War. South Australia appointed its Public Service Commissioner under the 1916 Public Service Act.[24] He was, like his Commonwealth counterpart, to be appointed for seven years. The first appointee was personally popular and achieved reforms; but he had to face powerful departmental heads and, like the Commonwealth Board, got bogged down in classification problems. In 1922 a Commission on the Public Service, the product of an economy drive, said that the Commissioner 'does not appear to have made any proper arrangements' for investigating the work of departments.[25] The government seems to have disallowed many of his salary recommendations, and never fully accepted the idea of an independent public service authority. Public service discontent probably helped Labor to come to power in 1924, and the new government passed the 1925 Public Service Amendment Act (partly based on the 1922 Commonwealth Act) by which more of the Commissioner's power passed to a Classification and Efficiency Board, consisting of himself as a chairman, and with one of the two other members appointed on the recommendation of the Public Service Association. For the next thirty-five years, the General Secretary of the Public Service Association was sent a copy of the Board's agenda for information and comment.[26] A distinguished Public Service Commissioner, L.C. Hunkin, a former Labor politician, was appointed in 1929 by a non-Labor government and was a major influence in South Australian administration for a generation; the 1925 Act had removed the condition that the Commissioner must be a public servant.[27]

In 1949, the Classification and Efficiency Board was replaced by a part-time Public Service Board, normally consisting of the Public Service Commissioner, a government nominee and a Public Service Association representative. This among other things fixed the pay of permanent staff, and recommended new posts to the Governor. The Public Service Commissioner controlled recruitment, recommended promotions, and became once more responsible for efficiency. In 1967 a further major reform took place in South Australia, when the full-time commissioner and part-time board were replaced by a full-time Public Service Board of three, and the Act was rewritten. The new Act made no provision for a staff representative.

The First World War led to rethinking in other States. In 1918, Tasmania replaced its board by a single Public Service Commissioner. The 1923 Act (section 10) gave him powers to deal with departmental economy and efficiency akin to those in the Commonwealth Act of the previous year. However, it also added to the agencies already excluded from central control, and the process of multiplying independent authorities continued till by the 1950s there were twenty-one different wage-fixing bodies within the relatively small Tasmanian government service.[28] In 1958, a three-man Public Service

Tribunal was set up to fix pay, including that of some employees outside the Public Service Act.

In Queensland, J.D. Story reported in 1919 on *The Classification of Officers of the Public Service*,[29] finding the same gap between theory and practice disclosed by Mason Allard in New South Wales and later by Ross in Victoria. He indicated, for example, that the section of the Queensland Act prescribing annual inspections was 'practically inoperative'. Following the 1920 Public Service Amendment Act, Story became sole Public Service Commissioner and held the post for nearly twenty years (in 1938 he became Vice-Chancellor of the University of Queensland, a position he retained till he was over ninety).

The Second World War and After

The Second World War had its main immediate impact on Commonwealth government where the number of departments more than doubled, and the number of civilian employees rose threefold. The Commonwealth service numbered about 47 000 in June 1939, and all but 10 000 of these were in the Post Office and the Customs Service. There were (even including these departments) under 9000 permanent officers in the top three divisions who might be regarded as available for administrative work, and many of these had been recruited at a low standard in the postwar years.[30] Inevitably there was much outside recruitment, and many major positions in the wartime service were filled by outsiders and officers seconded from the States (some of both groups stayed in the Commonwealth service after the war). In this operation, the public service authority was largely bypassed. 'Wartime civilian administration resembled a more primitive way of waging war in which a number of departmental chiefs assembled and led their own hordes in a common cause, some preferring to stay and hold the peacetime fort and others branching out into highly enterprising forays'.[31] Many of the wartime organisations were set up under National Security regulations and were independent of Public Service Board control. This had permanent effects. For example, about one-third of the Assistant Secretaries appointed between 1939 and 1952 had entered the service from outside as 'lateral recruits', and they were particularly well-represented in the main policy-making departments.[32]

After the war, the Commonwealth Public Service Board was returned to its full strength of three, with more staff and money and a new interest in improved recruitment techniques, training, organisation and methods, staff relations. It tried to reassert its authority over the departments. However, no full-scale inquiry into the public services was undertaken, either at Commonwealth or State level; and by the 1950s, though the new Board had important achievements to its credit, the post-war changes seemed to have worked themselves out. A new government tried to make cuts in the bureaucracy, there were besetting pay problems, and the recruiting situation was poor, partly the result of full employment and a bad press. In 1959, the Boyer Committee on Public Service Recruitment reported;[33] though its main recommendations had a dismal reception, it was a portent. The appointment two years later of a new Board Chairman, Frederick Wheeler, a former senior Treasury and I.L.O. official (and later Secretary to the Treasury), led to a renewed period of activism, especially in the field of pay and classification. However, in some ways the early and mid-1960s remained a stagnant period in government administration. The quality of recruitment picked up only slowly, earlier deficiencies began to reflect themselves in shortages of talent for promotion, and there was little impetus for reform from the government. More recent changes are discussed in other chapters. The most significant perhaps was the spate of inquiries into the public services and into government administration generally in the 1970s that produced the Coombs Report in the Commonwealth, the Bland reports in Victoria, the Corbett report in South Australia, and the Wilenski report in New South Wales. Public service reviews are also in progress in Western Australia and Tasmania.

Public Service Boards, Powers and Duties

The powers and duties of Public Service Boards are mainly to be found in the relevant statutes. They may broadly be listed as follows,[34] though there are important variations in their extent:
1. Administration and enforcement of the Public Service Act, including making regulations under the Act.
2. Policy-formation and research on personnel questions.
3. Recruitment, selection and placement of public servants.
4. Establishment and staff control, or recommending the number and classification of positions needed in the departments.
5. Making or approving promotions.
6. Determining salaries and conditions of service, a function that may be shared with arbitration authorities or other tribunals.
7. Helping to improve efficiency and economy in departmental management; by such means as: devising and applying measures and checks of efficiency, training, encouraging the use of improved methods, and so on.
8. Hearing appeals on certain questions.
9. Maintaining personnel records and statistics, and making an annual report to parliament.
10. Last but not least, advice to the Prime Minister/Premier and the government on matters sent to them for an opinion. This may include advice on administrative aspects of cabinet submissions, proposals for changing the organisation and functions of departments, top appointments (where they are not made by the public service authority itself), and so on. Cabinets may, of course, get advice wherever they please; often in the Commonwealth and in New South Wales and some other

States they have been happy to consult the public service authority on such matters.

Commonwealth

The Commonwealth Public Service Board consists of a chairman and two commissioners, appointed by the Governor-General for a term 'not exceeding five years', but eligible for reappointment, and usually reappointed if they wish. Their salaries are fixed by statute and specially appropriated. There are statutory disqualifications from office, but otherwise their removal is subject to disallowance by parliament. Though they can be appointed from outside the service, nearly all the commissioners since the war have been Commonwealth public servants, many of them senior members of the board's staff or former permanent heads. For administrative purposes the board is related to the Prime Minister's Department, makes its annual report to parliament through the Prime Minister, and the chairman has direct access to him. It controls recruitment, though it has delegated part of this to the departments. The creation of posts is reserved to the Governor-General 'on the recommendation of the Board, after the Board has obtained a report from the Permanent Head' (section 29 (1)). So the government is the final authority for establishments; it has usually accepted the board's recommendations, though at times, as in 1951 and again in the 1970s, it has imposed its own staff ceilings. The board is also responsible for the classification of positions. It negotiates most salary scales, though these are also subject to arbitration. Only the board can dismiss an officer.

It is not in as strong a position in relation to the departments as the New South Wales Board. Section 25 (2) of the Commonwealth Public Service Act provides that:

The Permanent Head of a Department shall be responsible for its general working and for all the business thereof, and shall advise the Minister in all matters relating to the Department.

The board has tended to accept the implied need to work by persuasion.[35] Promotions are made by departments, though subject to appeal; in the case of some positions, especially senior ones, the appeal is to the board itself. Permanent headships are a matter for the Prime Minister, though there is provision for consultation with the board's chairman and others (see Chapter Twelve). Section 17 of the Act gives the board the duty of devising 'means for effecting economies and promoting efficiency in the management and working of Departments', including examining their business and exercising 'a critical oversight' of their activities, but these are not, as in New South Wales, executive powers. It advises the permanent head of its suggestions, and if he does not concur, it can do no more than report to his minister or (as a last resort) to parliament. In its whole history the board has made only one report to Parliament under section 17, and that was half a century ago.[36] In line with this, it has tended to respect the permanent head's primary responsibility for departmental management, and has mainly worked by encouraging departments to make use of its advice (it has very occasionally threatened to do a management audit, and has power of entry into departments). On major changes in the machinery of government, such as the decision to create new departments, the board has often had some influence, but sometimes very little. In two important respects, the Commonwealth Public Service Board has more extensive scope than most State authorities. The first is that a larger percentage of Commonwealth employees is under the Public Service Act than in most States. Secondly, Commonwealth legislation creating new statutory authorities commonly requires them to seek board approval of terms and conditions of service (see Chapter Five).

The senior officers are known as First Assistant Commissioners and Assistant Commissioners. The former title is given to the heads of the five main divisions, departmental structures, management systems and efficiency, pay and conditions, recruitment and staff development, and planning, legislation and projects. As a large part of the Commonwealth service works away from Canberra, the board maintains offices in the State capitals and in the Territories, headed by a high-level Regional Director, with important delegated powers to recruit, inspect, make certain appointments, and so on.

New South Wales

The New South Wales Public Service Board is statutorily the most independent and powerful of all Australian Public Service Boards and Commissions. Its four members are appointed until sixty-five, normally from persons already in State government employment, and may be removed from office, apart from certain statutory disqualifications, only by resolution of each House of Parliament. Their salaries are fixed by statute and specially appropriated. Appointments to most public offices are vested by the State Constitution in the Governor-in-Council, but they are also subject to the Public Service Act, unless there is express statutory enactment to the contrary. Appointments under the Act, including permanent heads, are subject to board recommendation; it controls all recruitment examinations and all promotions. It may dismiss officers or reduce them in status and salary for disciplinary offences. It also has power to determine pay, and may enter into agreements with staff associations and unions.

Equally extensive are its powers to manage and control the service. It can make regulations for classification of officers and their work; for promotion, transfer and exchange of officers; for the recruitment of temporary employees; for leave; and generally for economy and efficiency. A striking sentence in the Public Service Regulations says: 'The Permanent Head of each Department shall be responsible *to the Board* [our italics] for the discipline, efficiency, and economic administration of the Department . . .' It may, and does, conduct special inquiries and has on occasion been asked by the cabinet to investigate and advise on the administration of agencies not subject to the Public Service Act. When holding an inquiry it has the powers of a royal commission. It has often had a large say in decisions to reorganise departments and reallocate functions and is generally consulted by the government on such matters. It is also regularly consulted on the staffing implications of new legislation. In a more general way, the board and especially its chairman, have been recognised as having an important co-ordinating role, expressed in forms such as the chairmanship of important committees at the official level, periodical meetings with permanent heads, or lunchtime gatherings of wider groups.

Its powers are subject to some limitations. A powerful minister may fight back, though the board has usually had the support of Premiers in its activities. As already indicated, there is one large area where it has no formal powers, that of the many statutory bodies which control their own staffing. It is also limited in its control of promotions by the restrictive provisions of the Public Service Act, and there is appeal machinery.

The influence of the New South Wales Board reached a new peak during the chairmanship of Wallace Wurth (1936–60),[37] a powerful defender of its prerogatives. In the 1960s, its inspectorate continued to grow, though there was also a trend towards delegating more authority to departments, and for the board to concentrate more on general policy and staff activities. Some senior officers now specialise in fields such as industrial relations, recruitment, staff development and so on, which form separate divisions. Five divisions each deal with a number of departments, and are responsible for general inspection. A Management Consultancy Division provides an advisory service to departments on management improvement, and also carries out 'management audits' of both departments and statutory authorities, as well as looking after an Administrative Research Unit. New South Wales has not accepted the Commonwealth view and that of the Coombs Report that management consultancy, efficiency auditing and the evaluation of 'programme effectiveness' should be tasks confided to three different sets of hands. The New South Wales Board's definition of management audit includes 'establishing whether the organization is effectively fulfilling the purposes for which it exists and achieving its objectives, and is being managed efficiently'. Departmental heads have also been asked to nominate senior officers as Productivity Officers to stimulate programme reviews, with first priority given to the 'elimination of irrelevant activities'.[38]

Victoria

Victoria has a less centralised system than New South Wales and governments have also been less willing to hand over power to an independent commission. The Public Service Board is mainly a product of the 1940 and 1946 Public Service Acts, as widely revised in 1974. At present it consists of a chairman, a government member and a service representative. The chairman serves until sixty-five, the others are appointed for terms not exceeding three years, but may be reappointed or re-elected. The service representative is elected by the permanent officers. The chairman's salary is fixed by statute, and all salaries of members are specially appropriated and (as in New South Wales) they may be removed from office only by parliamentary resolution, apart from the usual statutory disqualifications.

The board has powers of decision in most staff matters. It makes most appointments; it classifies officers and fixes most salaries and conditions of service. Many Victorian public servants have no access to arbitration, and the board is the final authority for wages and conditions of service, subject to disallowance by parliament; and in this particular respect it is more powerful than other public service authorities. It hears charges against officers. Permanent heads have power to make provisional promotions, as in the Commonwealth.

A Promotions Appeal Board hears appeals for most positions, the Public Service Board itself for senior officers. The latter is charged with the critical oversight of service efficiency, and is required to bring to the notice of permanent heads needed improvements in organisation and management. The government retains the power, after report by the board, to control the creation of new positions; it also appoints permanent heads, 'after reference of the matter to the Board' (there are some statutory exceptions to this latter rule).

An important limitation on its powers is the relatively large number of government employees not under the Public Service Act. The number under the Act (June 1976) was only 30 134 out of a total of over 190 000 State government employees in the many statutory authorities and elsewhere, including police and teachers, who also have their own tribunals on pay and employment conditions. Such uniformity of pay and conditions as exists between these various groups is maintained almost wholly by informal contact; the personal role of the chairman as a point of consultation and co-ordination can sometimes be important. One's impression is that the Public Service Board of Victoria has not in the past had the weight and authority of the Commonwealth and New South Wales Boards, nor the same backing from most governments (though the 1974 Act may have opened a new era in this respect). It is hard to imagine the chairman of either of these boards being accused of breach of parliamentary privilege, as the Chairman of the Victorian Public Service Board was in 1968, for at first refusing to give the Public Accounts Committee access to a management consultant's report on the Public Works Department; it is true that the charge was quickly dropped.[39]

Other States

In Queensland the State Constitution and Public Service Act vest supreme control of the Public Service in the Governor in Council. The three-member Public Service Board recommends to the Governor in Council on permanent appointments, including some promotions, and on the establishment and classification of positions, salaries, etc. Recommendations are submitted through the relevant minister; where they concern more than one department, or relate to the public service generally, through the Premier. If approval is not given, the matter may be sent back to the board for reconsideration.

The replacement of a single commissioner by a board in 1968 fulfilled a promise made years earlier; the opportunity was finally taken when the last commissioner retired. The new commissioners are appointed for terms not exceeding seven years, subject to reappointment. Their pay and tenure during this period are subject to similar guarantees to those of other Public Service Boards. The chairman is designated 'permanent head' of the Department of the Public Service Board, and as such may exercise certain powers of his own, including some relating to employees not under the Public Service Act. Permanent heads of departments have certain powers to nominate officers for promotion, with an appeal to the board. It recommends most other appointments; in the case of permanent heads, it advises the government. Salaries are in practice mainly fixed by arbitration awards or registered agreements, covering not only regular departments but also employees of statutory authorities. A larger percentage of government employees than in other States are subject to the Public Service Act. The Governor in Council, on the board's recommendation, may declare that any of his powers under the Act shall be exercised by the board or by the minister concerned. Considerable delegation has in fact taken place (in the case of education, almost all powers are delegated to the Minister for Education and the Director-General).

The Public Service Board of South Australia consists of three commissioners appointed for fixed terms not exceeding five years. It fixes pay and controls most personnel matters, including appointments other than permanent headships; however, on many matters there has been increasing delegation to departments. Detailed responsibility for departmental efficiency lies with permanent heads, but the board has important powers to advise, to monitor performance, and to report on the level of efficiency achieved.

In Tasmania a single Public Service Commissioner survived until 1973, but the effectiveness of his work was limited by various factors outside his control. Finally, Tasmania followed the other States in replacing him by a Public Service Board, the three members of which are appointed for terms not exceeding five years. The Public Service Tribunal was abolished, so the board now deals with pay; an Arbitrator hears appeals from its determinations. Like the commissioner, the board recommends appointments and promotions, and has powers to promote good management.

In Western Australia, the Public Service Commissioner was also replaced in 1970 by a Public Service Board of three. The government rejected a proposal that one of these should be an elected representative of public servants. It has recently (1978) rewritten its Public Service Act.

Membership and Tenure

A high degree of permanency attaches in practice to the tenure of most board members, unless they prefer otherwise, as this has been thought necessary to protect their independence and preserve continuity of policy. Commissioners are nearly always appointed from the public service or other government employment. The Chairman of the Commonwealth Board (1978) was a former Secretary of the Department of Finance. His predecessor was a senior Foreign Affairs officer; and his predecessor had been a permanent head, who returned to a permanent headship. The Chairman of the New South Wales Board had spent much of his service career with the board; his predecessor had been President of the Metropolitan Water Board, and earlier Under Secretary of the State Treasury and an officer of the Public Service Board. The Victorian Chairman was previously Auditor-General, but had earlier served with the Board.

If there is a board, this raises the problem of relations between its chairman and the other members. In New South Wales, the chairman has often been very powerful, and the Public Service Act provides (subject to some procedural safeguards) that if he disapproves of a board decision, 'the matter shall be determined according to the deliberate judgment of the chairman, irrespective of the decision of the other members'. In such cases he has to, and any other member may, forward reasons for his stand to the Premier; but this power of veto has very rarely, if ever, been used. In the Commonwealth the chairman appears distinctly *primus inter pares*, and for some purposes, such as permanent head appointments, has an independent role, but all board decisions are by majority vote. Generally two members of a board form a quorum. Not much is known about the way that boards subdivide and delegate their work in practice; there may be no regular meetings of the board as such, and its approval may mean simply approval by two members, including the chairman on major issues. Some have a weekly meeting, as does the Commonwealth board; in other cases the board may be in more continuous session and deal with more matters of detail. Some statutes make formal provision for delegation of powers to the chairman or more widely. One suspects that boards work best where the leadership of the chairman is clearly recognised, possibly even better where he has at least one really able deputy prepared to play the role of critical but loyal first lieutenant.

The Role of the Public Service Authorities

In other countries it has been rare to find as much power concentrated in the central public service authority as exists in the more powerful Australian boards, in particular, the combination of powers over recruitment and conditions of service, with those regarding management and efficiency.

Relations with the Treasury or Department of Finance

Financial management is bound to impinge on staff problems, as wages and salaries are an important part of government expenditure, so the Treasurer inevitably takes an interest in staff needs and costs. Where should the line be drawn in these matters? In Australia the situation varies. In general the main powers over staff matters rest with Public Service Boards, though the budgetary agency's power to check departmental estimates always gives it some voice, and in some States it has a powerful role in establishments. In the Commonwealth, the main power has usually rested with the board, though the cabinet is the final authority for establishments and up to the 1950s staffing limits were in fact imposed by the Treasury as part of the Estimates. In 1951 and several times in the 1970s, the government imposed its own staff ceilings and for a while kept a close check on them.[40] Funds have, of course, to be available to meet the cost of staff increases in any department, and the provision of these remains the prerogative of the Minister for Finance. But this power does not seem to have been used so as to quarrel with the Public Service Board. The same is true in New South Wales.

Some writers have argued that the Treasury or Department of Finance with its concern for the economical performance of governmental functions in general, is the department that should properly be concerned with the economical use of manpower, as used to be the case in Britain, even if detailed questions of recruitment and appointment are left to a separate personnel authority. Critics of the Civil Service Department in Britain have feared that it may lack the Treasury's weight in relation to the larger and more powerful departments, and may find it harder to attract a first-rate staff (unless there is a conscious programme of giving good people a spell in personnel work), or to obtain the backing of a really strong minister. Others fear that a specialised personnel agency, without wider concerns, tends to make personnel work a way of life, and that its staff may come to lack contact with the substantive issues of government. Similar criticisms have been made of some Public Service Boards. One role the Treasury has played in Britain is as a testing-ground for promising young public servants, who can be given a wide range of interesting and demanding work, and later placed in other agencies. Public Service Boards can also play this role, and have sometimes done so, but it is less easy for them. However, there are also some powerful arguments against Treasury control of staff questions. The main one is that personnel management, and wider questions of departmental organisation, require specialised and creative attention of a kind that financial departments, with all their other concerns, are unlikely to provide.

Relations with Other Agencies

The administrative history in the early part of this chapter has been written very much from a Public Service Board angle; it has been hard to avoid the implication that the health of the public service has varied directly with the strength of the public service authority. Yet we know far too little about Australian administrative history to draw so firm a conclusion. Nor can we safely conclude much about the relative efficiency of ministerial departments, as compared with those statutory authorities over which Public Service Boards have often had little or no power.

What is the broad case for and against a central personnel authority? The role of Public Service Boards has been described in various ways, as (i) impartial defender of the merit system against politicians and patronage; (ii) efficient central manager, and formulator of personnel policies, co-ordinating employment conditions and reaping the economies of scale and specialisation; less often, but sometimes (iii) as spokesman for the public service, seeing that its legitimate interests have a single voice to speak for them.[41] The Coombs Report thinks that an 'important purpose of the Board's independent status' is 'to protect standards of administrative performance' and to guard against undue pressure either for economy or for new programmes unaccompanied by the means to implement them.

On the first point, the Commonwealth Public Service Board represents a fairly sweeping victory for the notion of the public service as 'self-regulating',[42] even though governments inevitably retain some controls over so expensive an item. Members of parliament have usually been glad to keep out of public service affairs, save when pressured by public staffs themselves. Attempts to bring outside influence to bear on individual grievances (say, a missed promotion) are now fairly easy to ward off. Industrial relations can still become 'political', but this will always be the case under any system. There are occasional government-inspired retrenchments; however, the effects of these rarely last long. The very top appointments are still mostly, as we have seen, within the patronage of government, including appointments to the Public Service Board itself; but there is no evidence that this power is nowadays greatly abused, at least not to the point of scandal.

It has even been said that Public Service Boards have succeeded so well in establishing the merit system, that they have worked themselves out of the job. Are they still necessary to protect the merit system? Many statutory bodies seem to get on well enough without their protection. No doubt (it may be argued) there is a residue of protection still needed, but not one that needs elaborate machinery, perhaps one that could be performed by a committee of permanent heads or tribunal or some such device. Certainly it is true that the main case for a central personnel authority must rest nowadays not on its protective but on its other roles.

What is the case for a central agency to 'manage' the public service? As Caiden puts it,[43] it is the case for avoiding competitive bidding for staff, and establishing uniform standards of pay and conditions; widening career opportunities and curbing inbreeding in sections of the service; and reaping the economies of scale in having a single agency for recruitment, training, certain management services, and so on.

The first is an important function of many boards, and there will no doubt be increasing demands for forms of co-ordination that also include government employees not under the Public Service Acts. Public service authorities also still function to widen career opportunities. It is true that for most public servants their career will lie in one agency. Many departments need to think more than they do about how their officers can be made contented, efficient and committed to the department's particular objectives, and it may be that control by a central personnel agency in some way hinders this process. But the 'closed shop' can also be stultifying, as is true in some statutory authorities, and Public Service Boards help to keep the doors open.

The boards at their best can also offer expert advice to governments, and give specialised attention to problems of recruitment, personnel management, departmental organisation and working methods. This is especially important where there are still backward units, either because they are small and inbred, or their senior staffs are narrow and unimaginative.

Yet there are critics of the present system, who think that the public services have become obsessed with the idea of uniformity. They argue that different sectors of government increasingly differ in their needs and demands, as we have added to the old regulatory notion of government the idea that government should be concerned with creative action in many complex and specialised fields. They say that recruitment and staffing problems need tackling with greater flexibility. They claim that if the principles of good management are to apply in the public sector then the real employer, the agency that determines the work to be done, should have more control over who is to do it and on what terms. A related argument recognises the important general management and policy functions of central personnel authorities, but adds that if they are responsible for too many run-of-the-mill personnel functions, this hampers them in their wider role; and also that an 'authoritarian' approach may inhibit acceptance of the Public Service Board as an expert adviser and counsellor. The Coombs Commission thought that Public Service Boards, like other co-ordinating bodies, should emphasise their 'educating and promotional functions, delegating greater responsibility for immediate decisions to the departments and agencies concerned, and limiting their active intervention to the conduct of spot checks and joint studies . . .'[44]

It was said earlier that one impulse behind the creation of central personnel authorities was the belief that personnel administration could be made a specialised task, separate from problems of government policy. But this is only a half-truth. The organising and staffing of a department must be sensitively adapted to its particular tasks, and the people responsible for this need to be fully aware of the changing priorities of government. Public service authorities have sometimes preferred to protect their independence and the rituals of their craft by separating themselves from these issues. They need their quota of specialists but also of lively public servants with experience at a senior level of other government agencies, who are interested in substantive questions of policy, and know what ministers and permanent heads are thinking, even if they also have to stand up to them from time to time.

Public service authorities have already recognised the merits of some of these arguments. One of the striking developments in personnel administration is the growth of supportive and advisory activities, designed to assist a department's own efforts to become more efficient, rather than to regulate and direct. In the New South Wales Board, for example, much of the work of Management Consultancy Division is of this kind, and expanding activities in in-service training and the counselling services of the Staff Development Division point in the same direction. The approach is reflected in the growth of groups including departmental and board representatives, such as the Personnel Management Group and the Management Services Group. The Commonwealth Board has a longer history of acting by advice and persuasion and its recent mythology is that it has to work by 'co-operation'. The Coombs Report thought that management consultancy would be best done by a largely rotating staff bought in for relatively short periods from the departments and the private sector.

Another emerging role for public service authorities is in the area of systematic review of, and advice to governments on 'machinery of government' aspects of public policies. The Coombs Commission suggested that an important area was manpower planning, and the further development of a system of forward manpower estimates for each government agency, which would be approved by the government along with the financial estimates. Within these, departments would be freer to vary structures and to classify particular positions, though it was recognised that the board would need to retain some power to review departmental decisions.[45] In the larger governmental units at least, perhaps we are moving to a situation where the central personnel agency sets broad policies and standards, has an important voice in major appointments and in pay and conditions, is a court of appeal, and a source of research, advice and review, but where employing units will be large and well-organised enough to handle many of their own problems. In such a case, there would be less reason for distinguishing between Public Service Act employees and those of many statutory authorities. Most government workers could be brought under the same broadly conceived statutes.[46]

There would still be a danger that the personnel agency would interpret its central role too passively, and it would certainly need strong backing at cabinet level. This may be why the British so long relied on the Treasury in staff matters and one reason why the Fulton Committee recommended a Civil Service Department, responsible to the Prime Minister, rather than a wholly independent commission; and some observers are already a little disillusioned with the Civil Service Department. In Britain (apart from recruitment) personnel administration has always been seen as a direct political responsibility. The Corbett Committee on the South Australian Service thought that the government should be able to issue written directives on policy to the Public Service Board, and this proposal has been endorsed by the cabinet.[47]

The 1962 McCarthy Report on State Services in New Zealand recommended that the Public Service Commission be given the status of a department responsible to the Prime Minister for its general management functions, though not for those relating to individual public servants. As it said:

> Ultimate responsibility for the efficiency of the State Services rests inescapably with the Government . . . We think it advisable now to dispose of the erroneous but common view that the Public Service Commission's chief function is to act as a personnel authority independent from political control . . . To be successful (in destroying patronage), the Commission had to be made completely independent of political control in *matters affecting individual public servants* (our italics). And so it was. But in ensuring efficiency and economy in wider matters of general organization and conditions of employment, it must act always as the agent of the Government, which has ultimate responsibility for these things. It has never been and could never be politically independent in performing this function.[48]

It is certainly the case that the strength or weakness of Public Service Boards in Australia has depended to a considerable degree on the amount of backing they have received from Prime Ministers and Premiers. Even the most powerful and independent of them finds its authority slipping away if deprived for any considerable period of this kind of political support. This implies that the board must pay considerable heed to the views of governments, even if the latter have no power to give written directives and the board from time to time rejects advice privately communicated or even occasionally issues a mild threat.

Some writers (including the Coombs Commission) still see advantages in the independent status of Public Service Boards. A few even complain that they do not capitalise enough on their independence, and become as free as judges in uttering comment and criticism. A board is (as one of them recently stated) 'able to defend its policies and practices without offending the principles of ministerial responsibility'.[49] The Commonwealth Board was criticised some years ago because it rarely let anyone know 'what it is thinking, what are its successes, what are its failures, and what are its ideas for tackling these problems'.[50] It has not fulfilled its statutory function of reporting on the efficiency of the public service. The reports of some boards are occasionally outspoken, though rarely in the manner of Duncan McLachlan. The Commonwealth Public Service Board has lately taken some guarded steps in this direction; in 1974 it criticised the Vernon Report on the Post Office after its recommendations had been accepted by the government; the 1977 Report was critical of the government's behaviour on staff ceilings.

Arguably public service authorities might stick their necks out in public a little more than they do. It would be unrealistic to expect them regularly to expose their criticisms of departmental administration, or their differences of opinion with ministers and governments, and there is no evidence that this would help them to do their work better. But they might be more forthcoming about the general considerations that affect their policies, and readier to stimulate discussion about the problems and possibilities of public employment.

Notes

1. The history of bureaucracy is, of course, much older. For a short account of European public service history, see Ernest Barker, *The Development of Public Services in Western Europe*, Cambridge University Press, Cambridge, 1944 (reprinted Hamden, Connecticut, 1966).
2. The report is reprinted in *Public Admin.* (London), XXXII, Spring 1954, 1–16, and in Report, (Fulton) Committee on the Civil Service, London, 1968, I, Appendix B.
3. cf. Emmeline Cohen, *The Growth of the British Civil Service, 1780–1939*, Allen and Unwin, London, 1941, 119–23; and H.W. Parris, *Constitutional Bureaucracy*, Allen and Unwin, London, 1969, ch 2, 5.
4. G.E. Caiden, 'The Independent Central Personnel Agency—the Experience of the Commonwealth Public Service of Australia', *Public Admin.* (London), 42, Summer 1964, 150; and *Com. Parl, Deb.* (H. of R.), Vol. I, 19 June 1901, 1302.
5. Report on the Victorian Civil Service, *Vic. Parl. Papers*, 1856–7, Vol. IV. On Hearn, see J.A. La Nauze, 'Hearn and "The Government of England" ', *Public Admin.* (Sydney) XXVI, 4, December 1976.
6. cf. R.S. Parker, *Public Service Recruitment in Australia*, Melbourne University Press, Melbourne, 1942, 21–2.
7. Its Railway Management Act of the same year had provided for an independent Board of Railway Commissioners. Some of the worse scandals concerned the railway system. See R.L. Wettenhall, *Railway Management and Politics in Victoria, 1856–1906*, RIPA, Canberra, 1961; Caiden, *Career Service*, 40; and Geoffrey Serle, *The Rush to be Rich: A History of the Colony of Victoria, 1883–1889*, Melbourne University Press, Melbourne, 1971, 33–5.
8. G.E. Caiden, *Career Service*, Melbourne University Press, Melbourne, 1965, 40–1.
9. On Eagar and Fraser, see *Australian Dictionary of Biography*, Vol. 4, Melbourne University Press, Melbourne, 1972.
10. Report, Royal Commission on the Civil Service, 1895, 30.
11. cf. K.W. Knight, 'Patronage and the New South Wales Public Service: the 1894 Royal Commission', *Aust. J. Pol. Hist.*, VII, 2, November, 1961. For a contemporary comparison of the impact of depression on the Victorian and New South Wales services, see A.G. Austin (ed.), *The Webbs' Australian Diary 1898*, Melbourne University Press, 1965, 67, 87.
12. *NSW Parl. Deb.*, Vol. 80, 9 October 1895, 1270.
13. First Sectional Report, Royal Commission on the Public Service, 1918, *NSW Parl. Papers*, 1918, Vol. IV. See also W.C. Wurth, 'The Public Service of New South Wales since 1895', *J. Royal Aust. Hist. Soc.* 45, 6, (1960), 299–301; and

G.L. Little, *Public Service Retrenchment in New South Wales*, Sydney, 1902 (in Social Science Pamphlets Vol. 25, Public Library of Victoria).

14. R.L. Wettenhall, 'The Public Service and Public Corporations in Tasmania', *Public Admin.* (Sydney), XVIII, 4, December 1959; and *A Guide to Tasmanian Government Administration*, Platypus Publications, Hobart, 1968, 216.

15. Austin (ed.), *op. cit.*, 64.

16. V. Subramaniam, 'The Evolution of Classification Practices and Patterns in Australia', *Public Admin.* (Sydney), XIX, 4, December 1960, 330.

17. First Sectional Report, Royal Commission on the Public Service, 1918, *NSW Parl. Papers*, 1918, Vol. IV, xv.

18. On the history and work of the board's inspectorate, see 'They Represent the Board', *Progress* (NSW Public Service Board), March 1969.

19. *Public Service Act*, section 7(1A).

20. cf. G.E. Caiden, 'The Early Career of D.C. McLachlan', *Public Admin.* (Sydney), XXII, 2, June 1963: and *Career Service*, 65.

21. On this period see Caiden, *Career Service*, ch. 6–7; and cf. L.F. Giblin, 'The Recruiting of the Public Service', *Public Admin.* (Victorian Regional Group), I, 2, December 1929.

22. Report into the Public Service, *Vic. Parl. Papers*, 1927, Vol. I.

23. Andrew Garran, 'Promotion and Salaries in the Victorian Public Service', *Public Admin.* (Sydney), XIX, 1, March 1960, 53; cf. F.A. Bland, *Planning the Modern State*, 2nd edn, Angus and Robertson, Sydney, 1945, 160.

24. G.N. Hawker, 'South Australia's First Public Service Commissioner', Public Admin. (Sydney) XXVI, 2, June 1967.

25. *ibid.*, 179.

26. Report, Committee of Inquiry into the Public Service of South Australia, Adelaide, 1975, 5.

27. On Hunkin, see Hugh Stretton, *Ideas for Australian Cities*, Adelaide, 1970, 145ff.

28. R.L. Wettenhall, 'The Public Service and Public Corporations in Tasmania', *Public Admin.* (Sydney), XVIII, 4, December 1959, 299.

29. Report, Royal Commission on Public Service, *Queensland Parl. Papers*, 1919–20, Vol. 1.

30. Paul Hasluck, *The Government and the People, 1939–1941*, Canberra, 1952, 482–90.

31. *ibid.*, 490.

32. H.A. Scarrow, *The Higher Public Service of the Commonwealth of Australia*, Duke University Press, Durham NC, 1957, 111–4. The figures exclude purely wartime departments; one-third of the outsiders came from the State services.

33. On the Boyer Report, see Caiden, *Career Service*, ch. 19–20. Some of its less important recommendations were embodied in the 1960 Public Service Amendment Act.

34. Adapted from the list in G.E. Caiden, *The Commonwealth Bureaucracy*, Melbourne University Press, Melbourne, 1967, 191–2.

35. Sir Frederick Wheeler, 'Some Observations on the Commonwealth Public Service Board as a Co-ordinating Authority', *Public Admin.* (Sydney), XXVI, 1, March 1967. There is a similar provision in the Victorian and South Australian Public Service Acts, more cautiously worded.

36. See Report, RCAGA, Appendix Vol. Four, 240.

37. See articles in the memorial issue of *Public Admin.* (Sydney) XX, 1, March 1961. For some aspects of service history in this period see W.C. Wurth, *op. cit.*, 305–11.
38. Report, Public Service Board of NSW, 1976–77, 13.
39. Jean Holmes, *The Government of Victoria*, University of Queensland Press, St Lucia, 1976, 15–16, 30.
40. For the history of 'staff ceilings', see Report, Royal Commission on Australian Government Administration, Appendix Vol. One, 118–22.
41. A good summary of the case for Public Service Boards is in G.E. Caiden, 'The Commonwealth Public Service Board', in H. Mayer (ed.), *Australian Politics: A Second Reader*, Cheshire, Melbourne, 1969, 590.
42. Caiden, *The Commonwealth Bureaucracy*, 167.
43. *loc. cit.*
44. Report, RCAGA, 389.
45. Report, RCAGA, 241–2, 392–4.
46. Report, RCAGA, 256–60.
47. Report, Committee of Inquiry into the Public Service of South Australia, Adelaide 1975, 15.
48. Report on the State Services in New Zealand, 1962, 3, 48. cf. R.S. Parker, 'Public Service Management in the Welfare State', *Public Admin.* (Sydney) XXII, 3, September 1963.
49. Annual Report, Commonwealth Public Service Board, Canberra, 1977, 99.
50. Caiden, in Mayer, *op. cit.*, 596.

Addendum

A projected new Public Service Act in New South Wales will provide for a Public Service Board appointed for five years and subject to government direction on certain matters. Departmental heads will no longer be formally responsible to the Board for efficiency and economy but the Board will have certain powers in relation to statutory authorities.

Chapter Twelve

Staffing the Public Service

Success in staffing is governed by a number of factors. The recruits must have skills suited to the organisation, and the right temperament and outlook. There are social and economic factors involved—in particular, the way the organisation is related to the general social, educational and economic structure of the country, its 'image', the status it enjoys and the opportunities it offers compared with its rivals. These will set limits to the kinds of people it can recruit, retain and use to best advantage.

Any organisation has, of course, a certain freedom of manoeuvre. It can choose its own selection techniques and up to a point get the skills and personality types that suit it. Less obviously, it can adapt its internal structures to take account of the changing structures of the world outside. This is not simply a question of pay and conditions, or of training schemes, though these are important. The structure will have to be related to the educational system, the degree of occupational mobility, as well as to more intangible social factors such as attitudes to authority, hierarchy, and to government in general. Many failures in staffing result from the belief that selection techniques, training, and pay are the only things that matter.

Recruitment

General Policy

The main tasks of those immediately concerned with recruitment are to find the right tests of competence; to prevent favouritism, that is, avoid selection on grounds unrelated to competence; and to get a reasonable share of the talent in the community. All this has to be related to the needs of the service. The latter is a complex criterion. First, needs from the bottom to the top have to be taken into account, as the people recruited will ultimately have to fill posts at all levels. A good recruitment system has to be related to the structure of the public service, to a good system of job classification, and be accompanied by provision for placement, training and promotion. Of course 'needs' are themselves fixed partly in relation to recruitment possibilities. Any public service is, and has to be, modelled partly on the kinds

312

of recruit it can get, so its notions of what it needs are partly a product of its own history.

The principle of open competition, subject to some minimum educational standard, has been interpreted in a number of different ways, some of which (though defensible) are not really open competition. It does not apply at all to a growing number of positions where specialist qualifications are required. A few of the highest official posts, especially on statutory boards and commissions, may be filled from outside by nomination. However, some form of open competitive entry is still the common method of recruiting, departure from which has usually to be specially justified. The Coombs Commission thought it should be redefined as 'procedures which rely on a careful assessment of those personal qualifications and capabilities likely to contribute to the efficient working of government administration, and which as far as possible preclude patronage, favouritism or unjustified discrimination', and extended to all statutory bodies.[1] Recruitment to administrative–clerical positions has been very much on the basis of State school examinations. The Commonwealth still uses these as a minimum standard, but a clerical selection test (CST) was introduced in 1961 to place candidates in order of merit. It includes tests in computation, checking errors, spelling, vocabulary, English usage and expression, reading comprehension and current affairs, as well as in quantitative thinking and critical interpretation of data. So some attempt is made to measure administrative–clerical skills.[2] In New South Wales marks in school examinations are the main criterion for the Administrative–Clerical Division, but there is also an interview and other forms of testing.

The main recruiting authority for the regular departments is the Public Service Board. Some departmental positions (on the Board's recommendation) may be exempted from the Public Service Act. For example, nearly a fifth of Commonwealth Public Service Act employees are 'exempt staff', mostly Fourth Division workers employed by the Defence Department, the Department of Construction and similar agencies.

Within the broad principle of open competition, Australian public service authorities have a good deal of discretion about recruitment policy. The Public Service Acts usually say little or nothing about standards, points of entry, the nature of examinations and selection methods, and other aspects of the recruitment process. This is left to the recruitment authority to fix. However, recruitment authorities are usually required to make these conditions public. There is nothing to prevent public service authorities from delegating much of the detailed business of recruitment to departments, and nowadays they often do so, especially for specialist recruits and temporary appointments. Board control is fully safeguarded where there are statutory provisions that new appointments to the service shall not be made without the recommendation of the public service authority. The New South Wales Public Service Act provides that:

1. The Board shall 'make regulations for the competitive examination of

persons desirous of admission into the Public Service' (section 27 (1); the Board may state that an examination is not required in certain cases.)
2. No permanent appointment of anyone not already in the Service shall be made 'except upon a certificate from the Board that such an appointment is required' (section 34 (2); the Board also controls temporary employees.)

Not all Australian Public Service Acts are so explicit, but in all cases there is a service-wide system of recruitment control. Some boards now require departments to make forward estimates of their needs, as a basis for future planning.

The prevailing theory for a long time was that of a 'closed service' recruited at or near the bottom, and from school, but it never wholly corresponded to Australian practice. There have been later-age recruits, especially to professional positions, some of whom moved into higher administration. Wars led to extensive recruiting of outsiders who sometimes stayed on after the war. There has also been increasing room for graduates. For a long time, the public services reconciled theory and practice by recruiting cadets and trainees from school, then giving them leave and generous assistance to attend full-time university and other courses, but bonded to serve for some years on graduation. This method was applied extensively to professional categories and to the teaching service, but rarely to administrative–clerical groups. However, the Commonwealth, and more recently the States, have found various ways and means of recruiting graduates to administrative–clerical positions without treating them in all respects as base-grade clerks; and the old kind of cadetship is becoming rare even for professional groups. Finally, if we consider government employment as a whole, many statutory boards and commissions do their own recruiting, sometimes with fairly flexible arrangements, though accepting the broad principle of open competition.

The old conception of a career service has been eroded in a different way, as a result of higher levels of employment and greater job mobility. In one State service, of the administrative–clerical recruits with the Higher School Certificate in 1972, only 35 per cent were still there five years later.

Graduate Recruitment

While the public services accepted the school examination system, they were slow to link entry with the more advanced levels of education. In the Commonwealth it was only after much argument that provision was made for the recruitment of non-professional graduates. Some services have recruited graduates for professional and technical posts since before the First World War, though many used the cadetship method described above. Only in the last few years have the State services made special arrangements in the administrative field, though some States have for many years granted fairly liberal study leave to allow officers to graduate or to obtain higher qualifications part-time while in the service.

An Administrative Class on the former English model never became a serious issue in Australia. Apart from the influence of democratic sentiment and the opposition of public service associations, the pattern of the public services was well established before the Australian universities became national institutions (as they were slow to do, though four of them were founded in the nineteenth century). The States dominated the recruitment scene until the Second World War, and their general atmosphere was inhospitable to the direct entry of Arts or Economics graduates. In any case, many of them were getting reasonably good recruits from school, and professional officers were playing an increasingly important role.

The Commonwealth government took a major step in 1933, when it authorised an amendment to the Public Service Act (section 36A) permitting the appointment of graduates to clerical vacancies in the Third Division.[3] The number was not to exceed 10 per cent of announced vacancies, and recruitment was to the base-grade salary range. A trickle of 'generalist' graduates into the service followed (see Table 12.1), which increased when the scheme was revived after the war. They mainly found their way to Canberra, to the diplomatic service and the growing economic departments. They were supplemented by other graduates who entered from outside later in life, especially during and immediately after the war, or who graduated while in the service. Wider use was also made of the power to recruit specialist graduates, who later formed part of the group from which higher posts could be filled. A variety of research officer positions appeared which offered higher pay and more interesting work.

Indeed, a fairly quiet revolution began, as a result of which over 90 per cent of First Division officers are now graduates and over 70 per cent of the Second Division. Many others hold diplomas representing significant amounts of higher education. In departments such as the Treasury and the Public Service Board, about half the Third Division staff are graduates or diplomates.

TABLE 12.1

Graduate Appointments to Third Division, Commonwealth Public Service, 1938–75*

	Administrative	Specialist	Total
1938–39	15	13	28
1948–49	80	111	191
1959	78	134	212
1969	437	447	884
1975	877	871	1748

* Based on Table in *Report*, Commonwealth Public Service Board, 1971, 131; 1975 figures are calculated from the Public Service Board Statistical Yearbook 1976. All figures refer to a twelve-month period. Figures for the first three years are later estimates.

In 1957, a Commonwealth Committee of Inquiry into Public Service Recruitment[4] was established, partly as a result of general concern about the standard of recruits. One of its recommendations was that there should be some direct recruitment of graduates, along with serving officers of promise, into a Second Division Training Grade, which would contain positions suitable for higher administrative training. The idea was attacked by staff associations, and received little official or political support. However, in 1960 the Public Service Act was amended to make graduate entry to administrative–clerical positions part of normal recruitment, though 'so far as is practicable . . . not more than one-tenth of the total number of persons so appointed in a year' (section 36 (1)). The government has since (1976) agreed to remove this not very onerous restriction.

For some years there has been provision for a special intake of high-quality graduates. In 1963 the Commonwealth Public Service Board began a scheme for Administrative Trainees, selected graduates who are placed in a special Third Division category for a year's training, including job-rotation; competition for these positions is now intense. Some departments have their own similar schemes. The Public Service Board now co-ordinates the recruitment of many graduates of higher quality, who are appointed as Assistant Research Officers. Other non-professional graduates enter under the same conditions as non-graduate recruits, and take the Clerical Selection Test. In 1975, 1748 graduates were recruited, of whom about one-third were 'technological' (science, engineering, medical and so on); another third had various 'arts' qualifications, and the rest mostly had economics (about one-fifth) and law degrees. About 30 per cent were women.

It has been argued that some graduate recruits have been excessively privileged, and that graduate training schemes have been less democratic than the Boyer plan, and the post-Fulton scheme in Britain, which both also made special provision for promising non-graduates already in the service. However, the Commonwealth has a more 'open' promotion system than most public services, and the board, like some State boards, has given considerable encouragement to non-graduate public servants to obtain higher qualifications. In 1975, 629 Commonwealth officers graduated while already in the service, either as full-time cadets and trainees or under study assistance schemes. Again, the British scheme does not seem to have found much suitable talent among non-graduates.

The Public Service Board of New South Wales as early as 1918 prepared draft regulations relating to graduates in arts, law and economics—they included a provision that such candidates should have taken courses in, or be examined in, such subjects as economics, statistics, and public administration. However, in the disappointing climate of the interwar years, these proposals got nowhere. The idea was briefly revived from 1938–41 in the form of full-time study leave after entry for a small number of 'administrative cadets'.[5] This scheme was not continued after the war, and it was not until

1967 that the Public Service Board experimented again. There is now a regular yearly recruitment of Graduate Clerks.

There have been similar moves in other States. For example, South Australia some years ago agreed to appoint undergraduates as trainee research officers on a part-time basis, with the student being paid for work done in the service during his university career. In 1967, it introduced a scheme of direct graduate entry to administrative positions, and an increasing number have been recruited into the Administrative Division. Victoria lagged behind for a long time, and as late as the early 1970s only 2.5 per cent of the Administrative Division were graduates, made worse by the fact that the division operated as a 'closed shop' for administrative appointments. However, this State has recently started a graduate recruitment scheme, and appointed over sixty graduates to administrative positions in the year 1975–76. Western Australia has been recruiting twenty or more graduates a year to its Trainee Graduate Assistant Scheme since 1970.

Foreign Affairs

Australia has no equivalent of the special statutes in some other English-speaking countries that treat the Foreign Service as a special case. Foreign Affairs officers are Public Service Act employees like other public servants. This has not prevented significant differences from appearing, partly the inevitable result of differences of environment and experience. The diplomatic service is a well-knit community with a strong professional sense, and has some of the characteristics of a 'career system', as defined below. Diplomatic trainees are all recruited as graduates and there has been little transfer at any level from other departments (there was more in the early days). This has been partly to keep the promotion ladder open, but also indicates some disbelief in its usefulness. Some attempts have been made to 'reintegrate' the diplomats, and to make transfer in and out of the department easier.[6] Within it the cult of the generalist is still strong, and it is common just when an officer has mastered a specialised job, 'to whisk him off to Rome'.

There are some non-career appointments as Ambassador or High Commissioner but this is rarer than was once the case. The Labor Leader of the Opposition managed to find only fifteen former Liberal–Country Party MPs and party officials who had been made ambassadors, high commissioners and consuls-general in the twenty-four years of Liberal–Country Party government between 1951–77.[7]

The recruitment of Foreign Affairs officers has been more elaborate than for other departments, involving a series of interviews and tests, and special arrangements for post-entry training.[8] The educational background of diplomatic recruits used heavily to over-represent the independent schools, and this is still reflected in the total character of the service. About 60 per cent of career diplomats have attended such schools, perhaps half of these schools of a socially prestigious kind.[9]

Lateral Recruitment

The Australian public services have accepted in principle the notion of 'lateral recruitment', or outside appointment to higher vacancies that cannot be filled efficiently by insiders. But most Public Service Acts make it clear that this is to be exceptional, and surrounded by safeguards. There are still fears, especially by staff associations, that it might reopen the door to patronage or reduce the chances of promotion from below. However, there are many signs of loosening-up in the States, some of whom are short of talent for key positions.[10]

In the Commonwealth service, it is possible to appoint outsiders in special circumstances. However, the department must satisfy the Board of the need to advertise the vacancy outside the service, and that there is no officer available in the service who is as capable of filling the position as the recommended appointee. In some cases, to protect the rights of inside applicants, the Board is represented on selection committees. In practice, outside appointments to senior positions have never been as uncommon as this might suggest. A number of senior officers before the Second World War came from outside, or from the States—partly a reflection of the lack of talent then inside the service; others were professional officers, lawyers, engineers, and so on, who had been moved to senior administrative positions. After the war, outsiders were fairly widely appointed in order to strengthen the higher administration, at first mainly people who had proved their ability in temporary employment during the war. The sections have been invoked more sparingly since for general administration, though they have been used to appoint technical and professional officers in a period of great expansion in professional and scientific work, and there was a considerable increase in lateral appointments to administrative positions under the Labor government of 1972–75; in 1975, 36 Second Division officers and 214 senior Third Division recruits entered in this way.

The Image of the Public Service

Everyone worries nowadays about their image, not least the Australian public services. The worry is a proper one, as there are several reasons why this is important. First, it affects recruitment. As the Boyer Committee said, this is related not only to pay and conditions, but also to 'the general estimation in which the service is held by the public and by prospective employees'.[11] It probably also affects morale, especially that of public servants with unspectacular jobs. 'They cannot console themselves with the reflection that comfortless though the task itself may be they have the esteem and gratitude of the public whom they serve'.[12] If the public service has widespread unpopularity, this affects the attitude of public servants. It may lead to loss of pride in their job, excessive worry about pay, promotion and status, defensiveness in the face of outsiders, and oversensitivity to legitimate criticism. It is true that most studies of morale have failed to show that personal job satisfaction is closely related to efficiency. However, pride in one's group or one's department does seem to be related to good work. In any case, the discouraged public servant, even if he works well, is likely to be a poor recruiting officer. Finally, it may affect other relations between the public service and the public, and relations between the public service and the political system. A public service with a poor image has a public that expects the worst, and never gives it the benefit of the doubt; it may also have to work harder to win the respect even of its immediate political masters.

Little study has been made of the image of the Australian public services. From the work of A.A. Congalton on occupational status,[13] it is clear that, in the 1960s at least, groups such as university students ranked public service careers below the established professions and equivalent careers in the private sector. Past surveys of such groups have revealed a double, on the face of it inconsistent, image of government employment, on the part of those hostile to it. On the one hand, there is the 'clerical' image of the public service, with its supposedly dull and often inefficient routines, form-filling, and regimentation, characterised mainly in terms of lack of power and initiative. But there is also a 'bureaucratic' image, characterised by excess of power, 'a tyrannical body of public servants bossing other people about . . . a formidable body against which the individual has little chance . . . government by officialdom . . . arbitrary administration . . . an unassailable body of impassive, though perhaps hardworking people.'

Where concrete examples were given, students drew them from transport services, education, postal services and customs officers. This illustrates the point that to most people the concrete image of the public service is formed by the few government activities with which they come into direct contact or constantly read about in the press. 'On the whole the least qualified members of the service must do one of the most difficult parts of the business, that of meeting the public as individuals.'[14] Otherwise the public service is anonymous and undifferentiated, a mass of deskworkers whose functions are ill-understood, part of an impersonal machine directed by powerful masters, whoever the latter may be. As mentioned in Chapter Seventeen, in the Access Survey of the Coombs Commission, Australian counter staff were shown to have a reasonably good image in the eyes of their clients. However, it is significant that when the same clients were asked, not about a particular recent contact in the public service, but to give their 'general impression . . . of all the people in government offices you've ever come into contact with', their perceptions became less favourable—only 61 per cent rated them 'courteous', 65 per cent 'efficient', 52 per cent 'sympathetic'.[15] Many attitudes to the public service seem to be stereotyped, not closely related to actual encounters.

Another Australian survey of student opinion has shown that the greater the student's knowledge of or contact with government, the better the image of public servants. The public service also has a better reputation with students of poorer socio-economic background. In general, Australian bureaucrats rate high in terms of honesty and qualification for the job, less well in terms of creativity or desire to serve the public.[16] To judge by Gallup Polls, Australians have marginally more regard for public servants than Americans. For example, 67 per cent of Americans think both that there are too many federal employees and that they work less hard than other people, as opposed to 54 per cent and 63 per cent of Australians respectively.[17]

Is the image of the public service improving? It is better treated by the Australian press than in the 1950s, when one fairly often saw press headlines such as 'Alarming Increase of Government Employees' or 'Special Homes for Public Servants in Canberra'. This suspicion seemed to wane in the more managerialist climate of the next decade; senior officials achieved sizeable gains in numbers, pay and prestige, and the level of recruits began to improve. After Labor returned to power in 1972, Canberra public servants once more became targets for abuse—'fat cats' in Mr Cameron's phrase. There was what the Public Service Board called 'an atmosphere of more than normal criticism from various quarters', but Labor also made government employment attractive to new talent.

One important fact is that the Australian public services have at last adjusted themselves to changes in the educational system. An occupational category inevitably has a better image with those groups who see that they or their children can make a good career in it. The Australian bureaucracy may always have had a better reputation with the social groups whose sons saw good prospects there, not the most vocal members of society. In some European public services, recruitment was traditionally related to an inegalitarian educational structure, in turn closely related to the class structure. Undemocratic as this was, it at least established the notion, which was slower to emerge in countries like America and Australia, that government service was a desirable career for the socially established and well-educated.

Equal Employment Opportunity

(i) Women   At one time married women could not be employed permanently in the Commonwealth service unless there were special circumstances; however, a fair number were exempted from the rule, and the marriage bar was removed in 1966. The New South Wales rule had always been more permissive, and that State has also removed all restrictions. Other States have done the same (South Australia in 1967, Queensland in 1969). Women have achieved equal pay.

In the Commonwealth service, all positions in the Second and Third Divisions are open to both men and women (save for a few reserved only for the latter), but there is still prejudice against the employment of women in some sectors.[18] Outside the teaching service, few women have risen to positions of major responsibility. The Second Division of the Commonwealth Public Service contains (1977) only sixteen women and it goes without saying that there is no female permanent head. However, the percentage of women in permanent posts in the Third Division rose from 5 per cent in 1960 to 20 per cent in 1977. In the case of statutory bodies, the government usually appoints the members, and the Labor government of 1972–75 set out to appoint more women, so that many now have a woman on the board; at the same time a good many of the complaints about discrimination against women have related to statutory authorities. There is an Office of Women's Affairs in the unfortunately named Department of Home Affairs, and special units in some other departments.

In New South Wales the 1977 Anti-Discrimination Act now forbids discrimination on grounds of sex, race and so on, and one of the tasks of the Women's Coordination Unit in the Premier's Department is to keep a register of women suitable for appointment to government bodies. Of Public Service Act employees 50 per cent are women, but they form only 7 per cent of employees in the main statutory authorities, and there was only one woman among the 272 top administrators surveyed in the Wilenski review. It is true that the turnover of women is higher but many males also leave—of the clerks recruited in 1972, only 38 per cent of males and 25 per cent of females were still employed five years later (if we look only at those with the higher school leaving qualification, retention rates for women were marginally better than those for men, though their promotion rate was slower).[19]

McLachlan, the first Commonwealth Public Service Commissioner, opined in 1920 that, as a general rule, 'women are physiologically unfitted to carry responsibility at an age when men are improving and developing their capacity in this respect . . . There are, however, in the Service positions of a clerical character specially suitable for women . . . in this connexion the work of record clerks may be mentioned'.[20] Remnants of this view persisted in Australia longer than in most countries. In Victoria women were excluded from the examination for the then Administrative Division until 1972, when two women took the examination and passed before the Board realised they were female candidates.[21]

(ii) Other groups   The Coombs Report commented generally on disadvantaged groups, including women, Aborigines, migrants and the handicapped. (In 1977, there were 1625 Aborigines employed in the Commonwealth public service, nearly all in the Fourth Division.) It thought that the government had 'a special responsibility to act as a wise and enlightened employer' in this area. It recommended among other things that an Office of Equality in Employment should be established within the Public Service Board to promote equality, bring to notice discriminatory practices and investigate complaints.

Promotion

The Australian public services have been more dependent than most on a good promotion system, as they were based on the notion that most non-professional recruitment should be to the base-grade. So there has been a special need to see that the abler recruits to the lower grades get proper opportunities to rise from the ranks, and do not leave the service or become ossified before this happens. This is necessary both to get talented leadership at the top, and to obtain a reasonably contented and efficient workforce lower down. It is not simply a question of creating career opportunities for the outstanding, which have not been lacking in the swelling public services of the 1960s and early 1970s, but also of discriminating more generally between the more and the less competent, so that every efficient officer sees that his or her abilities and hard work are being recognised.[22]

'General service' and 'career' systems

A useful distinction is that between what have been called in America 'general service' and 'career' systems.[23] The nearest approach to the former is the old American conception of a merit system in which the service was thought of simply as a structure of jobs to be filled, and there was a set of competitive procedures for filling these positions, designed to find 'the right man for the job'. In America, it has been by law a completely open system, with entry in theory possible at any level to the best man, as determined by objective procedures, operated or supervised by a central personnel authority. Its nearest Australian equivalent, in theory at least, has been the Tasmanian service.[24] A modified version is to have a good deal of service-wide competition for advertised higher vacancies, as in the Commonwealth.

At the other extreme, in the fully developed 'career system', employment is thought of as a progressive, often planned, development, emphasising the man rather than the position. The career system developed in the armed services, notably for commissioned ranks and has spread from there to a few other sectors. In a full career system, an officer is recruited from the start on the basis of potential for a complete 'career' in the particular organisation, not just because he can adequately perform the vacancy to be filled. There may even be special pre-entry training with the organisation in mind. In any case, for the officer concerned, the career system and the organisation are closely linked—he thinks of himself as a 'member' rather than as an 'employee', and this is encouraged by paternalistic personnel methods and well-developed professional standards. Rank may tend to belong to the man, related to the level he has reached in his career, rather than to the particular job he is doing. Promotion is less closely related to particular job vacancies, though it may at certain levels be highly competitive. Assignments may be based on careful career planning.

Career systems seem to work best with elite groups. Some of their advantages are obvious; they are hospitable to career planning, promote institutional loyalty among the officers concerned, and in some ways are more flexible. In other ways they may be inflexible, because of the fixed career expectations built into them—they may promote resistance to outsiders, institutional conservatism, and an indisposition to accept assignments outside

the 'system' as these may hinder promotion within it.* They are also open
to accusations of privilege by those excluded from the system. It is perhaps
significant that in a recent survey over 70 per cent of Third Division
Commonwealth public servants said 'No' to the question: 'Would you like
a system in which people who show special ability would have a career
mapped out for them, rather than the present system where the person chooses
the jobs he applies for and has to compete against others for them?'; and
the selectively recruited graduate was only a bit more enthusiastic for career
planning than the run-of-the-mill Third Division officer.[25]

'In practice, no organization which aims to be both efficient and humane
can be at either extreme.'[26] Effective armies have to be seen as structures
of jobs as well as of men; effective public services, and business enterprises,
have to be seen as offering broad long-term career opportunities to individuals, even if these are not clearly mapped out. The Australian public
services are career services in this sense, and contain within them one or
two semi-developed 'career systems', such as the diplomatic service; a few
departments or sections of departments have something of the morale and
sense of belonging of a 'career system'. There is still dispute about how
far the public service should resort to career planning, how far establish
or preserve the principle of open or service-wide competition for higher
appointments, and so on.

Assurance and Promise: The Place of Seniority

Most public servants seek some combination of what (following Dr Caiden)
we may call 'assurance' and 'promise'. They expect a reasonable and
progressive reward for competent service, what has been called an 'average
career'. At the same time, they look for special recognition of outstanding
merit. Seniority as a criterion for promotion is often criticised, and for the
most part rightly. However, the seniority principle at least gives some
assurance to a competent officer that, even if he is not selected out of turn,
his merits will not be forgotten and his continued service recognised. It is
definite and enables a man to calculate his promotion prospects. It is objective.
It helps to give an employee a sense of status. The relevant prospects and
status are within a particular group of positions felt by the officer concerned
to be 'homogeneous'; it has been suggested that part of the problem of
seniority arises from the need to protect status and prospects within such
groups, while giving 'fair opportunities for all who so wish, to acquire new
abilities or capacities which would enable them to move clearly out of one
seniority group and into another'.[27]

Another justification of seniority is where discrimination on a merit basis
is hard to make, perhaps because the sector is one in which exceptional talent
has not much chance to show itself; or where there is close correlation between

---

* Even a career agency highly motivated to change, such as a scientific research establishment,
  can be institutionally highly conservative.

merit and seniority, where, for example, experience is what mainly counts
—though relevant experience is often inaccurately measured by service
seniority, and most inaccurately by seniority in a particular branch. A
seniority system also tends to flourish where there are widespread fears of
favouritism, or a strongly egalitarian tradition. In such cases frequent
departures from it may be so offensive to widely shared canons of fairness,
or lead to such minor increases in efficiency, that they may not be
worthwhile.

One way of attempting to satisfy egalitarian feelings is to adopt (as some
services have done) a sort of 'volunteer' system, or equality of competitive
opportunity—to advertise positions widely, and put the onus on the individual
to apply. Its main difficulty is the paperwork that it involves, and its tendency
to create a class of chronic applicants. A recent Chairman of the Commonwealth Public Service Board opted firmly for open competition for
promotions, at least so far as serving officers are concerned, as opposed to
a 'single, central, authoritarian assessment of management potential. Instead,
our system provides constant opportunities for officers to present their claims
for advancement and, over their career lifetime, to have these claims
considered by a variety of assessors'. They must 'compete vigorously and
constantly', largely in terms of capacity to cope with the higher responsibilities of the particular vacancy, rather than of 'assumed general abilities'.[28]
Officers are able to use their initiative in choosing the vacancies for which
they feel themselves best fitted.

He does not deny that 'assumed general abilities', sometimes based on
paper qualifications, also count, and should do so. However, the system he
describes assumes that officers in the competitive game have been given fair
opportunities in their employment situation to acquire abilities and demonstrate capacities.

The Pyramid

Any promotion system will leave a good many people discontented, or at
least disillusioned. Because organisations are pyramids, with the number of
positions decreasing as one moves upwards, most people find themselves
getting left behind by more successful competitors. Fortunately for job
satisfaction, people retire, die or otherwise cease to bother; and, in an
expanding organisation, the pyramid is constantly swelling. In Australia, the
public services in recent years have expanded fast enough to give many public
servants their chance; indeed, some public servants have seemed to get better
chances than they deserve. But this may now be changing.

There is also the safety-valve of movement to another organisation outside
the public service, or to another department inside the service. The public
service is not one pyramid, but a series of pyramids, and there are better
opportunities in some than others. Any promotion system has to pay some
regard to the possibilities of interagency and inter-occupational transfer. The
Australian notion of a career service has always implied some movement

of this kind; all the same, some Australian public services have suffered through excessive departmentalism or categorisation of jobs between which transfer is difficult. There are 'closed shop' departments or sections of departments. In 1973, in the Commonwealth service, 17 per cent of promotions to Third Division positions were from other departments, but 5 per cent or much less in the Taxation Office, Customs and Excise, Immigration, Repatriation (now Veterans' Affairs), and the Post Office.[29]

Promoting Authority and Promotion Appeals

The Public Service Acts were originally designed to give the public service authorities 'remarkably full control' over promotions.[30] In the States the Public Service Board is still normally the promoting authority, but its actual role and discretion varies. Sometimes it is laid down that the permanent head makes a provisional promotion, or the initial nomination, and there is generally provision for a promotions appeal board. Some States have succeeded in exempting certain senior appointments from the appeals system, and left the final voice with the Public Service Board.

In New South Wales the Public Service Act originally gave the Board complete discretion about promotions, but amendments and later legislation have complicated the situation, which is still in a case of flux. Section 19 of the Act allows an officer to appeal to the Board itself if he is dissatisfied with any of a large category of decisions affecting him, including promotion decisions. For the most senior posts, this is the only form of appeal. For many other positions, there is at present an appeal to Promotions Appeal Tribunals, three-men bodies with chairman and employer and employee members. In 1976–77, of 230 appeals heard, 37 were allowed; 234 were withdrawn before or at the hearing. Appeals may be made either on ground of superior efficiency, or of equal efficiency and greater seniority. (The Crown Employees Appeal Board used to deal with promotion appeals, but now only deals with one or two special groups, such as Water Board and certain police appeals.) The Bowen Committee of Inquiry into the Appeal Rights of Government and Quasi-governmental Employees is reviewing the whole problem.

Under the original Commonwealth Act, the Public Service Commissioner recommended promotions, after report from the permanent head. The first Commissioner thought this unwieldy, and recommended after he retired that the power to promote should lie with departments. After some political controversy, initial promotion was entrusted to permanent heads, but such promotions were provisional and subject to appeal to the Public Service Board. Publicity to 'provisional promotions' has been given ever since by reporting them in the *Commonwealth Gazette*, whether the position was originally advertised or not.

Some criticisms of this procedure were made by staff associations, and it was alleged that Board officers might be reluctant to quarrel with departmental decisions. The Bailey Report[31] recommended that three-man committees should hear promotion appeals, made up of one departmental and one staff representative, with a chairman appointed by the Public Service Board; and this became law in 1945. Promotions Appeal Committees were set up in each State and in Canberra, which finally determine most appeals. In the case of interstate appeals and certain higher-paid positions, the committee's decision takes the form of a recommendation to the Board, which has the final say. An officer may appeal on ground of superior efficiency or (more commonly) on ground of equal efficiency and greater seniority; the Coombs Commission has recommended that the latter ground be abolished.[32]

This system has some high costs in terms of man-hours and organisational upset. In 1975, over 4500 provisional promotions, about a sixth of the total, were appealed against and Appeal Committees conducted thousands of interviews on these and related matters. Of these, 551 appeals (12.1 per cent) were successful; even Second Division promotions can be contested. However, it is a flexible system, and additional committees can be created if the work piles up. Procedures are informal; appeals are held in private and no legal assistance is allowed. Whatever its demerits, an appeals system undoubtedly makes senior officers take care in recommending promotions (they may have to justify their actions), and it offers some reply to staff suspicions that 'they' are liable to overlook talent or to appoint the man the supervisor likes (on irrelevant grounds). Even with such appeals, only 45 per cent think the promotion system 'fair' (another 17 per cent were 'not sure').[33]

Criteria of promotion

The Australian public services have made statutory provision for promotion by merit. Most Public Service Acts provide for promotion according to 'relative efficiency', and only if rival candidates are deemed to be equally efficient, 'relative seniority'. The Boyer Committee on the Commonwealth Service recommended in 1959 that even this loophole for seniority be deleted.[34] This recommendation was not accepted by the Commonwealth, but the 1967 South Australian Public Service Act did so, and the Coombs Commission has once more recommended that the Commonwealth do the same.[35] Western Australia has now abolished all seniority rights.

No reliable assessment is available of how much seniority counts in practice. The raw figures, where they are available, are bound to be misleading. One State Public Service Board used regularly in its annual reports to say that, for example, '56 per cent of all promotions were not made in accordance with order of seniority'. But this tells one little about the situation in particular departments or levels of the service; nowadays there are meritocratic sectors, co-existing with others where seniority still counts for a good deal, sometimes officially so. For example, in some statutory authorities such as the New South Wales Public Transport Commission, the usual practice (1977) was still that the most senior applicant in the branch was promoted, provided they reached some acceptable standard. Even when this does not apply to the most senior jobs, it may still mean that individuals, however able, have virtually no chance of a senior position till they are forty. In a recent survey of the Commonwealth service, about a quarter of the sample thought seniority still 'very important' in determining promotions, and over 70 per cent thought it had some importance. In New South Wales, 30 per cent said promotion was based mainly on seniority, and another 50 per cent said it counted equally with ability (of course, this included people whose experience went back before the 1974 Act).[36] It is especially important to encourage merit in services where there is no surplus of able people and where some earlier recruits may be less able than recent ones.

Efficiency is commonly defined as 'special qualifications and aptitude for the discharge of the duties of the office to be filled, together with merit, diligence and good conduct'. This was the 1902 Commonwealth formula, which became standard with minor variations in most State services. There is nothing particularly scientific about this formula (what is 'merit'? why does 'qualifications' precede 'aptitude'?), but it seems to have worked fairly well in practice. It is clear that such a definition raises many questions, for example: how far should relevant experience count, as against general capacity and aptitude? How far should the promotion system take account, not only of efficiency in the particular position to be filled, but of capacity for development and 'promotability', aptitude for prospective vacancies higher up in the department? A good promotion scheme must provide early opportunities to people with the capacity to rise really high in the service. In practice ways seem to have been found of taking aptitude for higher posts into account in making promotions. In 1960 the Public Service Act was amended to provide that whenever a permanent head decides, and the Board approves, 'efficiency' in relation to a vacancy shall 'be deemed to include special qualifications and aptitude for the discharge of the duties of higher offices in the Department'. The Coombs Report has recommended a more thorough redefinition.[37]

In the Commonwealth, seniority is service-wide and in most cases based on date of appointment to the service. In most States it is based on a service-wide job classification or grade. However, in New South Wales seniority is based mainly on salary; for many years it was also not service-wide or even department-wide, but highly sectionalised, so there were over 450 separate seniority lists. This had the effect of making it harder for a specially fit applicant from another part of the service to compete with the best candidate already serving in the section within which the vacancy occurred, and it also narrowed the scope for appeal. A not wholly successful attempt to change this situation was made in 1974.[38] There is a good deal of sectionalised seniority also in statutory bodies in all States, some of which have developed very rigid promotion systems.

Methods of Promotion

In Australia examinations now have a very limited place in determining fitness for promotion.[39] The modern view is that, if the field of 'eligibles' is to be restricted in some way, to insist on candidates obtaining some outside qualification such as a diploma or university degree; or if there is an in-service examination, at least to demand a properly organised course of in-service training. It can be dangerous to rely too much on outside paper qualifications, and this may be one of those swings of the pendulum which could swing back. The in-service test as an instrument of promotion has partly become discredited because of the type of examination used; perhaps in due course there will be a return to more sophisticated kinds of testing.

Qualifying barriers governing promotion and transfer apply to positions requiring vocational qualifications, such as architects, engineers, geologists, lawyers and so on. Advanced training of a more liberal kind may be required for some positions; this may take the form of a salary barrier laying down the maximum salary that may be paid to an unqualified officer.

Otherwise, promotion is largely at the discretion of the promoting authority, subject to any system of appeals that may exist. As indicated earlier, in the Commonwealth service, the formal responsibility for promotions is vested in permanent heads of departments, though such promotions are provisional and subject to appeal by disappointed candidates. The main personnel records of individual Commonwealth public servants are kept in his department; the Board also keeps a central record, but this is not used for the qualitative assessment of individuals.[40] Where the Public Service Board is the promoting authority, the extent of actual Board control has varied considerably from querying an occasional proposed promotion, to drawing the relevent Board inspector closely into the discussions in the early stages, before an official recommendation is made. One may naturally expect the Board to take the closest interest in key positions.

In making initial recommendations for promotion, the views of the candidates' immediate supervisors will clearly be of the first importance. Some State services, and particular departments and agencies in other services, make regular use of staff reporting and may select officers for promotion partly on this basis, but it has not become standard practice in most Australian departments. Sometimes there are selection or interviewing committees, especially where vacancies are widely advertised. The Coombs Report endorsed the Commonwealth Board's view that vacancies should, whenever practicable, be advertised, and that selection should be by committee, which might well include a staff representative 'and on some occasions a representative from outside the department'.[41] Little use is made of special selection techniques, such as aptitude tests or 'executive selection' procedures, for promotion. There is still a good deal of emphasis on informal methods of assessment, and some scepticism of standardised methods of evaluation.

There are considerable differences of practice about advertising vacancies. In New South Wales the traditional practice has been to fill most vacant positions without advertisement, only inviting applications from outside the relevant group if there was no one within it regarded as meeting the requirements of the position; but the policy of 'open competition' for promotions has been gaining ground, and far more positions are now advertised than formerly. In the Commonwealth service there is (as mentioned earlier) a tradition of promotion on a 'volunteer' basis; that is, the onus is on the individual public servant to go out after any advertised position for which he has the minimum educational qualifications. Advertising is at the permanent head's discretion. Vacancies are often advertised in the *Commonwealth Gazette*; in any event (as stated earlier) the provisional promotion is published in the *Gazette*, and can be widely appealed against. In Queensland, all vacancies where promotion is subject to appeal are advertised in its *Government Gazette*.

Mobility

How far such variations in practice influence actual interdepartmental mobility would be hard to determine. Other factors affect mobility, such as seniority rules, restrictive insistence on 'qualifications', the rate of service growth, the available supply of talent, departmental habits (some departments and statutory authorities are particularly 'inward-looking'), and who makes the actual promotion. The Commonwealth system of promotions makes it hard for the Board to operate a policy of 'career planning' for individuals, even if it wanted to, though it does not seem to prevent individual departments from having such policies. However, the advertising of positions, combined with an appeal system, does at least give every public servant the feeling that he has a chance, though he may be left unsatisfied by the final decision. Perhaps it is possible to achieve this result in other ways, as New South Wales is currently trying to through its assessment centre (see below).

In some Australian public services the obstacles to a reasonable amount of mobility are still considerable. This not merely limits the experience of potential senior officers but, especially where opportunities for advancement vary greatly between departments, or sections of departments, can lead to frustration and waste of talent. The Coombs Commission sees an important place for the Public Service Board in 'planned mobility', within and between departments, and between Commonwealth and other employment. This has been largely left to take care of itself, but now things are changing. A shortage of experienced talent is developing at the top of the service as the post-war intake retires; greater movement will help to develop good senior officers and to spread talent more fairly. Public service growth will probably be slower, and mobility is some substitute for promotion in maintaining job interest, but mobility will decline as promotion declines unless counteracting steps are taken. There is already a fair amount of inbreeding in the Commonwealth service—over three-quarters of Third Division officers appointed between 1962 and 1974 (and remaining in the service) were in the latter year still in the department they had first joined. In the Commonwealth 17 per cent of promotions were to other departments (1975), in New South Wales 11 per cent (1976).[42]

It is true that the case for mobility can be overstated. So far as good work depends on specialised experience or loyal commitment to particular objectives, it may be desirable that many public servants should find their career in one agency, or section of an agency. Some public service authorities are sceptical about moving people about to 'broaden their experience'. It sometimes results in an officer moving on just when he is becoming really useful. It can also mean that senior staff do not have to live with the long-term results of their own errors. On the other hand, departments do need new blood from time to time, and where it is desired to produce a race of senior officers with general administrative and policy skills, or to promote a sense of unity, broadmindedness and common understanding in the service, variety of experience is very important.

Higher Appointments and Permanent Headships

There is a rather startling sentence in the Coombs Report about higher appointments. 'The Commission considers that the practice followed in the United Kingdom of maintaining . . . lists of possible candidates for higher appointments, supported by information about their qualifications, experience and performance, could prove valuable in Australia.'[43] The Public Service Board should keep such lists, including possible 'outsiders', so that it could advise both departments and statutory authorities about higher appointments.

It may be surprising to some readers that this is not already done, or not done with any consistency. But, as explained earlier, the Commonwealth service has not been enamoured of career-planning, certainly not across departments; and this has been fortified by the Board's limited role in promotions (New South Wales has done more). Now attitudes are changing.

The Board has, of course, always had a special role where permanent heads are concerned. Commonwealth permanent heads are appointed by the Governor-General on the recommendation of the Prime Minister. In the States, practice varies; in some States, including New South Wales, they have been appointed on the recommendation of the Public Service Board. In New South Wales the government has very rarely intervened in permanent head appointments—there seem to have been only one or two such cases since 1920. In Victoria and Queensland, there is provision for reference to the Board* but the government preserves its discretion. In South Australia the Board may call for applications, but the government has unqualified power to appoint. None of the Acts precludes the appointment of outsiders, though certain conditions may have to be satisfied.

The Commonwealth introduced new procedures in 1976 amendments to the Public Service Act. The details are fairly complex,[44] but the main features are as follows:

---

* There are a few statutory appointments to permanent headship in Victoria where this does not apply.

1. The Prime Minister and the Minister concerned get lists of recommended candidates from a small *ad hoc* committee of permanent heads led by the Public Service Board Chairman, who may also submit his own report.
2. The Prime Minister may then insist on advertisement (Mr Fraser has said that this is 'most unlikely'), and the Prime Minister or the Minister may also suggest further names for the list.
3. The Prime Minister makes the final recommendation, but if the individual is not on the final list of the committee or of the Board Chairman, or not already a permanent head, appointment must be for a fixed term up to five years, with eligibility for reappointment. If the governing party changes, such an appointment may be ended at any time; if a career public servant is involved, he or she may choose between reappointment elsewhere and early retirement.

The Board now has an Executive Staffing Unit to assist the Chairman in advising on senior appointments.

This formula resulted from long discussions after the government changed in 1975. Previous governments were free to appoint whom they wished to permanent headships, though they often consulted the Board; all permanent heads once appointed had the same rights, and were hard to displace. This caused no great trouble as long as ministers were generally ready to accept the appointments of their predecessors, and as long as outside appointments were rare. However, the Labor government of 1972–75 took the advice of the Board less than its predecessors, and made more changes (see Chapter Ten).

Indeed 'permanent' can be a misleading word. Even in 1965, at a time of great governmental stability, Commonwealth permanent heads had only occupied that position in their existing department for an average of 5.5 years; in mid-1975 it was only 2.7 years. It has been commonly held that a departmental head cannot be removed from his position without his consent, unless his department (and hence his position) is abolished. But the Commonwealth and South Australia have both now in different ways made possible a new class of removable permanent heads, and Tasmania has made a fair number of senior appointments on contract. In any case, departments are now regularly abolished and reconstituted under new names—or even under the old ones. In March 1971 the Prime Minister's Department was 'abolished' and immediately replaced by a new Department of the Prime Minister and Cabinet, with a different permanent head.[45] The Department of Administrative Services was abolished and recreated on 22 December 1975, with a new permanent head, and new functions. An interesting variant occurred in New South Wales in 1925, when J.T. Lang tried to displace the permanent head of the Treasury by splitting the job in two; the Public Service Board accepted this under duress, but the officer concerned decided instead to resign from the service (some years later he became State Premier).[46]

Even apart from this, it is usually hard for a permanent head to resist transfer in practice if his Minister and the Prime Minister both want to move him, though there have been one or two cases where a permanent head has held out. The Coombs Report thinks that if compulsory transfer takes place, it should be a decision of the Prime Minister and only after consultation with the panel that advises him on selections.[47] It also agrees with many submissions that permanent heads should normally expect to be moved after five to seven years in one department, though not with the recommendation of the South Australian Committee of Inquiry that they should all have fixed-term contracts. The Report argues that, apart from anything else, such a system 'would introduce a degree of rigidity . . . which governments could find highly inconvenient and an impediment to the execution of their policies. A fixed term may have the effect of lengthening the period a person should serve, just as it may arbitrarily cut a period of service too short.'[48]

The Department of Foreign Affairs already has something approaching a 'convention' of periodical shifts. Seven of the last eight permanent heads moved out well ahead of time. The Department is, of course, fortunate in having many prestigious overseas posts to which ex-permanent heads can be appointed. Sir Arthur Tange moved out in 1965 to become High Commissioner for India, then returned to Canberra in 1970 as Secretary to the Department of Defence.

The problem is to find some balance between flexibility and such reasonable security as helps a permanent head to give objective advice to his minister, and not to be 'tempted, even subconsciously, to withhold or moderate unpalatable advice for fear of incurring displeasure and putting his job at risk'.[49] Part of the rationale of 'permanency' among senior officers is that they should be encouraged to examine issues on their merits, as though their own futures were not involved. Of course, this is a matter of degree. It has become clear that a Commonwealth permanent head who seriously upsets his minister can often be got rid of, and when this does not happen, it is often because the officer concerned is able to mobilise political support from various quarters. Some people in Canberra argue that permanent heads and other senior bureaucrats already 'play politics' hard, and that the situation in this respect would not much differ if it were made still easier to shift them. Another argument is that courage, integrity and independence of mind are a product more of individual character than of job security. If this were so, we would still have to ask what kind of system is most likely to promote the choice of senior officers with the qualities we desire. Evidence on this matter is not plentiful, but in my view suggests some caution about changing the existing system. Certainly ministers, especially new ministers, tend to be poor choosers of top officials; this is not mainly because they play politics, but because they have little sense of the administrative requirements of the role, and are liable to be impressed by a spectacular personality, an agile mind, or a person with some specific expertise or knowledge which they admire but which is not necessarily relevant to managing a large organisation.

In general, there is a case for more formality and orderliness in making senior appointments within the public services. These are vital decisions which are likely to affect the fortunes of the department concerned for many years to come. I quote a relevant comment made to me by a Commonwealth government adviser with wide experience outside the public service:

> Quite recently I have been involved (partially) in the selection of . . . [a very senior officer]. In confidence I am bound to say that the procedure that has been adopted would not be acceptable for the appointment of a junior lecturer at a university. In senior appointments there appears to be far too much reliance on word of mouth reports and on the views of an inner circle of senior permanent heads.

There also seems no reason why the performance of permanent heads should not be periodically reviewed. The Corbett Committee in South Australia thought that, like everyone else, they should be annually assessed.[50]

Background of the Higher Public Service

Commonwealth

Information about the background of higher public servants is very incomplete, and what is said below has been pieced together from various sources. At least we can demonstrate that there are important routes to senior positions other than entry from school at base grade, followed by steady promotion. In December 1975, 72 per cent of officers in the First and Second Divisions of the Commonwealth service were graduates, and a further 13 per cent had other higher qualifications. Some of these degrees and diplomas had been obtained after joining the service, but around half the degrees had been obtained before appointment. About 10 per cent had higher degrees.

A 1975 survey of 746 senior officers showed that about two-fifths had received their secondary education at non-government schools, about half of these at Roman Catholic schools. Roman Catholics were somewhat over-represented in relation to population in the Third Division, but under-represented in the Second Division, and among the selective graduate entry of recent years; perhaps it is worth noting that over 40 per cent of public servants originally recruited in the select categories of Administrative and Foreign Office Trainee professed 'no religion'.[51] Other up-to-date information is harder to come by. An earlier survey of the senior public service showed that 22 per cent were the sons of manual workers, a relatively high figure compared with most countries.[52]

In 1975 all but one of twenty-eight Commonwealth permanent heads were graduates. Seventeen had degrees in economics or commerce, or arts degrees with a strong 'economics' element—good evidence of the predominance of economists in the senior ranks of the Commonwealth service. Only five had had a substantial career outside government service. However, many permanent heads had a good deal of experience in other government agencies.

Seventeen had served in two or three agencies besides the one they headed, and all but four or five in at least one other department, though only about a quarter had significant experience in co-ordinating departments such as the Treasury or the Public Service Board. Their average age on appointment as permanent head was forty-eight.[53] A fair number of young permanent heads have been appointed. Of 130 such appointments between 1950–73, 48 were under fifty and 5 were less than forty when appointed.

States

For most States, up-to-date information is scantier. A 1956 survey of 213 senior State officers with significant administrative responsibilities showed that, in both New South Wales and Victoria, under half were graduates, and this included a good many who had graduated after entering the service. The same percentage as in the Commonwealth sample mentioned above (22 per cent) were of working-class parentage. The main difference from the Commonwealth group was the much larger number of professionally trained officers in administrative positions; three-quarters of the sixty 'graduates on entry' were qualified in law, medicine, engineering, agriculture, architecture and so on. The great majority of non-professional degrees had been obtained by part-time study while in the service. Of a 1959 sample of New South Wales senior officers, about 40 per cent had degrees.[54]

The percentage of non-professional graduates in senior positions has certainly increased since then, though no revolution has taken place. The 1977 Senior Officer Survey[55] in New South Wales examined the background of the 272 senior officers earning more than $28 000 (excluding medical staffs). Of these officers, 55 per cent had degrees, and half were graduates when recruited; over 90 per cent had some form of higher qualification, as compared to 78 per cent in 1959. Most senior officers had still obtained their higher qualifications while in the service, though this includes people on full-time cadetships.

However, the New South Wales service is one of the better educated State services. The 1959 survey made comparisons with Queensland to the latter's disadvantage. At that time very few senior officers in Queensland had a degree, outside the professional group and a small number of ex-teachers who had moved into higher administration. In a number of States the best educated senior administrators have been those who have come up the professional ranks. In South Australia only a few years ago 82 per cent of senior administrators who had come up the professional route were university-educated, as compared with 47 per cent of the others, and the latter mostly held degrees taken part-time after entering the service.[56] However, the situation in that State has been changing rapidly, and an up-to-date survey would show a higher level of academic qualifications. In South Australia lately there has been much more lateral recruitment, and a number of senior officials now have inter-State, overseas, and Commonwealth Public Service backgrounds. An imperfect sample of permanent heads in South Australia

(1976) showed an average age on appointment of around forty-five; and three-quarters of them were graduates.

Only two of the New South Wales officers in the 1977 Senior Officer Survey came from non-English speaking countries, and there was only one woman. The median age of entry to the service was eighteen, but about a quarter entered after the age of thirty. Of Public Service Act employees, 24 per cent had worked at some time in the Public Service Board, and a smaller group in the Treasury—they had moved around more than senior employees of statutory authorities, who were more likely to have spent most of their career in the one agency.

A 1977 survey of permanent heads of major New South Wales departments showed that 90 per cent had degrees or other higher qualifications. Most had attended State high schools, and about half had entered the service from school, obtaining any further qualifications while in the service. Of the degrees held, about half were in arts, economics, education and the rest science degrees or professional qualifications (law, engineering, veterinary science).[57]

Types of Public Servant

Some Differences between Government Agencies

To some extent, different government agencies attract and generate different types of person, at least outside the more routine jobs. This process has some advantages, as true commitment to any work tends to shape a human being in its image. We often denounce, with reason, inbreeding in certain sectors —in statutory authorities, Foreign Affairs, or State Education Departments; but too much ease of transfer can reduce commitment. A department needs new blood but it also needs people who treat its problems as their own particular concern and interest. Some government agencies with high morale are those that run a little 'career service' of their own; this is also true of some stagnant departments. It is not easy to generalise.

Countries vary in this respect. In the United States the career bureaucracy is somewhat fragmented—senior officers in different departments tend to be different types. In the United Kingdom, the existence of an Administrative Class has helped to make the whole group of senior civil servants more homogeneous.[58] Australia is perhaps in the middle. Something akin to an administrative class has developed in the Commonwealth service, in the 1250 or so officers of the First and Second Divisions, 70 per cent of whom are in Canberra. However, more of them have come up the 'professional' line than in Britain, and they have a somewhat more heterogeneous social, educational and career background. This, and the relative newness of the service and its very rapid growth, have left Australian senior administrators with a weaker sense of unity and professional independence than their British counterparts. Though they are important figures in their own departments, and there is often a good sense of corporate feeling within departments, they seem to engage in more inter-departmental rivalries, and to carry less collective weight.[59] Nor was there ever a single department as dominant as the old British Treasury, able to nurture the idea of a Head of the Civil Service. Commonwealth permanent heads rarely met collectively until 1977, when a new Public Service Board chairman convened a series of meetings.

Allowing for such national differences, in all services the various agencies tend to develop differences of administrative 'style' and 'philosophy', which affect recruitment or which new recruits absorb. These differences partly arise from the sorts of problem and task involved, so that the people in Defence, Foreign Affairs, Treasury, Social Security are readily identifiable as different types. Little study has been made of this, but a few broad differences are worth noting:[60]

(i) Departments have different 'publics'   A department may deal mainly with primary producers, or (as do social welfare agencies) with under-privileged people, or (Foreign Affairs) with overseas governments and diplomats. These varying publics will need different treatment, and suggest different patterns of organisation. The public may have discretion to refuse the transaction or the department may, as with taxation, have compulsory powers. The public may vary in size, status (Foreign Affairs has a high-status public), attitude (they may be ignorant of, hostile to, accept resentfully, or welcome what the department does) and in need for technical skills or for personal treatment.

Public servants in social service agencies, for example, have to take special care to see that those most in need do not get neglected because they are often unaware of their rights, are shy and inarticulate or awkward to deal with, or lack the skills needed to make use of the services offered. This may encourage such public servants to adopt a more 'personal' approach, and a tendency to interpret clients' needs for them. Other departments have much more active clienteles, used to pressing their demands; or the public directly dealt with by the agency may not be the same as the public that is supposed to benefit from its work. The Trade Practices Commission or a pollution control agency mainly deals with private organisations restricting competition or damaging the environment; the government has not intervened in order to help them in their endeavours, but to benefit a broader and invisible public at large. A complex balancing act may be involved, as the public agency 'still must attend to the requirements of the group being regulated, especially when it needs to utilise persuasion as well as coercion, and it is the regulated group with which it directly deals'.[61]

(ii) There are departments (and units within departments) more concerned with policy-making, others more with 'operations'   An example of an 'operative' task would be one the functions of which were regulatory and based on legal powers. Much work in a taxation department is of this kind. Though there may be significant areas of discretion, there can be fairly precise definitions of duties and work can be governed largely by instructions given from above. Promotion will tend to be more by seniority. Large policy changes

may be abnormal, and often effected by legislation and new regulations. The high-level jobs tend to be managerial, concerned with making a large organisation run smoothly, and improving working methods, or concerned with interpretation of the law or drawing up rules for its implementation. A similar case would be a service organisation providing standardised social security benefits.

At the opposite extreme are departments with a strong policy-making element, such as the Department of Foreign Affairs, working under changing conditions. It is harder to have clear job definitions, the responsible jobs tend to shape themselves more to the individuals concerned. There may be separate branches dealing with different broad regions of the world, with the United Nations, international law and treaties, and so on; and within them officials with more specialised functions, dealing with Indonesia or Papua New Guinea. But the concerns of different units overlap and ease of communications, informal consultation, *ad hoc* meetings of senior officers, become more important. These factors are reflected in the qualities required of officers, in promotion criteria, and so on. There are also relatively more senior and middle level positions and fewer purely routine ones, though there is a great deal of routine even in Foreign Affairs.

(iii) Regulatory and Service Agencies   Some writers distinguish between agencies primarily concerned with enforcing rules and with arbitration, and those that provide a direct service to the public. In the former case, the agency may be unconcerned with, or even actively opposed to, expanding its powers; service agencies are more likely to believe in growth. 'It is usual for agencies responsible for building roads or providing welfare services to believe that an increase of their activities is highly desirable'.[62] The regulatory function may be very varied—from law and order, to elections, tax collection, public health. It may be routine or highly discretionary.

A special case of a regulatory agency is one concerned with regulating and co-ordinating the work of other government agencies—such as the Treasury/Department of Finance or the Public Service Board. They tend to see themselves as austere departments of principle, detached guardians of the public weal, withstanding the selfish pressures of the 'departments of interest', concerned only with their own narrow clienteles.[63]

(iv) Production and Business Agencies   Government agencies concerned with a physical product or which sell goods and services on the market have special features. Men with technical, professional and business skills may play an important role. Departments of Works and Construction, and Main Roads Departments, are examples of agencies concerned with a physical product. Engineers and architects are important, though managerial as well as professional skills are involved. An agency of this kind, if reasonably well-run, can often attract enthusiasm and loyalty, as achievement is concrete and measurable, and visible technological advances are often involved. Most government enterprises are organised in a special way, as statutory authorities

(see Chapter Five). They can be more flexible in their personnel arrangements if they wish. Here it should be easiest to apply tests of productivity and efficiency in the use of resources.

Generalists, Specialists and Professionals

One common way of categorising public servants is as 'generalists' and 'specialists', or sometimes as 'administrators' and 'professionals'.[64] These terms can lead to great confusion, as there are a number of different ways of defining them.

(i) Definitions   The literature of public administration until recently paid little attention to the important group of professional officers in public employment. 'Professionals' are usually defined in terms of (i) educational qualifications; and (ii) the work content and designation of posts currently occupied.[65] Thus a 'professional' in the fullest sense is someone who has acquired a higher education of a specialised kind, and whose duties require reasonably clear-cut special skills and technical knowledge. The word is sometimes used restrictively to include only prestigious and well-accepted qualifications, as in law and medicine, where there is also a long-recognised profession outside the public service; other groups, such as engineers and architects of equivalent education, now belong to this category. But the notion of professional qualifications could be extended to include 'quasi-professions' such as psychologists, statisticians and some highly trained categories of social worker; and the notion of professional work could be broadened in a similar way. One sometimes talks of 'professional' diplomats, meaning public servants of high status who practise a specialised skill, though it may be based on higher education of a more general kind. There is a certain logic in doing this, as in terms of group behaviour such specialists are often not so different from the recognised professionals. However, some specialist groups differ from professionals in the fullest sense, either because most or all are government employees (so they do not have a large outside profession to identify with, or appeal to), or because their status is lower. Both of these considerations apply to teachers. Diplomats have high status, but no outside counterparts. Like officers of the defence forces, they form a kind of 'public service profession', a 'career service within the service'.[66]

Sometimes the contrast is made between professional specialists and administrative generalists. A 'generalist' can also be thought of in terms of educational background and work. Often the word is used to refer to public servants whose education and experience have not involved any recognised professional training, and who are also engaged on work of a general administrative kind. This distinction is useful, though insecure in various respects.[67] Many so-called generalists, though they may not have had a professional education, have (either by education or experience or both) acquired specialised skills or knowledge of a semi-technical kind. This clearly applies, for example, to public servants working in personnel, financial and economic fields, and to the growing number involved in specialised management services, but it also applies to a wider range of public servants who have become highly expert in dealing with a particular field of work, whether it be sales tax legislation or social security benefits. If they are not professionals, it is hard not to call many of them specialists.

However, important groups of public administrators are generalists, in the sense that they are supposed to be capable of dealing with a wide range of public affairs. A good deal of their work could best be termed 'co-ordination'. At one level they are facilitators, who administer the conditions under which the various specialists work and produce their results: they perform the housekeeping routines and the secretarial function of seeing that decisions are properly recorded, processed and implemented. At another level they may do the job of mediator or liaison officer, keeping various groups in touch with one another, and sometimes arbitrating their differences. There are financial constraints on expert initiatives and one characteristic task of the generalist administrator is the allocation of resources between competing uses. At the highest level they may be arbiters or initiators of policies and programmes, assisting ministers in the final political decision that reconciles conflicting demands. This kind of administration also involves special skills —one may speak of specialists in policy formulation, or of experts on how to get things done within a public service environment. There is even a limited sense in which the higher public service as a whole constitutes a profession, with its own expertise and standards.[68]

(ii) Professionals in the Australian Public Service The status of the professional officer has varied between countries and over time. In the British civil service, the administrative generalist still dominates the scene. In the United States professional and specialist bureau chiefs have traditionally played an important role, and in France many top directorates are held by technicians, especially engineers. In Australia too the professional officer has had higher status than in Britain.[69] There are various historical reasons for this, including the greater concentration of government on the physical development of the country, the generally higher status of the professionally trained, and lower status of the arts graduate. However, these national approaches seem nowadays to be losing some of their distinctiveness, though important differences remain.

In Australia, both professional and non-professional officers can in theory reach most of the highest administrative posts. The Commonwealth and some States have no separate professional division; but even States with one have made it no obstacle to administrative preferment. All the same, frictions and rivalries between professional officers and others have existed. The former have tended to form coherent groups, making their own salary claims or seeking to preserve their own primacy in certain departments or branches. Generalist officers have sometimes developed 'a collective, tacit solidarity in keeping specialists at bay',[70] and there is some lack of understanding between agencies where generalists and specialists respectively are dominant.

In State services where most administrative–clerical officers have been school-leavers, the professionals have often been the best educated and most intelligent public servants, and they have risen to many of the most influential and best-paid positions. The history of this has not yet been written. We may note Bourke's comment in discussing the career of a distinguished New South Wales public servant who retired in 1961, that 'he presided over a Public Service that during his time was largely converted from a clerically to a professionally led service',[71] and Subramaniam's observation that: 'Even in 1907, professionals occupied 48 per cent of the Commonwealth positions above the third class, and in 1922 this rose to 72.1 per cent.'[72] In South Australia one recent survey indicated an inner administrative elite or 'top thirteen', twelve of whom were professionally trained, 'and with similar backgrounds: professional father, private school, tertiary degree, and then lateral entry to the public service'.[73] Encel has described in broad terms the attempt to avoid some of the consequences of a closed service, of which the rise of statutory corporations (themselves often run by the professionally trained) was one reflection.[74] Professionalism once established propagated itself, and also encouraged professional yearnings among other groups—so 'educationists' came to dominate Education Departments, dubiously professional categories swelled the professional divisions of some States, and there began a general search for some symbol of proficiency, certificate, diploma, nowadays degree, as an index of merit.

On the other hand a number of factors, including the narrowness of much professional training and the conservatism of many organised professions, as well as their natural interest in sticking to their last, have affected both the desire and capacity of professional officers to undertake higher administration and management. At any rate, in many Commonwealth sectors, and some sectors of State administration, the less narrowly specialised officer seems lately to have acquired the ascendancy. In an era of more complex policy-making a minister may often prefer as a senior administrator someone who speaks something closer to his own language, who is prepared to interpret technical advice and accommodate it to other considerations, and who has moved about more and had varied experience. The economist–public servant has played an important role in this process.

There are two problems about relations between these various groups. One is the relative access to the highest positions in the public service of officers with different educational and service backgrounds. The other is the problem of working relations between officers in professional-type posts and in administrative positions. Working relations between the two groups vary a good deal as between government agencies. Some may be dominated by an administrative group, with professionals playing a subordinate or advisory role. Others may have an administrative top, below which professionalised branches come into their own, and operate with a good deal of independence in their own field. In others, some professional group may dominate the department.

But this crude typology is very misleading as an account of the realities. For example, as we have already mentioned, a group of administrative officers may have a career, skills and attitudes such that they themselves come to have something of a 'professional' cast. Some government agencies contain more than one professional group, either competing groups, or a dominant group or groups with the others seen as ancillary. A Department of Works in which civil engineers have ruled the roost, may also contain architects and other kinds of engineer. A State Health Department may have medical officers of different kinds, psychiatrists, dental officers, research workers, and 'emerging' professional groups such as child guidance officers and trained social workers. In such agencies, one important source of tension may be between different professional groups. Some professionals tend to be specialised to a particular government agency, as are geologists and geophysicists in the Bureau of Mineral Resources, others can move more readily between government agencies. Some (e.g. medical officers) have a large private sector in which they can seek alternative professional employment, others (e.g. agricultural scientists) a much smaller one.

(iii) Professional Attitudes   Some writers wish to define the professional, not simply in terms of education and career pattern, but also in relation to attitudes and degree of autonomy in the work situation. It has been argued that professionals have a characteristic set of attitudes, which are reinforced where the profession is strongly organised inside or outside the service. These have been held by critics to include:[75]

1. A drive to raise or maintain status by expanding or protecting career channels, work areas, pay, and so on.
2. Emphasis on the substance of their own work and how it differs in kind and level from other fields, disinterest in its relation to other fields or in explaining and justifying their judgments to outsiders.
3. An anti-political outlook, in particular the belief that persons concerned with the ambiguities of bargaining and compromise are interfering and rather corrupt amateurs.
4. An anti-bureaucratic outlook, which tends to equate administration with form-filling, and to underrate problems of communication, co-ordination and mobilising many different resources to meet a particular situation. They may accept bureaucracy if they themselves control it; or seek autonomy, and defer only to superior professional competence or colleague control.

Professional officers often maintain links with the profession outside; they may spend part of their professional life with it, attend professional conferences, and keep up with, sometimes contribute to, its literature. Some writers distinguish between 'cosmopolitans' (who see themselves more as part of the wider professional community outside and move more readily from organisation to organisation) and 'locals' (who identify more with the particular organisation).

Most of these characteristics, if they exist, seem to differentiate professionals in degree rather than kind from other mortals; and there are important differences between the various kinds of professional. The research scientist seems to worry more about 'autonomy' than, say, the design engineer.[76] The latter is used to working to deadlines, to making decisions without having all the information, and to having his task defined for him to a considerable degree by somebody else. Certain types of specialist have a broader training and more concern with policy issues, as do some town planners. The actual work of a professional officer may be largely administrative, as when he is at or near the top of a sizeable hierarchy. There are many fields where a professional can only get promotion beyond a certain level by deserting his specialist interests and becoming an administrator—which may or may not please him. His professional skills may be useful in increasing his understanding of the work of, and smoothing his relations with, professional and technical subordinates. On the other hand, his skills may tempt him to believe that he knows everything, especially dangerous if he has been an administrator long enough to be suffering from technological obsolescence, or if (as is generally the case nowadays) his expertise is only in a small part of the total field covered by the department.

A place where one commonly meets tension between administrators and professionals is the scientific research establishment. Part of this may arise from personality differences, especially the scientist's demand for autonomy and impatience with bureaucratic procedures. But there are also tensions arising from the very nature of organisations. Managers of organisations tend to seek accountability, predictability, and so on. They are less willing than scientists to accept gambles, vague budgeting or failures to meet deadlines. In addition, senior administrators tend to be more sensitive to public expectations, more politically conscious, more concerned to see results that will be valued outside, and so on. All such generalities are uncertain. The 'narrow specialist' is a stereotype that may not bear examination or generalisation—for example, in a recent unpublished survey of professionals in the British civil service, G.R. Curnow found many who were sensitive to wider issues of administration and policy. Some of the narrowness of professional groups could be disposed of by attempts to broaden professional education, an effort which, though it is starting, has not proceeded far in Australia.

(iv) Current Trends   As we have indicated, the senior ranks of the Australian Public Services include large numbers of officers with a professional training. Of the higher qualifications held by Second Division officers in the Commonwealth service in 1970, over one-third were in fields such as science (15 per cent), engineering (13 per cent) and medicine (5 per cent). Another 20 per cent were in economics and commerce, 16 per cent in arts,

12 per cent in accounting, 8 per cent in law. In terms of career, about two-thirds of the Second Division came from 'administrative' areas, about one-third from 'professional' areas.[77]

One view of current world trends is that we are entering a new age of professionalism. The rise of the scientist and the computer, the new managerial revolution, the technology of war, and other complex fields of government, from urban planning and environmental control to energy policy, are (it is said) creating problems beyond the capacity of the old generalist administrator, and which also challenge old notions of administrative hierarchy. In times of rapid change and technological complexity, co-ordination cannot be achieved in the old ways, we have to depend much more on good lateral communications and the 'mutual interdependence of highly developed specialisms'.

At the same time, others have observed counter-tendencies, very evident in the Commonwealth service, where the increased intake of good non-professional officers since the Second World War has acted as an effective counterbalance to professional influence. One difficulty with the preceding argument is that, even if true, it makes the old-style specialist, with his status consciousness and habit of drawing precise boundaries round jobs, as out-of-date as the old-style generalist. The case for the generalist administrator is not disposed of by attacks on bureaucratic formalities and hierarchies. Indeed an important part of this case has precisely been that organisations need people skilled in easy communication across boundaries, who are alive to the need for interdependence because their 'professional ethic' takes in many different fields and levels of work and who are committed to the interests of the concern as a whole, a focus of resistance to particularistic commitments and decisions made on narrow grounds. There is also the fact, as we have seen, that many administrators have become experts in some special field.

Some writers in other countries attribute part of the rapid increase of government expenditure in recent years to the power of the professional bureaucrats (from the military and defence scientists to highway engineers and educationists and the Welfare Establishment), working closely with their private sector supporters and colleagues at other levels of government to promote expansion in their particular field. This situation may be accentuated if the professionals are strongly entrenched in statutory authorities with some independence.

Frictions between professional and non-professional public servants may be on the decline in Australia, partly because both are becoming better educated, partly because the closer linkages between technical and non-technical issues in government are drawing them together into closer working relationships. One reflection of this is an increasingly collegial atmosphere in the better departments, and various attempts to create a better working partnership by setting up mixed teams to deal with particular projects or problems. It also seems to be clearly recognised that higher administrative posts in the public services will need to draw on individuals with both professional and non-professional backgrounds.

Staff selection

Expectations and Resources

How best to select and develop officers with administrative potential is an important issue, but it might be useful first to consider what one is looking for. From the time an administrative position is created, certain expectations are held about how the occupant of the position is to behave. In meeting these expectations, the individual filling an administrative position uses certain resources, including personal resources. Accordingly, one could decide what one is looking for by studying the expectations people have of an administrator, or the resources the latter must have available, or both.

As was pointed out earlier (see Chapter One), there are two main types of expectation regarding public service administrators: (1) That they will advise. They are expected to advise more senior administrators, and at the highest level, responsible ministers, on the formation and amendment of policy, and on appropriate legislative measures and departmental arrangements for carrying out policy; and to report on the results of policy so administered, as a basis for considering further improvements or changes. (2) That they will manage. They are expected to direct and co-ordinate the activities of the staff engaged in carrying out accepted policy.

R.S. Parker some years ago provided a useful summary of the kinds of activity involved in administrative work:
1. Policy matters: discerning the more important general questions or problems arising out of the work of the branch, seeing their implications for the future as well as for the present, and for the country as a whole as well as for the department.
2. Formulating practicable and, if necessary, detailed proposals for actions; foreseeing the probable results of such proposals, including their effect on public opinion.
3. Taking responsibility when required for the adoption of such proposals, and organising and supervising their execution.
4. 'Paper work'—analysis of complicated material, including figures, and accurate and intelligent presentation of results; writing clear, brief, informative and acceptable letters and minutes.
5. Dealing with people inside and outside the department—discussing in committee, in conference or tête-à-tête for the purpose of reaching a decision; putting a point of view or obtaining information; managing and enlisting co-operation of subordinate staff; briefing superiors; negotiating with and interpreting the policy of the department to individuals or organisations.[78]

In the Australian public services, administrative officers concerned with the executive and managerial work involved in the last three of these categories are the more numerous group.

The usefulness of describing an administrative position in terms of general expectations, such as 'advisory' or 'managerial', has been challenged on the ground that many of the expectations attaching to each job are unique. On the other hand, some public services have expected their senior officers to become part of a service-wide system. This was part of the thinking behind the former Administrative Class in the United Kingdom, and was held to be one reason for the use of Treasury patronage to fill higher positions. The system aimed at having top civil servants in Whitehall operate as a team, but such a team may have the dangerous characteristic of being composed too much of mutually agreeable members.

The other approach to identifying potential is in terms of personal resources. Long lists of personal qualities required by an administrator or business executive may be culled from the literature, but many of them seem to be the product of armchair speculation, and are variations on the theme expressed in the old Scouts' Manual.

Trusty, loyal and helpful,
Brotherly, courteous, kind,
Obedient, smiling and thrifty,
Pure as the rustling wind.

As a reaction to this sort of exercise, researchers have turned in recent years to more empirical study, and specific measures of intellectual ability, personal characteristics and biographical data have been correlated with ratings of executive success. On the whole the results have been disappointing. A typical case is an investigation into the careers and characteristics of a hundred leading American executives, which showed that the only common feature of their careers was that each was making more money than the average for his age group within two years of joining his company.[79] A study of New South Wales and Queensland higher public servants arrived at the same sort of conclusion—the budding permanent head got his first major promotion at an age well ahead of his contemporaries.[80] This kind of data can be interpreted in two very different ways. One may conclude either that traits resulting in later success were evident at an early age, or that fortuitous early promotion put the lucky official in the limelight, or both.

Selection Procedures

One way of classifying selection procedures is on the basis of the length of time a candidate's behaviour is observed.[81] Thus if an organisation can only spare a few minutes for the process of observation, an appraisal interview can be used. If a few hours are available, a psychological test might be used as well. In an 'assessment centre' situation, a simulated work problem might be added, especially if a day or two is available. If the organisation is prepared to extend the period of observation to several years, it becomes possible to throw the candidate into a real job and rate actual performance.

Interviewing is the time-honoured method in Australia of assessing contenders for administrative positions. In a career service, however, the members of a selection committee do not necessarily have to rely mainly on the evidence before them in the interview situation. The applicant has usually been working as a public servant for a number of years, and colleagues and supervisors have evaluated performance. Therefore, a committee often uses the interview as a means of integrating information acquired from each applicant's past and present associates. Of course, this is harder if some applicants come from outside the service, and public services have not given enough thought to this problem. Their methods sometimes seem very casual and unsystematic to an outsider. Face-to-face confrontation also gives the committee some idea of superficial social capabilities, and an impression of the person behind the summary of qualifications and experience extracted from the job application. It is useful to ask why the interview is taken so seriously in the public service, because there is a great deal of evidence as to the unreliability of this method of assessment.[82] Nevertheless, it has been generally concluded that we will have to put up with it until something better comes along, and in the meantime make some attempt to get rid of some of its more unsatisfactory features.

Psychological tests are more useful in assessing individuals who are strangers to the organisation, or who are doing work that has not yet presented them with the types of problem or responsibility that they would face in an administrative position. It is not usual to find psychological tests being used in Australia to evaluate a candidate who is a known quantity. All the same, tests of specific intellectual functions have been used with some success overseas to predict the administrative ability of candidates from both inside and outside the organisation. The Administrative Judgment Test has proved to be the most consistently effective of the 'objective' methods used by the United States Civil Service Commission. It consists of a number of non-technical problems in administration prepared by experienced administrators. Each question has five suggested answers, one of which is widely regarded by good administrators as the best of the five.

After the appraisal interview, and the psychological test, the next stage is to combine the two, and add a 'simulation' of the actual work situation. Simulations are a distinctive feature of the assessment centre approach. These may be group-based or individual-based. In one group test, a problem of a mildly controversial nature is posed. Proceedings may begin with a free, leaderless discussion; then leaders are appointed, in rotation, to steer the group through a committee session. The best known assessment centre programmes in current operation are the ones introduced by D.W. Bray in the Bell group of companies and the British Civil Service Selection Board procedures. The Department of Foreign Affairs uses similar methods for its recruits.[83] In 1970, a Personnel Assessment Centre was established by the New South Wales Public Service Board to provide for in-depth evaluation of officers. It has been attended (1978) by over eight hundred volunteers, of whom more than a hundred have been chosen for the Executive Development Programme.

The most appropriate test of an officer's administrative potential is to promote him and see how he performs. But what happens if this test shows that he is unsuitable? In some parts of the world the problem has been solved by liquidation, but in Australia a promotion decision is not so readily reversible. A compromise arrangement is the appointment of an officer to a position where conditions are a sort of dress-rehearsal for bigger things. There may be a series of positions particularly useful as testing grounds for the next generation of top administrators. A basic problem is how to assess the performance of individuals in these testing situations. Is this to be done formally or informally?

An informal system has traditionally operated at senior levels of the British civil service. The Treasury in the past occupied a position of unique importance, now inherited by the Civil Service Department. It had much of the responsibility in practice for appointing the most senior departmental officials (permanent heads and deputies); it played an important part in arranging transfers of all administrative class officers between departments, and in short, was responsible for 'career planning' in the upper ranks of the service. Many leading officials had a spell in the Treasury itself, to which they had at some stage been posted from other departments, especially if they showed promise of an outstanding career. This enabled some central assessment of on-the-job capabilities.

Informal systems with some of these features were noted in an interesting study of the New South Wales and Queensland Public Services in the early 1960s.[84] Attention was drawn to the existence of *cadre* groups—officers not yet occupying the top jobs in the service, yet who seemed to be specially marked for promotion. In New South Wales, the two most important groups were Public Service Board inspectors and budget inspectors; in Queensland the *cadres* included audit inspectors and private secretaries to ministers. The survey showed that a high proportion of officers in these proving grounds had advanced rather swiftly to top administrative positions in the service, or to posts in statutory authorities. Other proving grounds exist but these are mainly confined to single positions in each department which, by tradition, have been the preserve of the 'heir apparent', as deputy headships have often been of permanent headships.

Some writers have advocated more use of understudying as a way of both testing and developing administrative potential. A 1955 Report of an Australian Capital Territory study group[85] thought that private secretaryships to ministers and senior officials should be deliberately used for this purpose. More recently, L.F. Crisp has argued that in the Commonwealth service the more promising young public servants often 'do not feel . . . they are being in any significant sense developed for and gathered into a "profession" with lively concern for . . . wider intellectual issues and interests'.[86] Among ways of remedying this defect, he advocates wider use of apprenticeship, such as tours of duty with a senior officer as his personal assistant, in the minister's office, with the secretariat of major committees and international conferences, or at major vantage-points in the policy-forming departments. He recognised that a few permanent heads already practised what he preached.

At the time of the 1955 Report, the Commonwealth Board saw 'obvious advantages' in such a scheme though they saw some disadvantages and difficulties, such as that 'the understudy may become the *alter ego* of his chief and be too close to him to develop his own personality. "Traditional policy" is not necessarily good policy.' They also pointed out that:

> At present . . . selections of private secretary (to a minister) may be made largely on the basis of personal preference of a minister and in order that such a scheme could become effective it would seem essential that a different concept of the private secretaryships would have to be accepted by ministers and by departments.[87]

There were moves in this direction in the 1960s, but conflicting conceptions of the role of a minister's personal staff have persisted (see Chapter Ten). The problems raised by Crisp are also acute in the States.

Staff Assessment Records

One important record used to assist in locating administrative potential is the confidential report on an officer's services, or staff report. A staff reporting scheme has been applied to lower and middle levels of the British service since 1922, and similar schemes exist in the United States. Although these have had their deficiencies, they represent a considerable advance on earlier practices. It is hard to escape the conclusion that, if there is to be a merit system of pay and promotion, then 'there must be some means of standardizing reports about the work of individuals, since there can be no fair choice except on the basis of comparison'.[88] In Australia, the Commonwealth Bank was one of the first statutory corporations to use standardised staff reporting. Some States, such as New South Wales and Western Australia, have introduced a standard form of staff reporting for clerical and administrative officers. Others have not yet tried this on a service-wide basis, although a few individual departments have established schemes.

The Boyer Report has this to say on the question of staff reports in the Commonwealth Service:

> It is both possible and also extremely desirable to improve present methods of assessing officers, at least within the limited field of administrative work . . . If reporting were regularly used . . . the potentialities of exceptionally able officers might be recognized early enough to give them the attention they deserve.[89]

Many years have passed since this observation was made, but the Commonwealth Service has so far not set up a comprehensive and universal system of staff reporting, though a few departments have had schemes and the Board has said that it was 'encouraging departments to introduce staff reporting schemes' while recognising that the 'requirements of departments differ and the staff interests need to be considered'.[90] Of course in the Commonwealth most promotions are initially the responsibility of permanent heads, not the Board. There has also been the belief that reporting systems should closely reflect actual job requirements, and it has been argued that these vary so much that no single system would be adequate. The amount of interdepartmental mobility has also been used as an argument against relying for selection purposes on staff reports prepared in many different agencies and sections of agencies in a scattered service.

The following uses of the staff report may be identified:
1. Personal development, work improvement through counselling and knowledge by the officer of 'where he stands'.
2. Salary administration, such as the determination of salary increments.
3. Information storage, evidence to form the basis of administrative decisions on promotions, transfers, etc.
4. Isolation of training needs.
5. Validation of assessment procedures that put the officer in his present position.

Multi-purpose reports have often been criticised for contributing to conflict in the organisation, and frustration in the individual. Confusion of these various objectives has led to much trouble in the past over the issue of whether reports should be open to the employee. There seems to be a general move towards recognising a staff right to access to most personal records. The Coombs Report argues that secrecy is not justified and bad for staff–management relations.[91] However, when reports are being used for selection and promotion, the reliability of ratings is likely to suffer if it is normal practice to communicate them to the individuals being rated. On the other hand for the first use mentioned above, open reports are essential.

Staff reporting schemes in the Australian public services are basically used for purposes of personal development and are 'open' schemes. A confidential system of staff reporting introduced by a New South Wales statutory corporation in 1968 was described by the Deputy Leader of the State Opposition as foreign to the Australian way of life.[92] Formal schemes typically apply to the lower administrative and clerical grades, and rarely seem to have any direct impact on the selection of officers for higher administrative work.

Personnel Inventories

'A glance round the lunchroom', quite literally, may be enough to identify administrative potential in a small or centralised organisation. However, with an increase in the size and dispersion of staff, there is likely to be a greater need for such things as 'personnel inventories' and 'replacement schedules'. In the United Kingdom it is the practice to maintain lists of possible candidates for higher appointments with information about qualifications, experience and performance, and in America the 'executive roster' became fashionable years ago. The United States Civil Service Commission has a computerised inventory of higher ranking federal employees but its practical help in aiding selection for top appointments is said to be meagre. In contrast to this the Commonwealth public service has tended to emphasise individual initiative. Although it nowadays provides a good many incentives and means for personal development, it has not aimed to manage careers. The Coombs Report thought that the Public Service Board should collect data on foreseeable vacancies, and on officers in senior posts or that the departmental head thinks may soon be ready for promotion to such posts, and also on suitable outsiders. The returns should indicate where it would help an individual's career to be transferred elsewhere or, for example, to have experience in a central policy or management agency such as the Department of the Prime Minister and Cabinet, the Public Service Board, or the Treasury/Department of Finance. The Board should also be able to interview such officers if it wished. The officer concerned would see any return made about him, and be able to add his own comments.

Training and Staff Development

History

Some sections of the public services have been slow to realise that experience can be supplemented in many ways that speed it up, systematise and sometimes correct it. The reports of Public Service Boards have for a long time stressed the importance of training. 'Effective training of officers . . . is an obligation which cannot be evaded without serious danger to future administration',[93] the Commonwealth Commissioner was writing in 1911. In his next report, he drew special attention to the work of the British Postal Institutes for the training of post office workers (an example soon to be followed by the Australian Postal Institute); and of the New South Wales and Victorian Railways Departments, pioneers in promoting the education of their employees. Some developments followed the First World War in the Post Office and other technical departments, Commonwealth and State. But little was done in the field of clerical or administrative in-service training. At this stage, emphasis seems to have been mainly on limited encouragement to attend evening classes by technical colleges, universities and other outside institutions. In 1928, for example, the Commonwealth began a 'free place' system in the universities for selected officers.

New South Wales had been early in the field with in-service examinations. Promotion examinations were envisaged in the 1895 Public Service Act, though it was a few years before they got going. However, little practical help was given in preparing for them. Some facilities were provided in 1909 for 'cadets' in the Department of Agriculture, to attend day lectures at the university and obtain degrees. Later other types of cadetship and traineeship were created, but this scheme was not widely extended until just before the Second World War. The New South Wales Board also encouraged clerical officers to obtain outside qualifications. Early in the century it stimulated the University of Sydney (and the Workers Educational Association) into providing educational facilities, originally for public servants, which served as a basis for some of the university's present courses. The University Department of Economics was established in 1906 partly as a result of the Board's representations.

It could still be written in 1941 that, for administrative officers, 'positive in-Service training, apart from sporadic instructions by senior officers in the immediate duties of the junior, is non-existent'.[94] The war stimulated training in many countries and spheres—including the army and industry as well as the public service. In Australia, the provision of courses for servicemen and ex-servicemen gave in-service training a chance to establish itself. The war also produced a new breed of senior official more receptive to such ideas; new government activities developed, which made training more necessary. In 1947, the Commonwealth Public Service Board requested all departments to initiate systematic plans for the training of new clerical staff. The larger Commonwealth departments now have their own training officers, while in the others some officer has usually had the training function added to his general functions, usually personnel. The Board itself runs courses centrally, especially for senior staff. Similar developments have taken place in the States. New South Wales was the first State in the field, with one of the Board's deputy chief inspectors becoming Director of Training and Examinations. Training is now, with other personnel services, under the Director of the Job Opportunity Division. A Staff Development and Training Officers Group was formed in 1969, to improve co-ordination, exchange information and identify training needs. The Board itself concentrates on courses common to many departments. Some of the larger departments have their own training officers, and nearly all departments of any size have a personnel officer with duties in this field, and a Staff Development Committee.[95] A recent survey of State government agencies, including statutory bodies, showed that they spent about $10 million a year on training.[96]

In Victoria a considerable development of formal training has taken place since 1958, when the Board set up a training section, now the Staff Development Centre. This was at first mainly at Board level, but each department is now encouraged as in New South Wales to set up a Staff Development Committee. The Board has discontinued its old central training programme, and plans only to conduct courses when a department asks for one. Other States have also made moves. Most training is on technical and occupational skills, especially in statutory authorities, or induction courses, with a handful of courses for supervisors. An Executive Development Centre was established in Western Australia in 1973.

Traineeships and Tertiary Education

As mentioned earlier, for a long time there was no parallel in Australia to the common overseas practice of recruiting large numbers of graduates, except in certain professional fields. However, the public services have for much longer recognised the value of higher education by providing study leave for serving officers, and more recently (in some cases) making some form of higher education a normal prerequisite for promotion to senior positions.

The fullest provision has been in the professional field. This has often taken the form of the traineeship or cadetship, by which selected candidates have been enabled to have a full-time university or college education, often generously financed, and then usually required to remain in the public service for a period after graduation, in accordance with a 'bond' to which a monetary penalty was attached. These schemes were specially popular with some State governments. New South Wales began to appoint professional trainees in the early years of the century, at first in fields such as agricultural and veterinary science and forestry. Later architecture, engineering, geology, librarianship, social work and various other fields were added. In 1977 there were over three hundred full-time professional trainees in New South Wales, not counting those sponsored by the Department of Education, or traineeships provided by statutory bodies, undertaking courses at universities, colleges of advanced education, and so on. But only eight new ones were awarded in 1977, as the service could now provide for its needs by recruiting ordinary unbonded graduates. Bonding was dying out.

Sponsored training of this kind has aimed to provide a good supply of able graduates for entry into professional fields, and to ensure that they start their career familiar with public service requirements. Similar cadetships have existed in the Commonwealth service since the 1920s. There has been some minor experiment with administrative cadetships on the same basis, but in general the public services preferred to recruit non-professional graduates after graduation, or to provide for serving officers by time off, and sometimes payment of fees, for part-time education.

A much larger number of public servants have been granted varying amounts of 'study leave' to attend courses, and others were undertaking courses without assistance (including some with 'leave without pay'). About 4000 New South Wales officers and employees were undertaking part-time studies in 1977. The Commonwealth has replaced its 'part-time free place' scheme by one which reimburses fees for subjects successfully passed, and provides up to five hours' leave with pay per week, which may be supplemented by leave without pay or on a 'make-up' basis. A few officers get full-time awards or complete the final year of a course as full-time students on salary. Over 11 000 officers were benefiting under one or other of these schemes in 1977, including 372 working for higher degrees. Several hundred more are studying on their own initiative or with leave without pay.

Victoria has 137 officers on full-time study leave with pay, and over 1500 with varying amounts of paid part-time study leave, often five hours a week.

Executive Development

In the mid-1970s the Commonwealth Public Service Board has become concerned about the emerging shortage of talent for top administrative positions, and in 1977 it launched a new Executive Development Scheme, designed to increase the supply of officers ready to meet the demands of higher administrative work. A fresh effort has been made to identify promising administrators, including professionals and public servants working away from Canberra. In 1978 about fifty middle-ranking officers will attend an intensive six-week residential course in management and policy studies, followed by a series of job-assignments in and outside the service. An Interchange programme has also been launched between Commonwealth and State services and with the private sector. The Coombs Report made general noises in favour of greater interdepartmental and other kinds of mobility, and job-rotation.[97] Apart from the residential course mentioned above, the Commonwealth Board also conducts Second Division seminars several times a year on broad topics such as the Coombs Commission recommendations, Australia's place in world affairs, departmental manpower planning; conferences for senior administrators on finance management and management development; specialist seminars for senior personnel managers and other groups.

In New South Wales anyone identified at the Personnel Assessment Centre as having administrative potential has the chance of taking part in a programme designed by an Executive Development Committee to meet his personal needs, involving attending courses and special job assignments. The Board has also organised a few exchanges with the private sector and with other States, usually for short periods of three or four months.

Establishment Control

Public Service Boards have no power to change the functions of departments which, as we have seen, are determined by the executive order of the government or by statute. However, most changes have staffing consequences, and here the public service authority plays an important role. Section 29 of the Commonwealth Public Service Act provides that the Governor-General 'may' create or abolish 'offices' (that is, positions in the service) 'on the recommendation of the Board, after the Board has obtained a report from the Permanent Head'. The classification of the office, once created, is solely the affair of the board. The latter may reject or modify a permanent head's recommendation, and the government usually accepts the board's view, though (as mentioned earlier) it sometimes imposes its own staff ceilings. Incidentally, the section 29 procedures are also the basis of 'tenure' in the public service, which is related to occupancy of an established position in a department. This raises problems if a department is abolished. The Coombs Report proposed some revision in the concept of tenure, which would in future be provided for in terms of appointment and be somewhat separated from office held.[98]

The Coombs Report also recommended the introduction of 'forward estimates' for manpower as well as finance (see Chapter Sixteen); under this ministers and their departments would negotiate for the manpower resources they wanted over the next three years, and these estimates, when approved by the cabinet, would become the basis for departmental planning. Such a process would involve closer co-operation between the Public Service Board and the Department of Finance than exists at present. It also raises many difficult problems of discovering what government priorities really are, and relating them in a meaningful way to manpower allocations, which few central personnel authorities in the world are equipped to tackle.

The board's power under section 29 is supplemented by its duty under section 17 to exercise critical oversight over the activities and methods of each department, and to devise means for effecting economies and promoting efficiency. A major change in staffing may be closely related to some structural change. The Commonwealth Public Service Board has no power to impose organisational changes if they are resisted by a department, but it can make recommendations; in particular, it can hinder changes it dislikes by refusing to recommend the positions necessary to implement the proposals. In each department there is an Establishments or Personnel Branch which is supposed to, and sometimes does, make a critical review of new staffing proposals within the agency, but it may of course prefer to act mainly as a post office and leave criticism to the Board.

There are many minor changes in staffing going on all the time in the departments, and more delegation to departments has been necessary. In some cases this involves creating a pool of positions in advance of needs. The department estimates its likely needs over the next year in various categories, and the board is given the argument in broad terms; it then creates the pool, from which the Department's Personnel Branch can provide individual positions as the need arises. To the Coombs Commission, the board proposed progressive devolution to the point where departments could create their own positions within manpower budgets approved for each major work programme. The Commonwealth Board has in fact already introduced a system of forward staffing estimates.[99]

Dismissal

We touch on this subject more briefly than it deserves, partly because there is so little to say. Disciplinary procedures have already been outlined in Chapter Ten. The general character of modern career services is such that it is virtually impossible to get rid of an inefficient staff member once he becomes 'established' unless his offences are flagrant (and sometimes not even then). As has been wisely said, much money and thought has gone into studying how to get people into organisations, but virtually none on how to get them out. Yet one of the common complaints of government administrators trying to improve the work of departments is the constraint imposed by the irremoveability of the incompetent.

The Coombs Commission had some mild words to say on the subject. It thought among other things that there should be ways of dealing with staff of 'limited efficiency', who could no longer meet the requirements of their position, even though it might be unfair to call them positively 'inefficient'; and that it should be easier to bring about management-initiated early retirements. The Fraser government's proposed legislation on this subject lapsed in 1977, and no further action has been taken at the time of writing. There is also a case for longer probationary periods, and for taking them more seriously.

Perhaps one should add that if white-collar employees in large organisations come to expect total security, even where their efficiency is demonstrably low or the demand for their services is ceasing to exist, they must not be surprised if similar demands spread to the total workforce.

Notes

1. Report, RCAGA, 177.
2. For discussion, see Report, RCAGA, Appendix Vol. Three, 223–46.
3. The cabinet of the day, which included one or two distinguished graduates like J.G. Latham, seems to have been partly influenced by the advocacy of the University Association of Canberra, whose main aim was to develop a university in Canberra. For a fuller account, see P.W.E. Curtin, 'Recruitment', in R.N. Spann (ed.), *Public Administration in Australia*, 1st edn, Government Printer, Sydney, 1959, 336–40; and Report, Commonwealth Public Service Board, Canberra, 1970, 198–204.
4. See its Report, 1959. Its chairman was Sir Richard Boyer, Chairman of the Australian Broadcasting Commission; an influential member was R.S. Parker, then Reader in Public Administration, Australian National University. For its other recommendations, see G.E. Caiden, *Career Service*, Melbourne University Press, Melbourne, 1965, 418–9.
5. See *1st Sectional Report*, Royal Commission on the Public Service, Sydney 1918, LXII. The proposed regulations and correspondence relating to the 1918 scheme are reprinted in F.A. Bland, *Government in Australia*, 2nd edn, Government Printer, Sydney, 1944, 149–152; and cf. S. Encel, *Equality and Authority*, Cheshire, Melbourne, 1970, 262, and R.S. Parker, *Public Service Recruitment in Australia*, Melbourne University Press, Melbourne, 1942, 107–8. On the 1938 scheme see F.A. Bland, 'Wallace Wurth and Public Service Examinations', *Public Admin.* (Sydney), XX, 3, September 1961, and K.W. Knight, 'Administrative Cadets in the New South Wales Public Service', *Public Admin.* (Sydney), XX, 4, December 1961.
6. Report, RCAGA, 267; and Appendix Vol. Three, 388–417.

7. *Com. Parl. Deb.* (H. of R.), V. 103, 16 February 1977, 116–7; cf. E.A. Lyall, 'Australia's Overseas Representation and Government Patronage', *Australian Outlook*, 23, 2, August 1969.
8. For a critical account, see Report, RCAGA, Appendix Vol. Three, 276–9.
9. Report, Department of External Affairs, 1967–68, 81; and Report, RCAGA, Appendix Vol. Three.
10. See for example 'The Swelling Ranks of Dunstan Men', *Canberra Times*, 2 February 1972. In Victoria in 1976 there were fourteen outside appointments to senior administrative positions. On New South Wales, see Interim Report, Review of New South Wales Government Administration, Sydney, 1977, 106.
11. Report, Commonwealth Committee on Public Service Recruitment, Canberra, 1959, 2.
12. Nigel Walker, *Morale in the Civil Service*, Edinburgh University Press, Edinburgh, 1961, 253, 263.
13. A.A. Congalton, *Status and Prestige in Australia*, Cheshire, Melbourne, 1969. In America, it seems that the more highly educated one is, the less one is attracted to public employment. See F.P. Kilpatric *et al.*, *The Image of the Federal Service*, Brookings Institution, Washington DC, 1964, 244.
14. W.J.M. Mackenzie and J.W. Grove, *Central Administration in Britain*, Longmans, London, 1957, 450.
15. Based on Table in Report, RCAGA, Appendix Vol. Two, 296; cf. *ibid.*, 222, 293, 326.
16. G.R. Curnow, 'Images of Bureaucracy', Department of Government, University of Sydney (mimeo).
17. *The Bulletin*, 20 August 1977.
18. For general attitudes to women, see S. Encel, N. MacKenzie and M. Tebbutt, *Women in Society*, Cheshire, Melbourne, 1974; on the public service, see Report, Commonwealth Public Service Board, 1975, 'Women in the Public Service'; Report, RCAGA, 186–7, 342–5, and references there given; and Interim Report, Review of New South Wales Government Administration, Sydney, 1977, ch. 13.
19. Information from Interim Report, Review of New South Wales Government Administration, Sydney, 1977, ch. 13.
20. *Report*, Commission on Public Service Administration, 1920, 76–7.
21. Jean Holmes, *The Government in Victoria*, University of Queensland Press, St Lucia, 1976, 48.
22. cf. B.B. Schaffer, 'Staff Conditions and Careers as a Problem of Management', *Public Admin.* (Sydney), XIX, 1, March 1960.
23. By F.C. Mosher, *Democracy and the Public Service*, Oxford University Press, New York, 1968, ch. 5.
24. P. Kelloway, 'Promotion Procedures in the Tasmanian Public Service', *Public Admin.* (Sydney), XXI, 3, September 1962, 276.
25. Report, RCAGA, Appendix Vol. Three, 60.
26. *The Civil Services of North America*, A Report by the [UK] Civil Service Department, HMSO, London 1969.
27. By Mr Barry Moore in an unpublished paper. See also the useful discussion of seniority in Interim Report, Review of New South Wales Government Administration, Sydney, 1977, 120 ff.
28. Sir Frederick Wheeler, 'Providing for Future Management Needs in the Commonwealth Service', *Public Admin.* (Sydney), XXX, 1, March 1971, 5.

29. Report, RCAGA, Appendix Vol. Three, 157.
30. R.S. Parker, *Public Service Recruitment in Australia*, Melbourne University Press, Melbourne, 1942, 51.
31. See Report, Committee of Inquiry into Systems of Promotion and Temporary Transfers, Canberra, 1945.
32. For this and other recommendations regarding promotion appeals, see Report, RCAGA, 206–13.
33. Report, RCAGA, Appendix Vol. Three, 'The Career Service Survey'.
34. *Report*, Committee on Public Service Recruitment, Canberra 1959, 17.
35. Report, RCAGA, 212.
36. Report, RCAGA, Appendix Vol. Three, 45; and Interim Report, Review of New South Wales Government Administration, Sydney, 1977, 115.
37. Report, RCAGA, 207.
38. cf. G.J. McCarry, 'Seniority: Will it Rule from the Grave?', *Public Admin.* (Sydney), XXXIV, 3, September 1975, 237.
39. For earlier practice in the use of promotion examinations, *see* R.S. Parker, *Public Service Recruitment in Australia*, Melbourne University Press, Melbourne, 1942, 80–105, and *Report*, Commonwealth Public Service Board, Canberra, 1970, 199–200.
40. For a controversy about 'computerised staff records', see *Australian Financial Review*, 2 December 1970.
41. Report, RCAGA, 207.
42. Report, RCAGA, Canberra 1976, Appendix Vol. Three, 188; Interim Report, Review of New South Wales Government Administration, Sydney, 1977, 130.
43. Report, RCAGA, Canberra, 1976, 395.
44. For a summary, see Report, Commonwealth Public Service Board, Canberra, 1977, 93; for a fuller account, see R.N. Spann, 'Ministers and Permanent Heads', in R.F.I. Smith and Patrick Weller, *Public Service Inquiries in Australia*, University of Queensland Press, St Lucia, 1978.
45. Sir Lenox Hewitt, the displaced head, has said that this device was 'invented' on this occasion. See RCAGA, Transcript of Proceedings, 29 April 1975, 2677–8. The department had previously (in 1968) been divided into two to find a permanent headship for Sir Lenox Hewitt.
46. Report, Public Service Board of NSW, Sydney, 1925, 5–7, *cit.* F.A. Bland, *Government in Australia*, 2nd edn, Government Printer, Sydney, 1944, 593–4.
47. Report, RCAGA, 101.
48. *ibid.*, 100–101.
49. *ibid.*, 100.
50. Report, Committee of Inquiry into the Public Service of South Australia, Adelaide, 1975, 64.
51. Report, RCAGA, Appendix Vol. Three, 80–81. Almost as many others were 'non-practising'.
52. S. Encel, *Equality and Authority*, Cheshire, Melbourne, 1970, 275.
53. Based on data supplied by the Public Service Board, supplemented by *Who's Who in Australia*.
54. See S. Encel, *op. cit.*, 282 ff; and B.B. Schaffer and K.W. Knight, *Top Public Servants in Two States*, University of Queensland Press, St Lucia, 1963. The latter survey excluded some senior professional positions.

55. I am indebted for these figures to the Commissioner, Review of New South Wales Government Administration, Professor P.R. Wilenski. The survey included statutory authorities.
56. D.C. Rodway, 'Characteristics of Administrators: A Study of Administrators in the South Australian Public Service', M.Econ. thesis, University of Adelaide, 1971.
57. Information from *Who's Who*, supplemented by private enquiry.
58. The Administrative Class has now (in name at least) been abolished. On it, see W.J.M. Mackenzie and J.W. Grove, *Central Administration in Britain,* Longmans, London 1957, Ch. 6.
59. cf. Report, RCAGA, 58.
60. For general discussion, see R.J.S. Baker, 'Organization Theory and the Public Sector', *J. Management Studies*, 6, 1, February 1969, and Peter Self, *Administrative Theories and Politics*, Allen and Unwin, London, 1972, 92–9.
61. Self, *op. cit.*, 94–5.
62. Self, *op. cit.*, 94.
63. See Leon Peres, 'Principle or Interest? Changing Roles within Australian Government', *Melbourne J. Pol*, 3, 1970.
64. For general discussion see F. Ridley (ed.), *Specialists and Generalists, A Selection of Readings*, US Government Printing Office, 1968; and N.C. Angus (ed.), *The Expert and Administration in New Zealand*, New Zealand Institute of Public Administration, Wellington, 1959.
65. cf. L.F. Crisp, 'Specialists and Generalists: Further Australian Reflections on Fulton', *Public Admin.* (Sydney), XXIX, 3, September 1970, 197. I am also indebted for some points to an unpublished paper by Dr G.R. Curnow.
66. On the characteristics of such 'career services', see the good discussion in F.C. Mosher, *op. cit.*
67. For doubts on the whole matter see Y. Dror, 'Specialists v. Generalists—a Misquestion', *Public Personnel Review*, XXXI, January 1970.
68. See L.F. Crisp, 'Public Administration as a Profession: Some Australian Reflections on Fulton', *Public Admin.* (Sydney), XXVIII, 2/3, June–September 1969; and R.N. Spann and G.R. Curnow, 'The Higher Civil Service as a Profession', *Quarterly J. Admin.*, IV, 3, April 1970.
69. V. Subramaniam, 'Specialists in British and Australian Administration: A Study in Contrast', *Public Admin.* (London), Winter 1963, and 'The Relative Status of Specialists and Generalists', *ibid.*, Autumn 1968.
70. Crisp, 'Specialists and Generalists', 207.
71. J.O.A. Bourke, 'Wallace Wurth as an Administrator', *Public Admin.* (Sydney), XX, 1, March 1961, 9; cf. A.J.A. Gardner, 'Specialists and the Administrative Career', *ibid.*, XXII, 1, March 1963, 31.
72. V. Subramaniam, 'Specialists and the Administrative Career: A Comment', *Public Admin.* (Sydney), XXII, 1, March 1963, 31.
73. Dean Jaensch, *The Government of South Australia*, University of Queensland Press, St Lucia, 1977, 139.
74. S. Encel, *op. cit.*, 249–57.
75. cf. the account in Mosher, *op. cit.*, 123 ff; P.M. Blau and W.R. Scott, *Formal Organizations*, Chandler Publishing Co., San Francisco, 1962, 60–74; and R.H. Hall, 'Professionalization and Bureaucratization', *Amer. Sociological Review*, 33, 1968, 92–104.

76. Don K. Price, *The Scientific Estate*, Harvard University Press, Cambridge, Mass., 1965, 122.
77. Based on *Reports*, Commonwealth Public Service Board, 1970, 118, 177; 1971, 74.
78. R.S. Parker, 'Executive Development in the Commonwealth Public Service', in R.N. Spann (ed.), *Public Administration in Australia*, 1st edn, Government Printer, Sydney, 1959, 426. It was based on a detailed job analysis of the work of middle-grade Administrative Class officers, undertaken by the UK Civil Service Selection Board.
79. R.M. Guion, *Personnel Testing*, McGraw–Hill, New York, 1965.
80. B.B. Schaffer and K.W. Knight, *Top Public Servants in Two States*, University of Queensland Press, St Lucia, 1963.
81. B.N. Moore, 'Identifying Administrative Potential', *Public Admin.* (Sydney), XXVII, 1, March 1968, 2.
82. For discussion, see R.L. Mason, 'Executive Selection', *Personnel Practice Bulletin,* June, 1962; and J.D. Tucker, 'On Dispensing with the Selection Interview', *Aust. Psychologist*, 5, 2, 1970.
83. D.W. Bray and D.L. Grant, *The Assessment Centre in the Measurement of Potential for Business Management*, Psychological Monographs, 625, 80, American Psychological Association, Washington DC, 1966; and B.N. Moore, *Personnel Assessment Centres in Britain and America*, NSW Public Service Board, Sydney, 1970. On the British arrangements, see also *Report*, (Fulton) Committee on the Civil Service, IV, 297–331. For an account of Foreign Affairs procedures, see Report, RCAGA, Appendix Vol. Three, 276–9.
84. Schaffer and Knight, *op. cit.*
85. See R.S. Parker, 'Executive Development in the Commonwealth Public Service', in R.N. Spann (ed.), *Public Administration in Australia*, 1st edn, Government Printer, Sydney, 1959, 441.
86. L.F. Crisp, 'Public Administration as a Profession: Some Australian Reflections on Fulton', *Public Admin.* (Sydney), XXVIII, 2/3, June–September 1959, 441.
87. Parker, *loc. cit.*
88. W.J.M. Mackenzie and J.W. Grove, *op. cit.*, 121.
89. *Report*, (Boyer) Committee on Public Service Recruitment, Canberra, 1959, 34–5.
90. *Report*, Commonwealth Public Service Board, 1976, 59.
91. Report, RCAGA, 202.
92. *Sydney Morning Herald*, 1 November 1968.
93. *Report*, Commonwealth Public Service Commission, 1911, *cit.* Bland, *Government In Australia*, 2nd edn, Government Printer, Sydney, 1944, 184.
94. R.S. Parker, *Public Service Recruitment in Australia*, Melbourne University Press, Melbourne, 1942, 250.
95. cf. *Human Resource Development: Handbook 1975–76*, Public Service Board of New South Wales.
96. Interim Report, Review of New South Wales Government Administration, Sydney 1977, 137.
97. Report, RCAGA, 396–8.
98. See Report, RCAGA, 242.
99. See for example Report, Commonwealth Public Service Board, 1976, 28.

Chapter Thirteen

Classification, Pay, Industrial Relations

When organisations grow beyond a certain point, they become more formal. The attempt is made to describe and analyse the various tasks that individuals are expected to perform, and to evaluate these in relation to one another. In the public service, this is called 'job classification', or 'position classification' or just 'classification'. Section 7 of the Commonwealth Public Service Act defines classification as: 'the arrangement of officers and positions in classes, and includes the allotment to officers and positions of salaries or limits of salary according to the value of the work'.

Problems of Classification

Jobs and Individuals

As the reference in the Commonwealth Public Service Act to 'officers and positions' indicates, an organisation can be considered from two points of view, as a group of persons, or as a group of jobs or positions. Correspondingly there are two ways of classifying the units, sometimes called the 'personal' or 'rank' method and the 'position' or 'job' method (the Americans call them 'rank-in-man' and 'rank-in-job'). At one extreme, one can start with the individuals and give them each a rank or title corresponding to a certain level in their career progression, as happens in the armed forces; and provide that this rank gives them a certain pay and status whatever job they are doing at any particular time. Alternatively one can treat an organisation not as a structure of individuals but as a structure of jobs.

In the Australian public services it is the position or group of positions —identified by a duty statement and an appropriate title—that is the object of classification, not the individual officer. The theory is that jobs should be described and evaluated without reference to the individuals who hold them. The latter's personal characteristics are not supposed to be relevant. *Positions* are classified not *people*. An officer is entitled to a grade and rate of pay only by virtue of the position he occupies. The position is graded on the basis of work performed and does not necessarily call for the full range of qualifications, experience or skills which the particular occupant may have.[1] This is broadly what happens in practice, though it is possible to make

360

some allowance for individual differences where classifications are broad and, especially in higher-level positions, an officer's personal merits can sometimes affect the classification of his job. There are a few groups, such as CSIRO and Atomic Energy Commission scientists, whose classification is on a personal basis, and where a personal assessment can result in individual scientists being moved up without there being any formal vacancy at the higher level.

There is in all public services a conflict between the need for comparability of standards in grading and pay and the inflexibility caused by a service-wide classification system. It is hard for an outside body like a Public Service Board to understand the character of every job in the various departments. Individual departments can often do this better, on the other hand some way is needed to stop them getting very much out of line with one another. This conflict is in some ways becoming more acute as public service tasks get more varied, and consequently the structures suited to them. Standard forms of grading seem especially unsuitable when applied to new types of organisation, such as project teams or research units or other kinds of work-group that do not follow regular patterns of bureaucratic hierarchy.

There are some higher-level and professional positions where the statement of duties cannot be drafted with as much precision as for other posts. Sometimes the only way to describe the duties of a senior officer may be in words such as 'responsible for (some broad activity)' or 'directs the work of a division/branch', or 'advises the permanent head'. Nor does it make sense to try to draw fine distinctions in cases where small differences between the duties of positions are clearly less important than the qualities of the individual officer. There are also an increasing number of specialists in the public service whose duties and responsibilities cannot be precisely defined, or vary with the particular individual appointed. It was considerations of this sort that led the Coombs Commission to recommend that departments should have more discretion in classification, with the Board setting and monitoring broad standards.

Divisional Classification

Positions are classified in two ways, by Division and by class or grade or work-level within a Division. The Commonwealth Public Service Act separates the Service into four divisions.[2] The First Division includes permanent heads of departments and such other officers as the Governor-General determines; it has become a very exclusive division, as policy has been to confine it almost entirely to heads of departments, and a few very senior statutory officers with 'permanent head' status.

The Second Division was to be composed of 'officers who, under officers of the First Division, are required to exercise executive or professional functions in the more important offices of the Service'.[3] It includes the top administrative staff below the permanent heads; for example, deputy secretaries, first assistant secretaries, assistant secretaries. The composition of the

Third and Fourth Divisions was left to the discretion of the Public Service Board. In practice the Third Division came to include most clerical and many professional positions, and the Fourth covered subclerical and manual grades, mostly (at the time) in the Post Office. This divisional classification came to be of little practical use. For the most part it lost any connection with recruitment and promotion. The lack of a clear line of distinction between Second and Third division positions also produced anomalies; a great deal of overlap developed and it became rather accidental whether a particular senior position was classified in one or other division.

The Boyer Committee on Public Service Recruitment tried to sort out some of these problems. It recommended that the Second Division become a group of administrators and policy-advising officers with some resemblance to the old United Kingdom Administrative Class, though freely open to promotion from below, and including lower-paid positions suitable for administrative training. Its particular recommendations were not accepted, but the attempt was made to reorganise the Second Division to give it a more meaningful character. The Commonwealth Public Service Board embarked in the 1960s on what it called 'an evolutionary process towards crystallizing the Second Division as a corps of top administrators and/or managers assisting and supporting the Permanent Heads by taking responsibility in a manner and to a degree which establishes an affinity between their responsibilities and those of the Permanent Head'.[4] This involved 'broadbanding' (reducing the number of classification levels within the Division) and encouraging mobility by creating a comparable structure of senior positions in each department. Positions not regarded as falling into the top administrative/managerial class were excluded from the Second Division, though it came to include professional officers with important policy-forming or management functions.

The Third Division continued to have a very wide spread from fairly senior officials to base-grade clerical officers. It includes many professional public servants—accountants, architects, engineers, and so on—and groups such as air traffic controllers and migration officers. Some 'broadbanding' has taken place there also. Entry nowadays requires at least the Higher School Certificate or equivalent. The Fourth Division contains 60 per cent of the service. It includes routine clerical workers such as typists and clerical assistants, a large artisan group, and other manual workers. Broadly it includes any position whose work at the base-grade does not require the Higher School Certificate, though it may involve trade certificates or other occupational skills.

In June 1977, the number of officers in the various Commonwealth divisions was as shown in Table 13.1.

The Coombs Commission has recommended that this divisional structure should be abolished, as useless and 'a source of caste and status'.[5] Some of this change, if it occurs, will be more nominal than real; the Commission still wants to retain departmental heads as a separate group, and also a Senior Executive Category which sounds very much like a Second Division.

TABLE 13.1

Number of Officers in Public Service Divisions

	Permanent	Temporary	Exempt	Total
First	30	—	1	31
Second	1 201	5	16	1 222
Third	59 042	1 680	668	61 390
Fourth	55 809	7 816	28 244	91 869
Total	116 082	9 501	28 929	154 512

In the States, there are also a number of broad divisions. New South Wales has five—Special (consisting of permanent heads), Professional, Administrative and Clerical, General (corresponding broadly to the Commonwealth Fourth Division) and Educational. New South Wales, like some other States, has retained a separate professional division. Its Administrative and Clerical Division covers the whole gamut of administrative–clerical jobs from deputy heads of departments, where these are not professionals, to base-grade clerical workers. The precise scope of the Professional Division is left to the Public Service Board, which has included within it not only professionally qualified officers in the narrow sense but also some other categories, including its own inspectors. The line between professional and administrative is in any case becoming harder to draw. The Board expressed itself some years ago in favour of abolishing the existing divisional structure, and replacing it by one more like that of the Commonwealth, and is now said to be not averse to getting rid of it completely.[6]

In June 1977 the number of permanent and temporary officers and employees in the New South Wales Divisions was as given in Table 13.2.

TABLE 13.2

New South Wales Division, 1977

Division	Number
Special	16
Professional	8 451
Administrative–clerical	22 900
General	40 152
Educational	3 647
Total	75 166

Classification within Divisions

There are two possible extremes in classifying positions within any particular division or major employment group. One is to have a few broad classes of position, the other is to have a great many classes. The first produces a simpler result. If a class or grade also includes within it an 'incremental scale', that is, salary steps up which officers progress more or less automatically by seniority, or subject to some simple efficiency bar, this is often well-liked, at least by lower-paid public servants. A simple classification system is sometimes regarded as more rational by those who argue that one cannot grade jobs finely, and that the attempt produces an immensely complicated situation, in which people are endlessly seeking minor promotion from one grade to another, or finding their career blocked by the variety of qualifications required for different types of employment. On the other hand it is argued that broadbanding of positions can produce too rigid a system; and, if combined with incremental scales, either reduces the incentive to be efficient (if the increments are automatic) or leaves too much power in the hands of the awarder of increments (if they are discretionary).

Most Australian public services started with a fairly simple system of classes, each with an incremental scale. In the early years of this century, for example, the Commonwealth had five broad classes in its clerical and professional divisions, and the lowest class had a nine-step scale. They were based on the Victorian classes. New South Wales had a somewhat larger number of grades, but the structure was still fairly simple.[7] This system broadly continued in Victoria, though there were some changes over the years. In the Commonwealth it was replaced by a system that attempted to classify each position precisely, resulting in a very large number of different classifications. Since the Second World War the Commonwealth has gradually been moving to a new variant of the old system, a process greatly accelerated by the Engineers' decisions of 1961–62. In New South Wales, the old structure has been replaced by one based on triennial agreements.

The elaborate Commonwealth system led to officers constantly seeking promotion to a different position classified at a somewhat higher salary, or trying to blackmail their departments into getting their position reclassified, to prevent them from moving. This was especially true after the Second World War, when there was an expanding service and a shortage of capable officers. The system also created a need for continuous review by the Public Service Board to remove anomalies. For some years after 1945, part of the task of fact-finding was taken over by classification committees set up to satisfy the public service associations—with a chairman representing the board, a departmental and a staff representative; more recently these have been superseded by direct negotiations between the board and staff associations, though the Coombs Report says that there may be a case for re-establishing them. But the main burden of reclassification after the war rested on the board itself, constantly under pressure from departments and their officers to have positions reclassified. Another problem was that in an inflationary period, salary scales were subject to constant change.

As a result the board made efforts to simplify the system, a process greatly speeded up in the 1960s. This involved a much more thoroughgoing analysis of departmental structures and employment groups, more systematic research into pay questions and the effort to present so convincing a case to staff associations and arbitration authorities that careful plans were not ruined by later arbitration decisions. A new pattern emerged, with two main features: a smaller number of classes of position and work levels within each employment category; and a system of category classification, so that many employment groups had their own individual structure of classifications.[8] There are now (1978) six standard salary levels in the Second Division and ten salary ranges in the clerical–administrative and related areas of the Third Division. Current policy is also to keep small the number of steps within each class, and to eliminate overlap of salaries between classes. The various broad employment categories in the Third Division are not classified in relation to one another within a single multi-point salary scale. Different employment groups now have their own individual and reasonably simple structure of classes. There is a large number of such structures.

This move was triggered off by arbitration decisions on engineers' salaries, which had the effect of raising them sharply. At the same time it was made clear by the Conciliation and Arbitration Commission that judgment was based on a special investigation of the engineering profession, and that other classes of employees were not 'as of right' entitled to increases based on existing relativities; their claims would need to be 'dependent upon proper proof of work value'. As a result, the Public Service Board reshaped its own thinking, and fixed separate scales for a large number of different employment groups.

> The employment group is best defined as one formed of positions the occupants of which perform a similar type of work. The occupants have usually undergone similar training, have developed similar skills, have obtained similar experience, and apply their training, skill and experience in a similar way to the work they undertake. The work of the group usually includes the direction and/or supervision of that particular type of work.[9]

This also made it easier to compare salaries with those of other employers, and to create classification structures relevant to normal career patterns, to training requirements, and so on. The net result has been that, though the number of salary levels or ranges in the whole service has increased, the number in each group has fallen, and this includes the very large group of officers engaged in administrative–clerical work.

Parts of the Fourth Division have been affected in the same way. However, in artisan-type positions, clear gaps between levels have existed for many years, and the same changes have not been needed. Types of position are closely related to outside occupations, and are almost all covered by arbitration awards.

Victoria and New South Wales avoided some of the Commonwealth's troubles, partly because of the less prominent role that arbitration has played in their public services. In Victoria, the old structure survived until recently, and since the Second World War public servants have been represented on the Public Service Board itself, so they have had less to gain by demanding some form of arbitration. The Victorian Public Service Board, as the salary-fixing authority, has been satisfied with nine classes for the Administrative Division. In the Professional Division a similar structure was greatly diversified, and there are now a large number of different categories with distinctive classifications. Since 1975 the divisions have been restructured and the former Administrative and Professional Divisions brought together as the Second Division, but the administrative classes and professional categories within the Division have continued as before. In New South Wales, the story is more complex and the State has experimented with many different systems. Currently, the structure is almost wholly determined by salary agreements between the board and staff associations. But an agreement typically provides for a basic incremental scale of at least ten years. Above these, are the so-called 'graded positions', positions to which a specific classification is allotted. The grades are fairly narrow for administrative–clerical officers, but broader in some professional areas. In the Administrative and Clerical Division there is at present (1978) a basic incremental scale, and above this twelve grades. There is some room within the incremental scale for recognising outstanding officers, in the form of accelerated progression.

Pay and Arbitration

In matters of pay and conditions, the public service is distinguished in some important ways from the private sector. A high degree of responsibility rests with the central personnel authority, which has among other things to try to preserve consistency over a very wide range of different groups. The public service is a career service, and in principle regarded as a unity. Where the Public Service Board is the main negotiator, it may also be harder to get the line managers involved in explaining the rationale of decisions. Pay is not influenced by normal considerations of profit, and operates within the fairly rigid system of classifications already described—it depends mainly on one's grade and seniority reached within the grade. In relation to any given position, it is usually impossible to strike individual bargains or to take account of the special merit or difficulties of a job.

Methods of Settling Disputes

There are three ways of settling a dispute over pay and conditions between employer and employees; by a trial of strength—strike, lockout, 'work to rule', wholesale dismissals, and so on; by negotiation between the parties, sometimes aided by a third party (conciliation or mediation); or by the decision of a third party, or arbitration.

In many countries trials of strength between public servants and their employers have been frowned upon as attempts to 'coerce the state'; in some, strike action by public servants is subjected to special formal limitations or legally banned. In Australia there have been special provisions such as the ban on strikes in section 66 of the Commonwealth Public Service Act (never invoked). Special restrictions on public servants have become harder to maintain as government activities have expanded and a larger percentage of the population have become government employees. In the Australian public services, trials of strength occasionally happen, but disputes are mostly settled in other ways.

The characteristic Australian way has come to be arbitration, through tribunals established by law. In many countries, this has not happened to the same extent. In Britain until recently procedures were almost wholly non-legal, the emphasis being on collective bargaining, negotiation between employers and employee organisations resulting in a collective agreement between the parties. This difference has been partly reflected in the public services. The British have for a long time made considerable use of Whitley Councils, which provide for continuous contact on a wide variety of issues between representatives of the 'staff' and 'official' sides of the service, at local, departmental and national levels; though there has also been some resort to arbitration.[10] In Australia, far more statutory machinery has developed for settling service disputes by arbitration. However, Australian public services have also resorted to negotiation and direct contact between staff associations and Public Service Boards.

In America, neither collective bargaining nor arbitration has traditionally found great favour with the federal government. The old view, now being modified, has been that the regulation of federal employment must rest solely with President and Congress. The American public services were slow to unionise— in 1962 only one-third of federal employees belonged to unions, though this had risen to 50 per cent by 1970, and is still rising. Collective bargaining has been slow to develop, partly because legislatures have traditionally fixed salaries (and the middle and lower grades have done fairly well out of this), but also because public attitudes to possible strikes in 'vital' services have been very unfavourable. There have also been fears that union activity would undermine the merit system, bring more politics into services where political pressures have always been harder to resist, and erode 'lateral recruitment'; that is, free entrance at any level if you are the best person for the job.[11] The last of these is certainly a legitimate fear.

Public services in all technologically developed countries have lately been influenced by some common factors, which have affected their attitudes to pay questions. The first is the growing size and complexity of the bureaucracy. The second is a high level of employment, which has made the security of public employment no longer such a special attraction (though it is still a real one) and has encouraged greater mobility between public and private sectors. The third is the problem of matching pay and conditions with those offered by outside employers for certain categories, such as top administrators and possessors of scarce professional skills. The fourth is a more general attitude, which seems to be growing, that public and private employment should be judged by similar criteria.

Pay Fixing in Australia

Most Australian employees in the private sector are covered by Commonwealth or State arbitration awards. Each State has its own arbitration system, Wages Boards in Victoria and Tasmania, Industrial Commissions in the other States. The Commonwealth Constitution also gives the Commonwealth parliament the power to make laws with respect to 'conciliation and arbitration for the prevention and settlement of industrial disputes extending beyond the limits of any one State'; as this has been given a broad interpretation, many disputes are now handled by the Australian Conciliation and Arbitration Commission, and many workers are covered by Commonwealth awards. By the 1930s, most States had given their own officers some access to the general arbitration system. The Commonwealth and some States have developed special tribunals to deal with public service disputes, but even where this has been the case, the general system of pay and arbitration has had important effects on their employees.

First, as in the Commonwealth, the Public Service Arbitrator is only concerned with certain categories of government employee, while some employees of statutory authorities have direct access to the general arbitration system. In other cases, private sector unions recruit government employees. There is a general tendency for industrial relations in public and private sectors to become more closely linked. This is reflected overtly in cases involving the joint hearing by the relevant arbitration authorities of claims covering both sectors; in closer relations between unions in the two sectors; in the fact that national wage decisions are reflected in public service pay, especially since wage indexation began.

Federal awards also influence pay in the States. Until 1920 the High Court held that federal awards could not bind the States as employers, but in that year the court decided otherwise, though the Commonwealth Conciliation and Arbitration Act gives the tribunal discretion to refuse to determine an issue which it considers should be dealt with by the States. This does not prevent federal awards from having indirect effects, either by setting the pace for general increases, or (more specifically) by affecting the decisions of the State arbitration authorities to which many State government employees have access. Conversely, State awards can be pacemakers for federal awards. More generally changes in the various public services and other sectors of government employment react on one another. The fact that most Commonwealth employees work in the States helps to keep pay in the different sectors from getting too far out of line.

(i) Commonwealth   The Commonwealth Public Service Board plays a major role in determining pay and conditions of service, though a veto must be reported to parliament and 'would be employed only in exceptional

circumstances and for very weighty reasons'.[12] The provision of funds to meet pay increases is the prerogative of the Treasurer, ultimately of Parliament. Some matters involve legislation (annual leave, pensions) or are handled at cabinet level, which has resulted in some notably generous provision of both holidays and superannuation. Rates of pay for First Division officers are fixed by a separate Remuneration Tribunal, which also deals with the salaries of politicians and judges. However, in normal circumstances the board has had a high degree of independence in determining pay and conditions.

Another limitation has been the growth of statutory authorities whose employees may not be under the Public Service Act, though a condition is often inserted in the statute that the Board's approval is needed in the fixing of salaries and conditions of service. In any case, where major industrial relations policies and practices are concerned the Board (and sometimes the Department of Employment and Industrial Relations) will be consulted.

Most important has been the development of arbitration. Public servants did not at first seek access to the Arbitration Court, but discontent grew among the newly formed staff associations, especially in the Post Office. In 1911 a Labor government gave Commonwealth public servants access to the court, which obtained a wide power to make awards on pay and other matters. D.C. McLachlan, the Public Service Commissioner, was not pleased with the results. In particular, he complained about the court's tendency to deal piecemeal with claims, without regard to their effects on the structure of the whole service.[13] McLachlan wanted the court's powers to revert to the public service authority. Instead the government provided in the 1920 Public Service Arbitration Act for a separate Public Service Arbitrator with power to determine public service pay and conditions. The Public Service Arbitrator is appointed by the Governor-General for seven years, renewable, and may be removed from office only by an address from both Houses of Parliament. He has great freedom to conduct cases 'without regard to technicalities or legal forms', but in practice has adopted substantially the procedures of an ordinary court, though in a less formal atmosphere. Compared with industrial arbitration generally, the procedures of the Arbitrator have been relatively simple and informal. His decision is binding on both parties, though an appeal is possible under certain conditions; and there is no time limit on the decision, it operates until repealed or varied.

Any organisation registered under the Conciliation and Arbitration Act may submit claims in respect of members who are Commonwealth government employees. So outside unions may lodge claims, as well as staff associations such as the Administrative and Clerical Officers Association (employees of a few statutory authorities, such as TAA and Commonwealth banking authorities, are outside the Arbitrator's jurisdiction). Applications to vary existing determinations may also be made by the Public Service Board or by a minister.

The existence of the Arbitrator has not removed the need for negotiation.

The 1920 Act placed great emphasis on the settlement of disputes by negotiation, and the Public Service Board has played a very important part in the making of pay offers and in bargaining with unions. The lodging of a claim is often a sign that ordinary negotiations have broken down, but even then the Arbitrator must call a conference to try and reach agreement between the parties, which may be followed by a 'consent determination'. The latter has been a common occurrence; in 1973–74 there were 233 consent determinations, though the number dropped sharply (to 57 in 1976–77) after the Public Service Board and Arbitrator came to work within the wage indexation principles of the Conciliation and Arbitration Commission. If agreement is not possible, the Arbitrator starts to hear evidence in public, following normal court procedure. However, the parties cannot be represented by lawyers, unless the latter are members or officers of the staff association or union concerned or (where the other side is concerned) are officers of the board or the department involved.

In his arbitrated determinations, of which there were 17 in 1975–76, the Arbitrator gives the reasons on which his decision is based. The determination is laid before parliament, and could be disallowed, though this has rarely happened. Since 1952 there are certain rights of appeal to the Australian Conciliation and Arbitration Commission, if the latter thinks that the public interest would be served. There is also now a procedure for reference direct, on similar grounds, without any prior adjudication by the Arbitrator. The latter may sometimes sit with the Commission when common issues are being heard.

A larger and more complex service raised the chances of delay in the arbitration process. The government has tried to meet this by giving more staff help, and in 1969 provided for Deputy Arbitrators, whose determinations need the concurrence of the Arbitrator. The Public Service Board also helped to reduce delay by improving its own procedures. Until the 1960s most major decisions on pay and conditions resulted from arbitration, but the Board then reasserted itself as a planner and negotiator in this area, and in special fields has also made use of joint working parties of management and staff representatives.[14] The situation has changed again since the 1975 National Wage Case decision of the Conciliation and Arbitration Commission, which outlined principles of wage indexation to cope with inflation. The Board and the Arbitrator have followed these guidelines, and have also used the Commission's machinery for dealing with anomalies and special problems. This has greatly reduced the number of pay claims, but also led to a few difficult cases, and there has been a greater disposition to appeal to the Commission about these. For the time being at least, the general arbitration system has once more become the major determinant of public service conditions, as it was before 1920. The Coombs Report has argued that the case made then for a separate Public Service Arbitrator no longer applies, and that most Commonwealth employees should return to the jurisdiction of the Commission.[15] It thinks that Parliament's power to disallow arbitrated pay determinations should be ended, as also the need for government approval of board decisions.[16] However, one member of the Coombs Commission argued forcibly that the government should have ultimate power over the pay of its employees, indeed should reserve for itself a power of direction to the Public Service Board on these matters.[17]

(ii) New South Wales   Under its original commission, the Public Service Board of New South Wales was solely responsible for determining salaries and gradings, in fact one of the main arguments for an independent board had been that it would introduce some system into this area. It has continued to fix pay and a wide range of service conditions (parliament reserves the final right not to vote the money). The salaries of the most senior officers under the Public Service Act are determined outright by the Board. However, certain limitations on its power over most salaries developed, though they left it the most important determiner of pay and service conditions.

The staffs of many statutory authorities are not under the Public Service Act, though these bodies are expected to confer with the board with the aim of keeping some uniformity. The terms and conditions of such employees are fixed by the authority concerned, or come under arbitration awards, industrial agreements, and so on. Another limitation has been the growth of arbitration as a means of settling pay disputes. As we have seen, Commonwealth public servants obtained access to arbitration in 1911. New South Wales public servants did so in 1919; and by 1935, most Australian public services had in some degree given their officers access to arbitration. However, the impact of this was diminished in New South Wales by the fact that most salaries have been determined by collective bargaining and covered by agreements between the board and staff associations. The Industrial Court normally keeps out of areas covered by current agreements, and the methods of negotiation involved in an agreement are now widely accepted. Within the Industrial Court system, a case may be heard by a Conciliation Committee, by a single judge of the Industrial Commission of New South Wales or by a full bench of the Commission, either originally or on appeal. The Conciliation Committees represent employers and employees, with a Conciliation Commissioner as chairman; they have been established for various sections of the public service and also for employees of statutory authorities.

A 1922 amendment to the Public Service Act allows the Public Service Board to 'enter into an agreement with any association or organization representing any group or class of officer or employee as to salaries, fees, allowances, and grades . . .' (section 14B). Such an agreement is binding on the board and on the association signing it, and also on all public servants in the relevant class or group, whether they are members of the association or not. An agreement usually has a currency of three years, though the board has been ready to vary it during its currency if satisfied that there are good grounds. However, it has always insisted that any such variation should only be by the consent of the parties.[18]

(iii) Other States and Authorities   In Victoria, many public servants have no access to arbitration. For a long time, the government of the day claimed a strong voice in fixing service conditions, with the public service authority merely recommending and advising. After the Second World War, the Public Service Board came to play a more important role, and now fixes most pay and conditions for government employees under the Public Service Act, subject to disallowance by Parliament. The presence of a public service representative on the board has helped to make this arrangement acceptable. However, there are a number of government employees whose employment is regulated by Wages Board determinations (with additional increments sometimes agreed to by the Government); and many more public employees than in New South Wales and the Commonwealth are employed by statutory authorities not covered by the Public Service Act.

Other States mostly ring the changes on the arrangements described above. South Australia and Western Australia both have Public Service Arbitrators. In Queensland, rates of pay have mainly been fixed by awards in proceedings before the Queensland Industrial Conciliation and Arbitration Commission, or by registered agreements with staff associations, covering not only the various public service grades but also other Crown authorities. In Queensland, even permanent heads' salaries are determined by the general industrial tribunal for the State.

We have already referred to some of the pay-fixing machinery for the large number of government employees not under the Public Service Acts. The main group of these—employees of statutory authorities in the States—are usually covered by awards of the general industrial tribunals of the States. Railway staffs are largely covered by federal awards, as are some other groups, such as employees of electricity undertakings in certain States. In Commonwealth statutory bodies, many employees are also covered by general awards.[19] There is also collective bargaining (as of banking authorities with the Commonwealth Bank Officers' Association). Many statutory authorities are subject to general approval of their terms and conditions of employment by the Public Service Board, as well as being subject to the Public Service Arbitrator. After wage indexation began in 1975, a Co-ordination Committee of officers from the Public Service Board and the Department of Employment and Industrial Relations was established to oversee the handling of all claims affecting Commonwealth staff.

Classification and Pay Criteria

Classification Criteria

There are two main tasks involved in classifying a position, job analysis and job comparison. Job analysis is concerned with determining and recording the essential components of a job and the qualities required of the occupant. It involves collecting information about the job (for example, drawing up statements of duties) and how it relates to other jobs, with the aid of charts and documents that describe the structure and processes of the organisation. This material has then to be analysed in terms of various criteria, such as: What is the most responsible duty of the position? How much individual discretion or judgment is involved? How much is the work supervised, checked, reviewed? What number and level of staff does the position supervise? What basic training and experience, or special aptitudes and skills, are needed? Where does it fit into the organisation structure? Job comparison involves using this analysis to fit the position into the general classification structure.

In fact both these tasks involve comparisons, with other positions in the same or comparable organisations or employment groups. Both involve judgment. The various factors cannot be precisely measured, and any check-list involving a number of different factors gives no clear guidance in cases where they may point in different directions (say, a job that involves a lot of intelligence but little supervision of other people). In general, it is easiest to compare within a single field of work; most sensible people think that no satisfactory way has been found of making such comparisons across a whole service, or between very different fields.

Pay Criteria

This is a very complex question, and all that can be attempted are a few general comments. Public service employment differs from much private employment in that pay depends on one's class or grade. Within any grade, there is usually no way of recognising individual merit or service or the special difficulties of a particular job, though some public authorities have developed provisions for 'merit loadings' or double increments or other ways of recognising special contributions—and they probably should do more of it. In New South Wales, for example, the Public Service Board has retained discretion to reward particular officers with outstanding qualifications or abilities, and has sometimes granted a further salary progression to officers because of lack of promotion available in their particular field of work.

'Fair comparison'[20] sums up most of what can be said in a general way about determining rates of pay, both the most relevant comparision as seen by reasonably independent and well-informed persons, and what is believed to be fair by the employees concerned. The latter has to be taken account of, as some levels of discontent lead to unacceptable losses in efficiency and incentive. Most public service authorities seem ready to make any comparisons that seem appropriate. Concepts about which there has been much recent discussion are 'job evaluation' and 'work value'. This is the notion that the 'value' of jobs can be assessed on the basis of the kinds of factors involved in job analysis: training and qualifications needed; attributes required in the performance of the job, such as mental and physical effort, and skill innate or acquired degree of discretion; and supervision involved and so on.

There is still dispute about how far job evaluation takes one in arriving at conclusions about pay.[21] It certainly makes easier the task of comparison between positions, helps in determining what are comparable occupations or levels of work, and may help management and workers to establish an acceptable and agreed job hierarchy.

However, modern public services cannot ignore 'market criteria' in determining what to pay their staff. One version of the market criterion is that the employer should pay 'what is necessary to recruit and retain an efficient staff'. This has a tough and businesslike sound, and is much in the minds of Public Service Boards. They have enough feedback from their recruitment branch to build up a fairly accurate picture of how effective their rates of pay are in recruiting various kinds of staff. Departmental heads and other senior officers are constantly bringing to their notice any problems in recruitment and efficiency and any undue numbers of resignations that may indicate more attractive salaries or conditions elsewhere. However, the notion of what is 'efficient' staff is not precise; there are no absolute criteria of efficiency, though one may be able to tell whether it is rising or falling.

A criterion that once had great appeal to public servants is that the public service should be a 'model employer'. This implies that it should give a lead in pay and conditions to the private sector. Arguments against this have been that in a high employment economy, and one where the public service represents a large sector of employment, it is inflationary; and that it tends to bring the public service into politics, by encouraging the belief that it can be used to bring about desirable changes in the social structure of the country. Whatever the merits of these arguments, Australian public services have on the whole aimed at being a 'good average employer', not a 'model employer'. The tendency has been to fix pay more and more by comparison with outside employment, and to adjust broad relativities to those ruling outside. However, it is also true that some groups have no proper outside counterparts, that relevant information may be lacking, and that special circumstances may have to be taken into account. In such cases, comparison with groups within the service with similar characteristics is relevant.

Similar considerations led the Priestley Commission on the British Civil Service[22] to lay down two principles:
1. The primary principle of civil service pay is fair comparison with the current remuneration of outside staffs employed on broadly comparable work, taking account of other conditions of service.
2. Internal relativities should be used as a supplement to the principle of fair comparison in settling civil service rates in detail, and may have to be the first consideration when outside comparisons cannot be made, but they should never be allowed to override the primary principle or to become rigid.

The Commission disliked the use of horizontal relativities, or comparisons between different occupational categories within the service, and saw no reason for freezing relative rates of pay in different occupations, without regard to outside demand. As a result of its recommendations a Civil Service Pay Research Unit was established. The Commonwealth Public Service Board also accepted the idea of pay research, but not of an independent body intervening as a third party in the pay debate. The Pay Information and Surveys Section advises the Board, not (as in Britain) a joint council representing both management and staff. The British unit suspended its work in 1975 at the start of the pay restraint policy but is to recommence in 1979, now with a board of outsiders to oversee its impartiality and efficiency.

Some of the difficulties of external comparison have already been mentioned. In some fields it may be hard to find comparable jobs outside the service. It can be argued that there is no true market price for certain kinds of labour, that what outside employers pay is itself influenced by public service rates, so that the public service is willy-nilly setting community standards in important fields of employment. Again, however one may discount certain relativities, they will remain important if employees think they are important, or the arbitrator does. The pattern of wages is a product of many different factors, market forces, custom, organised power, ideology (including current notions of 'wage justice') and persuasion; of short-run tactics as well as well as longer-term strategies and underlying trends.

Public Service Unions

Government employment is highly unionised, and public service unions go back at least to the 1880s. The Public Service Association of South Australia was founded in 1885.[23] About the same time similar unions were functioning in Victoria and New South Wales, though the records of the Public Service Association of New South Wales begin only in 1899, when it already had 1500 members. The first issue of its organ, *The Public Service Journal* (now *Red Tape*), appeared in January 1900. A number of postal and teachers unions were also founded in the 1880s and 1890s. Indeed, government staff associations led the way in organising white-collar workers. As public service unions began to get access to compulsory arbitration, and were able to negotiate awards for their members, their growth was encouraged, and they were also aided by the preference to unionists shown by Labor governments.

This chapter does not deal with unions solely concerned in fields covered by statutory corporations, such as transport and electricity supply, the structure and behaviour of which do not seem to have differed much from comparable bodies in the private sector (government airways and naval dockyards have had to cope with strong and sometimes militant unions). Most public service unions seem to have been conservative bodies, probably mainly a reflection of their white-collar character. They have rarely used the strike weapon, though they have not been averse to other forms of political pressure, and they have not been deterred by the ban on strikes in some Public Service Acts—as mentioned earlier, the Commonwealth Act (section 66) makes public service strikes illegal, but has not been invoked despite recent tendencies to resort to direct industrial action. There were one or two strikes in the years after the First World War,[24] then a long gap until signs of renewed militancy appeared in the late 1960s and after, when there were a number of postal strikes, some State teachers held short stoppages, and there were a few overtime bans. In 1977 a postal dispute provoked the Commonwealth Employees (Employment Provisions) Act, which increases the government's power to stand down, suspend or dismiss employees during a dispute. Staff associations have on occasion tried to influence elections. In 1961 Administrative and Clerical Officers Association (ACOA) members ran a campaign in a federal electorate against the sitting member, a minister, but the executive defeated a branch proposal for a repetition in 1963. In 1966 ACOA asked its members to vote for federal candidates who supported its claim for four weeks' annual leave.[25]

There is nothing to prevent public service unions from affiliating with outside bodies, though generally a majority of members have been opposed to links that might indicate political bias, and staff associations have preferred political lobbying to political alignment. A few unions with public service members are affiliated to the Australian Council of Trade Unions (ACTU), mainly blue-collar workers and unions with a large outside membership.

Commonwealth

There are thirty-seven staff organisations with membership confined to Commonwealth employees, but the Public Service Board has dealings with over seventy as public servants are also members of many outside unions, such as the Federated Clerks Union.[26] O'Dea distinguishes these two groups as 'house' and 'outside' associations.[27] These two groups sometimes have overlapping fields, as do the ACOA and the Clerks Union; and may conflict or co-operate, or do both simultaneously.

The largest staff associations are the Australian Postal and Tele-communications Union (APTU—47 000 members) and ACOA (48 000).[28] Other large 'house' associations are the Professional Officers Association (POA) and The Australian Public Service Association (Fourth Division Officers). Some individual professional groups have established their own organisations, especially since the Second World War—such as the Association of Professional Engineers, Australia (1948), which is an 'outside' association, and the Commonwealth Professional Surveyors Association (1965), a 'house' association. This large number of unions has been encouraged by the permissive provisions of the Arbitration Acts. However, most public servants are in one of five main bodies, all with over 15 000 members. There are one or two unregistered staff associations, such as the Second Division Officers Association. The Coombs Report thinks there are too many unions, and that many of them are over-centralised.

Staff associations have for many years participated in personnel adminis-tration. Representatives sit on disciplinary appeal boards, and are also active at departmental level especially on matters of staff welfare and amenities, and occasionally on wider questions. Their activities in relation to arbitration and promotion appeals are mentioned elsewhere. They have 'ready access to the official side at all levels and make good use of their contacts'.[29] As indicated earlier, there has been nothing as formal as the British Whitley Council System, in which staff and official sides sit together in a whole system of joint consultative bodies, local, departmental and national. However, some departments and statutory authorities have experimented with staff councils, and there is the Joint Council, a statutory body which first met in 1947. It has (1978) nineteen members, nine from the staff association, eight senior officers, and two Public Service Board representatives, one of whom is chairman—this has often been the Chairman of the Board. In form it is an advisory committee to the Board, and gets little publicity, though it has sometimes been influential. It sits twice a year, but also operates through subcommittees. It may consider any 'matters of general interest in relation to the Commonwealth Service', but has mainly dealt with employment questions, other than pay (which by agreement it does not discuss). The Coombs Report thought its scope should be expanded to include statutory authorities, and that departmental consultative councils should be set up somewhat on Whitley lines, though leaving a good deal of departmental discretion as to structure and scope.[30]

There is also a Council of Australian Government Employee Organisations (CAGEO) which grew up after the First World War to represent staff associations in matters of common concern. It was for a long time loosely structured, but was reconstituted in 1969 with provision for a full-time secretariat, and since then has been more active. Its membership was widened, and its name has since been changed to the present one. Its affiliated membership is about 267 000. A Council of Professional Associations (CPA) was established in 1954. There is also the Australian Council of Salaried and Professional Associations (ACSPA) which claims to represent white-collar workers generally, and to which some public service associations are affiliated.

Some State bodies

In New South Wales, the largest unions covering Public Service Act employees are the Public Service Association (PSA) of New South Wales (39 700) and the New South Wales Teachers Federation (44 000). There are separate associations for professional officers, and for other government employees such as police and fire brigades. The New South Wales Teachers Federation is affiliated with the ACTU, but this is exceptional among State white-collar unions. As in the Commonwealth, staff associations in the States play a significant role in personnel administration. A distinctive feature in New South Wales arises from the importance long given to collective bargaining, which has involved continuous contact between the public service and unions.

The New South Wales Teachers Federation was formed in 1919, by the union of two earlier bodies (teachers unions go back to the 1890s). Its official objectives and activities have since the 1930s had a more radical flavour than those of the PSA, and it has engaged in a good deal of political campaigning. The Federation has also obtained representation on a number of appointments and promotions committees of the Department of Education. It has fought for many years for an Education Commission on which it would be represented and such a body now seems likely to be established.[31]

Other States also have a general service union, such as the Victorian Public Service Association, the Civil Service Association of Western Australia and the Queensland State Service Union. Queensland like New South Wales has a Professional Officers Association, but with a much larger membership. An Australian Public Service Federation and Australian Teachers Federation exist, to which staff associations from various States are affiliated, and which are media for consultation between the State associations.

Attitudes

White-collar unions have traditionally been regarded as less militant than manual unions, and as having a more 'professional' or 'responsible' attitude to work and a closer identification with employers. This attitude may be changing, and may in any case be harder to sustain in large-scale government agencies. It has been said of Australian public servants that they 'tend to have much more working class attitudes than equivalent white-collar workers in private enterprise'.[32] Whether this be true or not, there are some special frustrations attached to white-collar employment in the public sector. Dr Sharp has suggested has suggested a number of reasons why these exist. First, 'there is no clear-cut employer . . . The boss is replaced by a hierarchical system of bosses, none of whom can really be the repository for our ill wishes and equally none of whom can assume the role of father.'[33] One reflection of this is delay sometimes in dealing with minor grievances. Secondly, the direct product of labour is often intangible, and sometimes hard to link psychologically with a final product. Thirdly, government employment probably enjoys lower social status than comparable work in the private sector.

There are some countervailing satisfactions—possibly less feeling than in some private firms 'that those who give the orders are motivated by personal considerations' and 'less of a gulf between those at the top and those at the bottom'. There is a greater sense of security (for those who like that) within a system governed by rules and with developed canons of fairness. However, as Dr Sharp added, security can also be a snare, tempting an employee to stay on in a frustrating job when it might have been better for long-run morale to go elsewhere. In any case, it is less important than it was in differentiating public and private employment. Public employment has probably lost some of its earlier attractions for the semi-skilled clerical worker, though it has been offering new opportunities to other groups.

Some of these conclusions were borne out in the Career Service Survey conducted for the Coombs Commission.[14] When Commonwealth public servants were asked to compare their job with a similar one outside the public sector, the most decisive advantages of the public service were seen to be security, and 'pay and conditions'. There was also some belief that 'treatment by seniors' and promotion prospects were better (but this was in a period of public service expansion). Reasonably positive attitudes to senior officers were also shown by the 76 per cent who thought that they could discuss problems with them, and the nearly 90 per cent who thought that their own section rated 'good' or 'excellent' in ease of getting to see senior officers. Only 61 per cent found their job satisfying; another 11 per cent were 'not sure'. Around two-thirds worked as part of a team rather than independently, over 10 per cent more than wanted to! The private sector seems to score highest among public servants for 'recognition of work well done', and the most often noted reason seen for people leaving the public service is uninteresting work. Over 90 per cent either disapproved of strikes over pay, or thought that they should be 'only a last resort'—roughly half each.

Still, public service associations have clearly been somewhat influenced by the general rise of activism in white-collar and professional groups. There are several reasons for this. One is the greater general belief that militancy pays. Another is changing general standards of 'respectable' behaviour—the old notion of the white-collar worker as staider and more responsible, with a higher sense of vocation, may have been somewhat eroded, or at least is not now seen as inconsistent with a bit more aggression. The increasing size of enterprises may be reducing identification with management. Greater awareness of what is happening in other organisations and groups increases everyone's desire to keep up with everyone else. Outside political groups are now also taking more interest in white-collar employees, partly because they represent a growing proportion of organised labour.

Staff Participation

There are some signs of pressure for more 'control from below', more staff participation in management, extending beyond the familiar areas of pay and conditions occupied by staff associations. There is current criticism of the 'dysfunctions of hierarchy', lack of communication between staff at different levels, rigid and unperceptive management, and so on. New South Wales teachers have pressed for an Education Commission, including teachers' representatives, to administer the school system, and the New South Wales government has moved in this direction. There have been demands for more democratic forms of self-government in the ABC, the press, the universities. They have come mainly from relatively well-educated white-collar workers, though the ACTU congress in 1977 adopted a policy on industrial democracy, and are preparing for negotiations with three large companies. In South Australia the Dunstan Government has cautiously adopted the cause, though the Premier has rejected the idea of legislation on the subject, and has said that worthwhile reforms depend on 'consensus support from all sides of industry'.[35] This is partly because some early initiatives attracted trade union hostility. There is a Unit for Industrial Democracy in the Department of Labour and Industry to help educate public servants in the concept, make recommendations and, with the Public Service Board, formulate programmes.

In New South Wales, the Public Service Board and the Review of New South Wales Government Administration have sent agreed proposals to the State Government, including joint consultative machinery in each major unit of a department, also with limited powers of decision, initially in areas such as internal training and aspects of working conditions, but not to extend to matters traditionally dealt with by unions. Projects for 'participatory management' will be encouraged in various agencies; the Board has its own worker participation unit.[36]

Some reformers have meant by more participation simply more consultation and wider delegations of power. But good as these may be, they do not necessarily promote control from below. Many intelligent leaders are keen to discover what their followers think, wish to improve their morale and sense of commitment, make them happier and busier by giving them more discretion in minor matters or experimenting with 'job enrichment', and they may find the techniques they use also convenient ways of spotting the promotable, identifying supporters and opponents, and consolidating the organisation against external threat. This has no necessary connection with widening the influence of lower personnel on major decisions, in that the same techniques can be used to reduce resistance and make control from the top more effective. So true believers in workers' control are not content with this, though they may support minor forms of participation as valuable training in skills and self-confidence and also as platforms for further demands. They want in some sense participation in major decisions, so that employees genuinely influence these decisions.[37]

Dahl has labelled the three main difficulties involved in applying such notions inside bureaucracies, the problems of competence, personal choice and affected interests.[38] The first is the problem of efficiency. Suppose, for example, departmental heads were chosen by, or were more under the control of their staffs, how far would this reduce managerial effectiveness, through delay, dilution of responsibility, or lack of expertise. And if it did, would this loss of efficiency be acceptable, or would it be compensated for by greater staff identification with the enterprise? A particular problem of establishing new devices to control power in bureaucracies is that they commonly lead to more bureaucracy.

The problem of "personal choice" might be put as follows: is more "participation" what most employees really want, compared with other ways of spending their time? Would it appeal only to minorities? Of course, as Dahl says, we should not reject self-management simply because it does not measure up to the highest ideals of participation, which failure is true of all forms of democratic association. Such evidence as there is also suggests that those who want to participate mostly prefer to do so in decisions that are perceived as immediately affecting them, such as working conditions and job security. Believers in participatory democracy are not over-impressed by such points, holding that they simply reflect the present authoritarian climate, the feelings of helplessness that it induces and the lack of worker experience of self-management.

An intractable problem, especially for government departments, is the issue of "affected interests". In government, the theory of internal democracy seems to conflict with the theory of external democracy, that government agencies should be instruments of policies fed into them from outside, through democratically accountable ministers. Some democrats argue that, if participation needs improving, the outside public and the clientele of government agencies come first. In government organisations the general public already does participate, very indirectly, through parliaments and ministers, and some outside groups do so through advisory bodies attached to the agency (see Chapter Five). Even so there are demands for improving the status of consumers of government and other services (see Chapter Seventeen). It is significant that the supporters of workers' control are often opponents of consumer control. The New South Wales Teachers Federation wants teachers well-represented on an Education Commission to run the school system; but its retiring president indicated in 1972 that he and the teachers rejected Education Department proposals that parents should be given more say at the local level. "He says teachers would welcome more discussion and co-operation with parents, but would resent amateurs dictating what they should do at school."[40] This is much the sort of reply that a businessman makes to demands for more worker participation in management. This is not an argument against participation, but it illustrates its complexities.

Some theorists of democracy have argued that the demand for participation, whether of workers or of consumers, has received too much emphasis; that the most effective check on leaders is not so much participation, as organised and legitimate opposition. So it has been argued that "collective bargaining is industrial democracy",[42] just as the struggle between organized political parties is the best guarantee of political democracy. On this view trade unions are the employee's protection against authoritarianism, as well as providing for participation in those matters that most directly affect him. One trouble about the analogy with politics is that major political parties are an opposition with some chance of becoming the government, while trade unions are not in this position in relation to business firms and government departments.

There is certainly some potential conflict between the orthodox industrial relations structure, in which the employee's interests are thought of as secured through his joining a trade union that presents a united front to the employer, and the participatory model in which the employee–employer distinction is continuously eroded. Much current discussion of participation fails to reckon with this fact, and this gives it a deceitful air.

There is also "voting with one's feet". Just as business competition is one good form of protection for consumers, so a free market for labour in a high employment economy is a major check on bureaucratic power. The rights and dignities of Australian government employees, as of workers generally, have been considerably enhanced by their greater freedom to go elsewhere if they dislike the local arrangements. Before the war it would have been inconceivable, as happened some years ago, that a group of discontented professional officers in the Commonwealth Public Service should have collectively advertised themselves as available for alternative employment. (Nor would they be likely to do so in 1979.)

Notes

1. Establishments Manual, Commonwealth Public Service Board, Canberra 1969, 20. For discussion, see Harold H. Leich, 'Rank in Man or Job? Both!', *Public Admin. Review*, Spring 1960; and O. Glenn Stahl, 'Of Jobs and Men', *ibid.*, July/August 1969.
2. There is no separate Professional Division in the Commonwealth Service. There was one before 1922, but it was abolished on the recommendation of McLachlan. For his reasons, see H.A. Scarrow, *The Higher Public Service of the Commonwealth of Australia*, Duke University Press, Durham, NC, 1957, 21–2.
3. Commonwealth Public Service Act, section 24(2).
4. Report, Commonwealth Public Service Board, Canberra, 1964, 10.
5. Report, RCAGA, 249.
6. Report, NSW Public Service Board, 1968–69, 21; Interim Report, Review of NSW Government Administration, Sydney, 1977, 128.
7. V. Subramaniam, 'The Evolution of Classification Practices and Patterns in Australia', *Public Admin.* (Sydney), XIX, 4 December 1960, 327.
8. See Report, Commonwealth Public Service Board, Canberra 1964, for the board's general thinking on simplifying classification structures. The subject is further discussed in the board's Report, Canberra, 1968, 20–29.
9. Report, Commonwealth Public Service Board, Canberra, 1970, 35.
10. See Henry Parris, *Staff Relations in the Civil Service: Fifty Years of Whitleyism*, Allen and Unwin, London, 1973. For critical comment on the rigidities of Whitleyism, see Report (Fulton) Committee on the Civil Service, London 1968, 1, 89, though the Committee and its Management Consultancy Group also thought that it made for a 'democratic, and largely trouble-free atmosphere' (Report, 11,8).
11. F.C. Mosher, *Democracy and the Public Service*, Oxford University Press, New York, 1968, ch. 6, has a good summary of American attitudes.
12. Sir Frederick Wheeler, 'Industrial Relations—A Public Service Point of View', *J. Industrial Relations*, 12, 2, July 1970, 149.
13. Report, Public Service Commissioner, 1916, 49 ff.; and see E.E. Crichton, 'The Development of Public Service Arbitration—I', *Public Admin.* (Sydney), XV, 2, June 1956.
14. R.J. Young, 'Trends, Attitudes and Responses in Public Employment', *Public Admin.* (Sydney), XXX, 2, June 1971, 167–8.

15. The Public Service Board had proposed that the Arbitrator should be replaced by an Australian Government Employees Industrial Tribunal within the general arbitration system.
16. Report, RCAGA, 277–80.
17. *ibid.*, 402–3.
18. The Board has also taken the view that it may increase the salary of an individual officer if necessary during the currency of an agreement.
19. For some account, see G.E. Caiden, *The Commonwealth Bureaucracy*, Melbourne University Press, Melbourne, 1967, 118–31; and Chapter Ten of this book.
20. This term is sometimes nowadays used with the narrower meaning of comparison with rates paid by other employers for comparable work.
21. See *Job Evaluation*, Report No. 83, (UK) National Board for Prices and Incomes, HMSO, 1968, which gives a good account of various problems and techniques. Chapter 8 is on 'Job Evaluation and the Civil Service', and discusses some dangers and difficulties. See also critical comment in R.J. O'Dea, *Principles of Wage Determination in Commonwealth Arbitration*, West Publishing Corp., Sydney, 1969.
22. W.J.M. Mackenzie and J.W. Grove, *Central Administration in Britain*, Longmans, London, 1957, 55.
23. It had a false start in 1881. For its early history, see G.N. Hawker, 'The Development of the South Australian Civil Service, 1836–1916', Ph.D. thesis, Australian National University, Canberra, 1967. For general comment on trade union development in the public services, see R.M. Martin, *Whitecollar Unions in Australia*, Australian Institute of Political Science Monograph, 1965; G.E. Caiden, *The Commonwealth Bureaucracy*, Melbourne University Press, Melbourne, 1967, ch. 11; *Career Service*, Melbourne University Press, Melbourne, 1965; and 'The Commonwealth Public Service Associations as a Pressure Group', *Aust. J. Pol. Hist.*, December 1964.
24. On public service strikes, see J. Iremonger *et al.* (eds), *Strikes: Studies in Twentieth Century Australian Social History*, Angus and Robertson, Sydney, 1973, especially articles on the 1903 Victorian Railway strike, the 1923 Melbourne police strike, and the 1968 NSW Teachers' Federation strike; G.E. Caiden, 'The Strike of Commonwealth Public Servants in 1919', *Public Admin.* (Sydney), XXI, 3, September 1962; and Frank T. De Vyver, 'The 1920 Civil Service Service and Teachers Strike in Western Australia', *J. Industrial Relations*, 7, 3, November 1965.
25. For earlier examples, both federal and State, see J.D.B. Miller, 'Public Service Associations and Politics', *Public Admin.* (Sydney), VI, 7, September 1947; V. Subramaniam, 'Political Rights of Commonwealth Public Servants', *Public Admin.* (Sydney), XVII, 1, March 1958; 'The Public Servant and Politics', in F.A. Bland (ed.), *Government in Australia*, Government Printer, Sydney, 1944; A. Wildavsky and D. Carboch, *Studies in Australian Politics*, Cheshire, Melbourne, 1958, 202–9.
26. See the list in Report, Commonwealth Public Service Board, Canberra, 1977, 128–9.
27. R.J. O'Dea, 'The Functions and Objectives of Staff Associations', *Public Admin.* (Sydney), XXX, 2, June 1971.
28. Membership figures for all unions are approximate as at December 1976. For useful facts, see D.W. Rawson, *A Handbook of Australian Trade Unions and Employees' Associations*, 3rd edn, Australian National University, Canberra, 1976.

29. Caiden, *The Commonwealth Bureaucracy*, Melbourne University Press, Melbourne, 1967, 269. Caiden gives a fuller account of the various modes of staff participation.
30. Report, RCAGA, 295–7.
31. On the Federation's history, see Bruce Mitchell, *Teachers Education and Politics*, University of Queensland Press, St Lucia, 1975.
32. W.J. Byrt, 'The Idea of a Promotions Appeal System', *Public. Admin.* (Sydney), XXV, 4, December 1966, 308.
33. I.G. Sharp, *Industrial Relations*, Commonwealth Public Service Board, Training Section booklet 17.
34. Report, RCAGA, Appendix Vol. Three, 1–189.
35. D.A. Dunstan, letter to *Australian Financial Review*, 6 April 1976, and in Christopher Jay, 'Spartans are at Adelaide's Walls', *Australian Financial Review*, 19 April 1978; cf. Peter Robson, 'Worker Participation in Australia', *Current Affairs Bulletin*, 54, 10, March 1978.
36. Interim Report, Review of New South Wales Government Administraiton, Government Printer, Sydney, 1977, 172–5.
37. On democracy as 'participation', see C. Pateman, *Participation and Democratic Theory*, Cambridge University Press, London, 1970, and H.S. Kariel (ed.), *Frontiers of Democratic Theory*, Random House, New York, 1970. On government agencies, see Frederick C. Mosher, *Democracy and the Public Service*, Oxford University Press, New York, 1968; the outline of pro's and con's in Mosher (ed.), *Governmental Reorganizations: Cases and Commentary*, Bobbs-Merrill, Indianapolis, 1967, 531–4; and Interim Report, Review of NSW Government Administration, Sydney, 1977, 168–71.
38. Robert A. Dahl, *After the Revolution?*, Yale University Press, New Haven, 1970, esp. 130–40. See also, Mosher, *Democracy and the Public Service*, ch. 1.
39. Dahl, *op. cit.*, 136.
40. *Sydney Morning Herald*, 17 February 1972.
41. W.W. Wirtz, *Labor and the Public Interest*, Harper and Row, New York, 1964, 57; cf. Hugh Clegg, *A New Approach to Industrial Democracy*, Blackwell, Oxford, 1960.

Part IV

SOME PROBLEMS OF POLICY AND MANAGEMENT

Chapter Fourteen

Policy-Making and Planning

The word policy has been used in many different senses.[1] For example, it may refer to political party programmes, long-term or short-term; to a government's announced programme or its actual pattern of actions (the foreign policy of the Fraser government); or to a particular decision or course of action. Wilfrid Harrison has said that the commonest use of the term 'refers to a course of action or intended course of action conceived as deliberately adopted, after a review of possible alternatives, and pursued or intended to be pursued'.[2] Austin Ranney has used this and other definitions to arrive at five components of a policy: (i) an object some aspect of the environment which it is intended to affect; (ii) a desired course of events; (iii) a selected line of action; (iv) a declaration of intent; (v) an implementation of intent. On this definition, a policy does not fully live up to its name unless it is implemented; that is, unless something actually happens. To put it differently, the idea of a 'policy' does seem to assume some deliberateness of intent, and some control over outcomes. In the case of public policy, a useful short definition might be a statement of intent that leads to a settled or definite course of action by a government agency or a holder of public office.[3] The action can include inaction, that is, deciding to do nothing. A policy statement may confine itself to laying down certain objectives, but it often also includes broad methods of reaching objectives, the 'strategy' or guidelines to be used in choosing courses of action. Thus in pursuing various educational objectives, it might be government policy to develop co-educational schools, or to give aid to independent schools, or to reduce class sizes, and there will be further specifications within these broad guidelines.

The Model of Rational Choice

One interesting question is how nearly one can expect the process of public policy-making to conform to the model of 'rational choice'.[4] Accounts of the latter vary, but most of them involve comprehensiveness and intellectual analysis. The decision-maker undertakes a careful and complete study of all the alternatives before him and all their possible consequences. He then ranks them according to his values, and chooses the one preferred. However, in practice public policy-making is usually not very like this.

One obvious departure from the model is that what looks from the outside like a policy may never have been 'decided' at all. Some so-called policies have not been decided, but happen, though one may later discern a pattern in what is happening (insofar as one can tell what is happening!). The British did not 'decide' to give up the Empire, or did so only at a late stage in the process. Most government is reactive, it does not look around for unachieved objectives, needs unmet or problems unresolved. There is often great resistance to taking decisions unless the environment gives an unmistakeable signal that decision is vital. Even when an intention is formed, the process of implementing it may convert it into something different, so the 'policy output' does not greatly resemble the statement of intent, and this may even cast doubt on the firmness or integrity of the original policy commitment.

Another point is that most public policy-making is not a matter of individual decision. An official has to convince other officials, and finally the minister, who may have to convince the cabinet. In almost all public decisions, many different individuals and groups are involved, so an important element is the resolution of differences. This may happen by persuasion. A significant component of the policy-making art is the power to persuade, which may include persuasion by the cogency of one's policy analysis, which in turn involves the ability to make proposals in terms understood by others, and to show how they relate to the objectives and values of others. This is in part a political skill, and one way in which policy-formulators need to be good politicians.

If persuasion fails or partly fails, compromise may be necessary. A public policy decision often expresses a compromise, something that no group thinks is best, but that is acceptable to most of those involved. Or a decision may be imposed by authority, and be implemented by the unconvinced or only partly convinced. Or there may be no firm and final decision, but only a vague formula; policy may be no more than 'a confluence of partial understandings among interested participants that change with the unfolding of events'.[5]

Allowing for all this, the effort at rational policy analysis is made in government, and rightly so. But there are other reasons why it fails to live up to the rational model.

Defining the Problem

Sometimes in government choosing the best answer to a problem is not as difficult as recognising what the problem is, and being able to formulate and define it. Just what is the 'Aboriginal problem' or the 'housing problem' or the 'problem of decentralisation'? Overt symptoms may be a poor guide to underlying factors, and may suggest wrong answers. Sometimes light is found by looking in some unexpected direction. Canberra was no part of a decentralisation strategy. All the same in the later 1960s the relative success of Canberra, and the relative failure of most State schemes for developing country towns, began to change the way in which the problem of decentralisation was stated and intelligent use of its example helped to evolve the notion of the 'growth-centre'. One characteristic of modern government is that much expertise is involved in recognising and correctly defining problems. The model of a good policy-maker may be not so much one who solves pre-established problems, but one who promptly identifies emerging problems.[6] A distinction is sometimes made between problems and dilemmas. A problem on this definition can be dealt with inside existing frames of reference, precedents and policies. A dilemma can only be coped with (if at all) by reformulating the issues, changing the focus of attention, 'seeing what the real problem is'. It needs the kind of insight that runs counter to the natural anticipations of the intelligence, and which seeks 'to find fault not with answers but with questions'.[7]

Choosing between Alternatives

Another stage in rational policy-making is considering the various alternative lines of action, and choosing between them. It includes collecting the facts, the more-or-less agreed data bearing on possible choices. This in itself may be so disillusioning that it drives one back to revising the objective or reformulating the problem.

But the main point is that much information may not be obtainable within the constraints imposed on policy-makers. Time may be too short; needed data are lacking, or conflicting; forecasting the future is difficult. In other words, public policy decisions involve costs and are made under conditions of uncertainty. The costs are the time and other resources spent in collecting relevant data and weighing their importance. The uncertainties are about what the facts are, what are the probable costs and benefits of different policies, what are the intentions of policy-makers in related fields. All this puts severe limits on the degree to which policy-makers can consider all the alternatives and their possible outcomes, and creates a considerable risk that they will fail to note some better option, or will miscalculate the outcomes. There is a temptation in such situations to produce a simplified answer for which there is good warrant in precedent, or which merely passes the buck. To give a very crude but common instance of the latter, an advisory committee set up to recommend policy in some field may propose that a new statutory agency be set up to develop the policies it should have developed itself, that a good deal of public money should be spent on the matter, and retire self-satisfied.

Simplification is, of course, necessary to produce answers at all. Only a few options can be analysed, and often inevitably in a rough and incomplete way. One form of simplifying is by factorisation—the task is subdivided and different parts handled by different people. Thus a department appraising the merits of a proposal will not try to weigh these in relation to alternative

projects of another department, or even to many of its own, but will leave
it largely to the budgetary authority to decide whether money is better
spent on this project than on others. This kind of segregation looks
undesirable, but much of it is inevitable. Within a department different
levels will be concerned with different aspects, some setting guidelines,
others collecting data within this framework. An organisation develops rules
and conventions to guide its members in which decisions they may take,
and by what criteria, whom they should consult, and so on.[8] This works
for standard problems, though it is liable also to produce standard answers
to non-standard problems. The general point being made here is that
policy-makers do not aim at anything like optimum rationality but set their
standards lower, at some 'acceptable' level—in Simon's words, they
satisfice, not optimise. What is regarded as acceptable depends on their
criteria of satisfaction, and a few general propositions about criteria of
satisfaction have been suggested.[9] One is that over time they tend to adjust
to the level of actual achievement; that is, what is regarded as satisfactory
comes to be reasonably close to what is achieved. However, once this
process is completed, aspiration levels tend slowly to rise. Aspirations are
also related to the achievement of other units with which we compare
ourselves (what sociologists call our reference groups). If, for example, we
are made aware that other comparable organisations or individuals are
getting better results than we are, this may cause an upward revision of
aspirations.

The role of comparison and imitation in administration has been little
studied, though it is quite common for organisations to assess the experience
of other organisations believed to be comparable (two common excuses for
inaction are: 'their problems are different', or 'they have already tried it and
failed'). Organisations often copy one another and evidence that some solution
has worked, or failed to work, in a roughly similar situation is not bad
evidence, especially in situations of uncertainty. Intelligent and systematic
comparative study could be a powerful technique of administrative improvement, and it is unfortunate that comparisons are so often superficial or based
on second-class information.

In various ways organisations can be planned to counter some of the
limitations discussed above. An important form of policy is 'policy-making
about policy-making', such as the creation of special machinery to define
objectives and identify problems, or to survey and develop resources, and
conduct other kinds of research. Procedures may be established to improve
prediction; thus an agency may make use of estimating procedures involving
the use of quantitative data and the calculation of future effects, from forward
estimating to cost-benefit analysis. There may be enforced procedures of
consultation and referral, in an effort to correct for possible bias or to avoid
parochial solutions to ramifying problems. Of course, insofar as a group
shares attitudes, group procedures can reinforce error as well as counter it.
Some writers have argued that good policy-making is closely related to good

'meta-policy-making' (policy-making about policy-making), including good machinery for processing and allocating problems, the existence of units specially devoted to thought and research about policy, the conscious development of knowledge resources, and so on.[10] Agencies that are poor meta-policy-makers are likely to be poor policymakers, or so it has been alleged.

Strategies of Policymaking

Lindblom and others have described some particular strategies of policy-making to cope with uncertainty, such as keeping one's options open, because one may know more later.[11] One may even deliberately choose an inadequate policy now, if this leaves open the chance of doing better in the future, in preference to a policy that appears to be soundly based but (if it turns out to be wrong) will be irreversible. There is also 'remedial' policy-making— if policy-makers 'cannot decide with any precision the state of affairs they want to achieve, they can at least specify the state of affairs which they want to escape', or the defects that need patching up. When it is hard to agree on or to define positive objectives, it may be wise to concentrate on eliminating conditions known to be bad. For example, it may be more sensible to get rid of bad Aboriginal housing than bother too much about the meaning of integration.

These strategies are examples of the seriality of much policy-making; often it is a series of steps in which periodical nibbling is a substitute for a good bite. Feasible new policies are often incremental, only marginally different from existing policies. This is because the effects of marginal changes are easier to forecast and because it is easier to persuade other people to agree to them;[12] possibly such changes are also easier to reverse if they prove mistaken. In practice policy-making rarely involves wholesale changes in direction, it usually consists more of sharpening or blunting the edge of existing policies, adding new items to a number of existing ones, or shifting priorities among the latter. Where a number of units of government are concerned, policy-making is less a matter of once-for-all solutions to problems, than a series of accommodations between the parties involved, what has been called 'partisan mutual adjustment'.[13] In some cases the best solution may simply be the one that can get the widest support.

This is a comforting theory in many ways, but unfortunately there are a number of areas where it does not appear to work. One of these is macro-economic policy, where piecemeal solutions seem to work badly; so, for example, income policies appear to have failed in various countries not so much because of inevitable tensions between the central policy-makers and the periphery, serious as these have been, but more because there has been no clear policy centre, and not enough policy co-ordination between the different economic agencies and interests involved.[14] Too little intellectual effort and consistency of purpose has gone into the policy-making process. Remedying one evil without thought of the consequences of one's actions in related fields is a kind of empiricism that is full of dangers where the interconnections are close and complex.

This may be a more serious criticism of incrementalist and pluralistic methods of policy-making than the commoner criticism that sometimes a major change is needed, which incremental methods cannot bring about. Incrementalism is not inconsistent with major change, one can often make at least as much change incrementally as in a more drastic way. It is arguable that incrementalism often promotes change or at any rate fruitful change; because its results are more calculable, it leads to fewer errors; because it suits cautious people and is less annoying to opponents, it makes change more acceptable. There is unfortunately a tricky problem about defining what is an incremental change as opposed to a drastic one, without being led into circularity.

Policy-making and the 'System'

Up to now we have mainly discussed policies as though they were a series of discrete choices, or decisions. But this kind of 'decision-making' approach has been criticised as giving too individualistic and voluntaristic an account of policy-making, and as ignoring the amount that is given in advance and not subject to deliberate choice.

First, there is often continuity of policy. A particular decision may really be based on previous commitments that now press with almost irresistible force in a certain direction. There are investments in well-established programmes which are difficult to change. There are also important institutional factors in decisionmaking, and preferences are often formed by the system within which choices are made. At the departmental level a public servant is helped how to decide, and whom to consult in deciding, by precedent. On many matters there will be an established departmental policy and procedures for dealing with certain kinds of question. The agency's structure is itself a set of precedents, of well-established processes and habits. There is institutional bias, and administrative systems, like political systems, have values and procedures built into them that operate consistently to favour some policies rather than others. 'Government behavior can be understood . . . less as deliberate choice and more as outputs of large organizations functioning according to standard patterns of behavior.'[15] To protect these standards the officers concerned do not always need to make positive decisions or recommendations. There can also be 'non-decision-making'.[16] Some considerations and demands are suppressed or maimed in their early stages, simply by failing to enter or to survive the processes of the system. Without conscious desire to ignore them, an organisation may act like a digestive system that rejects what it cannot cope with, or absorbs it only in greatly modified form. (A corollary of this is that a change in structure, or in staffing and financing, may bring about a change of policy, as well as vice versa.) In a more extended sense, the 'system' includes the whole governmental structure and its social and economic environment. This supplies certain kinds of information and not other kinds; represses certain sorts of demands and encourages others. Notions of what is possible or practicable are partly formed in this way. There is an interesting potential field of study which has been called 'problem formation', the study of how issues enter the governmental system in the first place.

Some administrative systems are more formal or formalistic than others, in the sense that the officially prescribed divisions between departments and the hierarchies within them have a preponderant influence in determining how things get done and whose voice counts. Australian administration would probably count as relatively formal in this sense. In America, the policy-making process seems to depend more on the building-up of informal relations cutting across the formally articulated structures. Of course, all reasonably efficient administrative systems partly depend on this process. A recent book has described the frequent need to build up particular decision networks, sometimes transient, sometimes more lasting, that cross the boundaries of formal hierarchies; and the 'reticulist' skills involved in knowing when and to establish these networks, which channels need activating, what information needs to be passed to whom, and so on. This is especially true when policy-making extends into intercorporate fields and impinges on the concerns of several different organisations.[17]

Also, as has been well-said, 'formality has more than one dimension'.[18] The British are relatively informal about the mechanics of public adminis-tration and about relations between trusted colleagues at various levels, but also have carefully articulated committee procedures for taking de-cisions. They like decorum, discretion, people who know their place and keep secrets. Americans may have far more form-filling and bureaucracy in certain respects, but also seem to leave more room for personal initiatives, invasion of one another's territory, the wide and informal consultation of 'outsiders'. On the other hand the transience of American top government executives may mean that their informal networks lack endurance and substance.[19]

There is another sense in which organisations may be said to influence objectives. Sometimes new policies are generated at lower levels within departments, perhaps by new groups entering them or by the public servants operating a service being brought, in the course of their day-to-day work, into consciousness of gaps in provision or situations not provided for.[20] In such cases policies may 'simply recognize and codify a process worked out over several years by people at humbler levels'.[21] Important changes of policy may be generated gradually within organisations, and only appreciated after they have happened. There exists an unpublished account of how an Australian technological institute wholly changed its character without a major policy decision being taken at any stage, partly by its staff introducing new courses and dropping old ones—had a policy decision been taken, the change might not have occurred! In various ways, if objectives breed organisations, organisations also breed objectives.

A Note on Systems Theory

At this point, a word on 'systems theory' as applied to administrative organisations might be relevant, as the theory is in part an expression of discontent with the model of organisations as structures designed to achieve the policies and objectives of their leaders. One can think of them instead as interacting groups of people with many and varied aims. The result of these interactions is an output or outputs, but not necessarily identical with anything purposed. Indeed, in order to survive, an organisation does not need to achieve its hypothetical policies or objectives; what it does need to do is to produce outputs that generate enough new inputs to keep the pattern of interaction going.

On this model, an organisation is a relatively stable system of interactions, with inputs that it transforms into outputs. It is an 'open system', that is, it depends on interchanges with an external world, or environment. If the environment values the output, it provides the basis for new inputs. The inputs include not only physical resources and labour but also new information, feedback about the environment and how the organisation is functioning in relation to it. Negative feedback tells an organisation that it is off course and enables it to take corrective action. Such a system also chooses its inputs, takes in only what it can make use of (in systems language, it has a 'coding mechanism'). This is a bare outline of one or two central notions of systems theory.[22]

There are limitations about this model. Systems theory has sometimes seemed to be preoccupied with the criterion of survival, but in human organisations there are also people who want them to be more efficient, to use their resources to better advantage—otherwise they had better die and be replaced by something else. The theory has sometimes directed attention too much away from purposive action, which does not square with much that one thinks one knows about human systems. It has also had difficulty in coping with the notion of organisational change.

However, the systems approach has a number of virtues. It reminds us of important ways in which organisations do acquire a momentum of their own, and their behaviour can be interpreted in survival terms. It also, like all useful models, calls attention to new and previously unsuspected relationships. A good example of this is the concept of 'membership'. A pioneer systems thinker, Chester Barnard, pointed to the difficulty of treating an organisation as a group of persons, as this assumes that we can clearly indicate who are the members of the organisation. From one point of view an organisation's clients and also its suppliers (usually thought of as outsiders) are members—it has to communicate with them, and induce them to contribute, or it will fold up. Conversely, its own employees cannot be assumed to be members. In one sense they are part of the environment, like clients and suppliers. Just as an organisation needs to induce inputs from the suppliers, so it needs to get inputs from its workers. To do this, it has to establish appropriate patterns of communication and inducements.

From this point of view an organisation is seen, not as a group of persons, but as a pattern of interactions, the precise boundaries of which are hard to define. It is the result of a process by which initial resources have been used to create incentives, which induce workers and clients and suppliers to contribute to it in appropriate ways.[23] This casts new light on the notion of membership and may lead, for example, to fruitful reflections about the similarities and differences between clients and employees. One may also be led to conclude that an organisation does not necessarily depend on its members accepting its objectives, but on their being induced to behave in certain ways, to produce an output (in pursuit of whatever goals they may happen to develop). Finally it may be that if we want to know who has the most power in an organisation, the question to ask is not, who sets the objectives? but: who controls the incentive system?

Planning

Planning is another awkward word to handle. In a broad sense it means deciding what to do, and is hardly distinguishable from policy-making. In this sense planning is going on all the time in administration, and there can be planning without a plan, or a distinguishable body of planners. But the word is often used to describe something more precise than 'policy', a systematic aspect of policy formation, 'systematic forethought'. It suggests model-building within the framework of broadly defined goals and objectives set for the planners, who then concern themselves with the construction of internally consistent models that try to describe inter-relations among the variables. This will not necessarily tell you what to do, but will highlight the possible consequences of alternative lines of action. An organisation with a 'plan' will have tried to define desired outputs, or alternative sets of these, as precisely as possible; estimated the resources available; formulated a reasonably precise programme that matches outputs and resources and indicates the various steps to be taken; and tried to forecast, and to suggest a strategy for coping with, major difficulties likely to be encountered.

A main purpose of a plan is to improve current decisions by ensuring that they are made with due regard to various future possibilities. A good plan also hinders 'non-decision-making', by exposing previously unsuspected needs to make certain decisions now, failure to decide which will have ramifying consequences.[23] This is one of the most unpopular features of planning. People used to think of a plan as a single firm set of recommendations, but it is now quite common for planners to outline a number of alternative plans, explaining the costs and benefits of each.

Most planning is 'partial' planning, in the sense that it only applies to some outputs, resources and programmes. It may relate only to a limited sector (defence or urban planning), or only operate in the case of certain processes (production planning, office planning). So-called planning may also fall short of the definition indicated above by, for example, concentrating on the end-product, and assuming that resources will be available; ignoring many options; confusing prediction and planning; forecasting a highly improbable future, or doing very little forecasting at all. Governments are often unwilling to publicise options, even when they have been considered. They like to look firm and decisive.

In the sense described above, planning is distinguishable from operations (to use military language), the carrying-out of the plan. But this distinction is often hard to maintain, as objectives and methods of attaining them may need constant modification in the light of changing circumstances, so that successful planning has to be a continuous process. If the people in closest touch with this feedback are those engaged in day-to-day administration, precise plans drawn up in divorce from operations may be unworkable. Secondly, a planning or policy unit, especially when it is imposed on an already existing agency by a well-meaning minister and is made up of outsiders, may be resented by the working administrators, all the more if its methods appear academic, leisurely or threatening.

On the other hand, it is hard in practice for operating staffs to find time and energy to think about the future; some kinds of planning may involve specialised quantitative skills; the more driving managerial types may be psychologically unfitted for a task that involves some withdrawal from immediate concerns, toleration of free speculation and debate, and envisaging of disruptive forms of change. It is sometimes argued that most senior public servants do not make good planners, because they are trained to concern themselves with the immediately practicable and politically acceptable. The practical administrator is often highly conscious of the need to simplify problems and seize upon the one or two essential points; the planner is freer to elaborate and to cost alternatives. However, it may be doubted whether good planning really requires very different talents from good administration —indeed, one of the problems is that 'those who are good at planning are likely to be good at opportunistic decision-making as well'.[24]

It is important in administration to make the necessary distinctions; there are situations in which fairly precise kinds of long-term advance planning are desirable, and ones where long-term plans have necessarily to be a bit vague and general, but within which more detailed short-term planning may be feasible; and so on. Thus in much capital budgeting, one may reasonably expect systematic long-term planning and the careful cost-benefit analysis of alternative proposals, in which specialised planning units may play a major role. In the area of foreign policy, the future is speculative and changeable, and planning must be correspondingly flexible, and fully aware of feedback problems; this does not mean that a planning unit will not work, but that it must be conceived of in a different way. Most planning and research units only work when many of the people concerned have a very special capacity for keeping in touch with the working officers of the organisation, for using their experience, and for learning how to formulate proposals in ways that seem relevant to day-to-day concerns, and do not pose too great a threat to the existing status system. At the same time planning is not the same thing as policy advice, it explores options in a freer and more independent fashion and is less concerned to produce an answer that is immediately acceptable. These complications help to explain why it is one of the hardest jobs on earth to produce good planners.

Of course, some so-called planning or policy units do not plan, they are more like intelligence or statistical units gathering data (which may include information on schemes used elsewhere) for the information of working administrators, or performing special pieces of research or even fairly routine tasks that the working administrators have not time to do themselves. At the other extreme, there may occasionally be a case for a detached unit engaged not in planning, but in speculative thought; such a unit must not desire to be, or look as though it is, influential in current policy options.

The notion that governments should have an overall plan into which all partial plans are fitted is probably unworkable. Governments, even in so-called planned economies, focus on a few partial plans for areas they consider specially important or which have caused special trouble. The implications of these for the rest of the system will be broadly assessed, especially their financial implications for the budget; and a limited number of alternative possibilities will have been considered. But the idea that the costs and benefits of such plans can be systematically weighed against many alternative and rival plans is an illusion, even in the computer age.

At lower levels planning can often be more systematic. Once there is a budget allocation for education, with some likelihood of continuity in time, and a broad set of objectives and policy guidelines, it is possible to have an approach to a long-term plan for, say, school buildings. As one descends the administrative scale, the constraints tighten and this makes good estimating and internally consistent planning easier. With severe and predictable constraints, it is easier to plan to do the best one can, though harder to do what one would like.

Policy and Planning Units

Australian government agencies have been slow to recognise the importance of the policy developing and planning functions. However, most Commonwealth departments now have policy groups, though the number of officers who spend their time mainly on this work is still fairly small. This is partly because of the well-founded belief that policies and plans are to some degree every senior administrator's concern, and it is dangerous to draw too firm a line around them.

Thus the Treasury has a long-established General Financial and Economic Policy Division. The Department of the Prime Minister and Cabinet has a strangely-named Operations Division (partly descended from Mr Whitlam's

Priorities Review Staff), which is concerned among other things with identifying 'priority program areas in need of review' and which has a Priorities Branch.

The Priorities Review Staff had been designed in 1973 to meet the need for a Prime Minister's think-tank, not preoccupied with immediate issues as his personal staff tended to be, and able to take a more detached view. It was largely modelled on the British Central Policy Review Staff and was intended to undertake periodical strategic reviews (to look back and see how the government's achievements measured up to long-term goals, and what seemed to have gone wrong), to raise policy issues that in its view were being ignored, and also to study and report on topics assigned to it. Though it produced a report on *Goals and Strategies*, which pointed to some 'issues for the future', its main and most successful work was on shorter-term issues, especially in mediating policy disputes between contending groups by offering its own well-argued views—on issues ranging from FM radio to child care policy. It included both public servants and staff brought in from universities and elsewhere. Its head, Mr Austin Holmes from the Research Department of the Reserve Bank, became a significant figure in the Prime Ministerial entourage, where he still was (now as Consultant Economist) in 1978.

The Coombs Report thought there was a case for a policy unit in the Prime Minister's Department, which could concentrate on issues of special urgency, but also help in developing guidelines for forward estimating and organise reviews of 'programme effectiveness' (see Chapter Eighteen).[26] It is also worth noting that one reason why the Coombs Commission laid such emphasis on regular forward estimates procedures was as a means of bringing ministers and officials together in a regular exercise in corporate planning and policy-forming, which would educate them in the planning process and encourage them to develop techniques of corporate planning in individual departments.

Various departments as well as those already mentioned have developed special policy and planning divisions. Thus, for example, the Department of Trade and Resources, and of Industry and Commerce, have Policy Development Divisions. The Department of Transport has a Strategic Planning and Resource Allocation Division whose functions range from the co-ordination of policy and planning advice on matters affecting a number of modes of transport, to developing medium and longer-range transport budgets and programmes. The Department of Aboriginal Affairs has a Planning Division to 'develop long range plans, formulate strategies and determine priorities, . . . conduct and commission relevant research . . . '. However, no one expects such units to monopolise the planning and policy functions, especially in departments such as Treasury and Prime Minister's, whose main *raison d'être* as departments is 'policy'. There are also from time to time important *ad hoc* units such as the study group created in 1977 under the chairmanship of Sir John Crawford to report on the problems of structural adjustment of manufacturing industry.

The dominant note of Canberra planning is probably the astringent one associated with economists, belief in rational thought about policy but fair scepticism of elaborate plans for coping with an uncertain future. When the Chairman of the New Zealand Planning Council talked recently to a Canberra conference about 'consultative planning', Mr Austin Holmes was reported as doubting 'the wisdom of all that consultative planning', of 'appeals to interest groups' which were more likely to lead to 'cosy agreements' between government and the powerful; he also questioned the effectiveness of most of the economic tools of central government in influencing the economy.[27] The cool note of this is not unfamiliar in Canberra.

Policy and planning units are rarer at State level, where governments have not in the past been planning-oriented. This has been partly the result of the hand-to-mouth character of federal financial relations and hence of State budgets, in part because many government agencies have been dominated by older types of specialists, such as engineers, or by effective but not well-educated administrators whose sophistication and tolerance for new-fangled ideas has been limited. Peter Wilenski's account is fair enough: 'While there is a strong emphasis in many departments and authorities on technical competence and getting the job done, there has not always been the same concern with thinking deeply about what the job itself should be'.[28] State ministers too have thought it was their function to make policy and the job of officials simply to carry it out, sometimes with the result that no one has made policy. However, a few special units exist—the following chapter mentions recent developments in Premier's Departments, starting with South Australia. In New South Wales the Department of Education has a Directorate of Planning Services, and the Public Transport Commission a Planning Division. A policy analysis group has been established within the Ministry of Transport.

Some work of a policy and planning kind is done within research units, and these have been accepted more readily in the States ('research' is a less menacing and pretentious notion than 'planning') as well as in Canberra. In certain fields the research and intelligence function was already well-recognised in the nineteenth century. In Victoria, H.H. Hayter from the 1850s onwards made Australian statistical reporting for a time the best in the world; in 1874 he became government statistician, with his own department, and began to publish the Victorian Yearbook. New South Wales had a statistics department by the 1880s; in 1887 T.A. Coghlan, the government statistician, published the first issue of the *Wealth and Progress of New South Wales*, and from 1895 a statistical handbook of 'the Seven Colonies'; these were the ancestors of the Australian Bureau of Statistics. Both men showed a broad interest in the measurement of social trends.

The character of modern research units varies greatly, and (as the Coombs Report says) many so-called Research Officers in the departments become over-involved in immediate problems. On the other hand there are long-established units such as the Research Department of the Reserve Bank of Australia, which has done much high-level economic investigation; and statutory bodies like the Industries Assistance Commission, whose main function is research and advice, and which employed over 340 Second and Third Division officers in 1976–77, of whom over 240 were graduates, and produced forty-six reports during the year. To protect the autonomy of the research function, special bureaus have been established by the Commonwealth government, the Bureau of Agricultural Economics, of Mineral Resources, of Transport Economics and the new Bureau of Industry Economics; though they are part of a regular ministerial department, each has its own Director and in this and other ways they are able to maintain their independence, while at the same time doing work relevant to the substantive functions of the department. Other departments have research directorates. There are departments such as the Commonwealth Treasury, which do a good deal of research, but where the permanent head says firmly: 'We do not have a research unit which we deliberately and specifically isolate from the day to day work of the department.'[29]

Research units are now fairly common at State level. In New South Wales, for example, the Department of the Attorney-General and Justice has a Bureau of Crime Statistics and Research 'to investigate the effectiveness of police, court and correctional methods; the causes and incidence of crime and the future needs of the State in controlling crime'. These terms of reference give it a clear policy orientation. The Department of Corrective Services has its own Research Division. The Department of Agriculture has a Division of Research Services and five Regional Research Directors operating centres that aim to be 'applied' and closely linked to extension services to farmers; several other divisions of the department have significant research functions. The Public Service Board has an Administrative Research Unit. Other agencies with research units and divisions include the Department of Motor Transport, Forestry Commission, State Pollution Control Commission and Department of Decentralisation and Development. Even Tourism has a Research Division; and there is a Bureau of Government Superannuation Research 'orientated towards the harmonious development of government and quasi-government retirement schemes', as the NSW Government Directory charmingly reports.[30]

Implementation

The definition of a policy quoted earlier included implementation. Some writers take the view that a policy does not fully live up to its name unless it issues in a line of action. There is a case for saying this. All the same it is useful to distinguish between policy and implementation, meaning by the latter all the problems that arise in executing a policy as intended. Of course, the action required by a policy decision may be more or less precisely specified. It may involve detailed steps that leave little room for discretion;

on the other hand the intention may simply be to move in some broad direction, in which case a wide variety of outcomes might all be perfectly consistent with the policy.

The work 'programme' is sometimes used to describe a more detailed kind of policy-making, where a definite goal has been set and it is clear what steps are needed to achieve it. Programmes might be said to have 'outputs', in the sense of benefits that can often be described in a fairly precise way; in contrast one might talk of the 'outcomes' of policies, including broader consequences and indirect effects.[31] However, there is no consensus in the literature about such definitions. Another word used earlier was a 'strategy', which suggests that not merely have objectives been set but some careful thought given to what instruments and procedures are likely to achieve them.

Impracticable Policies

Deficiencies in implementation can often be traced back wholly or partly to the policies themselves. Most obviously, some are less practicable than others, so a failure in execution really represents a failure in policy-making. The policy may have been drawn up in ignorance of the relationships involved in the situation to be changed, or without regard to available resources. As was noted earlier, plans drawn up in divorce from operations are likely to be unworkable for this kind of reason.

Symbolic Policies

Sometimes the so-called policy is mainly intended to have a symbolic role, and a large discrepancy between policy and outcome causes no surprise. A State Minister for Health might say if asked that the primary aim of a government mental hospital was to cure its patients. But suppose one were to find a handful of doctors, few of them with psychiatric training, looking after several thousand inmates, most of whom were elderly or had spent many years in hospital, one could reasonably conclude that the 'real' objectives were custodial, or that the hospital was really an old people's home; or one might say that the government really had no policy, but was just letting various things happen.[32] This is an extreme case, though close to the realities of some Australian States in the 1950s. Most organisations have some divergencies of this kind and it is not usually a case of conscious deception. The formal or announced goal is symbolic—it says what policy should be in a better world, not what it is at present. This may improve morale, though a large and continuing gap between theory and practice is more likely to lower morale than raise it.

Another example would be a government that declared that its social welfare policy was to concentrate benefits on those most in need, but which at the same time maintained a number of programmes that did not achieve this object. Here many factors may be involved in the ambiguities of policy —symbolism and ideology, political convenience, and underlying social factors that tend to bias the distribution of welfare services even by well-intentioned governments.

Operational and Non-operational Policies

Another case is where formally approved policies are too vague or ambiguous to be much guide to implementation—that is, they are not operational, in the sense of helping to guide choice between alternative courses of action. The decision to 'improve the housing of lower-income groups' or to 'defend Australia' would be a policy of this kind. The statute governing the former Tariff Board said that it could recommend assistance for industries that were economic and efficient. It was left to the judgment of the Board how this vague policy should be interpreted in making its reports.

Some ambiguity in policies may be inevitable or convenient. It helps governments and their agencies to accommodate diversity under a cloak of unity. One problem of policy analysis is that ministers often try to avoid committing themselves about difficult policy choices. Vagueness also makes it easier to adapt administration to changing circumstances, as has been true of some of the ambiguities in immigration policies, where many decisions about quotas, financial assistance, and so on have been made departmentally, and this has sometimes enabled changes to occur which might not have been possible had they been announced as new government policies.

Of course, even when officially announced policies are stated in very general terms, there are usually also ministerial or departmental guidelines which give administrators something more definite to work to. Occasionally one can set precise targets, and units with such targets have certain problems simplified. They can more readily concentrate effort on the most efficient ways of reaching them, and be more easily checked up on if the targets are not achieved. To the extent that policies remain vague, outcomes are more likely to be determined by a variety of bargains and compromises among the many participants in implementation. On the other hand, the attempt to avoid ambiguity may often lead to pedantic over-precision or legalism, or to the setting of measurable quantitative goals that lose sight of qualitative factors.

Priorities

Similarly a government agency may be given a number of clear policy objectives, but no guide as to what to do when they conflict, or all make claims on limited resources. The aims of government economic policy might be 'full employment plus stable prices plus an annual growth rate of 5 per cent'. Each may be a roughly measurable objective, but there may be no indication as to which should be sacrificed, and to what point, should they conflict. This would make it hard to say how successfully it was being implemented. Often it is impossible in such circumstances, apart from being politically inconvenient, to draft a policy statement that sorts out the priorities attached to the various objectives. Policy-making in this case is certainly serial

—indeed, a series of nudges, 'a little more of X this year, even at some expense (if necessary) to Y'.

One might illustrate the point in more detail by taking the recent case, already mentioned in Chapter Five, of the Industries Assistance Commission, which succeeded the Tariff Board in 1973. The Commission was to hold inquiries and report on matters 'affecting assistance to industries', and 'other matters' that might be referred to it; and it was to

> have regard to the desire of the Australian Government . . . to improve and promote the well-being of the people of Australia, with full employment, stability in the general level of prices, viability in external economic relations, conservation of the natural environment and rising and generally enjoyed standards of living, and, in particular, to . . .
> (a) improve the efficiency with which the community's productive resources are used;
> (b) encourage those economic activities . . . which contribute to improving . . . efficiency . . . ;
> (c) facilitate adjustment to changes in the economic environment by industries and persons affected by those changes;

and so on. There were other guidelines, but it is unnecessary to give the full list; the main point is not merely their inevitable vagueness, but the fact that they contain no guidance about what to do when the different considerations conflict. The most that could be said in general of the listed items is that they have a certain 'free-trade' and 'free-market' flavour about them.

This has been of political importance more than once, and particularly in 1976–77, when the Commission's recommendations for reducing tariff protection conflicted sharply with the more protectionist stance of the government. In April 1976, the Minister for Business and Consumer Affairs said that he had asked the Commission to pay more attention to the social, regional and employment consequences of its recommendations; this is the kind of 'nudge' referred to above, and it was later alleged that the Commission had failed to take due note of it, but how would one clearly establish this? The Commission certainly referred to such matters in its reports, though it was sceptical about predicting the employment consequences of particular protection levels.

As mentioned in Chapter Five, there was a crisis in August 1977 after the Commission had recommended cuts in the protection levels of the footwear, textile and clothing industries, at an awkward moment for the government, which foreshadowed additions to the Act to make the guidelines more explicit, and give them a more protectionist flavour (though it was not put as bluntly as this). It will be interesting to see the result. New guidelines are inevitably a shaky way of influencing the actions of a body that may well, in its own opinion, already be paying due regard to the various considerations and priorities that the government has in mind.

Here is another example. A British government directive during the Second World War read somewhat as follows, that 'only essential peace-time production is to be provided for. Military items are to be given a lower priority when they cater only for the European theatre and new items of equipment are not to be manufactured unless a serious loss of efficiency would be involved in not providing them'. Implementing this directive would be impossible except to someone in touch with the whole context—what had gone before, what other clues there were to present intentions, how sharp a series of new nudges was intended.

It is not uncommon for formal policy-makers to choose to avoid this issue of priorities, and leave many conflicts to be settled lower down; sometimes they are in fact settled by budget or manpower allocations. But they have to be decided in some way or other.

The bearing of all this on implementation is clear; if policy directives are hard to interpret, whether through unavoidable or deliberate vagueness or sheer inefficiency, the public servants who 'implement' policy will also in fact be making policy by default. Even if they are broad supporters of various government policies, they may rate them differently on their own scale of priorities, think other matters more important or urgent, or simply see the policies from a different perspective.

Organisations with a number of aims sometimes try to simplify the problem of priorities by treating one or two major goals as 'primary' and the rest as constraints. In a simple case, if quantity and quality of output are two values, they may treat quantity as the primary goal, subject to some minimum level of quality. Indeed groups often work more effectively if they have a clear primary goal—those that pursue many different objectives, with no clear rank-order, may come to lack a sense of purpose. The effectiveness of modern governments suffers through the distraction of many and varied tasks; they might do better to set themselves fewer things to do and concentrate on doing them well (itself easier said than done). At the same time, just as there is sometimes a case for keeping policies flexible, as in situations where innovation is highly valued, so there is sometimes one for letting organisations stay pluralistic (at some cost in certain respects) rather than imposing on them a spurious and constricting 'unity of purpose'.[33]

Also, a single-purpose department may be efficient in its own terms, but narrow in its outlook. Conservationists are made unhappy when, as quite often happens, government agencies are responsible only for a single resource —it may be rivers, forests, soils, wildlife, minerals—or for a single resource-use.[34] They tend to become over-committed to their particular objective, and lose sight of its place in the larger scheme of things.

Commitment

This reminds us that there may be variations in the degree of commitment to a policy—the penalty seen as involved in acting otherwise than intended, or the incentive to persist in the face of difficulties.[35] Policies with low commitment are clearly less likely to be implemented, not only because the policy-makers will be prone to give them away if challenged, but because they will bother less to convey their intentions firmly to the implementers, and the latter will be more inclined to kick over the traces. If those who carry out policies need commitment as well as those who make them, that involves attention also to their incentive to persevere, and may reinforce to policy-makers the need for consultation with those likely to implement their policies. This, as we said earlier, was desirable to make sure that the policies are practicable, but it can also help to improve the co-operation of implementers by increasing their sense of commitment. Just as lack of commitment exposes a policy to challenge at the implementation stage, so a high degree of commitment eases the later stages. Sometimes an early policy decision based on quite a narrow input of information and interests can generate enough commitment to put a strict limit on the influence of later inputs, even if the latter raise considerable doubts about the wisdom of the decision, or represent important opposing interests.[36]

A related variable is how far a policy-decision has really ended the conflict about what policy should be. Sometimes opponents of the decision try to open at the implementation stage the battles that they lost at the policy-making stage. This is a particularly attractive strategy where the policy decision has been made in broad terms, leaving many ambiguities at the edges, details to be filled in, legislation to be drafted, budget appropriations to be made.

Consents and Feedback

One recent study of policy implementation has highlighted the importance of the number of consents, or 'clearances', needed along the way.[37] Let us say that four separate individuals or groups are required to give consent to successive stages of the process of implementation, and let us suppose that there is an 80 per cent probability of each consent being given, this already reduces the probability of programme completion below half. The prevalence of this kind of veto power varies with types of political system —it is strong in very pluralistic systems of government such as the American, and of some importance in Australia, especially in federal relations. Consent can, of course, vary in degree; there can be lukewarm support or muted opposition, expressed in delay or attempts to modify parts of the scheme rather than unambiguous veto. What we are really talking about are needed acts of compliance, which can be reluctant or tardy, as well as not forthcoming at all. For some urgent or closely interlocking schemes, delay can amount to defeat, or the price of agreement may involve bargains that greatly change the character of the outcomes; sometimes one failure or a series of comparatively small failures in a sequence of linked activities can bring about disaster. One problem of modern government is that the greater interdependence of policies tends to multiply the number of related decision points, so that the success of any one decision often depends on more consents, and a few non-compliant sectors can seriously damage the whole system.

A common motive behind the creation of new agencies to get new policies off the ground is to by-pass an existing multiplicity of decision points. But, unless such an agency can be guaranteed very special and continuing political support, the move may well do more harm than good. The new agency may alienate the by-passed, attract envy by its privileged status, suffer in its early days from lack of administrative experience and develop in its later days the same ills as the system that it was designed to circumvent.

This does not mean that there is no case for a special unit to 'keep at' (in Caiden's phrase) the implementing departments and agencies, in particular to monitor their activities and to make sure that the policy-makers are adequately informed about what is going on, and what unforeseen problems are arising. Bureaucracies have many devices, not only for hindering changes they do not support, but for concealing what they are really up to. So there is often a need for some unit with strong political backing that is there to see that those necessary ingredients of any reform—persistence and perseverance—are encouraged. Feedback and evaluation in the shape of regular reviews and reports on progress, is an important element in good implementation procedures.

It often appears that there are a few key points at which opposition is likeliest. If these can be identified in advance, action can be taken to neutralise them. There are cases where the retirement or transfer of one or two key actors has greatly eased implementation problems; sadly there are as many cases where changes in the participants remove people important to the success of changes at a critical time. The relation between implementation and mobility is full of interest. In systems where ministers and even officials come and go, it becomes harder to locate responsibility for failures of implementation, as of policy-making.

The final stage of 'consent' in implementation is, of course, having a clientele or public ready to play its appropriate role as co-operator with the services provided by the organisation (see Chapter Seventeen).

Time pressures

Where implementation is concerned, there are always time lags.[38] By the time a policy comes to be implemented, circumstances have often changed in ways hard to predict. In recent years in economic policy this has even meant that, by the time a particular policy comes to be implemented, the opposite is what the situation demands. Aircraft arrive too late for their roles, new growth centres start to develop as the population needed to support them fails to materialise, plans made with one government in mind fail to be implemented by its successor, cost-inflation makes a commitment more expensive than the most pessimistic estimate. The World Bank is said to have used a 'coefficient of administrative friction' in appraising projects; that is, the average discrepancy observed in a given sector between original estimates and final outcomes.[39]

New Models of Policy-making

The reader may conclude from this discussion that public policy-making is far from living up to a rational model of choice, and is very much conditioned by unclear objectives, lack of time, low aspirations, incrementalism, compromise, built-in bias, non-compliance and other gaps between policy and performance. This assumption is correct. It is sometimes argued that incrementalism is peculiarly appropriate to the conservative and pragmatic outlook of Australian policy-makers, with their distaste for looking far ahead or making long-term plans, and scepticism about favourable outcomes.

This appeared a more comfortable doctrine some years ago than it does now, when important ares of policy seem less amenable to the incremental, piecemeal approach. Some recent writers, while accepting many of the points made above, are the same time fearful that they may be used to justify myopic, conservative, purely reactive government. They seek a model of policy that restores the possibility of vision, foresight and active choice. We end this chapter by mentioning two of them. Their writings are hard to summarise, and not all that easy to understand. But it may be useful to give at least a crude notion of what they are after.

The easier to read is Geoffrey Vickers.[40] He denies that the only model of a rational policy-maker is one who aims at pre-established objectives. In part he uses the kind of model mentioned earlier in discussing systems theory —an organisation maintaining its equilibrium and 'surviving' by responding to warning signals from the environment and taking corrective action. But the Vickers equilibrium is a moving equilibrium, and success in maintaining it depends crucially on two active elements in the system. The first is the capacity of policy-makers to make 'appreciative' judgments, to identify in good time emerging problems—problems that present themselves as a complex mixture of fact and value, not as some neatly definable objective. The second is the extent to which they set themselves to learn from one situation in dealing with the next. One definition of a bureaucracy is 'an organization that cannot correct its behaviour by learning from its errors';[41] and one point of encouraging more conscious policy-making and planning within an organisation is to develop greater self-consciousness about the policy process, including a sharper eye for new issues and better ways of checking why things have gone wrong. Meyerson and Banfield argued many years ago that what was needed for better planning was not more 'research', but experiment—actually to do something, and carefully appraise the results. [42] We have said little in this chapter on policy evaluation, and attempts to measure the effectiveness of policies, though it is touched on in Chapter Eighteen.

The second writer is Amitai Etzioni.[43] 'What is needed for active decision-making is a strategy that is less exacting that the rationalistic one but not as constricting in its prespective as incrementalism.' This he calls a 'mixed-scanning' strategy. As a soldier is taught first to 'scan the whole field in a rough, non-discriminating way for some obvious sign of danger', then may proceed bit-by-bit within the new context, so the active policy-maker alternately raises and lowers his vision, incrementing for most of the time but periodically reviewing the field and, if necessary, making a new fundamental decision. A possible implication is that the hardest lesson to learn is when to shift eye-levels in this way, when to do the many small things and when the one big thing.

Notes

1. See R.S. Parker, 'Policy and Administration', *Public Admin.* (Sydney), XIX, 2, June 1960, reprinted in R.N. Spann and G.R. Curnow, *Public Policy and Administration in Australia: A Reader*, Wiley, Sydney, 1975, 144–50.
2. In J. Gould and W.L. Kolb, *A Dictionary of the Social Sciences*, Tavistock, London, 1964, 509.
3. Austin Ranney (ed.), *Political Science and Public Policy*, Markham Publishing Co., Chicago, 1968, 7; cf. J.E. Hodgetts, 'The Civil Service and Policy Formation', *Canadian J. Econ. Political Science*, XXIII, 4, November 1957, 469.
4. On rational choice, a concept explored by economists and decision-theorists, see David Braybrooke and Charles E. Lindblom, *A Strategy of Decision*, Free Press, New York, 1963, ch. 3.
5. Hugh Heclo and Aaron Wildavsky, *The Private Government of Public Money*, Macmillan, London, 1974, 373.
6. cf. Geoffrey Vickers, *The Art of Judgment*, Chapman and Hall, London, 1965.
7. Bernard Lonergan, *Insight: A Study of Human Understanding*, Longmans, Green, New York, 1957, 19.
8. R.G.S. Brown, *The Administrative Process in Britain*, Methuen, London, 1970, ch. 7, discusses this point well.
9. See J.G. March and H.A. Simon, *Organizations*, Wiley, New York, 1958, 182–3; and J. Feldman and H.E. Kanter, 'Organizational Decision Making', in J.G. March (ed.), *Handbook of Organizations*, Rand McNally, Chicago, 1965, 632–4. These are stated as normal assumptions, likely to be true when data are not changing too rapidly. In unstable situations, there may be very odd reactions to stress.
10. See Y. Dror, *Public Policymaking Re-examined*, Chandler Publishing Co., San Francisco, 1968. For discussion, see V. Subramaniam, 'Two Complementary Approaches to Macro-decision Making', *Public Admin.* (Sydney), XXX, 4, December 1971.
11. See C.E. Lindblom, *The Policy Making Process*, Prentice–Hall, Englewood Cliffs, NJ, 1968, 24–6; and cf. D. Braybrooke and C.E. Lindblom, *A Strategy of Decision*, Free Press, New York, 1963, and Lindblom, *The Intelligence of Democracy*, Free Press, New York, 1965.

12. On incrementalism, see C.E. Lindblom, 'The Science of Muddling Through', *Public Admin. Review*, XIX, Spring 1959, 79–88, reprinted in A. Etzioni (ed.), *Readings in Modern Organizations*, Prentice–Hall, Englewood Cliffs, NJ, 1969; and Braybrooke and Lindblom, *op. cit.* For critical discussion, see Dror and Lindblom, in *Public Admin. Review*, XXIV, 3, September 1964, also reprinted in the Etzioni reader.

13. Braybrooke and Lindblom, *op. cit.*

14. I owe the point to John Corina.

15. G.T. Allison, *The Essence of Decision*, Little Brown, New York, 1971, 67.

16. See P. Bachrach and M.S. Baratz, *Power and Poverty, Theory and Practice*, Oxford University Press, New York, 1970, especially ch. 3.

17. J.K. Friend, J.M. Power and C.J.L. Yewlett, *Public Planning: The Intercorporate Dimension*, Tavistock Publications, London, 1974; cf. Hugh Heclo, *A Government of Strangers: Executive Politics in Washington*, Brookings Institution, Washington DC, 1977, on the scope and limitations of informal networks in Washington.

18. David Henderson, 'Under the Whitehall Blanket', *The Listener*, 17 November 1977.

19. Heclo, *op. cit.*, 107.

20. cf. Oliver Macdonagh, *A Pattern of Government Growth, 1800–1860*, MacGibbon and Kee, London, 1961, especially chs 15, 16.

21. D.V. Donnison and V. Chapman, *Social Policy and Administration*, Allen and Unwin, London, 1965, 246.

22. For further readings, see F.E. Emery (ed.), *Systems Thinking*, Penguin, Harmondsworth, Middlesex, 1969.

23. See C.I. Barnard, *The Functions of the Executive*, Harvard University Press, Harvard, 1938; cf. H.A. Simon, *Administrative Behavior*, 2nd edn, Macmillan, New York, 1957, ch. VI, 'The Equilibrium of an Organization'; J.G. March and H.A. Simon, *Organizations*, Wiley, New York, 1958, ch. 4; and P.B. Clark and J.Q. Wilson, 'Incentive Systems: a Theory of Organizations', *Admin. Science Quarterly*, 6, 2, September 1961.

24. J.K. Friend and W.N. Jessop, *Local Government and Strategic Choice*, Tavistock, London, 1969.

25. M. Meyerson and E.C. Banfield, *Politics, Planning and the Public Interest*, Free Press, Glencoe Illinois 1955, 277.

26. Report, RCAGA, 383.

27. As reported in *Canberra Times*, 31 January 1978.

28. Interim Report, Review of New South Wales Government Administration, Government Printer, Sydney, 1977, 4.

29. Sir Frederick Wheeler, Transcript of Evidence to RCAGA, 28 November 1974.

30. Directory of Administration and Services, Government of NSW, Government Printer, 1977, 170.

31. cf. Hugh Heclo, *Modern Social Politics in Britain and Sweden*, Yale University Press, 1974, 4, gives a slightly different version.

32. The example is Etzioni's.

33. cf. Peter Self, *op. cit.*, 30–1, 68–9.

34. L. Peres, 'Ecology, Conservation and Politics', a paper presented at the Conservation Conference, Australian National University, Canberra, June 1970.

35. See P.H. Levin, 'On Decisions and Decision Making', *Public Admin.* (London), 50, Spring 1972; and cf. A. Dunsire, *Administration: The Word and the Science*, Martin Robertson, London, 1973, 211–2.

36. P.H. Levin, *Government and the Planning Process*, Allen and Unwin, London 1976, discusses an English decision to build a New Town from this point of view.
37. Jeffrey L. Pressman and Aaron B. Wildavsky, *Implementation*, University of California Press, Berkeley, 1973, xvi, 107.
38. See on this Christopher Hood, *The Limits of Administration*, Wiley, London, 1976.
39. *ibid.*, 191.
40. Geoffrey Vickers, *The Art of Judgment*, Chapman and Hall, London, 1965; see also *Value Systems and Social Progress*, Pelican, Harmondsworth, Middlesex, 1970.
41. M. Crozier, *The Bureaucratic Phenomenon*, Tavistock Publications, London, 1964, 187.
42. *op. cit.*, 282.
43. A. Etzioni, *The Active Society*, Free Press, New York, 1968. See also 'Mixed-scanning: A 'Third' Approach to Decision-making', *Public Admin. Review*, 27, December 1967.

Chapter Fifteen

Co-ordination

When a number of units are producing goods and services interdependently, so that the activities of one are conditional on those of another, they have to be related to one another. 'Co-ordination' usually refers to the problem of relating units or decisions so that they fit in with one another, are not at cross-purposes, and operate in ways that are reasonably consistent and coherent.

However, this description covers two rather different processes. Sometimes a group of people are agreed on aims, but act in inharmonious ways because of ignorance. In this case, co-ordination refers to getting rid of involuntary inconsistencies of behaviour and giving coherence to a group of activities. People want to co-operate, but they need help to co-operate efficiently. Many kinds of 'administrative co-ordination' take this form. On the other hand, incoherence may arise from conflict over objectives and policies. In that case co-ordination is a way of getting some people to change their objectives. The two processes are often hard to separate in practice, as almost any method of co-ordination tends to affect both efficiency and policy. When it is said that certain activities should be co-ordinated in the interests of efficiency, we do well to remember that co-ordination is rarely a policy-neutral activity, but often 'the process by which the co-ordinated are made to ... conform to the policy of the co-ordinator'.[1] In government, co-ordination is often a way of channelling activities in accordance with political priorities. Even when people appear to agree on an objective, some may give it low priority or think that they should have the right to interpret its meaning in practice, or have the right to make the crucial decisions. Here again co-ordination means someone getting their own way.

The need for both kinds of co-ordination varies with the situation. Sometimes different activities are so loosely related that they can proceed in a relatively autonomous way, and it is best simply to leave various initiatives to flower, without trying to impose some arbitrary order on them. But there are other cases where there is so much overlapping and so many interdependencies, that it becomes vital to the efficient use of resources that activities should be integrated. Similarly there are situations where policy

411

conflicts are rare or mild, so no great effort has to be made about conflict-resolution. An ideal combination from this point of view would be an organisation where each individual could be given a cabbage patch and left to get on with the job, and where there was also a high level of consensus about the value of growing cabbages.

Administrative Conflict

In government there is always a good deal of conflict between departments. First, they are all competitors for limited resources, so that budget and manpower allocations are one important area where conflicting demands arise. Secondly, there may be conflicts over who should control some field of policy or range of tasks. Thirdly, there may be differences of opinion about what policy should be.

Of course, these conflicts also go on within departments. But an established department has often developed various ways of containing internal conflict, through a clearly developed authority system, control of promotions, various ways of promoting loyalty and identification, and so on. The Coombs Report says that 'an effective performance of the co-ordinating function entails developing . . . an awareness of the need for discipline, an acceptance of the constraints which make it necessary, and an active involvement in the processes by which it is applied'.[2] It is usually easier to promote this kind of co-operative feeling within a single government agency than towards the wider system of which it forms part. Some departments, especially those with a strong professional bond, develop powerful internal loyalties, often accompanied by fierce resistance to interference from outside.

Another point is that attitudes to the legitimacy of administrative conflicts vary. There is often a belief that administrative conflicts are always bad and ought not to occur. Organisations have a stake in pretending that there is consensus even when there is not. This tends to make conflicts illegitimate, to push them below the surface, and possibly hinder their working-out and fruitful resolution. Unfortunately, like many arguments in administration, this one is double-edged; pretending that conflicts do not exist, or should not exist, is one method of smoothing them away. It is often said that in British government administrative conflict is regarded unfavourably, as a sign of breakdown of the system, but that in the United States it is much more acceptable and even regarded as an indication of administrative health. Australia is perhaps between the two, though all such generalisations are hazardous. Attitudes to conflict are linked with differences of national culture, but there are also important institutional factors. For example, a federal system encourages administrative conflict, the Westminster model of cabinet government to some extent represses it—Australia has both. Ideology is important. People who believe that administration is inevitably 'political', an arena for the battles of different interests or for the dynamic enterprises of newly emerging forces, find the idea of conflict more agreeable and creative than those who think that the administration should be the neutral instrument or the guardian of some over-arching 'public interest'.

It is common to think of the public sector as a series of government agencies, each regulating or otherwise acting on the outside world. But it is increasingly common in government to find that achieving some policy aim involves one government agency influencing the actions of another government agency.[3] In Australia there are many obvious examples in Commonwealth–State relations, but it is equally the case at any given level of government. In Chapters Eleven and Sixteen, we discuss the controls that Public Service Boards and Treasuries exercise over the spending departments. However, the network of interorganisational influence is far more complex than this; one department is concerned with another for a huge variety of purposes, from building and purchasing and 'common service' activities, to the effects of one economic agency's policies upon those of another, or on foreign policy. It has even been suggested that it is often 'easier for a public agency to change the behaviour of a private organization than of another public agency',[4] or in other words that governments may find it easier to regulate the private sector than to regulate themselves.

This may be an extreme view, but there are many examples of failures of co-ordination in the government sector, and many 'private empires' such as some of the great statutory corporations have been, or the Department of Veterans' Affairs with its own network of hospitals and cash benefits. In this chapter we shall explore various types of co-ordination that exist within Australian government (some have already been covered in early chapters), and their possibilities and limitations.

Types of Co-ordination

One recent account of co-ordination defines it as those adjustments by which 'the adverse consequences of any one decision for other decisions in the set are to a degree and in some frequency avoided, reduced, counterbalanced or outweighed.'[5] This definition brings out the fact that co-ordination rarely leads to complete harmony and consistency, if only because it is itself often a costly process, and we can only spend a limited time co-ordinating what we do, as opposed to doing it.

Many people think of co-ordination as an activity involving the direct use of authority by some individual or group, what we may call hierarchical co-ordination. But this can be a misleading way of looking at the problem, especially in organisations with a complex set of interdependencies.[6] In such cases the direct use of authority to resolve inconsistencies, important as it sometimes is, has great limitations. It may be better to provide for co-ordination by the careful advance programming of activities, establishing procedures and routines for complex sequences of tasks. A schedule is established that says who is to do what and when. In this sense, co-ordination is part of planning, 'co-ordination by plan', built into the system in advance.

A clear example is some complex kind of assembly line or an automated factory.

But this answer is only possible where the pattern of interdependencies, even if complex, is reasonably stable and predictable. The more it is subject to unpredictable change, the harder it is to plan ahead. This is often true in government. In this case, relating different activities has to take the form of 'co-ordination by feedback', involving the constant flow of new information, both to report the new conditions and to indicate the adjustments needed to take account of them. Too much effort to plan in advance will simply lead to great inflexibility. At the same time, co-ordination by feedback raises many problems.

Communications

There are various ways of dealing with these problems. One is to improve the information flow. Co-ordination partly depends on good communications. Consider a group of people with common aims who nevertheless behave in ways quite inconsistent with the achievement of these aims, such as a body of amateur removal men trying to get a large piece of furniture through a small door. This does not happen only because the individuals concerned lack skill, but also because of poor communications between them. A lacks knowledge of B's proposed next move, B does not know what is expected of him by C, and so on. There are often situations where we can only take advantage of the division of labour by also building up an elaborate network of communications. In administration the flow of information is often more important than the flow of instructions—indeed it can sometimes take its place, as when a researcher readily accepts knowledge of the work of others as important to his own, and adjusts his activities accordingly.

One reason why it is often hard to work a new organisation properly is that there has developed no regular structure of mutual expectations and store of knowledge by reference to which particular communications can be interpreted. Even quite a small and simple group, such as a committee, works better when its members know one another reasonably well and even better when they have acquired experience of discussing the same subject together. This is one reason why physical propinquity is important for officials and departments that have much to do with one another. Of course, organisational distance is not only a factor of physical distance. Functional separation may be as important, as with various kinds of specialist; or status differences; or contacts too shortlived for mutual assessments or relationships of trust to develop.

Recent attempts to increase the flow of information within administrative systems have had valuable results. There is more awareness of the need for promoting ease of communications, and for statistical returns, information services, house journals, library services and so on. However, it is misleading to say that 'lack of communication' is what causes problems, as though a mere increase in quantity would solve them. There can be too much as well as too little communication. Costs are attached to sending and receiving information—it takes time and uses scarce resources. Too much information may also confuse people or make them anxious, or divert their attention from what is significant; sometimes an information channel is used precisely to do this, as in some public relations. Indeed, an essential feature of an organisation is that it restricts communication channels. At a party (in theory) anyone can talk about anything to anyone else, though in practice guests are 'organised' by time constraints, social conventions and their hosts. A government department restricts this free intercourse by laying down formal patterns of interaction; the requirement is that each officer should have the data appropriate to his role. When the extra cost of a bit of information exceeds the extra advantage of having it, it should not be provided, a fact often ignored by people who insist on detailed returns without asking what trouble it costs to prepare them, and how much use of them will be made when prepared. However, in changing situations, making sure that everyone has the 'right' information is a problem of the greatest complexity, as what is 'right' may vary with each case.

Self-containment

Another answer to the problem of co-ordination is to try to reduce the need for it by, for example, breaking down the organisation into more self-contained units. There is often some choice between giving each person a cabbage patch, which may minimise co-ordination problems but sacrifice economies of scale and specialisation; or organising people more elaborately, at the cost of making co-ordination harder. It is also possible to divide up work in ways designed to promote consensus, and to minimise policy conflicts. For example, one can try to build the structure as far as possible on naturally felt recognitions of mutual dependence; that is, not impose too many relationships that cut across the grain, and that will raise in their turn horrendous problems of control. One way of resolving a conflict in government, as in the economy, is to divide up the market. This involves mutual recognition that potentially conflicting groups have each a territory that will not be invaded by the others, the drawing of a frontier. It is a strong force in preserving departmentalism, and up to a point a necessary one, in order to limit co-ordination problems.

The Stages of Co-ordination

Co-ordination is often thought of as something carried out by a specialised co-ordinating body. Fortunately much of it happens piecemeal and even without great deliberation. In practice the need for more over-all forms of co-ordinating machinery only starts being taken seriously when piecemeal solutions have ceased to work, especially when resources are short and there is a widely felt need to reduce uncertainties about decisions being taken in different sections. Many forms of co-ordination take place without much thought, by the relatively spontaneous adjustments of some people to others.

Even when it involves more deliberate action, this action is often taken by one or more of the units themselves. In acting or deciding, we often take special care to see that our actions fit in with those of others. When we do, we are 'co-ordinating', and many kinds of joint activity depend greatly on this kind of awareness and disciplined collaboration that has some grasp of and regard for the total outcome of the enterprise.

Another kind of co-ordination takes the form of negotiation and bargaining among units behaving roughly as equals, to try and find a solution that accommodates them all. This is the sort of activity engaged in by an interdepartmental committee.

A further stage is when, in this joint activity, one unit comes to be regarded as having a special responsibility for improving co-ordination, but without having any formal power of veto or coercion. It plays, so to speak the role of chairman, or *primus inter pares*, a term often applied to Prime Ministers and Premiers. Indeed this is one role that a good Prime Minister or Premier plays. As well as being a leader taking initiatives, he is also chairman and co-ordinator of the cabinet, trying 'to combine diverse ambitious and competitive and sometimes conflicting talents into a coherent whole; to balance and to reconcile'.[7] A particular government agency or minister may come to have this kind of co-ordinating responsibility, especially where their main function overlaps with the concerns of many other departments.

A good example is the Department of Foreign Affairs, whose role is 'essentially one of co-ordination'.[8] There are two main reasons for this. In the first place, international and domestic affairs have many points of mutual interaction, so that an important task of the Department of Foreign Affairs is to bring home the international implications of domestic matters that are primarily the concern of other departments, it might be Aboriginal affairs or resources policy, or almost any issue one could name. Secondly, the Department of Foreign Affairs has to see that reasonably consistent overseas policies emerge from the various government agencies directly concerned with foreign countries. This has largely to be done through consultation, as the Department has no formal powers over other agencies. In some matters, such as the conduct of ordinary diplomatic business and aid for developing countries, it is in charge, though it will consult with other agencies as necessary. Other fields of international relations are the responsibility of the Departments of Defence, Trade and Resources, Immigration, and so on, but the Department of Foreign Affairs will expect to be consulted, and also has its own Defence Division and Economic Division to advise it on foreign policy aspects of these fields (conversely, the Department of Defence has a Strategic and International Policy Division, one of whose tasks is to 'handle defence aspects of international relations'). The Secretary to the Department of Foreign Affairs sits on the Defence Committee that advises the Minister for Defence. The Department also provides the chairman and secretariat for a number of interdepartmental committees in its field—in the mid-1970s it was convenor of around twelve, including the interdepartmental committees (IDC's) on the law of the sea, and on Japan.[9]

A more general co-ordinating function of the Department of Foreign Affairs is to act as the main official channel of communications to other governments and to international bodies on matters concerning Australia's overseas interests. Key overseas staff from other departments are sometimes attached to its embassies, and it co-ordinates delegation briefs for most overseas conferences. Foreign Affairs only provides about half of Australia's overseas representation—the rest come from the departments mentioned above, such as the Trade Commissioner Service of the Department of Trade and Resources.

Another recent example is Commonwealth government policy towards industry, which is the concern of several ministers and departments, especially Industry and Commerce, Business and Consumer Affairs, and Productivity. The Prime Minister announced in 1977 that he had asked the Minister for Industry and Commerce 'to undertake an over-riding responsibility in this area and to co-ordinate particularly policy developments within the three departments concerned'.[10] It was not clear that minister concerned would have any formal powers over the other departments, though he had the advantage of being in the cabinet, while they were not. Certainly his permanent head had no authority over theirs. The Coombs Commission suggested that there might be some grouping of related departments in 'functional clusters under the responsibility of one senior Cabinet minister, who would be in charge of one of the departments in the group',[11] and the arrangements just described may be intended as an example of this. A slightly different case arose in 1978 when the Department of Social Security was given responsibility for developing plans and policies in the broad field of health and welfare, and also for the review of existing policies and programmes. A special Social Welfare Policy Secretariat was created within the department to carry out this responsibility. This is getting closer to giving it some formal powers in the fields of the Departments of Health, Veterans' Affairs, Aboriginal Affairs, and so on, though of a 'staff' not a 'line of command' kind; its minister is also in the cabinet, and theirs are mostly not.[11a] It should be added that experience with such co-ordinating ministers and units has not always been happy in other countries, and it will be interesting to see how well these schemes turn out in Australia.

A further stage is where the co-ordinating agency acquires some definite authority over the area and the units it is to co-ordinate. Thus there may be a minister with some authority over several related fields, though the latter each have their own minister or statutory board in immediate charge of them; or there may be a co-ordinating commission with certain powers. In some cases, the co-ordinating authority may be small in numbers, and be concerned with major policy questions, but a minster may occassionally be the apex of an elaborate structure of co-ordination.

Thus the main role of the Ministry of Transport in New South Wales is 'to assist the Minister for Transport and Highways in the implementation, evaluation and co-ordination of transport policy and development in New South Wales'.[12] It had a staff of only 78 in 1976, whereas the statutory bodies that operate the main transport services employ over 60 000. In Canberra the Department of Defence a few years ago had only a small staff of its own, and co-ordinated (mainly through a network of committees) the then existing Departments of Army, Navy and Air Force, which still had their own ministers. Then the Department of Defence began to build up its own staff, and there were also placed under its control various specialised sectors previously the responsibility of the three services. By 1971 it had a staff of over 1600. Two years later the three service departments were abolished, and the Defence Minister assumed direct charge of their functions. In one sense he ceased to be a co-ordinating minister, but only in the sense indicated above. Much co-ordination has, of course, still to go on within the unified department; for example, there are still Air Force, Army and Navy Offices, headed by their own Chiefs of Staff, who have the command of their own forces and help to advise the minister, though they may be over-ridden and are required to consult with the Chief of Defence Force Staff on major matters.

We have briefly explored a variety of methods of co-ordination before mentioning the major formal co-ordinating bodies—cabinets and their committees, Public Service Board, Treasury or Department of Finance, and Prime Minister's and Premier's Departments. There is a good reason for this. It is important to bring out the fact that co-ordination can only to a limited degree be imposed authoritatively from above and that much of it depends on the units concerned developing a variety of co-operative, bargaining and mutually informing relationships.

Over-all Co-ordination

However, there are certain broad questions on which the need has been felt for an over-all co-ordinating body. These questions are of three main types —concerning administration (especially the use of manpower), finance and policy.

In the administrative field, Public Service Boards have certain powers designed to promote the more rational organisation of the various parts of the governmental machine (see Chapter Eleven), though they have not always been given the degree of support that they need for this task. We have also referred (in Chapter Four) to various common service agencies or 'overhead units' that serve the needs of other departments, citing them as examples of process specialisation. In doing so, we were thinking of the advantage of concentrating certain skills and techniques in one department. The case for this is reinforced if such agencies also play an important co-ordinating role, for example, if they satisfy a need for greater uniformity.[13] Thus a body such as the Australian Bureau of Statistics exists to co-ordinate the data collected by or for government agencies generally, and as between States and

Commonwealth, as well as to encourage the use of the best statistical skills and techniques.

Financial co-ordination is necessary to allocate money in due proportion among the many activities of governments, and to keep their total expenditure within available resources. The Treasury or Department of Finance, and ultimately the cabinet, are responsible for making this allocation; the former advise on general economic and financial policy, and relate the expenditure plans of the departments to one another through the Estimates (see Chapter Sixteen). Since much of the money spent by the States is raised through the Commonwealth, there are intergovernmental agencies, notably the Premier's Conference and the Loan Council (see Chapters Seven and Eight), that also play a part in this allocation.

Financial and manpower allocations are closely related to policy co-ordination, since they depend on or often constitute decisions about the relative value and urgency of different programmes. Hence Treasuries may play an important role in policy co-ordination, and sometimes Public Service Boards; in New South Wales the Public Service Board has been a knowledgeable and respected adviser of governments on many policy questions. All governments are helped in policy formation by the Prime Minister's or the Premier's Department, and some of these have become very important agencies in recent years. Their work is discussed below.

There are various problems about central co-ordinating agencies. As mentioned earlier, this kind of co-ordination can be a costly process—it takes up much of the time of able men, and also tends to duplicate staff. If the Department of the Prime Minister and Cabinet (for example) wishes to play this role, it has to use high-level staff to preside over, or attend, many interdepartmental committees; and it needs to duplicate the expertise to be found in other powerful departments, so as to be adequately briefed on the various matters that it is trying to co-ordinate.

A problem about powerful co-ordinating agencies is that in certain ways they may add to co-ordination problems. For example, one of the tasks of a Public Service Board is to co-ordinate the personnel activities of other departments; but the relations between the board and the departments also create new interdependencies and possibilities of conflict and disharmony. This is a truth often neglected by those who think that problems can be solved by the creation of new agencies to co-ordinate some field of activity. They forget that this will raise a new problem of how the new agency fits in with the departments it is supposed to co-ordinate, as well as with other agencies co-ordinating the same departments for other purposes. The multiplicity of co-ordinating agencies often tends to diffuse control and further complicate the system. Thus if someone argues that there are so many different agencies concerned with aspects of economic policy, that it is necessary to have a Department of Economic Planning to act as co-ordinator, one should pause to consider whether such an agency might not become just one more operator in an already overcrowded field.

The significance of this is increased when account is taken of what has been said already about conflict-resolution. One of the great sources of conflict in government is between co-ordinating departments and departments that object to being co-ordinated. A co-ordinating agency is likely to develop its own vested interests and characteristic outlook, possibly very different from that of a department concerned with substantive issues, which resents the imposition on it of what it regards as pointless procedural rules or impracticable policy objectives.

There is the related point made by the Coombs Report, that co-ordinating bodies with authoritative powers such as Public Service Boards and Treasuries may engage in too much externally imposed discipline, and not work enough by co-operation. Indeed the report regards its 'emphasis on the primary responsibility of the individual department or agency for efficient use of resources, and the consequential changes in the role of the co-ordinating authorities, particularly the Treasury and the Public Service Board' as 'perhaps the most significant changes envisaged by the Commission.'[14] The main point is that external discipline over departments has costs because it tends to diminish the sense of responsibility of the agencies controlled, and often leads to tension and hostility. It is better if by some means the various units of government can be brought to see the value of working together, and of voluntarily accepting certain disciplines.[15] Hence a co-ordinating body or group should regard itself as having an 'educating and promotional' role.[16]

Some of this may be a little starry-eyed, and one may suspect that government departments will continue to need a sharp eye kept on them where manpower and money are concerned. Conflicts or potential conflicts are sometimes severe enough for a fairly sharp form of imposed co-ordination to be thought necessary. Consider the case of limited resources. If the government for policy reasons wants sharply to reduce the budget deficit it may find it necesary to impose rigid expenditure limits and staff ceilings on each department. Being a hatchetman is not very creative and may cause more trouble than it is worth in the long run, but that does not dispose of its short term value. Some people would defend it even in the long run, arguing that the interest of many government agencies in maximising inputs (or minimising outputs where they pay few of the costs involved) is sufficiently great for a high degree for control by Treasuries and so on to be permanently necessary. The fact that the latter may in many ways be arbitrary and inefficient controls is not conclusive, if the alternative is even more irrational. Still, the general point that the Coombs Report is making remains true.

The Cabinet as Co-ordinator

The role of most cabinets as co-ordinators and resolvers of conflict is limited. Ministers do not in practice have much sense of collective responsibility for policy, and are rarely well-informed enough about, or willing to give much attention to 'detailed policy formulation in collective arenas';[17] nor have they learned to make proper use even of those central agencies that on paper seem partly designed to serve the whole cabinet, such as the Commonwealth Department of the Prime Minister and Cabinet. The Coombs Report points out that contacts between ministers are actually fewer nowadays than they were in the days when departments were smaller, and ministers less busy. It is true that a certain unity is enforced by the fear of losing office.

The Whitlam government of 1972–75 is a good example of the weaknesses of cabinets as co-ordinators. Its very size (twenty-seven members) made it a poor vehicle for resolving major policy issues, even had that accorded with the Prime Minister's style. So it rarely engaged in general debate, nor was it supplied with the materials for such debate. Ministers attended largely as spokesmen for their own departments. The same is true of many other cabinets, even much smaller ones than this. In such circumstances policy co-ordination either does not happen, or it gets done by someone else— perhaps the Prime Minister or Premier, or a variety of smaller groups of ministers and officials called into existence by the Prime Minister or Premier.

Liberal–National Country Party governments seem to have done a little better. In the 1950s they experimented with inner cabinets, and in 1956 Menzies adopted substantially the present arrangement, of a cabinet with around half the ministers inside, the others called on only when their own field or responsibility was under discussion. There have been few smaller groups of much consequence, though some Prime Ministers have had two or three other influential ministers whom they have regularly consulted; sometimes for a period a ministerial group such as the 1975 Cabinet Expenditures Review Committee (CERC) of the Whitlam government has played an important role. From mid-1975 onwards this five-man committee was for some months the major decision-making body, working closely with a parallel Officials Committee.

Cabinet Committees

Whatever the limitations of cabinets as co-ordinators, they have a good many decisions to take; so it seems natural enough to relieve the strains by delegating some work to smaller cabinet committees, including the ministers most directly concerned. Where there is a distinction between 'cabinet' and 'ministry', such committees may include some ministers not in the cabinet. This has happened in Australia, and both standing and *ad hoc* committees have been established at Commonwealth and State level.

However, attempts to create a full-scale system of standing committees have more than once ended in failure. It is easy for such bodies to complicate the works rather than ease the pressures. Fitting them into the weekly timetable is often difficult, in the press of other business. If their decisions lack authority, this may lead to their discussions being duplicated in the full cabinet, and their members will come to regard them as a waste of time. The Prime Minister may try to avoid this by acting as chairman of important committees, but this adds to his burdens, and he (and other ministers) may also come to feel that the system restricts his own freedom of action. A committee system is always rather unwieldy and slow, it depends on finding consensus (no easy job with some cabinets) and it is not suited to emergencies (of which governments may have a good many). It probably only works well if there is some kind of inner cabinet of a few powerful and like-minded ministers pushing things along, seeing that the committees are well run and have power to act in a good many matters, or if the committees deal mainly with relatively minor or specialised matters that can be fairly easily separated from the main flow of cabinet business.

The first important Commonwealth experiments with standing committees took place during the Second World War.[18] After the war, the Chifley government seems to have made successful use of committees and Menzies also experimented with standing bodies in the early days of his post-war ministry. Under successive non-Labor governments, the standing committee system seems to have declined in importance. However, the Foreign Affairs and Defence Committee which Menzies created remained in existence, though often inactive. Menzies had earlier set up a General Administrative Committee to deal with more routine items of business and a Legislation Committee to review draft bills before they were introduced into Parliament and to arrange the parliamentary programme. All three exist today.

In 1972, the large Whitlam cabinet planned to make more systematic use of standing committees than its predecessor. It began with five committees, Economic, Foreign Affairs and Defence, Urban and Regional Development, Welfare, Legislation;[19] the Prime Minister was chairman of the first three. They did not fulfill the hopes placed on them, partly for reasons already stated. Some became too big and unwieldy, especially the Economic Committee. The Foreign Affairs and Defence Committee met very infrequently; the others had largely faded out by 1974, except for the Legislation Committee, which was doing a useful task that could more readily be delegated, and most of whose decisions did not go to the cabinet for confirmation. In the later stages of the Whitlam government, more use was made of small *ad hoc* committees and of groups formally outside the cabinet committee framework, though related to it, such as the Cabinet Expenditures Review Committee mentioned earlier, which had a powerful say in vetoing expenditure proposals.

The Fraser government has also created a system of standing committees, and (so far as can be judged from outside) seems to be using it more successfully than its predecessor, though it looks rather complicated on paper. In 1978 there were ten main committees—Planning and Co-ordination, Foreign Affairs and Defence, Intelligence and Security, Machinery of Government, Monetary Policy, Wages Policy, Government Purchasing, Social Welfare Policy, General Administrative, and Legislation. The Prime Minister is chairman of the first five, and seems to keep firm control over agendas and referrals, Mr Lynch (Industry and Commerce) of four, and Mr Sinclair (Primary Industry) of the last. They and Mr Anthony (Deputy Prime

Minister and Minister for Trade and Resources) and Mr Howard (Treasurer) are all members of the nine-man Planning and Coordination Committee, whose task is to facilitate the co-ordination of the government's medium and long-term activities. Membership varies between seven and eleven, except for the General Administrative Committee which deals with 'matters not involving major policy initiatives or of significant economic or financial consequences', and which is a kind of second-tier cabinet of nineteen members, including all the ministers outside the cabinet proper as well as some in the cabinet. The cabinet gave up its Economic Committee because 'it touched on so many portfolios that it became akin to Cabinet itself'.[20]

Ministerial Committees and Officials

The best-recognised role of officials at meetings of the cabinet and other ministerial committees is to attend to take the minutes and record decisions (most States do not like officials at ministerial meetings even in this capacity). Here is an account of Commonwealth procedures in 1975:

> The recording of Cabinet decisions was done by officers of the Department of the Prime Minister and Cabinet. Three officers (including the Secretary of the department) usually attended and sat at three small tables at corners of the rooms . . . [Sometimes this] could entail asking the Prime Minister to clarify points or using breaks in the session to take informal soundings . . . In some cases where confusion reigned they still had to produce something that looked as if Cabinet had made an implementable decision. Post-cabinet consultations could involve the Prime Minister and several ministers and heads of departments . . . Decisions were circulated before the Prime Minister had seen them, but if there was any argument about a decision he would have the final say . . . Where decisions could be subject to various interpretations, the views of the recording officers were extremely influential.[21]

Apart from this, the participation of officials in ministerial committee work may be of various kinds. They may as individuals prepare papers. They often form an officials' committee, meeting separately to assist the ministerial committee with information and advice. They may be called in to the committee itself to provide information or to give advice on a particular matter. More rarely they may attend with ministers, to brief them and possibly also take some part in general discussion. The last of these was not uncommon during the Chifley Labor government; the Prime Minister encouraged ministers to bring officials to meetings of cabinet committees. 'Occasionally the Cabinet room looked as though a popular seminar were being held.'[22] Chifley seems to have had a special talent for handling this kind of group, and there were two other factors not easy to reproduce now —one was the much smaller size of the system, the other a greater degree of community of feeling in the 'official family', partly built up during the war.

The practice of officials attending cabinet committee meetings with ministers continued for a time in the Menzies period, then faded out.[23] There were thoughts of reviving it in 1972 but this came to nothing. It seems even to have remained rare for public servants to be called in to ministerial discussions to deal with specific points. Ministers have not in general favoured the idea of officials attending cabinet committees on a regular basis. This is partly because ministers are political creatures, and their debates tend to become political debates, in which they find the presence of officials inhibiting. Mr Crean (Commonwealth Treasurer, 1972–74) has

> described a couple of occasions on which Sir Frederick [Wheeler, Secretary to the Treasury] was invited to attend Cabinet. The thing was a flop because some colleagues kept blowing off on the thesis that the Treasury was out to nobble the Government.[24]

The present Prime Minister (1978) has made it clear that, if an official should attend a cabinet meeting, it would be 'to inform, not to debate', and once having given his information, he would normally withdraw.[25] It is said that the presence of officials makes some ministers feel insecure, as they do not wish to be shown up to their colleagues as less effective than their officials. Yet a Canadian permanent head has said that greater participation of public servants in ministerial committees there has given ministers more influence on policy and officials less; it has led to more 'probing of officials by ministers; less monolithic advice from the bureaucracy; more consideration of issues beyond departmental boundaries; and a greater ability of ministers to send a matter back to a department for further work or for the development of a different proposal'.[26]

In Australia it has seemed easiest for ministers and officials to come together 'to work out a package', to develop joint policies in a crisis or on some specific matter, as did the committee of the Chifley era that processed GATT (the General Agreement on Tariffs and Trade). It is harder for joint committees to sustain a continuing existence covering some general policy area. All the same it is rather baffling why permanent heads and other senior officials have not participated more in ministerial discussions. Certainly anyone who believes that greater attention needs to be given to the interdependencies of decision-making, both across departments, and as between policy-making and implementation, should encourage the development of more joint ministerial–official committees, and moves in this direction should not be inhibited by rigid views about the line between policy and administration. The Coombs Report has developed this point—it argues that the presence of officials at cabinet committees 'can frequently provide ministers with additional resources and bring under notice administrative matters'.[27] In its proposals for forward estimating, it makes considerable provision for joint bodies of this kind. Under the Fraser government, there seems to have been some revival of the practice of senior officials sitting in on cabinet committee meetings, at least 'to provide on the spot advice on specific issues, though such attendance is more likely at meetings of short term committees set up to examine particular matters'.[28]

It was mentioned earlier that a commoner device in Australia has been to have separate official committees working in parallel with committees of ministers, and supporting them with information and advice. Thus, alongside the Machinery of Government Committee of the Commonwealth Cabinet, there is (1978) a small Permanent Heads Committee. Some people are apprehensive that the official committees 'will not only predigest issues but also remove them substantially from ministers' control',[29] but there seems no evidence that they are such dangerous animals.

Interdepartmental Committees[30]

Below the level of the cabinet and its associated ministerial and official committees, there are many committees designed to bring together senior officers from different departments. These are commonly called inter-departmental committees (IDCs for short), but they may also have titles like 'working party', 'study group' and so on. The basic reason for their establishment is that many issues overlap a number of government agencies, and there is a need for more administrative co-ordination or for better co-ordination of policy-making. They may be standing committees, like the Defence Committee, that sometimes remain in existence for many years; or *ad hoc* committees set up to advise ministers on a particular problem.

Between June 1974 and December 1975 there existed at least 180 Commonwealth IDCs, in about equal numbers standing and *ad hoc*.[31] Only a third were initiated by ministers, more commonly the initiative was at the official level, with one of the major departments (say Foreign Affairs, Prime Minister's or Treasury) faced with an overlap situation and seeking a way to resolve the problem or sort out a conflict. Sometimes the officials concerned may get together to keep the matter away from the government. A fairly typical IDC would have representatives from five or six government agencies, often including the Prime Minister's Department and the Treasury. The members would rarely be permanent heads, but usually Second Division or top Third Division officers. IDC reports are hardly ever published, and even their existence may be kept secret.

Some IDCs deal with fairly straightforward matters of administrative co-ordination, such as those convened by the Department of Administrative Services (say, on car parking facilities), or committees to co-ordinate the building needs and programmes of government agencies. Others may be concerned with important forms of policy negotiation and the setting of guidelines for future relations between departments, or be like the 'troika' (permanent heads of Finance, Treasury and Reserve Bank Governor) that determines, within a formula laid down, variations in the Australian exchange rate. Terms of references may be specific, or very vague. Thus an IDC on Japan set up in 1970 with cabinet approval was asked 'to examine how policy towards Japan might best be co-ordinated',[32] and to report on the policy implications of nine objectives. This was broad enough for different departments each to see it in a different light, as suited their interests. Foreign Affairs thought it should be a major policy formulator, Trade saw it simply as a means of exchanging views and information. Cabinet had indicated that it would consist of permanent heads or their deputies, but in several cases this did not happen. A department can signal its view of an IDC by who it sends along. Departments commonly think of their IDC members as delegates, there to argue the departmental brief, not to develop views of their own; one symptom of this is a ready disposition to change their representatives. In the case of the IDC on Japan, only one member attended all seven meetings; and its successor, the Standing IDC on Japan (1971–74) had 139 participants at its nineteen meetings, 80 of whom attended only one meeting each, and only 6 of whom attended more than half.

The Coombs Commission was a forum for much criticism of IDCs as instruments for policy formulation. The Department of Foreign Affairs submission said that they were often not only cumbersome and slow, 'but their recommendations are ultra-cautious, merely reflecting the lowest common denominator of agreement. In many cases, their written reports are too long, complex and imprecisely phrased, being designed to paper over differences in the search for a fragile consensus.'[33] A Report to the Coombs Commission agreed that IDCs had considerable limitations as instruments of policy-making. They were better at administrative co-ordination, but even there the same results could often be obtained in more informal ways.[34]

It is probably true that a committee of departmental delegates is not a good source of clear and unambiguous policy advice, or good at settling serious conflicts, or producing major new initiatives. However, Painter and Carey argue that this is not necessarily the only purpose of such an IDC —its main purpose ought to be regarded as to get departments working together more effectively, and such an aim might be achieved even if the group only succeeds in clarifying differences of view and areas of disagreement, or in bringing out the implications of some proposed policy for existing departmental programmes and practices. This is a way of saying that we should not expect too much from IDCs as a co-ordinating device, or more generally that we should not think of co-ordination as an all-or-nothing affair.

Some people would like to draw a clearer distinction between the ordinary IDC which public servants attend as representatives of their departments, and the Task Force, to which officials and other members are appointed as individuals having relevant skills and knowledge. The Coombs Report suggests that in some policy areas more use of the latter is desirable, in which the group would clearly be expected to come up with well-thought-out and agreed-upon policy recommendations.[35] The composition of an IDC, as of other committees, can sometimes be manipulated. Thus in 1977 the Treasury was not represented on the IDC set up to report on the future role of the Industries Assistance Commission, presumably because it was thought likely to oppose any reduction in the power of the latter, which the government appeared to want.[36]

The Department of the Prime Minister and Cabinet

One consequence of the greater modern need for policy co-ordination, and the failure of existing instruments to achieve it, has been the growing power of the Department of the Prime Minister and Cabinet, and of some State Premiers' Departments. The former's role is defined in very broad terms, as: 'policy advising for the Prime Minister; secretariat services to Cabinet and its Committees; co-ordination of Government Administration; policy and program development and evaluation . . . '[37] It is also a main channel for relations with the State governments.

This description already indicates that it is in an important sense the Prime Minister's Department (which was in fact its official title until 1971), especially where policy is concerned; if we compare it with the British Cabinet Office, it is much more the instrument of one man, and its broad charter gives the Prime Minister a good deal of freedom to use it as he wishes.

A Prime Minister's Office was created in the Department of External Affairs in 1904. A separate Prime Minister's Department was established in 1911, but for many years its main concern was relations with the United Kingdom and with the Australian States. It also acted, as it still does, as the department to which independent statutory authorities such as the Public Service Board and the Auditor-General were loosely attached. Its role as a general co-ordinating body started to develop in a modest way during the Second World War, when its Secretary began to attend cabinet meetings to record decisions. After 1949 it became a full Cabinet Office, engaged in drafting and circulating agenda, handling submissions to cabinets and cabinet committees, recording decisions and passing these on to ministers. This role has itself given the department an important means of bringing order to cabinet business and exerting various other kinds of influence. The Secretary to the Prime Minister's Department became the official in closest touch with cabinet proceedings, often an interpreter to departments of cabinet thinking, a source of guidance and promoter of compromise. He was also in a good position to become adviser to the Prime Minister on everything from the membership of committees to the attitudes of various departments or the best tactic for achieving some policy objective. This kind of co-ordinating role, especially as a quiet and conservative umpire and persuader, was well-handled by Sir John Bunting, who headed the department (with a short interregnum) from 1959 to 1974. A later permanent head has claimed that it still operates in a lower-key way in cabinet business than the British Cabinet secretariat, which 'interferes far more' in, for example, the drafting of cabinet submissions.[38] Even if true, this is not inconsistent with the Australian department being more powerful in other ways.

When Mr Gorton became Prime Minister in 1968 he wanted a department that was more of a policy initiator, a channel through which the Prime

Minister could get expert advice that would increase his personal influence over policy. Bunting remained as Cabinet Secretary, but a Treasury officer was made Secretary of a separate Prime Minister's Department; other new staff were imported, the Economic Division was expanded and new divisions appeared for external relations and defence, and for welfare. However, this phase was shortlived. When Gorton resigned in 1971, the department received its present title and Bunting returned to his former role.

After the Whitlam government came to power in 1972, it at first sought policy initiatives from new agencies and units rather than from existing departments, and no one seemed much bothered about the problem of co-ordination. Though the department expanded, it also found itself flanked by influential newcomers, in the personal staff of the Prime Minister's Office, the Priorities Review Staff, and elsewhere. However, by late 1974 the Prime Minister felt the need for a more regularised, at the same time active, source of policy co-ordination and initiative. Bunting was replaced by an outside appointee, Mr John Menadue, and other effective senior appointments were made and their capacities expertly deployed. As a result the department considerably increased its influence on policy, through such means as comment on cabinet submissions by other departments, the co-ordination of advice in particular policy areas, increased representation on interdepartmental committees, some initiatives of its own, and the oversight of cabinet decisions already taken.

This new role has been extended under Mr Fraser and the department has acquired some of the flavour of an American Presidential Office, allowing for differences in national temperament. Menadue was in due course replaced by a permanent head with long experience in economic departments; his successor in 1978 was an old hand in the Prime Minister's Department. Its main divisions include the Cabinet Division, to service the cabinet and its committees; a number of substantive divisions, each mainly concerned with the co-ordination of advice in the various policy areas—Welfare; Economic; Trade and Industry; International; Resources and Development; and so on. There is also a Parliamentary and Government Division dealing with Executive Council matters and relations with Parliament—from the programming of legislation to briefing the Prime Minister on parliamentary questions—and which also services the Premiers' Conferences. The Operations Division has the task of identifying, in consultation with other branches, the priority programme areas in need of review, of undertaking selected reviews, and maintaining documentation on the government's general strategy.

Perhaps the greatest recent change in the department's position has been associated with the decline in power of the Treasury, especially since the latter was divided in 1976. In the Menzies era the Treasury emerged as virtually the only general policy co-ordinator, as the cabinet committee system decayed and the Prime Minister's Department claimed only a modest role. Now the latter is not only a major general co-ordinating department, but is important in economic policy-making and in the budgetary process and expenditure reviews, with a sizeable and capable staff of economic advisers of its own, some of them recruited from the Treasury. It has intervened in a number of other areas of special interest to the Prime Minister, for example, it became much involved in the co-ordination and presentation of the government's uranium policy. In 1977 one of its Deputy Secretaries chaired the IDC which enquired into the Industries Assistance Commission. In 1977, the central divisions of the department employed 573 public servants, of whom 43 were Second Division Officers. The ability of the department to have a say in virtually any field of policy, and its closeness to the Prime Minister, give it important natural advantages over its competitors. However, such power has still to be used selectively to be effective; and a department with a relatively small staff in any particular field will often be at some disadvantage in relation to the senior officers of other major departments, each with their command over special expertise, and experience and control of important channels of policy implementation. It is important for such a department to concentrate on a few things, and not try to 'second guess' other departments on too many issues. Otherwise, instead of being a useful co-ordinator and unifier of government, it could end by slowing everything up. The Coombs Commission thought that departmental positions should be filled partly on rotation from other departments, which would develop the talents and broaden the outlook of promising officers, prevent it becoming too entrenched and powerful at the expense of other agencies, and also promote understanding of the need for co-ordination in departments generally.[39]

A related issue is how far such a department is at the disposal of the Prime Minister, how far of ministers generally. One way it can serve the latter, apart from the usual work of the Cabinet Division, is for each policy division to develop links with a cabinet committee, to make sure that the committee has the relevant information and departmental views on the issues before it. The Coombs Report favoured this, and said moves were already being taken in this direction. It has been argued in the past that the department can perform this kind of co-ordinating role best if it is regarded as 'neutral', not with strong policy predispositions of its own.

The Department of the Prime Minister and Cabinet is only one of a number of units linked with the Prime Minister. First, over the years a number of new functions of government have been placed initially in agencies under the wing of the Prime Minister, though later often hived off elsewhere (this has happened to environmental protection, government support for the arts, Aboriginal affairs, women's affairs).[40] Secondly, one or two statutory authorities which have been given an exceptional degree of autonomy are associated with the Prime Minister, such as the Public Service Board, the Auditor-General's Office and the Commonwealth Ombudsman. The first two of these also have an important co-ordinating function in their own field. Thirdly, there are other staff units of the Prime Minister, including his personal staff. While in some respects the Prime Minister's Department has become a staff unit of the Prime Minister, it is important to distinguish this kind of 'institutionalised staff unit',[41] manned by career public servants and with its own formal structure, from the personal staff assistance now available to the Prime Minister, more of whom come from outside the public service, and whom he can use as flexibly as he pleases.

Co-ordination within States

There have been some bad examples of lack of co-ordination at the State level. In particular many States have lacked effective central units, other than the Premier himself, especially in the fields dominated by statutory authorities. This has reflected itself in unco-ordinated capital works programmes, transport and land use planning. The growth of *ad hoc* federal interventions in State affairs (discussed in Chapters Seven and Eight) has sometimes reinforced this lack of co-ordination.

State cabinets seem rarely to have played an important co-ordinating role. Ministers tend to be dominated by the concerns of their own departments, and some State cabinets are probably too large for effective work; a number of them have doubled in size since the Second World War. States have often depended on having a strong and active Premier. Premier's Departments have developed (the New South Wales Premier's Department dates from 1909) and in recent years one or two have come to play a major co-ordinating role—before that Premiers usually relied on their personal influence and their control of the Treasury to effect needed co-ordination.

The South Australian Premier's Department used to be mainly concerned with providing a secretariat for the Premier, but its staff grew from 12 in 1965 to 203 in 1975. It now includes a Cabinet Secretariat, a Policy Division, an Economic Intelligence Unit, a Media Co-ordination Unit, and an Arts Development Branch. The Policy Division undertakes research and reports on policy proposals as requested, and this has become a major task of the department. It also services the Planning and Priorities Advisory Committee, whose members are the Minister for Planning, the Under Treasurer, the Chairman of the Public Service Board and the Permanent Head of the Premier's Department, with two other permanent heads and the Premier as chairman.

More recently, the New South Wales Premier's Department has expanded its co-ordinating functions, especially under the Wran government of 1976. (Some of the units attached to it are listed in Chapter Three.) Its Cabinet and Parliamentary Division advises the Premier on cabinet matters, services the cabinet and its committees, and 'co-ordinates the activities of departments in relation to the preparation of legislation'. The recently created Policy Co-ordination, Analysis and Research Division is intended to play a similar role to its South Australian counterpart, and is responsible 'for co-ordination and analysis of aspects of Government policy, programmes and undertakings'.[42]

State cabinets also make use of cabinet committees. All have made use of *ad hoc* committees from time to time, to report on a particular current issue. Thus two recent cabinet 'subcommittees' in New South Wales have been concerned with the problems of the Newcastle dockyard and with expressways. Some cabinets have also experimented with standing committee systems. When Mr Lewis became Premier of New South Wales in 1974 he set up five standing committees of four or five ministers each, and himself chaired a Policies and Priorities Committee. Senior officers in the Premier's Department acted as committee secretaries. This committee system has been praised by the former Under-Secretary to the Premier's Department,[43] but other observers found it unnecessarily complex and productive of delay. One important effect seems to have been to curb the power of the Premier in certain areas, though this might have happened anyway after the reign of Sir Robert Askin. The latter had taken many decisions on his own initiative, and in particular had settled most budgetary questions by direct discussion with Treasury officials. The Policy and Priorities Committee came to play a more important role in such matters (see Chapter Sixteen). Though Mr Wran appeared to have let the system lapse when he first took office as Premier in 1976, the cabinet committee system has since been reinstated, including the Policies and Priorities Committee.

In Victoria Mr Hamer between 1974 and 1976 constructed an elaborate structure of cabinet committees, crowned by a Policy and Priority Review Committee chaired by the Premier, and a parallel Policy and Priority Review Board (which the Premier also chaired), including senior officials and private sector representatives. A State Co-ordination Council was also established in the Premier's Department, to advise the Premier on major planning and development proposals, and the Department has a Research and Policy Division.

There are a large number of IDCs in the States, both standing and *ad hoc*. Thus in the mid-1970s (to mention a few at random) New South Wales had IDCs on the care of the aged, dental health, grain transport, the planning and development of port facilities and the protection of coastal lands. There is a State Development Co-ordinating Committee, which includes the heads of the major State departments and agencies. It may be convened by any minister and deals with problems relating to development projects on which it had been asked to report. The Inter-Departmental Standing Committee on the Handicapped, advising on the co-ordination of services and grants to other organisations, includes such New South Wales Departments as Youth and Community Services (which provides the staff), Health Commission, Education, Treasury; it is in turn advised by regional committees and by a Consultative Council on the Handicapped which also represents outside groups. The Urban Transport Advisory Committee (URTAC) representing the main agencies concerned with transport and planning has some achievements to its credit.

Special co-ordinating machinery has also developed in the States to cover particular fields, or to settle conflicts and promote joint action between State and Commonwealth agencies (some devices used for this latter purpose are discussed in Chapter Eight).

Thus the development of the irrigation areas in the Murray–Murrumbidgee basin has involved the co-operation and co-ordinated action of many State and Commonwealth agencies. To regulate the Murray's total flow there is the River Murray Commission, a joint agency of the Commonwealth and three States. State water authorities have had to co-operate with many other agencies. In New South Wales the work of the Water Resources Commission (formerly Water Conservation and Irrigation Commission) has involved co-operation with the State Department of Lands in developing holdings for settlement; with the Commonwealth's Snowy Mountains Authority on problems of diverting Snowy waters into the Murray and Murrumbidgee systems and its effect on irrigation; with elected local councils and land boards in the irrigation areas; with the CSIRO and State Departments of Agriculture on soil surveys, irrigation research and extension services; with the Forestry Commission and Rural Bank; and with many private citizens' associations concerned with development of these areas.

In some States there are special kinds of co-ordinating authority. In Queensland, the Co-ordinator-General's Department under the Premier has in recent years played a very important role in appraising major investment projects, and the Co-ordinator-General has been described as the most powerful official in the State. In New South Wales the State Pollution Control Commission has the task of co-ordinating the activities of all public authorities in this field, and in certain circumstances may direct other agencies to take anti-pollution measures. In the field of New South Wales transport, as well as a co-ordinating Ministry and an important interdepartmental committee (the Urban Transport Advisory Committee) there is a Traffic Authority representing relevant government agencies, but with a full-time director and statutory powers over road closures and traffic systems.

The various State planning authorities. (see Chapter Nine) have an important co-ordinating role, as many departments and agencies are involved in land use planning. So the planning authority's plans have to tie in with those of other agencies concerned with transport, housing, water and sewerage, education, hospitals, and so on. It is extremely hard to prevent the latter working in watertight compartments. Even if the planning agency has wide statutory powers, it has some natural disadvantages—urban planning is not a powerful technology, in the sense that the advantages of any particular plan (or even of planning itself) can be shown in conclusive way. So a planning agency is often at a disadvantage in relation to a highly developed technology, such as highway or water engineering. Nor does it usually in Australia have any money to give away to which conditions might be attached, or any functional responsibility of its own (such as housing) which might give it extra weight. So its effectiveness depends very much on strong political and public support, which is not often forthcoming.

Co-ordination and Power

This should remind us about a very important aspect of co-ordination already referred to—that it is often concerned with getting the co-ordinated to do what they do not (initially at least) want to do. Its success depends greatly on how far the co-ordinator possesses superior resources and skills, and these include access to political support from the government, relevant interest groups, and so on. Control of some solid resource, such as Finance, is very important to a co-ordinating body. This raises interesting issues, which we cannot pursue here, about what influences 'the capacity to co-ordinate', in the phrase of Leon Peres.[44] As he says, insofar as power is a scarce commodity, and co-ordination is a function of power, a reasonable hypothesis might be that co-ordinating capacity is scarce. A co-ordinating unit without the resources for 'hard' co-ordination may need to practise 'soft' co-ordination, for example, try to call attention to unsolved problems, to create a good climate for discussion and the exchange of information, then perhaps develop attractive policies and by degrees mobilise support for them. This chapter will not have been successful if it has not conveyed some sense of the manifold ways of achieving better co-ordination. All of them may have to be used, and choosing the right mixture is a problem of the greatest difficulty in modern government.

Notes

1. Leon Peres, 'A Note on the Trend Report', *Public Admin.* (Sydney), XXIII, 3, September 1964, 253; cf. Jeffrey L. Pressman and Aaron B. Wildavsky, *Implementation*, University of California Press, Berkeley, 1973, 134–5.
2. Report, RCAGA, 389.
3. cf. J.Q. Wilson and P. Rachal, 'Can the Government Regulate Itself?', *The Public Interest*, 46, Winter 1977, 3–14.
4. *ibid.*, 4.
5. C.E. Lindblom, *The Intelligence of Democracy*, Free Press, New York, 1965, 154.
6. For discussion, see J.G. March and H.A. Simon, *Organizations*, Wiley, New York, 1958, 25–9, 158 ff.
7. Report, RCAGA, 379–80.
8. *ibid.*, 333.
9. Based on RCAGA 1974 survey.
10. Prime Minister, quoted in *Australian Financial Review*, 20 December 1977.
11. Report, RCAGA, 78.
11a. However the relevant ministers do belong to a Social Welfare Policy Committee, and the Secretariat works to this cabinet committee, and a parallel committee of permanent heads.
12. *The Government of New South Wales: Directory of Administration and Services, 1977–1978*, Government Printer, Sydney, 1977, 339.

13. cf. P. Self, *Administrative Theory and Politics*, Allen and Unwin, London, 1972, 137.
14. Report, RCAGA, 410.
15. *Ibid.*, 356, 389.
16. *Ibid.*, 389.
17. M. Painter and B. Carey, *Politics between Departments: The Fragmentation of Executive Control in Australian Government*, University of Queensland Press, St Lucia, 1979.
18. On ·the war, see P. Hasluck, *The Government and the People, 1939–1941*, Australian War Memorial, Canberra, 1952, ch. 11; on Chifley, see L.F. Crisp, 'Central Co-ordination of Commonwealth Policy-Making', *Public Admin.* (Sydney), XXVI, 1, March 1967.
19. A Forward Estimates Committee was also established, but quickly died. For a fuller account of their failure, see Report, RCAGA, Appendix Vol. Four, 195–6.
20. J.M. Fraser, 'Responsibility in Government', *Aust. J. Public Admin.*, XXXVII, 1, March 1978, 10. (The Prime Minister's Garran Oration.)
21. R.F.I. Smith, in Report, RCAGA, Appendix Vol. Four, 204–5.
22. L.F. Crisp, *Ben Chifley*, Longmans, London, 1960, 258.
23. See 'Commonwealth Policy Co-ordination', *Public Admin.* (Sydney), XIV, 4, December 1955; L.F. Crisp, 'Central Co-ordination of Commonwealth Policy-Making', *Public Admin.* (Sydney) XXVI, 1, March 1967; and R.F.I. Smith, 'Australian Cabinet Structure and Procedures', in Report, RCAGA, Appendix Vol. Four, 190–211.
24. Interview in *The Age*, 30 May 1975.
25. J.M. Fraser, *op. cit.*, 11.
26. G. Robertson, 'The Prime Minister, The Cabinet and the Privy Council Office', in W.D.K. Kernaghan (ed.), *Bureaucracy in Canadian Government*, 2nd edn, Methuen, Toronto, 1973, 57.
27. Report, RCAGA, 383.
28. J.M. Fraser, *loc. cit.*
29. Report, RCAGA, Appendix Vol. Four, 197.
30. See Painter and Carey, *op. cit.*, from which much of this section is drawn.
31. Based on an RCAGA survey by Mr Bernard Carey, and the figures were almost certainly incomplete. There is no official list of IDCs.
32. See T.V. Matthews, 'The IDC on Japan (1970–71)', in Report, RCAGA, Appendix Vol. Four, 293–300.
33. As quoted in *The Australian*, 22 November 1974.
34. See Report, RCAGA, Appendix Vol. Four, 337, 306.
35. Report, RCAGA, 386; cf. Appendix Vol. Four, 338.
36. See *Australian Financial Review*, 31 August 1977.
37. *Commonwealth Government Directory*, Canberra, 1977, 217. On it, see also F.A. Mediansky and J.A. Nockles, 'The Prime Minister's Bureaucracy', *Public Admin.* (Sydney), XXXIV, 3, September 1975; L.F. Crisp, 'Central Co-ordination of Policy-Making', *Public Admin.* (Sydney), XXVI, 1, March 1967; and Crisp, *Australian National Government*, 3rd edn, Longmans, Hawthorn, Victoria, 1973.
38. Alan Carmody, interview in *The Age*, 11 October 1977.
39. cf. Report, RCAGA, 382–3.
40. Report, RCAGA, 380; and cf. Chapter Three of this book.

41. The phrase is Peter Self's; see *Administrative Theories and Politics*, Allen and Unwin, London, 1972, 124.
42. *The Government of New South Wales: Directory of Administration and Services, 1977–78*, Government Printer, Sydney, 1977, 227, 228.
43. B.R. Davies, 'The Impact of a Cabinet Review', *Aust. J. Public Admin.* XXV, 1, March 1976. I have been greatly assisted by reading G.R. Pratt's unpublished M.Econ. thesis, 'Organisational Change in New South Wales Government Agencies', Department of Government, University of Sydney, Sydney, 1978.
44. L. Peres, 'So Where's the Co-ordination Capacity Coming From?', in R.F.I. Smith and Patrick Weller (eds), *Public Service Inquiries in Australia*, University of Queensland Press, St Lucia, 1978, ch. 17.

Chapter Sixteen

Budgeting and Financial Management

The financial objectives of government agencies have traditionally been seen as different from those of business. Most governmental units do not aim at profit, but at financing services that parliament and the government have decided to provide. The budgetary and financial system exists partly to ensure the government's accountability to parliament for its financial activities, to see that monies voted by the legislature are not misused. Hence government budgeting and accounting procedures differ from those of business, though there is an approach to commercial practice in government business enterprises.[1]

One important difference is that the funds allotted to government are to a significant extent 'temporary' funds, available for expenditure within a set period. Annually each of the seven governments in Australia submits budget documents to its legislature. These show receipts and payments during the preceding year, estimate future expenditure and make proposals for financing this. Presentation of the annual budget is one of the major events in the parliamentary year. It is much more than an outline of the government's past and proposed financial dealings. It is a plan, indicating how the government intends to carry into effect its political, social and economic aims. The estimates of expenditure are the best expression available of government priorities. Similarly proposals for financing expenditures reflect opinions about how the 'burden' should be shared among different sections of the community.

The budget is also a good example of the intermingling of planning and control. A budget is a plan; but the budgetary process can also act as a control, a device for checking up on departmental spending and taking corrective action. This is true even while the budget is being prepared. The pre-budgetary contacts with government agencies are one of the main ways in which the Treasury or Department of Finance can judge what is happening and advise the government on possible courses of corrective action. Once the budget exists, there is a further process of controlling expenditure, so that it conforms to the plan.

Nowadays it is common for monthly comparisons of actual transactions to be compared with the expected monthly pattern according to the estimates, and for serious differences to be investigated to see what action is required. The plan itself may need to be revised to take account of miscalculations or changing circumstances. Opportunities for saving, or the need for supplementary expenditures, arise and these adjustments go on throughout the year. Parliamentary approval of additional expenditure is generally sought in one package, the Additional Appropriation Bills passed around May. Occasionally substantial changes of the budget plans of some governments, though not in New South Wales, are made through a Supplementary Budget. In any case, changes of government policy or of economic conditions in the months after the budget considerably affect the overall balance. There is nothing surprising about this, nor is it necessarily a sign of incompetence.

Financial planning and control are basic to government, as money is the only common measure to which government activities can be reduced. The best way of approaching the selection of alternatives is often to express them in terms of money costs and benefits. There can be a surprising amount of resistance to this, either on the ground that the costs and benefits are immeasurable, or even (in the case of some social services) that it is immoral to attempt to measure them. This leads to much avoidable irrationality. One difficulty about operating budgetary controls is that, for full effect, they need relating both to centres of responsibility, and to clearly defined programmes. The first is needed to check on people, the second to check on task-achievement.

Some writers would criticise what we have said so far, on the ground that it assumes that budgeting is, at any rate in principle, a rational process, one by which the benefits of different courses of action can be objectively evaluated by a central agency. From another viewpoint budgeting can be seen as largely the outcome of political bargaining between interested parties, and of other similar processes.[2] Believers in the potential rationality of budgeting sometimes advocate more unified control of the process, by the Treasury or some other agency. Others may see the same increase of control as a political move, the effect of which will be to help some interests at the expense of others.

Budget Formulation

In budget preparation there are three main levels of responsibility. The first is departmental; the second is that of the budget agency; the third in Australia is the level of cabinet and parliament. Preliminary estimates of resources and requirements are made by the operating departments and agencies. The budget agency reviews these estimates through consultations with the departments and combines them into a preliminary budget for submission to cabinet. Ministers may separately submit proposals to cabinet in relation to new programmes. Cabinet determines the final budget put to the legislature. This bold outline conceals many procedural variations, and differences in budgetary philosophy and approach.

The Departments

The departmental organisation for preparing draft estimates is often fairly simple.[3] In small departments the finance officer normally has all the necessary data at hand, and can readily consult other officers to settle doubtful points; even in the larger departments his general knowledge and experience enable him to estimate accurately many items of revenue and expenditure. In doing so he, with the permanent head and one or two other senior public servants, will draw on reports by divisional or branch officers outlining any special needs or circumstances affecting their part of the department's activities. The assistance of technical branches will be especially important where capital budgeting is concerned. If the department is organised on a regional basis subsidiary estimates will be needed for activities at the regional level; this seldom creates difficulties in the Australian States, where regional agencies rarely have much independence, although this is now changing in a few fields, such as the health regions in New South Wales. Some departments have an estimates committee, which looks at the final drafts before they go to the Treasury.

The Role of the Treasury or Department of Finance

Most interest centres on the second level of budget preparation, that of the central budget agency. In the States this department is the Treasury; the Commonwealth now has two departments, the Treasury and the Department of Finance, and it is the latter that handles the details of the budget expenditures and non-tax revenues, the former is more concerned with general budgetary and economic policy and taxation measures. The functions of these departments vary in detail between governments, but include: advising on general financial and economic policy; controlling expenditure and revenue collection; managing the public debt; preparing tax and loan proposals; prescribing rules for government accounting. So the Treasury or Department of Finance is in part a department like other departments, with its own special tasks, but it is also responsible for controlling and co-ordinating the expenditures of other departments, and for advising the Treasurer or Minister for Finance and (through him) the cabinet on such questions.

The structure of the two Commonwealth departments reflects these functions. The Commonwealth Treasury is organised in five divisions, General Financial and Economic Policy, Overseas Economic Relations, Revenue Loans and Investment, Financial Institutions and Foreign Investment. The first is concerned with broad aspects of domestic economic policy, including taxation, monetary and budget policy, and research into problems of economic efficiency and growth. The second is responsible for external economic policy, including balance of payments issues, relations with international economic bodies, and so on. Revenue Loans and Investment handles government borrowing, and financial relations with the states and local government. Financial Institutions is concerned with banks and other financial organisations and activities, Foreign Investment with advice on regulating overseas investment in Australia. The Department of Finance also contains five Divisions—Accounting and Supply, General Expenditure, Defence and Works, Social Security, Transport and Industry—all concerned with detailed aspects of the traditional 'Treasury' function of examination, review, evaluation and monitoring of government expenditure proposals and programmes. Accounting and Supply is also responsible for preparing the government accounts and prescribing rules for departmental accounting. The General Expenditure Division is a co-ordinator and policy adviser on overall public expenditures, in the short-term and in relation to medium-term forward estimates.

The structure of State Treasuries is simpler. The best-developed, the New South Wales Treasury, is headed by an under secretary, who is also Comptroller of Accounts and State Co-ordinator of Works. There are two deputy under secretaries and two assistant under secretaries. The four main branches are Accounts, Administrative, the Budget Branch, the work of which is discussed below, and the Economist's Branch, established in 1969 to meet the growing demand for reviews of current economic trends, of Commonwealth–State financial relations, capital works programmes, and taxation policy. It has, for example, prepared background materials for Premiers Conferences and meetings of Commonwealth–State Treasury officers. Various State taxation offices and one or two other agencies are responsible to the Treasurer and maintain close links with the Treasury.

Most functions of finance departments involve activities all through the year. For example, new government or departmental policies may be considered by the cabinet at any time; many will have financial and economic implications, so the Treasurer or Minister for Finance will be called upon to advise on such policies. In Britain there is a longstanding rule that no proposal involving additional expenditure can be circulated to cabinet by a minister until it has been discussed with Treasury officers. Nothing quite so binding exists in Australia, and practice seems to depend more on the attitude of the Prime Minister or Premier. However, the central budget agency usually comments on submissions, and in most cases the department concerned will have already discussed the programme with it at the official level. Much negotiation and modification may have gone on before the matter ever reaches cabinet level, and a programme been given provisional approval well before it appears as a new item in the annual estimates. Broad trends are continuously watched and the government told how things are going. Treasury officers will be closely involved in interdepartmental committees and discussions on schemes with financial implications.

When Treasury or Department of Finance officers look at new proposals, they are concerned with problems that the department might have neglected. 'Sometimes there is a danger that a proposal, which apparently is fairly cheap initially, may open the way for excessive government expenditure by making a commitment that is open-ended or by creating a precedent'. The budgetary agency 'also likes to be sure that the costs of a programme are not deliberately understated'.[4] Much of the energy of a central budgetary agency is devoted to keeping expenditure down, so it inevitably gets the reputation of being 'negative'. This is reinforced by the volume of work it has to deal with. Spending ministers and departments can often afford to devote more time to their own favourite schemes than Treasuries can to opposing them, so Treasuries sometimes become associated in the minds of others with critical reports, dealing sharply and perhaps cogently with proposals designed to commit governments in new, complex and possibly expensive ways, but short on constructive suggestions for alternatives. A Coombs Commission Task Force suggested that a larger staff would give the Commonwealth Treasury more scope for a detailed look at long-term policy issues, and 'might also encourage further internal pluralism'. But the role of central budget agencies has not been such that they are perceived as a source of new spending initiatives; when departments seek their advice, they seem to do the best they can to give it.

This kind of activity gives the central financial department great power, especially where it combines the function of controlling expenditure with that of being chief adviser on economic policy. This is buttressed by the fact that these departments tend to attract some of the ablest public servants. One illustration of the growing importance of the Commonwealth Treasury (before its recent split) is that the number of First and Second Division public servants employed there grew from nine to fifty-two between 1951 and 1974.[5] A 1975 sample survey indicates that many senior officers had spent all or much of their career in the one department, but this has been said to present a misleading picture. A 1977 study of 157 middle to top Department of Finance staff showed 64 who had served only in the Treasury or Department of Finance, or been there at least ten years.[6] Treasuries have certainly liked in the past to build up a 'professional' staff and have benefited from having a capable and well-trained group of officers, able to build up an extensive knowledge of public finance in Australia and elsewhere, and a wide experience of the budgetary problems of other departments. Some would have liked to see more movement between them and the outside world.

In the Treasury or Department of Finance, the expenditure proposals of each department are dealt with by a fairly small but senior group of officers. The work of budget analysis depends greatly on the building up of personal contact between officers of the central budget agency and the departments, and where possible the creation of relationships of trust between the two. The methods used to choose and train such staff are important factors in determining how the system works in practice.

One limitation on the comprehensiveness of the budgetary process, especially in the States, is the number of statutory authorities outside the scope of normal Treasury control (see Chapter Five). The annual budget covers the expenditures of some statutory bodies, but many of these earn their own revenues and provide for expenditure from them without the money ever passing through any fund controlled by the Treasury or Department of Finance. Another area at least partly outside normal budgetary control is that relating to Commonwealth grants to the States and Loan Council decisions (see Chapter Seven). These are settled at meetings of the Premiers Conference and Loan Council, usually in June, although some specific purpose grants are reserved for later decisions as part of the Commonwealth budget. However, Commonwealth policy tends to prevail on these occasions, and the Commonwealth financial departments will have had an important say in formulating this policy.

In Australia, the most highly developed arrangements for budget formulation are those of the Commonwealth and New South Wales governments. Practice in the other States varies; in some the machinery and procedures associated with budget preparation are still of a simpler kind partly because of the smaller size of their budgets. However, the Commonwealth Grants Commission has had a powerful influence on the budgetary policies and practices of the smaller States (see Chapter Seven). It has led these States into keeping a sharp eye on the budgets of New South Wales and Victoria, and made them improve their own procedures.

New South Wales[7]

When the draft estimates of each New South Wales department have been endorsed by the permanent head and the minister they go (normally in July) to the Budget Branch of the Treasury, which has the initial responsibility for incorporating them into a broad budgetary plan. This involves first an item-by-item scrutiny of each set of estimates. Treasury inspectors hold discussions with departmental officers concerning their 'bids' for expenditure during the year.[8] Reports are then prepared on each department's requirements, with recommendations for such changes as are thought appropriate. This 'first revise' is in turn reviewed by senior Treasury officials, who will also need to take account of some major policy issues. For example, if the overall budget result still looks like showing an excess of expenditure over revenue, corrective measures will be needed. It may be necessary to cut departmental allocations further, or to consider raising taxes and other charges levied by the State. Senior Treasury officers lay down ground rules for a 'second revise', which is usually done by the budget inspectors without further consultation with departments. Out of this emerges the recommendations made to the Treasurer, and he and the Premier can then consider the general form of the budget. At this stage, other ministers may once again get into the picture. The Premier and Treasurer make final decisions on allocations, and an Allocation Letter goes to each minister. In recent budgets, some role in these discussions has also been played by the economic advisers on the Premier's ministerial staff.

In adjusting the revenue side of the budget, Australian State governments have had less room for manoeuvre than the Commonwealth government or than their counterparts in the Canadian and American federal systems. This is because their dependence on Commonwealth grants has placed a larger part of their revenues outside their own control. It has also induced them to spend all they get, and to try to balance their budgets on a year-to-year basis and to avoid running surpluses or deficits. There may be a change if the Fraser government's plan to restore more financial independence to the

States succeeds. 'This will require the acceptance of new attitudes to budgeting, recognizing that variations in revenue from year to year are likely to be more marked than before . . .'[9]

On the expenditure side, too, many items are uncontrollable, or thought to be so. They concern virtually inescapable commitments, the fruit of past policies and legislation, and the margin of readily adjustable expenditure is often small. If we look at New South Wales government expenditure for 1976–77,[10] there was the intractable deficiency ($331 million) of the Public Transport Commission; accumulated loan liability to the Commonwealth was nearly $4000 million, involving an annual interest commitment close to $300 million. Much of the $1005 million education bill and the $427 million health bill was the inevitable consequence of past policy decisions. Yet these already formed a very large slice of total current expenditure from Consolidated Revenue of $2939 million.

After expenditure allocations have been fixed, ministers in New South Wales arrange for revision of the detailed estimates to conform with the allocations determined. Some latitude is allowed to departments in deciding where to make cuts, though it is usual to specify allocations for a fairly large number of items and to indicate some proposals that should be wholly omitted. This is partly designed to ensure that departments do not reduce their overall vote to the approved total simply by cutting the provision for definite commitments such as salaries, which would then have to be supplemented later in the year. It does, however, also strengthen considerably the Treasury's control over the activities of the operating departments.

The Commonwealth

A somewhat similar process takes place at Commonwealth level, as outlined in Table 16.1, and allowing for the fact that Commonwealth budgetary agencies have to pay more attention than the States to the requirements of general economic policy, how far the budget should run a deficit, and so on.

TABLE 16.1

Commonwealth Budget Timetable

Month	Current Year	Prospective Year
Oct.		Cabinet considers broad Forward Estimates guidelines
		Forward Estimates circular requesting estimates sent out to Departments and Authorities
Jan.–Feb.	Current year revised Estimates received late January, examined by Department of Finance, Report submitted in early February	Forward Estimates figures received and scrutinised by Finance

TABLE 16.1 *continued*

Month	Current Year	Prospective Year
March	Departments submit Additional Estimate requirements for the remainder of the financial year; Requirements examined by Finance, presented to cabinet in April	Forward Estimates Report presented to cabinet; cabinet decides on reviews to be undertaken, and specifies guidelines
April–early May	Further revised Estimates received early May; examined by Finance and report made to cabinet or ministers	Finance and departmental officials prepare reviews of options for outlays and papers presented to cabinet; cabinet in a series of meetings determines funding for the coming year for a number of existing programmes
Late April–May	Additional Estimates Bills for current year submitted to Parliament; passed generally in late May	Supply requirements for the prospective year submitted and checked by Finance, then submitted to cabinet
		Supply Bills tabled in Parliament in May and passed in late May or early June
		Departments provide draft Estimates to Finance in late April or early May. These take into account cabinet decisions made in the Forward Estimates process
May–June		New policy submissions received from ministers
		Finance Divisions examine draft Estimates received and prepare submissions for cabinet
June		Premiers Conference and Loan Council meetings
		Announcement of some State grants and loan allocations
July	End of year result available four to five days after 30 June	Cabinet consideration of the budget
July–Aug.		Budget papers prepared
Aug. (2nd–3rd Tuesday)		Budget presented in parliament
Sept.–Nov.		Budget debates—Appropriation Bills passed by 30 November

The Role of the Cabinet

It must not be supposed that politicians are unimportant in determining budgetary outcomes—indeed, it is clear enough that cabinets and particular powerful ministers sometimes bring about policy changes with large financial implications, and which may be very unwelcome to Treasuries. The actual budgetary role of cabinets varies considerably over time, between States, and as between them and the Commonwealth. The scope of cabinet discussions will be partly fixed by the personality and political strength of the finance minister, partly by the degree of customary reliance on the professional skills of Treasury or Department of Finance. In some States the Premier regularly also holds the portfolio the Treasurer. Between 1940–76, the leader of the government was also Treasurer for the whole period in Victoria, for almost the whole time in South Australia and Western Australia; for nearly thirty years in New South Wales, and over twenty years in Tasmania; on the other hand, under five years in the Commonwealth, and under two in Queensland. When the two posts are combined, cabinet review of the Estimates may be limited. Often a well-established Premier has been able to make most budgetary decisions alone, with the aid of his senior Treasury officers. This dominance has been heightened by the Premier's leading role in negotiations for financial aid at Premiers' Conferences. In such cases ministers may simply be given a statement setting out departmental allocations already decided; a few special matters may be put to cabinet, but that body may not review the draft budget in detail, though it makes the policy decisions needed to bring the budget into balance, especially on the revenue side. Of course through the year the cabinet considers new policy proposals, and their financial implications; each member of it will also be well-informed about the allocations for his own department. According to W.A. Townsley, in Tasmania 'cabinet does not touch and perhaps does not see the consolidated revenue budget. The Treasurer consults individual ministers and senior officials with respect to loan allocations.'[11] In Victoria and Western Australia the Premier seems to settle most budgetary matters in direct discussion with the Treasury.

In New South Wales, there have been some important changes in procedure in recent years. Sir Robert Askin had settled most contentious issues by direct contact with the Treasury. When Mr Lewis succeeded him in 1974, the cabinet acquired a Policy and Priorities Committee which was used to review budgetary policy. Since then, the New South Wales Treasury has had to undertake more extensive paper work to justify its budgetary proposals. In New South Wales the Premier had usually been Treasurer until 1976, when the new Labor Premier, Mr Wran, appointed a separate Treasurer, but has taken a very active role in budget formulation and financial policy and established a ministerial advisory unit as a source of economic advice (including advice on budgetary policy). In Queensland cabinet review of the budget proposals has at times been fairly extensive and it has been customary for some years to allocate the Treasury portfolio to the minor party in the non-Labor coalition government. Even in this situation the Treasurer's position is likely to be strong. He will be thoroughly briefed on the implications of possible decisions about varying expenditure and revenue levels, and his officials will be consulted as particular issues come up during the cabinet's deliberations. While minor adjustments are possible it will usually be difficult for a minister to obtain a greatly improved allocation, as this can normally be only at the expense of another department.

In the Commonwealth, no Prime Minister has also been Treasurer since Chifley (1945–49), so the Treasurer has had to cope with a Prime Minister who may have his own views (and who has his own powerful department). The financial predominance of the federal government not only makes its budgetary decisions of major significance in influencing the general economic climate, but gives the Commonwealth more freedom to vary its budgetary policies. This increases the likelihood of widely differing views on policy.

So it is common for the Commonwealth Prime Minister and other important ministers to help weigh the relative merits of a number of alternative budgets. A finance minister who has to defend his policies very fully in cabinet, or cabinet committee, or to the Prime Minister, is not necessarily placed at a disadvantage, though he may be. He can use the opportunity to educate his colleagues in the economic facts, as seen by his department. One description is as follows, though it must be remembered that details vary with the personalities involved, and this account also predates the establishment of a separate Department of Finance:

> Usually, the Cabinet first makes a review of the general economic situation and determines the broad policy it is to follow on the Budget . . . Expenditure estimates are put forward by the Treasurer, and by other Ministers if they wish, for Cabinet review. Attention is especially drawn to matters involving new policy or to those cases where the Treasury [now Department of Finance] and the Departments are unable to agree on the best estimate for an existing item of expenditure. Submissions on the revenue estimates assess revenue at existing taxation rates. The Treasurer introduces taxation proposals, showing how much more/less revenue would be if the proposals were accepted, and the Cabinet reaches agreement on the form of taxation measures. Finally, the Budget Speech is settled by the Treasurer in consultation with the Prime Minister . . .[12]

Actual procedures have varied over the years. Thus in 1972 a major role in budget-making seems to have been played by two small cabinet committees, on revenue and expenditure. The 1975 budget was based on much preliminary work by a small Cabinet Expenditures Review Committee chaired by the Prime Minister and serviced by a parallel committee of officials led by a senior officer from the Department of the Prime Minister and Cabinet. The general tendency in recent years has been for the cabinet review to become a two-stage affair. The first meetings are now part of the 'forward estimates' process (see below). Cabinet considers budget prospects as indicated by the Forward Estimates Report and other papers presented in March. This may lead to wide-ranging reviews of existing programmes, along broad cabinet guidelines. The nature of these has varied. In 1976 and 1977 a Committee of Officials, drawn from Treasury/Finance and the Department of the Prime Minister and Cabinet, was asked to identify options for reducing the forward estimates. In 1978 the cabinet asked for review papers from these departments and from relevant spending departments, which it considered between April and June.

The second set of meetings—so-called 'Budget Cabinet'—is in July, an intensive series spread over about two weeks. Ministers consider the Treasurer's submissions, the latest advice on economic prospects, any proposed new policy options, and unsettled expenditure questions. The Estimates are accompanied by recommendations from the Minister for Finance for endorsement. Revenue decisions are usually made towards the end of this process. An interesting feature of recent budgets has been the more important part played by the Department of the Prime Minister and Cabinet; it appears likely in the future that no single department will have the same dominance as the old Treasury.

Most matters on the expenditure side will usually have been virtually settled by the time the cabinet receives the budget. 'Disagreed bids' generally represent only a small portion of total budget outlays.[13] In 1977 the total difference at issue was about $8 million out of a total of over $26 thousand million. The system creates considerable pressures to achieve agreement at the official level, partly because ministers fear the demands on their time of quarrels on minor issues. Of course, it must be remembered that what is being argued about at this stage is provision for policies already approved. Most major spending programmes and all proposals for new initiatives will have been considered in the earlier forward estimates reviews.

Of course if the cabinet really wants to put on a bigger squeeze, there is nothing to prevent it. However, much ongoing expenditure is the result of past commitments and decisions, from interest on loans, social security payments and public service salaries to expenditures arising out of firm political promises, such as grants to the States, defence spending, and so on. Even those items in ongoing programmes that could be varied, will often not be, or only marginally; there is an inbuilt tendency in budgeting to concentrate argument on new proposals, and to resist the reopening of previously settled questions. It is true that in recent years there have been one or two important *ad hoc* reviews of existing commitments. The Whitlam government in 1973 appointed the Coombs Task Force on Continuing Expenditure Policies, which recommended cuts in some expenditure programmes to make room for the new government's plans; it worked with the close co-operation of the Treasury.[14] The Fraser government has adopted a firm policy of reducing the rate of growth of Commonwealth expenditure, and this involves a more concerted effort to review existing programmes. This includes the annual reviews described above in relation to the budget process, which have tried to identify programmes that might be reduced or discontinued. The Prime Minister also announced at the time of the split between Treasury and Department of Finance that the Department of the Prime Minister and Cabinet would be given additional resources to undertake, with these two departments, reviews of programme 'effectiveness'. There are also the new responsibilities of the Auditor-General for auditing efficiency (see Chapter Eighteen).

Some reformers would like to see a much more regular and systematic review of performance and priorities incorporated into the State budget cycles. For example, in one State it has been recommended that each minister should report early in the year on 'priorities, needs and options', on the basis of which the Treasury would prepare papers on issues and choices in the current budget. The Premier and Treasurer would then have guidelines prepared for the departments, so that the latter would have a clearer context in which to prepare estimates. The guidelines would also indicate existing programmes in need of review.[15] We mention below the Coombs Commission proposals for forward estimating, which make some similar points, and parts of which have been embodied in recent Commonwealth procedures. There is some evidence that such relatively sophisticated exercises are hard to incorporate in the normal budget cycle, and schemes of this kind may be asking too much of those concerned, especially of ministers and cabinets. Assessing priorities and taking firm decisions about options is demanding and time-consuming work. This is not to say that the budget processes and documents cannot be improved, so as to be more intelligible to politicians and the public, and to assist in more rational decision making by ministers and cabinets; and that periodical reviews of ongoing expenditures in particular fields should not take place on a more regular basis. One step in the direction of greater budget flexibility was taken by the Commonwealth cabinet in 1976–77; it was directed that when ministers approve allocations for certain expenditure items, they should also fix limits to the levels of outstanding commitment for later years. This does not of course apply to expenditures whose future amounts are pre-determined by the legislation itself, such as social security benefits, but is useful for project-type expenditures.

The Line-Item Budget and its Limitations

It was fashionable a few years ago to see the root of the trouble in the 'line-item' budget characteristic of government operations. The line-item budget is characteristically concerned with 'inputs', the objects (materials, equipment, manpower, etc.) that government departments must procure in order to carry out their functions. For example, expenditures in Australian budgets are grouped mainly by organisational unit (department and sometimes subdepartment) and, within these, under headings such as: salaries, maintenance, postal expenses. The itemisation in terms of inputs begins with the preparation of the estimates and culminates in the final document presented to Parliament, which forms the basis of its detailed appropriations (for a specimen page of the New South Wales Estimates, see Table 16.2). This makes it clear when more money is being sought for each item of input, also which units spent more than was authorised. It is quite a good means of checking regularity and honesty, but the reasons for the variations are less apparent. It is very difficult to use such information to assess the relative importance of the objectives for which funds are sought.

Programme Budgeting

As a consequence there is some attractiveness about the notion of a 'programme budget' (or 'performance budget')[16] that tries to provide systematic answers to questions about the objectives of government agencies, the programmes by which they seek to achieve them, and the resources that each programme requires. In a programme budget, the expenditure side is set out in terms of programmes, groups of activities related to some objective of government. Each programme is broken down according to the agencies involved in its accomplishment, and so as to facilitate the measurement of costs and performance. Information about inputs, the central feature of the line-item budget, is presented in terms of the use to which these are put in the carrying out of governmental programmes. The Hoover Commission in the United States thought that:

> Such an approach would focus attention upon the general character and relative importance of the work to be done, or upon the service to be rendered, rather than upon the things to be acquired, such as personal services, supplies, equipment, and so on. These latter objects are after all, only the means to an end. The all-important thing in budgeting is the work or service to be accomplished, and what the work or service will cost.[17]

Many people have been attracted by the idea of formulating a budget that expresses the operations of a government according to its outputs rather than its inputs. They have argued that such a budget could be a significant management tool, as well as making legislative review more meaningful. Agencies would need to clarify their objectives, and group their activities in terms of programmes related to these. One could find out what resources were being used for each programme, and get a better notion of what the government's actual priorities were. It would make for more rational choice between alternative programmes, and it would help the decision to modify or abandon a particular objective, if the full cost of achieving it were known. It would assist forward planning; one idea associated with programme budgeting is more use of forward projections of expenditure, so that the full implications of a long-term programme become visible.

The concept of the programme budget is not without its severe critics. It is easier to talk about defining the objectives of government than actually to do so (hence current American disillusionment with the hopes once placed

TABLE 16.2

New South Wales Estimates: A Specimen Page

MINISTER FOR EDUCATION

Sub-heads under which this Expenditure will be Accounted for	1978–79 Estimate	1977–78	
		Appropriation	Expenditure
DEPARTMENT OF EDUCATION— PRIMARY EDUCATION	$	$	$
Salaries and Payments in the Nature of Salary			
A1. Salaries, Wages and Allowances, as per Schedule, page 142	356 600 000	312 690 000	320 203 430
A2. Payments for Leave on Retirement, Resignation, etc.	4 860 000	4 800 000	4 667 128
A3. Overtime	1 000	2 000	236
$	361 461 000	317 492 000	324 870 794
Maintenance and Working Expenses			
B1. SUBSIDIARY STAFF CHARGES— Meal Allowances	100	100	2
B2. EXPENSES IN CONNECTION WITH BUILDINGS— Rent, Rates, etc.	2 250 000	1 960 000	1 961 654
Maintenance, Alterations, Additions and Re- newals	17 500 000	18 000 000	18 696 991
Cleaning	1 073 000	850 000	926 162
B3. SUBSISTENCE AND TRANSPORT EXPENSES— Travelling, Removal and Subsistence Ex- penses	1 330 000	1 020 000	1 183 258
Motor Vehicles—Running Costs, Main- tenance, Hire and Insurance	45 500	29 000	37 485
Freight, Cartage and Packing	225 000	266 000	212 326
B4. GENERAL EXPENSES— Postal Expenses	416 000	600 000	374 014
Fees for Services Rendered	1 000	1 000	....
Stores, Provisions, Furniture, Equipment, Minor Plant, etc. (including Main- tenance and Repairs)	8 700 000	7 950 000	8 242 678
Minor Expenses not elsewhere included ..	100	100	29
$	31 540 700	30 676 200	31 634 599
Other Services			
C1. Nursery Classes and Nursery Schools— Wages and Materials in connection with preparation of meals for very young children	138 000	140 000	124 997
C2. Payments for Conveyance of Children to School	31 290 000	27 000 000	28 582 651
C3. School Telephone Expenses	985 000	925 000	949 453
C4. Allowances for primary pupils in non-State Schools	18 550 000	16 150 000	16 486 983
C5. Provision for Special Assistance to Disadvantaged Schools	3 350 000	3 100 000	4 045 602
C6. Grants to Schools in lieu of Subsidies ..	661 000	560 000	552 385
$	54 974 000	47 875 000	50 742 071
Total—Department of Education—Primary Education $	**447 975 700**	**396 043 200**	**407 247 464**

Source: Estimates 1978–79, p. 135.

on programme budgeting). Many government objectives are inevitably vague and imprecise, hard to define and to measure progress towards. Even some reasonably concrete and measurable types of activity have widespread repercussions on other activities which are hard to reduce to precise terms, though it may be a good idea to try. For example, the location of a major road or an airport has effects on other forms of transportation, on industrial location, population movement, job opportunities, amenities, and so on.

Secondly, no form of budgeting exempts government from the political process and the policy decisions that emerge from it. Government objectives are not things fixed and known. Operationally they are outgrowths of 'the policies we can agree on', of the political support that can be obtained for them; and political support has it costs, often as inescapable as economic costs. Of course, it may still help to try to clarify these objectives, and to enable choices to be made in fuller knowledge of the costs involved. We should encourage the attitude of mind that sees the need for periodical re-examination of aims, for the careful weighing of alternatives when decisions are taken, the determined effort to quantify benefits and costs and to take a longer-range view, while recognising that it is not the natural bent of politicians (or of humanity in general).

A subtler criticism is that programme budgeting is not as politically neutral as it purports to be, that it has political consequences, in tending to reduce the pluralism of decision-making and to concentrate power in budget offices and a few major departments. Its more extreme supporters have also been accused of ignoring the limitations on human rationality, in particular, where they promote the notion that one can have a 'zero-base budget', in which every existing expenditure is weighed against every competing alternative, as though one could start with a clean sheet each time. It is plausibly argued that this is an impossible exercise, and that it is more realistic to think of government programmes in incremental terms, to assume that most existing activities are relatively fixed constraints. One can then concentrate on improving rationality at the margin, especially where new expenditures are involved; and also have periodical shake-ups of the kind represented by the Coombs Task Force on Continuing Expenditure Policies.

There are various other problems. To provide the necessary figures may require sweeping changes in accounting methods and machinery; there may be conflict between the requirements of programming and those of execution, as when the unit responsible for carrying out a programme is not coterminous with the programme itself and cannot therefore be fully held to account for its management; there may be a need to maintain the control of regularity and honesty in the expenditure of public funds that is facilitated by the line-item budget.

There has been some interest in programme budgeting in Australia.[18] Conferences and seminars have been held, and there has been a good deal of discussion at the official level. A few government agencies conduct their internal budgetmaking on something which approaches a programme basis, even where the budget is later translated into the normal form. Interesting developments are also taking place in related ways of improving rationality, such as the 'forward look' (the long-term survey of particular fields of expenditure), the functional grouping of estimates and accounts, and cost-benefit analyses of certain projects. It may well be that the more viable elements of programme budgeting will gradually be incorporated into existing budgetary systems, even though the full gospel be rejected.

A functional classification was first used in the Commonwealth budget statements of 1973–4. Under each heading, outlays are analysed into categories which are intended to bring together expenditures with common objectives or purposes, and show the allocation of resources between broad areas of Commonwealth involvement, regardless of which department is responsible for the expenditure. Thus 'total outlays' are subdivided into major functional groupings such as Defence, Education, Health, Social Security and Welfare, Housing, and so on. Within these an attempt is made to show outlays on major programmes, so far as the data are available. But the headings are very broadly defined, and the information provided is of little or no use for evaluation, though they show the broad expenditure implications of current programmes. The figures are mainly derived by reclassifying existing appropriation data and the detailed estimates are still presented in the traditional way. The Annual Budget Papers presented to parliament in 1974 and 1975 included a special paper which (in 1975) was described as 'a comprehensive statement of Australian Government Programmes concerned with urban and regional development'. It included housing, local government, roads, water and sewerage, and so on. But this was a concession to the Department of Urban and Regional Development's desire to have its own budget, and disappeared with the demise of that department.

Forward Estimates

We have already referred to forward estimating. In 1971 the Commonwealth Treasurer announced that all departments would in future prepare for the government's consideration expenditure estimates for a further two years beyond each budget year (the Treasury had been making informal projections since the mid-1960s). This is also beginning in some States. The clearest value of forward estimates is to help economic management and government policy-making by showing the implications of current programmes for future changes in government spending. Where forward estimates are expected to include the cost of new policy proposals as well as of ongoing activities, as do the Commonwealth's, for example, they become a much more sophisticated and difficult operation. Up to now forward estimating in Australia has been an interesting experiment, but the three-year estimates have not been treated as binding, nor regarded as a firm basis for departmental planning. For the States a particular problem is lack of Commonwealth assurance on future General Loans Allocations. (In one or two exceptional cases, notably the universities, approved triennial programmes have at certain periods enabled forward planning to take place.) Such estimates run the risk of being so loosely made that they become useless exercises, ignored for practical purposes. It is difficult to get governments to commit themselves for several years ahead. On the other hand, three-year estimates of a binding character are sometimes said to foreclose the future and inhibit change, especially downward change.

It is clear that forward estimating has a future, even if efforts to date have been of limited scope. The Fraser government in 1976 asked for forward estimates for one year only, 'no more than an early indication of budget bids',[19] as part of the two-part budgetary process described above. However, in 1977 and 1978 departments were again required to provide three-year forward estimates, and these are submitted to the Department of Finance in January, though the main focus so far as the budget process is concerned is on the preliminary estimate for the first of the three years.

Forward estimates (it is argued) make governments and departments more alive to future commitments and the need to provide for new expenditure proposals, perhaps by requiring offsets elsewhere. The annual budget has too limited a time-scale to show up the long-term implications of government programmes. It encourages politicians to concentrate on short-term issues of budgetary policy, a tendency to which they are anyway over-inclined. The Coombs Report attaches great importance to the development of forward estimating as an annual exercise, in which ministers as well as officials play a full part, ending in a set of Forward Estimates on a three-year basis, for both finance and manpower, endorsed by the cabinet and so becoming a basis for future planning.[20] The Report envisages departments working within initial guidelines laid down by the cabinet on policy priorities and the proportion of the national income and manpower that the government plans to use for government purposes. It sees the whole exercise as one of corporate planning and bargaining that will help to make cabinets a central mechanism for determining resource priorities and also promote a greater sense of self-discipline among government agencies, 'the development of a consensus about the facts and . . . a hard-won agreement emerging from tough negotiation about the action which should flow from that consensus'.[21] The Report argues that departments at present see expenditure cuts too much as the arbitrary actions of outsiders, often reflecting not their priorities, nor even those of the government, but of the budgetary officials. A task force is at present (1978) looking into this proposal. When he announced the Treasury split in November 1976, the Prime Minister stressed the importance of forward planning, and the new Department of Finance has assumed the responsibility for forward estimates.

The British introduced five-year forward estimates in the 1960s. These are prepared by departments, reviewed by the Public Expenditure Survey Committee (PESC), a committee of public servants, and by cabinet, then published as a White Paper.[22] Some believe that this exercise in corporate forward planning has helped to promote rationality, if not greater self-discipline, but 'others are more sceptical; they argue that once a programme is accepted it is difficult to cut',[23] and that the Treasury could be tougher when it dealt with each department separately. PESC has been supplemented by Policy Analysis and Review (PAR), a process of selective review of government programmes to see whether they are achieving their aims and whether their resources are being used effectively.

Budget Authorisation

The second stage is authorisation by the legislature of the Budget presented by the government. The procedures are not discussed here in detail,[24] but some points should be noted. British and Australian legislatures may not originate bills providing for the expenditure of public monies, the initiative in financial legislation rests with the government. It is the latter's responsibility to produce a coherent financial programme; its passage is made a matter of confidence, and the government will accept few, if any, amendments. Once parliament has passed the Annual Appropriation Acts, the government may spend the appropriated funds until the end of the financial year for which they are provided.[5]

This does not mean that parliamentary debate on the financial programme is unimportant, and there are various ways in which parliamentary scrutiny of the budget might be improved. As things stand, few members are informed enough about the content and significance of the estimates to take advantage of the opportunity to debate them. Although parliament may not be an appropriate body to make detailed amendments to a budget, it should be able to examine the broad financial proposals and to discuss their implications. Instead, debate tends to move in a disconnected way from point to point, as members air their personal grievances and ride their hobby-horses. The Commonwealth Senate has been experimenting with a number of Estimates Committees since 1970, which departmental officers attend. Ministers and, through them, their officials may be asked for explanations of particular items, and the committees report to the Senate. The results have not been impressive. The House of Representatives, at the urging of the Prime Minister, created a Standing Committee on Public Expenditure in April 1976 with wide powers to examine the estimates and other matters related to government expenditure. It has twelve members, and can appoint sub-committees, call witnesses, examine files, and obtain assistance from Department of Finance and Public Service Board officials and so on.[26] The committee had prime ministerial support as a new avenue for checking departmental efficiency, and its first members included some able persons. How it will develop remains to be seen. Some people argue that parliaments have very rarely been effective controllers of public expenditure and that it is doubtful whether they can play this role; on the other hand the British

Select Committee on Expenditure has on occasion managed to bring to light some bad cases of error and mismanagement.

Implementation

With the passing by parliament of the Appropriation Act and other measures needed formally to authorise the budget, the way is clear for implementing the proposals embodied in the estimates. This third phase of the annual financial routine involves the collection of revenue, raising of loans, expenditure of authorised amounts, the banking arrangements necessary for the receipt, custody and payment of funds, the recording of transactions and the keeping of accounts.

The basic methods by which a government's financial business is conducted are normally defined in an Audit Act or similar statute and Treasury regulations made under the Act. A detailed account of the machinery and procedures applying in New South Wales is given by Campbell;[27] an essentially similar system operates in the other States, and at the federal level (where for Treasury, read Department of Finance). In general it sees the Treasury as the centre to which all governmental collections flow and from which all payments emanate. In fact, receipts are issued and cheques drawn by other departments and agencies; but monies received will ultimately find their way into the Treasury bank accounts, and funds to meet cheques drawn by the operating departments will be provided from those accounts.

Few receipts and payments today pass directly over the Treasury's counter. Most collections are handled through departmental public revenue accounts, having two special features: they may be opened by the Treasurer; and cheques drawn upon them must be for the purchase of bank drafts in favour of the Treasurer. Most expenditures pass through departmental drawing accounts into which payments may be made only by the Treasury. These accounts have overdraft limits authorised by the Treasury, against which departments draw cheques and then seek Treasury reimbursement. Broadly speaking, the financial machinery that has evolved allows for the decentralisation of the work of collecting and disbursing public monies but at the same time maintains a high degree of central control by ensuring that: all receipts are transmitted to the Treasury; only such monies can be paid out as are made available by it; and departmental spending is confined to amounts provided by parliamentary appropriation or by special approval of the Treasurer.

In Australia the Treasury or Department of Finance exercises strong control over all departments by virtue of its general responsibility to ensure that appropriations are not overspent, to conduct the government's banking and other financial arrangements, and to review and report on the overall financial position from time to time during the fiscal period. Most Treasuries maintain 'control' accounts from which they can at any time readily ascertain expenditures incurred by departments, and this facilitates central supervision.

Increasingly in recent years they have actively promoted contact with departments, and have not confined themselves to co-ordinating the draft estimates after they have been received. As indicated earlier, few proposals for additional or expanded services made at the time departmental estimates are prepared have to be investigated *ab initio*. Most have been discussed and probed during the year, some informally, others following written approach to the Treasurer, or through committees on which it is represented. By various means its sphere of influence has gradually extended right into the departments.

Its officers in the normal course of their work examine departmental reports, budget papers and financial statements of other governments as well as their own; they have access to reference material and can readily obtain information directly concerned with particular problems encountered in their day-to-day activities; they are able to build up an extensive knowledge of governmental administration and develop a much greater awareness of current developments than is usual among public servants. This places them in a favourable position in their negotiations with departmental officers.

Paradoxically too, the financial dominance of the Commonwealth has served to enhance the status and importance of State Treasuries. A case has regularly to be made to the Commonwealth for revenue funds and to the Loan Council for borrowing allocations and a great deal hangs on the decisions. A comprehensive brief must be prepared before each Premiers Conference and Loan Council meeting and most of the necessary spadework is done within Treasuries. This aspect of their activities brings their officers into close contact with major financial and economic policy-making and keeps them prominently under notice of the Premier and senior public servants.

The degree of freedom allowed to departments in determining the detailed allocation of the funds granted to them varies between the different units of government. For example, in some States departments have considerable freedom. In New South Wales the Treasury 'exercises considerable control over the internal break-up of each department's total annual expenditure allocation'.[28] Some observers advocate that departments should have more flexibility in spending within the total allotted to them. More financial delegation (it is argued) would give greater scope for genuine budgeting by the various administrative units, setting their own financial priorities, as some statutory authorities are already able to do; and this might promote economical working. It is certainly true that very detailed budgetary allocations, in which each unit is given fixed non-transferable amounts to spend on each item, remove the incentive for skilful internal financial management. In New South Wales provision is made for 'inter-item' transfers between individual items within a particular vote but Treasury approval is required before expenditure on any individual item is exceeded.

The inflexibility of the system should not be exaggerated. Many statutory authorities are partly or wholly financed from 'one-line' appropriations (see Chapter Five), though that is not always as flexible as it sounds. Even for departments there are usually procedures that make some flexibility possible. For example, where Commonwealth departments want to spend more on one item and save on another, the Minister for Finance generally looks on this favourably; there are ways by which appropriations for particular items can be supplemented, as from the Advance to the Minister for Finance or from the Additional Estimates approved by parliament during each year. It is also worth noting that more than half Commonwealth expenditures, such as pensions and other benefits, are authorised by Special Appropriation Acts, some of which authorise expenditure without time limit and which do not need voting annually; in such areas the department concerned has little or no flexibility anyway.

Appraisal

That the public accounts should be subject to review by parliament is a natural corollary of the principle of legislative sovereignty in financial matters. The authority to impose taxation and sanction expenditure needs supplementing by some means of checking whether the funds authorized by Parliament for expenditure on specified governmental activities have been applied only to the approved ends.

Historical Background

Machinery for this form of parliamentary review came late in the series of moves by which the British parliament sought financial supremacy, partly because effective appraisal procedures depended on reform in other financial arrangements. Although after 1688, the expenditures of the armed services were required to be voted annually, their estimates were not presented in detail to parliament, nor were the votes for the civil departments. The comparatively small non-military expenses of government were met from the Civil List, out of which the monarch's personal expenses were also defrayed. Parliamentary consideration of national expenditure as a whole was restricted to occasions when the monarch overspent the Civil List grants and sought additional funds. It was only by degrees between 1760 and 1830 that departmental expenditures were taken off the Civil List and annual parliamentary appropriations were introduced. On the revenue side it was customary to assign fees and the proceeds of particular taxes to individual departments, each of which kept accounts relating to its own activities.

This cumbersome arrangement persisted until 1787, when Pitt established the consolidated fund method of financing governmental expenditure, by which the proceeds of all taxes were paid into a common fund and departments received allocations from the fund to cover expenditure authorised by parliament. The creation of the Consolidated Fund 'broke the disorder caused by assigning particular taxes to special purposes and . . . provided the means of infinite expenditure control through comprehensive appropriation schedules'.[29]

The rest of British budgetary machinery was mainly a nineteenth-century creation. After 1830, the expenses of civil government were finally separated from the monarch's personal expenses. The classification of supply votes gradually became more detailed in a series of changes after 1824. The reform of the Exchequer, involving abolition of sinecures and obsolete systems of accounting, was virtually completed by moves made in the mid-1830s. The position of Comptroller and Auditor-General finally emerged in 1866, after the amalgamation of the Exchequer and Audit departments.[30]

Audit procedures had also developed slowly throughout this period. The first appropriation audit, aimed at ensuring that all departmental expenditures were in accordance with the purpose of the relevant parliamentary votes and that the total amounts approved were not exceeded, did not come until 1832. The Admiralty was the department concerned, but the system was not further extended until 1846, when the War and Ordnance Offices were required to submit accounts. The obligation to present accounts and submit to audit was made universal by the 1866 Exchequer and Audit Departments Act. With its passing, the essential features of the present financial system—the preparation of a more or less comprehensive plan, the authorisation of that plan by the legislature, the carrying out of the plan, and the rendering of an accounting to the legislature at the end of the fiscal period—were in existence.

The Auditor-General

Among British governmental practices that have passed almost intact to Australia are the basic features of the system of financial control, though a number of weaknesses in budgetary and audit control remained in the nineteenth century and later.[31] A Colonial Auditor was appointed in New South Wales in 1824 but the tenure powers and duties of the office of Auditor-General in that State were not defined by statute until 1870. Each government now appoints an Auditor-General responsible to parliament for auditing the accounts of government departments and most statutory authorities and who reports annually to parliament. Normally each Auditor-General holds office until he reaches sixty-five and may be removed from his post only at the request of both houses of parliament.[32] This, along with the fact that his salary is specially appropriated, is designed to free him from ministerial control and to enable him to report independently to the legislature. He and his officers have extensive powers in such matters as access to departmental files, calling for explanations from officials, and imposing surcharges on officers responsible for loss of public monies. The Auditor-General cannot, however, compel departments to adopt a certain course of action. His duty is to criticise, make suggestions, and draw attention to any breach of law or regulation; it is the Treasurer's responsibility to issue any necessary directions. If the Treasurer is not prepared to act on the suggestions made, the Auditor-General's remedy is to bring the matter to the notice of parliament, either in his annual report on the public accounts, or in a special report, leaving it to parliament to take whatever action it considers necessary.

A large part of the work of the Auditor-General is concerned with 'regularity' in spending, with ensuring that expenditures have been duly appropriated and incurred only on the purposes for which they were authorised. This is an essential function, but one with obvious limitations. It is true that the reports of Australian Auditors-General have often gone beyond the scope of the public accounts themselves; and the work of auditors, particularly when examining departmental procedures, may bring to light examples of inefficiency. For example, in his 1976–77 Report, the Commonwealth Auditor-General spoke of a 'deterioration in administrative efficiency' in some departments during the year, pointed to a few examples, and added that departments often complained that this had arisen from or 'been aggravated by, shortage of competent staff'.[33] But he did not commit himself to reasons or try to suggest remedies. Indeed there has been little development of the Auditor-General's role to include an 'efficiency audit' aimed at checking the desirability of expenditures and disclosing waste and extravagance, as distinct from illegal or irregular financial practices. This is not, of course, to say that no efficiency auditing goes on above the departmental level; for example, some Public Service Boards have special responsibilities in this regard. This topic is further discussed in Chapter Eighteen, especially the Commonwealth decision to extend the Auditor-General's powers in this field.

The Public Accounts Committee

The Public Accounts Committee is one potentially significant device for parliamentary review of the government's financial dealings. In the British House of Commons such a committee has existed since 1861, and has a good reputation. The Commonwealth parliament had a comparatively unsuccessful Joint Parliamentary Committee of Public Accounts between 1913 and 1932. Since it was re-established in 1951, it has had a more substantial record of achievement, at least in the early days under Professor F.A. Bland.[34] A number of States have similar bodies. Formally, the committee's main functions are to examine the public accounts as reported upon by the Auditor-General, to comment on any item, and to make suggestions about the form of the accounts. On the whole, the Commonwealth committee has interpreted its functions broadly and has inquired into a number of issues bearing on administrative efficiency. It has little staff of its own, and less formal contact with the Auditor-General than the British Committee; but it has had some expert advice from the Auditor-General's Office and the Treasury, has heard evidence from senior officials and reported to Parliament; its reports are published. The Treasury prepares minutes (also published) containing the replies of the agencies and indicating any action being taken on the reports. The committee is a fact-finding and reporting body, and has no executive powers. Its members are drawn from both House of Representatives and

Senate and include both government backbenchers and opposition represent-atives.

After some early successes, it declined greatly in force and often had neither the chairman nor staff needed to conduct an incisive and thorough-going enquiry. As with many Australian parliamentary committees, member-ship has often been regarded as a chore, rather than a chance to do useful work or build a reputation, and the relatively small size of parliaments means that there has been less backbench talent on which to draw. Parliament has taken little notice of its activities. There appeared in 1976–77 to be some evidence of revival. The Commonwealth Joint Committee on the Parlia-mentary Committee System recommended that the Public Accounts Commit-tee and the Expenditure Committee (see above) be replaced by a House Standing Committee on Public Administration concerned with administrative efficiency. The idea of such a committee was supported in general terms by the Coombs Commission.[35]

The Treasury and Economic Policy

The Commonwealth and State Treasuries have usually been incomparably the most influential economic departments, not only in co-ordinating and controlling expenditure, but in general economic policy. Rivals have some times developed, but Treasuries have had great staying power. The Com-monwealth Department of Trade, especially under Sir John McEwen, was an important rival in the 1960s. Between 1972 and 1975, the former Department of Urban and Regional Development tried, without great success, to become a major economic department. Since then the main contender has been the Department of the Prime Minister and Cabinet; while the Commonwealth Treasury itself, having angered two successive governments by 1976, has been weakened by bisection.[36]

There have been periodical suggestions that the financial control functions of the Treasury should be separated from its responsibilities for general economic management and policy. The reason given may be that the combination gives a single department too much power, or that the proper performance of the one function makes more difficult the carrying out of the other—thus it may be said that a Treasury cannot be the impartial critic of the cost of proposals, while it is also promoting its views about the policy involved in those proposals; or that it cannot concentrate on major issues of economic development and planning while it is also involved in the detail of 'the saving of candle-ends'.

The Coombs Commission considered the idea of dividing the economic policy function of the Treasury from that of financial control, but did not recommend it. Its main reason seems to be that the making of the budget is so central to the government's economic policy, that a separate economic policy department with no part in budgetary control is likely to be ineffective. However, it thought that there should be a greater contribution to economic policy-making from other departments, while recognising the danger that 'given the scarcity of good quality economic staff, the effect of dispersing them between several agencies may well be to reduce their effectiveness'.[37] A very large number of Commonwealth departments already have economic policy and advice inputs. The Commission also saw the possibility of some rough distinction between 'relatively short-term macro-economic management' as the main Treasury responsibility, and the consideration of longer-term structural changes in the Australian economy, where a separate department might be useful, as 'a source of forward looking economic intelligence', and to which bodies such as the Industries Assistance Commission might be attached.

This proposal was received with no great enthusiasm, though Labor has since promised a Minister for Economic Development. The Fraser Government preferred at first to expand the policy-making and budgetary role of the Department of the Prime Minister and Cabinet, and then in December 1976 also did what the Coombs Report had thought unwise—created a Department of Finance largely concerned with the review of expenditure and the preparation of budget estimates, with a separate Department of the Treasury for economic policy advice and general economic management. It is a pity that the name Treasury has thus been separated from what was traditionally the main function of that department, so-called 'Treasury control' of departmental spending. But we live in times when even conservative governments have scant respect for history.

Notes

1. For discussion of some differences between government and commercial accounting, see W.R.C. Jay and R.L. Mathews (eds), *Government Accounting in Australia,* Melbourne, 1968, 39–46, 185–203.
2. cf. Aaron Wildavsky, *Budgeting: A Comparative Theory of Budgetary Processes,* Little Brown, Boston, 1975, ch. 1.
3. For estimates procedures in a Commonwealth department, see Patrick Weller and James Cutt, *Treasury Control in Australia,* Ian Novak, Sydney, 1976, 56–8.
4. Weller and Cutt, *op. cit.,* 87.
5. Weller and Cutt, *op. cit.,* give a short account of the recent history of the Treasury; see also L.F. Crisp, 'The Commonwealth Treasury's Changed Role and Its Organisational Consequences', *Public Admin.* (Sydney), 20, 4, December 1961, reprinted in R.N. Spann and G.R. Curnow, *Public Policy and Administration in Australia: A Reader,* Wiley, Sydney, 1976.
6. Weller and Cutt, *op. cit.,* 38; and data presented in evidence to the House of Representatives Standing Committee on Expenditure, 1977 (to be published).
7. Procedures for capital works programmes and estimates are not examined here; for some discussion, see Chapter Seven; and, on Commonwealth procedures, Report, RCAGA, Appendix Vol. Four, 105–7.

8. See Interim Report, Review of New South Wales Government Administration, Government Printer, Sydney, 1977; and K.W. Knight, 'Formulating the New South Wales Budget', *Public Admin.* (Sydney), XVIII, 3, September 1959, 238–53, reprinted in Jay and Mathews, *op. cit.*

9. Premier of Western Australia, cit. *Com. Parl. Deb.*, (H. of R.), V. 105, 2 June 1977, 2420.

10. See Report of the Auditor-General, 1976–77.

11. W.A. Townsley, *The Government of Tasmania*, University of Queensland Press, St Lucia, 1976, 133.

12. 'The Parliament: Financial Procedures', prepared by the Commonwealth Public Service Board, reprinted in Jay and Mathews, *op. cit.*, ch. III.

13. cf. Patrick Weller, *The Treasury and the Politics of Advice*, University of Tasmania, 1977, 2–3, for a Labor government budget; and Weller and Cutt, *op. cit.*, 67.

14. Report, Task Force on Continuing Expenditure Policies, Canberra, 1973.

15. Interim Report, Review of NSW Government Administration, Government Printer, Sydney, 1977, 45–6.

16. These terms are here used interchangeably, though it is possible to prepare a budget in programme form which would contain little in the way of objective measures of performance. Performance budgeting is an extension of the concept of programme budgeting, adding a work measurement element. Programme budgeting is often referred to as PPB or PPBS, and is sometimes called 'output budgeting'. For further discussion, see K.W. Knight and K.W. Wiltshire, *Formulating Government Budgets: Aspects of Australian and North American Experience*, University of Queensland Press, St Lucia, 1977, ch. 4.

17. Commission on Organization of the Executive Branch of the Government, *Budgeting and Accounting*, Washington, DC, 1949, 8–9.

18. In 1969 two Commonwealth Treasury officers and a Public Service Board officer studied the use of programme budgeting in America, Canada and Britain. The Post Office and the Defence Department have conducted their own investigations; and see the annual Defence Reports for a description of the five-year 'rolling' defence programmes. Australian references include: *Planning, Programming, Budgeting and Control in the Australian Post Office*, APO, Melbourne, 1970; *Programme Budgeting*, Treasury working paper, Australian Government Publishing Service, Canberra, 1972, James Cutt, 'Programme Budgeting; Panacea or Mirage?', *Public Admin.* (Sydney), XXXIII, 1, March 1974, 24–35; Weller and Cutt, *op. cit.*, 68–70, 118–44, describe current PPB practice in some Commonwealth agencies, not amounting to much. See also J.C. McMaster and G.R. Webb (eds), *Australian Project Evaluation: Selected Readings*, Australia and New Zealand Book Co., Sydney, 1978.

19. Weller and Cutt, *op. cit.*, 73.

20. See Report, RCAGA, Canberra, 1976, chs 3, 11.

21. *ibid.*, 363.

22. See Aaron Wildavsky, *Budgeting*, Little Brown, Boston, 1975, ch. 19; and Hugh Heclo and Aaron Wildavsky, *The Private Government of Public Money*, Macmillan, London, 1974, 198 ff.

23. Weller and Cutt, *op. cit.*, 17; cf. Wildavsky, *op. cit.*, 380.

24. Commonwealth procedures are briefly outlined in 'The Parliament: Financial Procedures', Commonwealth Public Service Board, reprinted in Jay and Mathews, *op. cit.*

25. Some 'special' appropriations do not lapse in this way, but their spending is governed by conditions laid down in the Act concerned.

26. See *Aust. Parl. Deb.*, (H. of R.), V. 98, 8 April 1976, 1496–9.

27. W.J. Campbell, *Australian State Public Finance*, Sydney, 1954. For a brief account of federal procedures, see 'Accounting for Revenue and Expenditure in the Commonwealth Government' (prepared by the Commonwealth Public Service Board) in Jay and Mathews, *op. cit.* See also V.M. Levy, *Public Financial Administration*, Sydney, 1972.

28. Knight and Wiltshire, *op. cit.*, 131.

29. Gordon Reid, *The Politics of Financial Control*, Allen and Unwin, London, 1966, 57.

30. cf. Basil Chubb, *The Control of Public Expenditure*, Oxford University Press, Oxford, 1952, 13. A good discussion of the audit function, with comparative material from other countries is given by E.L. Normanton, *The Accountability and Audit of Government*, Manchester University Press, Manchester, 1966.

31. See Arthur McMartin, 'The Treasury in New South Wales, 1786–1836', *Public Admin.* (Sydney), XVII, 3, September 1958: Campbell, *op. cit.*, 21: and P.N. Lamb, 'Geoffrey Eagar and the Colonial Treasury of New South Wales', *Aust. Econ. Papers*, September 1962, and 'The Financing of Government Expenditure in New South Wales, 1856–1900', Ph.D. thesis, Australian National University, Canberra, 1963.

32. On the work of the Auditor-General, see Campbell, *op. cit.*, ch. 2; Jay and Mathews, *op. cit.*, ch. IV; *Manual of Government Accounting in New South Wales*, Government Printer, Sydney, 1967, ch. 11; and Report, RCAGA, Appendix Vol. Four 153–89, which includes overseas comparisons.

33. Report of the Auditor-General, Canberra, 1977, 143.

34. cf. David N. Reid, 'The Parliamentary Joint Committee of Public Accounts', in Jay and Mathews, *op. cit.*, ch. V.

35. Report, RCAGA, 113–4.

36. On Labor conflicts with the Treasury, see *National Times*, 9–14 September 11–16 and 18–23 November 1974 (articles by John Edwards) and 21–26 April 1975.

37. Report, RCAGA, 302.

Chapter Seventeen

Public Administration and the Public

There are various ways of looking at the administrator's relations with the public. Here we shall mention four, which may be called public relations, information, access and participation.

'Public Relations' suggests a manipulative approach, in which the administration takes the initiative in getting people to believe or do what suits the government or the public service. The other words raise wider questions, such as how far a democratic society requires from administrators attitudes and procedures that encourage public knowledge of, access to, interest and participation in government. Jeremy Bentham, the great English administrative reformer, first gave currency to 'publicity' as a major prerequisite of good administration. For him the opposite of good publicity was secrecy, whereas the opposite of good public relations is giving a bad impression. Bentham thought that bad administration should be made to give a bad impression, which would encourage its improvement.

'Information' refers here to making available factual information, explanation and argument. This may be volunteered by the government, or only dragged out, given under pressure of some sort. It may be of a 'public relations' kind and provided because it suits the administration to do so; it may be a means by which an outside individual or group can make the government serve their interests better. Then it becomes part of the problem of access, of how citizens can improve their approach to government, in order to take advantage of the goods and services available to them. For example, problems of information and access are both involved in grievance procedures, the means by which individuals may obtain redress for alleged failings in administrative decisions that affect them unfavourably. (see Chapter Six). But they also raise wider issues that are discussed later in this chapter.

'Participation' is the act of sharing in the formulation or implementation of policies. It goes further than the 'right to know', or the 'right to access', and implies some real power to influence policy outcomes, to have a say in the allocation of resources. A minimum definition of this 'right to influence' would be that the outside groups and individuals most nearly affected by some change have a claim to help in shaping proposals affecting them. However, some supporters of greater participation want to go much further

463

than this, and wish to see fundamental changes in the policy-making structures of government to make them more participatory.

Public Relations and Information Services

From the administrator's point of view, relations with the public have many aspects. First, a public servant may be aware of the need to tell the public how to make use of the service offered. A simple case is a railway timetable; a much more complex one would be making an under-privileged group aware of a new social service available to them. Secondly, an administrator may want to get information from the public that is needed in the department, from hard data (such as census returns, incomes, changes of address) to soft data, such as their likely attitude to some proposed change; or it may be information on what information they need, like the $150 000 survey planned by the Commonwealth government in 1978 to discover what migrants need to know about most. Finally, the aim may be to persuade the public, change their attitudes, try to convince them that they are being fairly treated or that the department is doing a wonderful job.

Even this brief account indicates that it is a complex business, not something that can be left to a public relations or information officer, but a task in which every public servant plays a part. It was said a decade ago of Australian public servants that they 'are not public relations conscious. They assume that if they do a good job, the fact is obvious to all (or at least to those that count), and that there is little need to waste public monies extolling their own virtues'.[1]

This was accurate when it was written, but there has been a considerable change since. As late as 1970, only eight Commonwealth departments had directors of information or public relations important enough to be listed in the Commonwealth Directory. It is true that there were already signs of change. Some States had opened centres for information and the sale of government publications. New South Wales has had a Government Information and Sales Centre since 1962 but (as the Wilenski report rightly says) most people still do not know that it exists, it has been obscurely located, and its function as an answering and referral service has remained under-developed. Government information and publishing services have not been well-organised in many States, and various proposals have been made for their improvement.[2]

However, by the 1970s indications of a new approach were apparent, especially among governments and ministers. In 1970 the South Australian Premier announced that he would seek to maximise the flow of information to the public, and the appointment of nine new public relations officers was reported.[3] In 1974 a press release from the new 'media co-ordinator' of the Dunstan government said that it was proposed to monitor all major news broadcasts and commentaries, so that government comment could be made where necessary. Mr Dunstan has had several journalists on his private staff, and South Australia has been said to run 'the most sophisticated public relations apparatus of any government in Australia'.[4] This was a sign of changing times, and the Commonwealth situation too had altered with the advent of a Labor government in 1972. A Department of the Media (a rarity in democratic societies, and since deceased) took over responsibility for government publishing and advertising, now the task of the Information Services Division of the Department of Administrative Services; it also seems at one stage to have tried unsuccessfully to 'corner' the public relations function by getting other departments to operate through it.[5] By 1977 the number of government departments listing Directors of Public Relations and the like had more than doubled, and a few had also acquired Media Officers. The Public Service Board austerely listed only a single officer, under 'Media Inquiries'. The Treasury listed no one.

In 1975 thirty-three of forty-three departments and statutory bodies to whom a Coombs Commission questionnaire was sent, had or were planning a specially designated information section. The existing sections employed at least eight hundred people and cost over $50 million a year. A good deal of the information supplied was 'propagandist in style and purpose', and mainly produced by journalists. School children were major customers. The Coombs Commission thought much of it was a waste of money, and made various suggestions, including the creation of an Information Advisory Council to advise on information policy and which might also monitor the relevance and objectivity of departmental publications.[6] The Commonwealth government has since appointed a task force of three public servants to assess the effectiveness of information services.

The concept of public relations reminds us that publicity can be a power resource, as is readily noted by critics of private sector advertising, though they often forget it when criticising bureaucratic secrecy. Greater readiness to release information can be selective, used so as to favour government, or to support some activities and groups at the expense of others. Also, as the Coombs report notes, snowing with information is 'a recognized technique of obfuscation'.[7] This should be borne in mind by those who criticise the public service for dwelling in the shadows, though it does not invalidate the criticisms. Too much stress on open government may just bring the good salesmen and specialists in the differential leakage of information to the top.

Freedom of Information

An Australian public servant has many restrictions placed on his freedom to give information to the public. There are stringent regulations regarding the disclosure of official information, sometimes backed by sanctions under the Crimes Act (see Chapter Ten). The traditional attitude has been that a government is entitled to keep secret the advice it receives and the grounds on which that advice is given, and what information is released is at the sole discretion of the minister.

In reply to this, it is nowadays commonly asserted that citizens have a right to know or to freedom of information. Individuals are entitled to know the criteria and procedures that departments use in exercising discretions affecting their rights. The public has a general right to be well-informed on facts and forecasts known to the government, and on what the latter plans to do, so as to widen opportunities for informed public discussion of government proposals; and (it is sometimes added) the public has a right to know the reasons why the government has acted in a certain way. The old theory was that citizens had recourse to their elected member of parliament; but even supposing this was once an adequate channel, this has long ceased to be the case. Parliament's power to extract information from ministers is itself limited, the greater complexity of government means that ministers themselves have less control and oversight over what public servants do. Hence some more direct right to obtain information is needed. Whether this be true or not, a continual questioning of government secrecy has become a feature of Australian politics in the 1970s, as it has in other countries. Things have greatly changed when the recently retired Chief Police Commissioner for the London metropolitan area can argue that government employees should 'be able to speak as freely about the maladministration and failure of government policies as about those of private corporations and other undertakings . . . '[8]

Decisions affecting individual interests

Many administrative decisions to resume land, to give or refuse a permission or a discretionary grant, and so on, directly affect the interests of individuals. They raise questions such as: What criteria does the department use in exercising discretions? What are the reasons for the decision? By what procedure was it reached? Some of these issues are discussed in Chapter Six, in relation to the power of courts to protect individuals, and the uses of administrative tribunals and Ombudsmen.

Public servants are often loth to give reasons for their decisions, as it adds greatly to the burdens of administration, and is an invitation to further correspondence and challenge. In a large bureaucracy, the reasons may also in practice have to be given by officers who did not themselves take the decision, and who may get them wrong! Some public servants do not find it natural or easy to take part in reasoned discussion, or publicly to defend decisions that they make—perhaps they are too accustomed to seeing themselves as the best judges of the public interest.

However, it is arguable that, even if ministers and their officials have to be given considerable discretion to do what they think best, at least they should state more fully their reasons for acting as they do. The need to explain administrative decisions may even in the long run help public servants themselves, as it promotes clearer definition of the policies they are supposed to be pursuing. The same applies to the 'internal law' or 'secret law' of government agencies, guidelines on how government policies are to be carried out, departmental interpretations of laws administered by the department, staff manuals and rule books provided for official guidance, and so on. Are there good reasons why most such information should not be available to the public?

Information on facts, plans and forecasts

This raises questions such as: Is the public supplied with enough factual information relevant to policy-making? Should governments consult more widely before decisions are taken? Should parliamentary committees or courts and tribunals have more power to call officials before them and to inspect government documents and files?

Australian governments do already publish much statistical and other information, but they are also reticent on many matters of fact. They prepare surveys and studies of a mainly factual kind which are treated as confidential and so escape comment and discussion.[9] Some government departments are not even required to publish an annual report, or do so uninformatively or belatedly. They have also tended to be reticent on future plans and proposals.

There have been important improvements in recent years, mainly associated with the Labor government of 1972–75. That government made greater use of task forces and committees of inquiry, publishing their reports as a prelude to legislation. It became commoner to publish the reports of standing advisory bodies before cabinet decisions were made.[10] There were more Green Papers or Discussion Papers, outlining government proposals, sometimes a number of alternative possibilities, for press and public debate before a final decision was taken. (There had been one or two precedents for this in the later 1960s, such as *Self-Government for the Australian Capital Territory*, published by the then Minister for the Interior in 1967, and the Report on *Selective Decentralisation* issued by the Development Corporation of New South Wales in 1969.) However, the importance of this procedure should not be exaggerated—it has had no major influence on policy-making. More departments were required to produce annual reports. There was a considerable increase in government publications generally, and in ministerial handouts, press briefings and conferences, departmental journals, sales outlets. The Department of Social Security is a notable case of an agency that became much freer with reports and documents, and started a journal, the *Social Security Quarterly*, which was to be 'edited in accordance with the highest standards of academic objectivity'; the official and other contributors were free to express their views 'as if they were contributing to an academic journal'.[11] The health insurance scheme was opened up for public discussion, thoroughly enough to give its opponents more than ample opportunities for criticism.

It is true that at least one department, the Commonwealth Treasury, published even less than it had done previously; in 1974 it suspended the annual White Paper on the Australian economy which had been a cautious vehicle for the Treasury view of economic developments, though this was an act of diplomacy (it was at odds with the government) not secrecy. In economic policy some of the most important acts of government, such as the 25 per cent tariff reductions of 1973, were determined in secret by very select groups of decision-makers. Economic policy and foreign policy are areas where governments understandably find it hard to be indiscreet, and where they can make a better case for secrecy than in some other fields. A pessimistic economic forecast which comes with government authority can be self-confirming through its reactions on the behaviour of others.[12] In some areas privacy is critical for the process of compromise and bargaining on which the peaceful settlement of conflicts rests, though the privacy needed may only be a temporary one.

There are some special Australian problems associated with open government, in a country unused to it and accustomed to the 'instant politics' of the *ad hoc* proposal and media and pressure-group over-reaction, and where political oppositions take an undeviatingly adversary public stance. However, we seem to be entering a period in which longer runs in policy-making are badly needed, and in which intelligent members of the public are becoming more concerned and assertive and possibly more sophisticated politically. This may in due course have its reactions on political habits, at least one hopes so in optimistic moments.

An eminent English public servant has argued that, if more effective public participation in policy questions is to take place,

> the public must be given, not only the raw data, but also their interpretation —with all their incompleteness and uncertainty—and the best estimate that can be made of . . . the considerations affecting policy. In recent years successive governments have been moving quite steadily in this direction: and if it continues there will be a growing field in which this work—the work of civil servants—will be put out for public information and discussion . . . To my mind there would be every advantage in the name of the civil servant responsible for such studies being known, and their being allowed to join in public debate on their own findings.[13]

In July 1977 the Head of the Home Civil Service in the United Kingdom wrote to department heads saying that in the case of future policy studies

> the background material should, as far as possible, be written in a form which would permit it to be published separately, with the minimum of alteration, once a ministerial decision to do so had been taken.[14]

though this was not intended to include the actual working papers by which governments reached particular policy decisions.

The need has also been argued for more formal provision for independent policy review of major plans, such as that to which metropolitan transport planning has been subjected in Adelaide, and which opponents of the Lake Pedder scheme of the Hydro–Electric Commission of Tasmania said should have taken place there; and for public hearings, at which objections can be heard before final policy decisions are taken. Australia has lagged behind countries such as Britain and Canada in this respect, though the situation has improved in recent years.

One innovation of the 1970s which illustrates some of the problems involved is the 'environmental impact statement' (EIS). These documents are now prepared by private developers and government departments, and indicate the anticipated physical, social and economic consequences of new development proposals, including possible alternatives and suggested measures to protect the environment. Though the various State and Commonwealth procedures differ, in general the relevant environmental agency may place the EIS on public display for some weeks and invite public comment, or in important cases encourage outside professional consultations or round table discussions with affected groups. In a few instances a formal public inquiry with courtlike procedures may take place. However, these matters are left to the discretion of the determining authority, for example, only a small percentage of all development proposals are even publicly displayed (many, of course, are of a minor kind) and there is considerable variety in the actual commitment of the various governments to environmental protection. Among the States, New South Wales has (1978) the most comprehensive legislation, while many environmentalists would regard Queensland, Western Australia and Tasmania as highly 'development-oriented' and having fewer legal safeguards. The public is undoubtedly consulted more than it used to be, but its formal role is still strictly circumscribed by government.

It is perhaps an encouraging sign that in 1978 the Australian Broadcasting Tribunal advertised for a journalist 'to encourage public participation in public inquiries by the . . . Tribunal into the granting of new licences and the renewal of licences for broadcasting and television stations and related matters . . . '.

Parliamentary and Party Committees

There is a related body of questions about how far parliamentary and party committees should have the right to question officials and to inspect government documents. The calling of public servants before such committees has now become accepted practice in Canberra,[15] if not in most Australian States, but governments reserve the right of ministerial veto. Government departments have also claimed Crown privilege in such matters as disclosure of documents, that is, they have claimed the right to preserve secrecy where disclosure would in the minister's view be contrary to the public interest. In 1976 the Fraser government laid down guidelines to apply to official appearances before party committees, and also on access by parliamentarians to public servants.[16] Such appearances were to be encouraged and there was to be the 'freest possible flow of factual and background material . . . consistent with preserving the necessary confidence of Government and maintaining the traditional political impartiality of officials', but appearances were subject to ministerial approval and officials were not to express views on policy or party-political matters. The government is (1978) considering similar guidelines for appearances before parliamentary committees.

There was a striking case of official outspokenness before a parliamentary committee in 1974. In March an Auditor-General's report on the Department of Aboriginal Affairs was tabled, which included strong criticism of the former minister and to some degree of the department. Among other things, the latter was said to have become aware of certain ministerial decisions involving expenditure only when the accounts were received. The parliamentary Joint Committee of Public Accounts began an inquiry and several departmental officers gave evidence.[17] The permanent head said that the former minister and his personal staff had tried to undermine his control of the department, and his criticisms were widely reported in the press. The minister made history by himself appearing before the committee to attempt to refute these allegations, though he was not cross-examined on his submission.

In July 1975 the Senate decided to call before it eleven senior officers and the Solicitor-General to produce documents and answer questions regarding the controversial $4000 million loan proposal of the Whitlam government. The Prime Minister wrote to the President of the Senate telling him that the public servants would attend, but each 'would be instructed by his Minister to claim privilege in respect to all questions upon the matters contained in the Resolution of the Senate and in respect of the production of all documents . . . relevant to those matters'.[18] He argued that this was clearly an inquiry into government policy, for which ministers and not officials were responsible, and that seeking to question the public servants concerned challenged the fundamental character of ministerial responsibility. This was stating the doctrine of official reticence, the view that information held by the government is its private property, in an uncompromising fashion. The question was raised whether a government's telling public servants not to provide information required of them by parliament did not constitute a breach of parliamentary privilege. The Senate Committee on Privileges, in its report of October 1975, was divided on this point, and no further light has been cast on this matter. Neither House of the Commonwealth Parliament has ever formally decided whether it accepts that its power to investigate is legally limited by Crown privilege.

Freedom of Information Legislation[19]

It has been argued that not only parliamentarians but the public in general have a right of access to government documents, subject to stated exceptions and to certain procedures being followed. Two exceptions often mentioned are confidential aspects of foreign policy and defence; and matters where an individual or group 'right to privacy' are involved, such as certain kinds of information about individual citizens and trade secrets. Countries such as Sweden have gone far in this direction. Official documents, with exceptions of the kind mentioned, are open to public inspection, and a regular procedure has been adopted for application to sight them.

In the United States the 1967 Freedom of Information Act (as amended in 1974) has gone part of the way. Federal agencies are required to publish certain kinds of document and to make others available for public inspection. There is a longer list of exemptions than in Sweden, including most files dealing solely with policy questions and most investigatory files of law-enforcement agencies, as well as defence and foreign policy matters that the executive government has specifically ordered to be kept secret, and matters the disclosure of which would 'constitute a clearly unwarranted invasion of personal privacy'. However, an individual denied information can sue the agency, and the onus is on the government to convince the court, which can inspect documents *in camera*, that the information has been properly classified as exempt. Sweden has a simpler procedure for challenging official rulings through the Ombudsman and administrative courts.

The American and Swedish approach to disclosure of information by individual public servants is broadly consonant with their general attitude to official documents. In America the severe restrictions on officials are confined to information involving internal or external security; there are other specific instances where federal officials are restricted in using official information, as in the tax field. The Swedish press law gives everyone, including public servants, the right to supply information to the press, though it is curtailed in a few fields. The American statute seems to have been favourably received in that country, though there has been concern at the large costs of administering it, and at its over-use by business firms for private gain.

The Whitlam government of 1972–75 planned to introduce a bill modelled broadly on the American one, but this did not happen, though an inter-departmental committee report was tabled in parliament in 1974. In 1976 the Coombs Commission supported the general idea, but made no explicit proposals and indeed was not very positive about the need for new legislation, as opposed to other kinds of government action to loosen things up, though one of its members produced a minority report and a draft bill.[20] Some countries have taken the arguable line that better results would be achieved by a firm government commitment to more 'open government', followed by regular parliamentary and administrative action to press for the release of more information. The Fraser government set up another committee which reported in late 1976;[21] legislation was promised but was not tabled until June 1978. It is considerably more cautious than the American law. First, it has a longer list of exemptions, including for example not only those mentioned above, including all cabinet papers, and 'internal working documents' that might disclose official advice, but also documents whose disclosure would 'prejudice relations between the Commonwealth and the States', or would be likely to have 'a substantially adverse effect on the national economy'. Secondly, although there is some provision for inspection of documents *in camera* by the Administrative Appeals Tribunal (see Chapter Six), under many exempted categories the minister's certificate that the matter is exempt must be accepted as conclusive. Other provisions that have turned out to be important in the United States, such as those regarding costs, are less liberal or are left to be covered under government regulations.

One problem area is information that reveals the attitude of particular officials on proposed lines of action, including confidential advice given to ministers. It is commonly argued that, if these deliberative processes of public administration are to be conducted frankly, public servants have a right to protect their written comments from public disclosure until a reasonably long period has elapsed after the decision (there is currently in Australia a '30-year rule'); this is, of course, apart from any duty they have not to disclose their own views publicly. It is claimed that one result of widespread public disclosure of files would be much greater caution in putting views on paper, to the detriment of efficient administration. The demand for more openness, and the apotheosis of officials who 'speak out', could lead in practice to more secrecy, and the restriction of consultation to a narrowing circle of reliable colleagues whose discussions leave no public trace. Of course one could argue that this has mostly happened already, and that the really confidential exchanges now take place in face-to-face contact or on the telephone. So opening the files will be of more limited use to the future historian or the current muckraker than some people realise.

A crucial question, even if we admit that there are competing claims between the need for secrecy and the 'right to know', is: who decides? If a government's claim that secrecy on some matter is in the public interest, or that it protects someone's right to privacy, clashes with the public's right to know, is the final decision to rest with a minister or public servant, or with an independent tribunal? Some overseas legislation, as we have seen, gives a court the major voice. The view of the recent Australian bill is that much more has to be left to ministers and that the minister should in important cases have final power to decide whether the release of a document would prejudice the public interest.

The same question has arisen in a somewhat different context, where government documents are relevant to some case brought in the courts. This matter was tested in the British House of Lords,[22] which decided that judges had the right to look at the documents in question themselves, and to determine whether the harm to the public interest involved in disclosure was greater than that involved in the frustration of the administration of justice. However, the case concerned a relatively minor matter (the dismissal of a probationary policeman) and it left many questions undecided.

It is arguable that the main contribution to open government in recent years has not been the result of any deliberate policy decision, but of some decay in the conventions of collective ministerial responsibility (always precarious in Australia) and also of public service neutrality, reflected in a greater disposition to personal comment by ministers and an increase in calculated leaks by both ministers and public servants.[23] The administrative leaks seem to have grown in the 1970s, first under the Whitlam government, then under Fraser. A series took place in the months after the 1975 election, provoking an investigation. The Fraser government reviewed security in government departments again in 1977, and has tried to tighten up procedures for handling papers, photocopying, and communicating with the press.[24] Modern technology has made it easier to copy documents. There is probably a general trend to more outspokenness and to somewhat greater politicisation of the public service. Public servants do not feel so guilty about indiscretions, and we are encouraged by modern political scientists and others to believe that everything is 'political'. No wonder that a few officials infer that they have a right, or even a duty, to let the press have some document of which they disapprove, or which they think may embarrass the government of the day. Also, the media coverage of Canberra increased in quantity and quality during the 1960s; a picture has been constructed of how things work that makes it easier to guess what is happening when a single key fact is revealed. Many journalists came to work as ministerial advisers in the 1970s, and now know the system from the inside, and have friends there.

A department may find support in the media as well as criticism. The press can be a weapon for a government agency or for an individual public servant when, for example, they think that something is going wrong but are prevented from saying so themselves by the regulations or by the conventions of official behaviour. This can be a dangerous game. An immediate cause of Mr Fraser's decision to carve up the Treasury in December 1976 is said to have been anger at a report in the Melbourne *Age*, believed to have come from a Treasury source.

Access

What obstacles are there to people getting the goods and services that government provides? If goods and services are sold, the main problem is to have the money to buy them. For most government services, other things are more important. One is the client's non-monetary resources—status, influence, knowledge, time, skill in establishing the right links with public agencies, or knowing how to enlist the help of the local member. The other main factor lies on the side of the government agency, its system for distributing its services. These two, the client's resources and the agency's distribution system, may reinforce or counterbalance each other.[25] For example, a system of appeals from agency decisions may positively favour the more resourceful client or the one who can afford to wait. On the other hand, the eligibility rules for a service may impose a means test designed to help the poor.

Even then the client has to know where and how to demonstrate eligibility. The rules may be in a strange language, need skill to interpret, impose a burden of documentation, or be costly in time spent in travelling or waiting. So what appears to help the client with fewer resources may actually disadvantage the one with fewest resources, including some migrants and

Aborigines. A subsidised health benefit plan designed for low-income families (since superseded) had 'complexities so great that they defeated not only potential beneficiaries but their social work advisers in voluntary agencies'.[26] A pamphlet designed to explain the scheme in simple terms required 137 questions and answers to cover the ground.

The responsibility for services may also be scattered among different agencies, with offices located in different places and sometimes hard to find, or forbidding in appearance. There may be great variations in service provision between areas, say, a surplus of hospital beds in the inner areas of big cities and a shortage in outer areas, as has been a common situation in some Australian State capitals. There may be long waiting times, or a discouraging counter staff. Actually Australian counter staffs did not come off too badly in an Access Survey Report to the Coombs Commission, based on interviews with a sample of staff and clients in five Commonwealth government agencies. Of the clients, 89 per cent thought them 'courteous' and 92 per cent 'efficient'; on the other hand only 74 per cent thought them 'anxious to help' and only 59 per cent 'sympathetic'.[27] A committee of officials has been reporting to the government on measures needed to improve counter staff services to the public.

Public Participation

'Participation' in government has come to have many meanings, but it is used here to mean having some genuine power to influence policy outcomes and the allocation of resources. Believers in more public participation in government have various aims—to increase the influence of the unorganised and so change the distribution of power, to improve policies by bringing more grassroots knowledge to bear on them, to educate the public politically, to increase the acceptability of public policies and reduce apathy and alienation. We have mentioned earlier various problems of staff participation—problems of 'competence', 'affected interests' and 'personal choice' (see Chapter Thirteen). These also arise in the case of public participation.

Some Problems of Participation

As to competence, one simple answer to the demand for more public participation in government decision-making is that the latter is a job for experts. If the public dislikes the broad trend of policy, its remedy is the ballot-box. This answer seems to involve a much too monistic view of government, and to ignore the fact that sections of the public, such as organised pressure groups, already participate in decision-making in fields that affect them, which sometimes results in resources going where they are least needed. It also over-estimates the 'expert' component in most government decisions, and also the capacity of so-called experts in many fields, and it underrates the public's competence or potential competence, especially on matters that engage them personally; certainly it underrates the competence of the more articulate and concerned, but often under-organised, sections of the public.[28]

The problem of 'affected interests' also arises. If outside interests are to be represented, which and to what degree? In many administrative contexts, the direct representation of consumers has the special difficulty that there is no 'natural constituency', often no way of choosing representatives except through government nomination or that of organised pressure groups, not quite the same thing as the elusive 'man or woman in the street'. Sometimes there is a constituency, as with the parents of children at a school, and these in fact have been encouraged to play at least a limited role in state schools (the ACT went further, and the Schools Authority established by ordinance in 1976 included three nominees of parents' and citizens' associations, as well as three representatives of the Teachers' Federation; there were also to be school boards with lay members). The organisers of the Regional Councils for Social Development had the idea of creating constituencies by electing councils at meetings of the general public, a device open to much manipulation, and not designed to give them minimal legitimacy in the eyes of better-established institutions (see Chapter Nine).

The problem of 'personal choice' is that most people may not wish to participate, or prefer to use their time in other ways. It is true that until the late 1960s the domestic actions of Australian governments aroused astonishingly little protest, save where they upset a few well-organised groups. But this situation has changed now that there are more articulate minorities, greater questioning of authority, increasing concern with environmental and welfare questions, and with the impact of planning decisions. A government committed to encouraging participation could probably do a fair amount to reduce apathy, which sometimes arises from feelings of helplessness or lack of knowledge about how public organisations work and how to apply effective pressure on them. Until recently Australian governments have rarely taken public consultation seriously, even in situations where it is most likely to be profitable (say, in planning a new housing area). Participation can be 'learned', but it needs time and money spent on it, and machinery for acquainting people with alternative choices, helping them to organise, and to learn to 'work the system', what types of action are open to them. Experiments in participation cannot be expected to succeed quickly, and demand a high level of integrity in those conducting them, one which conceivably will not be forthcoming in most cases. They can also be expensive —to give an overseas example, the Community Health Councils set up to encourage consumer participation in the British National Health Service may cost around $6 million in direct and indirect costs.[29]

The Commonwealth Labor government of 1972–75 made one or two efforts in this direction, though the main thrusts of policy expressed what might rather be described as a Fabian belief in the efficiency of centralist government. We have mentioned in Chapter Nine the experiments of the Australian Assistance Plan with Regional Councils for Social Development.[30]

The former Social Welfare Commission, which originated the Councils, saw itself as having a particular mandate to encourage 'consumer and volunteer involvement in welfare'.[31] There have been a number of other experiments, such as the Albury–Wodonga Consultative Council, though it has had to meet its 'constituency' problems by making a majority of members nominees of local councils in the area. The 1972 legislation in South Australia for Community Councils for Social Development does not provide for, nor intend, consumer representation.

There is no point in burking the difficulties, compounded in Australia by weaknesses in the structure of government below State level[32] and by the highly bureaucratic and unionised character of some State services, even where more public participation might otherwise seem feasible, as in the case of education. Supporters of participation sometimes spoil their case by implying that they have some new unpolitical remedy for our ills. Organisers of new forms of popular influence will continue to have some personal axe to grind, participation will always be likely to help those who do not most need helping, and much so-called participation will continue to be manipulative.

All the same it is easy to be cynical and there are some genuine possibilities of a more participative society taking better informed decisions, raising the sights of its members, and helping towards a more responsible and better integrated community. The Brotherhood of St Laurence in Melbourne has tried out a number of radical ideas in social policy with poor families, including a Family Centre Project committed to de-professionalising the relation between social worker and client, and planned so that the families ultimately controlled the project.[33] It has been an exercise in what some regard as a contradiction in terms, 'structured participation', in which the creation of participatory arrangements was itself to be a gradual process, rationally assessed at each stage, yet given a clear priority as an objective in cases of doubt.

Participation, Pressure Groups and Politics

Access and participation can be differential for groups as well as individuals. The point was made earlier that one difficulty about greater public participation in government is that, in many administrative situations, there is no 'natural constituency', no easy way of choosing representatives of the public. The simplest way out of this problem is to rely on already organised groups. Some pessimists have argued that more stress on public participation and public access, at any rate within existing bureaucratic structures, will only increase the power of the more vocal and better-organised.

As we have already indicated, many of the motives of those concerned with improving participation are high-minded, concerned with redistributive public policy or with helping the inarticulate and underprivileged to defend their interests. Sharpe has distinguished between this kind of 'community participation' and 'instrumental participation', which is 'essentially a much more prosaic demand of those affected by public policy to have a say in the determination of that policy'.[34] The latter is not necessarily egalitarian or community-minded, and is much more concerned with power-relationships than democratic values. It is indeed the case that more and more outside organisations are interested in the decisions of governments and attempt to influence them; and, knowing the power of the public service, they try to exert influence at the administrative as well as the political level. There is nothing wrong about this. Much government would not be possible without such groups, which among other things simplify the administrator's task of obtaining the information about facts and attitudes needed to make good decisions. An important function of pressure groups is to negotiate; but they also play an ideological role, in projecting particular images of themselves, of other groups and of society in general. Many of them are represented on the hundreds of advisory committees (see Chapter Five) that now assist government.

The most obvious influences that a modern government has to expect are those coming from producer groups—trade associations, trade unions, farm groups. But there are also professional associations, such as the Australian Medical Association; bodies representing Aborigines, ex-servicemen, pensioners; and reformist and conservationist groups that claim to have a disinterested concern with some area of public policy. Producer groups have the readiest access to government, being better organised, richer, more clearly representative of their members, often more knowledgeable and with more concrete and immediate objectives than other groups. The government has recently been giving financial help to Aboriginal, environmental and consumer groups to help them with running expenses and payment for professional assistance in the attempt to counter some of their natural disadvantages.[35]

In recent years the techniques of many outside groups have changed. What used often to be negative attitudes to government, expressed in public protest, have been supplemented or replaced by a more positive desire to 'co-operate' with government and to influence its actions from within. Major economic groups have set up offices in Canberra, and many of them employ ex-public servants to assist in negotiations; groups with Canberra offices include the Confederation of Australian Industry (CAI), the Australian Industries Development Association (AIDA), the Australian Mining Industry Council (AMIC), the Metal Trades Industry Association. Departments interested in a particular area of policy often find it useful to remain in a regular consultative relationship with outside interests, and may even encourage them to form a group for purposes of mutual information and negotiation. This can become too 'cosy' a form of inter-elite contact, so it is perhaps fortunate that as older groups tend to regularise their government contacts, new groups spring up from time to time to revive more open forms of pressure.

The 1972 change of government in Australia led to a shake-up in the 'old boy networks' and producer groups could no longer assume that their former links with the administration gave them reliable access to government thinking; the latter was in any case subject to more changes, causing greater uncertainty. Some groups, such as the Australian Mining Industry Council, openly clashed with Labor's Department of Minerals and Energy. But the Labor government retained or rebuilt many formal and other links with such groups. It is sometimes said that Labor governments need, or think they need, more formal contacts with business and farming groups, as non-Labor governments do with trade unions, precisely because the ministers have fewer good informal contacts. (Some Liberal Prime Ministers have relied more for advice on a few trusted friends in the business world than on organised business groups, and may even regard the latter with mild contempt.) It was, after all, the Whitlam government that first gave Australian industry its own department in Canberra.

Some believers in participation hold the view that it is only through such pressures that genuine participation is possible. Participation cannot be engineered by do-gooding elites but arises 'when clients with grievances begin to do something about them'.[36] The real obstacles to participation do not lie in particular government structures, but in the more fundamental difficulties that some groups have in organising through lack of money, cohesion, experience and faith in their capacity to influence the situation. Even when groups concerned with consumer welfare develop, their bargaining power tends to be low, and they suffer from the non-involvement of most of their potential supporters. Representation in such groups is often self-selective, the members mainly represent themselves.

It remains an open question how many people are really interested in extending participatory democracy as such. The main supporters tend to be those who are dissatisfied with present government policies, who hope to change these policies in favourable directions by invoking new forms of popular pressure. It is not clear how they would react if increased participation led to policy outcomes of which they disapproved; there is sometimes an act of faith that (in the long run, at least) this would not happen.

Finally, demands for more information, better access, more participation are demands for power, and raise significant political questions.[37] Control of information is a source of power, as is control of other scarce resources. 'The scarcest commodity in the civil service is information, and like all scarce commodities it is not freely exchanged . . . Therefore those with a knack of finding out what is going on are off to a headstart'.[38] The same is true of participation. Also, the old theory of public participation in government, that it mainly operated through an elected parliament to which ministers were responsible, in part reflected the view that there was some overriding 'public interest' of which legislature and governments were the main representatives and arbiters. For those who still hold to this view an important issue is: how is this public interest to be represented in the proposed new world of responsive public administration? How can the public genuinely participate more in public administration without at the same time fragmenting it, multiplying points of delay and obstruction, and creating a climate even more unfavourable than the present one for responsible decision-making? Against this, a pluralist school of thought sees multiple bargaining and variety as fundamental to democratic administration, and is not worried by fragmentation. It believes that it is more important for public servants to be responsive to their various clients than to their political masters; and that out of all this, all that can truthfully be called the interests of the public will be faithfully served. There is a third group that seeks to reconcile these two positions by holding that a society of better-informed and more efficacious citizens will also be one of more widespread consensus and trust.

Notes

1. G.E. Caiden, *The Commonwealth Bureaucracy*, Melbourne University Press, Melbourne, 1967, 47.
2. See for example Interim Report, Review of New South Wales Government Administration, 257.
3. *The Australian*, 15 June 1970.
4. Andrew Clark, *National Times*, 12 May 1975.
5. Bruce Juddery, *At the Centre*, Cheshire, Melbourne, 1974, 195.
6. Report, RCAGA, 351, 353.
7. *ibid.*, 350
8. Sir Robert Mark, *In the Office of Constable*, as quoted in *The Times*, 9 October 1978.
9. See examples in J. Spigelman, *Secrecy: Political Censorship in Australia*, Angus and Robertson, Sydney, 1972. Some of the items referred to have since been released, partly due to the work of Mr Spigelman.
10. See J.J. Spigelman, 'Open Government in the Seventies', in Report, RCAGA, Appendix Vol. Two, 159–60.
11. John Lleonart, 'Open Government in the Department of Social Security', *ibid.*, 187. But see also *Canberra Times*, 3 December 1977.
12. The Coombs Commission thought, for example, that the quarterly national income forecasts of the Treasury should remain confidential, though available on a restricted basis to some other departments. See Report, RCAGA, 304.
13. Sir William (now Lord) Armstrong, 'The Role and Character of the Civil Service', British Academy Lecture, London, 1970, 15.
14. See article in *The Times*, 17 August 1978, and Lord Croham, 'Is Nothing Secret?', *The Listener*, 7 September 1978.
15. On party committees, see Patrick Weller, 'Public Servants and the Briefing of Party Committees', *Aust. J. Public Admin.*, XXXVI, 2, June 1977.
16. *Com. Parl. Deb.* (H. of R.), V. 102, 9 December 1976, 3591–2.
17. 162nd Report, Joint Committee of Public Accounts, *Inquiry into the Financial Administration of the Department of Aboriginal Affairs*, Canberra, 1977.
18. *Com. Parl. Deb.* (Senate), V. 64, 15 July 1975, 2729–30.
19. See Geoffrey Hawker, 'The Administrative Implications of Freedom of Information Legislation', *Aust. J. Public Admin.*, XXXVI, 2, June 1977. I have been helped by an unpublished paper by Senator Alan Missen.
20. Report, RCAGA, Appendix Vol. Two, 1–156.

21. *Policy Proposals for Freedom of Information Legislation*, Report of Inter-departmental Committee, Canberra, 1976.
22. *Conway* v. *Rimmer* (1968), A.C. 910.
23. On collective responsibility, see S. Encel, *Cabinet Government in Australia*, 2nd edn, Melbourne University Press, Melbourne, 1974, ch. 12.
24. See, for example, *The Australian*, 15 July 1976; and press references in *National Times*, 16 and 23 May 1977.
25. The discussion here draws heavily on B.B. Schaffer, 'The Theory of Access', a paper delivered to the RCAGA seminar, Canberra, 1974.
26. ACOSS, 'Report on Accessibility of the Health Services', reprinted in R.N. Spann and G.R. Curnow (eds), *Public Policy and Administration in Australia: A Reader*, Wiley, Sydney, 1975, 508.
27. 'Access to Government Services', Report, RCAGA, Appendix Vol. Two, 22, 293 (There is a small unexplained discrepancy in different versions of the last figure.)
28. For relevant discussion see T.V. Matthews, 'Interest Group Access to the Australian Government Bureaucracy', Report, RCAGA, Appendix Vol. Two, 353–65, and references therein; P. Loveday, 'Citizen Participation in Urban Planning', in R.S. Parker and P.N. Troy (eds), *The Politics of Urban Growth*, Australian National University Press, Canberra, 1972, 129–48.
29. R. Klein and J. Lewis, *The Politics of Consumer Representation*, Centre for Studies in Social Policy, London, 1976, 157, *cit.* Erica Bates, *Aust. J. Public Admin.* XXXVII, 1, March 1976, 91.
30. There have been attempts to learn from this experience, such as Leonard Tierney, *From Vague Ideas to Unfeasible Roles*, Department of Social Studies, University of Melbourne, Melbourne, 1977; see also D.L. Jayasuria, *Australian Assistance Plan: Western Australian Evaluation Report*, Department of Social Work, Perth, 1975; Adam Graycar and others, *Australian Assistance Plan: Preliminary Report on Developments in South Australia and Northern Territory*, Flinders University, South Australia, 1974.
31. 1st Report, Social Welfare Commission, Canberra, 1973, 14.
32. For a case study of a local council's efforts to encourage citizen participation in planning, see Ron Davine, 'Citizen Participation in Planning: A Case Study of Artarmon', *Aust. Planning Institute J.*, April 1970, 46–50.
33. See Michael Liffman, *Power for the Poor*, Allen and Unwin, Sydney, 1978.
34. L.J. Sharpe, 'Instrumental Participation and Local Government', in J.A.G. Griffith (ed.), *From Policy to Administration*, Allen and Unwin, London, 1976, 122.
35. Matthews, *op. cit.*, 333, 350; see also 347, for a list of pressure groups with offices in Canberra.
36. Martin Painter, in H. Mayer and H. Nelson (eds), *Australian Politics: A Fifth Reader*, Cheshire, Melbourne, 1979.
37. cf. Cameron Hazlehurst, 'The Information Dimension', in C. Hazlehurst and J.R. Nethercote (eds), *Reforming Australian Government: The Coombs Report and Beyond*, RIPA and Australian National University Press, Canberra, 1977, 131; Hazlehurst, *Rights to Know*, Department of Political Science, University of Tasmania, 1977; and E.F. Kelly and R.L. Wettenhall, 'Policy Analysis and the "New Public Administration" ', *Public Admin.* (Sydney), XXXII, 4, December 1973, 404–13.
38. Samuel Brittan, 'The Irregulars', in R. Rose (ed.), *Policy-making in Britain*, London, 1969, 336.

Chapter Eighteen

Administrative Reform, Accountability and Efficiency

One of the new emphases in writing about administration is the demand for innovation, creativity and responsiveness to changing needs among administrators. The old neutral model of the administrative system assumed a fairly stable world, or one where the occasional change was injected into the administrative system by politicians requiring that some specific reforms be implemented. But now the administration itself is expected to be like the churches, *semper reformanda*, engaged in continual self-renewal. It is pressed to become 'proactive rather than reactive'[1], anticipating troubles rather than responding to them, whether this be in urban problems or defence.

In some respects Australian public administration has responded not too badly to this demand for self-reform. We have discussed changes in recruitment and staffing policies, budgeting, machinery of government, in earlier chapters. In fields such as organisation and methods, automatic data processing, and so on, the pace of change has also been fast.[2] There have been notable improvements in the working environment of administrators, and Australian public servants must now be among the best-housed in the world. The most successful areas of self-reform could be characterised in three ways—they have been areas where evolutionary change has been possible, as in graduate and lateral recruitment, or changes that have involved no great shock to the existing power and status system, or the technological benefits of which have been fairly obvious. They have also been made easier by taking place in a period of fairly steady growth in public service numbers and pay.

The point has often been made that public services are not wedded to inertia, but perhaps better fitted to cope with evolutionary changes than ones involving a sharp break; as Sir Arthur Helps put it in the last century, Improvement rather than Reform. Bureaucracies have a strong sense of continuity and their hierarchical structure promotes conformity. 'Those who think too freely . . . tend to be told that they need time to mature, or that they need more time to become "reliable" '.[3] It is sometimes argued that this would change if there was more participative management, and a greater attempt to involve the staff in decisions; but this is a still untested proposition, and the opposite could well be true, it could reinforce conservatism. For example, Mosher in his study of administrative reorganisations could find no correlation between the participation of subordinates and success or failure. Sometimes consultation worked best; sometimes it was better to present the staff with a *fait accompli*.[4] What seems to be more important is a longer-term history of good internal relations and trust. As Peter Bailey adds, this is especially true of changes that might involve a reduction in government activity. Indeed, one of the most difficult kinds of administrative reform is that which involves cutting out an existing institution or function; it is much easier to add a new agency than to get rid of an old one. Bureaucracies are used to dividing up the market, and are usually well organised to defend their present market share. This is supported by the 'remarkable system of checks and balances' that exists within Australian government administration,[5] where most new moves require wide consultation, with many opportunities for formal veto or appeal.

There is also the problem in many areas of public administration that it is difficult to measure the costs and benefits of reform. This makes it hard to state a conclusive case for some particular degree of change, or even sometimes for a particular direction of change. An organisation processing a material product can innovate more readily because the advantages of an improved technique or product change are more clearly demonstrable than those of an administrative or social change. This also helps to explain why it is easier to promote changes in office methods than larger changes of structure; not only are fewer vested interests involved (this is not always the case), but the benefits of change can be more unambiguously demonstrated. A study of ten reforms in urban public services in the 1960s suggests that the novelty and scope of the recommendations affected their acceptability less than the reversibility and testability of the change.[6]

Of course, uncertainty does not always lead to conservatism, it may also promote susceptibility to fads and fashions. So in administrative reform, as in social reform, one may get swings of the pendulum—the benefits of large-scale being preached at one time, followed by the gospel that 'small is beautiful', periods of integration succeeded by ones of pluralistic disintegration, or oscillation between demands for functional rationality and concern for a holistic approach to particular clienteles and communities.

We have already mentioned that it is hard to measure the effectiveness of administrative reforms. This difficulty is added to by the fact that the effects of many changes take a fair number of years to work themselves out, by which time many other things will have altered. There is also the general problem of measuring administrative efficiency, referred to later in this chapter.

The Sources of Change and Reform

One rough distinction that is sometimes made is between endogenous and exogenous sources of change, ones that originate from within the system, and ones that come from outside it. Some administrative reforms arise from new needs of which public servants themselves become aware—from techno-logical advances to gaps in welfare provision—or from new demands arising inside the organisation, as for more participation. Others come from outside political or clientele demands, or changes in the environment (say, in the rate of economic growth), or through the reports of outside committees of inquiry. However, this distinction is not as clear as it may look at first sight, as many changes are the result of a coalescence of internal and external pressures. We discuss below the 'outsider-insider' distinction as applied to reports on administrative reform.

A related distinction is similar to that made by Helps between improvement and reform. It is the distinction between the kind of 'natural' change that is happening all the time inside government as a result of normal feedback processes and the entry of new personnel, and 'artificial' change deliberately induced from outside, which may be part of some more fundamental project of social reform, or which may be unwelcome to the recipients. Gerald Caiden even suggests we reserve the words 'administrative reform' for the latter, for 'the artificial inducement of administrative transformation against resistance',[7] which may (among other things) involve a new moral impetus. This is clearly relevant to some situations, though it involves a very pessimistic estimate of the vested interests inside an existing system. There is a different view, that we should try as far as possible to build on existing foundations even where far-reaching changes are necessary. Thus it could be argued that two important preliminary activities of would-be reformers are; first, to list the so-called obstacles to reform and ask how they might be converted into supports; secondly, to ask what have been the greatest successes and failures in reform, especially in the recent past, and to try to learn the necessary lessons and to build on success.

A number of writers have challenged the view that administrative reform is necessarily a slow process—a conservative assumption largely accepted by the recent Coombs Commission—and argued that 'you can change institu-tions quickly if you really want to. It is simply a matter of will in a relatively small number of decisive points.'[8] On this view, bringing about reform is mainly a matter of being clear about what you want to do, what (if you are not yourself the decision-maker) political will for change can be aroused, and what the wider public will respond to, or at least acquiesce in. It is easier to say this than to do it. For example, it has never been quite clear what those who have criticised the Coombs Commission for its conservatism and continued adherence to the Westminster Model would have put in the latter's place. One of the Coombs Commissioners has even maintained that 'no public service enquiry since 1852 has produced, in any established western democracy, more than changes at the margin',[9] a proposition that I have not had time to test. He has also argued that although some other recent inquiries in Australia and overseas were set up with the idea of making far-reaching changes, they 'have not been able to come up with recommendations of that kind', even when given broad terms of reference.

Whatever one's views about these controversies, proposals for change obviously stand a better chance if they are broadly in the direction of prevailing currents, either outside or inside the system. Thus the emphasis of the Glassco Commission in Canada (1960–63) on better business management in government was in accordance with existing general trends and widespread outside beliefs about deficiencies in public administration. In Britain the Fulton Committee's criticisms of the Administrative Class went down well in the anti-elitist mood of the later 1960s, just as the Boyer Committee's more cogent advocacy of an administrative class in Australia had on the whole suited Canberra a decade earlier; it is true that even in these cases the actual changes following the reports, though important, only took place in modified form. It has been suggested that it might be better for administrative reformers to concentrate on assessing and predicting the forces to which their organisations will in due course be compelled to adapt, 'and quietly to encourage the development of these' where their effects appear desirable, rather than to stake too much on initiating change from within.[10]

Some Recent Inquiries

This chapter deals with some recent committees and commissions of inquiry that have concerned themselves with administrative reform. Such bodies have an old history in Australia (some are mentioned briefly in Chapter Eleven), since J.T. Bigge was appointed in 1819 by the British government as Commissioner to inquire into the Administration of New South Wales.[11] Each generation from the 1850s onwards produced a crop of inquiries, but the enterprise petered out in the 1920s, and was succeeded by almost half a century when such outside investigations largely ceased, until a series of new committees and commissions was appointed between 1973 and 1976, starting with the Corbett Committee appointed by the Labor government in South Australia in May 1973.

The reasons for this are complex. The reforms of the 1920s and (in the Commonwealth) the changes brought about by the Second World War seem to have generated the minimal satisfaction with the state of the public services needed to fend off critics. In general it is fairly rare for administrative organisations to be brought to some conspicuous and major public test, despite minor irritations. For one thing, politicians tend to regard administrative problems as dull and unromantic, so it may take a striking event to produce a major change. There was a flicker of Commonwealth 'reformism' starting with the Murray Report on the Universities (1957) and which included the Boyer Committee on Public Service Recruitment, but it largely petered out with the unacceptable Vernon Report. An important precipitating fact or for the recent series of inquiries was the advent of a Commonwealth Labor government in Canberra in December 1972, but this itself was a reflection of unease with current social performance which had also begun to affect Commonwealth and State non-Labor governments in the early 1970s.

Many of the recent schemes for administrative reform in Australia bring out the crucial importance of personalities and changes of leadership. A change of government can upset the applecart, not only because parties change, but people change. The Coombs Report was to have been tailored for Mr Whitlam, and had to be partly retailored for Mr Fraser. The 1974 New South Wales review was probably the product of Sir Robert Askin's impending retirement and a bid for power by Mr Lewis. The Corbett Report in South Australia was very much a product of the Dunstan era. The 1977 New South Wales review may be classed as 'early Wran'. But it is not only the personalities of Premiers that matter, or of the Commissioners of Inquiry. Particular senior officials may play a crucial role. For example, in New South Wales the appointment of a new Under Secretary of Lands and a new Chief Commissioner of the then Water and Irrigation Commission, both in early 1975, seem to have been crucial in settling some of the character of controversial changes in machinery of government. As is well-known, the impending retirement of a senior administrator is often an appropriate moment to initiate the reorganisation of a government agency.

However, it should perhaps be stressed that most of the inquiries discussed below were not set up by governments specially anxious to promote radical experiment. In general, they were at least as concerned with improving the efficiency and keeping down the cost of an existing administrative machine which had for some years been growing fairly fast, certainly in absolute terms, and in some areas relatively to the private sector. (Even in the case of the Whitlam government most of its more radical experiments were in fact launched by the time the Coombs Commission was set up in 1974, even if this was not fully realised in all quarters at the time.)

The recent reports and inquiries referred to in this chapter are as follows:

Commonwealth
1. Report (Coombs) Royal Commission on Australian Government Administration, Canberra 1976
2. (Bland) Administrative Review Committee, 1976—no published reports

New South Wales
1. Machinery of Government Review, 1974—no published reports
2. Interim Report, (Wilenski) Review of New South Wales Government Administration, 'Directions for Change', Sydney 1977

South Australia
Report, (Corbett) Committee of Inquiry into the Public Service of South Australia, Adelaide 1975

Victoria
Reports, (Bland) Board of Inquiry into the Victorian Public Service, Melbourne 1974–5 (four reports).

As their short titles indicate, these bodies mostly had broad terms of reference—in the case of the Coombs Commission, almost unmanageably broad. This is not necessarily an advantage, as major administrative change sometimes occurs by stealth or at least by precedent-setting in particular cases. Wettenhall has pointed out that some of the more narrowly based British inquiries, as into electricity and broadcasting, probably achieved a good deal more in developing and popularising the concept of the 'public corporation' (see Chapter Five) than a committee more broadly concerned with machinery of government would have done.[12]

There seems to have been a general tendency to reduce the membership of administrative inquiries in Australia in this century—the norm has been the three-man or even one-man inquiry. Even though the Coombs Commission had only five members, given its wide terms of reference, this increased the difficulty of getting a set of recommendations that (as someone has put it) 'speak with a loud clear voice'. This is especially true where a body is of somewhat variegated composition, where the chairman is more used to playing his own hand than seeking consensus from a group of equals, and where the process of delimiting the field and arriving at conclusions on various points does not proceed in an orderly fashion. However, as we have already indicated, there are difficulties about speaking in a loud clear voice about the broad problems of public administration in the 1970s, when there are many plausible competing voices and no obviously simple answers to questions. Sir Henry Bland as a one-man Board and Professor Wilenski as a one-man Commissioner had (formally speaking) no one but themselves to persuade, at least about the contents of their reports, so it was to be expected (especially given their personalities and predilections) that they would present reports with sharper outlines, and speedily— both produced a first major report less than a year after being commissioned.

If actual memberships of recent inquiries were small, the larger nineteenth-century commissions would have envied some of them their research staffs and consultants. The Coombs Commission set a wholly new standard in this matter, with a secretariat and research section of over seventy, some fifty projects commissioned from consultants, five task forces and three other advisory bodies. However, it is significant that business management consultants played a much smaller part than was the case with the Canadian Glassco Commission.[13] The South Australian inquiry began with only one secretary and an adviser, but soon had a research staff of five and some part-timers. The 1977 New South Wales Review had three full-time research officers, two secretaries and considerable part-time help, and the Public Service Board and an outside body conducted a number of surveys for it (five years earlier the part-time Barnett Committee on Local Government Areas and Administration in New South Wales had almost no effective staff assistance save on purely routine matters).

Committees of inquiry have commonly wasted much time on formal public hearings, a waste not usually compensated for by much extra information or 'legitimacy'. The Coombs Commission (and the Barnett Committee) were notable offenders; most of the other recent inquiries have been more sensible, and relied mainly on their own research, on written submissions, and personal private interviews supplemented by a few informal hearings or seminars. The Glassco Commission in Canada decided not to hold public hearings but rather produce an interim report to outline problems and arouse interest—perhaps it erred too much in the other direction, and some deficiencies in its recommendations have been attributed to lack of awareness of the views of interested groups. The Canadian inquiry also seems to have organized its research better than the British Fulton Committee on the Civil Service or the Coombs Commission, which both fell into the trap (though Coombs did much better than Fulton) of not being able to take full account of it in preparing the report. The Coombs Commission produced some interim documents in the way of task force reports and discussion papers but in a haphazard way, and they had inadequate feedback on the main recommendations, though the commission had the excuse of having to wind up operations somewhat more quickly than expected. There was also a little 'action research', experimental and pilot projects to test innovatory methods of administration, but this got off the ground too late to yield significant results. One was the NOW project referred to in Chapter Four.

Outsiders and Insiders

The work of committees of inquiry of the kind described is often equated with the notion of an 'outside look' at government administration. First, it should be said that such a body is by no means the only way of bringing outside expertise to bear on organisations. Australian governments have begun to exploit in very varied ways the possibilities of research through outside groups and individuals. Departments make use of outside consultants, often with departmental officers also as part of the team, in everything from ADP, work measurement schemes, transportations survey and market research, to ways of improving Aboriginal living standards. More use has been made of research units in universities and the Australian National University in particular has become an important centre for government-aided research in urban studies, federal relations, and so on. The New South Wales Public Service Board established an Administrative Research Unit in 1964, some of whose officers were seconded from other departments, others recruited from universities. The unit is guided by an Administrative Research Committee, composed of senior university staff, who help to isolate problems needing research, to formulate priorities and to guide research activities. Some of its more influential early reports include those on Administrative Potential (which recommended the creation of the present Assessment Centre) and on Community Health Services (an important step in the movement for regionalisation of State health services). It has more recently been studying topics such as: Public Service Growth, Equal Employment Opportunity, Community Participation, and bread-and-butter topics such as sick leave policies and the form and content of the Public Service Board's annual report.

This is an 'inside' body, but one on which considerable influence has been exercised by outsiders. It may help to remind us that the distinction is often one of degree rather than kind. The recent committees of inquiry also illustrate this. In the Corbett Report an important role was played by a public service member of the committee, Mr R.D. Bakewell, then Director of the Premier's Department. The leader of two of the inquiries, Sir Henry Bland, was a former Commonwealth permanent head, as were Professor Wilenski and Dr Coombs; the latter had also been Governor of the Reserve Bank, and he had another senior public servant on his five-member Commission. Two of the other three members of the 1976 Bland committee were public servants.

The problem of combining outside and inside research and advice is not simple, even when the aim is primarily to obtain an expert judgment, not to mollify interests. The case for an outside look is not confined to the situation where internal expertise is clearly lacking. Organisations by their nature limit the attention of their members, and also create vested interests in certain types of response. Those closest to a problem are often most inclined to stress the practical difficulties of coping with it; those insiders affected for the worse by a particular solution will tend to oppose it, not only out of self-interest, but because their situation has conditioned them into not seeing that solution as viable. The inadequacies of the inside look may generate arguments in favour of the outside look, the consultant, the committee of inquiry, or the research and planning unit, uninvolved in the day-to-day concerns and biases of the working administrator. Such people have their own limitations of vision; their virtue is not necessarily that they see the problem more clearly, but at least they may see it differently, unless the insiders call for advice from outsiders like themselves (as sometimes happens). Mosher finds that outside inquiries tend to be more comprehensive, critical (there is an inbuilt motive to criticise), long-winded, and expensive; and more inclined to recommend structural changes or imitations of other organisations. Outsiders also stress how things should be after change rather than how to change them. Insiders tend to produce shorter and clearer reports, focussed on specific problems, knowledgeable about feasibility and strategies for implementation, but minimising self-criticism.[14]

Some problems are recognised and solved more successfully from outside an organisation than inside. But the opposite may be true; or the outside may see the problem more clearly, but the inside solve it better once it has been formulated. So an administrative reform committee may help to formulate basic problems, even if all their particular solutions are not accepted. It is an interesting question which kinds of administrative problem lend themselves most readily to formulation or solution by outside investigators, by internal research units, and so on. On many administrative questions, outsiders 'very rarely know enough to hit the mark exactly . . . they supplement, and do not replace, criticism from within the service itself'.[15] Of course, much in their reports is often based on internal critical appraisals which their existence helps to provoke; the Coombs Commission gave the

Commonwealth Public Service Board a good chance to formulate its own recommendations for change (the latter seems to have learned a lesson from the British Treasury's aloofness from the Fulton Committee).

The 1974 Machinery of Government Review in New South Wales is the clearest example of the 'insider' or 'in-house' approach to administrative reform.[16] The review was overseen by a cabinet sub-committee, under which were several study groups, each chaired by a minister and consisting mainly of government servants. Associated with this was the close link between the making and implementation of recommendations. This was partly because Mr Lewis, who initiated the inquiry, had become Premier while it was proceeding, but also because 'most of the political trade-offs, exchanges and bargaining . . . had already occurred in the study groups and sub-committee',[17] and many of the reporters were also important implementers. A third characteristic of the review was that it went on with little publicity. Finally, it was speedy and cheap.

In some ways the 1974 review was a special case, because of its unusual concentration on machinery of government questions, the structure and functions of government agencies. Most previous inquiries had been concerned with public service personnel questions. Machinery of government is a difficult area for an outside committee to deal with. There are several reasons for this (see also Chapter Four), but important ones are that major changes in structure tend to raise public policy issues, and to promote much infighting about departmental prerogatives; and their advantages are rarely clear enough to make the arguments for change conclusive. On the other hand, the more minor changes are going on all the time, and no once-for-all solution is likely to be adequate.

There are some other advantages of an internal review such as that undertaken in New South Wales. First, it is educative. It brings ministers into firsthand touch with administrative problems, and makes senior officials think about their own organisations. More than that, by their involvement in the study of agencies other than their own, it promotes awareness of other parts of the service. Secondly, this very involvement increases the chances of implementation, as many of those who have to carry out the proposals have already been involved in making them. Finally it costs less—though it is hard to calculate the concealed costs of taking the officials off other work. True, the work was completed quickly and that has also been claimed as an advantage, though others have argued that it meant some necessary background research was not done. In particular, ministers could spare little time for continuous work and must have had to make a good many decisions without much preparation—the same may well have been true of some permanent heads.

Criticisms of this kind of review also include the claim that, as so many vested interests were involved in the reviewing, there were many problems that it could not deal with, and many recommendations were superficial kinds of 'bureau-shuffling', eliminating a few obvious anomalies and overlaps, but not tackling major problems or looking very far into the future. To this extent the results would bear out Mosher's conclusions about the limitations of internal reviews.[18] But this criticism may be exaggerated. It is true that the review did not achieve much in eliminating unnecessary functions or agencies, which had been one aim. But some of the reshuffling was important, such as combining Transport and Highways under a single minister, and there were other significant results, as in the field of standing cabinet committees. The review also seems to have hastened the process by which the great statutory corporations have been subjected to more overall policy co-ordination.

Acceptability and Implementation

More significant perhaps are other factors that bear on the acceptability and implementation of reform proposals. Many people conceive of a committee of inquiry as an unpolitical body which is supposed to produce 'impartial' or 'expert' recommendations, hand them over to whoever commissioned the investigation, and then disband. But there is an alternative model of an inquiry that, even if it consists of outsiders, works closely with the government (possibly also with the opposition) to see how far the political will exists for reform, and on what issues; and, as well as making recommendations, advises on their implementation.

The first of these can take various forms. In different ways the Bland Inquiry in Victoria and the Corbett Committee in South Australia both had important links with, and the support of the Premiers. In New South Wales Mr Lewis himself presided over the 1974 review, and Mr Wran doubtless helped to initiate the Wilenski review. The Coombs Commission obtained a good deal of Public Service Board 'co-operation' but gained least advantage from its political connections, especially after 1975, though it seems to have paid some attention to pleasing the new government in its final report; this certainly benefited in acceptability by being more moderate in tone than the Discussion Papers had led many people to expect. It is usually thought that stress on political acceptability will lead to a conservative report, but this does not necessarily follow. One reason that so-called radical reports are unacceptable is that they do not rate acceptability as a great virtue and so make little effort to find out what elements of a radical programme can most profitably be stressed. The Corbett report cheerfully admitted that its report would 'be seen by many of its readers to be, on the whole, a conservative one'.[19] One suspects that it somewhat underplayed its novelty, as it in fact included one or two fairly radical proposals, such as the appointment of permanent heads on seven-year contracts.

This also raises questions about what audience a report is written for. If its main proposals are to be digested by politicians they should appear somewhere in short and fairly simple form (the Coombs Report may have failed here). The British Fulton Report was more readable though superficial. If the ideas are to reach the public service they need to have a pragmatic and unsatirical tone (one wonders, for example, whom the cartoons in the Wilenski Interim Report were intended to influence). If the report is to influence long-run thinking as well as bring about shorter-term change, the broad principles that underlie it must be firmly enunciated.

Finally there is the question of strategies for implementation. We have already mentioned these in the case of the 1974 New South Wales review. The Coombs Report included a proposed strategy for implementation, though one not free from ambiguity.[20] Among other things, it recommended that the cabinet should approve 'in principle' the main recommendations, and direct that action be taken to give effect to these; and that a ministerial committee should help to expedite reforms, helped by a small staff and with power to set up task forces. Perhaps it was a lot to ask of any government to accept over three hundred recommendations 'in principle'. A government could perhaps have committed itself to the 'main thrust' of the report (though that was not too easy to identify). The 1975 change put this out of court anyway, just as it ended any chance that the commission itself or its staff would play an implementing role. But the advent of the Fraser government has not been as disastrous to the report as some feared, though the proposals are being dealt with piecemeal and a period of public service cuts is not one favourable to administrative experiment. Responsibility for implementing the report is vested in the Machinery of Government Committee of the cabinet, served by a committee of permanent heads and a small unit in the Prime Minister's Department; there is also special machinery within the Office of the Public Service Board.[21] By late 1976, less than five months after the report was formally presented, the Prime Minister was able to announce various decisions, including approval in principle for efficiency audits, some extension of forward estimating procedures and various working parties and task forces, one of which reported on the implementation of efficiency auditing in 1977[22] and legislation was foreshadowed. A report was made to the House of Representatives in November 1977 on matters that specially concerned the Public Service Board, including decisions about staff rotation, the Interchange Program (see Chapter Twelve) and so on.[23] An experiment in regional co-ordination recommended by the Coombs Commission is also being undertaken. All this is not so bad when one considers that (as Curnow says) politicians have little incentive to devote great energy to administrative reform, rarely a matter on which public reputations are built or destroyed.[24]

One implementation strategy is to allow the report-writers themselves to play a part in executing their report. This happens most naturally where the report itself is an inside job, as with the 1944 review in New South Wales. A halfway house is perhaps represented by the Corbett Inquiry where *inter alia* the academic chairman has since joined the Public Service Board. The Wilenski review on New South Wales has drawn on past experience, positive and negative, and the single commissioner has been appointed not only to report but to 'advise on the implementation of such improvements as the

Government decides upon'. The intention seems to have been that the initial reporting would itself be a focus for discussion rather than a body of firm and specific recommendations; the aim was 'to produce desirable changes in the government administration rather than simply an addition to public administration literature'.[25] The Interim Report is not in fact so different from earlier documents of the kind as this quotation might suggest. As Corbett has pointed out, every inquiry faces the dilemma that it would like to test out its ideas on various people before coming to firm conclusions, but also fears that the responsible authorities may be annoyed by this or jump to wrong conclusions, as happened with some discussion papers of the Coombs Commission.[26] Delay may also give time for opposition forces to gather strength.

Content of Recommendations

In spite of various differences of emphasis among the recent reports on administrative reform, they tend to have some common themes. The first of these might be summarised as the need for accountable management. As it was most starkly put by the Coombs Commission, 'the realities of contemporary government require that the bureaucracy be seen as exercising some powers in its own light',[27] and it is held to follow that

1. Departments should be clearly seen as having greater responsibility for their own affairs ('let the managers manage'), and correspondingly departmental heads be more clearly accountable for their efficiency, and so on down the line.
2. Central personnel and financial departments should interfere less in detail but establish broader controls, but there should be provision for 'efficiency audits' and tests of effectiveness.
3. New statutory authorities should be created only when exceptional circumstances justify them, and will be less needed if departments are more efficient and flexible. More generally, there tends to be too great a proliferation of government agencies.

These proposals are sometimes to be found alongside a rather different notion that could be called the need for greater political responsibility. This is sometimes related to accountability by saying (for example) that more accountable management means that it will be easier for parliaments and ministers to know what it is going on, and to take the necessary corrective action. But the stress on the link between politics and administration can also lead in a different direction by suggesting, as the Coombs Report does, that

4. Ministers should be able to become more involved in departmental operations if they wish, and, more generally, no clear line can or need be drawn between politics and administration, and there is a case for more co-operative work between ministers and officials.

Another theme of several reports is the need for greater responsiveness— broadly that public services tend to be too closed, centralised, hierarchical, impersonal, not responsive enough either to their clients, or to their own staff. Out of this arises recommendations such as that

5. Public services should become more 'representative', at least by removing obvious forms of discrimination in recruitment and promotion.
6. There should be greater mobility both within the various government agencies and services, and between government and other sectors.
7. More attention needs paying to decentralisation, and to other means of improving public 'access', including access to information.
8. There should be greater consultation with employees and a general encouragement of more participatory forms of management.

There are other important themes in certain reports such as

9. The need for better recognition of the forward planning and research function in government agencies.

Some of these proposals for reform are liable to conflict with one another.[28] For example, my own experience is that organisations that reap the benefits of participation, decentralisation, team-work, initiative and so on, are liable also to be ones in which it is harder to impose clear tests of accountability for error and inefficiency. There is also a potential conflict between the doctrine that ministers should involve themselves more closely in adminis-tration and the view that senior officials should be made more clearly accountable. As the Coombs Report itself admits,

> On the one hand, if ministers involve themselves in decisions to a degree necessary for them to accept responsibility for them, officials are likely to feel less personally responsible and the outcome may therefore be less efficient. On the other hand, attempts to acknowledge and give precision to the responsibility of officials and to hold them accountable for its exercise may be seen as weakening direct ministerial responsibility and therefore political control.[29]

We have said a good deal in earlier chapters about the politics–administration continuum, and about problems of participation and access, so the rest of this chapter will be mainly concerned with some general issues of accountable management.

Responsibility and Accountability

Responsibility and accountability are two words often encountered in discussions of administrative reform; and all of us are in favour of them.

Administrative responsibility sometimes refers to relations with the outside world. This 'external responsibility' is what is referred to in questions such as how the responsibility of public servants to parliament could be improved. Officials also have their own area of responsibility within an organisation. Responsibility is 'to' others 'for' certain activities. An officer is responsible for certain functions, which may be written in job descriptions or statements of duties or just taken for granted. It is often hard in practice to spell out just what specific list of things an administrator is responsible for, and what is their relative importance as they compete for scarce time. In many cases responsibility may have to be seen, not so much in terms of specific tasks to be done, as of progress towards certain goals, both through his own actions and those of his subordinates. It is responsibility for getting things done by others, and may be very unclear about the edges. Incidentally such an officer's 'authority' may be even less clearly defined than his responsibilities—in government administration some powers may be precisely stated, such as who makes appointments or authorises payments, but over a large range it is not possible to give clear definitions of authority, or (in the catchphrase) to guarantee 'powers commensurate with responsibilities'. In modern organisations 'no administrator can be given in advance, as a matter of right, all the resources, clearances and other forms of co-operation that are needed for him to discharge his responsibilities'.[30]

It is clear that the notion of responsibility is complex, and this is further borne out when we look at its other face, 'responsibility to'. What cash-value does this have? Here we may also introduce the word 'accountability'. A simple meaning of responsibility to some individual or group might be that one is accountable to a superior if some result is not achieved, or some procedure not followed. An individual may be deemed accountable or answerable if there is a procedure by which he can be 'controlled', in the sense of called upon to report on and to justify his performance, and rewarded or penalised according to the judgment on it.[31] Though this kind of accountability exists, its actual incidence is uncertain, partly because it implies that there are adequate arrangements for the information flow on which judgments of performance are based. There is an element of mythology about this version of responsibility, especially in more senior positions, where inefficiency may be quite hard to pin down (or to pin down firmly, so that one's judgment is convincing to third parties), and where the sanctions are often obscure.

Responsibility is in fact a broader and vaguer notion than accountability. Hart has distinguished 'liability–responsibility' from 'role–responsibility', where the primary meaning of the latter is having an assigned task, probably 'duties of a relatively complex or extensive kind, defining a "sphere of responsibility" requiring care and attention over a protracted period of time'.[32] One may be accountable or answerable for such a responsibility, but it also implies a large area of discretion—indeed, it is hard to see how one could be held accountable for complex tasks unless one also had considerable discretion in carrying them out. On the other hand 'liability–responsibility' essentially involves answerability, and it could even be answerability for someone else's failure where one had no knowledge that the action was being taken, something like the older conception of ministerial responsibility for departmental errors.

We have up to now been talking as though responsibility is always 'to' a defined person or group. But there is the further complication that it may be deemed to exist to more than one person or group, just as in practice accountability is not just a requirement imposed by a hierarchical superior, one may also in practice be brought to account by peer groups or 'from below', by customers or clients.[33] For example most people would say nowadays that a permanent head has a responsibility to 'the government' as well as to his own minister, and may find himself in a dilemma if his minister is clearly not carrying out government policy. A specialist officer may on certain matters feel responsible to the head of a technical branch, though the formal line of authority runs through an administrative superior. To make the story still more complex, some people equate an official's responsibilities to his expected roles, what is 'expected of' him by others. If this is so, responsibility may be not only to superiors, but also to colleagues, and to subordinates, and to the agency's clientele, to all of whom an official is expected to be 'responsive'. One could in principle give a description of the role of an administrative officer, as a supplement to a formal statement of duties, which would set out his relationship to a whole series of other role-players in the form of: 'I rely on them to . . . They rely on me to' perform various tasks or move towards certain objectives.[34]

Some writers conclude from this that responsibility has to be seen in a pluralistic way, and we must openly recognise that a truly responsible official is responsive to expectations and demands coming from many different quarters. I do not want to argue the merits of this here,[35] but only to point out that it further complicates the use of the word 'responsibility'. Indeed an important virtue of the old orthodox view that the responsibility of officials means accountability to their superiors, ultimately the minister, is that it is simple. In principle at least, it can be stated in a not-too-ambiguous way, and some canons of accountability established which one can broadly judge are being lived up to or not. Alternative theories tend to be vaguer and woollier, and their cash-value harder to assess in cases of doubt and difficulty. A person who claims to be responsible to everyone may contrive to be responsible to no one.

However, it is certainly true that organisations depend a good deal on subjective feelings of responsibility, and that these include a sense of responsibility towards colleagues and clients, as well as loyalty to the purposes of the department as the public servant understands them. Here again the word may be used in various senses. It may imply conscientious adherence to professional standards, a strong sense of duty and integrity. Taking a decision responsibly can also imply a prudent care for consequences, as opposed to arbitrary or rash decision-making. This 'subjective responsibility' is related in complex ways to an officer's objective responsibilities as seen by his superiors, or his colleagues. Much so-called 'responsible government' has in practice always rested on the professional standards and traditions of the public service in these respects, rather than on formal accountability to a superior. In practice to make accountability work at all involves a good deal of 'self-policing', especially of the mutual control kind that imposes peer-group norms on individuals.[36] A danger of 'peer-group control' is that it can decay into bureaucratic collusion, but the strict external policing of a function can also sometimes end in complicity between the policers and policed. The danger of collusion is less where the persons concerned have a strong sense of responsibility and professional standards: or something to gain from checking or criticising their colleagues; or where self-government is reinforced by the threat of its withdrawal if abused; or more generally by greater open-ness in government (see Chapter Seventeen).[37]

To take the first of these, there are those who lay great stress on this notion of a responsible bureaucracy, the 'self-government of the public service profession', and it is an attractive and important ideal; and a kind of self-government achieved by some professional and not-so-professional outside groups. (It would be interesting, for example, to compare the self-policing of British housebuilding standards by the interests involved through the National Housebuilding Council and without cost to the government, with the expensive attempts at bureaucratic control through the New South Wales Builders Licensing Board.)[38] Of course there are other difficulties with certain kinds of professional peer group; professionalism may set high standards and even increase listening capacity but (as has been said) it also increases distance from the source of the noise. This is the argument of those who say that some sorts of 'responsiveness' depend more on shared culture or mutual understandings with the public served than among the officials themselves; hence the case for a 'representative bureaucracy', and a 'kin police', and the view that middle-class bureaucrats are naturally insensitive to lower-class (or upper-class) problems, or even that bureaucracy as such imposes a culture of its own that renders it systematically incapable of dealing with some kinds of issue. The case is not proven, but it needs mentioning.[39]

As already said, mutual control can also operate through one individual or group having something to gain from checking another, the so-called doctrine of 'countervailing power'. It is certainly true that some democratic control and accountability is secured in this way, as through conflicts between departments, and the principle of 'divide and rule' is an old one in government, though it often has costs that outweigh its benefits.

So people control one another through ·their consensus as well as their conflicts, from below as well as from above, and there are all kinds of other apparent paradoxes about responsibility and accountability. We have mentioned one paradox earlier—of the Coombs Commission wanting a greater involvement of ministers in departmental management and a closer partnership between ministers and officials generally, but at the same time wishing public servants 'to be seen as independently influential in policymaking, therefore to be held directly accountable for their actions'[40]. This is really part of a more general dilemma. Many of the sorts of responsibility we have been discussing involve not just doing one's own carefully defined task but also acknowledging interdependence; having concern for policy, for what is happening elsewhere in the organisation or to one's colleagues or to the public, or some desire that one's own efforts should be part of a co-ordinated effort. Yet a good deal of talk about accountability implies the attempt to draw sharp boundaries, so that each can be clearly answerable for his own sector. No doubt both have their place; it is also not hard to imagine situations in which attempts to improve accountability would promote the dodging of responsibility (and doubtless vice versa).

Efficiency and Effectiveness

The purpose of accountable management is often said to be to improve efficiency and effectiveness. The Benthamite language of efficiency[41] has penetrated most sectors of modern life including government. As one local authority told the Barnett Committee on New South Wales Local Government, 'it is the responsibility of the Council and its staff to ensure that the use of money, manpower, equipment and methods are utilized to the maximum efficient optimum'. The demand for more efficiency in government seems unambiguous when it is kept as abstract as this. Once we descend into detail, it becomes less obvious what is being talked about.

Definitions

'Efficiency' has often been associated with 'economy', and this is reasonable, as they are different ways of talking about the same thing. One aim of the 1895 Act that created the Public Service Board of New South Wales was to 'ensure the establishment and continuance of a proper standard of efficiency and economy in the Public Service', and the Board were given important powers to this end. Some other Public Service Acts have similar provision. But 'efficiency and economy' represent not two aims, but one. They only seem different if one forgets that minimising costs (the popular idea of economy) has no meaning except in relation to a given output, just as maximising output is always in relation to given costs. Both terms are properly used to express a relationship between an organisation's input and its output. Broadly speaking, an efficient organisation is one that achieves the level of output desired at the lowest possible cost—that is, with minimum use of scarce resources; this is also an economical organisation. 'Economy' can also be used to mean cutting costs at some expense to performance; fortunately we have a third word, 'effectiveness', to describe the converse, improving performance even with some addition to costs.

More precisely, it is common to distinguish 'effectiveness' from 'efficiency' where the former is used to refer, not to the relation between input and output, but between desired and achieved output. So one can say that a department is 'effective' if it achieves some desired objective; that is, if it is a success at doing whatever it is trying to do. Sometimes government agencies are oriented towards effectiveness rather than efficiency, and at times this is appropriate, for example, where achieving an aim has an importance that outweighs even a sizeable increase in the costs of doing so. 'Survival' is one example of a desired aim to which the costs have been claimed to be irrelevant, or largely so. A related case is where what looks like inefficiency is an inevitable outcome of the aims that governments have set themselves. Thus much criticism of waste in schemes to aid Aborigines has been countered by the argument that success in achieving the final objective is both very important and involves running many risks and making experiments that have a more than normally high chance of failure, so that what seems inefficient may be a necessary condition of ultimate effectiveness. This kind of controversy is always hard to settle, and illustrates the practical difficulty of drawing the line between measuring efficiency and questions that touch on policy itself.

If efficiency concerns the relation between input and desired output then, to talk sensibly about it, we have to know first, what is the desired output; and secondly, how to measure progress towards it, and what costs are involved. In many fields such measurement techniques have been and are being developed. They often have fancy names, and the practical details vary, but almost all can be summarised as attempts to focus more clearly on the outputs of an organisation, and to measure more precisely progress towards them, and the costs of that progress.

Outputs

One especially intractable problem in government administration is identifying and defining outputs, including establishing quantitative indicators of outputs.[42] While inputs can often be measured in terms of money costs, outputs may be hard to measure objectively, even where they can be broadly identified. For example it is far easier to measure the value of labour and materials devoted to education than to measure the performance of the educational system (especially when some educators resent the effort to do so). As a result the emphasis in government has often been on controlling inputs—staff, salaries, purchases, and so on—and on financial audit, so-called 'fiscal accountability', to check on the regularity and legality of expenditures.

Even where an administrative unit can define and measure its own output, it may still be unclear what relation this has to final output (the output that reaches the public). The officials concerned may enthusiastically and 'efficiently' push paper around to no real purpose, encouraged by the fact that their intermediate objectives are easier to reduce to measurement than the final goals they are supposed to serve, and live up to the usual tests of good management. Another problem is that organisations are multi-product. They produce a variety of final outputs that compete with one another for scarce resources, some of which are easier to define and measure than others. Again there arises the danger of concentrating on measurable outputs at the expense of less readily measurable but possibly more important ones. In this as in other fields, hard data drive out soft data.

Many administrative decisions also have indirect effects. Achieving some aims may unwittingly damage others. This happens even in fairly simple questions of the organisation and methods sort, where there are human relationships involved. The problem is much more acute where it is a question of improving the efficiency of the police, or of urban planning, or of universities.

The answer to such problems is not to give up the effort to measure efficiency but to keep a sense of proportion, and in particular to calm neurotic fears of making qualitative judgments where quantitative ones are unavailable or inadequate; and also to try hard to devise ways of measuring the less easily measurable. The latter has been one of the aims of activities such as cost-benefit analysis and intelligence-testing, and invariably earns them much abuse from ignorant, prejudiced or ideologically committed quarters; they are, of course, perilous enterprises and need intelligent criticism as well as support.

Another important limitation of defining efficiency in terms of 'desired outputs' is that it assumes that the levels of output chosen are the best ones. However, the outputs chosen by an organisation may not be the best for those on whose behalf they are produced. It is a common error of much managerialist talk of efficiency to think of desired outputs or objectives as somehow established according to internal criteria, not by signals from clients. Yet it is not socially efficient to produce the wrong outputs, those undesired by the customers, or less desired than some alternative combination, even if they are being produced as cheaply as possible. Productive efficiency is not the same as social efficiency, or 'allocative efficiency'. In private business this broader concept of allocative efficiency is sometimes said to be achieved through a competitive market that ensures the non-survival of organisations that produce undesired outputs, however efficiently. There is controversy about the effectiveness of this solution, but few will deny the existence of the problem; and even if the market deals with it badly, government may do even worse.

Responsibility for Efficiency

As we have seen in earlier chapters, responsibility for particular aspects of administrative efficiency has been vested by statute in various controlling bodies. These typically include a Public Service Board, a Treasury or Department of Finance, and an Auditor-General's Department or Office. The legislature sometimes also creates a more direct avenue of control by establishing a Public Accounts Committee or an Expenditure Committee.

Public Service Boards have varying degrees of responsibility in this field. However, together they cover less than half of government employment in Australia: and some are also restricted, by custom if not by character, in the role that they play. For example, though the Public Service Act clearly gives the Commonwealth Public Service Board power to conduct efficiency audits, it has been very reluctant to assume this responsibility, and the Coombs Report agreed with this. One ground was that it could not be 'wholly objective' in assessing departmental efficiency as much of what departments do might result from the Board's own decisions on staffing, or on its advice as management consultants.[43] Secondly, the Board's role as consultant in 'management improvement' was said to depend on co-operative relations that might be damaged if the Board were also to make public criticisms of departments.[44] Here a distinction is implied between external audit, which is essentially the presentation of critical information on past costs and outcomes (though this information may be used to improve future performance), and management consulting ('where the activity of the external agency extends to the design, prescription and examination of alternatives, and possibly also to the actual implementation of alternative structures and processes').[45] There is, of course, no clear line between the two activities; and in New South Wales the Public Service Board has regarded itself as concerned with efficiency audit as well as management consultancy, and with assessing effectiveness. Its Management Consultancy Division conducts management audits, including audits of some statutory authorities, and the reports are considered by a cabinet subcommittee, including the Board Chairman, Treasury Under Secretary and a representative of the Premier's Department as co-opted members.[46]

Treasuries and Departments of Finance have in one sense had more extensive control than public service authorities, as they cover a wider range of government employment. But (see Chapter Sixteen) the emphasis of Treasury control has been very much on inputs, with only superficial attention being given to efficiency as defined above, though the cost-effectiveness of projects has now started to receive more attention both by Treasuries and departments.[47]

Auditors-General are concerned with an even more extensive range of government agencies. But, as we have seen, though they have publicised some obvious examples of extravagance and waste, they have mainly been concerned with the regularity and legality of financial transactions. In countries such as America, France and Western Germany efficiency auditing has become an accepted part of the audit authority's responsibility.[48] The Coombs Report recommended that this function be given to the Commonwealth Auditor-General, as an officer of prestige and recognised impartiality, with established access to government agencies and a special status as an independent officer reporting to parliament. It also thought that there should be a parliamentary committee on administrative efficiency linked to the Auditor-General, possibly as an extension of or substitute for the Public Accounts Committee.[49] The government has legislated on the former recommendation, and Queensland has given its Auditor-General extra powers.

Some writers regard efficiency auditing as a fairly natural extension of the Auditor-General's existing power to check the regularity of government expenditure, but there is some exaggeration about this. The Auditor-General himself has freely admitted that it will involve the introduction of a wide variety of new skills into the Audit office, including experts in administration and management, and that to put the new function on its feet will take four or five years.[50] Neither does the Auditor-General's close relation to the legislature seem to be a convincing argument, though it enables supporters of the proposal to argue that efficiency audits under such auspices will also improve accountability to parliament. R.S. Parker may be right when he says that any such outcome would involve a vast change in the existing habits of MPs, and a considerable erosion of present conceptions of party solidarity. It is more likely that the Auditor-General's efficiency audits will become just another example of peer-group control, by which some public servants check up on others, with 'all the latent potentialities . . . for mutual bureaucratic accommodation rather than mutual scrutiny and criticism',[51] though as we have seen, peer-group control can be a most useful device.

The whole concept of efficiency auditing probably needs more criticism than it is currently getting. It is superficially an attractive idea to combine rigorous *ex post* (after the event) checking-up on efficiency with greater freedom from the existing relatively inflexible *ex ante* (before the event) checks and regulations of personnel and budgetary controllers, or niggling attempts to monitor current performance. But *ex post* reviews have some sizeable disadvantages. They cannot cope with irreversible errors as expressed in the proverb about 'shutting the stabledoor after the horse has bolted'. Another problem is that of devising suitable sanctions to punish poor performers, which democratic governments have never been good at doing, and on which the Coombs Commission found no cogent things to say. And is the apportionment of blame to become a matter for discussion in parliamentary committee reports and elsewhere? If the principle of accountable management is accepted, there will be strong pressure for this. What Wheare has said about the 'anonymity' of public servants is relevant here, that what its opponents really object to is not facelessness but immunity. If public servants are blamed but not named, they do not even have the minister's punishment of bad publicity, and it also leads to doubts about whether they have really been made to suffer for some act of maladministration.[52] Of course, a public servant's career often does suffer as a result of his mistakes, though unfortunately not the really important mistakes of a long-term kind that take years to show themselves, and sometimes nowadays an official is named as well as blamed (see Chapter Ten). Yet there are many problems about this in a collective enterprise, where it may often be unfair to attempt to fix the responsibility clearly on one person, as some observers felt in a recent New South Wales case. As the Coombs Report itself says: 'In a large and complex organisation which deals with issues requiring time-consuming consideration, decision-making tends to become diffused, incremental and impersonal and it becomes difficult to pin-point its precise locus'.[53] There is also the question of an individual officer's, or for that matter a department's, right of reply.

Ex post checks on efficiency also, as we have seen, raise difficult problems of measurement of performance. This is easiest when the setting of standards can be made reasonably precise, and where compliance with them can be checked by a reasonably simple inspection and reporting system. In many situations it may not be possible to lay down precise standards or guidelines, or only at considerable cost to initiative and flexibility. The Commonwealth Public Service Board when it looked into forward staff estimating is said to have found that in 1976–77 about a quarter of departmental programmes were at the time adaptable to assessments of 'productivity', though that does not mean that output indicators could not be developed for others.[54] It is significant that there is a scarcity of actual published examples of efficiency audits in the public sector, at least of a major kind.[55] There is the problem that the information on which to base judgments of poor performance may be more readily available for some activities of an individual or group than others. Some activities with a low importance in the total spectrum may be much more visible than other more important matters, and their non-performance be far more likely to attract unfavourable notice. It is, for example, by no means an infallible test of a good permanent head that he should be a good 'resource manager', though success there may be roughly measurable. The quality of his policy advice, his negotiating skills and capacity to find acceptable solutions to problems, may be at least as important, but harder to assess from outside. Actually even in matters such as financial and staff administration, many crucial outputs are difficult to measure.

> As with comparable functions like budgeting and planning, it is character-istic of personnel administration that its contribution can rarely be measured objectively when it is at the level of greatest effectiveness, but its value is more easily determinable when it neglects its more important function.[56]

Mandell is making the point that the most important task of personnel and budgetary staffs may be to advise the line administrator, but this is just where it is least possible to measure results. At any rate, it has till now (and not without some justice) been the

> well-entrenched orthodoxy of Australian Government administration that efficiency is best promoted at the planning stage, that it is a function of adequate organization for the task involved and that subsequent remedial action is at best of marginal value. This view is often buttressed by the observation that control by review has never been successfully used as a general tool for promoting efficiency anywhere in the world.[57]

Evidence on this last point seems to be lacking. However, the general point is simple to grasp. Where measures of specific performance are difficult or impossible, checks on efficiency may have to be broader, and concerned more with controlling the general trend of activities. Consider the work of senior administrators or members of a scientific research establishment. Checks are certainly needed to see that they are working efficiently. But it is not possible to lay down a clear standard output for them, or easily measure the quantity and quality of their actual output. Nor if we had this information, would we necessarily know much about how to improve the situation.

Also the type of controls used may have to be very different. Often the most effective type of control of senior staff is simply to take great pains in appointing good people to key positions. 'In the whole organisation . . . there are about two hundred people who take on themselves the decisions which make or mar the success of the business as a whole . . . The biggest job of top management is to ensure the quality of this two hundred.'[58]

Then there are the sorts of controls of efficiency that have been called 'field controls', because they pervade the whole field of an individual's activity, influencing him in many subtle ways of which he may be quite unaware. Pay and promotion schemes may be arranged so as to satisfy feelings of justice, and encourage effort in the right direction. Rewards and penalties may be internalised, by encouraging staff to develop standards of proper behaviour of feelings of loyalty to the department. As we have seen it is arguable that the most effective check on bureaucratic efficiency is a strong feeling for professional standards and professional ethics, leading among other things to much self-policing.

If permanent heads and other senior officers do not have such standards, it is very hard to bring them to book; and if it takes a large new bureaucracy in the Auditor-General's Office to do so, the cure may be worse than the disease. In any case the very skills that cause an individual to rise within a large organisation often also make him adept at muddying the waters if threatened; and his colleagues are likely to help him, if a threat to him seems to threaten them also. One should not underestimate the collective solidarity of departments in the face of external criticism, and the extent to which people will decide to hang together rather than separately.

This is not a reason for abandoning the concept of efficiency checks. Some activities are measurable, or can be made so. Some agency should certainly be able to ask if a department has been implementing policy in a reasonably efficient and economical way, and to make a public report; and minister and permanent head, and possibly other senior officers, should be able to take part in the ensuing debate. It is all best seen as part of the wider business of more openness of government, more 'publicity' in Jeremy Bentham's sense. All the various devices are worth trying but in a spirit of modest scepticism about the final efficiency of any one of them.

Measuring Effectiveness

It is common nowadays to draw a distinction between 'efficiency auditing', which (as indicated earlier) is concerned with whether an organisation is using its resources economically in achieving its outputs, and reviews of 'programme effectiveness' or programme 'auditing' or 'evaluation', which try to estimate the success of the department in doing what it is trying to do, the degree to which it is reaching desired objectives. This may often be an even harder task. The Coombs Report proclaimed the need for it but gave it almost no attention, nor have other inquiries. It has been asserted that the Auditor-General should be able to examine efficiency without getting involved in 'political judgments', and that the more value-laden task of reviewing the effectiveness of continuing programmes could best be done from within the Department of the Prime Minister and Cabinet.[59] At the same time it was recognised that the two tasks would need to be closely related, but the report went into no detail on this.

The Working Party on Efficiency Audits has also mentioned the difficulty in practice of separating issues of efficiency and effectiveness.[60] For example, if one wants to know whether desired outputs are being obtained at minimum cost, one needs to know how far actual outputs accord with desired outputs. This is not difficult in the case of operations and procedures where there are well-established criteria, but this is often not the case—as the Working Party says, to be efficient some administrative activities involve not only speed and timeliness, but also equity and consistency.

Effectiveness reviews would presumably involve not simply asking how far some agency was achieving its objectives, but also what light this cast on the need for alternative strategies, or even on whether the objectives themselves were attainable, or some programmes should be run down. There are also questions about how far one is still talking about *ex post* review, how far of continuous assessment or monitoring of certain programmes, or of *ex ante* planning and replanning. The Coombs Report gives one example, Aboriginal affairs, where it thinks that progressive reassessment of programmes is needed, a process in which the Department of Aboriginal Affairs would collaborate and in which research should be encouraged to develop 'measurable indicators of various components of welfare'.[61] This would clearly be a very much more continuous and intensive affair than the occasional outside look at how some other agency was living up to its professed aims.

In the Prime Minister's statement announcing the splitting of the Treasury in November 1976, the summary of the functions of the new Department of Finance included 'participation in evaluation of the effectiveness of expenditure programs in meeting Government determined objectives'.[62] It was also stated that 'there will be a strengthening of the existing resources available in the Department of the Prime Minister and Cabinet for the evaluation of the effectiveness of government programs. Regular evaluations will be undertaken of major sectors of government services.' The Department would also develop further its capacity to advise 'on forward planning, priority setting and the strategic planning of government initiatives . . . closely associated with accelerated development of the forward estimates system'.

A problem about the more precise specification of objectives involved in programme evaluations is not merely that it may be technically difficult, but it may not suit ministers or governments politically; they often prefer to keep policies vague (see Chapter Fourteen). Governments that take effectiveness reviews seriously seem to combine them with the efficiency audit function, and to give the head of the department a prestigious role, as has the President of the German Audit Office.[63]

Conclusion

In this final chapter we have only been able to touch on some general aspects of administrative reform and the pursuit of greater efficiency and effectiveness in government. Perhaps it is appropriate to end with one or two very broad reflections, especially as this is a period in which words like 'efficiency' and 'administration' have for many people an inhuman flavour.

Indeed, one way of summarising some recent criticisms of Government Administration or Public Administration as an activity, and as an academic subject, is to interpret them as attacks on efficiency as a value. The pursuit of efficiency (it is said) has been only too successfully carried on, so far as it involves manipulating and processing people and things in bureaucratic ways. But it may be an ineffective or even injurious criterion when it comes to satisfying real social needs or meeting demands for greater participation in government or improving the quality of life.[64] Chesterton summarised one kind of criticism over seventy years ago. 'When everything about a people is for the time growing weak and ineffective, it begins to talk about efficiency . . . Vigorous organisms talk not about their processes, but about their aims.'[65] Similarly we have been told in recent years that we should concentrate more on Public Policy, not Public Administration, and be concerned with the outputs of modern government rather than the means by which they are produced.

There are other reasons why the study of the institutions and procedures of government has been unfashionable in many quarters. One is the belief that it is the 'informal' side that is really important, that there is so great a gulf between the realities of power and influence and the descriptions of formal institutions, as to make the latter misleading as well as dull. The institutional approach has also been criticised because it seemed to carry with it a conservative implication that certain forms and procedures were sacred and immutable. Nevile Johnson has given a good answer to this kind of criticism. Forms and procedures are not immutable, but they are an inevitable part of government; and just as in Politics, one cannot begin to understand the act of individual voting except in the context of the party and constitutional structures within which it takes place; so one can have no grasp of the conduct of ministers and public servants without understanding the constraints that administrative structures and processes lay on them; and not only the constraints, but also the opportunities that these institutions provide for decision and action. Structures and procedures facilitate action as well as impede it, one cannot act at all except in a world where most things are fixed in advance and one can take them largely for granted. Also, as Johnson says, if institutions are studied critically, they throw great light on the values and standards of the society in which they exist, since they are not neutral machines, but exhibit 'continuing relationships which have a normative content'.[66]

As for the quest for greater efficiency and effectiveness in government, if it simply meant concern with the latest technological gimmickry, or inventing new names for old pursuits (Organisational Dynamics, or what you will), or bothering more about pennypinching than human waste, criticism of it would be justified. But the rationale of the quest for Administrative Reform lies in the fact that resources are still scarce in relation to human needs and demands, and these resources need husbanding. Efficiency in government implies pursuing desired social ends, whatever these may be, with the minimum of waste, and what rational objection can there be to that?

There is an even greater need for studies of the effectiveness of government. There is an increasingly influential school of thought, on both sides of the political fence, which doubts whether social welfare goals are necessarily promoted by the continued expansion of the government sector. Some growth in the cost of government services is to be expected where population is increasing and where greater affluence creates a higher demand for some collective goods and services and where the average voter can probably still use government as a means of redistributing some welfare in his direction; but public services also grow as a result of expansive forces generated within governments and bureaucracies unrelated to any public benefits accruing, or because their true cost to the public is concealed by the way they are financed. There is also a problem of 'overload', the danger of governments taking on more than they can cope with. Hence some services may be oversupplied, others undersupplied, or (because of overload) supplied inefficiently, at higher cost than necessary, or ineffectively, to the wrong people or in other ways not calculated to achieve the aim desired. So one of the most important tasks of modern governments is to govern themselves; that is, to co-ordinate and assign priorities to their own interventions. Another is to widen the search for 'social indicators', the attempt to set goals so that achievement can be better measured against costs. How far such self-control and sophisticated calculation can be relied upon remain two great unknowns in trying to assess the desirable future role of government in Australia, as in other societies.

Notes

1. G.E. Caiden, 'New Patterns in American Public Administration', *Public Admin.* (Sydney), XXIX, 3, September 1970, 260.
2. For a valuable summary of developments in these fields, see Barry Moore, 'The Quest for Efficiency', in R.N. Spann (ed.), *Public Administration in Australia*, new edn, Government Printer, Sydney, 1973, 501–13.
3. Peter Bailey, 'Can Public Administration Cope?' *Aust. J. of Public Admin.* XXXVII, 1, March 1978, 55.
4. F.C. Mosher (ed.), *Governmental Reorganizations*, Bobbs–Merrill, New York, 1967.

5. Bailey, *loc. cit.*
6. P. Szanton, 'Innovation in U.S. Urban Public Services: Ten Case Studies', Rand Corporation 1973, cit. Richard Rose (ed.), *The Dynamics of Public Policy*, Sage Publications, London, 1976, 241.
7. G.E. Caiden, *Administrative Reform*, Allen Lane, London, 1970, 1.
8. Cameron Hazlehurst, 'The Information Dimension', in Cameron Hazlehurst and J.R. Nethercote (eds), *Reforming Australian Government: The Coombs Report and Beyond*, RIPA and Australian National University Press, Canberra, 1977, 128.
9. Peter Bailey, 'Why We Can't Do Without the Public Service', in *Bureaucracies,* University of New South Wales Occasional Papers No. 3, 1977, 31.
10. Barry Moore, in an unpublished paper on 'The Management of Change'.
11. See article on Bigge in *Australian Dictionary of Biography*, I, Melbourne University Press, Melbourne, 1966; on the history of public service inquiries, see Chapter Eleven above, and R.L. Wettenhall, 'A Brief History of Public Service Inquiries' in R.F.I. Smith and Patrick Weller (eds), *Public Service Inquiries in Australia*, University of Queensland Press, St Lucia, 1978.
12. *op. cit.*, 26.
13. cf. J.E. Hodgetts, *The Canadian Civil Service*, University of Toronto Press, 1973, 25.
14. Mosher, *op. cit.*, 506 ff.; cf. Mackenzie and Grove, *op. cit.*, 219–21.
15. C.H. Sisson, 'The Civil Service', *Spectator*, 6 March 1971.
16. See articles by H.D. Dickinson and G. Gleeson, Barry Moore, and B.R. Davies, in *Public Admin.* (Sydney), XXXIV, 1 and 2, March and June 1975; and *Aust. J. Public Admin.*, XXXV, 1, March 1976.
17. Ross Curnow, 'The New South Wales Machinery of Government Review', in Smith and Weller, *op. cit.*
18. Mosher, *op. cit.*, 507.
19. Report, Committee of Inquiry into the Public Service of South Australia, 13.
20. Report, RCAGA, 412.
21. Trevor Mathews, 'Implementing the Coombs Report: The First Eight Months', in Smith and Weller, *op. cit.*
22. Report, Working Party on Efficiency Audits, Canberra, 1977.
23. *Com. Parl. Deb.* (H. of R.), 4 November 1977, 2934–6.
24. Ross Curnow, 'The New South Wales Machinery of Government Review', in Smith and Weller, *op. cit.*, 125.
25. Interim Report, Review of New South Wales Government Administration, Sydney, 1977, 315.
26. D.C. Corbett, 'The How and Why of Public Service Enquiries', Australian National University Seminar Paper, mimeo., Canberra, 1974.
27. Report, RCAGA, 13.
28. For discussion, see R.N. Spann, 'The Coombs Doctrine', in Hazlehurst and Nethercote, *op. cit.*, 78–86.
29. Report, RCAGA, 13.
30. B.M. Gross, *The Managing of Organizations*, Free Press, New York, 1964, I, 305.
31. Report, RCAGA, 11 n.2. Some writers distinguish 'accountability' from 'answerability', cf. K. Baier, 'Responsibility and Freedom', in R.J. De George (ed.), *Ethics and Society*, Anchor, New York, 1966.
32. H.L.A. Hart, *Punishment and Responsibility*, Clarendon Press, Oxford, 1968, 212–3.

33. cf. D.C. Hague, W.J.M. Mackenzie and A. Barker (eds), *Public Policy and Private Interests: The Institutions of Compromise*, Macmillan, London, 1975.
34. I owe the wording to Mr Barry Moore.
35. cf. F.C. Mosher, *Democracy and the Public Service*, Oxford University Press, New York, 1968, especially 7–10. A classic controversy on the subject was the Friedrich–Finer one reprinted in D.C. Rowat (ed.), *Basic Issues in Public Administration,* Macmillan, New York, 1961.
36. cf. D.C. Hague, W.J.M. Mackenzie and A. Barker (eds), *op. cit.*
37. *ibid.*, 31; ch. 2 gives a good account of various methods of administrative 'control' on these lines.
38. cf. Anthony Barker, in *ibid.*, 333–55, and Peter Samuel, *The Bulletin*, 18 April 1978, citing a paper by Ted Lieper of the Australian National University.
39. cf. J.D. Kingsley, *Representative Bureaucracy*, The Antioch Press, Yellow Springs, Ohio, 1944, the pioneer work; V. Subramaniam, 'Representative Bureaucracy: A Reassessment', *American Political Science Review*, 61, 4, December 1967; and Martin Albrow, *Bureaucracy*, Pall Mall, London, 1970, 112, 117.
40. R.S. Parker, 'What Can Be Said for the Coombs Commission?', in Hazlehurst and Nethercote, *op. cit.*, 61.
41. Bentham did not use the word in its modern sense, but invented much of the language associated with it. 'Efficiency' as a word is said to have come into vogue in the period of criticism of British administration associated with the Crimean War. It had another run for its money as national efficiency in the early 1900s, when the Germans were thought to be good at it.
42. cf. R.N. Spann, 'Reflections on Efficiency', *Public Admin.* (Sydney), XIX, 4, December 1960, reprinted in R.N. Spann and G.R. Curnow, *Public Policy and Administration in Australia: A Reader*, Wiley, Sydney, 1975.
43. Report, RCAGA, 48.
44. For discussion, see J.R. Nethercote, 'Efficient Allocation of Resources within the Public Service', in Hazlehurst and Nethercote, *op. cit.*
45. James Cutt, 'Accountability, Efficiency and the Royal Commission on Australian Government Administration', *Aust. J. Public Admin.*, XXXVI, 4, December 1977, 334.
46. Interim Report, Review of New South Wales Government Administration, 69–72.
47. For recent departmental case studies, see J.C. McMaster and G.R. Webb (eds), *Australian Project Evaluation: Selected Readings*, Australia and New Zealand Book Co., Sydney, 1978.
48. See E.L. Normanton, *The Accountability and Audit of Governments*, Manchester University Press, Manchester, 1966.
49. Report, RCAGA, 49–50, 110–14.
50. Report of the Auditor-General, Canberra, 1977, 269, 290; and cf. Report, Working Party on Efficiency Audits, Canberra, 1977.
51. R.S. Parker, 'What Can Be Said for the Coombs Commission?', in Hazlehurst and Nethercote, *op. cit.*, 63.
52. K.C. Wheare, 'Crichel Down Revisited', *Political Studies*, 23, 2–3, 1975, 405.
53. Report, RCAGA, 11.
54. Neil V. Walker, 'Effectiveness and Efficiency: Problems of Assessment', *Aust. J. Public Admin.*, XXXVI, 4, December 1977.
55. Cutt, *op. cit.*, 337.

56. Milton Mandell, in F.M. Marx (ed.), *Elements of Public Administration*, 2nd edn, Prentice–Hall, New York, 1959, 500.
57. J.R. Nethercote, 'Efficient Allocation of Resources Within the Public Service', in Hazlehurst and Nethercote, *op. cit.*
58. Geoffrey Heyworth, in G.E. Milward (ed.), *Large-scale Organisation*, Macdonald and Evans, London, 1950, 177.
59. Report, RCAGA, 49.
60. Report, Working Party on Efficiency Audits, Canberra, 1977, para. 39; as cited in Brian Kimball's review, *Newsletter*, RIPA (ACT Group), December 1977.
61. Report, RCAGA, 342.
62. *Com. Parl. Deb.* (H. of R.), V. 102, 18 November 1976, 2899.
63. Cutts, *op. cit.*, 345.
64. For representative attacks, see the articles in Dwight Waldo (ed.), *Public Administration in a Time of Turbulence*, Chandler Pub. Co., Scranton, 1971, and Frank Marini (ed.), *Towards a New Public Administration*, Chandler Pub. Co., Scranton, 1971.
65. G.K. Chesterton, *Heretics*, John Lane, London, 1905, 17.
66. Nevile Johnson, 'The Place of Institutions in the Study of Politics', *Political Studies*, 23, 2–3, 1975, 158.

Further References

Most relevant books and articles are noted in the references for each chapter, but a few words on general reference material may be helpful.

The *Official Year Book of Australia* (referred to shortly as *Year Book Australia*), published by the Australian Bureau of Statistics (as are the various State Year Books) is a mine of useful information on Australian government. It includes some details about developments in administration and public policy.

Annual Reports of the Commonwealth and State Public Service Boards contain information about changes in public services and sometimes also in the organisation of departments. For statistics, see also the (Commonwealth) Public Service Board *Statistical Yearbook*. Other official government publications are listed quarterly and annually in *Australian Government Publications*, National Library of Australia. One of special value is the *Commonwealth Government Directory*, which gives information on the organisation and functions of Commonwealth departments, statutory authorities and other agencies, including names of senior officers, members of committees, and so on. Some States have similar directories.

The *Commonwealth Record* is an official (and inferior) weekly chronicle of government events and pronouncements, which displaced the *Australian Government Digest* (1972–75, quarterly, then *A.G. Weekly Digest* in 1975), which displaced the still more useful *Australia in Facts and Figures*.

Other sources of information are:

Australian National Bibliography (weekly, with monthly, quarterly and annual cumulations), National Library of Australia.

Bibliography of Administrative History, Royal Institute of Public Administration, Victorian Regional Group, 1966—on Victorian administration.

F.A. Bland, *Government in Australia*, 2nd edn, Government Printer, Sydney, 1944, contains many extracts from government reports, with an historical commentary.

D.H. Borchardt, *Check List of Royal Commissions, Select Committees and Boards of Inquiry*, Wentworth Press, Sydney—five volumes have so far appeared, Commonwealth 1900–50, 1950–60, New South Wales to 1960, Tasmania to 1959, Victoria to 1960.

Concise Guide to the State Archives of New South Wales, Archives Authority of NSW, Sydney, 1970 (and supplements).

Consolidated Index to (Commonwealth) Parliamentary Papers, 1901–49, Canberra, 1955, consolidates the first five indexes. *Sixth General Index to Parliamentary Papers*, Canberra 1966 covers 1950–61. There are also Annual Indexes.

Consolidated Index to Minutes of Proceedings and Printed Papers, New South Wales Legislative Council, Sydney, 1956 onwards, is still incomplete but four volumes cover 1874–1954. Some other States have printed Consolidated Indexes to Parliamentary Papers: for example, South Australia, 1857–1961 (five vols), Tasmania 1856–1967 (two vols), Western Australia 1870–1956 (two vols).

R.L. Cope (ed.), *Government Publications in Australia: Papers on Their Use and Understanding*, Parliamentary Library, 3rd edn, Sydney, 1972.

Jean Craig (ed.), *Bibliography of Public Administration in Australia 1850–1947*, Department of Government and Public Administration, University of Sydney, Sydney, 1955.

J. Finlayson, *Historical Statistics of Australia: A Select List of Official Sources*, Department of Economic History, Australian National University, Canberra 1970.

Joint Committee of Public Accounts, 155th Report, has an *Index, 1st to 146th Reports of the Committee*, Canberra, 1976.

K.W. Knight, *The Literature of State Budgeting in Australia, Canada and the United States of America: A Survey and Select Bibliography*, University of Queensland Press, St Lucia, 1970.

R.D. Lumb, *The Constitutions of the Australian States*, 4th edn, University of Queensland Press, St Lucia, 1977.

H. Mayer and others, *A Research Guide to Australian Politics and Cognate Subjects,* Cheshire, Melbourne, 1976, includes sections on Government Publications; Public Administration and Policy; Public Finance and Expenditure.

Joanna Monie and Adrienne Wise, *Social Policy and Its Administration: A Survey of the Australian Literature 1950–75*; Pergamon Press, Sydney, 1977, includes social services, education, public health, urban planning and local government.

D. Pike and B. Nairn (eds), *Australian Dictionary of Biography*, Melbourne University Press, Melbourne, 1966 onwards, includes many biographies of administrators and public servants.

Report, Royal Commission on Australian Government Administration, Canberra, 1976. There are also four Appendix Volumes, containing valuable research reports. An Index to the Report was published separately by the Royal Institute of Public Administration, GPO Box 1657, Brisbane.

Union List of Higher Degree Theses in Australian University Libraries, University of Tasmania Library, Hobart—published periodically. A cumulative edition to 1965 exists, and supplements since then.

R.L. Wettenhall, *A Guide to Tasmanian Government Administration*, Platypus Publications, Hobart, 1968, is the fullest guide to any State administration, and includes interesting departmental histories.

E. Zalums, *Bibliography of South Australian Royal Commissions, Select Committees and Boards of Inquiry 1857–1970*, Flinders University, Bedford Park, 1975.

E. Zalums, *Western Australian Government Publications: A Bibliography*, 2nd edn, National Library of Australia, 1971.

Journals

The *Australian Journal of Public Administration*, Sydney, 1937 onwards (called *Public Administration* until 1976), quarterly, contains many valuable articles. There is a separately printed Consolidated Index to the end of 1966; 1967–76 are covered in a supplementary index printed in the December 1977 issue of the journal. The journal includes regular surveys of administrative developments.

Among other journals publishing articles of special interest to students of Australian government administration is the *Australian Quarterly*, Australian Institute of Political Science.

Some regional groups of the Royal Institute of Public Administration publish newsletters containing notes and short articles; for example, the *Newsletter* of the ACT Group, quarterly; and the *Bulletin* of the South Australian Group.

An independent publication at present edited by Dr G. Hawker of the Canberra College of Advanced Education is the *Policy Studies Newsletter.*

A number of government agencies and local government associations publish specialised periodicals and broadsheets, many of which are listed in *Serials in Australian Libraries: Social Sciences and Humanities*, National Library of Australia, with regular supplements. Other useful guides to periodical literature are *Apais*, National Library of Australia, a subject index to current periodicals and newspaper articles, monthly with annual cumulations; and *Newspapers in Australian Libraries: A Union List*, 3rd edn, National Library of Australia, 1975, part 2 of which deals with Australian newspapers.

INDEX

Aboriginal affairs, 39, 54, 60, 85, 91–2, 208, 321, 417, 474–5, 498, 504
Access, 162–3, 463, 473–4
Accountability, 16, 493–7
Administration defined, 17–22
Administrative and Clerical Officers Association (ACOA), 367
Administrative Appeals Tribunal, 161, 471
Administrative Arrangements Orders, 49
Administrative courts and tribunals, 158–61
Administrative reorganization, ch. 4
see also Machinery of Government
Administrative Research Unit, 300, 400, 487
Administrative Review Committee, 97–8, 148, 485
Administrative Review Council, 161
Administrative work, nature of, 17–22, 338–9, 344–5
Advisory bodies, 60–75, 145–9, 199
see also Committees of Inquiry, Royal Commissions
Aged, care of, 195
Agreements, 192, 196, 201, 203–5
see Federal relations
Agricultural Economics, Bureau of, 52, 203, 400
Agriculture, 69–70, 77, 350, 400
see also Primary Industry, Department of
Agricultural Council, 199 200
Allard, Mason, 291, 292–3
Albury-Wodonga Development Corporation, 65, 71, 118, 204, 225, 476

Arbitration, 36
Commonwealth, 121, 159, 365, 368, 370
N.S.W. 366, 368, 371–2
Other States, 365–6, 368, 371, 372
Assessment of administrative potential, 344–50, 353, 487
Atomic energy, 65, 129, 136, 144
Attorney-General, 70, 88, 89, 155, 206, 252, 259, 286, 288, 400
Auditor-General, 47, 138, 457–9, 499, 503–4
Australia Council, 64, 85, 203
Australian Conciliation and Arbitration Commission,
see Arbitration
Australian Assistance Plan, 168, 196, 229, 475–6
Australian Broadcasting Commission (ABC),
see Broadcasting
Australian Bureau of Statistics,
see Statistical services
Australian Capital Territory (A.C.T),
see Canberra
Australian Government Administration, Royal Commission, 16, 19, 43, 86, 92, 97, 102, 108, 115, 134, 147, 148, 149, 230, 269, 271, 305, 306, 307, 313, 326, 327, 330, 332, 349, 350, 353, 354, 355, 361, 362, 364, 370–1, 377, 379, 398, 399, 412, 417, 420, 424, 426, 429, 447, 452, 459–60, 465, 471, 483, 485, 486, 490, 491, 492, 493, 496, 500, 501, 503
Australian Government Publishing Service, 60

Australian Industry Development Corporation, 68, 129, 134, 135, 138, 139
Australian Loan Council,
see Loan Council
Australian National Airlines Commission,
see Trans-Australia Airlines
Australian Shipping Commission, 67, 129,
133, 139–40
Australian Transport Advisory Council,
200
Authority, 99–100, 104–5
attitudes to, 35–6

Barling, Joseph, 291
Bentham, Jeremy, 290, 463, 503
Bigge, J.T., 484
Bland, F.A., 458
Bland, H.A., 115, 135, 281, 485, 486, 488,
490
Board, Peter, 37
Borrowing,
see Loan Finance
Boundary activities, 22
Boyer Committee,
see Recruitment
Brisbane City Council, 128, 217, 232
Broadcasting, 65, 102–3, 129, 131, 133,
135, 138, 141, 286, 379
Brown, Harry, 294
Budget,
see Treasury
Bunting, John, 277, 427, 428
Bureaucracy, 36, 100–1
costs of, 101–3
Burke, Edmund, 286
Burns, Tom, 102
Business administration, contrasted and
compared,
see Public Administration

Cabinets and cabinet committees, 44–6,
59–60, 69, 420–5, 430–1, 444–7,
450
see also Ministers
Caiden, G.E., 483
Canada, 289, 424
Canberra, 61–2, 76, 93, 226–7, 251
see also National Capital Development
Commission

Civil aviation, 194
see also Trans-Australia Airlines
Classification, 360–6
Clientele, 91–2
Coghlan, T.A., 291, 399
Colleges of Advanced Education,
see Universities and Colleges
Collegiality, 52–3
Colonial Secretary, 251–2
Committees,
Commonwealth–State, 193, 194, 199–
203
Interdepartmental, 416–7, 425–7, 431,
471
of Inquiry, 97, 161, 316, 325
Parliamentary, 43–4, 142–3, 156–7,
453–4
see also Advisory Bodies, Cabinet, Pub-
lic Accounts Committees, Royal
Commissions
Common service functions, 89, 106–7
Commonwealth Bank, 128, 348
see also Reserve Bank
Commonwealth Banking Corporation, 68,
129, 134, 135
Commonwealth Constitution, 165–9
amendment, 166–7
Commonwealth and State powers, 165–
6, 169
Concrete Pipes Case, 169
Engineers' Case, 167
financial provisions, 168–9
referenda, 166–7
social services, 166
see also Federal relations, Grants, High
Court, Loan Council, Uniform taxation
Commonwealth government activities,
growth of, 53–5
contrast with States, 75–8
Commonwealth Grants Commission, 120,
180, 238, 441
see also Grants
Commonwealth Hostels Ltd., 124
Commonwealth Parliament,
see Parliament
Commonwealth Public Service,
see Public Service

Commonwealth Scientific and Industrial Research Organisation (CSIRO), 58, 66, 77, 122, 131, 136, 138, 199, 203
Commonwealth–State Councils,
see Committees
Communications, 414–5
Conciliation,
see Arbitration
Consolidated Revenue Fund, 456
Construction,
see Works
Continuing Expenditure Policies, Task Force on, 147, 448
Consultation,
see also Public service associations, Whitley Councils
Consumer affairs, 70, 206
Coombs, H.C., 279, 446, 486, 488
see also Australian Government Administration, Royal Commission
Co-ordination, 27, 51, 82–3, 208, 226, 228, ch. 15
Corbett committee (S.A.), 332, 333, 485, 488, 490, 491
Corporate Affairs Commission, 70
Corrective Services,
see Prisons
Council-Manager system, 126, 232, 243
Council of Australian Government Employee Organisations, 377
County councils, 216, 220, 223, 235
Courts, 36, 59, 69, 154, 161, 162–3, 166, 204
see also Administrative courts, Arbitration, High Court, Land and Valuation Court
Crown Employees Appeal Board (N.S.W.), 257, 325
Cumberland County Council,
see County Councils
Cumpston, J.H.L., 294
Curnow, G.R., 269

Dahl, R.A., 380
Deakin, Alfred, 288, 292
Debt, Government,
see Loan Finance

Decentralization, 39, 71, 106–9, 125, 127, 225
see also Delegation, Regionalism
Defence, 154
Department of, 62, 416, 417, 418
Delegated legislation, 153–7
Delegation, 106–8
see also Decentralization
Departments, 49ff
definition, 50
organization of, 51–3, 84
Commonwealth, 49, 60–8
growth of, 53–5, 86
State, 69–75
growth of, 55–7
see also Ministries
Development Corporation (N.S.W.), 127, 146
Discipline and dismissal, 257–8, 354
Division of work, ch. 4
Dror, Y.

Economic policy, 77–8, 83–4, 88, 399, 402, 406, 419, 438, 459–60
Economists in public service, 36, 279, 316, 333, 399
Economy,
see Efficiency and Economy
Education, 53, 62–3, 71, 91, 95, 147, 200, 203, 208, 399
see also Universities and Colleges
Efficiency and economy, 80, 287, 289, 292, 298, 299, 354, 497
defined, 497
effectiveness and efficiency, 497–8, 503–4
Efficiency audits, 500–4
Electricity authorities, 125, 128, 136, 137
Employee representation,
see Participation
Employment, Government, 33, 54, 56, 76
Environment, 75, 88–9, 144
Australian, ch. 2
Equality in employment, 320–1
Establishment control, 353–4
Estimates, 437–47, 453, 455
see also Treasury
Etzioni, A., 405
Executive Councils, 49, 59, 69, 130, 153

Executive development,
see Training and staff development
Expenditure, government, 170–2
local government, 235
Export Finance and Insurance Corporation, 67, 129, 140
External Affairs,
see Foreign Affairs

Federal Constitution,
see Commonwealth Constitution
Federal Court, 161
Federal relations, 14, 37, 105, chs. 8–9, 405
Agreements, 192, 196, 201
current trends, 170, 210–2
co-operative federalism, 189ff
Commonwealth–State contrasts, 75–8
disparities between States, 175, 179–80
overlapping and duplication, 105, 207–8
role of officials, 37, 208–10
transfer of functions, 166–7, 173
see also Committees, Commonwealth Constitution, Uniformity of laws
Federal–State finance, 170–87
Finance,
see Federal–State finance, Loan Council, Treasury
Finance, Department of,
see Treasury
Fire Commissioners (N.S.W.), 133
First Division
see Permanent Heads
Foreign Affairs, Department of, 53, 94, 270, 346, 416, 427
Forestry, 125, 131, 200
Fourth Division, 362
Fraser, Malcolm., 281, 471
Freedom of Information Acts, 470–3
Fringe areas, 95
Fulton Report,
see United Kingdom civil service
Functions, government
grouping of, 87–94
growth in, 33

Government Administration defined, 16–17, 22–30
see also Public Administration

Government, attitudes to, 34–5
Government Insurance Offices, 116, 126, 131, 134, 136
Grading,
see Classification
Graduates in public service, 255, 314–7, 333–5
Grants, Commonwealth, 176–82
local government, 178, 179, 234–5, 237–8
Greenwood, Gordon, 210
Gulick, Luther, 87

Hancock, W.K., 35
Hayter, H.H., 399
Harbour Trusts, 123, 128, 132
see also Maritime Services Board
Health, Commonwealth Department of, 64, 86
N.S.W., 52, 228
Victoria, 52
Health Commissions, 52, 71, 228
Health Insurance Commission, 118
Health Ministers, Conference of, 202
Health services, 52, 196, 273, 401, 487
see also Hospitals
Hearn, W.E., 288
Helps, Arthur, 481
Heydon, Peter, 272
Heyes, Tasman, 272
Hierarchy, 14, 100
costs of, 103–4
High Court, 159, 166, 167–9, 176, 177, 193, 203, 368
"Hiving-off", 107–8
Hodgson, W.R., 294
Holman, W.A., 197
Hospitals, 195, 202, 401
Housing, 35, 75, 128, 129, 240
Hudson, William, 37

Immigration, 64, 86–7, 402, 416
Implementation, 18, 400–8
Incentives, 104
Incrementalism, 25, 391–2
Industrial Courts,
see Arbitration
Industries Assistance Commission, 61, 117, 121–2, 400, 403, 426, 429, 460

Information services, 463, 464–9
Innovation, 22, 25
In-service training,
    see Training
Interchange Program, 353, 491
Inter-Departmental Committees,
    see Committees
Interdependence, 15
Interest groups, 476–8
Inter-Government Relations, Advisory
    Council for, 199
Inter-State Commission, 203
Interviewing, 345–6

Job analysis, 372–3
Job classification,
    see Classification
Joint Coal Board, 67
Joint Council, 377
Judges, role ol, 36
    see also Courts

Labour and Industry, Department of
    (N.S.W.), 72
Lalor, Peter, 253
Lands, Department of (N.S.W.), 72
Land and Valuation Court, 159
Law and Administration, 18, 89–90,
    263–4
Legal aid, 196–7
Lindblom, C.E., 391
Loan Council and loan finance, 68, 182–7,
    198, 440–1, 455
Local government, 125, ch. 9
    Acts, 154
    areas, 216, 219–227, 239
    committees, commissions, 126, 147
    Departments of, 56, 72, 125, 234, 239
    development of, 216–9
    elections, 231, 232
    employment, 249
    finance, 178
    functions, 154, 215, 234, 235–6
    officials, 219, 233
    statistics, 216
    see also County councils, Regionalism,
        Urban planning

Machinery of Government, 58ff, 96–8
    Haldane Report on (1918), 97, 109

Management, 20–2
Management services, 21, 51
Manpower planning, 354
Maritime Services Board (N.S.W.), 124,
    132, 137
Marketing boards and schemes, 65–6, 70,
    120, 127, 193
McLachlan, D.C., 293–4, 321
McLeay, Alexander, 252
Melbourne City Council, 217, 231
Melbourne and Metropolitan Board of
    Works, 128, 225–6
Metropolitan government,
    see Urban planning
Metropolitan Waste Disposal Authority,
    126
Metropolitan Water Sewerage and
    Drainage Board (N.S.W.), 58, 125,
    126, 132, 134, 137, 222, 225
Minerals and Energy, 93, 175, 191–3, 200
Mines, Department of (N.S.W.), 73
Ministers, role of, 47–9, 127–8, 141–2,
    264–8
    Assistant ministers, 45
Ministerial staffs, 269, 278–80, 347, 348,
    430, 441, 444, 464
Ministries, 51, 55, 71, 74
Mobility, 329–30
Monash, John, 37
Mosher, F.C., 81
Municipalities,
    see Local government
Murphy, Frank, 294

National Capital Development Com-
    mission (N.C.D.C.), 61, 91, 118, 129,
    144
National debt,
    see Loan finance
National Development, Department of,
    65, 93, 191, 259
National Health and Medical Research
    Council, 200–1
National parks, 146
Neutrality, 256–7
New South Wales, 105, 145, 156, 157,
    175, 197
    cabinet, 45, 138
    departments, 50, 69–75, 97, 227–8

local and regional government, 216, 217–9, 228, 231, 235, 497
public enterprise and statutory bodies, 116–7, 123–7, 131, 135, 136–8, 141, 142
public service, 251, 253–4, 289–91, 292–3, 313–4, 316–7, 321, 328, 330, 346, 348, 351, 363, 366, 377–8, 380, 500
see also Treasury and under individual agencies
New Zealand, 162
Non-departmental agencies, 57–8, 60–75, ch. 5
see also Advisory bodies, Statutory authorities
Northern Australia, 65, 93, 129, 175, 251
Nuclear energy, see Atomic energy

O'Connor, C.Y., 37
Offshore oil and gas, 191–3
Ombudsman, 162
Open Government, see Secrecy

Parker, R.S., 27
Park trusts, 126
Parliaments, 43–4, 59, 68, 142–4, 155–7, 259, 501
budgetary procedures, 453–4
see also Committees
Participation, 104–5, 132–3, 379–82, 463, 474–9
Pay, see Salaries
Peres, Leon, 94, 122, 433
Permanent Heads, 36–7, 48, 134, 266–71, 330–3, 336–7, 348, 361, 369
Personnel administration, chs. 11, 12
see also Establishment control, Recruitment, Training, etc.
Pharmacy Boards, 126
Pipeline Authority, 65, 118, 193
Planning, 21, 395–400
see also Urban planning
Pluralism, 13–4
Police, 205, 248, 257, 291

Policy and policymaking, defined, 387
policy and administration, 17–9, 263–8, 270–1
Politics and administration, 17–9, 23, 25, 26, 94–5, 258–60
impact of government changes, 276–81
Political rights of public servants, 258–63
Postal and telecommunications services, 54, 55, 129, 132, 134, 135, 140
Premiers' Conference, 183, 197–9
Premier's Departments, 46, 73, 85, 430, 500
Pressure groups, see Interest groups
Primary Industry, Department of, 65–6, 199
Prime Minister and Cabinet, Department of the, 46, 66, 85, 97, 197, 281, 331, 350, 397–8, 419, 427–30, 491, 504
Prices Justification Tribunal, 61, 121
Priorities Review Staff, 398
Prisons, 74
Professionals in public service, 28–9, 248, 333–5, 338–44
Programme budgets, 447–51
Promotion, 255, 321–33
appeals, 325–6
criteria and methods, 326–9
Public Accounts Committees, 43, 143–4, 458–9
Public Administration defined, 16–22
private sector compared, 22–30
Public comment, right of, 260–3
Public corporations, see Statutory authorities
Public health, see Health
Public relations, 463, 464–5
Public servants, anonymity, 260–3
defined, 247–8
legal status, 248
neutrality and changes of government, 256–7, 274–81
rights and obligations, 256–8
social background, 315, 317, 320–1, 333–5, 342–3

see also Politics and administration,
Political rights of public servants
Public service,
character of, 255
growth and statistics of, 248–50,
286–97
image of, 318–20
see also Graduates, Mobility, Per-
manent Heads, Promotion, Re-
cruitment, Second Division
Public Service Acts cited:
Commonwealth, 353, 354, 360
Public Service Act, 1902, 292
Public Service Arbitration Act, 1920,
369
Public Service Act, 1922, 258
Public Service (Amendment) Act,
1960, 316, 327
New South Wales,
Civil Service Act, 1884, 289
Public Service Act, 1895, 290
Public Service Act, 1902, 291
Public Service (Amendment) Act,
1919, 293
Public Service (Amendment) Act,
1922, 371
Public Service (Amendment) Act,
1955, 293
Public Service (Amendment) Act,
1974, 327
Other States,
Queensland, 291, 296, 302
South Australia, 295
Tasmania, 295–6, 302
Victoria, 289, 294, 300
Western Australia, 302
Public service associations, 258, 375–9
Public Service Boards, 58, 134, 255, 257,
297–8, 350, 499–500
Commonwealth, 96–7, 121, 132, 135,
250, 294, 296–7, 298–9, 354, 362,
368–71
New South Wales, 251, 289–90, 293,
299–300, 351, 352, 500
Queensland, 134, 296, 301–2
South Australia, 295, 302
Tasmania, 295–6, 302
Victoria, 294, 300–1
Western Australia, 302

Public Transport Commission (N.S.W.),
58, 74, 124, 136, 399
Public Trustee, 47, 70, 126, 205
Public Works, Department of (N.S.W.), 74

Qantas Airways Ltd., 67, 114, 124
Quangos, 30
Queensland, 175, 181, 199
departments,
local and regional government, 217,
218, 219, 228–9, 231, 232, 235
public enterprise and statutory bodies,
123, 128
public services, 251, 291, 296, 329, 330,
372, 378
Treasury, 185, 444–5
see also Brisbane City Council

Railways, 122–3, 131, 140–1
Commonwealth, 128
New South Wales, 123, 131
other States, 123, 140–1
see also Public Transport Commission
(N.S.W.)
Rates, local, 235, 236–7
Recruitment, 312–8
Boyer Committee, 37, 316, 326, 348,
362, 484
examinations, 313
history of, 253–5, 292, 294, 296–7
lateral recruitment, 255, 296, 318
see also Graduates, Wastage rates
Regionalism, 92–3, 227–31
Regulations and Ordinances, Senate Com-
mittee on, 43
Repatriation,
see Veterans Affairs
Research, 66, 399
see also Commonwealth Scientific and
Industrial Research Organisation
Reserve Bank of Australia, 129, 131, 133,
134, 135, 141, 169, 400
see also Commonwealth Bank
Responsible government, 34
Responsibility, 16, 493–7
River Murray Commission, 65, 201
Roads, 58, 120, 125, 337
Robson, W.A., 158
Ross, Wallace, 294

Royal Commission Reports,
  Public Service Administration (C'wealth) (McLachlan), 1920, 293–4
  Public Service (N.S.W.), (Littlejohn), 1895, (Allard), 1918, 290, 292–3
  Public Service (Vic.), 294
  Economies (C'wealth) (Gibson), 1920, 294
  Greater Sydney (Cocks), 1914, 222
  Local Government Areas (Clancy), 1946, 221
  Rating, Valuation and Local Government Finance (Else-Mitchell), 1967, 237
  see also Australian Government Administration, Royal Commission on
Rural Bank of N.S.W., 125, 126

Salaries, 363–75
  see also Arbitration
Sawer, Geoffrey, 174
Science,
  see Research
Second Division, 248, 251, 296, 361–2, 365
Secrecy, 260–1, 465–73
Self, Peter, 25, 106
Sharkansky, Ira, 144
Sheehan, H.J., 294
Simon, H.A., 390
Snowy Mountains scheme, 65, 201
Social costs, 24
Social security, 51, 67, 159, 266, 337, 417
Social services, 35, 74, 91, 95, 168, 194–7, 336, 337, 475–6
  committees and commissions, 147
  Commonwealth–State powers, 166, 168
  expenditure, 172, 182
  local government and, 215, 219, 224, 229, 235–6
  voluntary bodies, 195–7, 476
Social Welfare Policy Secretariat, 67, 417
South Australia, 50, 128, 175, 208, 464–5
  local government and planning, 217, 221, 222, 226, 229
  public services, 251, 253, 291–2, 295, 317, 330, 372, 380
  see also Corbett committee

Specialization,
  see Division of work
Specialists,
  see Professionals
Speight, Richard, 37
Spill-over effects, 24, 181
Staff associations,
  see Public service associations
Staff problems,
  see Personnel
Staff reporting, 348–50
Staff representation,
  see Participation
State Brickworks (N.S.W.), 74, 124
State capitals, 38–9
State Dockyards (N.S.W.), 74, 124
State enterprises,
  see Statutory authorities
State government, 38–9, 49, 68–75, 430–2
  functions and powers, 33–4, 75–8
  see also under separate States
State Planning Authority (N.S.W.), 223–4
Statistical services, 108, 207, 209, 399, 418
Statutory authorities, boards and corporations, 29, 48, 57–8, ch. 5
  advantages, 118–22
  composition and staff, 130–6
  control, 121, 135, 141–5
  defined, 113–4
  finance, 114, 136–41
  Commonwealth, 117–8, 128–30, 138–40, 369
  New South Wales, 116–7, 123–7, 131, 136–8, 141, 142
  other States, 115–6, 127–8, 141–2
Statutory instruments, 154, 156
  see also Delegated legislation
Story, J.D., 37
Strikes, 375–6
Superannuation, 205, 369, 400
Sweden, 107–8
Sydney County Council, 125, 126, 137
Sydney Cove Redevelopment Authority, 125–6
Sydney Farm Produce Market Authority, 126
Systems theory, 19

Tariffs,
see Industries Assistance Commission
Tasmania, 167, 175, 444
local government, 216, 217, 231, 232
public enterprise and statutory bodies, 128
public service, 251, 253, 254, 291, 295–6, 322, 330, 331
Tate, Frank, 37
Taxation, 176–8
Boards of Review, 159
Commonwealth, State, local, 178
uniform taxation, 167, 176–7
Teachers' Federation, 53, 377–8, 379, 381
Television,
see Broadcasting
Tertiary Education Commission,
see Universities and Colleges
Third Division, 362, 365
Thomson, E. Deas, 252
Tourism, 65, 74, 202
Town planning,
see Urban planning
Trade, Department of, 26, 67, 85, 86, 250, 416, 417
Trade unions,
see Public service associations
Training and staff development, 350–3
Trans-Australia Airlines (TAA), 67, 114, 130, 131, 135, 138–9, 141
Transport Commissions, 127
see also Public Transport Commission (N.S.W.)
Transport Economics, Bureau of, 67, 203, 400
Transport, Ministry of (N.S.W.), 74, 125, 142, 399, 417–8
Treasury and Department of Finance, 63, 68, 88, 90, 94, 281, 347, 350, 397, 419, 438, 459–60, 500, 504
budget formulation, 437–53
cabinet and, 444–7
Consolidated Fund,
Forward Estimates, 442–3, 445–6, 451–3
"hiving off", 108
officials, 331
role of, 337

Commonwealth, 198, 250, 426, 438, 442–4, 446, 473
N.S.W., 185–7, 209, 441–2
other States, 185–7, 209
see also Programme budgets, Federal–State Finance, Loan Council
Turnover,
see Wastage rates

Ultra Vires, 154–5
Uniformity of laws, 169, 205–7
Uniform taxation, 167, 176–7
United Kingdom, 33–4, 143, 269, 345, 452–3
civil service, 105, 259, 271, 286–8, 335, 347, 348, 350–1, 484, 489, 490
United States, 160, 259, 271–2, 335, 346, 348, 351
Universities and Colleges, 120
Murray Report, 147, 484
Tertiary Education Commission, 62, 146, 203
Urban and Regional Development, Department of, 15, 53, 91, 230, 451
Urban planning, 220, 223–7, 432

Vernon Committee of Economic Inquiry, 148, 185, 484
Veterans Affairs, 68, 85, 91, 195, 413, 417
Vickers, Geoffrey, 407
Victoria, 156, 175, 191
departments, 55
local government and planning, 215, 217, 225–6, 229, 231–2, 235
public enterprise and statutory bodies, 115–6, 123, 127–8, 135, 141–2
public service, 251, 253, 288–9, 294, 317, 321, 330, 351, 353, 365–6, 372, 378, 485

Waldo, Dwight, 99
Wastage rates, 314
Water Resources Commission (N.S.W.), 125
Weber, Max, 100
Western Australia, 157, 162, 175, 191
local government and planning, 217, 221, 229, 236

public enterprise and statutory bodies, 127, 128, 132, 133
public service, 251, 291, 297, 317, 330, 348, 351, 372, 378
Wettenhall, R.L., 97, 142, 143
Wheare, K.C., 501
Wheeler, Frederick, 268, 297, 324
Whitham, E.G., 120, 211, 229, 276–81, 471, 478
Whitley Councils, 377

Wilenski, P.S., 105, 135, 279, 321, 399, 464, 485, 486, 488, 491–2
Women in public service, 231, 320–1
Works, Commonwealth Department of, 90–1, 286
see also Public Works, Department of (N.S.W.)
Wurth, W.C., 37
Wyndham, Harold, 37